Hungary

written and researched by

Norm Longley

with additional contributions from

Tim Burford, Charles Hebbert and Dan Richardson

ROUGH
GUIDES

www.roughguides.com

Contents

Bathing matters colour section following p.144

Food and drink colour section following p.368

◄◄ Man in

Prague

CZECH REPUBLIC

Brno

AUSTRIA

SL

Zvolen

VIENNA

R. Danube

BRATISLAVA

Balassagyarmat

Nové Zámky

BÖRZSÖNY HILLS

CSERHÁT

Hegyeshalom

Mosonmagyaróvár

Szob

Komárno

Esztergom

Vác

Győr

Komárom

Tata

Szentendre

Sopron

Csorna

M1

Lake Fertő

Tatabánya

BUDAPEST

Aszod

KISALFÖLD

M0

Kőszeg

Pápa

M7

Lake Velence

M5

Szombathely

Sárvár

Celldömölk

Székesfehérvár

Veszprém

Graz

BAKONY HILLS

Dunaújváros

Szentgotthárd

Sümeg

Balatonfüred

Tapolca

Tihany

Siófok

Zalaegerszeg

Keszthely

Lake Balaton

Lenti

Fonyód

Dunaföldvár

SLOVENIA

Kiskőrös

Ljubljana

Nagykanizsa

Kalocsa

Varazdin

Kaposvár

Dombóvár

Kiskunhalas

Csurgó

Szekszárd

R. Danube

Zagreb

MECSEK HILLS

Pécs

SÁRKÖZ

Baja

Szigetvár

Barcs

Mohács

CROATIA

Harkány

Villány

Siklós

N

SER

0   50 km

Osijek

Banja Luka

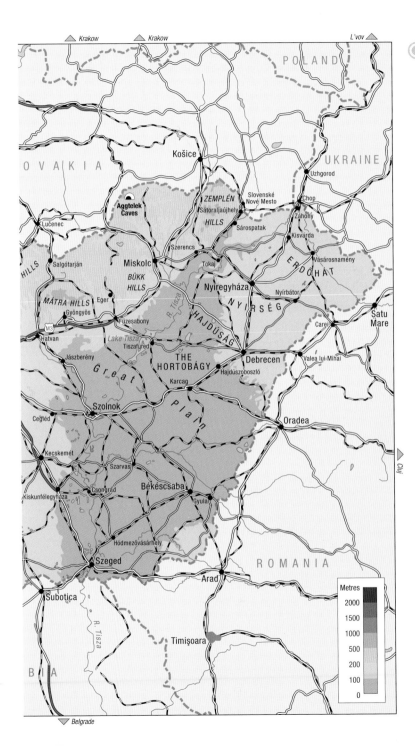

POLAND

OVAKIA

UKRAINE

Košice

Uzhgorod

ZEMPLÉN

Slovenské
Nové Mesto

Chop

Aggtelek
Caves

Sátoraljaújhely

Zahony

Lučenec

HILLS

Sárospatak

Kisvárda

Szerencs

Vásárosnamény

HILLS

Salgótarján

Miskolc

Tokaj

ERDŐHÁT

*BÜKK
HILLS*

Nyíregyháza

Nyírbátor

MÁTRA HILLS

Eger

R. Tisza

N Y Í R S É G

Gyöngyös

Satu
Mare

Füzesabony

H A J D Ú S Á G

Carei

M3

Hatvan

Lake Tisza
Tiszafüred

Debrecen

Valea lui Mihai

Jászberény

G r e a t

THE
HORTOBÁGY

Hajdúszoboszló

Karcag

▷ Cluj

Szolnok

Cegléd

P l a i n

Oradea

Kecskemét

Szarvas

Kiskunfélegyháza

Csongrád

Békéscsaba

Gyula

Hódmezővásárhely

ROMANIA

Szeged

Arad

Subotica

R. Tisza

Metres
2000
1500
1000
500
200
100
0

Timişoara

B I A

Belgrade

Introduction to
Hungary

A relatively small, landlocked nation of just over ten million people, Hungary is perhaps one of Europe's least understood countries, a land possessed of so much more than spas and goulash. Having served for centuries as a bulwark against Ottoman Turkish expansion in Europe, it then endured a lengthy period under Habsburg rule, before its emergence from forty years of Communist rule and an awkward transition to western-style democracy and a capitalist market economy. For visitors the country embraces a range of terrific destinations – not least the beautiful, and very hip, capital city, Budapest – alongside a wonderfully diverse range of landscapes, including one of Europe's largest lakes, Balaton, and the beguiling expanse of the Great Plain.

Right at the heart of Europe, Hungary was likened by the poet Ady to a "river ferry, continually travelling between East and West, with always the sensation of not going anywhere but of being on the way back from the other bank"; this seems especially evident in the Hungarians' strong identification with the West, and simultaneous display of fierce pride in themselves as Magyars – a race that transplanted itself from Central Asia. Following a brave and bloody uprising against Soviet rule in 1956, Hungary effected a move towards so-called "Goulash Communism", which represented a moderate deviation from the hard-line Socialist principles practised elsewhere in the Eastern bloc. Indeed, the country embarked on reforming state socialism long before Gorbachev, making the transition to multi-party democracy without a shot

▶ Pécs

being fired, while the removal of the Iron Curtain along its border set in motion the events leading to the fall of the Berlin Wall. The ensuing spread of glossy Western capitalism, particularly in the capital, brought very mixed blessings indeed for Hungarians – many of whom saw their living standards fall sharply. The country's accession to the European Union in 2004 – which was broadly favoured by most Hungarians – brought a fresh sense of optimism, though a series of economic and political crises since then has only served to deepen tensions among the wider population. Although EU membership appears to have made little tangible difference to the lives of Hungarians, the country has seen its profile raised, resulting in an upsurge in the number of visitors keen to discover the undoubted charms of this relatively little-known nation.

Fact file

• Hungary, covering an area of 93,000 square kilometres, lies in the Carpathian basin in the heart of Europe. Two-thirds of the country is flatland, the greatest single area being the Great Plain, or *puszta*, which sprawls across the eastern half of the country. The remainder is undulating terrain, with only one mountain, Mount Kékes in the Northern Uplands, topping 1000m. There are nine national parks spread around the country, the largest of which is the Hortobágy on the Great Plain. Hungary has Central Europe's largest and warmest lake, the Balaton, two major rivers – the Danube and the Tisza – and over a thousand natural springs.

• On October 23, 1989, Hungary became an independent republic once again. The 1989 constitution set in place a parliamentary system of government, elected every four years, with the prime minister at its head. The head of state, the president, is elected every five years. Having been admitted to NATO in 1999, Hungary finally achieved its greatest political goal in 2004 when the country joined the European Union.

• With few natural resources, Hungary's economy is driven largely by its manufacturing industry. Foreign investment is amongst the highest of the former Communist countries.

• The population of the country currently stands at just over ten million, one fifth of whom live in Budapest. It is estimated that over five million Hungarians live outside the country, a large number in Transylvania, Romania.

Whilst Budapest deservedly takes centre stage, there is much more besides; gorgeous Baroque towns stand cheek by jowl with ancient castles and fortresses, while nature asserts itself spectacularly in the form of Lake Balaton, the thickly forested Northern Uplands, and the immense sweep of the Great Plain, not to mention one of the grandest stretches of the great Danube River. Aside from the country's extraordinary concentration of thermal spas, there is a wealth of other activities available, including watersports, horseriding, cycling and hiking, while nearly two dozen wine regions offer the chance to sample a range of quality wines little known beyond its own borders.

Where to go

he capital, **Budapest**, dominates the country in every sense – administratively, commercially and culturally. Divided into two distinct parts by the River Danube – the historical Buda district on the elevated west bank, and the grittier but more dynamic Pest district on the eastern side – the city boasts a welter of fine museums and churches, coffee houses, Turkish baths and Roman ruins, as well as some splendid architecture and a diversity of entertainment unmatched in many Central or Eastern European cities.

The most obvious attraction after Budapest is the magnificent **Danube Bend**, one of the most spectacular stretches of this immense river. Sweeping its way north out of the capital, the river passes through the delightful town of Szentendre on the west bank – a popular day-trip from the capital – before moving serenely on through historic Visegrád and up to Esztergom, the centre of Hungarian Catholicism. Southwest of Budapest, **Lake Balaton**, with its string of brash resorts, styles itself as "the Nation's Playground", and contains Europe's largest thermal bath at Hévíz, and some splendid wine regions, notably around the Badacsony Hills on the north shore and Balatonboglár on the southern shore.

Encircling Balaton and encompassing the area west of the Danube, **Transdanubia** has the country's most varied topography, from the flat, rather monotonous landscape of the northern Kisalföld to the verdant, forested Orség in the southwest. The region also claims some of the country's finest towns and cities, most notably Sopron with its atmospheric Belváros (inner town), and the vibrant city of Pécs, with its superb museums and Islamic architecture. Further south, the vineyards around Villány and Siklós – Hungary's first wine road – yield some of the country's finest wines.

The mildly hilly mountain ranges of the **Northern Uplands**, spreading eastwards from Budapest, offer Hungary's best opportunities for leisurely

Hungarian architecture

Hungary's architectural legacy rivals that of any country in Central or Eastern Europe, thanks in part to centuries of competing rulers and faiths – Romans, Ottomans and Habsburgs amongst others. The capital, Budapest, embraces an abundance of styles, from its grand, neo-Gothic Parliament building to the fabulous Art Nouveau zoo and Ottoman bath houses. Many outlying towns and cities, too, boast architectural treasures – notably Pécs, with its fine mosques, the Baroque towns of Győr and Sopron, and Kecskemét and Szeged, both of which showcase splendid Secessionist structures. The countryside, too, reveals some wonderful vernacular architecture, particularly in Northern Uplands villages such as Hollókő, and Fuzér and Hollóháza in the Western Zemplén, which are characterized by folksy dwellings set against a landscape of low rounded hills. Hungary's religious architecture is no less prominent, with an enormous Neoclassical basilica in Esztergom, a Gothic-era monastery at Pannonhalma, and magnificent synagogues in Budapest and Szeged all to the fore, while the enchanting medieval wooden churches in the isolated northeastern corner of the country are mini-masterpieces of ecclesiastical architecture. Wherever you are in Hungary, there's a good chance you'll come across the work of Imre Makovecz, whose exuberant structures, designed using raw materials, have made him a somewhat controversial household name.

pursuits, including hiking, cycling and even skiing. The region is also home to the country's most fantastic natural wonder, the Aggtelek Caves, whilst the more sparsely populated northwestern region, the Zemplén range, will appeal to castle enthusiasts and those seeking to get off the beaten track. The Uplands are also famed for their wine centres, the most renowned being Eger – an enchanting town in its own right, showcasing some marvellous Baroque architecture – and Tokaj.

The area south of the Uplands is dominated by the vast, flat swathe

▲ Parliament, view of the dome with spires, Budapest

of land known as the **Great Plain**, bisected by Hungary's other great river, the Tisza. Covering almost fifty percent of the country, the Plain doesn't have the clear-cut attractions of other regions, but it can be a rewarding place to visit. Szeged, close to the Serbian border, is the area's most appealing centre, with some delightful architecture and perhaps the country's most beautiful synagogue. Further east, its rival city Debrecen serves as the jumping-off point for the archaic Erdőhát region and the mirage-haunted Hortobágy *puszta*, home to a fantastic array of wildlife.

When to go

Most visitors come in the summer, when nine or ten hours of sunshine can be relied on most days, sometimes interspersed with short, violent storms. The humidity that causes these is really only uncomfortable in Budapest, where the crowds don't help; elsewhere the climate is agreeable. Budapest, with its spring and autumn festivals, sights and culinary delights, is a standing invitation to come

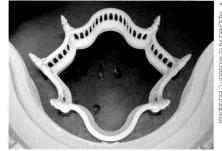

▼ Applied Arts Museum, Budapest

out of season. But other parts of Hungary have little to offer during the winter, and the weather doesn't become appealing until late spring. May, warm but showery, is the time to see the Danube Bend, Tihany or Sopron before everyone else arrives; June is hotter and drier, a pattern reinforced throughout July, August and September. There's little variation in temperatures across the country: the Great Plain is drier, and the highlands are wetter, during summer, but that's about as far as climatic changes go. The number of tourists varies more – popular areas such as Szentendre and Tihany can be mobbed in summer, but rural areas receive few visitors, even during the high season.

Average monthly temperatures

	Jan	Feb	Mar	Apr	May	Jun	Jul	Aug	Sep	Oct	Nov	Dec
Budapest												
Temp (°F)	29	30	42	52	61	67	72	68	63	53	42	34
Temp (°C)	-2	-1	6	11	16	19	22	20	17	12	6	1
Debrecen												
Temp (°F)	27	32	41	51	60	66	70	70	61	51	41	34
Temp (°C)	-3	0	5	10	16	18	21	21	16	10	5	1
Miskolc												
Temp (°F)	27	27	37	48	57	65	68	67	63	48	37	35
Temp (°C)	-3	-3	3	9	14	17	20	19	17	9	3	2
Szeged												
Temp (°F)	31	33	42	52	61	65	70	68	64	53	41	35
Temp (°C)	-1	1	6	11	16	17	21	20	18	12	5	2

17

things not to miss

It's not possible to see everything that Hungary has to offer in one trip – and we don't suggest you try. What follows is a selective taste of the country's highlights: outstanding buildings, natural wonders and colourful festivals. They're arranged in five colour-coded categories, which you can browse through to find the very best things to see and experience. All highlights have a page reference to take you straight into the guide, where you can find out more.

01 Danube Bend Page **162** • One of the most enchanting stretches of the River Danube sweeps its way up from Budapest before twisting dramatically through a forested valley towards Slovakia – the views are best appreciated from atop Visegrád Citadel.

02 **Watersports on Lake Balaton** Pages **195** & **216** • Siófok and Keszthely are just two of the resorts where you can sail, windsurf, slide or, of course, swim.

04 **Aggtelek Caves** Page **352** • Take a tour through the largest, and one of the most amazing, stalactite cave systems in Europe.

03 **Pécs** Page **294** • Vital and absorbing, the city of Pécs has one of the most significant collections of Turkish buildings in this part of Europe.

www.roughguides.com

06 Budapest Spring Festival
Page **132** • The capital's premier annual arts festival hosts a matchless line-up of music, theatre and film, as well as a grand parade.

05 Hortobágy National Park
Page **418** • You'll find blue-skirted cowboys, rodeo shows and a diverse collection of wildlife – water buffalo, corkscrew-horned sheep and wild boar – in Hungary's largest national park; there's also excellent bird-watching.

08 Hiking in the Bükk Hills
Page **329** • These lovely, beech-covered hills in the Northern Uplands are Hungary's prime hiking region, with trails to suit walkers of all abilities.

07 Busójárás Carnival
Page **308** • Masked "busó" figures dressed in animal hides parade through the town of Mohács and in boats across the Danube in this awesome spectacle.

09 Folk and Gypsy music Page **458** • Don't pass up the chance to experience the ubiquitous, irrepressible sounds of Hungarian folk and Gypsy music.

10 Wine cellars Pages **306** & **357** • You shouldn't leave Hungary without visiting one of its famous wine cellars, the best of which are located on the Villány-Siklós wine road and in the Tokaj-Hegyalja region.

11 Eger Page **335** • Atmospheric Uplands town strewn with gorgeous Baroque architecture and famed for its local red wine, "Bull's Blood".

12 Paprika See *Food and drink colour section* • The foodstuff most commonly associated with Hungary is not quite the fiery stuff of legend but it is an integral part of the Magyar kitchen.

13 Sopron Page 258 • Pretty town, close to the Austrian border, featuring a spectacular Belváros brimming with absorbing museums and architecture.

14 Esterházy Palace Page **268** • Once one of the most opulent palaces in Europe, this eighteenth-century Baroque and Rococo masterpiece is still the most beautiful in the country.

16 Thermal baths See *Bathing matters* **colour section** • There's no better way to relax than in one of Budapest's magnificent Turkish baths or one of the many countryside spas.

15 Hollóko Page **327** • Nestling in the heart of the Cserhát Hills, a visit to this exquisitely preserved village – a World Heritage Site – is a must for its architecture and folk customs.

17 Várhegy, Budapest Page **99** • Historic Castle Hill is the capital's defining feature, a long, elevated plateau spotted with bastions, churches and some fine museums.

Basics

Basics

www.roughguides.com

Getting there

BASICS | Getting there

Flying is the easiest way to reach Hungary, with several airlines now flying direct from airports in the UK and Ireland, as well as direct flights from the US and Canada. There are presently no direct flights from Australasia or South Africa. Travelling overland from the UK takes around a day by train and a day and a half by bus, although with an InterRail or Eurail pass you can take in Hungary as part of a wider European trip. Another option is to drive, a journey of over 1700km, best covered over a couple of days.

Airfares are highest from June to August, and drop during the "shoulder" seasons – March to May and September to October. The best prices are found during the low season, from November to February, excluding Christmas and New Year when prices are hiked up and seats are at a premium.

You can often cut costs by going through a **specialist flight agent**, who in addition to dealing with discounted flights may also offer student and youth fares and travel insurance, rail passes, car rentals, tours and the like. Some agents specialize in **charter flights**, which may be cheaper than scheduled flights, but departure dates are fixed and withdrawal penalties are high.

Flights from the UK and Ireland

Flying to Budapest (approximately 2hr 30min from London) has never been easier or cheaper, particularly with the proliferation of low-cost operators in recent years. At the time of writing **easyJet** goes from Gatwick and Luton, and **Wizz Air** from Luton only. **Ryanair** has flights from Bristol, East Midlands and Glasgow Prestwick. **Jet2** has summer-only flights from Manchester to Budapest. Tickets with these airlines go for

an average of £50 return, or sometimes even less, including tax. However, as flights fill up quickly, you'll need to book a couple of months ahead during summer; moreover, the earlier you book, the cheaper the ticket is likely to be.

In addition, **British Airways** and the Hungarian national airline **Malév** fly direct daily to Budapest from Heathrow and Gatwick. From **Ireland**, Aer Lingus and Malév fly daily between Dublin and Budapest, and Ryanair has five flights a week from Dublin. Scheduled fares from London start at around £200 in high season and £120 in low season, and from Ireland around €250 in high season and €150 in low season.

Flights from the US and Canada

Delta Airlines fly non-stop from New York to Budapest all year round, while **Malév** runs non-stop services from New York and Toronto between May and September – flight times are around eight and a half hours from New York and nine and a half hours from Toronto. From the **east coast** of the US expect to pay around US$750 low season and US$950 high season; and from the **west coast** around US$900 low season and US$1300 high season.

roughguides.com

Find everything you need to plan your next trip at @www.roughguides.com.
Read in-depth information on destinations worldwide, make use of our unique trip-planner, book transport and accommodation, check out other travellers' recommendations and share your own experiences.

From **Toronto**, expect to pay around Can$900 in low season and Can$1300 in high season.

Alternatively, you can use one of the **European carriers** to fly you into a major European hub and continue your journey from there. **Lufthansa**, for example, offers low-season midweek return fares to Budapest (via Frankfurt) from around US$650 from New York and US$850 from West Coast cities, rising to around US$950 and US$1250 respectively during high season. From Canada, Lufthansa (via Frankfurt) offers return fares from around C$1250 low season, and C$1600 high season.

Flights from Australia, New Zealand and South Africa

There are no direct flights to Hungary from Australia or New Zealand so you'll have to change airlines, either in Asia or Europe, although the best option is to fly to a Western European gateway, such as London, Paris or Frankfurt, and get a connecting flight from there. A standard return **fare** from eastern Australia to Budapest via London, with **Qantas**, is around Aus$2800 high season and Aus$2200 low season. The same routings apply for flights from New Zealand, with a standard return fare from Auckland, with **Air New Zealand**, from around NZ$3500 high season, and NZ$2800 low season.

Similarly, there are no direct flights to Hungary from South Africa. A standard return fare from Johannesburg to Budapest via Frankfurt or Vienna (with **South African Airways** or a leading European airline) is around ZAR9000 in low season or ZAR10,000 in high season.

Trains

Travelling by **train** to Hungary is likely to be considerably more expensive than flying, though it can be a leisurely way of getting to the country if you plan to stop off in other parts of Europe along the way. The shortest

---

Six steps to a better kind of travel

At Rough Guides we are passionately committed to travel. We feel strongly that only through travelling do we truly come to understand the world we live in and the people we share it with – plus tourism has brought a great deal of **benefit** to developing economies around the world over the last few decades. But the extraordinary growth in tourism has also damaged some places irreparably, and of course **climate change** is exacerbated by most forms of transport, especially flying. This means that now more than ever it's important to **travel thoughtfully** and **responsibly**, with respect for the cultures you're visiting – not only to derive the most benefit from your trip but also to preserve the best bits of the planet for everyone to enjoy. At Rough Guides we feel there are six main areas in which you can make a difference:

- Consider what you're contributing to the **local economy**, and how much the services you use do the same, whether it's through employing local workers and guides or sourcing locally grown produce and local services.
- Consider the **environment** on holiday as well as at home. Water is scarce in many developing destinations, and the biodiversity of local flora and fauna can be adversely affected by tourism. Try to patronize businesses that take account of this.
- Travel with a purpose, not just to tick off experiences. Consider **spending longer** in a place, and getting to know it and its people.
- Give thought to how often you **fly**. Try to avoid short hops by air and more harmful night flights.
- Consider **alternatives to flying**, travelling instead by bus, train, boat and even by bike or on foot where possible.
- Make your trips "**climate neutral**" via a reputable carbon offset scheme. All Rough Guide flights are offset, and every year we donate money to a variety of charities devoted to combating the effects of climate change.

journey from London's St Pancras International to Budapest takes around nineteen hours; a standard second-class return ticket on this route, incorporating Eurostar, will cost around £350. Eurostar trains depart more or less hourly (roughly 6am–7.30pm) from St Pancras through the Channel Tunnel to Paris Gare du Nord (1hr 50min). Arriving in Paris, you take a TGV (from Gare de l'Est) to Munich and then an onward connection to Budapest. Going via Brussels, Cologne and Vienna is slightly cheaper, but involves more trains and takes around 24 hours.

Deutsche Bahn is the best option for making seat reservations on continental trains, and its website (see p.24) is an excellent resource for checking railway timetables, while the website of **The Man in Seat Sixty-One** (see p.24) is an excellent source of information on most aspects of rail travel in Europe. The best printed source for timetables is Thomas Cook's red-covered European Rail Timetable, which details schedules of the main Hungarian train service; the same publisher also produces the useful Rail Map of Europe.

Rail passes

If you're taking in Hungary as part of a wider trip, then you might consider the **InterRail Pass** (ⓦ www.interrail.net). These are only available to European residents (or those who have been resident in a European country for at least six months), and you will be asked to provide proof of residency before being allowed to buy one. They come in over-26 and (cheaper) under-26 versions, and cover thirty countries, of which Hungary is one.

There are now two types of pass. The old zonal pass has been replaced with a **Global Pass**, covering all thirty countries (one month of continuous use costs €599 for over 26s/€399 for under 26s; 22 days' continuous €469/309; 10 days in 22 €359/239; 5 days in 10 €249/159). InterRail Passes do not include travel between Britain and the Continent, although holders are eligible for discounts on rail travel in Britain and Northern Ireland and cross-Channel ferries, as well as reduced rates on the London–Paris Eurostar service.

The other InterRail scheme is the **One-Country Pass** (formerly the Eurodomino

pass), which allows you to travel for a certain number of days during a one-month period depending upon which pass you buy. For Hungary it is as follows: eight days in one month costs €139 for over 26s/€90 for under 26s; six days in one month €119/77; four days in one month €89/58; three days in one month €69/45.

Eurail passes

Non-European residents qualify for the **Eurail Pass** (ⓦ www.eurail.com), which must be bought before arrival in Europe (or from RailEurope in the UK). The **Global Pass** allows for unlimited rail travel in Hungary and twenty other countries, and is available in increments of fifteen days (€511 for over 26s/€332 for under 26s), 21 days (€662/429), one month (€822/535), two months (€1161/755) and three months (€1432/933). There is also a **Flexipass** which allows for either ten (€603/393) or fifteen days' travel (€792/515) within a two-month period. The **One-Country Pass** allows unlimited first-class train travel on any five days within fifteen (€76/57), or any ten days within one month (€105/71), within Hungary.

Furthermore, there's the **Select Pass**, which allows travel in three (from €211), four (from €235) or five (from €260) bordering countries over a selected period of time (5, 6, 8 or 10 days within a two-month period); and a Regional Hungary-Romania Pass (from €133), which allows unlimited free first-class train travel on five, six, eight or ten days within two months within these two countries.

Buses

The **bus** journey from London to Budapest takes around 28 hours and is extremely hard going. A standard return fare (valid for six months) with Eurolines costs around £110, but regular promotional offers can bring this down to as low as £70. The buses are air-conditioned and have on-board toilets. The usual route is to take the ferry across the Channel to Calais and then via Brussels and Vienna – there is also a stop in Győr.

By car

Driving to Hungary from London, a distance of some 1500km, can be a pleasant proposition. However, it's really only worth considering if you are going to travel in Hungary for an extended period, or want to take advantage of various stopovers en route. Once across the Channel (see p.24), the most direct **route** to Budapest is from Ostend, travelling via Brussels, Aachen, Cologne, Frankfurt, Nürnberg, Linz and Vienna. It can be covered in 24 hours, but you should really allow a couple of days in case you meet delays. Detailed printouts of the route can be obtained from the Michelin website (ⓦ www.viamichelin.com).

Note that it is compulsory to buy a motorway sticker (*matrica*) if you are driving on Hungarian motorways (see p.27) – you can do so online ahead of travelling, or at one of the petrol stations in Austria shortly before the border, which should reduce any waiting. See p.26 for details about driving within Hungary.

Airlines, agents and operators

Airlines

Aer Lingus ⓦ www.aerlingus.com.
Air France ⓦ www.airfrance.com.
Air New Zealand ⓦ www.airnz.co.nz.
British Airways ⓦ www.ba.com.
Delta ⓦ www.delta.com.
easyJet ⓦ www.easyjet.com.
Jet2 ⓦ www.jet2.com.
KLM (Royal Dutch Airlines) ⓦ www.klm.com.
Lufthansa ⓦ www.lufthansa.com.
Malév Hungarian Airlines ⓦ www.malev.hu.
Qantas Airways ⓦ www.qantas.com.
Ryanair ⓦ www.ryanair.com.
South African Airways ⓦ www.flysaa.com.
Wizz Air ⓦ www.wizzair.com.

Agents and operators

General operators

North South Travel UK ☎ 01245/608 291, ⓦ www.northsouthtravel.co.uk. Friendly, competitive travel agency, offering discounted fares worldwide. Profits are used to support projects in the developing world, especially the promotion of sustainable tourism.
STA Travel US ☎ 1-800/781-4040, UK ☎ 0871/2300 040, Australia ☎ 134 782, New Zealand ☎ 0800/474 400, South Africa ☎ 0861/781 781; ⓦ www.statravel.com. Worldwide specialists in independent travel; also student IDs, travel insurance,

car rental, rail passes, and more. Good discounts for students and under-26s.
Trailfinders UK ☎ 0845/058 5858, Republic of Ireland ☎ 01/677 7888, Australia ☎ 1300/780 212; ⓦ www.trailfinders.com. One of the best-informed and most efficient agents for independent travellers.

Specialist operators

Adventures Abroad US ☎ 1-800/665-3998 or 604/303-1099, ⓦ www.adventures-abroad .com. Adventure specialist offering Budapest and countrywide tours but mostly longer, multi-country and multi-city tours.
Avian Adventures UK ☎ 01384/372 013, ⓦ www .avianadventures.co.uk. Seven-day autumn bird-watching tours in the Bükk and Hortobágy national parks (£1345), and an eleven-day trip combining Slovakia (£1550).
Classic Journeys US ☎ 1-800/200-3887, ⓦ www.classicjourneys.com. Eight-day, two-city tours of Prague and Budapest from US$3595.
Cox & Kings UK ☎ 020/7873 5000, ⓦ www .coxandkings.co.uk. Upmarket cultural trips to Budapest: a four-night break starts at £520, while there's a ten-night trip (from £2345) that also goes to Vienna and Prague; prices include flights, transfers and breakfast.
Danube Travel Australia ☎ 03/9530 0888, ⓦ www.danubetravel.com.au. Regional specialist whose offers include weekly spa packages in Budapest (from A$699 per person including half board and some treatments but not flights).
Eastern Eurotours Australia ☎ 1800 242 353 or 07/5526 2855, ⓦ www.easterneurotours .com.au. Package tours to Budapest and multi-city tours including Vienna and Prague.
Exodus UK ☎ 0870/240 5550, ⓦ www.exodus .co.uk. Range of tours including self-guided cycling trips from Vienna to Budapest (8 days £530/15 days £950), and a fourteen-day multi-country tour with some walking (£1100).
Explore Worldwide UK ☎ 01252/760 000, ⓦ www.explore.co.uk. Ten-day multi-country tours (£1050), including cycling (with spa and vineyard visits) in Hungary, Austria and Slovenia and a walking tour in the Czech Republic and Slovakia – the Hungary leg includes a visit to Budapest and moderate walking in the Northern Uplands.
Great Escapes UK ☎ 0845/330 2084, ⓦ www .greatescapes.co.uk. Good-value Budapest city breaks, starting at £280 for a four-night trip including flights from the UK.
HF Holidays UK ☎ 0845/458 0120, ⓦ www .hfholidays.co.uk. Eight-day cycling tours,

including Vienna to Budapest via Lake Balaton (£670), and a wildlife and spas trip on the Great Plain (£650).

Kirker Holidays UK ☎020/7593 2288, ⓦwww.kirkerholidays.co.uk. Three-night cultural breaks in Budapest in a four-star hotel from £423 per person, including flights from the UK. They can book opera tickets and arrange walking tours of the city.

Martin Randall Travel UK ☎020/8742 3355, ⓦwww.martinrandall.com. Well-respected art, architecture and music tours. Prices for a seven-day trip are from around £1500, which includes flights from the UK, hotels, transfers, excursions, concert tickets and some meals.

Naturetrek UK ☎01962/733051, ⓦwww.naturetrek.co.uk. Eight-day natural history tours (£1100 upwards) from this well-regarded operator, including various seasonal bird-watching trips in the Bükk and Hortobágy national parks, and a butterfly holiday in northeastern Hungary.

Osprey City Holidays UK ☎0845/310 3031, ⓦwww.ospreyholidays.com. Two-night Budapest city breaks in one of three excellent and central hotels from £240 per person, including travel from London Heathrow.

Ramblers Holidays UK ☎01707/331 133, ⓦwww.ramblersholidays.co.uk. Eight-day moderate-difficulty walking tour (£800) of the Bükk hills in the Northern Uplands, which also includes three nights in Budapest.

Regent Holidays UK ☎0117/921 1711, ⓦwww.regent-holidays.co.uk. Long-established Eastern European specialist offering three-night Budapest city breaks (from £292 including flights) and tailor-made itineraries.

Thermalia Travel UK ☎0870/165 9420, ⓦwww.thermalia.co.uk. Spa holiday specialist offering weekend stays and longer at four-star thermal resorts in Budapest and Héviz, centred around health and fitness. A range of packages.

Vamos Travel UK ☎0870/762 4017, ⓦwww.vamostravel.com. Excellent small company offering a wide range of possibilities, including three-night Budapest city breaks, opera and ballet packages, and stag weekends.

Rail contacts

Deutsche Bahn ⓦwww.bahn.de. The German national rail website is the best source of international timetabling information.

European Rail UK ☎020/7619 1083, ⓦwww.europeanrail.com. Independent specialist offering a range of European rail tickets, including InterRail.

Europrail International Canada ☎1-888-667-9734, ⓦwww.europrail.net. Eurail and country passes.

Eurostar UK ☎0870/518 6186, outside UK ☎+44/1233 617 575; ⓦwww.eurostar.com. High-speed train links from London St Pancras to Paris, Lille and Brussels.

The Man in Seat Sixty-One ⓦwww.seat61.com. Excellent website detailing routes, timings and fares across Europe.

Rail Europe UK ☎0844/848 4064, ⓦwww.raileurope.co.uk; US ☎1-888-382-7245, Canada ☎1-800-361-7245, ⓦwww.raileurope.com; Australia ☎03/9642 8644, ⓦwww.raileurope.com.au; New Zealand ☎09/377 5415; South Africa ☎011/628 2319, ⓦwww.raileurope.co.za. Wide range of European passes, including InterRail, and Eurostar tickets.

Bus contacts

Eurolines UK ☎0871/781 8181, ⓦwww.nationalexpress.com/eurolines.

Ferry and Channel Tunnel contacts

Eurotunnel UK ☎0870/535 3535, ⓦwww.eurotunnel.com. Drive-on, drive-off shuttle trains for vehicles from Folkestone to Coquelles, near Calais.

Norfolkline UK ☎0870/870 1020, ⓦwww.norfolkline.com. Dover to Dunkerque

P&O Ferries UK ☎0871/664 5645, ⓦwww.poferries.com. Dover to Calais.

Sea France UK ☎0871/663 2546, ⓦwww.seafrance.com. Dover to Calais.

SpeedFerries UK ☎0871/222 7456, ⓦwww.speedferries.com. Dover to Boulogne.

Stena Line UK ☎0870/570 7070, ⓦwww.stenaline.co.uk. Harwich to Hook of Holland.

Getting around

Although it doesn't break any speed records, public transport in Hungary is, on the whole, clean, cheap and reliable – most towns are easily reached by train, whilst there's a similarly comprehensive bus network. The country's predominantly flat landscape makes both driving and cycling highly appealing propositions, enabling you to visit anywhere you please, and in your own time.

By rail

The centralization of the **MÁV** rail network means that many cross-country journeys are easier if you travel via Budapest rather than on branch lines where services are slower and less frequent. **Timetables** displayed in stations are in yellow (for departures) or white (for arrivals), with the different types of fast trains picked out in red. By far the fastest are the **InterCity** ("IC" on the timetable) trains, which run express services between Budapest and all the larger towns; don't be misled by **Express** trains (marked "Ex" on timetables) – although they stop at major centres only, and cost ten percent more than *gyorsvonat* and *sebesvonat* services, which stop more regularly, they are still pretty slow. The slowest trains (*személyvonat*) halt at every hamlet along the way, and since the fare is the same as on a *gyorsvonat*, you might as well opt for the latter. It's not worth using inter-national trains for journeys within Hungary, since they are expensive and not always faster.

Most trains have first- and second-class sections, and many also feature a buffet car (indicated on timetables). **Second-class** trains have PVC seats and can be uncomfortable and crowded. **First class** offers slightly more comfort. International services routed through Budapest have **sleeping cars** (*hálókocsi*) and **couchettes** (*kusett*), for which tickets can be bought at MÁV offices in advance, or sometimes on the train itself. **Bicycles** (*bicikli*) can be carried on most passenger trains (you have to buy a separate bicycle ticket, which is around 25 percent of the full ticket price); look for the bicycle pictogram on the timetable. Some trains have special carriages with stands for bikes; otherwise, you must go to the first or last carriage.

If you're planning to travel extensively by rail, it's worth investing in the chunky **timetable** (*Hivatalos Menetrend*; 850Ft; note that the larger format version has no extra information), which also has details of the

---

Hungarian transport terms

Finding out travel information (*információ*) can be your biggest problem, since transport staff rarely speak anything but Hungarian, which is also the only language used for notices and announcements (except around Lake Balaton, where German is widely spoken). The following should be useful for **deciphering timetables**. *Érkezőjáratok* (or *érkezés*) means "**arrivals**", and *induló járatok* (or *indulás*) "**departures**".

Trains or buses **to** (*hova*) a particular destination leave from a designated **platform** (for example *vágány 1*) or **bus stand** (*kocsiállás*); and the point of arrival for services **from** (*honnan*) a place may also be indicated.

Some services run (*közlekedik*, *köz.* for short) *munkaszüneti napok kivételével naponta köz* – **daily, except on holidays**, meaning Sunday and public holidays; *munkanapkon* (*hetfőtől-péntekig*) *köz* – **weekdays, Monday to Friday**; *munkaszüneti napokon köz* – **on holidays**; or *09.30-tól délig vasárnap köz* – **on Sunday 9.30am–noon**. *Átszállás* means "**change**"; *át* "**via**"; and *kivételével* "**except**".

narrow-gauge lines. It is available from the MÁV office in Budapest at VI, Andrássy út 35 (☎1/322-8082) and most of the larger train stations. You can also check train information, in English, on ⓦwww.elvira.hu.

Tickets

Tickets (*jegy*) for domestic train services can be bought at the station (*pályaudvar* or *vasútállomás*) on the day of departure, although it's possible to reserve them up to sixty days in advance. You can break your journey once between the point of departure and the final destination, but must get your ticket validated within an hour of arrival at the interim station. **Fares** are calculated by distance travelled, although the type of train involved will also be reflected in the price; to give you some idea, a journey of 100km, travelling second class on an Express train, will cost around 1600Ft (a return is exactly double); the same journey travelling first class will cost around 2000Ft. A **one-way ticket** is *egy útra*, and a **return**, *retur* or *oda-vissza*. If you're found travelling without a ticket you will incur a **fine** of 2000Ft, on top of the fare itself.

Seat bookings (*helyjegy*), in the form of a separate numbered bit of card, are obligatory for services marked ® on timetables (mostly international or Express trains), and optional on those designated by an R. It is advisable to book a seat on InterCity trains, especially those going to Lake Balaton in the summer, but otherwise it is not necessary. Bookings can be made up to two months in advance at any MÁV office. It's best to buy tickets for **international trains** (*nemzetközi gyorsvonat*) at least 36 hours in advance, since demand can be high. The central MÁV ticket office in Budapest, which handles bookings, gets very crowded during summer so be prepared for a long wait.

Concessionary fares on domestic services are available for children under 6 (free) if they don't occupy a separate seat, and for children aged between 6 and 14 (50-percent discount).

By bus

Buses from Budapest are generally comfortable, though the stock in the rest of the country can be quite ropey. Regional **Volán**

companies run the bulk of Hungary's **buses**, which are called *busz* (pronounced "boose" as in "loose", *not* "bus", which means "fuck" in Hungarian). **Fares** are calculated by distance travelled; to give you some idea, a 100km trip costs around 1400Ft. Schedules are clearly displayed in bus stations (*autóbuszállomás* or *autóbusz pályaudvar*) in every Hungarian town. Arrive early to confirm the departure bay (*kocsiállás*) and to be sure of getting a seat. For long-distance services originating in Budapest or major towns, you can buy tickets with a seat booking up to half an hour before departure; after that you get them from the driver, but you risk standing throughout the journey. You can also reserve seats up to sixty days in advance at the station. Services in **rural areas** may be limited to one or two a day, and tickets are only available on board the bus. As on trains, children under 6 travel free unless they occupy a separate seat, and there is a 33-percent discount for children up to the age of 10; otherwise there are no concessions.

By boat

Between April and October the Mahart company (ⓦwww.mahartpassnave.hu) operates domestic and international **passenger boats** on the section of the Danube running through the capital, between Budapest and Esztergom (via Szentendre and Visegrád), while Balaton Shipping (ⓦwww.balatonihajozas.hu) operates ferry services on Lake Balaton (where there is also a car ferry between Szántód and Tihany-rév operating March–Nov).

By car and motorbike

Although road traffic has increased significantly in recent years and many minor roads are still in relatively poor condition, **driving** in Hungary can be both an attractive and hassle-free option. Motorways and dual carriageways are generally in good condition, as are most single-lane roads, although country roads tend to be busy and much less pleasant.

Hungary's roads fall into four categories. Hungary's motorway network, which is still being extended, consists of the M1 to the border with Austria at Hegyeshalom; the M3 to Nyíregyháza in the northeast (branching off the M3 is the M30 to Miskolc and the M35 to Debrecen); the M5 south to Kecskemét and Szeged; and the M7 to Balaton and through to the border with Croatia. The M0 is the ring motorway around the capital, of which the stretch between the M1 and the M3 is complete. To travel on all the motorways (except the M0) you will need to purchase a **vignette** (*Matrica*), available from most petrol stations and currently costing 1530Ft for four days, 2550Ft for ten days and 4200Ft for a month. A system of mobile patrols and electronic number-plate readers enforces the scheme, and there are steep fines for those travelling on a motorway without a vignette. Some, but not all, rental-car companies provide one, so check first.

Lesser **highways** (numbered with a single digit from one to eight) radiate from Budapest like spokes in a wheel, linked by **secondary roads** identified by two or three digits (the first one indicates the highway which the road joins; for example, roads 82 and 811 both meet Route 8 at some point). Lastly, there are unnumbered, bumpy **back-country roads**, which tourists seldom use. **Pedestrian zones** (found in many towns and shaded light blue on maps) are indicated by "Restricted Access" signs – *kivéve célforgalom*.

More generally, Hungarian driving habits often leave much to be desired, a particular danger being the tendency to overtake at absurdly dangerous moments. **Pedestrians**, meanwhile, should never assume that a car will stop for them on a pedestrian crossing; drivers in Hungary will often do anything to avoid having to slow down and make way for pedestrians, swerving around them instead or screeching to a sudden halt. The usual precautions apply when it comes to the potential for theft: never leave valuables inside the car and always lock it, even if you're just popping into a shop for five minutes.

Petrol stations (*benzinkút*), many of which are now open 24 hours, can be found everywhere, even in the most rural backwaters – expect to pay around 250Ft per litre of unleaded (*olómmentes benzin*). Typical **parking** costs are around 120Ft for one hour, though in Budapest and in some of the

resorts around Balaton you can expect to pay double this amount. Information on nationwide **driving conditions**, albeit in Hungarian or German only, can be obtained from ÚTINFORM (☏1/322-7643); conditions in Budapest are monitored by FŐVINFORM (☏1/317-1173).

Rules and regulations

Speed limits for vehicles are 130kph on motorways, 110kph on highways, 90kph on other roads and 50kph in built-up areas. The most important **rules** are the prohibitions against repeatedly switching from lane to lane on highways, using a hand-held mobile phone whilst driving, and sounding the horn in built-up areas unless to avert an accident. It is also compulsory for driver and passengers to wear seatbelts, to use dipped headlights during the day when driving outside built-up areas, and to keep a triangular breakdown sign, spare bulbs and a first-aid box in the car. Children under the age of 12 are forbidden to travel in the front seat. At crossroads, vehicles coming from the right have right of way, unless otherwise indicated by signs, and pedestrians have priority over cars turning onto the road. Remember that trams *always* have right of way, and that some traffic islands serve as bus or tram stops. On highways and secondary roads it's illegal to reverse, make U-turns, or stop at islands. **Drinking and driving** is totally prohibited. The police are no longer empowered to levy on-the-spot fines, so should you find yourself in receipt of a penalty, this must be paid at the post office.

Accidents should be reported to the Hungária Biztosító international motoring department at Budapest XI, Hamzsabégi út 60 (☏1/466-8800; Mon–Fri 8am–4pm) within 24 hours; if someone is injured the police must also be notified (☏107). For breakdowns call the Autóklub Segélyhívó **24-hour breakdown service** (☏188) anywhere in the country, run by the **Hungarian Automobile Club** (Magyar Autóklub or MAK).

Car rental

Renting a car is easy provided you're 21 or older, and hold a valid national driving licence. You can order a car through rental agencies in your own country, which sometimes works out cheaper, particularly if you book online. Most of the major companies have an outlet in Budapest (see "Listings" in the Budapest chapter), including the airport, as well as in some of the major cities.

Car rental **costs** are not particularly cheap; expect to pay around €45–50 upwards for a day (unlimited mileage), the rate decreasing the longer the rental period. There's little difference in price amongst the major companies, but you might find that local companies offer better deals. Credit cards are usually required for a deposit. Before signing, check on any mileage limits or other restrictions or extras, as well as what you're covered for in the event of an accident. You may be able to take the car into neighbouring countries, although most companies charge extra for this.

Car-rental agencies

Alamo ⓦ www.alamo.com.
Apex ⓦ www.apexrentals.co.nz.
Auto Europe ⓦ www.autoeurope.com.
Avis ⓦ www.avis.com.
Budget ⓦ www.budget.com.
Dollar ⓦ www.dollar.com.
Enterprise Rent-a-Car ⓦ www.enterprise.com.
Europcar ⓦ www.europcar.com.
Europe by Car ⓦ www.europebycar.com.
Hertz ⓦ www.hertz.com.
Holiday Autos ⓦ www.holidayautos.co.uk (part of the LastMinute.com group).
Irish Car Rentals ⓦ www.irishcarrentals.ie.
National ⓦ www.nationalcar.com.
SIXT ⓦ www.sixt.com.
Thrifty ⓦ www.thrifty.com.

Hitchhiking

Hitchhiking (*autostop*) is widely practised by young Magyars, and is considered pretty safe. However, as anywhere, it's a potentially risky business and if you do decide to travel this way, you should take all sensible precautions.

Cycling

Given the generally flat terrain, and the light winds and low rainfall from July until the end of September, **cycling** is a good way to get around Hungary. There's a growing number of cycle paths in the country, indicating an increasing awareness of the cycling community. However, there are several caveats for cyclists: they are not allowed on main roads (with single-digit numbers) or on some secondary roads in "peak hours" (7–9.30am and 4–6pm). In towns, there are sunken tramlines and slippery cobbled streets to contend with.

There is a series of very enjoyable touring routes, ranging from the serene calm of Lake Balaton to the more rugged and demanding Bükk Hills, which is more suited to mountain-bikers. However, the 290-kilometre route along Hungary's western border, from Lake Fertő in the north down to the Őrség region, is regarded as one of the most scenic and varied. Generally speaking, May and September – when the weather is at its most appealing and the roads are free from the tourist hordes – are the ideal cycling months.

If you wish to transport your bike by train, look out for the bicycle or luggage symbols in the timetable; you'll have to pay a small charge. See p.38 for more cycling information.

Accommodation

The variety and quality of places to stay in Hungary have increased radically in recent years. Hotels aside, competitively priced pensions and guesthouses are widely available, while, for those with less cash to spend, there are enough private rooms, hostels and, in summer, college dormitories to go around, and many towns have reasonably central campsites. All in all, it shouldn't prove difficult to find somewhere that suits your tastes and budget. Reservations for all types of accommodation are advisable during high season (June–Aug), but particularly if you're on a tight budget or bound for somewhere with limited possibilities.

Hotels and pensions

Hungarian **hotels** (*szálló* or *szállóda*) are classified according to a **five-star grading system**, although this gives only a vague idea of prices, which can vary dramatically according to the locality and the time of year. Moreover, the ratings are not always the best guide to standards, as some places officially meet the basic criteria in terms of facilities, but are in fact poor. Prices in Budapest and the Balaton region are on average around 15–25 percent higher than in other areas, though rates can drop by as much as thirty percent in those hotels on Balaton that open over the **winter**. **Breakfast** is usually, but not always, included in the price.

Budapest now has a range of hotels to match just about any major city in Europe, and it's here that you'll find the vast majority of the country's five-star establishments. These invariably possess all the facilities you'd expect from a luxury hotel, whilst four-star establishments don't lag too far behind in the ultra-comforts stakes, boasting immaculately appointed, often beautifully furnished, rooms with satellite TV and internet access (in many cases wi-fi), and pristine bathrooms. Many also house a swimming pool, fitness suite, sauna and other leisure facilities. You'll certainly find these latter facilities as standard in the growing number of spa and wellness hotels opening up around the country. Three-star places are, generally speaking, reliable with perfectly adequate facilities, though, compared to some of the pensions about, many do not represent decent value for money. Further down the ladder, you're in hit-or-miss territory when it comes to two-star hotels, whilst you're definitely better off forsaking a one-star (which are now few and far between) for private accommodation or a hostel/dormitory. Single rooms are more difficult to come by, particularly in high season, and **solo travellers** are likely to end up paying for a double.

Private (often family-owned) **pensions** are appearing in ever greater numbers in towns

Accommodation price codes

Accommodation in this guide is graded according to the price bands given below. Note that prices refer to the **cheapest available double room in high season**. Out of season rates can fall by as much as thirty percent. For dormitories in hostels, the price per bed has been given. Note that many places now post current room rates in euros, even though you pay in forints.

❶ €15/4000Ft and under
❷ €16–25/4001–6500Ft
❸ €26–35/6501–9000Ft
❹ €36–45/9001–11,500Ft
❺ €46–55/11,501–14,500Ft
❻ €56–70/14,501–18,500Ft
❼ €71–85/18,501–22,500Ft
❽ €86–100/22,501–26,000Ft
❾ €101/26,001Ft and over

and villages throughout Hungary, where they often undercut hotels with the same star rating. While some are purpose-built, with a restaurant on the premises, others are simply someone's house with a TV in the living room and a few rooms upstairs. There's no correlation between their appearance and title – some style themselves *panzió* (or *penzió*), others as *fogadó*. Some pensions coexist with bungalows and a campsite to form a tourist complex, and quite a few are near a thermal bath or swimming pool, with restaurants and sports facilities, too.

Private rooms

Hostels aside, taking a **private room** (termed *Fiz*, short for *fizetővendégszolgálat*) is often the cheapest option available, particularly if two of you are sharing; expect to pay around 4000Ft/€15 for a double room and 3000Ft/€12 for a single, though, as with hotels, prices are rather inflated in Budapest and around Lake Balaton. The common practice is to charge thirty percent extra if you stay fewer than three nights, while a general lack of single rooms means that **solo travellers** often have to pay for the price of a double. Many Tourinform offices have good listings of private accommodation, and they can often advise on places, though they do not usually book them. This can usually be arranged by local tourist agencies such as Balatontourist, or simply by knocking on the door of places displaying *szoba kiadó* or *Zimmer frei* signs, which abound along the west bank of the Danube Bend, both shores of Lake Balaton, and in thermal spas throughout Hungary.

As a rule of thumb, a town's Belváros (inner sector) is likely to hold spacious apartments with parquet floors, high ceilings and a balcony overlooking a courtyard, whereas in the outlying zones you'll probably be housed in a charmless, high-rise modern development. Some, though not many, places may also offer **breakfast**, though this is not usually included in the price. By offering a small amount of money, you may also be able to use the washing machine. It's also possible to rent whole **apartments** in some towns

and resorts, also bookable through the same agencies.

Village homestays

Village tourism (*falusi turizmus*) – farmhouse-style accommodation in villages – is a thriving sector in Hungary, and something many smaller villages are being encouraged to partake in. Currently, the most popular areas for village tourism are in the Northern Uplands and the Őrség and Tisza regions. While the scheme offers the opportunity to stay and socialize with a Hungarian family, the downside is that the majority of places are in extremely remote areas and, unless you have your own transport, often very difficult to reach. Accommodation is **graded** according to a sunflower classification system; four sunflowers, the highest grade, denotes a house where rooms have private bathroom or shower/toilet. The majority of places, however, offer shared bathrooms and toilets, either with other guests and/or the hosts. Expect to **pay** around 4000–5200Ft/€15–20 for a double bed per night; meals are not usually included in the price but many households are willing to cook a meal on request. Tourinform and local tourist agencies can provide details, or you can contact the **Hungarian Federation of Rural Tourism** in Budapest at Király utca 93 (☎1/352 -9804, ✉agroturizmus@t-online.hu), which produces a brochure listing all homestay accommodation in the country.

Hostels and dormitories

Hungary has a good range of **youth hostels** (*Ifjúsági Szálló*), though these are largely the preserve of Budapest and the larger towns and cities; rural ones are still pretty thin on the ground. You can expect to pay around 2600–4000Ft/€10–15 for a dorm bed in Budapest, slightly less elsewhere. Some are official IYHF hostels, for which you'll need a membership card issued by the national hostel organization in your own country (see opposite), though, in practice, many hostels in Hungary don't insist on one. Many hostels, including all of those in Budapest, are open year round, and **reservations** for any hostel in the country can be made through the

Hungarian Youth Hostels Association Travel Section (ⓦ www.youthhostels.hu), which also produces a handbook listing all hostels around the country.

There are two other kinds of official **tourist hostels**: *túristaszálló*, generally found in provincial towns, and *túristaház*, located in highland areas favoured by hikers. Both are graded "A" or "B" depending on the availability of hot water and the number of beds per room. *Túristaszálló* rates range from 1600Ft/€6 to 3000Ft/€12 – the former for a bed, the latter for a double or triple room. In *túristaház*, which rarely have separate rooms, a dormitory bed goes for 1300–2000Ft/€5–8. It's generally advisable to check first with the local Tourinform office regarding availability.

In many towns, you can also stay in vacant college **dormitories** for about 2600Ft/€10 a night. Generally, these accept tourists over the whole of the summer vacation (typically July & Aug) and in some cases at weekends throughout the year. You're best off checking with Tourinform first, but otherwise you can just turn up at the designated college (*kollégium*) and ask if there are any beds available.

Youth Hostel Associations

UK and Ireland

Youth Hostel Association (YHA) UK ☎01629/592 700, ⓦ www.yha.org.uk.
Scottish Youth Hostel Association ☎0870/155 3255, ⓦ www.syha.org.uk.
Irish Youth Hostel Association ☎01/830 4555, ⓦ www.anoige.ie.
Hostelling International Northern Ireland ☎028/9032 4733, ⓦ www.hini.org.uk.

US and Canada

Hostelling International–American Youth Hostels US ☎1-301/495-1240, ⓦ www.hiusa.org.
Hostelling International Canada ☎1-800/663-5777, ⓦ www.hihostels.ca.

Australia, New Zealand and South Africa

Australia Youth Hostels Association ☎02/9281 9444, ⓦ www.yha.com.au.
Youth Hostelling Association New Zealand ☎0800/278 299 or 03/379 9970, ⓦ www.yha .co.nz.

Campsites and chalets

There's a good spread of **campsites** (*kemping*) throughout Hungary, with by far the greatest concentration around Lake Balaton. These range across the spectrum of "de luxe" to third class. The better places usually have an on-site restaurant and shops, whilst quite a few boast sporting facilities such as a swimming pool and tennis courts; second- or third-class sites often have a nicer ambience, with lots of old trees rather than a manicured lawn and acres of campers and trailers. Expect to pay around 800Ft/€3 per person per night (twice that around Lake Balaton during the summer), plus a basic ground-rent fee, and an extra charge for a vehicle. There are **reductions** of 25–30 percent during "low" season (Oct–May), and during the high season for those with an international camping carnet (see below). Children up to the age of 14 also qualify for fifty-percent reductions. The majority of sites are open from April or May to September or October, with a few open all year round; it's advisable to ring ahead at the more popular sites, particularly those around Balaton. While a few resorts and towns have semi-official **free campsites** (*szabad kemping*), **camping rough** is illegal, although young Hungarians sometimes do it in highland areas where there are "rain shelters" (*esőház*).

If you're planning to do a lot of camping, an **international camping carnet** is a good investment. The carnet gives discounts at member sites and serves as useful identification. Many campsites will take it instead of making you surrender your passport during your stay, and it covers you for third-party insurance when camping. In the **UK and Ireland**, the carnet is available to members of the AA or the RAC, or to members of the **Camping and Caravanning Club** (☎024/7669 4995, ⓦ www .campingandcaravanningclub.co.uk), the **CTC** (☎0870/873 0061, ⓦ www.ctc .org.uk), or the foreign touring arm of the same company, the **Carefree Travel Service** (☎024/7642 2024), which provides the carnet free if you take out insurance with them. In the **US and Canada**, the carnet is available from home motoring organizations, or from **Family Campers and RVers** (FCRV;

☎1-800/245-9755 or ☎716/668-6242, ⓦwww.fcrv.org).

Rates for renting **chalets** (also called bungalows) or *faház*, literally "wooden houses", vary hugely according to amenities and size (they usually sleep 2–4 people), whilst rates are often doubled in July and August around Balaton. The first-class chalets – with well-equipped kitchens, hot water and a sitting room or terrace – are excellent, while the most primitive at least have clean bedding and don't leak. An

alternative source of accommodation is **holiday homes** or **workers' hostels** (*üdülőház*), which proliferate around resorts. Traditionally, these buildings were reserved for trade-union members, and even today many still reserve a large proportion of their rooms for workers. Standards are similar to those of a two-star hotel, though they can vary from the grim to the respectable; some operate as fully functioning hotels, some have just a handful of rooms available, whilst others do not accept tourists at all.

Food and drink

Even under Communism, Hungary was renowned for its abundance of food: material proof of the "goulash socialism" that amazed visitors from Romania and the Soviet Union. Nowadays, there is more choice than ever, particularly in Budapest, where first-class restaurants abound and almost every world cuisine is available.

For foreigners the archetypal Magyar dish is "goulash" – historically the basis of much **Hungarian cooking**. The ancient Magyars relished cauldrons of *gulyás* (pronounced "gou-yash"), a soup made of potatoes and whatever meat was available, which was later flavoured with paprika and beefed up into a variety of stews, modified over the centuries by various foreign influences. Hungary's Slav neighbours probably introduced native cooks to yogurt and sour cream – vital ingredients in many dishes – while the influence of the Turks, Austrians and Germans is apparent in a variety of sticky pastries and strudels, as well as recipes featuring sauerkraut or dumplings. Another influence was that of France, which revolutionized Hungarian cooking in the Middle Ages and again in the nineteenth century. For a **glossary** of food and drink terms see p.469.

Breakfast, snacks and sandwiches

As a nation of early risers, Hungarians like to have a calorific **breakfast** (*reggeli*).

Commonly, this includes cheese, eggs or salami together with bread and jam, and in rural areas is often accompanied by a shot of *pálinka* (brandy) to "clear the palate" or "aid digestion".

A whole range of places purveys **snacks**, notably *csemege* or **delicatessens**, which display a tempting spread of salads, open sandwiches, pickles and cold meats; in a few, you can eat on the premises. For other sit-down nibbles, people patronize either *bisztró*, which tend to offer a couple of hot dishes besides the inevitable salami rolls; *snackbár*, which are superior versions of the same, with leanings in the direction of being a patisserie; or *büfé*. These last are found in department stores and stations, and are sometimes open around the clock. The food on offer, though, is often limited to sausages – including those comprising parts of the lung or liver (*hurka*), and the greasier version filled with rice (*kolbász*).

On the streets, according to season, vendors preside over tables of *kukorica* (corn on the cob) or trays of *gesztenye* (roasted chestnuts). Fried-fish (*sült hal*) shops are common in towns near rivers or lakes. *Szendvics* (sandwich), *hamburger* and *gofri* (waffle) stands are mushrooming in many towns, as are Chinese fast-food and Turkish kebab joints, which offer further cheap alternatives. Another popular munch is *lángos*: the native, mega-size equivalent of doughnuts, often sold with a sprinkling of cheese and soured cream. For fresh fruit and produce, head to the local outdoor **market** (*piac*) or market hall (*vásárcsarnok*), where people select their fish fresh from glass tanks, and their mushrooms from a staggering array of *gomba*, which are displayed alongside toxic fungi in a "mushroom parade" to enable shoppers to recognize the difference.

No list of snacks is complete without mentioning **bread** (*kenyér*), which is so popular that "Hungarians will even eat bread with bread", as the old saying has it. White bread remains the staple of the nation, but in many supermarkets, especially in Budapest, you can usually get a range of brown (*barna*) and rye (*rozs*) breads.

Restaurants and meals

Hungarians have a variety of words for their finely distinguished **restaurants**. In theory an **étterem** is a proper restaurant, while a **vendéglő** approximates to the Western notion of a bistro, though in practice the terms are often used interchangeably. The old word for an inn, **csárda**, now applies to posh places specializing in certain dishes (for example, a "Fishermen's inn", or *halászcsárda*, serves fish), restaurants alongside roads or with rustic pretensions, as well as to the humbler rural establishments that the name originally signified.

Traditionally, Hungarians take their main meal at **lunchtime**, although the old

tendency for restaurants to have fewer dishes available in the evenings has now disappeared.

You'll find many restaurants, at least those in the more touristy areas, with bands of musicians playing at lunchtime and in the evening, their violin airs and melodic plonkings of the cimbalom (see p.458) an essential element of the "scene". While some restaurants offer a bargain set menu (*napi menü*) of basic dishes, the majority of places are strictly à la carte. You'll probably be asked if you want a **starter** (*előételek*) – generally a soup or salad, though nobody will mind if you just have one of the dishes offered as the **main course** (*főételek*) or, alternatively, order just a soup and a starter. Bread is supplied almost automatically, on the grounds that "a meal without bread is no meal". **Drinks** are normally listed on the menu under the heading *italok*. For a two-course meal with wine, expect to pay around 2500–4000Ft/€10–15 in an average restaurant, twice that in downtown Budapest.

Most places have **menus** in German, and increasingly, English, a language of which most waiters and waitresses have a smattering. However, look out for those places that give you a menu without prices, a sure sign that they're expensive, or plan to rip you off – get the waiter to bring you a menu with the prices listed, or leave. A service charge is rarely included in the bill (but do check carefully) and so the staff depend on customers **tipping** – ten percent of the total is customary, if you think it's merited. **Overcharging** is not uncommon, so again, check that bill assiduously. Be warned that if you say "thank you" as you hand the money over, this implies that they can keep the change.

Opening times

It's difficult to generalize, but as a rule **restaurants** are open from around 11am until 11pm. However, it is worth remembering that many places still close early, around 10pm, especially outside the capital.

Cafés are a bit less straightforward: patisserie-type places generally operate from 9/10am to 6/7pm, but many cafés double up as bars so close at 10 or 11pm, while others stay open until 1/2am. In listings we indicate places that are not open on a certain day and/or close particularly early, say 4/5pm in the afternoon.

Unfortunately, standards of service still leave much to be desired, even in many Budapest restaurants, with a certain lethargy afflicting many waiting staff.

Vegetarian food

Despite the emergence of *vegetarianus* restaurants in Budapest, and a growing understanding of the concept, **vegetarians** are still poorly catered for. Although an increasing number of restaurants offer vegetarian dishes, many of these are depressingly predictable, and it's only in the more upmarket places that the choices become anything like tempting. You can find yourself on a diet of vegetables or cheese fried in breadcrumbs; these are known as *rántott gomba* (mushrooms), *rántott karfiol* (cauliflower), or *rántott sajt* (cheese), and – if you are lucky – *padlizsán* (aubergine), *zukkini* (courgette), or *tök* (pumpkin). *Gomba paprikás* (mushroom paprika stew) is also OK if it is cooked in oil rather than in fat. Alternatively, there are eggs – fried (literally "mirror" – *tükörtojás*), soft-boiled (*lágy tojás*), scrambled (*tojásrántotta*), or in mayonnaise (*kaszínótojás*) – or salads, though in winter these are often of the pickled vegetable variety. Even innocuous vegetable soups may contain meat stock, and the pervasive use of sour cream and animal fat in cooking means that avoiding animal products or by-products is difficult. However, greengrocers (*zöldségbolt*) and markets sell excellent produce which, combined with judicious shopping in supermarkets (for pulses, grains, etc), should see you through.

Coffee houses and patisseries

Many Hungarians like to kick-start the day with **coffee**, followed by further intakes at various intervals throughout the day, usually in the form of tiny glasses of *kávé*: super-strong, served black and sweetened to taste, this is a brew that can double your heartbeat. **Coffee houses** were once the centres of Budapest's cultural and political life – hotbeds of gossip where penurious writers got credit and the clientele dawdled for hours over the free newspapers. Sadly this is no longer the case, but you'll find plenty of unpretentious *kávéház* serving the

beverage with milk (*tejeskávé*) or whipped cream (*tejszínhabbal*), should you request it. Ordering a cappuccino can be a very hit-or-miss affair as they vary dramatically in quality wherever you go, with the worst efforts consisting of little more than a regular coffee with a dollop of whipped cream unattractively slumped on top.

Tea-drinkers are in a minority here, perhaps because Hungarian **tea** with milk (*tejes tea*) is so insipid, although *tea citrommal* (with lemon) is pleasantly refreshing. However, there are a growing number of **teahouses** (*teaház*) about, serving a terrific range of teas from around the world, as well as all manner of other beverages.

Most coffee houses have some pastries on offer, although you'll find much more choice in the **patisseries** (*cukrászda*), which pander to the Magyar fondness for sweet things. **Pancakes** (*palacsinta*) **with fillings** – *almás* (apple), *diós* (walnuts), *fahéjas* (cinnamon), *mákos* (poppy seeds), *mandulás* (almonds) or *Gundel*-style, with nuts, chocolate sauce, cream and raisins – are very popular, as are strudels (*rétes*) made with curds and dill (*kapros túrós rétes*), poppy seeds (*mákos-rétes*) or plums (*szilvás rétes*). Even the humble dumpling is transformed into a *somlói galuska*, flavoured with vanilla, nuts and chocolate. But the frontrunners in the rich and sticky stakes have to be chestnut purée with whipped cream (*gesztenyepüré*); coffee soufflé (*kapucineres felfújt*); baked apple with vanilla, raisins and cream (*töltött alma*); and the staggering array of **cakes**. The average **cukrászda** displays a dozen or more types, including *dobostorta* (chocolate cream cake topped with caramel) and the pineapple-laden *ananásztorta*.

If you're still not satiated, there's **ice cream** (*fagylalt*), the opium of the masses, sold by the scoop (*gombóc*) and priced low enough that anyone can afford a cone. The most common flavours are *vanília*, *csokoládé*, *puncs* (fruit punch), *citrom* and *kávé*, though mango, pistachio and various nutty flavours can be found too. And finally there's *metélt or tészta* – a rather unlikely-sounding but quite tasty dessert of chopped sweet noodles, served cold with poppy seeds or some other topping.

Drinking

Hungary's climate and diversity of soils are perfect for **wine** (*bor*), though cold winters mean that reds are usually on the light side. In the last few years the wine market has really begun to take off, and, though good vintages are still cheap by Western standards, prices are rising steadily. In bars and most restaurants you can either buy it by the bottle (*üveg*) or the glass (*pohár*). There are 22 wine-growing regions in the country, the best of which are Villány, Eger, Tokaj, Szekszárd and the Balaton. They even manage to grow grapes on the sandy soils around Kecskemét, at the edge of the Great Plain, but the wines from there are of poorer quality. Overall, though, standards are constantly rising as more vineyards try to win the right to label their bottles *minöségi bor* (quality wine), the equivalent of *appellation contrôlée*.

Wine bars (*borozó*) are ubiquitous and far less pretentious than in the West: the wine served is often pretty rough stuff, and there's usually a cluster of interesting characters round the bar. True devotees of the grape make pilgrimages to the extensive **wine cellars** (*borospince*) that honeycomb towns like Tokaj and Eger. By day, people often drink wine with water or soda water, specifying a *fröccs* or a yet more diluted *hosszú lépés* (literally, a "long step"). Wine can be sweet (*édes*), dry (*száraz*), semi-sweet (*félédes*) or semi-dry (*félszáraz*). Hungarians enjoy the ritual of **toasting**, so the first word to get your tongue around is *egészségedre* (EGG-aish-shaig-edreh) – "cheers!". When toasting more than one other person, it's

grammatically correct to change this to *egészségünkre* ("cheers to us!"). Hungarians only consider it appropriate to toast with wine or spirits. A simpler version that will get you by is *szia* (see-ya) for one person, and *sziasztok* (see-ya-stock) for more people.

As long as you stick to native brands, **spirits** are also cheap. The best-known type of *pálinka* – brandy – is distilled from apricots (*barack*), and is a speciality of the Kecskemét region, but spirits are also produced from peaches (*öszibarack*), pears (*körte*) and any other fruits available. This is particularly true of *szilva* – a lethal spirit produced on cottage stills in rural areas, allegedly based on plums. Hungarians with money to burn order whisky (*viszki*) to impress, but most people find its cost prohibitive.

Bottled **beer** (*sör*) of the lager type (*világos*) predominates, although you might come across brown ale (*barna sör*) and draught beer (*csapolt sör*). Hungarian beer production is almost totally in the hands of the big international breweries. Western brands like Tuborg, HB, Wernesgrünner and Gold Fassel are mostly brewed under licence in Hungary, while you can also find imported Czech brands like Urquell Pilsen and Staropramen. The old Austro-Hungarian beer Dreher has made a comeback in the hands of South African Breweries. Other brands to try are Arany Ászok, a very cheap light beer, and Pannonia Sör, a pleasant hoppy beer from Pécs. **Beer halls** (*söröző*) range from plush establishments sponsored by foreign breweries to humble stand-up joints where you order either a small glass (*pohár*) or a half-litre mug (*korsó*).

Festivals

The Hungarian calendar is replete with marvellous festivals and events, and whilst most of the bigger ones take place in Budapest, you'll find plenty happening throughout the rest of the country too. Naturally enough, most festivals take place over the summer, but if you're visiting any other time, you shouldn't have too much difficulty in tracking down some kind of event; Tourinform can fill you in on what's happening.

A festival calendar

Most Hungarian festivals typically feature a varied programme of classical and contemporary music mixed with art and theatrical performances, but there are many other uniquely "Hungarian" events taking place. **Wine festivals** are an integral and immensely enjoyable part of the festival scene, with each wine-producing centre staging its own celebration at some time during the year (typically between May and Oct); the key ones occur in Balatonboglár, Eger, Kőszeg, Szekszárd and Tokaj. Great fun, too, are the many varied **food festivals** which take place around the country, particularly in towns across the Great Plain such as Baja, Békéscsaba, Makó and Szolnok. **Historical pageants**, such as those at Gyula, Sümeg, Veszprém, and, most notably, Visegrád, are extremely popular, as are the **equestrian shows** with their "rodeo" atmosphere and amazing displays of horsemanship at Hortobágy, Kiskunság, Nagyvázsony and Szántódpuszta.

It is also worth knowing about the tradition of **name-day (névnap) celebrations**, which are as important to Hungarians as birthdays are in other countries. Customarily, the celebrant invites relatives and friends to a party, and receives gifts and salutations. Lest you forget someone's name-day, tradition allows congratulations to be rendered up to a week afterwards. The following festivals are covered in greater detail in their respective chapters.

February

Busójárás Carnival Mohács, end of Feb. Hungary's biggest winter festival sees displays of masked revellers re-enacting ancient

spring rites and ritual abomination of the Turks. See p.368.

March–April

Anniversary of the 1848 Revolution Countrywide, March 15. Wreaths are laid at monuments around the country to commemorate the revolution against the Habsburgs.
Budapest Spring Festival Last two weeks in March. Hungary's largest and most prestigious arts festival is an intensive programme of orchestral and chamber music, jazz, theatre, film and lots more; it's run in conjunction with ten other towns and cities across the country. See p.132.
Hollókő Easter Festival Easter weekend. The locals don their colourful finery to participate in authentic interpretations of old folk music, dancing and handicraft demonstrations, not least the famous painted eggs. See p.328.
Mediawave International Film and Music Festival Győr, last week in April. Superb alternative gathering, at the core of which is an enterprising programme of film, while there's also music, dance and movement theatre, literary events and conferences. See p.251.

May

Gizella Days Veszprém, beginning of May. In honour of the first Hungarian queen, there are concerts, folk-dancing, medieval markets and horse shows in the castle district and elsewhere throughout town. See p.232.
Balaton Festival Keszthely, mid-May. The lake's premier cultural happening is a week-long festival of classical concerts, theatre programmes and art exhibitions, some of which take place down by the lakeside itself. See p.221.

June

Bartók + International Opera Festival Miskolc, mid-June. Prestigious operatic festival featuring the work of Bartók alongside that of a different composer each year. See p.351.

Danube Carnival Budapest, mid-June. Rock and pop concerts, folk and contemporary dance troupes and classical musicians from Hungary and neighbouring countries. At several venues.

Győr Summer Mid-June to mid-July. Long-running festival of music, dance and theatre, some of which takes place on a water stage. See p.251.

Pécs Weeks of Art and Gastronomy Mid-June. A fantastic array of mini-festivals related to art, food and music. See p.302.

Sopron Festival Weeks Mid-June to mid-July. Month-long arts festival in the town's squares and courtyards, plus musical programmes in the nearby Fertőrákos Caves. See p.264.

July

Siófolk International Festival Siófok, first week of July. Folk and dance music featuring dance troupes from all over the world. See p.199.

Fish Soup Festival Baja, second weekend in July. The town's huge main square is taken over by hundreds of bubbling cauldrons containing all manner of soups and casseroles to be devoured over two days. See p.378.

International Palace Games Visegrád, second week of July. Rousing historical pageant with jousting, archery and lots of other medieval shenanigans held within the grounds of the old Royal Palace. See p.161.

Beethoven Nights Martonvásár, July. Outdoor concerts performed by the National Philharmonic Orchestra in the beautiful park of the Brunszvik castle. See p.186.

Gyula Castle Theatre Summer Season July–Aug. Fabulously entertaining programme of performing arts (drama, opera, ballet and puppetry) and music (classical, jazz and folk) taking place in the castle courtyard and on a floating stage on the nearby lake. See p.406.

Szeged Open-Air Festival July–Aug. Hungary's oldest and largest open-air theatre festival is a high-class affair, with music, drama and dance on numerous stages in Szeged's vast main square. See p.401.

Anna Ball Balatonfüred, end of July. Open-air events, cultural programmes and a sparkling ball in the sumptuous Anna Grand hotel to round things off. See p.207.

August

Eger Baroque Festival Beginning of Aug for three weeks. Terrific programme of dance and classical

music, as well as jugglers, craftsmen and stall-keepers lining the streets. See p.341.

Flower Carnival Debrecen, mid-Aug. The only event of its type in Central and Eastern Europe, this vibrant festival culminates in a colourful array of floats in the main square on Aug 20. See p.417.

Máriapócs Aug 15 and Sept 8. Religious pilgrimage in this small village in Eastern Hungary attracting thousands.

St Stephen's Day Countrywide, Aug 20. Honouring the death of Hungary's patron saint and "founding father", with day-long celebrations, the biggest of which is in Budapest with craft fairs, folk dancing, river parades and a spectacular fireworks display to round things off.

Sziget Festival Budapest, mid-Aug. Now firmly established amongst the premier pop and rock festivals in Europe, this marathon six-day bash attracts some of the world's biggest and best artists. See p.132.

Jewish Summer Festival Budapest, last week in Aug. Evenings of classical and Klezmer music, opera, dance, as well as film and literary events in the Dohány utca synagogue, Budapest Jewish Museum and other venues. See p.133.

September

Debrecen Jazz Days Debrecen, end of Sept. The oldest and best jazz festival in the country, with performances by both local and international stars. See p.417.

Goulash Festival Szolnok, first or second weekend of Sept. Hungary's most famous dish is celebrated in this convivial food-fest, which includes cooking competitions, lots of wine, folk dancing and a handicrafts market. See p.410.

Wine-Song Festival Pécs and the Villány-Siklós wine region, last weekend of Sept. One of Europe's premier festivals for male choir and vocal bands, run in conjunction with wine evenings. See p.302.

October

Budapest Autumn Festival Budapest, mid-Oct. Second only to the Spring Festival, this features programmes from the world of contemporary arts, including some excellent film screenings. See p.132.

Kolbasz Sausage Festival Békéscsaba, end of Oct. Another fabulous gastronomic festival, this time celebrating the spicy Csaba sausage, plus lots of wine-tasting for good measure. See p.405.

Sports and outdoor activities

Hungary has a stronger sporting pedigree than most people appreciate, and although the glory days of the national football team are long gone, there have been notable Olympic Games successes in recent years. The most prestigious and high-profile sporting event in the Hungarian calendar is the Formula One Grand Prix in Budapest each August.

Hungarian sport first came to international prominence thanks to its magnificent **football** (*labdarúgás*) team of the 1950s. In particular, it was a 6–3 demolition of England at Wembley in 1953 that alerted the wider footballing world to the marvellous Magyars. Whilst football might still be the nation's favourite sport, standards have declined alarmingly in recent years, with the international team struggling lamely, and unsuccessfully, to qualify for major tournaments and domestic football suffering from lack of finance and too few quality players to make it the thrilling spectacle it once was.

In the **Olympic** arena Hungary has achieved outstanding success, and is consistently in the top ten in the Olympic Games medals standings, an extraordinary feat given the size of the country and its hitherto limited resources. Its top-medalling sport is fencing, and its most successful Olympian, the little-known Aladár Grevich, who won seven gold medals in the sport between 1932 and 1960. These days, the country's sporting success is mostly confined to the pool, courtesy of the consistently superb water-polo team, which captured Olympic gold in Sydney in 2000, Athens in 2004, and Beijing in 2008.

Cycling

Hungary affords plentiful opportunities for cycling enthusiasts, from the easier, flatter routes on the Great Plain and around Lake Balaton, to the more challenging, hilly routes of the Northern Uplands, a more attractive proposition for mountain bikers.

The National Tourist Office produces a **cycling map**, available from Tourinform offices, which features twelve recommended routes, ranging from two to seven days' duration, as well as a list of hotels and guesthouses which offer a range of services to cyclists. There are also several other dedicated cycling maps available, the best of which is the 1:250,000-scale *Cycling Around Hungary* (Frigoria), which also includes sights of interest, accommodation and cycle maintenance and rental shops. If cycling in Budapest, then get hold of the free *On a Bike in Budapest* map from Tourinform. It is possible to **rent bikes** (by the hour, day or week) in most large towns and many of the Balaton resorts from private operators and certain campsites (details are given where appropriate in the Guide). Bike shops are fairly common, with repair shops in most larger towns, including several in Budapest.

For more **information** on cycling in Hungary contact the Hungarian Cyclists' Federation in Budapest, at Vadász utca 29 (☎1/206-6223), or the Hungarian Mountain Bike Association at Visegrádi utca 50 (☎1/339-9289).

Horseriding

Hungarians profess a lingering attachment to the horse – their equestrian ally since the time of the great migration and the Magyar conquest – and the horse-herds or *csikós* of the Plain are romantic figures of national folklore. Most native **horses** are mixed breeds descended from Arab and English thoroughbreds, crossed in recent years with Hanoverian and Holstein stock. The adjective most commonly used to describe their character is "spirited". In the competitive field, Hungary has produced some fine carriage drivers who have won a succession of individual and team gold medals at European and World Championships.

The current popularity and growth of equestrianism in Hungary is reflected in the number of schools (over 500) offering **riding programmes**. Schools, many of which have English-speaking guides, are graded according to a horseshoe classification system, with the highest, five, being a school of distinguished quality. Programmes available range from summer riding camps for children to riding adventure tours for the more experienced lasting anywhere between one and ten days. There are also expeditions by **covered wagons** (*cigany kocsi*), which tourists drive and navigate across the *puszta* (Great Plain) and Northern Uplands. Although there are schools all over the country, the greatest concentration is on the Great Plain, around Lake Balaton and in the Northern Uplands. A one-week adventure tour starts at around €650, with tutorage, meals and lodgings included in the **price**. Many schools also offer additional recreational activities such as swimming and tennis as part of the package. Saddlery is provided, but you'll need your own riding clothes. Note that many schools will not accept you if you are not fully insured.

The Hungarian Equestrian Tourism Association in Budapest (☎1/455-6183, ⓦwww.equi.hu) has the most comprehensive file on riding schools in Hungary, and can advise on the range of programmes available. In addition, many Tourinform offices stock a glossy brochure in various languages detailing over 200 equestrian programmes throughout the country.

Hiking

The most beautiful areas for **walking** are the Börzsöny, the Bükk, the Bakony and the Pilis, though all the wooded hill regions in Hungary are crisscrossed with walking **trails**, which are signed with coloured stripes and symbols on trees, stones and buildings. At 1100km, the National Blue Trail is a roughly circular route which takes you through just about every region of the country, whilst, at 105km, the Red Trail is a considerably shorter route through the delightful western Őrség region.

Maps (*turistatérkép*) are available from most Tourinform offices and bookshops; walking paths are shown as red lines, with a letter above them to tell you what colour the stripes on the trees or boulders are: Z = green, K = blue, S = yellow and P = red.

Most paths are marked with stripes or crosses, but some are marked with a coloured circle (circular routes), a square (leading to a building or village), a triangle (leading to a peak), or an L-shape (leading to a ruin).

Some of the more popular areas, such as the Börzsöny, to the east of the Danube, north of Budapest, have basic **accommodation** called *túristaház* or *kulcsosház* (see p.31), but it's wise to book in advance; the Tourinform offices carry a list of phone numbers. If you plan to do some extensive walking in the country, then a useful companion is the **pocket guidebook**, *Walking in Hungary* (Cicerone), which details over thirty routes through Uplands areas.

Other sports and activities

Notwithstanding the ubiquitous spas, **swimming** is hugely popular with Hungarians and most towns and cities have at least one indoor and one outdoor pool, whilst during the summer many retreat to the suitably clean and shallow waters of **Lake Balaton**. Here a host of other watersports can be enjoyed, including **windsurfing** (*szörf*) and **sailing** (*vitorlázás*); equipment can be rented from the *kölcsönzo* at the main Balaton boat stations and at nearby Lake Velence.

Whilst still in its infancy, golf is rapidly gaining in popularity in Hungary, and there are now around a dozen courses (a mix of 9 and 18 holes) scattered throughout the country, though these are mostly confined to the area around Budapest and the Transdanubia region – expect to pay around 15000Ft/€55 for eighteen holes. Racquet sports are also popular, with **tennis** (*tenisz*) leading the way; however, public courts are at a premium and so you'll probably have to go to the more upmarket hotels in Budapest and main resorts to find available ones. Few **squash** (*fallabda*) courts exist outside Budapest. Hungary's topography rules out any dramatic or lengthy slopes, but that doesn't stop enthusiasts from **skiing** in the Mátra Mountains and the Buda Hills. A final possibility is to pop along to the local **sports hall** (*sportcsarnok*), where facilities are usually of a fairly decent standard.

Travel essentials

Addresses

These usually begin with the postcode, which indicates the town or city and locality. The most common terms are *utca* (street, abbreviated to *u.*), *út* (or *útja*, avenue), *tér* (or *tere*, square) and *körút* (ring boulevard). You may also encounter *rakpart* (embankment), *sétány* (promenade), *híd* (bridge), *köz* (lane), *hegy* (hill) and *liget* (park). Town centres are signposted *Belváros*, *Városközpont* or *Centrum*. A *lakótelep* is a high-rise housing estate.

Children

From a practical point of view, travelling with children in Hungary will present few problems. Most of the better-quality hotels are well equipped to cope with children, whilst many restaurants should be able to provide high chairs. Quite a few restaurant menus now incorporate a selection of dishes for kids, though these are invariably a bit samey, while in many places you can also ask for small child's portions (*kisadag*). All supermarkets are well stocked with nappies, baby food and other essentials.

The real challenge will be keeping the youngsters entertained. Whilst Budapest has plenty of attractions for kids (see p.140), you'll have to use your imagination a little more once outside the capital. The most obvious attraction is Lake Balaton which, with its numerous **beaches** and clean, shallow waters, is ideal for young children. Some beaches also have water slides and various other play facilities. Hungary also has some wonderful **narrow-gauge trains** (detailed throughout the book), which are frequently full of screeching kids, while boat trips along the Danube are another possibility. A reliable fall-back option is the trusty **zoo**, and whilst Hungarian zoos can be rather tatty affairs, kids are sure not to mind. Some larger towns and cities, such as Pécs and Kecskemét, have excellent **puppet theatres** which parents will probably enjoy as much as their offspring. Especially worth

looking out for are those summer festivals which stage puppet shows, including the one in Pécs. More generally, many of Hungary's excellent festivals have plenty going on to keep kids entertained.

Children under the age of 6 get to travel free on all **public transport**, with further discounts offered to those between the ages of 6 and 14. Children under the age of 12 are forbidden to ride in the front seat of a **car**. Some **museums** offer discounted entry rates to children.

Costs

Although Hungary is not the bargain destination it once was, it's still excellent value on the whole. If you're on a tight **budget**, you could get by on 8000Ft (around £25/€30/$40) a day, staying in a hostel or private accommodation (around 3000–4000Ft), eating in cheap diners (1000–2000Ft per meal) and using public transport. Those on a moderate to mid-range budget (cheap to mid-range hotel, better restaurants plus car rental) can expect to spend around £70/€85/$110. If you're on a higher level of spend (the best hotels and restaurants, plus car rental), count on spending upwards of £100/€120/$150. Some costs can also vary according to where you are in the country. In Budapest, and to a lesser degree around Lake Balaton, they are appreciably higher than elsewhere, and you can expect to pay around a third more for a cup of coffee or a meal there as opposed to one of the other towns.

Museum admission charges are reasonable, the typical fee being around 500–600Ft/€2–3, although some of the major attractions (such as the Esterházy Palace in Fertőd or the Festetics Palace in Keszthely), and many of the Budapest museums, charge in excess of 1000–1500Ft/€4–6. Expect to pay for car rental what you would pay in most other

European countries. If you're planning to stay in Hungary for any length of time, you could invest in the **Hungary Card** (⊛www .hungarycard.hu; 7200Ft), available from all Tourinform offices, which offers a good range of countrywide discounts, including reductions on certain hotels and restaurants, museum entrances, public transport and special events. The **Budapest Card** (see p.59) offers similar discounts in the capital.

Tipping is standard practice when paying for meals, drinks and taxi fares (though not when paying for drinks at a bar counter); ten percent or thereabouts is fine, unless the service was not worth it. In restaurants, include the tip when you are paying the bill – say the amount you want to pay and they will give you the change – or give the tip to the staff rather than leaving it on the table. Note that ten percent may have quietly been added to the bill, in which case you don't have to leave more. It's also customary to tip bath attendants who unlock your cubicle (100–200Ft is usual), and even medical staff in hospital. If you expect change back, don't say *köszönöm* (thank you) when handing over payment, as it will be assumed that you want the change to be kept.

Crime and personal safety

Hungary is one of Europe's safest countries, and it's very unlikely you'll have any problems. However, although violent crime is extremely rare, the threat of theft is present, particularly in Budapest where pickpocketing, car theft and scams directed at tourists are not uncommon. Unfortunately, the incidence of racist attacks is also increasing, with the Hungarian Roma bearing the brunt of physical assaults.

Since the 2006 riots that made international headlines (see p.451), a small nationalist (even neo-Nazi) hardcore has made regular appearances on Budapest's streets in protests against the Socialist government. In 2007 and 2008 they attacked the Gay Pride march, and their red-and-white striped flags, the fascist *Árpád sáv*, are on the fringe of demonstrations held on national holidays, especially March 15 and October 23, when they often head towards the hated state TV building on Szabadság tér, where the Soviet war memorial whips up their fury (see p.81).

The police

The Hungarian **police** (*rendőrség*) have a milder reputation than their counterparts in other Eastern European countries, and are generally keen to present a favourable image. During the summer, **tourist police** patrol the streets and metro stations of Budapest mainly to act as a deterrent against thieves, and to assist in any problems tourists may encounter. As police occasionally ask to inspect **passports and visas**, you should carry your documents with you. Most Hungarian police have at least a smattering of German, but rarely speak any other foreign language. To contact the **police**, call ☎107; they have a setup with Tourinform to provide translators should this be necessary. Alternatively, you can call the English-speaking 24-hour Police Hotline (☎1/438-8080).

Scams

Parts of Budapest, notably Vaci utca in the Belváros, are notorious for "**consume girls**", who target solo male foreigners. A couple of attractive young women (they're not difficult to spot) will approach you, get talking and, without wasting any time, "invite" you to a bar of their choice. A few drinks later, you'll find yourself presented with a bill somewhat bigger than you bargained for and be strong-armed into paying up. The bars, and the waiters who work in them, are an integral part of the scam, so bids for escape or complaint are futile, but if you ever do find yourself caught up in such a situation then report it to the police.

Even if you disregard pick-ups and avoid places offering the "companionship of lovely ladies", there's a risk of gross overcharging at restaurants or bars which don't list their prices. Be cautious, and always check how much things cost before ordering. If you do get stung, try insisting that you'll only pay in the presence of the police. To register a complaint for any scam contact the Bureau of Consumer Affairs, József krt 6 (☎1/459-4800).

Electricity

The Hungarian system runs on 220 volts. Round two-pin plugs are used. A standard continental adapter enables the use of 13-amp, square-pin plugs.

Entry requirements

Since Hungary signed up to the Schengen agreement in 2007, citizens of the 24 Schengen states can enter Hungary with just an ID card and stay for up to ninety days. Citizens of the UK, Ireland, US, Canada, Australia and New Zealand, and most other European countries, can enter Hungary with just a passport and stay for the same period. South African citizens will need to apply to their local Hungarian consulate for a visa (€60), though note that visas valid for another Schengen country are also valid for Hungary.

Hungarian embassies and consulates abroad

Australia and New Zealand Embassy: 17 Beale Crescent, Deakin, Canberra, ACT 2600 ☎02/6282 3226, ⊛www.mfa.gov.hu/emb/canberra; consulate: Suite 405 Edgecliffe Centre, 203–233 New South Head Rd, Edgecliffe, Sydney, NSW 2027 ☎02/9328 7859, ⊛www.mfa.gov.hu/cons/sydney.
Canada Embassy: 299 Waverley St, Ottawa, Ontario, K2P 0V9 ☎613/230-2717; consulate: 425 Bloor St East, Suite 501, Toronto M4W 3R4 ☎416/923-8981; ⊛www.mfa.gov.hu/emb/ottawa.
Ireland Embassy: 2 Fitzwilliam Place, Dublin 2 ☎01/661-2902, ⊛www.mfa.gov.hu/emb/dublin.
South Africa Embassy: 959 Arcadia St, Hatfield, Pretoria 0083 ☎012/342-3288, ⊛www.mfa.gov.hu/emb/pretoria.
UK Embassy 35b Eaton Place, London SW1 8BY ☎020/7235-2664, ⊛www.mfa.gov.hu/kulkepviselet/uk/hu
US Embassy: 3910 Shoemaker St NW, Washington DC 20008 ☎202/362-6730, ⊛www.huembwas.org/; visa enquiries ☎202/362-6737. Consulates: 223 East 52nd St, New York, NY 10022 ☎212/752-0669, ⊛www.mfa.gov.hu/cons/newyork; 500 North Michigan Ave, Suite 750, Chicago IL 60611 ☎312/670-4079, ⊛www.mfa.gov.hu/cons/chicago; 11766 Wilshire Blvd, Suite 410, Los Angeles, CA 90025 ☎310/473-9344, ⊛www.mfa.gov.hu/cons/los_angeles.

Customs

Visitors over the age of 16 are allowed to bring 200 cigarettes (or 250g of tobacco, or fifty cigars), one litre of wine and one litre of spirits into Hungary. There is no import duty on personal effects, though items like laptop computers and video cameras, which are judged to have a high resale value, are liable to customs duty and 25 percent VAT unless you can prove that they are for personal use. Duty-free export limits for tobacco and alcohol are the same as the import limits.

Health

No inoculations are required for Hungary. Standards of public health are good, and tap water is safe to drink. All towns and some villages have **pharmacies** (gyógyszertár or patika), which normally open Monday to Friday from 9am to 6pm, and on Saturday from 9am until noon or 1pm; signs in the window give the location or telephone number of the nearest all-night (éjjeli or ügyeleti szolgálat) pharmacy.

In **emergencies**, dial ☎104 for the Mentők ambulance service, or get a taxi to the nearest **hospital** (kórház). Hungary's national health service (OTBF) provides free emergency treatment in any hospital or doctor's office for citizens of the EU who have the free European Health Insurance Card (EHIC; ⊛www.ehic.org.uk), but there is a charge for drugs and non-emergency care. Unfortunately, the standard of hospitals varies enormously. Low morale among medical staff and shortages of beds testify to poor wages and the general underfunding of the health service. It is standard practice to tip doctors and medical staff, and unfortunately this is sometimes the best way of ensuring good treatment.

For non-urgent treatment, tourist offices can direct you to a local **medical centre** or doctors' surgery (orvosi rendelő), and your embassy in Budapest will have the addresses of foreign-language-speaking **doctors** and **dentists** who will probably be in private (magán) practice.

Sunburn (napszúrás) and insect bites (rovarcsípés) are the most common **minor complaints** for travellers; sunscreen and repellent are available locally. Mosquitoes can be annoying, but the bug to beware of in forests around Budapest is the kullancs, a tick which bites and then burrows into human skin, causing inflammation of the brain. The risk of one biting you is fairly small, but if you get a bite that seems particularly painful, or are suffering from a high temperature and stiff neck following a bite, it's worth having it checked out as quickly as possible.

Insurance

Before travelling to Hungary you'd do well to take out an insurance policy to cover against theft, loss and illness or injury. Before paying for a new policy, check whether you are already covered by your home insurance policy or private medical scheme. A typical travel insurance policy usually provides cover for the loss of baggage, tickets and – up to a certain limit – cash, as well as cancellation or curtailment of your trip. Specialist travel insurance companies offer various levels of cover, or consider the travel insurance deal we offer (see below). If you need to make a **claim**, you should keep receipts for medicines and medical treatment, and in the event you have anything stolen, you must obtain an official statement from the police.

Internet

Internet access is readily available in just about every town in Hungary, although connection speeds vary and only some have keyboards labelled in English. **Wi-fi** is becoming increasingly widespread, and certainly in the better hotels this is now almost a standard facility. Elsewhere, you'll find quite a few cafés, even in the smaller towns, with wireless hotspots. The website Ⓦwww.hotspotter.hu/en lists places in Budapest offering access both for free

(*ingyenes*) and for a fee (*térítéses*), as do listings magazines such as *Pesti Est*. Expect to pay 300–500Ft per hour online.

Laundry

Self-service launderettes (*mosoda*) are still pretty rare, even in Budapest, but there are a few companies offering service washes such as Top Clean, which has many locations in the capital. Otherwise there is the competent but expensive Hungarian-American Ametiszt, with quite a few outlets throughout the country. Staying in private lodgings, you may be allowed to use your host's washing machine for a small cost.

Living in Hungary

Teaching English has traditionally been the main opportunity for **work** in Hungary, and now, more than ever, language teaching is big business. This is reflected in both the growing number of native speakers working in Budapest and in the number of schools to have opened up outside the capital in recent years.

The most reputable **language school** in Hungary is International House, which has schools in Budapest, at Vermező út 4 (Ⓣ1/212-4010, Ⓦwww.ih.hu), and Eger, at Mecset utca 3 (Ⓣ36/413-770); their minimum requirement is a CELTA or TESOL qualification, and preferably one year's experience. They offer a range of teacher training qualifications in Budapest. There are also teaching opportunities at the British Council, 1075 Madách Imre út 13–14 (Ⓣ1/483-2020, Ⓦwww.britishcouncil.hu), whose minimum requirements are a CELTA and two years' experience.

Study and work programmes

If you fancy taking up the challenge of **learning Hungarian**, or wish to brush up on your existing language skills, there are several schools in Budapest catering for foreigners, the best being the Hungarian Language School at VIII, Bródy Sándor utca 4 (☎1/266-2617, ⓦwww.magyar-iskola.hu). The school runs a comprehensive range of short- and long-term courses, from beginners to advanced, as well as organizing cultural programmes and workshops.

There are also several organizations arranging summer **work camps** or **exchange programmes** in Hungary for people from a large number of countries. Eager to publicize their cultural achievements and earn foreign exchange, the Hungarians also organize **summer courses** in everything from folk art to environmental studies. Hungary's major **summer school** is at Debrecen University (☎52/532-594, ⓦwww.nyariegyetem.hu), which has been running for decades and whose main programme focuses on the Hungarian language and the country's history and culture. Other study subjects include photography (at Vác), fine arts (Zebegény), Esperanto (Gyula), Baroque recorder music (Sopron), jazz (Tatabánya), orchestral music (Pécs and Kecskemét), music-teaching by the Kodály method (Esztergom and Kecskemét), folk art (Zalaegerszeg) and nature studies (Keszthely). Fees include room and board and various excursions and entertainments. Courses typically run for two or four weeks, with a two-week course, including full-board accommodation, costing around €600. They've also got a branch in Budapest, at V, Báthory utca 4.II.1 (☎1/320-5751, ⓦwww.summerschool.hu/bp).

AFS Intercultural Programs US ☎1-800/AFS-INFO, Canada ☎1-800/361-7248, UK ☎0113/242 6136, Australia ☎1300/131 736, NZ ☎0800/600 300, SA ☎11/447 2673; ⓦwww.afs.org. Intercultural exchange organization with programmes in over fifty countries.

BTCV (British Trust for Conservation Volunteers) UK ☎01302/388 883, ⓦwww.btcv.org.uk. One of the largest environmental charities in Britain, with a programme of national and international working holidays (as a paying volunteer).

Council on International Educational Exchange (CIEE) US ☎1-800/40-STUDY,

ⓦwww.ciee.org. Leading NGO offering study programmes and volunteer projects around the world.
Earthwatch Institute US and Canada ☎1-800/776-0188, UK ☎01865/318 838, Australia ☎03/9682 6828; ⓦwww.earthwatch.org. Scientific expedition project that spans over fifty countries with environmental and archeological ventures worldwide.

Mail

Post offices (*posta*) are usually open Monday to Friday 8am to 6pm and Saturday 8am to noon in most towns, and until around 4pm on weekdays (closed Sat) in smaller places. In Budapest you'll find several offices functioning around the clock. Mail from abroad should be addressed "poste restante, posta" followed by the name of the town; tell your friends to write your surname first, Hungarian-style, and underline it; even this may not prevent your mail being misfiled, so ask them to check under all your names. To collect mail, show your passport and ask "*Van posta a részemre?*". For express mail or packages, all the major **courier** companies, including DHL, Fedex and TNT, have offices in Budapest. **Stamps** (*bélyeg*) can be bought at tobacconists or post offices, though the latter are usually pretty crowded and very few staff speak English. Stamps cost around 150Ft for postcards within Europe, and 170Ft for further afield. Note that letters and postcards have different rates, so don't buy a job lot of stamps.

Maps

You may want to supplement the maps in this book with Hungarian **town plans** (*várositérkép*), which also detail main sights and tram and bus routes. These maps cost between 300Ft and 400Ft and are available from Tourinform offices, local tourist agencies or bookshops (*könyvesbolt*). If you're travelling by car, the *Magyar Auto Atlasz* is a must. Available from bookshops, it contains **road maps** and plans of most towns (though some of the street names may be out of date). Tourinform also issues a variety of useful, free road maps, including one showing Budapest's one-way streets and bypasses. Many Tourinform offices, as well as bookshops, stock **hiking maps** (*turistatérkép*) covering the highland regions, which should be purchased in advance wherever possible, as they may not be available on the spot; see p.39 for more on hiking.

Media

Hungary has a long tradition of lively print media, and there are several main broadsheets available, in addition to a range of English-language papers, though these are confined to the capital. Television coverage, meanwhile, differs little from that in other European countries, with foreign cable and satellite television having made huge inroads in recent years.

Generally speaking, Hungarian **television** is pretty dismal, with state TV (MTV) screening a dreary diet of game shows and low-budget soaps from morning to night. In addition, there are numerous commercial channels such as TV2, the German-Belgian owned RTK Klub and Duna TV, a state-supported channel geared to Hungarian minorities abroad, though these are little better. It is for this reason that many Hungarians subscribe to satellite channels, with whole apartment blocks sharing the cost of installation. Most half-decent hotels have some form of satellite TV, though in many cases they will feature German channels only; only in the classier hotels will you find the full satellite package.

Competing with the largest circulation broadsheet **newspaper**, *Népszabadság* (formerly Communist, but now avowedly Socialist), is the liberal-conservative leaning *Magyar Nemzet*. In addition, there are, of course, plenty of tabloids doing the daily rounds of sensationalism. There's now a proliferation of Budapest-based English-language weeklies, including the highly readable *Budapest Times* (Ⓦ www.thebudapesttimes.hu), which also has good cultural content; the *Budapest Sun* (Ⓦ www.budapestsun.com), a rather lightweight, newsy rag with entertainment and events listings; and the *Budapest Business Journal* (Ⓦ www.bbj.hu), which covers mainly business and politics. In addition, the *Budapest Week* (Ⓦ www.budapestweek.com) is a comprehensive online arts and entertainments weekly with excellent listings sections as well as a useful classifieds section. In Budapest you can find most of the **English** broadsheet papers in the classier hotels, some newsagents and in the street kiosks, though, inevitably, you'll pay a premium. You could also drop into the British or American cultural centres in Budapest, which usually have a reasonable stock of recent newspapers and magazines. Whilst not in English, *Pesti Est* is a useful free weekly listings pamphlet available from tourist offices and hotels in most towns and cities throughout the country.

There are plenty of private **radio** stations, but for news, most listeners tune into foreign stations, especially the **BBC World Service** (Ⓦ www.bbc.co.uk/worldservice), **Radio Canada** (Ⓦ www.rcinet.ca), and **Voice of America** (Ⓦ www.voa.gov).

Money

Hungary's unit of currency is the **forint** (Ft or HUF). The forint comes in notes of 200, 500, 1000, 2000, 5000, 10,000 and 20,000Ft, with 5, 10, 20, 50 and 100Ft coins (1Ft and 2Ft coins were withdrawn from circulation in 2008 and amounts are rounded up – or down). Note that many places (particularly hotels in Budapest) quote their prices in euros. At the time of writing, the **exchange rate** is around 320Ft to the pound sterling, 260Ft to the euro and around 220Ft to the US dollar; for currency rates check out Ⓦ www.xe.com or www.oanda.com. It's relatively easy to get forints before you travel – you can buy them at exchange offices, or in the UK at post offices, but you will probably have to order them in advance.

As a rule you're best off changing money in **banks**, which you can find just about everywhere and which are generally open Monday to Friday between 9am and 3 or 4pm. Otherwise, you can change money at private exchange offices, also found in most towns, or at tourist agencies, such as Ibusz. Very few places charge commission. There are also an increasing number of **Automatic Currency Exchange Machines**, where you insert your foreign currency in return for forints, a convenient method if there is nowhere open. The exchange rate is usually the same as that offered in banks.

If taking **cash**, a modest amount of low-denomination euros is advisable, though dollars and pound sterling are also accepted in most places. ATMs are now widespread, and even in the smaller towns you'll have no problem tracking one down. Credit cards are accepted just about everywhere, including many hotels, restaurants, shops and petrol stations. Note that if your debit or credit card won't work in a particular ATM, it is worth trying another – not all of the smaller banks are connected to the right global clearing system.

By far the most recognized travellers' cheques are American Express, whether sterling or dollars. Although it may not be required in all instances, make sure you have your passport when changing traveller's cheques (or cash). Also note that, in some banks, you may have to show the receipt from the issuing bank, or another cheque to prove continuity of serial numbers.

Opening hours and public holidays

Shops are generally open Monday to Friday from 10am to 6pm, and on Saturdays from 10am to 1pm; grocery stores and supermarkets open slightly longer hours at both ends of the day. The shopping malls are open Monday to Saturday 10am to 8pm or 9pm, and Sunday 10am to 6pm. There are also a growing number of 24-hour shops (signed "non-stop", "0–24" or "*éjjel-nappali*").

Museums are generally open Tuesday to Sunday 10am to 6pm, and in winter 9 or 10am to 3 or 4pm, though some of the smaller ones may close down altogether out of season. Hungary's **thermal baths** are usually open daily from 8 or 9am to 6 or 7pm, although some open at 6am – as most of the baths in Budapest do. Office hours are usually Monday to Friday from 8am to 4pm. There are, of course, exceptions to the above – all specific opening times are detailed throughout the Guide. For the opening hours of post offices, banks and pharmacies, see the relevant entries in this section. Most things in Hungary shut down on the **public holidays** listed below. When these fall on a Tuesday or Thursday, the Monday before or the Friday after may also become a holiday, and the previous or next Saturday a working day to make up the lost day.

Public holidays

January 1 New Year's Day
March 15 Independence Day
March/April Easter Monday
May 1 Labour Day
August 20 St Stephen's Day
October 23 National holiday
November 1 All Saints' Day
December 25 Christmas. (Since celebrations start on Christmas Eve, many shops will be closed the whole day, and by the afternoon everything closes down.)
December 26

Phones

In towns and cities, calls can be made from public phones with 10, 20, 50 and 100Ft coins (minimum call 20Ft), though **cardphones** are far more common and it's worth keeping a phonecard (*telefonkártya*) to hand; cards currently cost 500Ft, 800Ft and 1800Ft and are available from Matáv (the Hungarian telecommunications company) shops, post offices, tobacconists and some hotels. The best card for international calls is the Barangaló card (1000Ft, 2000Ft and 5000Ft), available from post offices, which offers excellent per-minute rates to countries worldwide. To call to a part of Hungary outside the area you are in, dial ☏06 (which gives a burring tone), followed by the area code and the subscriber's number.

If you want to use your home mobile phone in Hungary, check with your phone provider first to see whether it will work in the country, and what the call charges will be; US cell phones need to be tri-band to work. If you want to buy a Hungarian **SIM card** (they cost about 1500Ft) try the outlets such as T-Mobile or Vodaphone, which both have pay-as-you-go offers. Hungarian **mobile phone** numbers begin with ☏06-20, 06-30, 06-60 or 06-70, followed by seven digits. Calling a mobile phone number, you have to dial all the numbers, unless you are calling from a phone on the same network, when you drop the first four digits.

When **calling Hungary** from abroad, dial your international access code, then 36 for Hungary, then the area code (omitting the initial zero where present) and the number. If the Hungarian number begins with 06, omit these two digits. **Within Hungary**, directory enquiries is on ☏198, international directory enquiries on ☏199.

Religion

The majority of the Hungarian population affiliates itself to the Roman Catholic Church, with the remainder comprising Reformed Protestant (Calvinist), Evangelical Protestant (Lutheran) and other, smaller groups such as Serb and Greek Orthodox. As in many other former Communist countries there has been a steady rise in religious interest, with the church playing a more visible role in everyday life, although, Christmas and Easter aside, it's rare to see churches full.

Getting into **churches** (*templom*), however, may be more problematic. The really important ones charge a small fee to see their crypts and treasures, and may prohibit sightseeing during services (*mise* or *istentisztelet*, or Gottesdienst in German). In small towns and villages churches are usually kept locked except for worship in the early morning and/or the evening (between around 6pm and 9pm). A small tip is in order if you rouse the verger to unlock the building during the day; he normally lives nearby in a house marked *plébánia*. Visitors are expected to wear "decorous" dress – that is, no shorts or sleeveless tops. In Budapest, several churches offer religious services in English (see Budapest "Listings").

Hungary has a fabulously rich Jewish heritage with over forty **synagogues** (*zsinagóga*) across the country, the most outstanding of which are in Budapest – where the Dohány utca synagogue is the largest in Europe – Pécs and Szeged. However, most of Hungary's synagogues were ransacked during World War II and subsequently left derelict or given over to other functions, and whilst a number have since been reopened and restored, many lie in a desperate state of neglect. Budapest is the only place which retains a sizeable Jewish community, but in most places with a synagogue or Jewish cemetery, it is easy to get directions, although you may have to ask around for a key.

Hungary's few remaining **mosques** (*djami*) now qualify as museums rather than places of worship; Pécs, as well as housing a number of other reminders of the country's Ottoman past, is home to the only intact mosque in the country.

The Hungarian terms for the main **religious denominations** are: *Katolikus* (Catholic), *Református* (Calvinist), *Evangélikus* (Lutheran), *Görög* (Greek Orthodox), *Görög-Katolikus* (Uniate), *Szerb* (Serb Orthodox) and *Zsidó* (Jewish).

Time

Hungary is one hour ahead of GMT, six hours ahead of Eastern Standard Time and nine ahead of Pacific Standard Time. A word of caution: Hungarians express time in a way that might confuse the Anglophone traveller. As in German, 10.30am is expressed as "half eleven" (written 1/211 or f11), 10.45am is "three-quarter-eleven" (3/411 or h11), and 10.15am is "a quarter of eleven" (1/411 or n11).

Tourist information

A large number of free brochures, maps and special-interest leaflets are produced by the Hungarian National Tourist Office, and distributed by its offices abroad and by Tourinform (ⓦwww.tourinform.hu) – the extensive, and excellent, network of tourist information centres within Hungary. As well as the

---

Calling home from abroad

Note that the initial zero is omitted from the area code when dialling the UK, Ireland, Australia and New Zealand from abroad.

Australia international access code + 61

New Zealand international access code + 64

UK international access code + 44

US and Canada international access code + 1

Republic of Ireland international access code + 353

South Africa international access code + 27

booklets on hotels and campsites, there are also useful brochures on cultural events and festivals, gastronomy and wine, health tourism, riding, cycling and activity holidays.

Within Hungary, **Tourinform** has an office in just about every town and city, and in some villages too. Invariably, these have an abundance of information on accommodation (although most do not book rooms), restaurants and activities, and many can also supply you with a free map. Inevitably, opening times vary greatly, depending upon both their location and season. Summer opening times (typically June–Aug) are, generally speaking, weekdays 8 or 9am to 6 or 7pm and weekends 10am to 4 or 5pm, and during the winter Monday to Friday only from 9am to 4 or 5pm.

In addition to Tourinform, you'll find local **tourist agencies** in most towns, many of which are regionally based and have a few branches in towns of close proximity; for example, Balatontourist, one of the biggest, has offices all around Lake Balaton. These are, though, primarily useful for booking **accommodation** in private rooms and apartments. Similarly, tourist agencies' opening hours vary enormously, with some even open until 8 or 9pm in the summer.

Hungarian tourist offices abroad

UK Hungarian National Tourist Office, 46 Eaton Place, London SW1X 8AL ☏ 020/7823 1055, ⓦ www.gotohungary.co.uk.
US Hungarian National Tourist Office, Commercial Counsellor's Office, 350 Fifth Ave, Suite 7107, New York, NY 10118 ☏ 212/695-1221, ⓦ www .gotohungary.com.

Government websites

Australian Department of Foreign Affairs ⓦ www.dfat.gov.au, ⓦ www.smartraveller.gov.au.
British Foreign & Commonwealth Office ⓦ www.fco.gov.uk.
Canadian Department of Foreign Affairs ⓦ www.international.gc.ca.
Irish Department of Foreign Affairs ⓦ www.foreignaffairs.gov.ie.
New Zealand Ministry of Foreign Affairs ⓦ www.mft.govt.nz.
US State Department ⓦ www.travel.state.gov.
South African Department of Foreign Affairs ⓦ www.dfa.gov.za.

Travellers with disabilities

Hungary has been painfully slow to acknowledge the needs of the disabled traveller, and, whilst progress is being made, don't expect much in the way of special facilities. Not surprisingly, Budapest is the one place where facilities are most advanced, with a number of hotels (albeit the more expensive ones) accommodating specially designed rooms, and an increasing number of museums providing ramps for wheelchairs. For information on public transport accessibility in Budapest, check the "Passengers with disabilities" section of the Budapest transport website, ⓦ www.bkv.hu, which lists routes where modern low-floored buses operate. The only accessible trams are the #4 and #6 on the Nagykörút. The Airport Shuttle bus is also accessible.

Outside Budapest, however, travellers with disabilities will have an even tougher time of it, although there have been some positive developments, such as at Lake Balaton, where several beaches have been fitted with lifts which can transport disabled people into the water. Furthermore, an increasing number of train stations are implementing ramps and lifts for disabled passengers so they can access platforms and carriages.

The **Hungarian Disabled Association** (MEOSZ), San Marco utca 76, 1032 Budapest (☏ 1/388-5529, ⓦ www.meosz .hu), which is also the regional office for Eastern Europe, is currently doing a terrific job of trying to raise the profile of disabled people's needs in Hungary. As well as advising on all aspects of coping with disabilities while in Hungary, they provide information on all tourist facilities in the country specifically equipped for the physically disabled, including hotels, museums, restaurants and transportation. MEOSZ also operates its own special transport service in Budapest whereby, for a fixed payment, a bus equipped with lift or ramp can take you to your chosen destination.

Guide

Guide

www.roughguides.com

1

Budapest

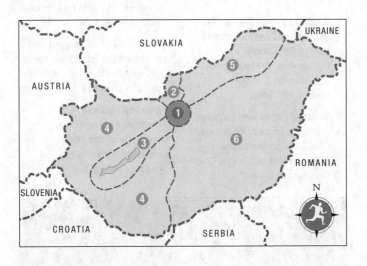

CHAPTER 1 # Highlights

✳ **Hungarian Railway History Park** The chance to ride and even drive a steam train is a big draw for all ages. See p.84

✳ **Zoo** The Art Nouveau animal houses and the chance to feed the camels and giraffes make this a very special zoo. See p.89

✳ **Jewish quarter** Explore the atmospheric neighbourhood behind the Dohány utca Synagogue, the focal point of Budapest's Jewish community. See p.92

✳ **Várhegy** Laden with bastions, mansions and a huge palace, Castle Hill preserves many medieval features, and a Cold War nuclear bunker. See p.99

✳ **Turkish baths** Experience unrivalled atmosphere and luxury in an original Ottoman bathhouse. See p.111

✳ **Coffee shops** This venerable Central European institution is alive and well in the streets of Pest. See p.120

✳ **Sziget Festival** Frenetic open-air rock and pop festival held in August. See p.132

✳ **Folk music** The swirling tunes of Hungarian folk music are brought to life in the city's folk clubs. See p.134

✳ **Music Academy** A magnificent showcase for some of the best classical music in the country. See p.136

▲ Fresco in the foyer of the Music Academy

Budapest

The importance of **BUDAPEST** to Hungary is difficult to overestimate. More than two million people live in the capital – one fifth of the population – and everything converges here: roads and rail lines; air travel; industry, commerce and culture; opportunities, wealth and power. Like Paris, the city has a history of revolutions – in 1849, 1918 and 1956 – buildings, parks and avenues on a monumental scale, and a reputation for hedonism, style and parochial pride. In short, Budapest is a city worthy of comparison with other great European capitals.

Surveying Budapest from the embankments or the bastions of Várhegy (Castle Hill), it's easy to see why the city was dubbed the "Pearl of the Danube". Its grand buildings and sweeping bridges look magnificent, especially when floodlit or illuminated by the barrage of fireworks that explode above the Danube every August 20, St Stephen's Day. The eclectic inner-city and radial boulevards combine brash commercialism with a *fin-de-siècle* sophistication, while a distinctively Magyar character is highlighted by the sounds and appearance of the Hungarian language at every turn.

Since the end of Communism, Budapest has experienced a new surge of dynamism. Luxury hotels and malls, restaurants, bars and clubs have all proliferated – as have crime and social inequalities. Though many Hungarians fear the erosion of their culture by foreign influences, others see a new golden age for Budapest, as the foremost world-city of Mitteleuropa.

The River Danube – which is never blue – determines basic **orientation**, with Buda on the hilly west bank and Pest covering the plain across the river. More precisely, Budapest is divided into 23 districts (*kerület*), designated on maps and street signs by Roman numerals; many quarters also have a historic name. **Pest** is where you're likely to spend most of your time, enjoying the streetlife, bars and shops within the **Belváros** (Inner City), and museums and monuments in the surrounding Lipótváros (likewise part of the V district), Terézváros (VI), Erzsébetváros (VII), Józsefváros (VIII) and Ferencváros (IX), demarcated by two semicircular boulevards – the **Kiskörút** (Small Boulevard) and the **Nagykörút** (Great Boulevard) – and radial avenues such as Andrássy út. Across the river in **Buda**, the focus of attention is the I district, comprising Várhegy and the Víziváros (Watertown); the XI, XII, II and III districts are worth visiting for Gellért-hegy, the Buda Hills, Óbuda and Rómaifürdő.

Some history

Though Budapest has formally existed only since 1873 – when the twin cities of Buda and Pest were united in a single municipality, together with the smaller Óbuda – the history of settlement here goes back as far as the second millennium BC.

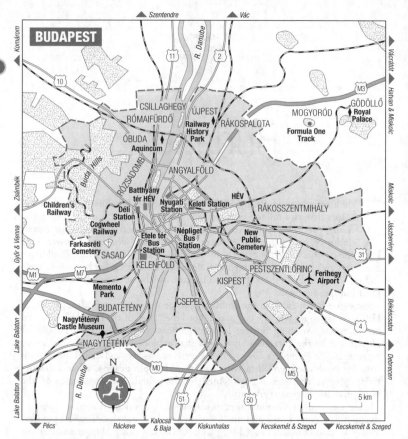

During the first Age of Migrations, the area was settled by waves of peoples, notably Scythians from the Caucasus and Celts from what is now France.

During the first century BC, the Celtic Eravisci tribe was absorbed into Pannonia, a vast province of the Roman Empire. This was subsequently divided into two regions, one of which, Pannonia Inferior, was governed from the garrison town of **Aquincum** on the west bank of the Danube; ruins of a camp, villas, baths and an amphitheatre can still be seen today.

The Romans withdrew in the fifth century AD to be succeeded by the Huns. Germanic tribes, Lombards, Avars and Slavs all followed each other during the second Age of Migrations, until the arrival of the **Magyars** in about 896. According to the medieval chronicler, Anonymous, while other tribes spread out across the Carpathian basin, the clan of Árpád settled on Csepel-sziget (Csepel Island), and it was Árpád's brother, Buda, who purportedly gave his name to the west bank of the new settlement. It was under the Árpád dynasty that Hungary became a Christian state, ruled first from Esztergom and later from Székesfehérvár.

The **development of Buda and Pest** did not begin in earnest until the twelfth century, and was largely thanks to French, Walloon and German settlers who worked and traded here under royal protection. Both towns were devastated by the Mongols in 1241 and subsequently rebuilt by colonists from Germany, who named Buda "Ofen", after its numerous limekilns. (The name Pest, which is of Slav origin, also means "oven".) During the fourteenth century, the Angevin kings from France established Buda as a **royal seat**, building a succession of palaces on **Várhegy**. It reached its apogee in Renaissance times under the reign of "Good King" Mátyás (1458–90) and his Italian-born wife, Queen Beatrice, with a golden age of prosperity and a flourishing of the arts.

Hungary's catastrophic defeat at Mohács in 1526 paved the way for the **Turkish occupation** of Buda and Pest, which lasted 160 years until a pan-European army besieged Buda Castle for six weeks, finally recapturing it at the twelfth attempt. Under **Habsburg rule**, with control exerted from Vienna or Bratislava, recovery was followed by a period of intensive growth during the second half of the eighteenth century. In the first decades of the following century, Pest became the centre of the **Reform movement** led by Count Széchenyi, whose vision of progress was embodied in the construction of the **Chain Bridge** (Lánchíd), the first permanent link between Buda and Pest, which had hitherto relied on pontoon bridges or barges.

When the Habsburg Empire was shaken by revolutions which broke out across Europe in **March 1848**, local reformists and radicals seized the moment. While Lajos Kossuth (1802–94) dominated Parliament, Sándor Petőfi (1823–49) and his fellow revolutionaries plotted the downfall of the Habsburgs in the *Café Pilvax* (which exists today in a sanitized restaurant form in central Pest), from where they mobilized crowds on the streets of Pest. After the War of Independence ended in defeat for the Hungarians, Habsburg repression was epitomized by the hilltop Citadella on Gellért-hegy, built to cow the citizenry with its guns.

Following the Compromise of 1867, which established the Dual Monarchy familiarly known to its subjects as the K & K (from the German for "Emperor and King"), the twin cities underwent rapid **expansion** and formally merged. Pest was extensively remodelled, acquiring the Nagykörút (Great Boulevard) and Andrássy út, the grand thoroughfare that runs from the Belváros to the Városliget (City Park). Hungary's **millennial anniversary celebrations** in 1896 brought a fresh rush of construction, and Hősök tere (Heroes' Square) and Vajdahunyad Castle at the far end of Andrássy út are just two examples of the monumental style that encapsulated the age. New suburbs were created to house the burgeoning population, which was by now predominantly Magyar, although there were still large German and Jewish communities. At the beginning of the twentieth century the cultural efflorescence in Budapest rivalled that of Vienna and its café society that of Paris – a *belle époque* doomed by World War I.

In the aftermath of defeat, Budapest experienced the Soviet-ruled **Republic of Councils** under Béla Kun, and occupation by the Romanian army. The status quo ante was restored by **Admiral Horthy**, self-appointed regent for the exiled Karl IV – the "Admiral without a fleet, for the king without a kingdom" – whose regency was characterized by gala balls and hunger marches, bombastic nationalism and anti-Semitism. Yet Horthy was a moderate compared to the Arrow Cross Fascists, whose power grew as **World War II** raged.

Anticipating Horthy's defection from the Axis in 1944, Nazi Germany staged a coup, installing an Arrow Cross government, which enabled them to begin the massacre of the **Jews** of Budapest; they also blew up the Danube bridges as a way of hampering the advance of the Red Army. The seven-week-long **siege of Budapest** reduced Várhegy to rubble and severely damaged much of the rest of the city, making **reconstruction** the first priority for the postwar coalition government.

As the **Communists** gained ascendancy, the former Arrow Cross torture chambers filled up once again. A huge statue of the Soviet dictator (whose name was bestowed upon Budapest's premier boulevard) symbolized the reign of terror carried out by **Mátyás Rákosi**, Hungary's "Little Stalin". However, his liberally inclined successor, **Imre Nagy**, gave hope to the people, who refused to tolerate a comeback by the hardliners in 1956. In Budapest, peaceful protests turned into a citywide **uprising** literally overnight: men, women and children defying Soviet tanks on the streets.

After Soviet power had been bloodily restored, **János Kádár** – initially reviled as a quisling – gradually normalized conditions, embarking on cautious reforms to create a "**goulash socialism**" that made Hungary the envy of its Warsaw Pact neighbours and the West's favourite Communist state during the late 1970s. A decade later, the regime saw the writing on the wall and anticipated Gorbachev by promising **free elections**, hoping to reap public gratitude. Instead – as Communism was toppled in Berlin and Prague – the party was simply voted out of power in Hungary.

While governments have come and gone since the historic election of 1990, Budapest's administration has remained in the hands of **Mayor Gábor Demszky**, who is on his fifth term in office at the time of writing. Despite allegations of corruption, he is widely acknowledged to have steered the city forwards without any major upsets, and secured state funding for a **fourth metro line**, running from Keleti Station in Pest to Étele tér in Buda. Scheduled for completion in 2012 but already over time and budget, its construction seems likely to be the headstone of his career as mayor of one of the great cities of Europe.

Arrival and information

Other than the airport, all **points of arrival** are fairly central and most within walking distance or just a few stops by metro from downtown Pest. The city's three metro lines and three main roads meet at the major junction of Deák tér in Pest, making this the main transport hub of the city. Depending on when and where you arrive, it's definitely worth considering either arranging somewhere to stay before leaving the terminal or station (there are reservation

---

Budapest addresses

Finding your way around Budapest is easier than the welter of names might suggest. Districts and streets are well signposted, and those in Pest conform to an overall plan based on radial avenues and semicircular boulevards.

Budapest addresses begin with the number of the district – for example, V, Petőfi tér 3 – a system used throughout this chapter. When addressing letters, however, a four-digit postal code is used instead, the middle digits indicating the district (so that 1054 refers to a place in the V district).

As a rule of thumb, **street numbers** ascend away from the north–south axis of the River Danube and the east–west axis of Rákóczi út/Kossuth utca/Hegyalja út. Even numbers are generally on the left-hand side, odd numbers on the right. One number may refer to several premises or an entire apartment building, while an additional combination of numerals denotes the floor and number of individual **apartments** (eg Kossuth utca 14.III.24). Confusingly, some old buildings in Pest are designated as having a half-floor (*félemelet*) or upper ground floor (*magas földszint*) between the ground (*földszint*) and first floor (*elsőemelet*) proper – so that what the British would call the second floor, and Americans the third, Hungarians might describe as the first. This stems from a nineteenth-century taxation fiddle, whereby landlords avoided the higher tax on buildings with more than three floors.

services at all of them), or stashing your luggage before setting out to look for a room. For all **departure** information, see the relevant sections of "Listings", at the end of this chapter.

By air

Ferihegy Airport, 20km southeast of the centre, has three passenger terminals. Ferihegy 1, which is closest to the city, serves as the terminal for no-frills airlines. Ferihegy 2A and 2B are on the other side of the airport, ten minutes' drive further out: 2A serves countries covered by the Schengen agreement (including Austria, Belgium, Denmark, Finland, France, Germany, Iceland, Italy, Greece, Luxembourg, the Netherlands, Norway, Portugal, Spain and Sweden), while Ferihegy 2B covers the rest of the world (the UK, US, Romania, etc). Terminal 1 handles both Schengen and non-Schengen traffic. The easiest and most expensive option for heading into the centre is the **airport taxi**, Zóna taxi, which charges a fixed fee to different zones (you'll pay around 5300Ft or €25 to the centre), and also offers return fares. Alternatively, Ferihegy's Tourinform offices (daily 8am–11pm) can help with booking an ordinary city cab for around 5000Ft. A cheaper option is the **Airport Shuttle** minibus (T1/296-8555, Wwww.airportshuttle.hu), which will take you directly to any address in the city. Tickets (2990Ft single, 4990Ft return; discounts available for groups of two or more) can be bought in the luggage claim hall or in the main concourse; you give the address you're heading to and then wait five to twenty minutes until the driver calls your destination.

   Public transport might be more inconvenient but it's not much slower, and it's certainly cheaper. Bus #200E departs every fifteen minutes from the stop between terminals 2A and 2B via terminal 1 to Kőbánya-Kispest metro station; from here, you can switch to the blue metro line to get to the centre. Total journey time is about thirty minutes from terminal 1 and 45 minutes from 2A and 2B, and both bus and metro tickets costs 290Ft each if bought from the newsagents in the terminals or from the machine by the bus stop. Buying a bus ticket from the driver on board costs 400Ft.

   The quickest and cheapest route into the centre is to catch a mainline train from the station across the road from Ferihegy 1, which takes you to Nyugati Station for a mere 300Ft (discounts with Budapest Card; see p.59); journey time is 22 minutes and trains leave every half hour; you buy tickets at the Tourinform desk inside the terminal building. Catching the train from Nyugati to the airport you can get tickets from the ticket offices by platform 13 – ask for tickets to Ferihegy. Trains to the airport are flagged on the departure board and leave on the hour and 35 past the hour. Ferihegy is the stop after Kőbánya-Kispest, and is very poorly signed.

By train

The Hungarian word *pályaudvar* (abbreviated "*pu.*" in writing) is used to designate a **train station**. Of the six in Budapest, only three are important for tourists, but note that their names, which are sometimes translated into English, refer to the direction of services handled rather than their location so that Western Station (Nyugati pu.) is north of downtown Pest, and Southern Station (Déli pu.) is in the west of the city; Eastern Station (Keleti pu.), however, is to the east of the city centre.

   Most international trains terminate at Pest's **Keleti Station**, on Baross tér in the VIII district. It's something of a hangout for thieves and hustlers, and there are plenty of police about checking people's ID. There are usually plenty of touts offering accommodation as international trains arrive. The most reliable of several hostel-booking agencies here is Mellow Mood (see p.71), whose office is to the right of the big glass doorways at the end of the station. It also organizes transport to its hostels, and should be able to offer other city information, too. Otherwise, head for the Tourinform office at Deák tér (see below). In summer there are long queues at the 24-hour left-luggage office by platform 6 (300Ft or 600Ft for 24hr depending on bag size, half that amount for 6hr).

On the northern edge of Pest's Great Boulevard, **Nyugati Station** has a 24-hour left-luggage office (same prices as at Keleti) next to the ticket office beside platform 13, but has no tourist office. To reach Deák tér, take the blue metro line two stops in the direction of Kőbánya-Kispest.

Déli Station, 500m behind the Vár in Buda, which has left-luggage facilities (same prices as at Keleti) but no tourist office, is four stops from Deák tér on the red metro line.

By bus

International buses and services from the Great Plain and Transdanubia terminate at the **Népliget Bus Station**, 5km southeast of the centre at Üllői út 131 in the IX district. Adjacent to Népliget train station, the bus station is six stops from Deák tér on the blue metro line. The station staff should be able to help you order a regular taxi, which will cost around 2000Ft to the centre – there is no fixed tariff for the ride from here.

The **Árpád híd Bus Station** in the XIII district (on the blue metro line) is the jumping-off point for buses to and from Szentendre and the Danube Bend; the **Stadion Bus Station** in the XIV district (on the red metro line) serves the Northern Uplands and the **Etele tér Bus Station** in the XI district (take buses #7 or #7E to the centre) serves the Buda hinterland. None of the city's bus stations has any tourist facilities.

By hydrofoil

Hydrofoils from Vienna dock at the **international landing stage**, on the Belgrád rakpart (embankment), near downtown Pest. They operate from April to October and are run by **Mahart** (☎1/484-4010 or 4050, ⓦwww.mahartpassnave.hu).

Information, maps and tours

Leaving aside the business of finding accommodation, the best source of **tourist information** in Budapest is Tourinform (ⓦwww.tourinform.hu), the National Tourist Office. The most central office at V, Sütő utca 2, just around the corner from Deák tér metro (daily 8am–8pm; ☎1/438-8080), has multilingual staff who can answer just about any question on Budapest or Hungary in general. However, it is often packed and the staff overstretched, so you might get more attention at the privately run Yellow Zebra, inside the courtyard just behind the Tourinform office (daily 9.30am–6.30pm; ☎1/266-8777, ⓦwww.discoverhungary.com). The same people run another office, Discover Budapest, behind the Opera House at Lázár utca 16 (Mon–Fri 9.30am–6.30pm, Sat–Sun 10am–4pm; ☎1/269-3843, ⓦwww.discoverbudapest.com). Alternatively, head for the Tourinform offices at VI, Liszt Ferenc tér 11 (daily: May–Sept 10am–10pm; Oct–April 10am–6pm; ☎1/322-4098); and in Várhegy on Szentháromság tér (daily 8am–8pm; ☎1/488-0475), which are both run by the Budapest Tourism Office (ⓦwww.budapestinfo.hu). There are also Tourinform offices in all three airport terminals.

It's a good idea to get hold of a proper **map** of the city at the earliest opportunity. The small freebies supplied by tourist offices give an idea of Budapest's layout and principal monuments, but lack detail. Larger, folding maps are sold all over the place, but their size makes them cumbersome. For total coverage you

The Budapest Card

If you're doing a lot of sightseeing, you might be tempted to buy a **Budapest Card**. For 6500Ft (48hr) or 8000Ft (72hr), it covers travel in most of the city, entry to over sixty museums, and affords discounts of up to fifty percent in some shops and restaurants as well as on some sightseeing programmes and cultural and folklore events. The card is available from tourist offices, hotels, central metro stations and at the airport, and comes with a booklet explaining where it can be used. Note that it's not valid for the Airport Shuttle minibus, the funicular that goes up to the castle or for tours of Parliament, but as most museums in Budapest now charge admission, it can represent good value. You can find more information on Ⓦwww.budapestinfo.hu/en.

can't beat the wirebound *Budapest Atlasz*, available in different sizes in bookshops, which shows every street, bus and tram route, and the location of restaurants, museums and suchlike.

There are several sources of English-language **listings information**: the free fortnightly *Budapest Funzine*, distributed in cafés and bars, is aimed at the expat market and has good background information on events, as well as listings for the art-house cinemas; the weekly *Budapest Sun*, which costs 399Ft at newsstands but can also be found in hotel lobbies, has a more comprehensive set of film listings in English; and the free monthly *Where Budapest* (available in hotels) has information on current events. The Hungarian-language listings bible, the weekly freebie *Pesti Est*, has extensive details of film and music events, and sometimes has an English section in the summer – it is widely available in bars.

If you're hard-pressed for time, you might appreciate a two- to three-hour **city bus tour**. These generally take you past the Parliament, along Andrássy út, across to the Várhegy and up to Gellért-hegy for panoramic photo opportunities. Of the many on offer, Ibusz runs three-hour trips for 6000Ft, and for 9200Ft will add on a visit to the Parliament building; tickets are sold at V, Ferenciek tere 10, in the centre (or online at Ⓦwww.ibusz.hu). Buda Tours (☎1/374-7070, Ⓦwww.budatours.hu) has a two-hour tour for 4000Ft, and in summer uses open-top buses; you buy tickets at VI, Andrássy út 2.

For a range of **walking tours**, including some which take in less obvious attractions such as Communist Budapest or the city's bars, try the Yellow Zebra or Discover Budapest offices (see opposite). Prices for three-and-a-half-hour tours go from 4000Ft (Ⓦwww.absolutetours.com). The same office handles **bike tours** (Ⓦwww.yellowzebrabikes.com), and tours on strange-looking two-wheel segways (Ⓦwww.citysegwaytours.com). All tours cost 4000–5000Ft – you need to book ahead only for the segway trips.

For information on being guided round the old Jewish area behind the Dohány utca synagogue see p.91.

City transport

Most of Budapest's backstreets and historic quarters are eminently suited to **walking** – and this is much the best way to appreciate their character. Traffic is restricted in downtown Pest and around Várhegy in Buda, and fairly light in the residential backstreets off the main boulevards, which are the nicest areas to wander around. (Pedestrians should be cautious of both car drivers and cyclists, who will rather swerve around you than stop.)

The city's **metro trains**, **buses** and **trams** reach most areas of interest to tourists, while the outer suburbs are well served by the overground **HÉV** rail network. Services operate generally between 5am and 11pm, and there are also night-time buses covering much of the city. Locals will tell you that standards are falling, and more cuts in services are certainly expected, but public transport is still efficient and covers most of the city.

There's a whole array of **tickets** available for use on public transport, but since validating your ticket can be complex and is easy to forget, it's best to get a **travel pass** if you're staying for more than half a day.

Tickets and passes

Standard single **tickets** valid for the metro, buses, trams, trolleybuses, the Cogwheel Railway (see p.117) and suburban HÉV lines (up to the edge of the city) cost 290Ft per journey and are sold at metro stations, newspaper kiosks and tobacconists. Metro tickets also come in a variety of other types, depending on whether you are changing trains and how many stops you want to go: a metro section ticket (240Ft) takes you three stops on the same line; a metro transfer ticket (450Ft) is valid for as many stops as you like with one line change. Tickets bought on board buses and trolleybuses (*helyszini vonaljegy*) cost 400Ft.

The standard single ticket is not valid on night buses: you have to buy a 400Ft *helyszini vonaljegy* separately – on board or from a ticket machine – unless you have a day or weekly pass (see below). **Books** of ten standard single tickets (*tíz-darabos gyüjtőjegy* – 2600Ft) are also available – these are still valid if torn out of the book but cannot be used on night services.

Tickets must be **validated** when you use them. On the metro and HÉV you punch them in the machines at station entrances (remember to validate a new ticket if you change lines, unless you have a metro transfer ticket); on trams, buses and trolleybuses, you punch the tickets on board in the small red or orange machines.

Day passes (*napijegy*) cost 1500Ft and are valid for unlimited travel from midnight to midnight on the metro, buses, trams, trolleybuses, the Cogwheel Railway and suburban HÉV lines; three-day passes (*turistajegy*) cost 3700Ft and weekly passes 4400Ft. **Season tickets** cost 5950Ft for two weeks and 9000Ft for a month, and are available from metro stations, but you'll need a passport photo for the accompanying photocard; there are photo booths inside the entrance of Deák tér and Moszkva tér stations.

Children up to the age of 6 travel free on all public transport. EU citizens over the age of 65 also travel free, but must show proof of age if challenged by inspectors. See p.48 for information on disabled access.

Bear in mind that there are active **pickpocket** battalions on the metro (especially the yellow line) and on the city buses and trams. Gangs distract their victims by

Just the ticket

It's worth bearing in mind that **ticket regulations** on Budapest's public transport are subject to regular changes, and the myriad rules make it easy to catch foreigners out – many readers have complained about the treatment meted out by inspectors who can be unpleasant and tend to be strict in levying 6000Ft fines for travelling without a valid ticket. If you feel you've been fined unfairly you can try taking your complaint to the office at Akácfa utca 18 (Mon–Fri 8am–5pm, Wed open till 6pm). You can find the latest information on tickets – and any changes in the ticket systems and prices – on the website of the **Budapest Transport Company** (BKV; ⓦ www.bkv.hu).

pushing them or blocking their way, and empty their pockets or bags at the same time. Also beware of bogus ticket inspectors "working" the transport system and demanding money from passengers. Genuine inspectors wear blue armbands saying *jegyellenőr*, and usually work in twos or threes.

The metro

The Budapest metro has three lines, usually referred to by their colour; they intersect at Deák tér in downtown Pest (see map below). From nearby Vörösmarty tér, the **yellow line** (line 1) runs out beneath Andrássy út to Mexikói út, beyond the Városliget. The **red line** (line 2) connects Déli Station in Buda with Keleti Station and Örs vezér tere in Pest; and the **blue line** (line 3) describes an arc from Kőbánya-Kispest to Újpest-Központ, via Ferenciek tere and Nyugati Station. A fourth line is under construction between Keleti Station and Etele tér: its completion is scheduled for 2012, but few expect it to be ready in time. Trains run at two- to twelve-minute intervals. There's little risk of going astray once you've learned to recognize the signs *bejárat* (entrance), *kijárat* (exit), *vonal* (line) and *felé* (towards). The train's direction is indicated by the name of the station at the end of the line, and drivers announce the next stop between stations.

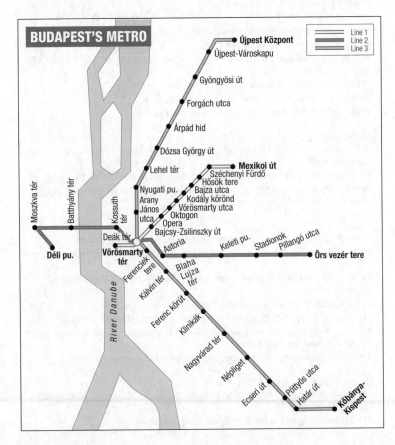

Buses, trams and trolleybuses

There is a good **bus** (*autóbusz*) network across the city, especially in Buda, where Moszkva tér (on the red metro line) and Móricz Zsigmond körtér (southwest of Gellért-hegy) are the main terminals. Bus stops are marked by a picture of a bus on a white background in a blue frame, and have timetables underneath; most buses run every ten to twenty minutes (*utolsó kocsi indul . . .* means "the last one leaves ..."). On busier lines express buses – with an E at the end of the number – run along the same route making fewer stops: for example, the bus #7E that runs along most of the route of the #7. **Night buses** have three-digit numbers beginning with a 9 and run every hour or half-hour from around midnight or whenever the service they replace finishes: so the #906 follows the route of the #6 tram on the Nagykörút from 12.30am, when the tram stops, until 4.15am.

Useful bus, tram and trolleybus routes

Buses
#7 Bosnyák tér–Keleti Station–Móricz Zsigmond körtér (via Rákóczi út, Ferenciek tere, *Gellért Hotel*, Rudas Baths).

#16A Moszkva tér–Dísz tér (Castle District).

#16 Erzsébet tér–Dísz tér (Castle District)–Bécsi kapu tér–Moszkva tér.

#26 Nyugati Station–Szent István körút–Margit-sziget–Árpád híd metro station.

#27 Móricz Zsigmond körtér–Gellért-hegy.

#65 Kolosy tér–Pálvölgyi Caves–Fenyőgyöngye restaurant at the bottom of Hármashatár-hegy.

#86 Southern Buda–Gellért tér–the Víziváros–Flórián tér (Óbuda).

#105 Apor Vilmos tér–Lánchíd–Deák tér–Gyöngyösi utca.

#116 Fény utca market–Moszkva tér–Dísz tér (Castle District).

Night buses
#906 Moszkva tér–Margit-sziget–Nyugati Station–Great Boulevard–Móricz Zsigmond körtér.

#907 Örs vezér tere–Bosnyák tér–Keleti Station–Erzsébet híd–Etele tér (Kelenföld).

#914 and **#950** Kispest (Határ út metro station)–Deák tér–Lehel tér–Újpest, along the route of the blue metro and on to the north and south.

Trams
#2 Margit Bridge–Petőfi híd (along embankment)–Közvágóhíd HÉV station.

#4 Moszkva tér–Margit-sziget–Nyugati Station–Nagykörut–Petőfi Bridge–Október 23 utca.

#6 Moszkva tér–Margit-sziget–Nyugati Station–Great Boulevard–Petőfi híd–Móricz Zsigmond körtér.

#19-41V Batthyány tér–Víziváros–Szent Gellért tér.

#47 Deák tér–Szabadság híd–*Gellért Hotel*–Móricz Zsigmond körtér–Budafok.

#49 Deák tér–Szabadság híd–*Gellért Hotel*–Móricz Zsigmond körtér–Etele tér bus station and Kelenföld train station.

#61 Móricz Zsigmond körtér–Villányi út–Moszkva tér–Hűvösvölgy.

Trolleybuses
#72 Arany János utca metro station–Nyugati Station–Zoo–Széchenyi Baths–Petőfi Csarnok–Thököly út.

#74 Dohány utca (outside the Main Synagogue)–Városliget.

The network of yellow (or the newer orange) **trams** (*villamos*) is smaller, but provides a crucial service round the Nagykörút and along the Pest embankment. **Trolleybuses** (*trolibusz*) mostly operate northeast of the centre near the Városliget. Interestingly, their route numbers start at 70 because the first trolleybus line was inaugurated on Stalin's 70th birthday in 1949. Trolleybus #83 was started in 1961, when Stalin would have been 83.

To get off buses, trams and trolleybuses, press the button above the door or on the handrail next to it before the bus reaches the stop, which alerts the driver. On a very few trams, such as #2, you may have to press the button next to the doors to open them.

Most new buses, trams and trolleybuses have dot displays that tell you the name of the next stop, and the driver may also mumble it.

HÉV trains

The green overground **HÉV trains** provide easy access to Budapest's suburbs, running at least four times an hour between 6.30am and 11pm. As far as tourists are concerned, the most useful line is the one from **Batthyány tér** (on the red metro line) out to **Szentendre**, which passes through Óbuda, Aquincum and Rómaifürdő. The other lines originate in Pest, with one running northeast from **Örs vezér tere** (also on the red metro line) to **Gödöllő** via the Formula One racing track at Mogyoród; another southwards from Boráros tér at the Pest end of Petőfi híd to Csepel; and the third from **Közvagóhíd** (bus #23 or #54 from Boráros tér) to **Ráckeve**.

Ferries and other options

Although **ferries** play little useful part in Budapest's transport system, they do offer an enjoyable ride. From May to September there are boats along the Danube between Boráros tér (by Petőfi híd) and Batthyány tér up to Jászai Mari tér and Rómaifürdő. These run every fifteen to thirty minutes between 7am and 7pm, and cost between 200Ft (for journeys from Pest across to the Margit-sziget) and 600Ft. Ferry tickets can be obtained from kiosks (where timetables are posted) or machines at the docks. Mahart (☏1/484-4013, ⊛www.mahartpassnave.hu), whose office is across the dangerously busy quayside road from Vigadó tér, also operates boats to Szentendre and the Danube Bend (see p.144 for details), and, along with other companies such as Legenda (☏1/317-2203, ⊛www.legenda.hu), runs sightseeing trips from the piers between Vigadó tér and Erzsébet híd.

In the Buda Hills, there's also the **Cogwheel Railway** (Fogaskerekűvasút, now officially designated as tram #60), the **Children's Railway** (Gyermekvasút), and the **chairlift** (*libegő*) between Zugliget and János-hegy (see p.118). Note that BKV tickets and passes are valid only for the Cogwheel Railway – for the others, you'll need to buy tickets at the point of departure or on board. Details for all of these are given on p.60.

Taxis

Budapest's registered **taxis** are cheap and plentiful, and are recognizable by their yellow number plates; make sure your taxi has a meter that is visible and switched on when you get in, and that the rates are clearly displayed. **Fares** begin at 300Ft, and the price per kilometre is around 250Ft.

Taxis can be flagged down on the street, and there are **ranks** throughout the city; you can hop into whichever cab you choose – don't feel you have to opt for the one at the front of the line if it looks at all dodgy. For a cheaper rate, order a cab by phone. The best companies are the established ones: Citytaxi (☎1/211-1111, ⓦwww.citytaxi.hu), whose cars have yellow shield logos; Főtaxi (☎1/222-2222), with a red-and-white chequerboard and oval lights on its car roofs; Tele-5-taxi (☎1/355-5555); and Volántaxi (☎1/466-6666); the first two are the most likely to have English-speaking dispatchers.

Foreigners are easy prey for **rogue taxi drivers**, so avoid unmarked private cars, and drivers hanging around the stations and airport. There are also a few fake Fő- and Citytaxis, sporting poor copies of their logos.

Driving

All things considered, **driving** in Budapest can't be recommended. Road manners are nonexistent, parking spaces are scarce and traffic jams are frequent, while the Pest side of the Lánchíd (Chain Bridge) and the roundabout before the tunnel under Várhegy are notorious for collisions – and careering trams, bumpy cobbles, swerving lane markings and unexpected one-way systems make things worse. In addition, access to the Castle District and parts of the Belváros are strictly limited.

In terms of **parking**, you might be better off leaving your car outside the centre and using public transport to travel in – there are park-and-ride facilities at most metro termini. If you must park in the centre, the best options are the underground car parks in Szent Istvan tér by the Basilica and underneath Szabadsag tér, both in Lipótváros. Parking on the street in the central districts costs 120–440Ft – you get a ticket from the nearest machine.

Cycling

Cycling is finally catching on in Budapest – cyclist numbers have risen sharply and cycle lanes are slowly appearing. It isn't easy riding: drivers are only beginning to be aware of cyclists and you also have to contend with sunken tram lines, bumpy cobbles and bad air pollution. Bikes are banned from the major thoroughfares and the **cycle routes** are still patchy – they don't link up to form a network yet. However, there are good routes out of town, such as along the Buda bank of the Danube to Szentendre and on up towards Slovakia. Tourinform has free cycling maps of Budapest. Bicycles can be carried on HÉV trains and the Cogwheel Railway for the price of a single ticket, but not on buses or trams.

Several places offer **bike rental**: try the friendly Bikebase, near Nyugati Station at VI, Podmaniczky utca 19 (moves to no.15 in winter; ☎1/269-5983, ⓦwww.bikebase.hu; daily 9am–7pm); Yellow Zebra, V, Sütő utca 2, in a courtyard behind the main Tourinform office (☎1/266-8777, ⓦwww.yellowzebrabikes.com; daily 9.30am–6.30pm), which also offers city cycling tours; or Budapest Bike at *Szóda* bar, VII, Wesselényi utca 18 (☎06-30/944-5533, ⓦwww.budapestbike.hu; daily 9am–midnight), which also organizes bike tours and rents mopeds. Bike shops that do repairs include Nella Bikes, off Bajcsy-Zsilinszky út at V, Kálmán Imre utca 23 (☎1/331-3184, ⓦwww.nella.hu); and the Bike Store, VI, Nagymező utca 43 (☎1/312-5073).

Accommodation

Budapest's **accommodation** has improved markedly in terms of availability, so much so that the surplus of rooms has eased the get-rich-quick price hikes that once afflicted the city. Rooms are most in demand at Christmas, New Year, the Spring Festival in March/April and the Grand Prix in August, when rates are marked up as much as twenty percent in some hotels. Even so, it should always be possible to find somewhere that's reasonably priced, if not well situated. Out of season, you can find excellent deals at many top hotels.

Budget travellers will find most **hotels** and **pensions** expensive even during low season (Nov–March, excluding New Year). The best alternative is a **self-contained studio flat or apartment** – especially for family groups. These have become more available in recent years, while the old cheap standby of a **private room** in a flat is getting very hard to find.

Hostels vary in price: some represent the cheapest accommodation in the city, while others are more expensive than private rooms. Another inexpensive option is **campsites**, where tent space can usually be found, even if all the **bungalows**, which some have, are taken.

Hotels and pensions

New hotels have been opening all over the city, and in every price category, with the more select boutique hotels such as *Lánchíd 19* and *Zara* offering a welcome touch of refinement. In this city of baths it is no surprise that several of the big hotels offer spa packages: the *Gellért* and the Margít-sziget hotels were built next to springs, while other five-star hotels in the centre have spa complexes. Hotels fill up quickly so it's best to **book** before leaving home or, failing that, on arrival through an agency or any airport tourist office. Hotel star ratings give a fair idea of **standards**, though facilities at some of the older three-star places don't compare with their Western equivalents, even if prices are similar. Almost all hotels vary their prices according to **season** – the price codes given below are what you can expect to pay in high season (but not Grand Prix prices). The city's **pensions** are slightly cheaper but offer a more personal service, and don't fall far short of small hotels in the facilities they offer.

Pest

Staying in **Pest** offers the greatest choice of hotels, and more in the way of restaurants and nightlife, but traffic noise and fumes are quite bad. Most of the outlying locations are easily accessible by metro. The prime spots are along the riverbank with views across to the Royal Palace, although all the prewar grand hotels were destroyed during the war, and their replacements don't quite have the same elegance. The more expensive places tend to be in the downtown area, with prices generally – though not always – falling as you go further out. Moving out of the centre, more hotels are grouped around the Nagykörút, the larger ring road, and the City Park.

Downtown

For locations, see the map on p.74.

Anna VIII, Gyulai Pál utca 14 ☎1/327-2000, ⓦwww.annahotel.hu. Located in a quiet road and with off-street parking, this hotel offers 42 small, fairly basic rooms – twin beds only – with TV and shower. Some rooms have a/c, and there are also apartments with double beds and baths. ❾

Hotel Art (Best Western) V, Királyi Pál utca 12 ☎1/266-2166, ⓦwww.bwhotelart.hu. A small hotel in a quiet backstreet. Rooms are quite cramped, but have a/c, minibar, phone and TV, and there's a sauna, fitness room and laundry service. ❾

Astoria V, Kossuth utca 19 ☎1/889-6000, ⓦwww.danubiushotels.com/astoria. Four-star vintage hotel which has given its name to the major junction in central Pest on which it's located. The good-sized rooms have a sofa, safe, minibar, phone and TV; half have baths while the rest have showers, and there are smoking and non-smoking floors. The hotel's *Mirror* restaurant has an excellent reputation and the coffee house (see p.121) is a popular meeting point. ❾

Four Seasons V, Roosevelt tér 5–6 ☎1/268-6000, ⓦwww.fourseasons.com /budapest. A magnificent restoration of this Budapest landmark has produced a new level of

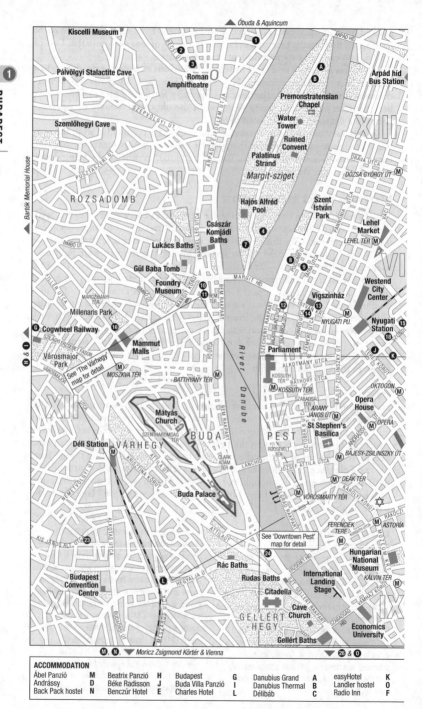

▲ Óbuda & Aquincum

Kiscelli Museum
Pálvölgyi Stalactite Cave
Roman Amphitheatre
Szemlőhegyi Cave
Árpád hid Bus Station
Premonstratensian Chapel
Water Tower
Ruined Convent
Palatinus Strand
Margit-sziget
RÓZSADOMB
Bartók Memorial House
Hajós Alfréd Pool
Szent István Park
Lehel Market
LEHEL TÉR
Lukács Baths
Császár Komjádi Baths
Gül Baba Tomb
Foundry Museum
Vígszinház
Westend City Center
Millenaris Park
Cogwheel Railway
Nyugati Station
NYUGATI PU.
Mammut Malls
See "The Várhegy" map for detail
Városmajor Park
MOSZKVA TÉR
BATTHYÁNY TÉR
Parliament
KOSSUTH TÉR
Opera House
OKTOGON
BUDA
Mátyás Church
VÁRHEGY
PEST
St Stephen's Basilica
Déli Station
Buda Palace
See 'Downtown Pest' map for detail
FERENCIEK TERE
ASTORIA
XII
Rác Baths
Hungarian National Museum
KÁLVIN TÉR
Budapest Convention Centre
Rudas Baths
International Landing Stage
Citadella
Cave Church
Economics University
GELLÉRT HEGY
Gellért Baths

River Danube

▼ Moricz Zsigmond Körtér & Vienna

▼ 26 & O

ACCOMMODATION

Ábel Panzió	**M**	Beatrix Panzió	**H**	Budapest	**G I**	Danubius Grand	**A**	easyHotel	**K**
Andrássy	**D**	Béke Radisson	**J**	Buda Villa Panzió	**I**	Danubius Thermal	**B**	Landler hostel	**O**
Back Pack hostel	**N**	Benczúr Hotel	**E**	Charles Hotel	**L**	Délibáb	**C**	Radio Inn	**F**

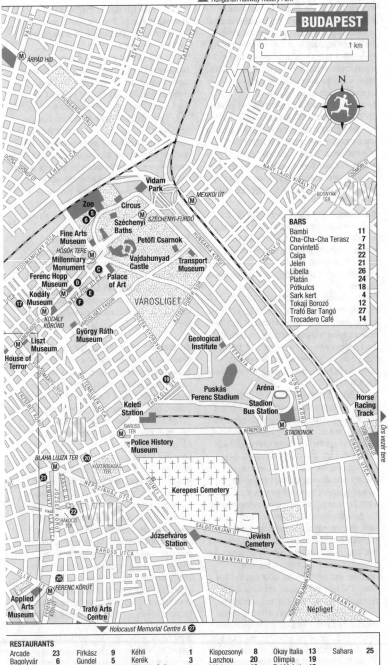

▲ Hungarian Railway History Park

BUDAPEST

0   1 km

N

Ⓜ ÁRPÁD HÍD

XV

VÁCI ÚT

BÉKE ÚTCA

PLÁTÁN UTCA

HUNGÁRIA KÖRÚT

LEHEL UTCA

DÓZSA GYÖRGY ÚT

NAGY LAJOS KIRÁLY ÚT

CSÖMÖRI ÚT

BOSNYÁK TÉR

XIV

Vidam Park

Ⓜ MEXIKÓI ÚT

Zoo
Ⓓ 5
Ⓓ 6

Circus

Ⓜ SZÉCHENYI-FÜRDŐ

Széchenyi Baths

Fine Arts Museum

Petőfi Csarnok

HUNGÁRIA KÖRÚT

THÖKÖLY ÚT

HŐSÖK TERE Ⓜ

Millenniary Monument

Vajdahunyad Castle

Transport Museum

PODMANICZKY UTCA

Ⓒ

Ferenc Hopp Museum

Ⓓ

Palace of Art

Ⓔ

VÁROSLIGET

Kodály Museum
17

Ⓜ
Ⓕ

VÁROSLIGETI FASOR

ATTOS DÜRER SOR

DÓZSA GYÖRGY ÚT

KODÁLY KÖRÖND Ⓜ

György Ráth Museum

RÓTTENBILLER UTCA

Liszt Museum Ⓜ

House of Terror

VÖRÖSMARTY UTCA

ERZSÉBET KÖRÚT

Geological Institute

STEFÁNIA ÚT

19

THÖKÖLY ÚT

Puskás Ferenc Stadium

Aréna

Stadion Bus Station

HUNGÁRIA KÖRÚT

Horse Racing Track

Keleti Station

BAROSS TÉR Ⓜ

KEREPESI ÚT

Ⓜ STADIONOK

Őrs vezér tere ▶

VII

BLAHA LUJZA TÉR Ⓜ 20

Police History Museum

KÖZTÁRSASÁG TÉR

21

NÉPSZÍNHÁZ UTCA

JÓZSEF KÖRÚT

RÁKÓCZI TÉR

22

RÁKÓCZI ÚT

VIII

Kerepesi Cemetery

FIUME ÚT

ÜLLŐI ÚT

SOMOGYI UTCA

BAROSS UTCA

SALGÓTARJÁNI ÚT

Józsefváros Station ◀

Jewish Cemetery

KŐBÁNYAI ÚT

25

Ⓜ FERENC KÖRÚT

Applied Arts Museum

Trafó Arts Centre

FERENC KÖRÚT

KÖNYVES KÁLMÁN KÖRÚT

KŐBÁNYAI ÚT

Népliget

▼ Holocaust Memorial Centre & ㉗

BARS

Bambi	11
Cha-Cha-Cha Terasz	7
Corvintető	21
Csiga	22
Jelen	21
Libella	26
Platán	24
Pótkulcs	18
Sark kert	4
Tokaji Borozó	12
Trafó Bar Tangó	27
Trocadero Café	14

RESTAURANTS

Arcade	23	Firkász	9	Kéhli	1	Kispozsonyi	8	Okay Italia	13	Sahara	25
Bagolyvár	6	Gundel	5	Kerék	3	Lanzhou	20	Olimpia	19		
Chez Daniel	17	Gusto's	10	Kisbuda Gyöngye	2	Márkus	16	Taj Mahal	15		

luxury in the city; the rooms have Art Nouveau-style fittings (even down to the beautiful radiators) and are excellently equipped; those overlooking the Danube naturally have the best aspect. Both the restaurants are excellent – the *kávéház* is slightly cheaper than the *Páva* but still a very good option – and the service throughout the hotel is superlative. Underground garage. ⑨

Kempinski Corvinus V, Erzsébet tér 7–8 ☎1/429-3777, ⓦwww.kempinski-budapest.com. A flashy five-star establishment on the edge of the Belváros, which counts Madonna and Lewis Hamilton amongst its past guests. Tastefully furnished rooms offer every luxury, right down to a phone extension in the bathroom. Swimming pool, sauna, solarium, fitness room and underground garage, and wi-fi throughout. ⑨

K&K Opera VI, Révay utca 24 ☎1/269-0222, ⓦwww.kkhotels.com. Smart, modern and fully a/c four-star hotel right by the Opera House, with underground parking. Its 206 rooms – all with minibar, TV, safe and phone – have been recently refurbished, and around half have baths, the others showers. ⑨

King's Hotel VII, Nagy Diófa utca 25–27 ☎1/352-7675, ⓦwww.kingshotel.hu. Its location in the old Jewish ghetto and its kosher restaurant next door makes the King's popular with Jewish visitors. It has 79 rooms with one to four beds, all a/c with fridge, safe and internet access. No-smoking rooms available. You have to pay in advance for Sabbath meals. ⑧

Le Méridien V, Erzsébet tér 9–10 ☎1/429-5500, ⓦwww.lemeridien-budapest.com. Originally built for the Adria insurance company at the turn of the twentieth century, this building housed the police headquarters in the Communist years until it was totally gutted and reopened as a luxury hotel in 2000 – a welcome rival for the *Kempinski* next door. It's magnificently furnished throughout, and the well-equipped rooms are perhaps the most tasteful in the city. Parking and swimming pool. ⑨

Mercure Museum VIII, Trefort utca 2 ☎1/485-1080, ⓦwww.mercure-museum.hu. Having established itself in an imaginatively transformed Pest apartment block on a quiet street behind the National Museum, the *Mercure* has now expanded into the next-door block and has 104 rooms. The new half is sleek and modern in design, but the older part has more appeal, set around a glass-roofed courtyard. This is the old breakfast/restaurant area – more pleasant than the new one. Rooms are small but well equipped, with en-suite bathrooms, hairdryer, satellite TV and minibar. Off-street parking available, and wi-fi throughout. ⑨

Pest VI, Paulay Ede utca 31 ☎1/343-1198, ⓦwww.hotelpest.hu. Pleasant hotel in an old Pest apartment block – the bared walls in the bar area and foyer reveal its eighteenth-century origins – and it's well situated in a small street across Andrássy út from the Opera House. Its 25 good-size rooms have a/c and TV, and a bath or shower. Breakfast is in the glass-covered courtyard. ⑨

Starlight Suiten V, Mérleg utca 6 ☎1/484-3700, ⓦwww.starlighthotels.com. Good-value hotel, given its location near the Lánchíd (right behind the *Four Seasons*), with 54 spacious smoking and non-smoking suites. The rooms are very simply furnished but are large and well equipped: each has a kitchenette with a microwave, two televisions (one in each room), a sofa and a writing desk. There is wi-fi access throughout, and services include a sauna, steam bath and fitness rooms. ⑨

Zara Boutique V, Só utca 6 ☎1/577-0700, ⓦwww.zarahotels.com. New four-star boutique hotel off the bottom of Váci utca close to the Main Market Hall. Its 74 rooms are very pleasingly furnished with smart, dark furniture set against light walls, and are well equipped. All have showers, and you can ask for double or twin beds. Wi-fi in the lobby. ⑨

Around the Nagykörút

Béke Radisson VI, Teréz körút 43 ☎1/889-3900, ⓦwww.danubiushotels.com/beke. See map, p.66. Large vintage hotel in a handy location on the Nagykörút near Nyugati Station. Its facilities include a sauna, pool, business centre, underground garage and a good café on the ground floor. The 239 rooms have four-star facilities, including a/c, minibar, TV and safe. ⑨

Corinthia Grand Royal VII, Erzsébet körút 43–49 ☎1/479-4000, ⓦwww.corinthiahotels.com. See map, p.74. Pleasant new five-star place on the main boulevard, with over 400 comfortable rooms and two good restaurants. This was once one of the grand prewar hotels, but for forty years the building was used as offices, while the ballroom acted as the very grand Red Star cinema. The rebuilding – only the facade is original, as you discover when you tap on the grand pillars in the foyer – has been beautifully executed, using original drawings; even the gorgeous ballroom is totally reconstructed (except for the chandeliers). The hotel has its own luxury spa complex at the back, dating from 1886. ⑨

easyHotel VI, Eötvös utca 25/a ☎1/411-1982, Bookings by internet only: ⓦwww.easyhotel.com. See map, p.66. The Easy empire has reached Budapest, bringing the same approach to this brand-new place near Oktogon as it uses on easyJet, where cheapness and simplicity rule. The a/c rooms are all no-smoking and have one bright orange wall. They come in two sizes: small (7–9 square metres, enough room for a bed and your bag, as long as it's not too big); and standard, which has slightly more space and even a couple of hooks. The en-suite shower/toilet has the feel of an airplane cubicle. In Easy fashion you pay extra for TV and internet access. There are two rooms with disabled access – and much more room – on the ground floor. Rooms start at €15, according to demand, but are usually €60–70. ❻

Medosz Hotel VI, Jókai tér 9 ☎1/374-3001, ⊛www.medoszhotel.hu. See map, p.74. Near Oktogon, this friendly hotel was a trade union hostel until 1989. Not much has changed – it's still an unappealing modern block from the outside, and the small rooms have the simple bathrooms and basic institutional furniture that resonates with Communist Hungary nostalgia – but the location, good prices and helpful staff make it a popular choice. Rooms have TV and twin beds – some have the two beds end to end so ask if you want yours next to each other. ❻

Beyond the Nagykörút

For locations, see the map on p.66.

Andrássy VI, Andrássy út 111 ☎1/462-2100, ⊛www.andrassyhotel.com. Housed in a fine Bauhaus building near the Városliget, the *Andrássy* offers five-star accommodation without the corporate feel. Most double rooms have balconies, baths and all mod cons, including safes big enough for your laptop, though the smaller Classic rooms have power showers and no balcony. Try for one away from Andrássy út, which is a busy thoroughfare. The *Baraka* restaurant has a good reputation, and the hotel has wi-fi access throughout and easy access to the Belváros. ❾

Benczúr Hotel VI, Benczúr utca 35 ☎1/479-5650, ⊛www.hotelbenczur.hu. Large, modern and functional hotel on a leafy street off Andrássy út, with a nice garden at the back and parking in the yard (850Ft extra). The 60 "superior" doubles in one wing are all no-smoking and come with shower, TV and a/c, while the slightly cheaper

"standard" ones that make up the other wing have fewer frills but do have baths – and are divided into smoking and non-smoking rooms. There are also some apartments for families. The hotel website says that Pope John Paul II was a guest, but don't ask to stay in the same room – he didn't sleep here. ❽

Délibáb VI, Délibáb utca 35 ☎1/342-9301, ⊛www.hoteldelibab.com. The *Délibáb* stands right on Hősök tere, within walking distance of the sights on Andrássy út and the City Park, and has excellent transport links too. Its rooms are simply furnished but pleasant: most are no-smoking, some have balconies, but none has a/c. Best to avoid the rooms looking towards the park over the busy Dózsa György út. ❼

Radio Inn VI, Benczúr utca 19 ☎1/342-8347, ⊛www.radioinn.hu. Spacious, simply furnished smoking and non-smoking apartments complete with a living room, TV, big twin beds and a small kitchen with two electric rings; no a/c, however. Situated in a leafy street by the Chinese and Vietnamese embassies, with a pleasant garden. ❼

Margit-sziget

Margit-sziget's two hotels cater for wealthy tourists who come for the seclusion and fresh air – and for the thermal springs that made this a fashionable spa resort around the turn of the twentieth century.

Danubius Grand and Danubius Health Spa Resort Margitsziget XIII, Margit-sziget ☎1/889-4700, ⊛www.danubiushotels.com/grandhotel, www.danubiushotels.com/thermalhotel. See map, p.66. Both hotels are at the northern end of the island and provide a very wide range of spa facilities from mud spas to massages, as well as medical and cosmetic services from pedicures to plastic surgery, and have wi-fi access (for a fee). Rates include access to the thermal baths, pool, sauna, gym and other facilities. The *Grand* is the island's original, *fin-de-siècle* spa hotel; rooms here have balconies and high ceilings, and have been totally refurbished, with period furniture. The *Health Spa* is the big modern one, with balconies offering views over the island. ❾

Buda

Buda has fewer hotels than Pest, with less choice in the mid-range in particular, though there are some cheaper places in the northern suburbs. Broadly speaking, Buda's hotels are in three main areas: the historic but expensive Várhegy and Víziváros; the Tabán and Gellért-hegy, which gets cheaper as you move away from the river; and the Buda Hills, within easy reach of Moszkva tér.

Várhegy and the Víziváros

For locations, see the map on p.100

Art'otel I, Bem rakpart 16–19 ☎1/487-9487, ⓦwww.artotel.hu. This boutique hotel combines eighteenth-century buildings – comprising beautiful, spacious rooms with original doors and high ceilings – with a modern wing overlooking the river, offering marvellous views. Rooms are well equipped (bright red dressing gowns are among the items provided). There's a wi-fi network all round the hotel, and the business centre offers internet use. ⑨

Astra I, Vám utca 6 ☎1/214-1906, ⓦwww .hotelastra.hu. Small hotel in a converted 300-year-old building at the foot of the Castle District near Batthyány tér. Twelve well-furnished rooms (including three apartments) with minibar and a/c. ⑨

Burg I, Szentháromság tér 7 ☎1/212-0269, ⓦwww.burghotelbudapest.com. Modern, small hotel right in the middle of the Castle District, opposite the Mátyás Church. The recently renovated rooms are all no-smoking, have en-suite bathrooms, a/c, minibar, safe and TV. Wi-fi throughout. ⑨

Hilton Budapest I, Hess András tér 1–3 ☎1/889-6600, ⓦwww.danubiushotels.com/hilton. By the Mátyás Church, with superb views across the river, this hotel incorporates the remains of a medieval monastery and hosts summertime concerts in the former church. Luxurious to a fault. Wi-fi all over, and smoking and non-smoking floors. Excellent special offers available. ⑨

Kulturinnov I, Szentháromság tér 6 ☎1/224-8102, ⓦwww.mka.hu. Well positioned for sightseeing in a large neo-Gothic building right by the Mátyás Church, and on the first floor of the Hungarian Cultural Foundation, which hosts cultural events, concerts and exhibitions. The quiet and spacious rooms have a minibar. Some rooms have a TV, and about half have a/c – but the thick walls offer some protection against the heat. Wi-fi throughout. Breakfast included. ⑨

Lánchíd 19 I, Lánchíd utca 19 ☎1/419-1900, ⓦwww.lanchid19hotel.hu. The Hungarian debut of the worldwide Design hotel chain lies just below the Royal Palace, close to the Chain Bridge. Its award-winning design – all the work of local architects and artists – includes such features as an exterior facade of moving panels, as well as stylish lobby furniture and glass walkways leading to the 45 well-equipped rooms, which have striking bathrooms and individual decor themed on a wedding, a film or the like. Wi-fi throughout. ⑨

St George Residence I, Fortuna utca 4 ☎01/393-5700, ⓦwww.stgeorgehotel.hu. Variously a medieval inn, art school and law court, this fabulous building has been immaculately restored to become one of the city's most characterful hotels; the 26 sumptuously decorated suites, all furnished in Grand Empire-style, are priced according to size but all essentially comprise a bedroom, bathroom (some with jacuzzi) and living room with a study corner and fully equipped kitchenette. A top location and cheerful, obliging staff make this a first-class stopover. ⑨

Victoria I, Bem rakpart 11 ☎1/457-8080, ⓦwww.victoria.hu. Small, very friendly hotel on the embankment directly below the Mátyás Church. The rooms have excellent views of the Lánchíd and the river, and are equipped with minibar, TV and a/c. Sauna and garage facilities. ⑨

The Tabán and Gellért-hegy

Ábel Panzió XI, Ábel Jenő utca 9 ☎1/209-2537, ⓦwww.abelpanzio.hu. See map, p.66. Perhaps the most appealing pension in Budapest, a 1913 villa with beautiful Art Nouveau fittings in a quiet street, 20min from the Belváros. There are just ten rooms, two with twin beds, so book ahead; discount if you pay in cash. ⑥

Charles Hotel XI, Hegyalja út 23 ☎1/212-9169, ⓦwww.charleshotel.hu. See map, p.66. On the hill up from the Erzsébet híd on the main road to Vienna, this friendly apartment hotel was one of the first of its kind in the city. It has 73 rooms and apartments (you can choose double or twin beds, bath or shower) which come with cooking facilities, minibar and TV; those facing the inner yard are better, as the road is very busy. Some of the cheaper rooms have no a/c. Wi-fi all over, and bikes available for rent. Parking costs €8. ⑥

Citadella I, Citadella sétány ☎1/466-5794, ⓦwww.citadella.hu. See map, p.74. Breathtaking views of the city from this hotel inside the hulk of the old citadel, but at the weekend the neighbouring disco can be a bit noisy. The entrance gate is beside the restaurant outside the walls – you'll need to press the buzzer. To get here, take bus #27 from Móricz Zsigmond körtér, then it's a 10min walk from the Busuló Juhász stop. The cheapest doubles have shared facilities, while for a little more you can get rooms with private showers or baths. ④

Gellért XI, Szent Gellért tér 1 ☎1/889-5500, ⓦwww.danubiushotels.com/gellert. See map, p.74. Large, light corridors and lots of character at this well-established hotel. The facade, especially when floodlit, is magnificent, and so is the thermal pool, to which residents have their own lift down (and free entry, which comes with a bathrobe). A large number of single rooms are available; all rooms are en suite. The cheaper rooms look on to the courtyard and don't have the views – or the sound of the trams, which blight the others, in spite of double glazing. The beer hall (*söröző*) serves good food, and the coffee shop is excellent. Note that impending renovation may close all or part of the hotel. ➌

Orion I, Döbrentei utca 13 ☎1/356-8583, ⊛www .bestwestern-ce.com/orion. See map, p.100. Small modern block in the Tabán district, just south of Várhegy. The simple rooms have TV and minibar – those at the front can be noisy – and guests can make use of a sauna. ➒

The Buda Hills

For locations, see the map on p.66.
Beatrix Panzió II, Szehér út 3 ☎1/275-0550, ⊛www.beatrixhotel.hu. Friendly eighteen-room

pension in the villa district northwest of Moszkva tér – take tram #61. There's a bar on the ground floor, a sauna, and parking too. ➏

Buda Villa Panzió XII, Kiss Áron utca 6 ☎1/275-0091, ⊛www.budapansio.hu. Up in the hills above Moszkva tér – it's a 10min ride from there on bus #156 (note that the last bus leaves about 10.45pm). This comfortable and friendly ten-room pension has a small garden that's perfect for relaxing in after a day's sightseeing, and a bar in the lounge on the first floor. ➏

Budapest II, Szilágyi Erzsébet fasor 47 ☎1/889-4200, ⊛www.danubiushotels.com/budapest. Cylindrical tower facing the Buda Hills, opposite the lower terminal of the Cogwheel Railway, 500m from Moszkva tér. Rooms come with a/c, TV and minibar, and there's a sauna, fitness room and business centre too. The lobby's decor is rather 1970s, but at least there are excellent views over the city from the upper floors. ➑

Hostels

If you don't have a tent, a dormitory bed in a **hostel** is the cheapest alternative – note that dorms tend to be mixed sex. Many hostels also have rooms at much the same price as private accommodation, but often with very basic student furniture. Still, at least there are no surcharges of the sort levied in private rooms for staying fewer than four nights, and the hostels offer 24-hour information from English-speaking staff at the reception desk.

Unless stated otherwise, the hostels listed below are open year-round. Student dormitories are open during July and August only, many of them located in the university area south of Gellért-hegy. You can't be sure of getting a bed in the hostel of your choice in summer without **booking** in advance.

The Mellow Mood group runs some excellent year-round hostels in the city and also handles some of the university accommodation open during the summer. Staff at its office in Keleti Station (daily: June–Aug 7am–midnight; Sept–May 7am–8pm; ☎1/343-0748 or 1/413-2062, ⊛www.mellowmood.hu), on the right of the glass doors at the far end as you arrive, can give information, make bookings and also organize transport to the group's hostels from the station.

Note that many of Pest's hostels are in residential blocks and frown on rowdy guests.

Pest

Astoria City VII, Rákóczi út 4.III.27 ☎1/266-1327, ⊛www.astoriacityhostel.com. See map, p.74. On the third floor (with a lift), this is a pleasant small hostel in the heart of the city, with two eight-bed dorms, one six-bed and one en-suite double room. The six-bed overlooks a quiet inner courtyard, the others to the noisy main road. They also have apartments in the same block, and rooms a few doors along. Prices include breakfast and internet access. Laundry service available. Dorm beds from €12, double ➍

Caterina VI, Teréz körút 30.III.28 ☎1/269-5990, ⊛www.caterinahostel.hu. See map, p.74.

Long-established hostel that has moved to a new venue, above the Művész cinema near the Oktogon, and although it's on the third floor with no lift, the small setup gives it a friendly feel. There are rooms of six, eight and ten bunk beds, as well as a room for three, and three apartments in neighbouring streets. The eight-bed room is the quietest, looking on to the courtyard – the others overlook the noisy boulevard. They have a laundry service, a kitchen and free internet access. Dorm beds from 2500Ft, including breakfast.

Green Bridge V, Molnár utca 22 ☎1/266-6922, ⊛www.greenbridgehostel.com. See map, p.74. Small hostel in a quiet street near the Danube in the Belváros. Run by a helpful young couple, it's on the ground floor and has rooms of five to eight beds, plus two double rooms. There's a laundry service, and free internet access and coffee. They can also book places on cave tours. Beds from €10, doubles ⑤

Mandragora VIII, Krúdy Gyula utca 12.I.7 ☎1/789-9515, Ⓦwww.mandragorahostel.com. See map, p.74. Relaxed small first-floor hostel on a quiet road a couple of streets behind the National Museum run by a friendly young couple with good English. Decoration is Indian-inspired, and there is use of kitchen, bikes for rent, wi-fi. One double room plus a six-bed and an eight-bed dorm. Cash only. Beds from €14, doubles ④

Marco Polo VII, Nyár utca 6 ☎1/413-2555, Ⓦwww.marcopolohostel.com. See map, p.74. Big, busy and clean hostel close to Blaha Lujza tér, with simply furnished four- and twelve-bed dorms with bunks, as well as 36 double rooms, and a bar in the cellar. IYHF cardholders get a discount. Dorm beds 4500Ft, doubles ⑥

Red Bus V, Semmelweis utca 14 ☎1/266-0136 Ⓦwww.redbusbudapest.hu. See map, p.74. Friendly and relaxed hostel on a quiet backstreet close to Deák tér, with rooms of two to five beds. Breakfast and use of the kitchen are included in the price; internet use and laundry service are extra. As it's set in a residential block, this is not a place for partying. See website for special offers; otherwise 3600Ft for dorm beds, doubles ④

Buda

For locations, see the map on p.66.

Back Pack XI, Takács Menyhért utca 33 ☎1/385-8946, Ⓦwww.backpackbudapest.hu. Charming 50-bed hostel with a shaded garden, about 20min from the centre (tram #49 or bus #7 to Tétényi út stop). The staff provide lots of information on the city, sport and fitness, and also organize cave trips. Dorm beds from 3000Ft, doubles ④

Landler XI, Bartók Béla út 17 ☎1/463-3621. One of the older hostels in the city, housed in the Baross Gábor Kollégium, near the Gellért Baths. Basic two- and three-bed rooms, with high ceilings and basins – shared bathrooms on the corridor. Open July & Aug only. A bed in a three-bed room is 3400Ft, two-bed rooms are 4000Ft per person or 5900Ft for single occupancy.

Private apartments and rooms

The days of grannies renting out rooms through Ibusz are generally in the past – nowadays it is far easier to find self-contained **studio flats** or **apartments**. You can rent these through agencies – such as Ibusz, V, Ferenciek tere 10, on the corner of Petőfi Sándor utca (Mon–Fri 9am–6pm Sat 9am–1pm; ☎1/501-4910, Ⓦwww.ibusz.hu), or the To-Ma agency at V, Október 6 utca 22 (Mon–Fri 9am–noon, Sat & Sun 9am–5pm; ☎1/353-0819, Ⓦwww.tomatour.hu) – or internet-based companies such as Budapest Lets (Ⓦwww.budapestlets.com), a UK-Hungarian venture managing about forty well-equipped properties, from one-room studio flats on Ráday utca to luxury apartments on Várhegy.

You can still rent a **private room** – through the two agencies above – the downsides being that you have less choice and you are less independent of the owners. Depending on location and amenities, **prices** for a double room start at 6000Ft a night, while apartments go from 8000Ft. Rates can be up to thirty percent higher if you stay fewer than four nights.

Camping

Budapest's **campsites** are generally well equipped and pleasant, with trees, grass and sometimes even a pool. They can get crowded between June and September, when smaller places might run out of space. It is illegal to camp anywhere else, and the parks are patrolled to enforce this.

The campsites listed here are all on the edge of the city on the Buda side, since the Pest ones are not very inviting.

Csillebérci Camping XII, Konkoly Thege Miklós út 21 ☎1/395-6537, Ⓦwww.csilleberciszabadido.hu. Large site up in the Buda Hills, with space for 1000 campers and a range of bungalows. Bus #90 from Moszkva tér to the Csillebérc stop or bus #90A to Normafa, then a short walk. Open all year.

Római Camping III, Szentendrei út 189 ☎ 1/388-7167, ⓦ www.romaicamping.hu. Huge site beside the road to Szentendre in Rómaifürdő (25min by HÉV from Batthyány tér), with space for 2500 campers. It also has wooden bungalows, and the price includes use of the neighbouring Rómaifürdőlido. Open all year.

Zugligeti Niche Camping XII, Zugligeti út 101 ☎ 1/200-8346, ⓦ www.campingniche.hu. At the end of the #158 bus route from Moszkva tér, opposite the chairlift up to János-hegy, this is a small, terraced ravine site in the woods with space for 260 campers and good facilities, including a pleasant little restaurant occupying the former tram station at the far end. April–Oct.

Pest

Pest is busier, more populous and vital than Buda: the place where things are decided, made and sold. While Buda grew up around the royal court, the east bank was settled by merchants and artisans, and commerce has always been its lifeblood. Much of its architecture and layout dates from the late nineteenth century, giving Pest a homogeneous appearance compared to other European capitals. Boulevards, public buildings and apartment houses were built on a scale appropriate to the Habsburg empire's second city, and the capital of a nation which celebrated its millennial anniversary in 1896. Now sooty with age or in the throes of restoration, these grand edifices form the backdrop to life in the **Belváros** (inner city) and the residential districts, hulking gloomily above the cafés, wine cellars and courtyards where people socialize. While there's plenty to see and do, it's the ambience that sticks in one's memory.

Away from the waterfront, you'll find that two semicircular boulevards are fundamental to **orientation**. The inner city lies within the **Kiskörút** (Small Boulevard), made up of Károly körút, Múzeum körút and Vámház körút. Further out, the **Nagykörút** (Great Boulevard) sweeps through the VI, VII, VIII and IX districts, where it is called Szent István körút, Teréz körút, Erzsébet körút, József körút and Ferenc körút respectively. Pest is also defined by **avenues** (*út*) radiating out beyond the Nagykörút – notably Bajcsy-Zsilinszky út (for Nyugati Station); Andrássy út, leading to the **Városliget** (City Park); Rákóczi út, for Keleti Station; and Üllői út, leading out towards the airport. As the meeting point of three metro lines and several main avenues, **Deák tér** makes a good jumping-off point for explorations.

The Belváros

The **Belváros** (Inner City) is the hub of Pest and, for tourists at least, the epicentre of what's happening – abuzz with pavement cafés, buskers, boutiques and nightclubs. Commerce and pleasure have been its lifeblood as long as Pest has existed, as a medieval market town or the kernel of a city whose *belle époque* rivalled Vienna's. Since their fates diverged, the Belváros lagged far behind Vienna's Centrum in prosperity; but the gap is fast being narrowed, at least superficially. It's now increasingly like any Western city in its consumer culture, but you can still get a sense of the old atmosphere, especially in the quieter backstreets south of Kossuth utca.

The **Kiskörút** (Small Boulevard) that surrounds the Belváros follows the course of the medieval walls of Pest, showing how compact it was before the phenomenal expansion of the nineteenth century. However, little remains from further back than the eighteenth century, as the "liberation" of Pest from the Turks by the Habsburgs in 1686 left the town in ruins. Some Baroque churches and the former Greek and Serbian quarters attest to its revival by settlers from other parts of the

▲ Nyugati Station   Hősök tere & the Városliget ▲

DOWNTOWN PEST

0 — 100 m

Museum of Ethnography
KOSSUTH TÉR
Parliament
KOSSUTH TÉR M
VÉRTANÚK TERE
Eternal Flame
ALKOTMÁNY UTCA
VADÁSZ UTCA
BÁTHORY UTCA
Bedő House
Glass House
HOLD UTCA
HAJÓS UTCA
Mai Manó House
JÓKAI UTCA
JÓKAI TÉR
OKTOGON M OKTOGON
VI
Holocaust Memorial
Soviet Army Memorial
US Embassy
TV Building
Post Office Savings Bank
SZABADSÁG TÉR
ZOLTÁN UTCA
Market Hall
TERÉZVÁROS
Operetta Theatre
LISZT FERENC TÉR
Liszt Music Academy
National Bank
ARANY JÁNOS UTCA
ARANY JÁNOS UTCA M
Opera House
OPERA M
Ernst Museum
ERZSÉBET KÖRÚT
VII
LIPÓTVÁROS
Academy of Sciences
OKTÓBER 6 UTCA
NÁDOR UTCA
Museum of Trade & Tourism
BAJCSY-ZSILINSZKY ÚT
ANDRÁSSY ÚT
PAULAY EDE UTCA
New Theatre
KIRÁLY UTCA
LÁNC HÍD
ROOSEVELT TÉR
Gresham Palace
JÓZSEF ATTILA UTCA
St Stephen's Basilica
Post Office Museum
ERZSÉBETVÁROS
Rumbach utca Synagogue
Orthodox Synagogue
Museum of Electro-technology
BKV Office
SZÉCHENYI RAKPART
N
VIGADÓ TÉR
VÖRÖSMARTY TÉR M
DEÁK UTCA
DEÁK TÉR M
Underground Railway Museum
Lutheran Museum and Church
RUMBACH UTCA
Dohány utca Synagogue & Jewish Museum
DOHÁNY UTCA
Kelet Station ▶
Vigadó
Servite Church
SZERVITA TÉR
Central Post Office
KÁROLY KÖRÚT
RÁKÓCZI ÚT
VIII
Cathedral of the Dormition
Párizsi Udvar
Franciscan Church
ASTORIA M
Eötvös Loránd University (ELTE)
Radio Building
Contra Aquincum
PETŐFI TÉR
Belváros Church
FERENCIEK TERE
FERENCIEK TERE M
Károlyi Garden
MÚZEUM KÖRÚT
BRÓDY SÁNDOR UTCA
JÓZSEFVÁROS
Ferenc Körút M
ERZSÉBET HÍD
MÁRCIUS 15 TÉR
BELVÁROS
Petőfi Literary Museum
Hungarian National Museum
MIKSZÁTH KÁLMÁN TÉR
Applied Arts Museum
St. Gellért Statue
Rudas Baths
Serbian Orthodox Church
KÁLVIN TÉR M
Szabó Ervin Library
REVICZKY UTCA
KRÚDY GY U.
BAROSS UTCA
International Landing Stage
SZENT GELLÉRT RAKPART
River Danube (Duna)
BELGRÁD RAKPART
ÜLLŐI ÚT
RÁDAY UTCA
Citadella & Liberation Monument
Cave Church
Great Market Hall
FŐVÁM TÉR
FERENCVÁROS
IX
GELLÉRT-HEGY
XI
SZABADSÁG HÍD
Economics University
Gellért Baths

RESTAURANTS

Alföldi	50
Belcanto	16
Bock Bisztró	C
Bouchon	4
Café Kör	25
Carmel	34
Csarnok	5
Eklektika	10
Falafel	18
Fausto's Osteria	43
Fészek	28
Fülemüle	45
Gerlóczy	44
Govinda	26
Hummus Bar	1 & 19
Il Terzo Cerchio	38
Kádár Étkezde	30

RESTAURANTS (CONTD.)

Károlyi	47
Két Szerecsen	17
Kis Mama Konyhája	55

Klassz	13
Köleves	31
Krizia	2
Lou Lou	27
M	21
Menza	11
Múzeum	46
Pomo D'Oro	23
Rézkakas	49
Soul Café	56
Trattoria Toscana	54
Trattoria Trattoria	53
Via Luna	8
Vapiano	41

ACCOMMODATION

Anna	N	Hotel Art	R
Astoria	P	Kempinski Corvinus	K
Astoria City hostel	M	K&K Opera	D
Caterina hostel	A	King's Hotel	H
Citadella	U	Le Méridien	J
Corinthia Grand Royal	C	Mandragora hostel	Q
Four Seasons	G	Marco Polo hostel	I
Gellért	V	Medosz	B
Green Bridge hostel	S	Mercure Museum	O
		Pest	E

Red Bus hostel	L		
Starlight Suiten	F		
Zara Boutique	T		

BARS

Action	51	Giero	14
Capella	52	Gül Baba Szeráj	15
Castro Bistro	37	Katapult	42
CoXx	38	Kiadó	3
Ellátó	32	Kuplung	24
		Le Café M	9
		Mélypont	48
		Morrison's	20
		Moyo	7
		Old Man's Music Pub	33

Paris-Texas	57
Piaf	6
Sark	29
Sirály	22
Sixtus	35
Spoon	36
Szimplakert	40
Szóda	39
Vian	12

Habsburg empire, but most of the **architecture** dates from the era when Budapest asserted its right to be an imperial capital, between 1860 and 1918. Today, first-time visitors are struck by the statues, domes and mosaics on the Neoclassical and Art Nouveau piles, which are reflected in the mirrored banks and luxury hotels that symbolize the post-Communist era.

Vörösmarty tér

The starting point for exploring the Belváros is **Vörösmarty tér**, the leafy centre of the district where crowds eddy around the portraitists, café tables and craft stalls that set up here over summer, Christmas and the wine festival. While children play in the fountains, teenagers lounge around the **statue of Mihály Vörösmarty** (1800–50), a poet and translator whose hymn to Magyar identity, *Szózat* (Appeal), is publicly declaimed at moments of national crisis. Its opening line – "Be faithful to your land forever, Oh Hungarians" – is carved on the pedestal. Made of Carrara marble, it has to be wrapped in plastic sheeting each winter to prevent it from cracking.

On the north side of the square is the **Gerbeaud patisserie**, Budapest's most famous confectioners. Founded in 1858 by Henrik Kugler, it was bought in 1884 by the Swiss confectioner Emile Gerbeaud, who invented the *konyakos meggy* (cognac-cherry bonbon) and sold top-class cakes at reasonable prices, making *Gerbeaud* a popular rendezvous for the middle classes. His portrait hangs in one of the rooms whose gilded ceilings and china recall the *belle époque*.

Beside *Gerbeaud*'s terrace is the entrance to the **Underground Railway** (Földalatti vasút), whose vaguely Art Nouveau cast-iron fixtures and elegant tilework stamp it as decades older than the other metro lines. Indeed, it was the first on the European continent and the second in the world (after London's Metropolitan line) when it was inaugurated in 1896. Visit the Underground Railway Museum at Deák tér (see p.78) to learn more about its history.

Váci utca

Running from Vörösmarty tér down towards the Great Market Hall – interrupted by Ferenciek tere, where you have to cross a pedestrian subway – **Váci utca** has been famous for its shops and **korzó** (promenade) since the eighteenth century. During the 1980s, its vivid streetlife became a symbol of the "consumer socialism" that distinguished Hungary from other Eastern Bloc states, but Budapesters today are rather less enamoured of Váci, leaving it to rely on tourists for its livelihood. Overpriced souvenir shops and cafés compete with hustlers, buskers and exchange bureaux. A few landmarks along the way might catch your eye, such as the scantily clad **Fisher-girl statue** on **Kristóf tér**, a small plaza running across to Szervita tér (see p.76), or the **Pest Theatre** (no. 9) on the site of the *Inn of the Seven Electors*, where the 12-year-old Liszt performed in 1823.

Váci's looks improve between Ferenciek tere and the Great Market Hall; though no less touristy, the old buildings and cobbled sidestreets have been tastefully face-lifted. Look out for the prewar **Officers' Casino** on the corner of Ferenciek tere (now a bank's headquarters); a sculptural **plaque** on the wall of no. 47, commemorating the fact that the Swedish King Carl XII stayed here during his lightning fourteen-day horseride from Turkey to Sweden, in 1714; and the nineteenth-century hulk of the **Old Budapest City Hall** at nos. 62–64, where the city council still holds its meetings.

Shortly after this, a left turn into Szerb utca will bring you to the **Serbian Orthodox Church** (daily 10am–4pm; 500Ft), built by the Serbian artisans and merchants who settled here after the Turks were driven out. Secluded in a high-walled garden, it's best visited during High Mass on Sunday (10.30–11.45am), when the singing of the liturgy, the clouds of incense and flickering candles create an unearthly atmosphere. A block or so south of the church, part of the **medieval wall** of Pest can be seen behind a children's playground on the corner of Bástya utca and Veres Pálné utca.

Szervita tér to Ferenciek tere

If the crowds on Váci utca deter you, a parallel route may suit you better. By turning off Váci at Kristóf tér, you can cut through to **Szervita tér** – named after the eighteenth-century **Servite Church**, whose facade bears a relief of an angel cradling a dying horseman, in memory of the Seventh Kaiser Wilhelm Hussars killed in World War I. Across the way are two remarkable buildings from the golden age of Hungarian architecture. No. 3 has a gable aglow with a superb **Art Nouveau mosaic** of *Patrona Hungariae* (Our Lady) flanked by shepherds and angels, one of the finest works of Miksa Róth (see p.93). The **Rózsavölgyi Building**, next door but one, was built a little later (between 1910 and 1913) by the "father" of Hungarian Modernism, Béla Lajta, whose earlier association with the National Romantic school is evident from the majolica bands on its upper storeys. On the ground floor is the Rózsavölgyi music shop, one of the oldest and best in the city.

From here, Petőfi Sándor utca runs south to **Ferenciek tere** (Franciscans' Square). The square itself has been swallowed up by the highway-style ramp of the Érzsébet híd, squeezed between a pair of *fin-de-siècle* office buildings, named the **Klotild Palaces** after the Habsburg princess who commissioned them. Still more striking is the **Párisi Udvar**, a flamboyantly eclectic shopping arcade completed in 1915. Its fifty naked statues above the third floor were deemed incompatible with its intended role as a savings bank, symbolized by images of bees throughout the building. The neglected arcade, with its hexagonal dome designed by Miksa Róth, is as dark as an Andalusian mosque and twice as ornate, and cries out for restoration.

The eastern side of Ferenciek tere seamlessly becomes **Kossuth Lajos utca**, which passes the **Franciscan Church** that gave the square its name. The relief on the church's wall recalls the great flood of 1838, in which over four hundred citizens were killed; it depicts the heroic efforts of Baron Miklós Wesselényi, who personally rescued scores of people in his boat. The junction of Kossuth Lajos utca with the Kiskörút is named after the **Astoria Hotel** on the corner, a prewar haunt of spies and journalists that was commandeered as an HQ by the Nazis in 1944 and the Soviets after the 1956 Uprising. Today, its Neoclassical coffee lounge is redolent of Stalinist chic.

To explore further, head south from the church past the dome of the university library till you come to another thoroughfare, named after Count Mihály Károlyi, the liberal politician who briefly led the government after World War I. Immediately to the right, on the corner, is the **Centrál Kávéház**, one of Pest's grand old coffee houses where, in the early twentieth century, writers and intellectuals lingered day and night. Károlyi's birthplace at no. 16 houses the **Petőfi Literary Museum** (Petőfi Irodalmi Múzeum; Tues–Sun 10am–6pm; 600Ft; Ⓦwww.pim .hu), showcasing the personal effects of Sándor Petőfi, the nineteenth-century revolutionary poet (see box, p.390), and later Hungarian writers, including Endre Ady's fedora and Mihály Babit's bomb-flattened typewriter. The mansion's garden, the **Károlyi-kert**, is a delightful haven within the Belváros with an agreeable restaurant (see p.125). It was here that Lajos Batthyány, head of the independent Hungarian government following the 1848 revolution, was arrested in 1849, and General Haynau, the "Butcher of Vienna", signed the death warrants of Batthyány and other rebel leaders after finishing his morning exercises.

Along the embankment

The **Belgrád rakpart** (Belgrade Embankment) bore the brunt of the fighting in 1944–45, when the Nazis and the Red Army exchanged salvos across the Danube. As with the Várhegy in Buda, postwar clearances exposed historic sites and provided an opportunity to integrate them into the environment – but the magnificent **view** of Buda Palace and Gellért-hegy is hardly matched by the row of modern hotels on the Pest side. While such historic architecture as remains can be seen in a fifteen-minute stroll between the Erzsébet híd and the Lánchíd, **tram #2** enables you to see a longer stretch of the waterfront between Szabadság híd and Kossuth tér in the north, periodically interrupted by a tunnel that's the first to be flooded if the Danube overflows its embankments, as sometimes happens in the summer.

The bold white pylons and cables of the **Erzsébet híd** (Elizabeth Bridge) are as cherished a feature of the panorama as the stone Lánchíd to the north or the wrought-iron Szabadság híd to the south. Of all the Danube bridges blown up by the Germans as they retreated to Buda in January 1945, the Erzsébet híd was the only one not rebuilt in its original form.

In the shadow of the bridge ramp, the grimy facade of the **Belváros Parish Church** (Belvárosi Plébánia Templom; Mon–Sat 7am–7pm, Sun 8am–7pm; free) masks its origins as the oldest church in Pest. Founded in 1046 as the burial place of St Gellért (see p.112), it was rebuilt as a Gothic hall church in the fifteenth century (his remains had been long shipped off to Venice), turned into a mosque by the Turks and then reconstructed as a church in the eighteenth century. By coming after Latin Mass at 10am on Sunday you can see the Gothic sedilia and Turkish *mihrab* (prayer niche) behind the high altar, which are otherwise out of bounds. The vaulted nave and side chapels are Baroque.

On the square beside the church, a sunken enclosure exposes the remains of **Contra-Aquincum**, a Roman fort that was an outpost of their settlement in Óbuda. More pertinently to modern-day Hungary, the name of the square, **Március 15 tér**, refers to March 15, 1848, when the anti-Habsburg Revolution began, while the adjacent **Petőfi tér** is named after Sándor Petőfi, the poet whose *National Song* – the anthem of 1848 – and romantic death in battle made him a patriotic icon. The **Petőfi statue** has long been a focus for demonstrations as well as patriotic displays – especially on March 15, when it is bedecked with flags and flowers. Beyond it looms the Greek Orthodox **Cathedral of the Dormition**, built by the Greek community in the 1790s and, more recently, the object of a tug-of-war between the Patriarchate of Moscow that gained control of it after 1945 and the Orthodox Church in Greece that previously owned it. The cathedral admits sightseers (Wed 2–5pm, Fri 1–5pm, Sat 3–8pm, Sun noon–5pm), and has services in Hungarian, accompanied by singing in the Orthodox fashion.

Just north of Petőfi tér, the gigantic **Marriott Hotel** is situated between the embankment and the street running parallel, Apáczai Csere János utca. On the Danube side of the *Marriott*, the concrete esplanade is a sterile attempt at recreating the prewar **Duna-korzó**, the most informal of Budapest's promenades, where it was socially acceptable for strangers to approach celebrities and stroll beside them. The outdoor cafés here, which boast wonderful views, charge premium rates.

Vigadó tér

Further north, the promenade crosses **Vigadó tér**, an elegant square named after the **Vigadó** concert hall, whose name translates as "having a ball" or "making merry". Inaugurated in 1865, this Romantic pile by Frigyes Feszl is encrusted with statues of the Muses and plaques recalling performances by Liszt, Mahler, Wagner, von Karajan and other renowned artists. Badly damaged in World War II, it didn't reopen until 1980, such was the care taken to recreate its sumptuous decor. At the time of writing, the hall was once again closed for refurbishment, and the reopening date uncertain.

Don't overlook the statue of the impish **Little Princess**, which has been sitting on the railings by the tram line since 1990. After dusk, you'll hardly notice that she isn't a person, if you notice her at all. By day, she looks like a cross-dressing boy in a Tinkerbell hat. Prince Charles was so taken by her that he invited her creator, László Marton, to hold an exhibition of his work in Britain. The nearby Vigadó tér **docks** are the point of departure for boats and hydrofoils to Szentendre, Visegrád and Esztergom on the Danube Bend (see Chapter 2).

Deák tér and Erzsébet tér

Three metro lines and several important roads meet at **Deák tér** and **Erzsébet tér** – two squares that merge into one another (making local addresses extremely confusing) to form a jumping-off point for the Belváros and Lipótváros. You'll recognize the area by two landmarks: the vast mustard-coloured **Anker Palace** on the Kiskörút and, by the metro pavilion on the edge of the Belváros, the **Lutheran Church**, which hosts some excellent concerts that include Bach's *St John Passion* over the fortnight before Easter. Next door, the **Lutheran Museum** (Evangélikus Múzeum; Tues–Sun 10am–6pm; 500Ft) displays a facsimile of Martin Luther's last will and testament, and a copy of the first book printed in Hungarian, a New Testament from 1541. In the 1990s, Mayor Demszky's plan to build a new National Theatre on Erzsébet tér was thwarted by the government, leaving a vast pit dubbed the "National Hole". Eventually filled in and tidied up, it now houses the *Gödör Klub*, an underground concert and exhibition venue, visible from above through a glass-bottomed pool.

Accessible via the upper sub-level of Deák tér metro, the **Underground Railway Museum** (Földalattivasút Múzeum; Tues–Sun 10am–5pm; 270Ft or one BKV ticket) extols the history of Budapest's original metro. The exhibits include two elegant wooden carriages (one used up until 1973) and period fixtures and posters, which enhance the museum's nostalgic appeal. The metro's genesis was a treatise by Mór Balázs, proposing a steam-driven tram network starting with a route along Andrássy út, an underground line being suggested as a fallback in case the overground option was rejected. Completed in under two years, it was inaugurated in 1896 – in time for the Millennial Exhibition – by Emperor Franz Josef, who agreed to allow it to bear his name, which it kept until 1918. The metro was the first on the European continent and the second in the world (after London's Metropolitan line), and originally ran from Vörösmarty tér as far as the Millennial Exhibition grounds at Hősök tere.

Lipótváros and beyond

Lipótváros (Leopold Town), to the north of the Belváros, started to develop in the late eighteenth century, first as a financial centre and later as the seat of government. Though part of the V district like the Belváros, it has quite a different ambience, with sombre streets of Neoclassical buildings interrupted by squares flanked by monumental Art Nouveau or neo-Renaissance piles. Busy with office workers by day, and something of a place to eat out at weekends, another source of vitality is the Central European University (CEU), funded by the Hungarian-born billionaire financier George Soros.

It makes sense to start a Lipótváros visit either with Roosevelt tér, just inland of the Lánchíd, or St Stephen's Basilica, two minutes' walk from Erzsébet tér. Most of the streets between them lead towards the set-piece expanse of **Szabadság tér**, whence you can head on towards Parliament – though the Kossuth tér metro station or tram #2 from the Belgrád rakpart will provide quicker access.

Roosevelt tér

At the Pest end of the Lánchíd, **Roosevelt tér** is blitzed by traffic, making it difficult to stand back and admire the magnificent Art Nouveau **Gresham Palace** on the eastern side of the square. Commissioned by a British insurance company in 1904, it's named after the financier Sir Thomas Gresham, the author of Gresham's law that bad money drives out good, whereby the circulation of coins of equal face value but different metals leads to those made of more valuable metal being hoarded and disappearing from use. The building was in an awful state when it was acquired by the Four Seasons hotel chain, but fears of a crass refurbishment have been dispelled by a loving restoration: authentic materials and even the original workshops were sought out to do the job. Today you can once again see Gresham's bust high up on the facade, and members of the public may walk in to admire the subtle hues of the tiled lobby and glass-roofed arcade with wrought-iron peacock gates and stained-glass windows by Miksa Róth.

Statues of Count Széchenyi (see p.267) and Ferenc Deák, another major nineteenth-century politician, stand at opposite ends of the square. The statue of the former isn't far from the **Hungarian Academy of Sciences** (Magyar Tudományos Akadémia), founded after Széchenyi pledged a year's income from his estates towards its establishment in 1825 – as depicted on a relief on the wall facing Akadémia utca.

While the Academy and the Lánchíd are tangible reminders of Széchenyi's enterprise, there is no reminder of Deák's achievement in forging an *Ausgleich* (Compromise) with the Habsburgs. This was symbolized by the crowning of Emperor Franz Josef as King of Hungary in 1867, when soil from every corner of the nation was piled into a Coronation Hill, on the site of the present square. Here the emperor flourished the sword of St Stephen and promised to defend Hungary against all its enemies – a pledge that proved almost as ephemeral as the hill itself. Eighty years later, the square was renamed Roosevelt tér in honour of the late US president – a rare example of Cold War courtesy that was never revoked.

▲ Gresham Palace

St Stephen's Basilica and Bajcsy-Zsilinszky út

St Stephen's Basilica (Szent István Bazilika; Mon–Fri 9am–5.15pm & 7–7.30pm, Sat 9am–1pm & 7–7.30pm, Sun 1–5pm; free) took so long to build that Budapesters once joked, when borrowing money, "I'll pay you back when the basilica is finished". Work began in 1851 under the supervision of József Hild, continued after his death under Miklós Ybl, and was finally completed by Joseph Krauser in 1905. At the inaugural ceremony Emperor Franz Josef was seen to glance anxiously at the dome, whose collapse during a storm in 1868 had set progress back. At 96m, it is exactly the same height as the dome of the Parliament building – both allude to the putative date of the Magyars' arrival in Hungary (896 AD).

In a **chapel** (April–Sept Mon–Fri 9.30am–4.30pm, Sun 1–4.30pm; Oct–March Mon–Fri 10am–4pm, Sun 1–4.30pm; free) to the left at the back is the gnarled **mummified hand of St Stephen**, Hungary's holiest relic. The Szent Jobb (literally, "holy right") is paraded with great pomp through the surrounding streets on August 20, the anniversary of his death, but at other times you can see it in the chapel by inserting 100Ft to illuminate the casket.

Although the **treasury** (same hours as the cathedral; 400Ft) is paltry compared to that at Esztergom's Basilica, you shouldn't miss the so-called **Panorama Tower** (daily: April–May 10am–4pm; June–Aug 9.30am–6.30pm; Sept–Oct 10am–7.30pm; 500Ft), reached by a lift to the base of the cupola, 65m up, and then another lift or a spiral stairway (mind your head on the joists) to the external walkway, which offers a grand **view** over the city, as well as the option of walking back down 302 stone steps. **Masses** are held in the basilica on weekdays (7am, 8am & 6pm) and Sundays (8am, 9am, 10am, noon, 6pm & 7.30pm).

At Szent István tér 15, just north of the Basilica, the **Museum of Trade and Tourism** (Kereskedelmi és Vendéglátóipari Múzeum; daily except Tues 11am–7pm; 600Ft; @ www.mkvm.hu) has several rooms devoted to fashions and ephemera from the *belle époque* and interwar eras, and sometimes hosts culinary events. The avenue running past the Basilica is named after Endre Bajcsy-Zsilinszky (1866–1944), a right-wing MP who ended up an outspoken critic of Fascism and was shot as the Russians approached. **Bajcsy-Zsilinszky út** is the demarcation line between the Lipótváros and Terézváros districts, running northwards to **Nyugati Station**, an elegant, iron-beamed terminal built in 1874–77 by the Eiffel Company of Paris. Beside the station, the **Westend City Center** is one of Budapest's largest malls, boasting four hundred outlets, an artificial waterfall and a rooftop **ice-skating rink** (daily 8am–10pm, Fri & Sat till midnight; 800–1000Ft depending on the time and day; @ www.jegterasz.hu).

Szabadság tér

For over a century, Lipótváros was dominated by a gigantic barracks where scores of Hungarians were imprisoned or executed, until this symbol of Habsburg tyranny was demolished in 1897 and the site redeveloped as **Szabadság tér** (Liberty Square). Invested with significance from the outset, it became a kind of record of the vicissitudes of modern Hungarian history, where each regime added or removed **monuments**, according to their political complexion.

In the early years of the twentieth century, Hungary's burgeoning prosperity was expressed by two monumental temples to capitalism: the **Stock Exchange**, whose designer, Ignác Alpár, blended motifs from Greek and Assyrian architecture and crowned it with twin towers resembling Khmer temples; and the **National Bank** across the square, its facade encrusted with reliefs symbolizing honest toil and profit. While the former became the headquarters of Hungarian Television after the Communists abolished the stock market, the bank still functions as such. An entrance at Szabadság tér 8 leads to a stylish **Visitor Centre**

(Mon–Fri 9am–4pm; free; ⊛http://english.mnb.hu) featuring curiosities such as the "Kossuth" banknotes that were issued in America during the politician's exile after the failed War of Independence, and notes denominated in billions of forints from the period of hyperinflation in 1946.

From 1921 to 1945, the square was dominated by the Monument to Hungarian Grief – consisting of a flag at half mast and four statues called North, South, East and West – in protest at the 1920 Treaty of Trianon, which awarded two-thirds of Hungary's territory and a third of its Magyar population to the "Successor States" of Romania, Czechoslovakia and Yugoslavia. After World War II, this was replaced by a **Soviet Army Memorial** commemorating the liberation of Budapest from the Nazis, with bas-reliefs of Red Army troops and tanks advancing on Parliament. Today, the Soviet obelisk is fenced off to protect it from vandalism by right-wing nationalists, who periodically erect a tent nearby, emblazoned "Give us back our flag!", coyly neglecting to mention the revanchist impulse behind the original monument.

Ironically, the Soviet memorial and the protest tent stand near the former headquarters of the Fascist Arrow Cross, and the **US Embassy** (now cordoned off for security), which for fifteen years sheltered Cardinal Mindszenty, the Primate of Hungary's Catholic Church, in the aftermath of the 1956 Uprising. Later, however, the US became embarrassed by his presence, as did the Vatican, who finally persuaded him to leave for Austria in 1971 (see box, p.167). Nearby is a statue of **General Harry Bandholtz** of the US army, who intervened with a dogwhip to stop Romanian troops from looting the Hungarian National Museum in 1919. The statue was erected in the 1930s, removed after World War II, and reinstated by the Communists prior to President George Bush's visit in 1989.

The Bedő House and Post Office Savings Bank

On Honvéd utca, behind the Soviet memorial, look out for the pistachio facade of the **Bedő House** (no. 3), a superb example of Hungarian Art Nouveau architecture, built by Emil Vidor in 1903. Recently restored after decades of neglect, it's now the **Museum of Hungarian Art Nouveau** (Tues–Sun 10am–5pm; 1100Ft), showcasing furniture, graphics and interior design – right down to the toilets in the basement – with a shop selling reproduction and original pieces, and the *Art Nouveau Café*. For more in a similar vein, turn right onto Báthory utca and right again onto Hold utca, where you can't miss the former **Post Office Savings Bank**, its tiled facade patterned like a quilt, with swarms of bees (symbolizing savings) ascending to the polychromatic roof, which is the wildest part of the building. Its architect, Ödön Lechner, once asked why birds shouldn't enjoy his buildings too, and amazing roofs are a feature of his other masterpieces in Budapest, the Applied Arts Museum (see p.97) and the Geological Institute (see p.90). Now an annex of the National Bank, its foyer is accessible during banking hours but the rest of the interior is only open to the public on European Heritage Day sometime in September (ask Tourinform for details).

From the Glass House to Vértanuk tér

Diagonally across the street from the Savings Bank is a wrought-iron **market hall** (Mon 6am–5pm, Tues–Fri 6am–6pm, Sat 6am–3pm), one of five opened on a single day in 1896, which still serve the centre of Pest – much less touristy than the Great Market Hall. Its rear entrance will bring you out on Vadász utca, not far from one of Budapest's least-known memorials to the Holocaust, at no. 29, across the street.

The **Glass House** (Üvegház; daily 1–4pm; free) was so-called after the extensive use of glass in its Modernist design and its erstwhile role as a glass showroom.

From 1944 to 1945, it was one of many properties in Budapest that were designated as neutral territory by the Swiss Consul Carl Lutz (see p.92), serving as a refuge for 3000 Jews and the underground Zionist Youth organization. An **exhibition** (to the right of the courtyard) explains how Lutz, Wallenberg and other "Righteous Gentiles" managed to save thousands of Jews from the SS and Arrow Cross death squads.

A few blocks from the Glass House, at the junction of Hold utca and Báthori utca, a lantern on a plinth flickers with an **Eternal Flame** commemorating Count Lajos Batthyány, the Prime Minister of the short-lived republic declared after the 1848 War of Independence, whom the Habsburgs executed on this spot on October 6, 1849. As a staunch patriot – but not a revolutionary – Batthyány is a hero for conservative nationalists, and his monument is the destination of annual marches on October 6.

The refrains and paradoxes of Hungarian history are echoed on **Vértanuk tér** (Martyrs' Square), between Szabadság tér and Kossuth tér, where a **statue of Imre Nagy** – the reform Communist who became prime minister during the 1956 Uprising and was shot in secret afterwards – stands on a footbridge, gazing towards Parliament. With his raincoat, trilby and umbrella hooked over his arm, Nagy cuts an all too human, flawed figure, and is scorned by those who pay their respects to Batthyány.

Kossuth tér

Lipótváros reaches its monumental climax at **Kossuth tér**, named after the leader of the 1848 Revolution, Lajos Kossuth, but also featuring a statue of an earlier hero of the struggle for Hungarian independence, Prince Ferenc Rákóczi II. The quote inscribed on the latter's plinth – "The wounds of the noble Hungarian nation burst open!" – refers to the anti-Habsburg war of 1703–11, but could just as well describe the evening of October 23, 1956, when crowds filled the square, chanting anti-Stalinist slogans at Parliament and calling for the appearance of Nagy – the prelude to the Uprising that night. An **eternal flame** burns in memory of those who died here on October 25, when ÁVO snipers opened fire on a peaceful crowd that was fraternizing with Soviet tank-crews.

Two more notable monuments can be seen in the vicinity. Immediately south of Parliament sits the brooding figure of **Attila József**, one of Hungary's finest poets, who was expelled from the Communist Party for trying to reconcile Marx and Freud, and committed suicide in 1937 after being rejected by his lover. His powerful, turbulent verse has never lost its popularity, and he earns his place here for his poem *By the Danube*. Further south beside the river is a poignant **Holocaust Memorial**: dozens of shoes cast in iron, marking the spot where hundreds of Jewish adults and children were machine-gunned by the Arrow Cross and their bodies thrown into the Danube. Before being massacred, they were made to remove their coats and footwear, which were earmarked for use by German civilians.

Parliament and the Museum of Ethnography

The Hungarian **Parliament** building (Országház; Ⓦ www.parlament.hu) makes the Houses of Parliament in London look humble, its architect Imre Steindl having larded Pugin's Gothic Revival style with Renaissance and Baroque flourishes. Sprawling for 268m along the embankment, its symmetrical wings bristle with finials and 88 statues of Hungarian rulers, surmounted by a dome 96m high (alluding to the date of the Magyar conquest; see p.438). One weakness in the design was the white limestone of the exterior, which has been degraded by the elements and pollution; since 1925 it has required almost constant cleaning and replacement.

For centuries, Hungarian assemblies convened wherever they could, and it wasn't until 1843 that it was resolved to build a permanent "House of the Motherland" in Pest-Buda (as the city was then called). By the time work began in 1885, the concept of Parliament had changed insofar as the middle classes were now represented as well, though over ninety percent of the population still lacked the right to vote. Gains were made in 1918, but they were soon curtailed under the Horthy regime, just as the attainment of universal adult suffrage in 1945 was rendered meaningless after 1948 by a Communist dictatorship, until the advent of democracy in 1990.

Tickets for **tours** of the interior in English (daily at 10am, noon & 2pm; free for EU citizens with passport, otherwise 2950Ft) and other languages sell out fast, once the ticket office opens at 8am. It's sited by Gate X on the Kossuth tér side, beyond the rope near the Eternal Flame, where visitors with tickets wait to be admitted; you'll need to ask the guards to let you cross the barrier. Statues, carvings, gilding and mosaics are ten a penny, lit by lamps worthy of the Winter Palace – but there are also cosy touches such as the individually numbered brass ashtrays where peers left their cigars smouldering in the lounge while they popped back into the chamber to hear someone speak; a good speaker was said to be "worth a Havana".

Besides the magnificent interior, visitors get to see **St Stephen's Crown**, the symbol of Hungarian statehood for over 1000 years. Its distinctive bent cross was caused by the crown being squashed as it was smuggled out of a palace in a baby's cradle; at other times it has been hidden in a hay-cart or buried in Transylvania, abducted to Germany by Hungarian Fascists and thence taken to the US, where it reposed in Fort Knox until its return home in 1978, together with the orb, sceptre and sword that comprise the **Coronation Regalia**. On a humbler note, there's also a **scale model** of Parliament made of 100,000 matchsticks, built by a patriotic family over three years.

Across the square at no. 12 stands a neo-Renaissance pile housing the **Museum of Ethnography** (Néprajzi Múzeum; Tues–Sun: 10am–6pm; 800Ft; ⓦwww.neprajz.hu), one of the finest museums in Budapest. Its permanent exhibition on **Hungarian folk culture** is fully captioned in English and thematically arranged, and although such beautiful costumes and objects are no longer part of everyday life in Hungary, you can still see them in regions of Romania such as Maramureş and the Kalotaszeg, which belonged to Hungary before 1920. Upstairs, temporary exhibitions can cover anything from Bedouin life to Hindu rituals, while in the weeks leading up to Easter and Christmas the museum puts on **concerts** of Hungarian folk music and dancing, and **craft fairs**.

Further out

Szent István körút, running from Nyugati Station to the Danube, marks the end of Lipótváros – but there are a few sights further out worth a mention. **Szent István Park**, opposite Margit-sziget, is the social hub of the old wealthy Jewish neighbourhood, with the finest flowerbeds in the city – an apt site for a **monument to Raoul Wallenberg**, who gave up a playboy life in neutral Sweden to help the Jews of Budapest in 1944. Armed with diplomatic status and money for bribing officials, Wallenberg and his assistants plucked thousands from the cattle trucks and lodged them in "safe houses", manoeuvring to buy time until the Russians arrived. Shortly afterwards, he was arrested as a spy and vanished into the Gulag, never to return. The monument itself was constructed in the 1950s but "exiled" to Debrecen before being stashed away for decades, only taking its rightful place in Budapest in 1999.

The Danube bank below the park, the Újpesti rakpart, is the site of the summertime **Budapest Beach** (Budapest Plázs; ⓦ www.budapestplazs.hu), which takes its cue from the Paris original. From May onwards the whole of the embankment facing Margit-sziget is closed to traffic and covered in sand and palm trees, recreating a seaside feel, and there are stages, live music, children's programmes and numerous food stalls and restaurants to keep beach-goers happy.

Inland, the engagingly hands-on **Hungarian Railway History Park**, or Hungarian Railway Museum (Magyar Vasúttörténeti Park; Tues–Sun: April–Oct 10am–6pm; late March & Nov to mid-Dec 10am–3pm; 950Ft, child 300Ft, family 1900Ft; ⓦ www.mavnosztalgia.hu), lurks in the freight yards of the XIV district. Its roundhouse and sidings house over seventy locomotives and carriages from 1870 onwards, including the Árpád railcar that set the 1934 speed record from Budapest to Vienna in just under three hours, and a 1912 teak dining carriage from the Orient Express. Between April and October (10am–4pm), you can **drive** a steam train (1000Ft), luggage cart (300Ft) or engine simulator (500Ft), ride a locomotive turntable (200Ft) or a horse-drawn tram (100Ft), or operate a model railway (200Ft). **Children's Day** (May 25) and **Transport Day** (June 7–8) see all kinds of events, with free admission for under-18s.

From April to October, the ticket price includes travel to the museum by vintage train from Nyugati Station (9.40am, 10.40am, 1.40pm & 3.40pm), for enthusiasts who don't mind being choked by diesel fumes for half an hour. Tickets are available from the MÁV Nosztalgia office next to platform 10 in the station. Otherwise, the park gates at Tatai út 95 are a short walk from the Rokolya utca stop, which is a longish ride by bus #30 from Keleti Station or Hősök tere.

Terézváros

Laid out in the late nineteenth century, **Terézváros** (Theresa Town), or the VI district, was heavily influenced by Haussmann's redevelopment of Paris, and at that time it was one of the smartest districts in the city. Under Communism, the area became pretty run-down, but the appeal of the old apartment blocks lining its streets is now bringing in the middle classes; the villas near the park have recovered their value and café society flourishes around Liszt Ferenc tér.

Andrássy út

Running in a perfect straight line for 2.5km up to Hősök tere on the edge of the Városliget, Budapest's longest, grandest avenue was inaugurated in 1884 as the Sugár (Radial) út but soon renamed **Andrássy út** after the statesman Count Gyula Andrássy. The name stayed in popular use throughout the years when this was officially Stalin Avenue (1949–56) or the Avenue of the People's Republic (1957–89), until it was formally restored. With its greystone edifices laden with dryads, its Opera House and coffee houses, the avenue retains something of the style that made it so fashionable in the 1890s, when "Bertie", the Prince of Wales, drove its length in a landau, offering flowers to women as he passed. The initial stretch up to the Oktogon is within walking distance of Erzsébet tér, but if you're going any further it's best to travel from sight to sight by the yellow metro beneath the avenue, or bus #4.

At Andrássy út 3 the **Post Office Museum** (Posta Múzeum; Tues–Sun 10am–6pm; 500Ft) occupies a fabulous old apartment, complete with parquet floors, marble fireplaces, Venetian mirrors, and frescoes by Károly Lotz; its owners fled to the US in 1938. Exhibits include a compressed-air mail tube, vintage delivery vehicles, and a display on the inventor Tivadar Puskás, a colleague of Thomas Edison, who set up the world's first switchboard and telephonic news service in Budapest in the early 1900s. Press #10 on the entry-phone to gain access to the building.

The **State Opera** (Állami Operaház) was founded by Ferenc Erkel, the composer of Hungary's national anthem, and occupies a magnificent neo-Renaissance pile built in 1875–84 by Miklós Ybl. It can boast of being directed by Mahler (who complained about the anti-Semitism in Hungary), hosting performances conducted by Otto Klemperer and Antal Doráti, and sheltering two hundred local residents (including Kodály) in its cellars during the siege of Budapest. Tickets for English-language **tours** of the interior (daily 3 & 4pm; 2600Ft) are available from the shop to the left of the foyer; see p.135 regarding tickets for performances. In a similar vein, don't miss the **New Theatre** (Új Színház) on Paulay Ede utca, off the other side of Andrássy, whose blue and gold Art Nouveau facade and foyer (by Béla Lajta) are superb.

One block beyond the Opera, Andrássy út is crossed by **Nagymező utca** – nicknamed "**Broadway**" because of the theatres and nightclubs on the street. During the interwar years, the best-known club was the *Arizona*, run by Sándor Rozsnyai and his wife Miss Arizona (which inspired Pal Sándor's 1988 film of the same name, starring Hanna Schygulla and Marcello Mastroianni); the Rozsnyais were murdered by the Arrow Cross in 1944. Their club was at Nagymező utca 20, in the former home of the Habsburg court photographer who lends his name to the bottle-green tiled **Mai Manó House** (Mai Manó Ház; Mon–Fri 2–7pm, Sat, Sun & holidays 11am–7pm; 700Ft; ⓦwww.maimano.hu), which features temporary photographic exhibitions in three separate galleries, and an excellent photographic bookshop on the first floor. Across the street, notice the **statue** of the composer **Imre Kálmán**, lounging on a bench outside the Operetta Theatre.

At Nagymező utca 8, on the far side of Andrássy, the **Ernst Museum** (Ernst Múzeum; Tues–Sun 11am–7pm; 600Ft; ⓦwww.mucsarnok.hu) is another venue for temporary exhibitions, affiliated to the Műcsarnok on Hősök tere (see p.88). It's worth a peek inside purely to see the building's Art Nouveau features by József Rippl-Rónai and Ödön Lechner, and also checking out the Art Deco lobby of the Tivoli theatre next door.

Further up Andrássy, two elongated squares lined with pavement **cafés** provide a vibrant interlude. On the left (north of Andrássy út) is **Jókai tér**, with a large statue of the novelist Mór Jókai, while across the road on **Liszt Ferenc tér**, the composer Liszt hammers an imaginary keyboard with his vast hands, blind to the drinkers and diners surrounding him. At the far end of the square, the **Music Academy** that bears his name (no. 8) contains a magnificent Art Nouveau entrance hall designed by Aladár Körösfői-Kriesch, and two gilded auditoriums whose glorious decor matches the quality of the music played there.

Continuing up Andrássy brings you shortly to the intersection with the Nagykörút (Great Boulevard) at the **Oktogon**, an eight-sided square flanked by eclectic buildings. With 24-hour fast-food chains ensconced in two of them, and buses and taxis running along the Nagykörút through the small hours, the Oktogon never sleeps. During the Horthy period it rejoiced in the name of Mussolini tér, while under the Communists it was called November 7 tér after the date of the Bolshevik revolution.

Beyond the Oktogon

You can't miss the **House of Terror** (Terror Háza; Tues–Fri 10am–6pm, Sat & Sun 10am–7.30pm; 1800Ft; ⓦwww.terrorhaza.hu), due to the ominous black frame surmounting this house at Andrássy út 60 – once the dreaded headquarters of the secret police. Dubbed the "House of Loyalty" by the Fascist Arrow Cross during World War II, it was subsequently used for the same purpose by the

Communist ÁVO (see box below). Opened in 2002 as a cross between a museum and a memorial, the House of Terror has been criticized by some for glossing over Hungary's role in the invasion of the Soviet Union, and its emphasis on Stalinist terror compared to the Holocaust (a subject treated in far more depth at the Holocaust Memorial Centre, see p.98). A video in the lobby repeatedly plays the image of a man weeping at the execution of 1956 insurgents, saying "this was their socialism". Perhaps balance is impossible in such a sensitive area, and the public treatment of the Stalinist years is at least a much-needed, if simplified, beginning.

The moment you step in through the spooky automatic door you're bombarded with funereal sounds and powerful images, starting with a Soviet tank and photos of ÁVO victims in the courtyard. An audioguide (1000Ft) can save you the trouble of reading the English-language sheets in each room, but the latter pack far more information. The displays begin on the second floor (you take the lift, then work downwards) with a couple of rooms dealing briskly with the murder of 600,000 Jews and Gypsies in the Holocaust, before moving on to the Soviet "liberation", deportations of "class enemies", rigged elections, collectivization, and other themes. The most harrowing part is the **basement**, with its reconstructed torture chamber and cells, where the music mercifully stops as the exhibits are allowed to speak for themselves.

A little further up Andrássy on the opposite side, the Old Music Academy at no. 67 harbours the **Liszt Memorial Museum** (Liszt Ferenc Emlékmúzeum; Mon–Fri 10am–6pm, Sat 9am–5pm; closed on national holidays; 800Ft; ⓦ www .lisztmuseum.hu), entered from around the corner at Vörösmarty utca 35, where the composer – who was the first president of the Academy – lived from 1881 until his death in 1886. His glass piano and travelling keyboard are the highlights of an extensive collection of memorabilia and scores. **Concerts** are performed here by young pianists every Saturday at 11am (800Ft; Budapest Card covers entry to the museum but concert tickets must be bought separately).

Another great Hungarian composer lends his name to the **Kodály körönd** (named Hitler tér during World War II), one of Budapest's most elegant squares, flanked by four neo-Renaissance mansions (one with gilt sgraffiti). At no. 1 on the northeast corner, the flat where Kodály lived until his death in 1967 is now the **Kodály Memorial Museum** (Kodály Emlékmúzeum; Wed 10am–4pm, Thurs–Sat 10am–6pm, Sun 10am–2pm; 600Ft; ⓦ www.kodaly-inst.hu), preserving his library, salon, dining room and folk-art collection.

Two fine collections of Asian art lurk just beyond the körönd. The **György Ráth Museum** (Tues–Sun 10am–6pm; 600Ft) displays lovely artefacts from all the great civilizations, in an Art Nouveau villa at Városligeti fasor 12 – reached via Bajza utca – whose garden contains a statue of the Hungarian Orientalist Sándor Kőrösi-Csoma, as a Buddhist monk. The **Ferenc Hopp Museum** (same hours;

The ÁVO

The **Communist secret police** began as the party's private security section during the Horthy era, when it betrayed Trotskyites to the police to take the heat off their Stalinist comrades. After World War II it became the 9000-strong Államvédelmi Osztály or **ÁVO** (State Security Department), its growing power implicit in a change of name in 1948 – to the State Security Authority or **ÁVH** (though the old acronym stuck). Ex-Nazi torturers were easily persuaded to apply their skills on its behalf, and its network of 41,000 informers permeated society. So hated was the ÁVO that any members caught during the Uprising were summarily killed, and their mouths stuffed with banknotes (secret policemen earned more than anyone else).

600Ft; @www.hoppmuzeum.hu) at Andrássy út 103 hosts temporary shows of Asian art from the same collection; you can buy a combined ticket for both for 1000Ft. From here, the final stretch of Andrássy út up to Hősök tere is lined with spacious villas set back from the avenue, mostly housing embassies.

Hősök tere and around

Laid out in 1896 to mark the thousandth anniversary of the Magyar conquest, **Hősök tere** (Heroes' Square) is appropriately grandiose. The **Millenniary Monument** at its centre consists of a 36-metre-high column topped by the figure of Archangel Gabriel who, according to legend, appeared to Stephen in a dream and offered him the crown of Hungary. Around the base are Prince Árpád and his chieftains, who led the Magyar tribes into the Carpathian Basin. As a backdrop to this, a semicircular colonnade displays statues of Hungary's most illustrious leaders, from King Stephen to Kossuth. During the brief Republic of Councils in 1919, when Hungary was ruled by revolutionary soviets, the square was decked out in red banners and the column enclosed in a red obelisk. In 1989, it was the setting for the ceremonial reburial of Imre Nagy and other murdered leaders of the 1956 Uprising (plus an empty coffin representing the "unknown insurgent") – an event which symbolized the dawning of a new era in Hungary. Today it's more likely to be filled with rollerbladers and skateboarders, for whom the smooth surface is ideal, and it's also used to host **events** such as the National Gallop or Army Day.

Museum of Fine Arts

To the north of the square, the **Museum of Fine Arts** (Szépművészeti Múzeum; Tues–Sun 10am–5.30pm; 1400Ft; @www.szepmuveszeti.hu) is the pan-European equivalent of the Hungarian National Gallery, housed in an imposing Neoclassical building completed in 1906. Most exhibits are labelled in English and a free floor-plan is available, but if you want more information you should go on an English-language **tour** (Tues–Sat 11am & 2pm from the lobby; free) or rent an **audioguide** (1000Ft). Besides its permanent collection, there are regular **temporary exhibitions** (1400–3200Ft; combined ticket 3600Ft) and cultural **events** on Thursdays (6–10pm; 3000Ft), as advertised.

On the **lower ground floor**, a hippopotamus-tusk wand carved with spells to protect a child presages the **Egyptian Collection**, chiefly from the Late Period and Greco-Roman eras of Egyptian civilization. Its highlights are four huge painted coffins and a child-sized one, a mummified crocodile, cat and falcon, and a tautly poised bronze of the cat-goddess Bastet. Across the lobby, the section entitled **Art around 1900** starts with **Symbolist** and **Decadent** works such as Franz von Stuck's *The Kiss of the Sphinx*, moving on through works by the Hungarian **Art Nouveau** masters József Rippl-Rónai and Károly Ferenczy to two iconic images by Oskar Kokoschka: *Veronica's Veil* and the poster *Der Sturm*.

The **ground floor** proper features an excellent **bookshop** (where you can have a poster of any picture in the museum printed for 9000Ft) leading to a wing used for **temporary exhibitions** (requiring a separate ticket), and several rooms devoted to **ancient Mediterranean cultures** from Etruria to Athens, mainly represented by jugs and vases. Before heading upstairs, visit the grand **Renaissance Hall**, used for hanging large allegorical works on loan from other museums; the **Baroque Hall** (often used for televised events), and the **Prints and Drawings Room** at the far end on the right, mounting temporary displays (free) drawn from the museum's holdings of work by Raphael, Leonardo, Rembrandt, Rubens, Dürer, Picasso and Chagall.

The museum's hoard of Old Masters is based on the collection of Count Miklós Esterházy, which he sold to the state in 1871. These works are organized into eight sections on the **first floor**, which are harder to navigate than you'd imagine due to a system of numbering main rooms with Roman numerals and smaller ones with Arabic digits. The **Spanish Collection** of seventy works is arguably the best in the world outside Spain, with seven El Grecos (most notably *Christ Stripped of His Garments* and *The Agony in the Garden*) in room V; five Goyas in room III, and Velázquez's *Peasants at Table* and Ribera's *Martyrdom of St Andrew* in room VI.

The **Italian Collection** is almost as impressive, with Raphael's "Esterházy Madonna" and a self-portrait by Giorgione (room XIX), Titian's *Madonna and Child with St Paul* and several Tintorettos (rooms XII and XX), plus a Veronese grandee (room XVII). The **German Collection** ranges from Kauffann's *The Wife of Count Esterházy as Venus* (room X) and darkly Gothic works by Cranach the Elder, Holbein's *Dormition of the Virgin* (room XI) and a *Young Man* by Dürer (room 14). Whereas the **Flemish Collection** has such gems as Van Dyck's *St John the Evangelist* (Room VIII), and the **Dutch Collection** an array of Brueghels, from Pieter the Elder's *Sermon of St John the Baptist* to Jan's *Garden of Eden with the Fall of Man* (room XII), the single room of **English art** can only muster a dull portrait apiece by Hogarth, Reynolds and Gainsborough.

For a change of mood, enter the section entitled **From Romanticism to Postimpressionism**, where room XII displays Courbet's wild landscapes and life-sized *Wrestlers*, and Rodin's sculpture *The Brazen Age*. Tucked away elsewhere you'll find *Lady with a Fan* by Manet (room 20), orchards and river-views by Renoir, Monet and Pissarro (room 21), Toulouse-Lautrec's *Ladies* and a little-known Gauguin, *Black Pigs*, from his Tahitian period (room 22).

The Palace of Art and Dózsa György út

On the south side of the square is the **Exhibition Hall**; (Műcsarnok Tues, Wed & Fri–Sun 10am–6pm, Thurs noon–8pm; 1400Ft; ⓦ www.mucsarnok.hu), also called the Palace of Art (not to be confused with the Palace of Arts, covered on p.99). A Grecian pile with gilded columns and a mosaic of St Stephen as patron of the arts, it was inaugurated in 1895. Its magnificent facade and foyer are in contrast to the four austere rooms used for **temporary exhibitions** (two or three at a time), often of modern art. It's possible to buy a combined ticket (1400Ft) valid for a month, which also covers exhibitions at the Ernst Museum on Nagymező utca (see p.85).

Dózsa György út, the wide avenue running off alongside the Városliget, serves as the setting for occasional **fairs** and **concerts**. In Communist times it was here that Party leaders reviewed parades from a grandstand, beneath a 25-metre-high statue of Stalin that was torn down during the Uprising, dragged to the Nagykörút and hammered into bits for souvenirs. After the re-imposition of Communist rule a statue of Lenin was erected in its place, which remained until it was taken away "for structural repairs" in 1989 and finally ended up in the Memento Park (see p.113). Three monuments mark the distance that Hungary has travelled since then. The **Timewheel** is the world's largest hourglass, a metal canister 8m in diameter that rotates 180° on the last day of each year, symbolizing Hungary's accession to the European Union in 2004. Where the Stalin statue once stood, the **Monument to the Uprising** is a forest of oxidized columns merging into a stainless-steel wedge, beside a Hungarian flag with a circle cut out, recalling the excision of the Soviet symbol in 1956 (this long strip alongside the park has been named Ötvenhatosok tere – Square of the 56-ers). Beyond this, a crucifix rises over the foundations of the **Virgin Mary Church** that the Communists demolished in 1951.

The Városliget

The leafy **Városliget** (City Park) starts just behind Hősök tere, where the fairy-tale towers of **Vajdahunyad Castle** rear above an island girdled by an artificial lake that's used for boating in the summer and is transformed into a splendid ice rink in winter. Like the park, the castle was created for the Millenniary Anniversary celebrations of 1896, so dramatic effects were the order of the day. This "stone catalogue" features replicas of the Chapel at Ják (May–Sept daily 10am–8pm; 100Ft) in western Hungary (see p.280) and two Transylvanian castles, enclosing a Renaissance courtyard that makes a romantic setting for evening **concerts** from July to mid-August.

In the main wing of the castle, the **Agriculture Museum** (Mezőgazdasági Múzeum; Tues–Sun 10am–5pm; 600Ft; Ⓦwww.mezogazdasagimuzeum.hu) traces the history of hunting and farming in Hungary. Its most interesting sections relate to the early Magyars and such typically Hungarian breeds of livestock as long-horned grey cattle and woolly pigs. Don't miss the hooded **statue of Anonymous** outside. This nameless chronicler to King Béla is the prime source of information about early medieval Hungary, though the existence of several monarchs of that name during the twelfth and thirteenth centuries makes it hard to date him (or his chronicles) with any accuracy.

Leaving the island by the causeway at the rear, you're on course for the **Petőfi Hall**; (Petőfi Csarnok Ⓣ01/363-3730 or Ⓦwww.petoficsarnok.hu for information), a 1970s "Metropolitan Youth Centre" that regularly hosts good concerts (outdoors in summer), films, parties, and a flea market at weekends. Accessible by a staircase around the back, the **Aviation and Space Flight Exhibition** (Repüléstörténeti és Űrhajózási kiállítás; April–Nov Tues–Fri 10am–5pm, Sat & Sun 10am–6pm; 800Ft) features some vintage planes and a space capsule. The museum is an offshoot of the **Transport Museum** (Közlekedési Múzeum; Tues–Fri 10am–5pm, Sat & Sun 10am–6pm; 800Ft; 1100Ft for both museums), 250m away on the edge of the park, which contains antique cars, mothballed steam trains and models galore – don't miss the model railway that runs every hour on the hour.

The Széchenyi Baths, Zoo, Circus and Vidám Park

On the far side of the park's main axis, Kós Károly sétány, the **Széchenyi Baths** (Széchenyi Gyögyfürdő; daily 6am–10pm; 2400Ft/2800Ft with locker/cabin) could be mistaken for a palace, so grand is its facade. Outside is a statue of the geologist Zsigmondy Vilmos, who discovered the thermal spring that feeds its outdoor pool and Turkish baths. This is perhaps the best venue for mixed-sex bathing, and in one of the large outdoor pools you can enjoy the surreal spectacle of people playing chess while immersed up to their chests in steaming water – so hot that you shouldn't stay in for more than twenty minutes. The best players sit at tables around the pool's edge (the late former world champion Bobby Fischer among them in the 1980s); bring your own set if you wish to participate.

Beyond the baths on the other side of Állatkerti körút, the **Municipal Circus** (Fővárosi Nagycirkusz; all year except Sept Wed, Thurs & Fri 3pm, Sun 11am & 3pm, Sat 11am, 3pm & 7pm; 1900–2800Ft; Ⓦwww.maciva.hu) traces its origins back to 1783, when the Hetz Theatre played to spectators on what is now Deák tér. To the right is **Vidám Park**, an old-fashioned fairground known as the "English Park" before the war (daily 11am–6pm, till 8pm July–Aug; weekdays adult/child 3900/2500Ft; weekends & holidays 3900/2900Ft; free for children under 100cm in height; Ⓦwww.vidampark.hu); the funfair was the setting for Ferenc Molnár's play *Liliom*, which inspired the musical *Carousel*.

Further down towards Hősök tere you'll find the delightful Elephant Gates of Budapest's **Zoo** (Állatkert; Jan, Feb, Nov & Dec daily 9am–3pm; March & Oct

Mon–Thurs 9am–4.30pm, Fri–Sun 9am–5pm; April & Sept Mon–Thurs 9am–4.30pm, Fri–Sun 9am–5.30pm; May–Aug Mon–Thurs 9am–6pm, Fri–Sun 9am–6.30pm; 1850Ft, child 1290Ft; ⓦ www.zoobudapest.com), which opened its doors in 1866. Its Art Nouveau pavilions by Károly Kós (dating from 1911) seemed the last word in zoological architecture, but it slowly stagnated until the 1990s, when a new director began long-overdue improvements. In 2007, the zoo proudly announced the world's first birth of a rhino conceived by artificial insemination, and the little rhino remains one of its top attractions. Don't miss the exotic **Elephant House**, resembling a Central Asian mosque, the **Palm House** with its magnificent **aquarium** below, or the **Bonsai garden**. Look out also for children's events and evening concerts, as advertised outside the main entrance; the children's corner is signposted "Állatóvoda". Note that the animal houses open one hour later and close thirty minutes before the zoo itself.

The stadium district

The **stadium district**, 1km south of Vajdahunyad Castle, is chiefly notable for the **Puskás Ferenc Stadium**, where league championship and international **football** matches, **concerts** by foreign rock stars and events such as the national dog show are held. Originally known as Népstadion ("People's Stadium") and built in the early 1950s by fifty thousand Budapestis who "volunteered" their labour, unpaid, it was renamed in 2002 after the legendary footballer and manager Ferenc Puskás (1927–2006), who captained the Mighty Magyars in their stunning triumph over England at Wembley Stadium in 1953, before defecting to forge a second career at Real Madrid.

To the west of the stadium is the smaller Kisstadion, while to the east Stalinist statues of healthy proletarian youth line the court that leads to the indoor **Papp László Sportaréna** (or Aréna), a mushroom-shaped silver structure which also hosts concerts and sporting events – Papp was the first boxer to win three Olympic gold medals (1948, 1952 and 1956). The intercity **Stadion bus station** completes this concrete ensemble.

Catching trolleybus #75 along Stefánia út, past the Aréna, you can admire the **Geological Institute** at no. 14, one of the major edifices in Budapest designed by Ödön Lechner. The exterior is as striking as his Post Office Savings Bank (see p.81) and Applied Arts Museum (p.97), with a gingerbread facade, scrolled gables and steeply pitched Transylvanian roofs patterned in bright-blue tiles, crowned by figures holding globes on their backs. By visiting its small **Geological Museum** (Földtani Múzeum; Thurs, Sat & Sun 10am–4pm; 400Ft), you can also see something of the interior, with its fairy-tale stucco and cobalt-blue stairways.

Erzsébetváros

Budapest's VII district, **Erzsébetváros** (Elizabeth Town), is the most atmospheric of Pest's inner suburbs, and the city's **Jewish quarter**. Its boundary with Terézváros runs down the middle of Király utca, which used to be a main thoroughfare before Andrássy út was built, and contained 14 of the city's 58 licensed brothels in the 1870s. After decades of shabby respectability under Communism, cafés, restaurants, design and furniture boutiques now herald its gentrification. Though not the most logical place to start exploring the Jewish quarter, the route here from the direction of Andrássy út makes a wonderful approach, as you zigzag through the backstreets. However, if you approach the area from the Kiskörút, as most people do, the obvious first stop is the Dohány utca (Tobacco Street) Synagogue.

This is the starting point for English-language **guided walking tours** of the quarter, run by Aviv (☎1/462 0477), departing daily except Saturday at 10.30am,

11.30am, 12.30pm & 1.30pm, with extra tours at 2.30pm and 3.30pm from April to October. The cheapest tour (1900Ft) simply covers the synagogue and memorial garden; another (2250Ft) includes the Jewish Museum, while the most expensive (2600Ft) also features the Rumbach utca Synagogue. For a fascinating personalized walking tour of the entire quarter, contact Eszter Gömöri (Ⓔ bp .cityguide@gmail.com), who charges €25 an hour. None of the prices cited include admission charges, where these apply.

The Dohány utca Synagogue and Jewish Museum

The splendid **Dohány utca Synagogue** (Dohány utcai Zsinagóga; April–Oct: Mon–Thurs 10am–5pm, Fri 10am–3pm, Sun 10am–6pm; Nov–March: Mon–Thurs 10am–3pm, Fri & Sun 10am–2pm; 1600Ft including the Jewish Museum) is one of the landmarks of Pest. Located only five minutes' walk from Deák tér, just off Károly körút, it is Europe's largest synagogue and the second biggest in the world after the Temple Emmanuel in New York, with 3600 seats and a total capacity of over 5000 worshippers. Built between 1854 and 1859 by a gentile architect, Ludwig Föster, its design epitomizes the Byzantine-Moorish style that was popular in the 1850s. The colours of its brickwork (yellow, red and blue) are those of Budapest's coat of arms, reflecting the patriotism of the Neolog community, a Hungarian denomination combining elements of Reform and Orthodox Judaism, which today accounts for eighty percent of Hungarian Jewry (the Orthodox and Hassid communities in the provinces having been all but wiped out in the Holocaust). In the 1990s the synagogue was restored at a cost of over $40 million, funded by the Hungarian government and the Hungarian-Jewish diaspora, notably the Emmanuel Foundation, fronted by the actor Tony Curtis, born of 1920s emigrants.

You have time to admire the gilded onion-domed towers while waiting to pass through a security check, before entering the magnificent **interior** by Frigyes Feszl, the architect of the Vigadó concert hall. Arabesques and Stars of David decorate the ceiling, the balconies for female worshippers are surmounted by gilded arches, and the floor is inset with eight-pointed stars. The layout reflects

▲ Dohány utca Synagogue

the synagogue's Neolog identity, with the *bemah*, or Ark of the Torah, at one end, in the Reform fashion, but with men and women seated apart, according to Orthodox tradition. On Jewish festivals, the place is filled to the rafters with Jews from all over Hungary, whose chattering disturbs their more devout co-religionists. At other times, the hall is used for concerts of classical or klezmer music, as advertised outside and on Ⓦ www.jewishfestival.hu.

The **cemetery** behind the synagogue only exists there because the Nazis forbade Jews from being buried elsewhere – one of many calculated humiliations inflicted on the ghetto by the local SS commander, Eichmann. Some 2281 Jews are buried beneath simple headstones, erected immediately after the Red Army's liberation of the ghetto on January 18, 1945. Beyond the cemetery looms the cuboid, domed **Heroes' Temple**, erected in 1929–31 in honour of the 10,000 Jewish soldiers who died fighting for Hungary during World War I. These days it serves as a synagogue for everyday use and is not open to tourists.

To the left of the main entrance and up the stairs is the **Jewish Museum** (Zsidó Múzeum). Notice a relief of Tivadar (Theodor) Herzl, the founder of modern Zionism, who was born and taught on this spot. In the foyer is a gravestone from the third century AD – proof that there were Jews in Hungary six hundred years before the Magyars arrived. The first three rooms are devoted to Jewish festivals, with beautifully crafted objects such as Sabbath lamps and Seder bowls, while the final one covers the Holocaust, with chilling photos and examples of anti-Semitic propaganda. Oddly, the museum says nothing about the huge contribution that Jews have made to Hungarian society, in every field from medicine to poetry. Upon leaving, turn the corner onto Wesselényi utca and enter the **Raoul Wallenberg Memorial Garden**, named after the Swedish diplomat who saved 20,000 Budapest Jews by lodging them in safe houses or plucking them from trains bound for Auschwitz (see p.444). The park's centrepiece is a **Holocaust Memorial** by Imre Varga, shaped like a weeping willow, each leaf engraved with the names of a family killed by the Nazis. Also within the grounds is the **Goldmark Hall**, named after Károly Goldmark, the composer of the opera *The Queen of Sheba*.

Other sights in the Jewish quarter

Fanning out behind the synagogue is what was once the Jewish **ghetto**, created by the Nazis in April 1944. As their menfolk had already been forced into labour battalions intended to kill them from overwork, the 70,000 inhabitants of the ghetto were mainly women, children and old folk, crammed into 162 blocks of flats – over 50,000 of them around Klauzál tér alone.

In happier times, each Jewish community within the quarter had its own place of worship, with a *yeshiva* (religious school) and other facilities within an enclosed courtyard invisible from the surrounding streets – as epitomized by the **Rumbach utca Synagogue** (Mon–Thurs 10am–4.30pm, Fri 10am–2.30pm, Sun 10am–5.30pm; 800Ft). Built by Otto Wagner in 1872, for the so-called "Status Quo" or middling-conservative Jews, it now belongs to the Neolog community and may be turned into a museum or cultural centre. Its octagonal Moorish interior – decorated in violet, crimson and gold – has yet to be fully restored after being ruined during the war. As a plaque outside notes, the building served as a detention barracks in August 1941, from where up to 1800 Slovak and Polish refugees were deported to the Nazi death camps.

En route from Dohány utca to the Status Quo Synagogue you'll cross Dob utca, where you'll see a **monument to Carl Lutz**, the Swiss consul who began issuing *Schutzpasses* to Jews, attesting that they were Swiss or Swedish citizens – a ruse subsequently used by Wallenberg. After the war Lutz was criticized for abusing Swiss law and, feeling slighted, proposed himself for the Nobel Peace Prize.

His monument – a gilded angel swooping down to help a prostrate victim – is locally known as "the figure jumping out of a window".

Just beyond Lutz's memorial, a grey stone portal at no. 16 leads into the **Gozsdu-udvar**, a 200-metre-long passageway built in 1904 and running through to Király utca 11. Connecting seven courtyards, it was a hive of life and activity before the Holocaust; after many years of dereliction, it has now been redeveloped as a luxury plaza containing flats and shops.

The kosher *Fröhlich* patisserie at Dob utca 22 is one of several Jewish businesses around **Kazinczy utca**, the centre of the 3000-strong Orthodox community, where Yiddish can still be heard. There's a butcher's in the yard of Dob utca 35 and a wigmaker at no. 31, while down to the right at Kazinczy utca 28 are a kosher baker and pizzeria, opposite the kosher *Carmel* restaurant. Almost next door to the last stands the **Orthodox Synagogue** (Mon–Thurs 10am–4.30pm, Fri 10am–2.30pm, Sun 10am–5.30pm; 800Ft), built by Béla and Sándor Löffler in 1913 in the Art Nouveau style, with a facade melding into the curve of the street, and an interior with painted rather than moulded motifs.

For something quite different, visit the **Museum of Electrotechnology** (Magyar Elektrotechnikai Múzeum; Tues–Fri 10am–5pm, Sat 9am–6pm; 400Ft) in a former electricity sub-station at Kazinczy utca 21. Its curators demonstrate the world's first dynamo (invented in 1859 by Ányos Jedlik) and other devices in rooms devoted to such topics as the history of light bulbs, or the Hungarian section of the Iron Curtain. Though the current was too weak to kill and the minefields were removed in 1965, patrols kept it inviolate until 1989, when the Hungarians ceased shooting escapees, thereby spelling the end of the Iron Curtain as a whole.

Beyond the Nagykörút

Where Dohány utca crosses the Nagykörút you'll spot the **New York Palace**, a venerable Budapest landmark. Named after the insurance company which commissioned the building in 1895, its magnificent coffee house was one of the great literary cafés of interwar Budapest. Under Communism the edifice housed a publishers, and its Beaux Arts facade – with a small Statue of Liberty high up on the corner – survived being rammed by a tank in 1956. Now reopened as a luxury hotel, its gilded and frescoed restaurant-cum-coffee house is worth a look even if you can't afford to eat there.

Further along Dohány utca the district changes, becoming more working class and tinged with Arab and Chinese influences as you near the **"Garment District"** around **Garay tér**, whose bustling old **market hall** has just been thoroughly modernized, which may squeeze out much of the market's old atmosphere. Take the metro to Keleti pu. to save yourself walking further than necessary to the **Miksa Róth Museum** (Róth Miksa Múzeum; Tues–Sun 2–6pm; 600Ft; Ⓦwww .rothmuzeum.hu) at Nefelejcs utca 26, in the backstreets to the north of Keleti Station. Located in the former home of this leading figure in the Art Nouveau movement, it shows the diversity of Róth's work in stained glass and mosaics, which can be seen in Parliament, the Gresham Palace and the Music Academy.

Józsefváros

Separated from Erzsébetváros by Rákóczi út, **Józsefváros** (Joseph Town) – the VIII district – is an amalgam of high and low life. While the Hungarian National Museum, Eötvös Loránd University and the Szabó Ervin Library on Múzeum körút make for a lively **student quarter**, its seedier hinterland beyond the Nagykörút – nicknamed "Chicago" between the wars – is still associated with vice and crime, despite efforts to clean it up. You can wander safely anywhere in Józsefváros by day, and between the Kiskörút and Nagykörút in the small hours, but elsewhere stick to main roads and avoid pedestrian underpasses after midnight.

Múzeum körút

Running from Astoria to Kálvin tér, **Múzeum körút** is a stately arc lined with trees, shops and grand buildings. Immediately beyond the East–West Business Centre by the Astoria junction stands the old faculty of the **Eötvös Loránd Science University** (known by its Hungarian initials as ELTE). It's named after the physicist Loránd Eötvös, whose pupils included many of the scientists who later developed the US atomic bombs at Los Alamos. Across the street, on Ferenczy utca, you can see a small crenellated section of the **medieval wall of Pest**. The wall gradually disappeared as the city was built up on either side, but fragments remain here and there – a larger chunk lurks in the courtyard of no. 21.

Staying on the outer edge of Múzeum körút, you'll find the **Múzeum Kávéház** at no. 12. One of the earliest coffee houses in Pest, its original frescoes and Zsolnay ceramic reliefs from 1885 still grace what has long since become a restaurant (see p.125). From here, you can wander down **Bródy Sándor utca**, beside the garden of the Hungarian National Museum. It seems an unlikely place for a revolution to start – yet this is where the Uprising began, outside the **Radio Building** at no. 7, when ÁVO guards fired upon students demanding access to the airwaves, an act which turned the hitherto peaceful protests of October 23, 1956 into a revolt against the secret police and other manifestations of Stalinism.

Hungarian National Museum

Like the National Library on Várhegy, the **Hungarian National Museum** (Magyar Nemzeti Múzeum; Tues–Sun 10am–6pm; 1000Ft; free on March 15, Aug 20 & Oct 23; ⓦ www.hnm.hu) was the brainchild of Count Ferenc Széchenyi (father of István), who donated thousands of prints and manuscripts to form the basis of its collection. Housed in a Grecian-style edifice by Mihály Pollack, it was only the fourth such museum in the world when it opened in 1847, and soon afterwards became the stage for a famous event in the **1848 Revolution**, when Sándor Petőfi (see box, p.390) first declaimed the *National Song* from its steps, with its rousing refrain "Choose! Now is the time! Shall we be slaves or shall we be free?" Ever since, March 15 has been commemorated here with flags and speeches.

By way of amends for losing the Coronation Regalia in 2000 (now on display in Parliament – see p.83), the National Museum has undergone a major refit, resulting in two new subterranean levels devoted to **medieval and Roman stonework** – the latter starring a second-century AD mosaic floor from a villa at Nemesvámos-Baláca in western Hungary. To the left of the ground-floor foyer, a darkened room displays King Stephen's Byzantine silk **coronation mantle**, which is far too fragile to be exhibited in the Parliament building. Equally impressive is the section to the right of the foyer, called **On the East–West Frontier**, which covers the pre-Hungarian peoples of the Carpathian Basin. Its highlights include three skeletons and grave goods from a 1600 BC cemetery, gold Germanic bangles and the **Nagyszentmiklós treasure**, a gorgeous 23-piece gold dinner service belonging to an Avar chieftain.

The main exhibition on the upper floor traces **Hungarian history** from the Árpád dynasty to the end of Communism. Béla III's crown and sword, a wall fountain from the royal palace at Visegrád, and a huge carved pew are among the treasures in the medieval and Renaissance section, which ends with a gallery of the oldest portraits in Hungary (omitting only the infamous "Blood Countess" Báthori). The Reform era and the *belle époque* are covered in rooms 11–18, followed by World War II and the Communist era in room 20. The last features a radio set dedicated to Stalin's 70th birthday, a scaled-down model of the Stalin statue torn down by crowds in 1956, and kitsch tributes to János Kádár, who reimposed Communist rule with a vengeance, but later liberalized it to the point that his successors felt able to abandon it entirely. Not to be missed are the **propaganda** films from the Horthy, Fascist and Stalinist eras, whose resemblance to each other makes the point.

Kálvin tér

Múzeum körút ends at **Kálvin tér**, a busy intersection with roads going to the airport, the east, and westwards across the river, where street fighting was especially fierce in 1956. It seems miraculous that the **Szabó Ervin Library** (Mon–Fri 10am–8pm, Sat 10am–4pm; closed July, reduced hours in Aug; free), on the corner of Baross utca, survived unscathed. Built in 1887 by the Wenckheim family – who enjoyed a near-monopoly on Hungary's onion crop – the library is well worth a look. At the main entrance on Reviczky utca, you can ask at the information desk about visiting the ornate fourth-floor reading rooms, reached by a lovely wooden staircase. Staff may ask you to register but will probably just wave you through.

Outside the library and facing Kálvin tér stands one of the few surviving monuments marking the hated Treaty of Trianon (see p.443): the so-called **Fountain of Hungarian Truth** (Magyar Igazság kútja). Erected in 1928, it honours the British press magnate Lord Rothermere, whose campaign against the treaty in the *Daily Mail* was so appreciated that he was offered the Hungarian crown. On June 4, the anniversary of the treaty's signing, nationalist and Fascist groups gather to pay their respects.

To the Nagykörút and Keleti Station

Behind the library lies an atmospheric quarter of small squares and parochial schools; formerly shabby, it's now buzzing with cafés and bars popular with students, and is promoted by the local council as "**Budapest's Soho**". Having face-lifted **Mikszáth Kálmán tér** and much of Krudy utca, the process of gentrification is set to cross the **József körút** – one of the sleazier arcs of the Nagykörút – to embrace **Rákóczi tér**, the locus of street prostitution until it was outlawed in 1999. At the time of writing, the square was fenced off for the construction of the new metro line, with its **market hall** a place for locals to shop and a centre for Chinese wholesalers – but the whole area may well move upmarket in the future.

While theatregoers bestow bourgeois respectability upon **Köztársaság tér** – the home of Budapest's "second" opera house, the **Erkel Theatre** (named after the composer of the national anthem, Ferenc Erkel) – the grittier side of life prevails at **Keleti Station** on Baross tér. As the station is Budapest's "gateway to the east", it's not surprising that Chinese takeaways and Arab shops are a feature of the area – as are frequent ID checks by the **police**, who patrol here in threes ("One can read, one can write, and the third one keeps an eye on the two intellectuals", as the old joke has it).

The Police History Museum

Handily for the police, their precinct HQ is only two blocks from the station, on Mosonyi utca. Tourists who'd never go there otherwise can visit the **Police History Museum** (Rendőrség-Történeti Múzeum; Tues–Sun 9am–5pm; free; Ⓦ www.policehistorymus.com) next door at no. 7, guarded by a dummy sentry. Since the exhibits are captioned in Hungarian only, you can easily miss the ideological cast of the display of uniforms and memorabilia, which harbours a tribute to the Communist border guards and militia, and CIA leaflets inciting the

Uprising. Be thankful you're not an exhibit in the other hall, where many displays depict murders and mutilations in horrific detail, unlike the staged – and very 1960s – crime scene with a sign listing key points for trainee investigators. Stuff on forgery and art theft in the 1980s begs the question why there's nothing about crime in Hungary nowadays. The show ends with a display of police uniforms from fellow forces in the EU, and there's also a shop selling police memorabilia, where you can have your fingerprints taken as a souvenir.

Kerepesi Cemetery

Five minutes' walk from the museum, along Fiumei út, you'll find **Kerepesi Cemetery** (Kerepesi temető; daily: April & Aug 7am–7pm, May–July 7am–8pm, Sept 7am–6pm, Oct 7am–5pm, Nov–March 7.30am–5pm; free), the Père Lachaise of Budapest, where the famous, great and not-so-good are buried. Vintage hearses and mourning regalia in the **Funerary Museum** (Kegyeleti Múzeum; Mon–Thurs 10am–3pm, Fri 10am–1pm; free) near the main gates illuminate the Hungarian way of death and set the stage for the necropolis. In Communist times, Party members killed during the Uprising were buried in a prominent position near the entrance and government ministers in honourable proximity to Kossuth, while leaders and martyrs who "Lived for Communism and the People" were enshrined in a starkly ugly **Pantheon of the Working Class Movement**; some have been removed by their relatives since the demise of Communism. Party leader János Kádár – who ruled Hungary from 1956 to 1988 – rates a separate grave, still heaped with wreaths from admirers.

Further in lie the florid **nineteenth-century mausoleums** of Kossuth, Batthyány, Deák and Petőfi (whose family tomb is here, though his own body was never found). Don't miss the Art Nouveau funerary arcades between Batthyány's and the novelist Jókai's mausoleums, nor the nearby tomb of the diva Lujza Blaha, the "Nation's Nightingale", whose effigy is surrounded by statues of serenading figures. Other notables include the composer Erkel, the confectioner Gerbeaud and three chess grandmasters whose tombs are engraved with the chess moves that won them their titles. A more recent addition is József Antall, the first post-Communist prime minister of Hungary, honoured by an allegorical monument with horses struggling to burst free of a sheet.

The New Public and Jewish cemeteries

Two more notable cemeteries lie further out in the X district of Kőbánya, 15km from central Pest, a 35-minute ride by tram #37 or #28 from Népszínház utca (near Blaha Lujza tér metro) to the main gates on Kozma utca. The **New Public Cemetery** (Új köztemető; daily dawn–dusk; free) is the final resting place of Imre Nagy and 260 others executed for their part in the Uprising, who were buried in unmarked graves in 1958. Any flowers left at **Plot 301** were removed by the police until 1989, when the deceased received a state funeral on Hősök tere. The plot is 2km from the main gates, with minibuses running there every twenty minutes. Near the graves, an ornate wooden gateway and headposts mark a mass grave now designated as a **National Pantheon** – as opposed to the Communist pantheon in Kerepesi.

The adjacent **Jewish cemetery** (Izraélita temető; Mon–Fri & Sun 8am–2pm; free) is the burial place of Ernő Szép (author of *The Smell of Humans*, a searing Holocaust memoir), as well as many rabbis and industrialists. Beside the wall on Kozma utca stands the dazzling blue-and-gold tiled Art Nouveau tomb of shopkeeper **Sándor Schmidl**, designed by Ödön Lechner and Béla Lajta. The gates to the Jewish cemetery are 700m up the road from the New Public Cemetery; tram #37 runs past.

Ferencváros

Pest's IX district, **Ferencváros** (Francis Town), was developed to house workers in the latter half of the nineteenth century, on the same lines as the more bourgeois Józsefváros. During the 1930s and 1940s, its population confounded Marxist orthodoxy by voting for the extreme right, who returned the favour by supporting the local football team **FTC** – popularly known as **"Fradi"** – which became the unofficial team of the opposition under Communism, subsequently known for its hooligan "ultras". The club's green and white colours can be seen throughout the district; its stadium is way out along Üllői út. (See p.139 for more on Fradi and the football scene in general.)

Initially, Ferencváros takes its tone from two institutions on Vámház körút, the section of the Kiskörút that separates it from the Belváros. The wrought-iron **Great Market Hall** (Nagycsarnok; Mon 6am–5pm, Tues–Fri 6am–6pm, Sat 6am–3pm) is as famous for its ambience as for its produce, with tanks of live fish and stalls festooned with strings of paprika downstairs and cheap eateries upstairs. Nearer the Danube, the **Economics University** (named after Karl Marx during Communist times) makes a fine sight from Buda at night, reflected in the river, and adds to the liveliness of the area by day. The building was originally Budapest's main Customs House (Vámház) – hence the name of the körút. A freestanding section of the **medieval wall** of Pest can be found off Vámház körút in the courtyard of no. 16, if the door is open.

Further inland off Kálvin tér (see p.95), **Ráday utca** hums with restaurants, cafés and bars, their pavement tables packed till after midnight, occasionally disturbed by stag parties. In late June/early July, the **Ferencváros festival** (FETE) sees concerts on Bakáts tér at the far end of Ráday, and other events in the neighbourhood, while the **Goethe-Institut** at no. 58 has its own programme of events throughout the year.

The Applied Arts Museum and Corvin Cinema

Grey, polluted **Üllői út** isn't an obvious place to linger, but there's much to see within a few blocks' radius of Ferenc körút metro. Take the signposted exit in the underpass to marvel at the **Applied Arts Museum** (Iparművészeti Múzeum; Tues 2–6pm, Wed, Fri, Sat & Sun 10am–6pm, Thurs 10am–10pm; 800Ft; Ⓦwww .imm.hu), the most flamboyant creation of Ödön Lechner, who strove to create a uniquely Hungarian form of architecture emphasizing the Magyars' Ugric roots, but was also influenced by Art Nouveau. Inaugurated by Emperor Franz Josef during the 1896 Millennial celebrations, it has a vast dome tiled in green and yellow and a portico with ceramic Turkic motifs on an egg-yolk-coloured background, from the Zsolnay porcelain factory in Pécs (see p.298). By contrast, the all-white interior is reminiscent of Mogul architecture: at one time it was thought that the Magyars came from India. The museum has a large collection but no permanent displays, instead mounting small exhibitions of its own material and major shows drawn from other collections.

Returning to the subway and crossing the Nagykörút, duck into **Corvin köz**, a U-shaped Art Deco maze of passages and apartment blocks surrounding the **Corvin Cinema**, from which teenage guerrillas (some as young as 12) sallied forth to battle Soviet tanks in 1956. Since the fall of Communism, they have been honoured by a statue of a young insurgent outside the cinema. Inside, the auditoriums are named after illustrious Hungarian actors or directors such as Alexander Korda – one of many Magyars who made it in Hollywood. From the cinema you can walk round the corner and along Práter utca to find a delightful statue of the **Paul Street Boys** – the heroes of Ferenc Molnár's eponymous 1906 novel – portraying the moment they are caught playing marbles in the yard of their enemies, the Redshirts. The most widely sold and translated Hungarian book ever, it's both a universal tale of childhood and a satire on extreme nationalism.

If you're wondering how locals were able to fight so well in 1956, the answer lies across Üllői út, where the Hungarian garrison of the **Kilián Barracks** was the first to join the insurgents, organizing youths already aware of street-fighting tactics due to an obligatory diet of films about Soviet partisans. It was in Budapest that the Molotov cocktail proved lethal to T-54s, as the "Corvin Boys" trapped columns in the backstreets by firebombing the front and rear tanks. Memorial plaques honour Colonel Pál Maleter and others who directed fighting from the Corvin Cinema.

Holocaust Memorial Centre

One block past the barracks, a right turn into Páva utca brings you to the **Holocaust Memorial Centre** (Holocaust Emlékközpont; Tues–Sun 10am–6pm; 1000Ft; ⓦwww.hdke.hu), more chilling than the House of Terror (see p.85); think twice about bringing children here. Like Libeskind's Jewish Museum in Berlin, the building is distorted and oppressive; darkened ramps resounding to the crunch of jackboots and the shuffle of feet lead to artefacts, newsreels and audiovisual testimonies relating the slide from "deprivation of rights to genocide". From 1920 onwards, Jews were systematically stripped of their assets by right-wing regimes with the participation of local citizens, and Gypsies forced into work gangs. The family stories and newsreel footage of the death camps after liberation are truly harrowing, accompanied by the roar and clang of a furnace being stoked. Visitors emerge from the bowels of hell to find themselves within a glorious and sunlit Art Deco **synagogue**, built by Leopold Baumhorn in the 1920s, which has been restored and incorporated in the memorial centre, itself designed by István Mányi.

On your way back to the metro, it's worth a detour onto Liliom utca to see another striking building – an old transformer plant turned into an outstanding contemporary arts centre, **Trafó** (see p.137 for details).

The Natural History Museum and Botanical Garden

A kilometre further down Üllői út just past the Klinikák metro stop, a left turn up Korányi Sándor utca brings you to the revamped **Hungarian Natural History Museum** (Magyar Természettudományi Múzeum; daily except Tues 10am–6pm; 600Ft, 1000Ft for temporary displays; ⓦwww.nhmus.hu). Though slightly out on a limb, it's worth the hike, especially if you have children, with lots of colour, wide-open spaces, and explanations in English. A hall dominated by a whale skeleton leads through to a fantastic **underwater room**, with colourful fish in salt- and freshwater aquariums – the mock seabed under the glass floor makes you feel as if you're walking on water. The first floor has lots of interesting displays on animals from around the world, while the top floor focuses on what Hungary is doing for the environment. The shop by the entrance sells an excellent range of animal-related souvenirs.

Across the road is a small **Botanical Garden** (Fűvészkert; daily 9am–5pm, greenhouses closed noon–1pm and from 4pm; 800Ft). Delightfully jungle-like, it derives part of its appeal from its rather run-down state.

The National Theatre and Palace of Arts

Spectacularly floodlit in blue and gold on the banks of the Danube, the National Theatre and Palace of Arts complex looks like the crowning jewel of Budapest's cultural life from a distance, being a three-kilometre ride from Deák tér (take tram #2 to the penultimate stop, Vágóhíd utca). Though still isolated by tracts of wasteland, the landscaping, outdoor bars and hip warehouse developments are colonizing the riverside from the Petőfi bridge outwards, gradually creating a whole new arts and leisure zone.

The **National Theatre** (Nemzeti Szinház; ⓦ www.nemzetiszinhaz.hu) resembles a Ceaučescu folly, its exterior and environs strewn with random architectural references and statuary. The Classical facade submerged in a water feature is a replica of the frontage of the original theatre on Blaha Lujza tér, torn down to build the metro in 1964 – seen by many as a Communist plot to undermine Hungary's identity – which condemned the company to a dump in the backstreets of Pest while the debate continued as to where this national institution should be housed. The fiasco of the "National Hole" on Erzsébet tér (see p.78) was followed by a scandal over the existing site, when it emerged that the minister in charge awarded the contract to the architect of his holiday home. Lacklustre performances since the theatre opened haven't helped.

Next door is the **Palace of Arts** (Művészetek Palotája; ⓦ www.mupa.hu), a vast edifice that is the new home of the excellent Philharmonic Orchestra and National Dance Theatre. No expense has been spared to make this a top venue; particularly in the concert hall, whose acoustics are so sharp that some orchestras are said to dislike it, as you can hear their mistakes. The Palace incorporates the **Ludwig Museum** or Museum of Contemporary Art (Kortárs Művészti Múzeum; Tues–Sun 10am–8pm; 1000Ft; ⓦ www.ludwigmuseum.hu), established in 1996 to build upon an earlier bequest by the German industrialist Peter Ludwig. The collection includes US pop art such as Warhol's *Single Elvis* and Lichtenstein's *Vicki*, as well as Picasso's *Musketeer with a Sword* and a *Sealed Letter* by Beuys. It also hosts **temporary exhibitions** by international artists, who sometimes personally conduct guided tours (Thurs at 7pm and Sat at 5pm; 1000Ft for under ten people; reserve 14 days ahead ☏ 1/555 3469, ⓔ guidedtour@lumu.hu).

Buda

Viewed from the embankments of the Danube, **Buda** forms a collage of palatial buildings, archaic spires and outsize statues, crowning craggy massifs. This glamorous image conceals more mundane aspects, but at times, in the right place, Buda can really live up to it. To experience **Várhegy** (Castle Hill) at its best, come early in the morning to visit the **museums** before the crowds arrive, then wander off for lunch or a soak in one of the Turkish baths, and return to catch street life in full swing in the afternoon. The outlying **Buda Hills** – accessible by chairlift and the **Children's Railway** – are obviously less visited during the week, while **Gellért-hegy**, with its superb views over the city, the **Rózsadomb** district and the **Roman ruins** of Óbuda and Rómaifürdő can be seen any time, but preferably when the weather's fine.

Várhegy

Várhegy (Castle Hill), often referred to simply as the **Vár**, is Buda's most prominent feature. A 1500-metre-long plateau encrusted with bastions, mansions and a huge palace, it dominates both the Víziváros below and Pest, over the river, making this stretch of the river one of the most majestic urban waterfronts in Europe. The hill's grandiosity and strategic utility have long gone hand in hand: Hungarian kings built their palaces here because it was easy to defend, a fact appreciated by the Turks, Habsburgs and other occupiers. Its buildings, a legacy of bygone Magyar glories, have been almost wholly reconstructed from the rubble of 1945, when the Wehrmacht and the Red Army battled over the hill while Buda's inhabitants cowered underground –

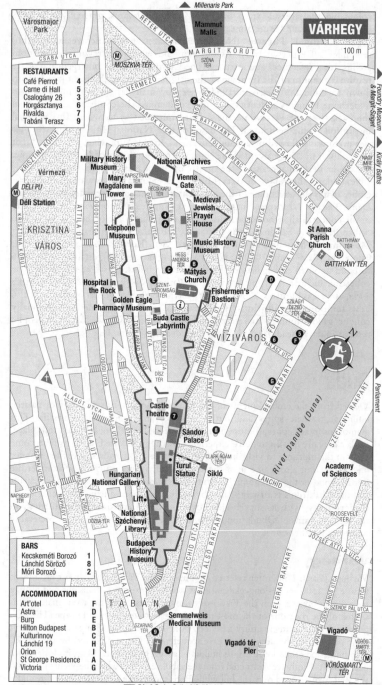

VÁRHEGY

0   100 m

RESTAURANTS
Café Pierrot	4
Carne di Hall	5
Csalogány 26	3
Horgásztanya	6
Rivalda	7
Tabáni Terasz	9

BARS
Kecskeméti Borozó	1
Lánchíd Söröző	8
Móri Borozó	2

ACCOMMODATION
Art'otel	F
Astra	D
Burg	E
Hilton Budapest	B
Kulturinnov	C
Lánchíd 19	I
Orion	A
St George Residence	G
Victoria	

the eighty-sixth time that it was ravaged and rebuilt over seven centuries, rivalling the devastation caused by the recapture of Buda from the Turks in 1686.

Though the hill's appearance has changed much since building began in the thirteenth century, its main **streets** still follow their medieval courses, with Gothic arches and stone carvings in the courtyards and passages of eighteenth- and nineteenth-century Baroque **houses**, whose facades are embellished with fancy ironwork grilles. Practically every building displays a *műemlék* plaque giving details of its history (in Hungarian only), and a surprising number are still homes rather than embassies or boutiques – there are even a couple of schools and corner shops. At dusk, when most of the tourists have left, pensioners walk their dogs and toddlers play in the long shadows of Hungarian history.

There are several **approaches** to Várhegy, mostly starting from the Víziváros (described on p.108). The simplest and most novel is to ride up to the palace by **Sikló** (see p.110 for details), a renovated nineteenth-century funicular that runs from Clark Ádám tér by the Lánchíd (Chain Bridge). Alternatively, you can start from Moszkva tér (on metro line 2) and either take buses #16, #16A or #116, leaving from the raised side of Moszkva tér, which terminate by the palace – or walk uphill to the Vienna Gate at the northern end of Várhegy. Walking from Batthyány tér via the steep flights of steps (*lépcső*) off Fő utca involves more effort, but the dramatic stairway up to the Fishermen's Bastion is worth the sweat. The most direct approach **from Pest** is to ride bus #16 from Erzsébet tér across the Lánchíd to Clark Ádám tér – giving you the option of taking the Sikló or staying on the bus and getting off at one of the stops on Várhegy.

Szentháromság tér

North of the palace lies the **Várnegyed** (Castle District), where, in medieval times, residence was a privilege granted to religious or ethnic groups, each occupying a certain street. Armenians, Circassians and Sephardic Jews also established themselves here during the Turkish occupation. The "liberation" of Buda by a multinational Christian army under Habsburg command was followed by a pogrom and ordinances restricting the right of residence to Catholics and Germans, which remained in force for nearly a century. In 1944, the Red Cross established safe houses here for Jewish refugees, some of whom remained hidden in caves after the others were forced into the ghetto. By the time the Red Army finally took Buda on February 13, 1945, only four houses on the hill were habitable.

The obvious starting point is **Szentháromság tér** (Holy Trinity Square), the historic heart of the district, named after an ornate **Trinity Column** erected in 1713 in thanksgiving for the abatement of a plague. To the southwest on the corner of Szentháromság utca stands the former **Town Hall** of Buda, which functioned as a municipality until the unification of Buda, Pest and Óbuda in 1873. Down the road at Szentháromság utca 7, the tiny **Ruszwurm patisserie** has been a pastry shop and café since 1827, and was a gingerbread shop in the Middle Ages. Its Empire-style decor looks much the same as it did under Vilmos Ruszwurm, who ran the patisserie for nearly four decades from 1884.

In the small park by the square, Tourinform can supply a free map of Várhegy and rent an **audioguide** for self-guided walks (3000Ft for 3hr). Nearby is a touch-friendly **scale model** of the Mátyás Church and Fishermen's Bastion, labelled in Braille for blind visitors.

The Mátyás Church

The square's most prominent feature is the neo-Gothic **Mátyás Church** (Mátyás templom; Mon–Fri 9am–5pm, Sat 9am–1pm, Sun 1–5pm; 700Ft; audioguide 400Ft), whose diamond-patterned roofs and toothy spires are wildly asymmetrical but nevertheless coherent in form. Officially dedicated to Our Lady, but popularly named after "Good King Mátyás", the building is a late nineteenth-century re-creation by architect Frigyes Schulek, grafted onto those portions of the original thirteenth-century church that survived the siege of 1686. The frescoes and altars had been whitewashed over or removed when the Turks turned it into a mosque. Ravaged yet again in World War II, the church was laboriously restored by a Communist regime keen to show its patriotic credentials, and the transition to democracy saw the sanctity of this "ancient shrine of the Hungarian people" reaffirmed – which means that visitors are expected to be properly dressed and respectfully behaved.

Entering the church through its twin-spired **Mary Portal**, the richness of the interior is overwhelming. Painted leaves and geometric motifs run up columns and under vaulting, while shafts of light fall through rose windows onto gilded altars and statues with stunning effect. Most of the **frescoes** were executed by Károly Lotz or Bertalan Székely, the foremost historical painters of the day. The **coat of arms of King Mátyás** can be seen on the wall to your left, just inside; his family name, Corvinus, comes from the raven (*corvus* in Latin) that appeared on his heraldry and on every volume in the famous Corvin Library.

Around the corner to the left, beneath the south tower, is the **Loreto Chapel**, containing a Baroque Madonna, while in the bay beneath the Béla Tower beyond the stairs you can see two medieval capitals, one carved with monsters fighting a dragon, the other with two bearded figures reading a book. The tower is named after Béla IV, who founded the church, rather than his predecessor in the second gated chapel along, who shares a double sarcophagus with Anne of Chatillon. Originally located in the old capital, Székesfehérvár, the **tomb of Béla III** and his queen was moved here after its discovery in 1848. Although Hungary's medieval kings were crowned at Székesfehérvár, it was customary to make a prior appearance in Buda – hence yet another sobriquet, the "Coronation Church".

The church also has a small collection of **ecclesiastical treasures** and relics, including the right foot of St János. The **crypt**, normally reserved for prayer, contains the red-marble tombstone of a nameless Árpád prince. Otherwise, climb a spiral staircase to the **Royal Oratory** overlooking the stained-glass windows and embossed vaulting of the nave; here votive figures and vestments presage a **replica of the Coronation Regalia**, whose attached exhibition is more informative about the provenance of St Stephen's Crown than that accompanying the originals, on display in Parliament (see p.82).

Mass is celebrated in the Mátyás Church daily at 7am, 8.30am and 6pm, and at 10am and noon on Sundays and public holidays. The 10am Mass on Sunday is in Latin with a full choir. The church is also a superb venue for **concerts** during the festival seasons, and evening organ recitals throughout the year. Details appear in listings magazines and on the church's own website, Ⓦ www.matyas-templom.hu. Tickets are available from any booking agency (see p.134).

The Fishermen's Bastion

After the Mátyás Church, the most transfixing sight is the **Fishermen's Bastion** (Halászbástya) just beyond, which frames the view of Pest across the river. Although fishermen from the Víziváros reputedly defended this part of the hill during the Middle Ages, the existing bastion is purely decorative. An undulating white rampart of cloisters and stairways intersecting at seven tent-like turrets symbolizing the Magyar tribes that conquered the Carpathian Basin, it was designed by Schulek as a foil to the church. The view of Pest across the river is only surpassed by the vistas from the terrace of Buda Palace, and the Citadella on Gellért-hegy. However, you might baulk at paying 400Ft to go up to the top

King Stephen

If you commit just one figure from Hungarian history to memory, make it **King Stephen**, for it was he who welded the tribal Magyar fiefdoms into a state and won recognition from Christendom. Born Vajk, son of Prince Géza, he emulated his father's policy of trying to convert the pagan Magyars and develop Hungary with the help of foreign preachers, craftsmen and merchants. By marrying Gizella of Bavaria in 996, he was able to use her father's knights to crush a pagan revolt after Géza's death, and subsequently received an apostolic cross and crown from Pope Sylvester II for his coronation on Christmas Day, 1000 AD, when he took the name Stephen (István in Hungarian).

Though noted for his enlightened views (such as the need for tolerance and the desirability of multiracial nations), he could act ruthlessly when necessary. After his only son Imre died in an accident and a pagan seemed likely to inherit, Stephen had the man blinded and poured molten lead into his ears. Naming his successor, he symbolically offered his crown to the Virgin Mary rather than the Holy Roman Emperor or the pope; she has since been considered the Patroness of Hungary. Swiftly canonized after his death in 1038, **St Stephen** became a national talisman, his mummified right hand a holy relic, and his coronation regalia the symbol of statehood. Despite playing down his cult for decades, even the Communists eventually embraced it in a bid for some legitimacy, while nobody in post-Communist Hungary thinks it odd that the symbol of the republic should be the crown and cross of King Stephen.

level – tickets from the machine nearby (students and OAPs get their half-price tickets from an office beside Tourinform) – as the free view from the lower level is just as good.

Between the bastion and the church, an equestrian **statue of King Stephen** honours the founder of the Hungarian nation, whose conversion to Christianity and coronation with a crown sent by the pope presaged the Magyars' integration into European civilization (see box above). The statue is reflected in the copper-glass facade of the **Budapest Hilton**, opposite, along with the church and the bastion. Incorporating chunks of a medieval Dominican church and monastery on the side facing the river, and an eighteenth-century Jesuit college on the other, the hotel bears a copy of the **Mátyás Relief** from Bautzen in Germany that's regarded as the only true likeness of Hungary's Renaissance monarch – who is shown being crowned by a pair of angels.

North towards Kapisztrán tér

If you're not in a hurry to reach the palace, it's worth exploring the northern reaches of the Várnegyed, whose streets abound in period details. A common medieval feature that's survived is the sedilia, rows of niches with seats, in the passageway to the inner courtyard. For an example, look no further than the *Fortuna* restaurant on Hess András tér, which occupies the site of Hungary's first printing press, set up by András Hess in 1473. Also notice the hedgehog relief above the door of the former *Red Hedgehog Inn* at no. 3, where Janissaries were billeted in Turkish times.

The **Music History Museum** (Zenetörténeti Múzeum; Tues–Sun 10am–4pm; 1000Ft; ⓦwww.zti.hu), at Tàncsics Mihàly utca 7, occupies the Baroque Erdödy Palace where Beethoven was a guest in 1800 and Bartók had his workshop before he emigrated. The collection ranges from a Holczman harp made for Marie Antoinette and a unique tongue-shaped violin in the classical section to hurdy-gurdies, zithers, cowhorns and bagpipes, as well as many Bartók scores and jottings.

Next door, **no. 9**, was once a barracks where the Habsburgs jailed Hungarian radicals such as Mihály Táncsics – after whom the street is named – but in an earlier age it was home to both Ashkenazi and Sephardic Jews, and called Zsidó utca (Jewish Street). The Ashkenazi community was established in the reign of Béla IV and encouraged by King Mátyás. Though you wouldn't think so from the outside, no. 26 contains a **Medieval Jewish Prayer House** (Középkori Zsidó Imaház; May–Oct Tues–Sun 10am–6pm; 400Ft) once used by the Sephardis. All that remains of its original decor are two Cabbalistic symbols painted on a wall, though the museum does its best to flesh out the history of the community with maps and prints – all the real treasures are in the Jewish Museum in Pest (see p.92).

Sparing a glance for the turbaned Turk's head above the doorway of no. 24, head on to **Bécsi kapu tér**, an inclined plaza named after the **Vienna Gate** that was erected on the 250th anniversary of the recapture of Buda. Beside it, the forbiddingly neo-Romanesque **National Archives** (no admission) guard the way to **Kapisztrán tér**, a larger square centred on the **Mary Magdalene Tower** (Magdolna-torony), whose accompanying church was wrecked in World War II. In medieval times this was where Hungarian residents worshipped; Germans used the Mátyás Church. Today the tower boasts a peal of bells that jingles through a medley by the jazz pianist György Szabados, which includes Hungarian folk tunes, Chopin's *Études* and the theme from *The Bridge on the River Kwai*.

Beyond is a **statue of Friar John Capistranus**, who exhorted the Hungarians to victory at the siege of Belgrade in 1456, which the pope hailed by ordering church bells to be rung at noon throughout Europe. It shows Capistranus bestriding a dead Turk and is aptly located outside the **Military History Museum**, located in a former barracks on the north of the square (Hadtörténeti Múzeum; April–Sept 10am–6pm; Oct–March 10am–4pm; closed Mon; 700Ft). This has gung-ho exhibitions on the history of hand-weapons from ancient times till the advent of firearms, and the birth and campaigns of the Honvéd (national army) during the 1848–49 War of Independence, but what sticks in the memory are the sections on the Hungarian Second Army that was decimated at Stalingrad – ask about seeing newsreel footage, as there are no regular shows. The entrance to the museum is on the Tóth Árpád sétány, a promenade lined with cannons and chestnut trees, overlooking the Buda Hills, which leads past a giant **flagpole** striped in Hungarian colours to the symbolic **grave of Abdurrahman**, the last Turkish Pasha of Buda, who died on the walls in 1686 – a "valiant foe", according to the inscription.

Országház utca and úri utca

Heading back towards Szentháromság tér, there's more to be seen on **Országház utca**, which was the district's main thoroughfare in the Middle Ages and known as the "street of baths" during Turkish times. Its present name, Parliament Street, recalls the sessions of the Diet held in the 1790s in a former Poor Clares' cloister at no. 28, where the Gestapo imprisoned 350 Hungarians and foreigners in 1945. No. 17, diagonally across the road, consists of two medieval houses joined together and has a relief of a croissant on its keystone from when it was a bakery. A few doors down from the former Parliament building, Renaissance sgraffiti survive on the underside of the bay window of no. 22 and a Gothic trefoil-arched cornice on the house next door, while the one beyond has been rebuilt according to its original fifteenth-century form.

The adjacent **Úri utca** (Gentleman Street) also boasts historic associations, for it was at the former Franciscan monastery at no. 51 that the five Hungarian Jacobins were held before being beheaded on the "Blood Meadow" below the hill in 1795. Next door is a wing of the Poor Clares' cloister that served as a postwar telephone exchange before being turned into a **Telephone Museum** (Telefónia Múzeum; Tues–Sun 10am–4pm; 400Ft), entered from Országház utca 30 on weekends and holidays. The curator of the museum strives to explain the development of telephone exchanges since Tivadar Puskás introduced them to Budapest in the early 1900s – activating a noisy rotary one that's stood here since the 1930s – and you're invited to dial up commentaries in English or songs in Hungarian, check out the webcam and internet facilities, and admire the personal phones of Emperor Franz Josef, Admiral Horthy and the Communist leader Kádár.

Further down the street on either side, notice the statues of the four seasons in the first-floor niches at nos. 54–56, Gothic sedilia in the gateway of nos. 48–50, and three arched windows and two diamond-shaped ones from the fourteenth and fifteenth centuries at no. 31.

The Hospital in the Rock and Buda Castle Labyrinth

Six to fourteen metres beneath the streets lie 10km of galleries formed by hot springs and cellars dug since medieval times. In 1941, a section was converted into a military hospital staffed from the civilian Szent János hospital, which doubled as an air-raid shelter after the Red Army broke through the Attila Line and encircled Budapest in December 1944. In the 1950s a nuclear bunker was added to the complex, maintained in readiness until 2000, a time capsule of the Cold War. English-language tours of the **Hospital in the Rock** (Sziklakórház; Tues–Sun 10am–8pm; Ⓦwww.sziklakorhaz.hu) run every hour till 6pm; one limited to the hospital (30min; 2000Ft), the other also featuring the bunkers (1hr; 3000Ft). Ramped throughout for wheelchairs and trolleys, its operating theatres contain 1930s X-ray and anaesthetic machines (used in the film *Evita*) and gory waxworks; bed sheets in the wards were changed every fortnight until 2000.

The ventilation system is run by generators installed in the **nuclear bunker** built in 1953, with charcoal air-filters, a laboratory for detecting toxins, atropine ampoules to be injected against nerve gas, and an airlock fitted when the bunker was enlarged between 1958 and 1962. To preserve its secrecy, fuel was delivered by trucks pretending to "water" flower beds on the surface, via a concealed pipeline. The entrance to the hospital is at Lovas út 4/b, on the rear hillside beyond the castle walls, reached by descending the steps at the end of Szentháromság utca and then walking 50m uphill.

Just downhill from the steps at Lovas út 4/a is a wheelchair-accessible entrance to the **Buda Castle Labyrinth** (Budavári Labirintus; daily 9.30am–7.30pm; 2000Ft; Ⓦwww.labirintus.com), a separate maze of **caves** that most visitors enter from Úri utca 9, at the top of Várhegy. The displays include copies of the cave paintings of Lascaux (Buda's caves also sheltered prehistoric hunters), and a "bravery labyrinth", where you have to make your way through a section of cave in total darkness. Masked figures and a giant head sunken into the floor enliven other dank chambers. There's a cup of warming tea at the end of the optional 25-minute tour.

South towards the palace

Heading south from Szentháromság tér towards the palace, you'll come to the intriguing **Golden Eagle Pharmacy Museum** (Arany Sas Patikamúzeum; Mon 10.30am–5.30pm, Tues–Sun 10.30am–6.30pm; 500Ft) at Tárnok utca 18. The first pharmacy in Buda, established after the expulsion of the Turks, its original furnishings lend authenticity to dubious nostrums including the skull of a mummy used to make "Mumia" powder to treat epilepsy; there's also a reconstruction of an alchemist's laboratory, complete with dried bats and crocodiles, and other obscure exhibits such as the small, long-necked Roman glass vessel for collecting widows' tears. The *Tárnok* coffee house, next door but one, occupies one of the few buildings on the hill to have kept its Renaissance sgraffiti – a red and orange chequerboard pattern covering the facade.

Both Tárnok utca and Úri utca end in **Dísz tér** (Parade Square), where the mournful Honvéd memorial presages the ramparts and gateways controlling access to the palace grounds. Ahead lies the scarred hulk of the old Ministry of Defence, while to your left is the **Castle Theatre** (Várszínház), where the first-ever play in Hungarian was staged in 1790 and Beethoven performed in 1808. The last building in the row is the **Sándor Palace** (Sándor Palota), formerly the prime minister's residence, where Premier Teleki shot himself in protest at Hungary joining the Nazi invasion of Yugoslavia. It is now the residence of the country's president, a figurehead who is elected by parliament rather than the electorate.

Next door, the upper terminal of the **Sikló** funicular (see p.110) is separated from the terrace of Buda Palace by a stately gateway and the ferocious-looking **Turul statue**, a giant bronze eagle clasping a sword in its talons. In Magyar mythology the Turul sired the first dynasty of Hungarian kings by raping the grandmother of Prince Árpád, who led the tribes into Europe. During the nineteenth century it became a symbol of Hungarian identity in the face of Austrian culture, but wound up being co-opted by the Habsburgs, and has today been adopted as an emblem by Hungary's skinheads.

From here, you can descend a staircase to the **terrace** of the palace, commanding a sweeping **view** of Pest. Beyond the souvenir stalls prances an equestrian **statue of Prince Eugene of Savoy**, who liberated Buda in 1686. The bronze statues nearby represent **Csongor** and **Tünde**, the lovers in Vörösmarty's drama of the same name.

Buda Palace

As befits a former royal residence, the lineage of **Buda Palace** (Budavári palota) can be traced back to medieval times, with the rise and fall of various palaces on the hill reflecting the changing fortunes of the Hungarian state. The first fortifications and dwellings, hastily erected by Béla IV after the Mongol invasion of 1241–42, were replaced by the grander palaces of the Angevin kings, who ruled in more prosperous and stable times. This process reached its zenith in the reign of Mátyás Corvinus (1458–90), whose palace was a Renaissance extravaganza to which artists and scholars from all over Europe were drawn by the blandishments of Queen Beatrice and the prospect of lavish hospitality; the rooms had hot and cold running water, and during celebrations the fountains and gargoyles flowed with wine. After the Turkish occupation, and the long siege that ended it, only ruins were left – which the Habsburgs, Hungary's new rulers, levelled to build a palace of their own.

From Empress Maria Theresa's modest beginnings (a mere 203 rooms, which she never saw completed), the Royal Palace expanded inexorably throughout the nineteenth century, though no monarch ever lived here, only the Habsburg Palatine (viceroy). After the collapse of the empire following World War I, Admiral Horthy inhabited the building with all the pomp of monarchy until he was deposed by a German coup in October 1944. The palace was left unoccupied, and it wasn't long before the siege of Buda once again resulted in total devastation. Reconstruction work began in the 1950s in tandem with excavations of the medieval substrata beneath the rubble, which were incorporated in the new building, whose interior is far less elegant than the prewar version, being designed to accommodate cultural institutions.

The complex houses the **Hungarian National Gallery** (Wings A, B, C and D), the **Budapest History Museum** (E) and the **National Széchenyi Library** (F) – the first two of which are definitely worth seeing and could easily take an afternoon. There are separate entrances for each.

The Hungarian National Gallery

Most people's first port of call is the **Hungarian National Gallery** (Magyar Nemzeti Galéria; Tues–Sun 10am–6pm; 900Ft for permanent displays, 800Ft for visiting shows; ⓦ www.mng.hu), devoted to Hungarian art from the Middle Ages to the present. It contains much that's superb, but the vastness of the collection and the confusing layout can be fatiguing. Though all the paintings are labelled in English, other details are scanty, so it's worth investing in a guidebook (3500Ft) or guided tour (3300Ft for up to five people; book a couple of days in advance on ⓣ 06-20/4397-326). The main entrance is on the eastern side of Wing C, overlooking the river, behind the statue of Eugene of Savoy. Don't buy a special ticket (500Ft) to see the separate **Habsburg crypt**, containing the tombs of several Habsburgs who ruled as palatines of Hungary up until 1849, until you've checked that a tour is scheduled, as they require at least 25 people (ⓣ 06-20/4397-331).

On the **ground floor** of the museum, marble reliefs of Beatrice and Mátyás and a wooden ceiling from a sixteenth-century church are the highlights of a **Medieval and Renaissance Lapidarium**, which you need to pass through to reach the fantastic collection of fifteenth-century **Gothic altarpieces** at the rear of Wing D. Notice the varied reactions to the *Death of the Virgin* from Kassa and the gloating spectators in the Jánosrét *Passion*. From the same church comes a *St Nicholas* altar as long as a limo and lurid as a comic strip. The pointed finials on the high altar from Liptószentmária anticipate the winged altarpieces of the sixteenth century on the floor above. To get there without returning to the foyer, use the small staircase near the altarpieces and turn left, left and left again at the top.

The **first floor** picks up where downstairs left off by displaying **late Gothic altarpieces** with soaring pinnacles. Much of the **Baroque** art in the adjacent section once belonged to Prince Miklós Esterházy or was confiscated from private owners in the 1950s. Don't miss Ádám Mányoki's portrait of Ferenc Rákóczi II, a sober look at a national hero that foreshadowed a whole artistic genre in the nineteenth century. This and other **National Historical art** fills the central block, where you'll be confronted by two vast canvases as you come up the staircase: *Zrínyi's Sortie* by Peter Krafft depicting the suicidal sally of the defenders of Szigetvár, and the *Reoccupying of Buda Castle* by Gyula Benczúr. At the end near Wing B, you'll find Sándor Lilzen-Mayer's *St Elizabeth of Hungary* offering her ermine cape to a ragged mother and child, and two iconic scenes by Bertalan Székely: *The Battle of Mohács*, a shattering defeat for the Hungarians in 1526; and *The Women of Eger*, exalting their defiance of the Turks in 1552. Wing B covers other trends in nineteenth-century art, with sections devoted to **Mihály Munkácsy** and **László Paál** – exhibited together since both painted landscapes, though Paál did little else whereas Munkácsy was internationally renowned for pictures with a social message – and **Pál Szinyei Merse**, the "father of Hungarian Impressionism", whose models and subjects were cheerfully bourgeois.

On the **stairs** to the floor above you'll pass three huge canvases by the visionary artist **Tivadar Kosztka Csontváry**, whose obsession with the Holy Land and the "path of the sun" inspired scenes like *Look Down on the Dead Sea* and *Ruins of the Greek Theatre at Taormina*. The **second floor** covers twentieth-century Hungarian art up to 1945, starting with the vibrant **Art Nouveau** movement off to the right of the atrium. Pictures by János Vaszary (*Golden Age*) and Aladár Körösfői Kriesch (founder of the Gödöllő artists' colony – see p.324) are set in richly hand-carved frames, an integral part of their composition. József Rippl-Rónai was a pupil of Munkácsy whose portraits went mostly unrecognized in his lifetime. Here you'll also find Csontváry's magically lit *Coaching in Athens at the Full Moon*.

Since all the Socialist art was evicted in the 1990s, the **third floor** has been used for temporary exhibitions of graphics or photos by Hungarian artists. On fine days, visitors can ascend to the palace's **dome** for a **view** of the city.

The Mátyás Fountain and National Széchenyi Library

The courtyard outside is flanked on three sides by the palace, and overlooks Buda to the west. In the far corner stands the flamboyant **Mátyás Fountain**, whose bronze figures recall the legend of Szép Ilonka. This beautiful peasant girl met the king while he was hunting incognito, fell in love with him, and died of a broken heart after discovering his identity and realizing the futility of her hopes. The man with a falcon is the king's Italian chronicler, who recorded the story for posterity. It is also enshrined in a poem by Vörösmarty.

A gateway guarded by lions leads into the **Lion Courtyard**, totally enclosed by further wings. To the right is the **National Széchenyi Library** (Országos Széchenyi Könyvtár; Tues–Sat 10am–8pm, closed mid-July to late Aug). Founded in 1802 on the initiative of Count Ferenc Széchenyi, the father of István (see p.267), it receives a copy of every book, newspaper and magazine published in Hungary. You can only visit the reading room on guided tours (200Ft; ☏1/487-8657) or with a reader's pass (6000Ft; passport required to apply). During library hours, a passenger **lift** (100Ft) in the adjacent building by the Lion Gateway – open to all – provides direct access to and from Dózsa tér, at the foot of Várhegy.

The Budapest History Museum

On the far side of the courtyard, the **Budapest History Museum** (Budapest Történeti Múzeum; mid-March to mid-Sept daily 10am–6pm; mid-Sept to Oct daily except Tues 10am–6pm; Nov to mid-March daily except Tues 10am–4pm; 1600Ft, audioguide 850Ft; Ⓦ www.btm.hu) covers two millennia on three floors before descending into the vaulted, flagstoned halls of palaces of old. Due to the ravages inflicted by the Mongols and the Turks there's little to show from the time of the Conquest or Hungary's medieval civilization, so most of the second floor is occupied by **Budapest in Modern Times**, an exhibition that gives an insight into urban planning, fashions, trade and vices from 1686 onwards, with items ranging from an 1880s barrel organ to one of the Swedish Red Cross notices affixed to Jewish safe houses by Wallenberg (see p.92). The **remains of the medieval palace** are reached from the basement via an eighteenth-century cellar. A wing of the ground floor of King Sigismund's palace and the cellars beneath the Corvin Library form a stratum overlaying the **Royal Chapel** and a **Gothic Hall** displaying statues found in 1974. In another chamber are portions of red marble fireplaces and a massive portal carved with cherubs and flowers, from King Mátyás's palace.

If you feel like walking down the hillside into the Víziváros, the river-facing route switchbacks past a Rondella and the former **Palace Gardens** (whose crumbling statues and terraces are on the World Monument Fund's list of endangered sites) to end up at the lower terminal of the Sikló. Aiming for the Tabán (see p.111), it's better to leave the castle grounds by the **Ferdinánd Gate** near the Mace Tower, from which steps run directly down to Szarvas tér.

The Víziváros

Originally a poor quarter where fishermen, craftsmen and their families lived, the **Víziváros** (Watertown) between Várhegy and the Danube was repopulated after the expulsion of the Turks by Croatian and Serbian mercenaries and their camp followers. Today it's a reclusive neighbourhood of mansions and old buildings meeting at odd angles on the hillside, reached by alleys which mostly consist of steps rising from the main street, **Fő utca**. Some of these are still lit by gas lamps and look quite Dickensian on misty evenings.

Batthyány tér and around

The district's main square, named **Batthyány tér** after the nineteenth-century prime minister, was originally called Bomba tér after the ammunition depot sited here for the defence of the Danube. Now home to a long-established market and the underground interchange between the red metro line and the HÉV rail line to Szentendre, it's always busy with shoppers and commuters. To the right of the market is a sunken, two-storey building that used to be the *White Cross Inn*, where Casanova reputedly once stayed. Many of the older buildings in this area are sunken in this way: ground level was raised several feet in the nineteenth century to combat flooding. The twin-towered **St Anne Parish Church**, on the corner of the square, sports the Buda coat of arms on its tympanum. Its interior is ornate yet homely, the high altar festooned with statues of St Anne presenting Mary to the Temple in Jerusalem, accompanied by a host of cherubim and angels, while chintzy bouquets and potted trees welcome shoppers dropping in to say their prayers.

To the Lánchíd and Sikló

Heading south along Fő utca from Batthyány tér, you'll notice a spiky polychrome-tiled church on **Szilágyi Desző tér**, where an inconspicuous plaque commemorates hundreds of Jews massacred beside the Danube by the Arrow Cross in January 1945, when Eichmann and the SS had already fled the city. Further on, you can see the old **Capuchin Church** featuring Turkish window arches, at no. 30 on the left-hand side, and the **Institut Français** at no. 17, which celebrates Bastille Day with an outdoor concert beside the Danube.

A block or two later you emerge onto Clark Ádám tér, facing the majestic **Lánchíd** (Chain Bridge), which has a special place in the history of Budapest and in the hearts of its citizens. As the first permanent link between Buda and Pest (replacing seasonal pontoon bridges and ferries), it was a tremendous spur to the country's economic growth and unification, linking the rural hinterland to European civilization so that Budapest became a commercial centre and transport hub. The bridge symbolized the abolition of feudal privilege, as nobles, hitherto exempt from taxes, were obliged to pay the toll to cross it. It also embodied civic endurance, having been inaugurated only weeks after Hungary lost the 1849 War of Independence, when Austrian troops tried and failed to destroy it. In 1945 it fell to the Wehrmacht, who dynamited all of Budapest's bridges in a bid to check the Red Army. Their reconstruction was one of the first tasks of the postwar era; the Lánchíd reopened on the centenary of its inauguration, and is now honoured with its own **Bridge Festival** (Hídünnep) in June.

The bridge was the brainchild of **Count István Széchenyi**, a horse-fancying Anglophile with a passion for innovation, who founded the Academy of Sciences and brought steam engines to Hungary, amongst other achievements. Designed by **William Tierney Clark**, it was constructed under the supervision of a Scottish engineer, **Adam Clark** (no relation), who personally thwarted the Austrian attempts to destroy it by flooding the chain-lockers. Whereas Széchenyi later died in an asylum, having witnessed the triumph (and subsequent defeat) of Kossuth and the 1848 Revolution, Adam Clark settled happily in Budapest with his Hungarian wife.

During his time in Budapest, Clark also built the **tunnel** (*alagút*) under Várhegy which, Budapesters joked, could be used to store the new bridge when

▲ The Lánchíd (Chain Bridge)

it rained. Next to the tunnel entrance on the river end is the lower terminal of the **Sikló**, a nineteenth-century **funicular** running up to the palace (daily 7.30am–10pm, closed every other Monday; 700Ft one-way, 1300Ft return; Budapest Card not valid). Constructed on the initiative of Ödön, Széchenyi's son, it was only the second funicular in the world when it was inaugurated in 1870, and functioned without a hitch until wrecked by a shell in 1945. The yellow carriages are exact replicas of the originals, but are now lifted by an electric winch rather than a steam engine. In the small park at its foot stands **Kilometre Zero**, a zero-shaped monument from which all distances from Budapest are measured.

To the Király Baths and Bem tér

From Batthyány tér, Fő utca runs north to **Bem tér**, named after the Polish general Joseph Bem, who fought for the Hungarians in the War of Independence. The statue of Bem with his arm in a sling was a rallying point for the crowds that marched on Parliament at the beginning of the 1956 Uprising. *Bambi*, at the junction of Frankel Leó utca, is a Budapest institution, retaining its 1970s furnishing and fierce waitresses (see p.120).

You can identify the nearby **Király Baths** (Király Gyógyfürdő; 1300Ft) by four copper cupolas, shaped like tortoise shells, poking from its eighteenth-century facade. The Király has separate days for men (Tues, Thurs & Sat 9am–8pm) and women (Mon, Wed & Fri 7am–6pm). Together with the Rudas, this is the finest of Budapest's Turkish baths, whose octagonal pool, lit by star-shaped apertures in the dome, was built in 1570 for the Buda garrison. The baths' name, meaning "king", comes from that of the König family who owned them in the eighteenth century.

Approaching the baths from the south, you'll pass the hulking Fascist-style **Military Court of Justice** at Fő utca 70–72, where Imre Nagy and other leaders of the Uprising were secretly tried and executed in 1958. The square outside has now been renamed after Nagy, whose body lay in an unmarked grave in the New Public Cemetery for over thirty years (see p.96).

A century ago, the neighbourhood surrounding Bem tér was dominated by a foundry established by the Swiss ironworker Abrahám Ganz, which grew into the mighty Ganz Machine Works. The original ironworks only ceased operation in 1964, when it was turned into a **Foundry Museum** (Öntödei Múzeum; Tues–Sun 9am–4pm; 400Ft). You can still see the old wooden structure and the foundry's huge ladles and cranes *in situ*, together with a collection of cast-iron stoves, tram wheels, lampposts and other exhibits. The museum is located at Bem utca 20, 200m from Bem tér, or barely a block from Margit körút.

The Tabán, Gellért-hegy and beyond

South of the Vár lies the **Tabán** district, once Buda's artisan quarter, inhabited by Serbs (known as *Rác* in Hungarian), and subsequently a seedy pleasure zone until the area was razed in the 1930s and replaced by an anodyne park that was later carved up by flyovers. Thankfully, the city planners spared Tabán's historic Turkish baths, and its traditions of lusty nightlife have been revived by the neighbouring outdoor bars.

The Tabán and its Turkish baths
In the more sedate reaches of the Tabán below the Vár, the **Semmelweis Medical Museum** at Apród utca 1–3 (Tues–Sun: March–Oct 10.30am–6pm; Nov–Feb 10.30am–4pm; Ⓦ www.semmelweis.museum.hu; free) honours the "saviour of mothers", Ignác Semmelweis (1815–65). He discovered the cause of puerperal fever (a form of blood poisoning contracted in childbirth) and a simple method for preventing the disease, which until then was usually fatal: the sterilization of instruments and the washing of hands with carbolic soap. Inside are displayed medical instruments through the ages, including such curios as a chastity belt.

An even better reason to come to the Tabán, though, is to visit its Turkish baths, where you can immerse yourself in history. The relaxing and curative effects of Buda's **mineral springs** have been appreciated for two thousand years. The Romans built splendid bathhouses at Aquincum, to the north of Buda, and, while these declined with the empire, interest revived after the Knights of St John built a hospice on the site of the present Rudas Baths, near where St Elizabeth cured lepers in the springs below Gellért-hegy. However, it was the Turks who consolidated the habit of bathing – as Muslims, they were obliged to wash five times daily in preparation for prayer – and constructed proper bathhouses which function to this day.

Two lie at the southern end of the Tabán by the Erzsébet híd bridgehead. The **Rác Baths** (Rác Gyógyfürdő), tucked away beneath Hegyalja út, retain an octagonal stone pool from Turkish times, but at the time of writing were closed as part of a major redevelopment that will turn them into a luxury spa hotel complex. Heading on towards the Rudas Baths, you'll pass the **Drinking Hall** (Ivócsarnok; Mon, Wed & Fri 11am–6pm, Tues & Thurs 7am–2pm), beneath the road to the bridge, which sells inexpensive mineral water from three nearby springs. Beyond the bridge, the **Rudas Baths** (Rudas Gyógyfürdő; 2200Ft) harbour a fantastic octagonal pool constructed in 1556 on the orders of Pasha Sokoli Mustapha. Bathers wallow amid shafts of light pouring in from the star-shaped apertures in the domed ceiling, surrounded by stone pillars with iron tie-beams and a nest of smaller pools for parboiling oneself or cooling down. The Rudas has separate days for mixed (Fri noon–4am, Sat 6am–5pm & 10pm–4am, Sun 6am–5pm), men-only (Mon & Wed–Fri 6am–8pm) and women-only (Tues 6am–8pm) bathing.

Gellért-hegy

Gellért-hegy is as much a feature of the waterfront panorama as Várhegy and the Parliament building: a craggy dolomite cliff rearing 130m above the embankment of the Danube, surmounted by the Liberation Monument and the Citadella. The hill is named after Bishop Ghirardus (Gellért in Hungarian), who converted pagan Magyars to Christianity at the behest of King Stephen. After his royal protector's demise, vengeful heathens strapped Gellért to a barrow and toppled him off the cliff, where a **statue of St Gellért** now stands astride a waterfall facing Erzsébet híd.

Before ascending the hill, take a look at the **Gellért Hotel** facing Szabadság híd, a famous Art Nouveau establishment opened in 1918, which Admiral Horthy commandeered following his triumphal entry into "sinful Budapest" in 1920. During the 1930s and 1940s, its balls were the highlight of Budapest's social calendar, when debutantes danced on a glass floor laid over its pool. The attached **Gellért Baths** (Gellért Gyógyfürdő) are magnificently appointed with majolica tiles and mosaics, and a columned, Roman-style **thermal pool**, with lion-headed spouts. To enjoy its waters (May–Sept daily 6am–7pm; Oct–April Mon–Fri 6am–7pm, Sat & Sun 6am–5pm; 2800Ft/3100Ft with a locker/cubicle), you must first reach the changing rooms by a labyrinth of passages; staff are usually helpful with directions. At the far end of the pool are steps leading down to the separate **thermal baths** (daily 6am–6pm), with segregated areas and ornate plunge pools for men and women. Tickets cover both sections, and towels, bathrobes, bathing caps and swimsuits can be rented. From May to August you can also use the **outdoor pools**, including one with a wave machine, on the terraces behind the main baths.

On the hillside opposite the entrance to the baths lies the sepulchral **Cave Church** (Sziklatemplom) where Mass is conducted by white-robed monks of the Pauline order – Hungary's only indigenous order (founded in 1256). The order once provided confessors to the monarchy, and had a monastery beside the church, until the whole order was arrested by the ÁVO at midnight Mass on Easter Monday, 1951, and the chapel was sealed up until 1989. Flickering candles and mournful organ music create an eerie atmosphere during services (daily 8.30–9.30am, 11am–noon, 4.30–6.30pm & 8–9pm), but tourists are only allowed to enter between times. Outside the entrance stands a **statue of St Stephen** with his horse.

From here, you can follow one of the footpaths to the summit – about a twenty-minute climb. The hillside, which still bears fig trees planted by the Turks, was covered in vineyards until a phylloxera epidemic struck in the nineteenth century. Kids will enjoy the long tubular **slides** on the hotel-facing slopes of the hill.

The Liberation Monument and Citadella

Whether you walk up or travel part-way by bus (#27 from Móricz Zsigmond körtér to the Busuló Juhász stop, followed by a 10min walk), the **summit** of Gellért-hegy affords a stunning **panoramic view**, drawing one's eye slowly along the curving river, past bridges and monumental landmarks, and then on to the Buda Hills and Pest's suburbs, merging hazily with the distant plain.

On the summit stands the **Liberation Monument** (Felszabadulási emlékmű) – a female figure brandishing the palm of victory over 30m aloft. Originally commissioned by Admiral Horthy in memory of his son – killed in a plane crash on the Eastern Front – the monument was ultimately dedicated to the Soviet troops who died liberating Budapest from the Nazis. Its sculptor, Zsigmond Kisfaludi-Strobl, substituted a palm branch for the propeller it was meant to hold and added a statue of a Red Army soldier at the base of the monument, to gain approval as a "Proletarian Artist". Having previously specialized in busts of the aristocracy, he was henceforth known by his compatriots as "Kisfaludi-Strébel" (*strébel* meaning "to climb" or "step from side to side"). The monument survived calls for its removal following the end of Communism, but its inscription was rewritten to honour those who died for "Hungary's prosperity", and the Soviet soldier was banished to the Memento Park (see below).

The **Citadella** or fortress behind the monument was built by the Habsburgs to dominate the city in the aftermath of the 1848–49 Revolution. When the historic Compromise was reached in 1867, Budapest's citizens breached the walls to affirm that it no longer posed a threat to them – though in fact an SS regiment did later hole up here during World War II. Today it has been usurped by a private company, charging visitors 1200Ft to set foot inside the walls (daily 8am–dusk) to view an outdoor exhibition on the hill's history since the Celtic Eravisci lived here two thousand years ago, and a dull re-creation of a **Nazi bunker** in a concrete cellar. There's also a hotel, reached by a separate entrance (p.70).

Farkasréti Cemetery

Two kilometres west of Gellért-hegy in the hilly XI district, the **Farkasréti Cemetery** (Farkasréti temető; daily 7.30am–5pm; free) is easily reached by riding tram #59 from Moszkva tér to the penultimate stop or by catching bus #8 from Március 15 tér in Pest. Among the 10,000 graves in the "Wolf's Meadow Cemetery" are those of **Béla Bartók** (whose remains were ceremonially reinterred in 1988 following their return from America, where he died in exile in 1945), his fellow composer **Zoltán Kodály**, and the conductor **Georg Solti** (who left Hungary in 1939 to meet Toscanini and thus escaped the fate of his Jewish parents). Less well known abroad are the actress Gizi Bajor, Olympic-medal winning boxer László Papp, and Hungary's Stalinist dictator **Mátyás Rákosi** (to avoid vandalism, only the initials on his grave are visible). Also look out for the many wooden grave markers inscribed in the ancient runic Székely alphabet.

But the real attraction is the amazing **mortuary chapel** by architect Imre Makovecz – one of his finest designs (1975) – whose wood-ribbed vault resembles the inside of a human ribcage, with a casket for corpses where the heart would be. Be discreet, as the chapel is in constant use by mourners. Anyone keen to see more of Makovecz's work should pay a visit to Visegrád (p.163.), north of Budapest.

Memento Park

One of Budapest's most popular attractions, the **Memento Park** or Statue Park (Szoborpark; daily 10am–dusk; 1500Ft; ⓦwww.mementopark.hu) brings together 42 of the monuments that once glorified Communism in the capital, to celebrate its demise. The park is way out beside Balatoni út in the XXII District, 15km southwest of the city centre; getting there involves taking bus #47-49v from Deák tér to Etele tér, and then a Volán bus from stand 7 or 8 towards Diósd-Érd, which takes ten minutes to reach the park. More expensive but simpler is the Memento Park bus that leaves from in front of *Le Meridien* hotel by Deák tér at 11am daily throughout the year, with an additional service at 3pm in July and August (3950Ft including entry to the park – tickets from the Volánbusz office across the road from the *Meridien*).

Built in stages (1994–2004) as an "unfinished project", the complex is an anti-temple to a bankrupt ideology. Visitors are greeted by a replica of the **Stalin grandstand**, from which Party leaders reviewed parades; the giant boots recall the eight-metre-high Stalin statue toppled in 1956. Beyond lies Witness Square, representing all those squares in Eastern Europe where people defied Communism. In the **Barrack Hall** you can watch *Life of an Agent*, a montage of ÁVO training films on how to bug or search premises and recruit informers. Across the way, the **Red Star Store** sells Lenin and Stalin candles, model Trabant cars and selections of revolutionary songs, which can be heard playing from a 1950s' radio set.

The park proper lies behind a bogus Classical facade framing giant statues of **Lenin**, **Marx** and **Engels**. Lenin's once stood beside the Városliget, while Marx's and Engels' are carved from granite quarried at Mauthausen, a Nazi concentration camp in Austria, later used by the Soviets. Inside the grounds you'll encounter the **Red Army soldier** that guarded the foot of the Liberation Monument on Gellért-hegy, and dozens of other statues and memorials, large and small. Artistically, the best are the **Republic of Councils Monument** – a giant charging sailor based on a 1919 revolutionary poster – and Imre Varga's **Béla Kun Memorial**, with Kun on a tribune surrounded by a surging crowd of workers and soldiers (plus a bystander with an umbrella).

The Tropicarium and Nagytétényi Castle Museum

Two more sights are located still further out in Buda. A must-see for kids, the **Tropicarium** (daily 10am–8pm; 1900Ft, child 1200Ft; ⓦwww.tropicarium.hu) is the largest aquarium-terrarium in Central Europe. Its saltwater section has an eleven-metre-long glass tunnel for intimate views of sand tiger and brown **sharks**, while the freshwater part has piranhas, mouth-breeding cichlids from Africa's Great Lakes, and an outdoor pool to show fish lying dormant when it freezes over. Even better is the mini-**rainforest** complete with macaws, marmoset monkeys, iguanas and alligators, kept steamy by a downpour with thunder and lightning effects, every fifteen minutes. The Tropicarium is in the Campona Shopping Centre, Nagytétényi út 37–43, in Buda's XXII district; take bus #3 from Móricz Zsigmond körtér or #14 or #144 from Kosztolányi Dezső tér.

Further out in the XXII district, the **Nagytétényi Castle Museum** (Nagytétényi Kastélymúzeum; Tues–Sun 10am–6pm; 600Ft; 800Ft for temporary exhibitions; ⓦwww.nagytetenyi.hu) is strictly for lovers of antique furniture. Its 28 rooms display furniture from the Gothic to the Biedermeier epochs, owned by the Applied Arts Museum; the most outstanding exhibit is a walnut-veneered refectory from Trencsen Monastery. In July and August, **historical dances** and **concerts** are held in the grounds (☏1/207-0005 for details). To get there, take bus #3 from Móricz Zsigmond körtér (30–45mins) or the Tropicarium (15min) to the Petőfi utca stop, cross the road and follow Hugonnay utca down past the children's playground to the *kastély*.

Around Moszkva tér and the Rózsadomb

The area immediately north of Várhegy is largely defined by the transport hub of **Moszkva tér** and the reclusive residential quarter covering the **Rózsadomb** (Rose Hill), but the **Millenarium Park** and Mammut malls have created a focus for the area, whose interest previously lay in the ambience of the Rózsadomb, Gül Baba's tomb in the backstreets, and easy access to the Buda Hills.

Moszkva tér and the Millenarium Park

Once a quarry, and subsequently an ice rink and tennis courts, the busy transport nexus of **Moszkva tér** (Moscow Square) has kept its name due to the sheer cost of renaming all the vehicles, maps and signs on which it appears. Among the useful services that run from here are the red metro; buses #16, #16A or #116 to Várhegy; bus or tram #61 to Hűvösvölgy; and trams #4 and #6 to Margit-sziget and Pest's Nagykörút. Trams #4 and #6 run along Margit körút, past the **Mammut malls** (fronted by a statue of the woolly beast), and can get you within walking distance of Gül Baba's tomb (see opposite).

The main attraction of the area lies behind the mall, where the site of the former Ganz Machine Works has been transformed into the **Millenarium Park** (daily 6am–11pm; free) with water features, vineyards and plots of corn to represent different regions of Hungary. Kids can be let loose on the fantastic **playground**, and visitors of all ages can enjoy the **performances** at the outdoor theatre, indoor and outdoor concerts and an ever-changing rota of **events** in the converted factory buildings; get details from the information centre (daily 10am–6pm; ℡1/336 4057, Ⓦwww.millenaris.hu) in Building G.

A big draw for those with kids or an interest in science is the **Palace of Miracles** (Csodák palotája; mid-June to late Aug daily 10am–6pm; rest of the year Mon–Fri 9am–5pm, Sat & Sun 10am–6pm; 1200Ft, family 3440Ft; Ⓦwww.csodapalota .hu) in Building D. This interactive playhouse is the brainchild of two Hungarian physicists and aims to explain scientific principles to 6- to 12-year-olds, using devices such as optical illusions, a bed of nails, a simulated low-gravity "moonwalk" and a "miracle bicycle" on a tightrope. Nearby in Building B, the **House of the Future** (Tues–Fri 9am–5pm, Sat & Sun 10am–6pm; 1500Ft, family 4500Ft) offers digital-based temporary exhibitions on futuristic themes.

The Rózsadomb

Budapest's most exclusive neighbourhood lies beyond smog-ridden **Margit körút** and the backstreets off Moszkva tér. If you're coming from Bem tér, consider a preliminary detour to the rather over-restored **tomb of Gül Baba** on Mecset utca, just above Margit körút (Tues–Sun: May–Sept 10am–6pm; Oct–April 10am–4pm; 500Ft). This small octagonal building is a shrine to the "Father of the Roses", a Sufi Dervish who participated in the Turkish capture of Buda but died during the thanksgiving service afterwards. Restored with funds from the Turkish government, the tomb now stands in a pristine little park with marble fountains and arabesque tiles. Carpets and examples of calligraphy adorn the shrine, which fittingly stands in a rose garden, surrounded by a colonnaded parapet with fine views.

The **Rózsadomb** (Rose Hill) itself is as much a social category as a neighbourhood, for a list of residents would read like a Hungarian *Who's Who*. During the Communist era this included the top Party *funcionárusok*, whose homes featured secret exits that enabled several ÁVO chiefs to escape lynching during the Uprising. Nowadays, wealthy film directors and entrepreneurs predominate, and the sloping streets are lined with spacious villas and flashy cars.

Heading downhill to the riverbank just north of Margit híd, you can find the Neoclassical **Lukács Baths** (Lukács Gyógyfürdő; Mon–Sat 6am–7pm, Sun 6am–5pm; 1700Ft/1900Ft with a locker/cabin), harbouring a mixed thermal pool and a small swimming pool. The courtyard leading to the baths is festooned with plaques of gratitude in different languages from those who have benefited from the medicinal waters. In 2008 a large thermal cave lake was opened up under the Lukács – though plans to open it to the public may take a while. The adjacent **Császár Komjádi Pool** (Császár Komjádi Uszoda; daily 6am–6pm; 1320Ft) has a Turkish bath-hall dating from the sixteenth century, plus an excellent modern outdoor swimming pool that gets covered over in winter; the entrance is on the embankment side.

Óbuda and Rómaifürdő

Óbuda is the oldest part of Budapest, though that's hardly the impression given by the factories and high-rises that dominate the district today, hiding such ancient ruins as remain. Nonetheless, it was here that the Romans built a legionary camp and a civilian town, later taken over by the Huns. Under the Hungarian Árpád dynasty this developed into an important town, but in the fifteenth century it was eclipsed by Várhegy. The original settlement became known as Óbuda (Old Buda) and was incorporated into the newly formed Budapest in 1873. The tiny old town centre is as pretty as Várhegy, with several **museums** worth seeing, but to find the best-preserved **Roman ruins** you'll have to go to the **Rómaifürdő** district, further out.

Óbuda

After its incorporation within the city, **Óbuda** became a popular place to eat, drink and make merry, with garden restaurants and taverns serving fish and wine from the locality. Some of the most famous establishments still exist around **Fő tér**, the heart of eighteenth-century Óbuda, with its ornate Trinity Column. While there's no denying the charm of their Baroque facades and wrought-iron lamps, many are simply trading on past glories; see p.127 for our pick of Óbuda's eating places.

There's more to enjoy from a cultural standpoint. Directly opposite the Árpád híd HÉV exit at Szentlélek tér 6, the **Vasarely Museum** (Vasarely Múzeum; Tues–Sun 10am–5.30pm; 800Ft; Ⓦwww.vasarely.tvn.hu) displays eyeball-throbbing Op Art works by Viktor Vasarely (1906–99), the founder of the genre, who was born in Pécs in southern Hungary, emigrated to Paris in 1930 and spent the rest of his life in France.

Around the corner at Fő tér 1, the Baroque Zichy mansion contains a courtyard seemingly unchanged since Habsburg times, at the back of which is the **Kassák Museum** (Kassák Múzeum; Wed–Sun 10am–5pm; 300Ft), dedicated to the Hungarian Constructivist Lajos Kassák (1887–1967) and featuring his paintings, magazine designs and possessions. Another door off the yard leads to the **Óbuda Museum** (Óbudai Múzeum; Tues–Sun 10am–6pm; 300Ft), a fascinating local history collection with reconstructed living rooms from a Sváb (German) community on the edge of Buda, and a middle-class household in thrall to Art Nouveau.

Across the square at no. 4, another Baroque mansion houses the charming **Kun Collection of Folk Art** (Kun Zsigmond Népművészéti Gyűjtemény; Tues–Sun 10am–5pm; 300Ft): peasant furniture, ceramics and textiles collected by "Uncle Zsigmond", as he was fondly known, who lived to the ripe old age of 107; the museum was his former apartment.

Whatever the weather, you'll see several figures sheltering beneath umbrellas just off Fő tér, life-sized sculptures by Imre Varga, Hungary's best-known living artist, whose oeuvre is the subject of the **Varga Museum** (Varga Imre Múzeum; Tues–Sun 10am–6pm; 500Ft) at Laktanya utca 7. Pathos and humour pervade his sheet-metal, iron and bronze effigies of famous personages, including Pope John Paul II and Bartók.

Roman remains

Óbuda's Roman remains lurk in a concrete jungle. On Flórián tér, 500m west of Fő tér, weathered columns rise amid a shopping plaza, while the old **military baths** (*thermae maiores*) are exposed in the pedestrian underpass beneath the Szentendrei út flyover. The largest ruin is a weed-choked, crumbling **military amphitheatre** (*amfiteátrum*) which once seated up to 13,000 spectators, at the junction of Pacsirtamező utca and Nagyszombat utca, 800m further south – accessible by bus #86 or by walking 400m from Kolosy tér, near the Szépvölgyi út HÉV stop.

North of Óbuda, the riverside factory belt merges into the **Rómaifürdő** (Roman Bath) district, harbouring a campsite, a lido and the ruins of **Aquincum**. Originally a settlement of camp followers spawned by the legionary garrison, Aquincum eventually became the provincial capital of Pannonia Inferior. The **ruins** (Tues–Sun: May–Sept 9am–6pm; late April & Oct 9am–5pm; Nov 10am–4pm; 900Ft; Ⓦwww.aquincum.hu) are visible from the Aquincum HÉV stop, a brief walk from the site. Enough of the foundation walls and underground piping survives to give a fair idea of the town's layout, with its forum and law courts, its sanctuaries of the goddesses Epona and Fortuna Augusta, and the *collegia* and bathhouses where fraternal societies met. Its bare bones are given substance by an excellent **museum** (opens at 10am, same ticket) and smaller exhibitions around the site. Its star exhibit is the **mosaic** of Nessus abducting Deianeira, which originally consisted of sixty thousand stones, selected and arranged in Alexandria before shipment to Europe. The **Floralia Festival** (May 17–18) and **Aquincum Summer** (mid-May to mid-Sept at weekends) see theatrical performances, crafts-making displays, mock gladiator battles and other events staged here.

The Buda Hills

Thirty minutes or less by bus from Moszkva tér, the **Buda Hills** provide a welcome respite from Budapest's summertime heat. While some parts can be crowded at the weekend with walkers and mountain-bikers, it's possible to ramble through the woods for hours and see hardly a soul during the week. If your time is limited, the most rewarding options are the **"railway circuit"** or a visit to the **caves** – though the Bartók or Kiscelli **museums** will be irresistible to some. Exploring the hills **by trail-bike** is a more ambitious option, if you've got a day to spare and the stamina. Velo-Touring (XI, Előpatak utca 1 ☎1/319-0571, Ⓦwww.velo-touring .hu) rents 21-gear bikes (3530Ft for 5hr; 23,500Ft deposit) and can advise on routes. Bikes can be carried on the Cogwheel and Children's railways.

The "railway circuit"
This is an easy and enjoyable way to visit the hills that will especially appeal to kids. The whole trip can take under two hours if connections click, or a half-day if you prefer to take your time. You begin at the lower terminal of the **Cogwheel Railway** (Fogaskerekűvasút, now designated as tram #60), which is two stops from Moszkva tér on tram #18 or #61 or bus #22, #56 and others heading up Szilágyi Erzsébet fasor; alight opposite the cylindrical *Budapest Hotel*. The train was the third such railway in the world when it was inaugurated in 1874, and was steam-powered until its electrification in 1929. Running every ten minutes or so (daily 5am–11pm; BKV fares and passes apply), its cogs fitting into a notched track, the train climbs 300m over 3km through the villa-suburb of **Svábhegy**; for the best view, take a window seat on the right-hand side, facing backwards.

From the upper terminal on **Széchenyi-hegy**, it's a minute's walk to the **Children's Railway** (Gyermekvasút). A narrow-gauge line built by Communist youth brigades in 1948, it's almost entirely run by 13- to 17-year-old members of the Scouts and Guides movement, enabling them to get hands-on experience if they fancy a career with MÁV, the Hungarian Railways company. Watching them solemnly wave flags and salute departures, you can see why it appealed to the Communists. Trains depart for the eleven-kilometre, 45-minute journey to Hűvösvölgy every 45–60 minutes (Tues–Sun 9am–5pm, June–Aug also Mon; 450Ft to any mid-station, 600Ft from terminus to terminus). In summer, they sometimes run heritage trains, pulled by a steam engine or vintage diesel loco, for which a 200Ft supplement is charged.

The first stop, **Normafa** (more quickly reached on bus #90 or #90A from Moszkva tér), is a popular excursion centre with a modest **ski-run** and sledging slopes. Its name (Norma-tree) comes from a performance of the famous aria from Bellini's *Norma* given next to an old tree here by the actress Rozália Klein in 1840. At the next stop, **Csillebérc**, kids and adults can enjoy an **adventure playground** (Mon–Fri 10am–6pm, Sat & Sun 9am–7pm; 1200–2800Ft per hr; ⓦ www.kalandpalya.com), with tree-top walkways and wire-slides – at Challengeland.

Alighting at **János-hegy**, one stop on, it's a fifteen-minute climb to the top of János-hegy (527m), the highest point in Budapest. The Romanesque-style **Erzsébet lookout tower** (daily 8am–8pm; free) on the summit offers a panoramic view of the city and the Buda Hills. By the buffet below the summit is the upper terminal of the **chairlift** or **Libegő**, meaning "floater" in Hungarian (May–Sept 10am–5pm; Oct–April 9.30am–4pm; closed every other Mon; 500Ft), which wafts you down over trees and gardens to the suburb of **Zugliget**, from where #158 buses return to Moszkva tér.

Wild boar, which prefer to roam during the evening and sleep by day, are occasionally sighted in the forests above **Hárshegy**, one stop before the terminus at Hűvösvölgy. **Hűvösvölgy** (Cool Valley) is a rapidly expanding suburb spreading into the hills and valleys beyond, also linked directly to Moszkva tér by the #56 bus. The **Art Nouveau bus terminus**, with its covered stairways leading to the train station, has been restored to its original elegance.

Caves, the Bartók house and other sights

The hills to the west of Óbuda feature a network of caves that are unique for having been formed by thermal waters rising up from below, rather than by rain water. Two sites offer guided tours (some English spoken) every hour on the hour, if there are five people. In both cases the starting point is **Kolosy tér** in Óbuda (accessible by bus #86 from Flórián tér or Batthyány tér, or bus #6 from Nyugati tér in Pest), from where you catch bus #65 five stops to the Pálvölgyi Cave, or bus #29 four stops to the Szemlőhegyi Cave. As the two caves are ten minutes' walk apart, it's possible to dash from one to the other and catch both tours within two hours.

The **Pálvölgyi Stalactite Cave** (Pálvölgyi cseppkőbarlang; tours hourly Tues–Sun 10am–4pm; 1250Ft) at Szépvölgyi út 162 is the more spectacular of the two labyrinths, discovered in 1904 by a quarryman searching for a sheep that disappeared when the floor of the quarry fell in. Half-hour tours start on the lowest level, boasting rock formations such as the "Organ Pipes" and "Beehive", before ascending a crevice to the upper level, ending at "Paradise", overlooking the hellish "Radium Hall" 50m below.

Quite different is the **Szemlőhegyi Cave** (Szemlőhegyi barlang; tours hourly Mon & Wed–Sun 10am–4pm; 1250Ft) at Pusztaszeri út 35, with less convoluted and claustrophobic passages and no stalactites. Instead, the walls are encrusted with cauliflower- or popcorn-textured precipitates. Discovered in 1930, the cave has exceptionally clean air, and its lowest level is used as a respiratory sanatorium.

A fifteen-minute uphill slog from the Szemlőhegyi cave, the **Kiscelli Museum** (Kiscelli Múzeum; Tues–Sun: April–Oct 10am–6pm; Nov–March 10am–4pm; 700Ft; ⓦ www.btmfk.iif.hu) occupies a former Trinitarian monastery at Kiscelli utca 108. Its collection includes the Biedermeier furnishings of the Golden Lion pharmacy which used to stand on Kálvin tér, sculptures and graphics by twentieth-century Hungarian artists, and antique furniture exhibited in the blackened shell of the monastery's Gothic church, which makes a dramatic backdrop for **concerts**, film shows and other events (see ⓦ www.kiscell.org). The museum can be reached by bus #165 from Kolosy tér or bus #60 from Batthyány tér.

Music lovers can make a pilgrimage to the **Bartók Memorial House** at Csalán utca 29 (Bartók Béla Emlékház; Tues–Sun 10am–5pm; 800Ft; ⓦ www.bartokmuseum.hu), which can be reached by taking bus #29 from the Szemlőhegyi Cave to the

Nagybányai út stop, or bus #5 from Moszkva tér to the Pasaréti stop and then a short walk. Bartók and his family lived in the villa from 1932 until they emigrated to America in 1940. Besides an extensive collection of Bartók memorabilia, you can see some of his original furniture and possessions, including folk handicrafts collected during his ethno-musical research trips to Transylvania with Zoltán Kodály. Chamber music **concerts** (tickets up to 2000Ft) are held here from March until June (℡1/394-2100 for information).

Before returning to Moszkva tér, it's worth a brief detour to see the delightful **Napraforgó utca housing estate**, built in 1931. Its 22 houses – designed by as many architects – embody different trends in Modernist architecture, from severe Bauhaus to folksy Arts and Crafts style.

Margit-sziget

A saying has it that "love begins and ends" on **Margit-sziget** (Margaret Island), for this verdant expanse just upriver from the city centre has been a favourite spot for lovers since the nineteenth century, though until 1945 a stiff admission charge deterred the poor. Today it is one of Budapest's most popular recreation grounds, its thermal springs feeding outdoor pools and ritzy spa hotels. There are two entrances to the island: from Árpád híd at the northern end and Margit híd to the south. Trams #4 and #6 stop at the southern entrance, tram #1 stops at the northern entrance, and bus #26 (from Nyugati tér, by Nugati pu. metro) runs up the middle of the island and finishes at the Árpád híd metro (both stations are on the blue metro line). Motorists can only approach from the north of the island, via the Árpád híd, at which point they must leave their vehicles at a paying car park. Near both entrances you can rent **bikes**, **pedaloes** and **electric cars**, which tend to be rather battered but will get you around. Runners will love the low-impact **jogging** path around the island's circumference.

Walking down from the tram stop on Margit híd, you'll find picnickers unloading cars and people streaming in to party in the woods or at outdoor bars and clubs like *Cha-cha-cha* and *Sárk kert* (see p.130). Revellers are greeted by a **fountain** that emits bursts of grand music, beyond which, off to the left, is the **Hajós Alfréd Pool** (known as the "Sport"; Mon–Fri 6am–3pm, Sat & Sun 6am–6pm; 1300Ft), named after the winner of the 100-metre and 1200-metre swimming races at the 1896 Olympics, who was also the building's architect. The main attraction here is the all-season outdoor fifty-metre pool, where the national swimming team trains on weekdays from 9am. Another venue, the **Palatinus Strand** (May–Aug daily 9am–7pm; 1800Ft, 2000Ft at weekends), lies nearly a kilometre further north. With a monumental entrance from the 1930s, it can hold as many as ten thousand people at a time in numerous open-air thermal pools, complete with a water chute, wave machine and segregated terraces for nude sunbathing.

Further north, an **outdoor theatre** (Szabadtéri Színpad) by a conspicuous water tower, hosts plays, operas, concerts and fashion shows over summer, and is a handy spot for a beer or snack. To the east stands a ruined **Dominican church and convent**; Béla IV vowed to bring his daughter up as a nun here if Hungary survived the Mongol invasion, and duly confined 9-year-old Princess Margit when it did. She apparently made the best of it, acquiring a reputation for curing lepers and other saintly deeds, as well as for not washing above her ankles. The convent fell into ruin during the Turkish occupation, when the island was turned into a harem. The **Premonstratensian Chapel**, northeast of the water tower, dates back to the twelfth century, when the order first established a monastery on the island. Two luxury **spa hotels** can be found beyond: the refurbished *fin-de-siècle Ramada*

Grand, with an inviting café and beer terrace, and the modern, less appealing *Thermal*. Beside the latter is a **Japanese Garden** with warm springs that sustain tropical fish and giant water lilies.

Eating and drinking

Hungarians relish **eating and drinking**, and Budapest is great for both. Though Magyar cuisine naturally predominates, you can find everything from Middle Eastern to Japanese food, bagels to Big Macs. The diversity of cuisine is matched by the range of outlets and prices – from de luxe restaurants where a meal costs an average citizen's monthly wage, to backstreet diners that anyone can afford.

Breakfast and brunch venues

A lot of bars are open from early morning, but the ones below distinguish themselves in what they offer. A popular development in the city's restaurant scene is **Sunday brunch**, usually an all-you-can-eat buffet for a fixed price. Brunch at *Gundel* (see p.126) is a great way to taste its cuisine without the usual formality, and will set you back 5800Ft; most of the top hotels also lay on a spread. Prices can be slightly higher there, but most of the hotels have children's play areas. Brunch usually starts around noon and lasts till about 3pm; booking is advisable.

In addition to the places below, three bars in Pest that are breakfast favourites are the *Sirály* on Király utca, which best captures the old coffee-house tradition of artists and writers sitting round reading newspapers, *Vian* on Liszt Ferenc tér (p.130) and the laid-back *Kiadó* nearby on Jókai tér (p.129).

Bambi I, Frankel Leó utca 2–4. See map, p.67. This excellent old bar not far from the Margit híd on the Buda side is also a good breakfast venue with its omelettes and coffee.

Nothin But the Blues VIII, Krúdy Gyula utca 6. Down in the streets behind the National Museum, it serves a full English breakfast of baked beans, bacon, Cumberland sausage and hash browns, with unlimited tea or coffee (1100Ft) – a rarity in Budapest – with tables outside.

Princess Outlets at the exits of metro stations all over the city. Sweet and savoury puff pastries to go – try a mushroom or cheese-filled *bürek*.

Sir Morik IX, Ráday utca 15. Another Pest café popular with neighbourhood expats for its range of freshly brewed coffees from around the world and for its croissants and pastries – which you have to carry to the tables outside if you don't want to perch on a stool indoors.

Coffee houses, cafés and patisseries

Daily life in Budapest is still punctuated by the consumption of black coffee drunk from little glasses, though cappuccinos and white coffee are becoming ever more popular. These quintessentially Central European coffee breaks are less prolonged these days than before the war, when Budapest's **coffee houses** (*kávéház*) were social club, home and haven for their respective clientele. Free newspapers were available to the regulars – writers, journalists and lawyers (for whom the cafés were effectively "offices") or posing revolutionaries – with sympathy drinks or credit to those down on their luck. Today's coffee houses and **patisseries** (*cukrászda*) are less romantic but still full of character, whether fabulously opulent, with silver service, or homely and idiosyncratic. However, the tendency to aim either at the rich business visitor and charge high prices (such as the *Lukács*) or lure in a younger clientele via loud music (such as the *Angelika*) is driving away the older regulars and cutting off these institutions from their roots.

▲ Central Kávéház

Pest

Astoria Kávéház V, Kossuth utca 19. See map, p.74. The *Astoria* hotel's *Mirror* coffee house/bar dates from the turn of the last century and is still a popular meeting place.

Art Nouveau Café, Bedő House, V, Honvéd utca 3. This restored Art Nouveau gem of a building just north of Szabadság tér is a delightful spot for a coffee break.

Azték V, in the Röser-bazár, a courtyard running between Károly körút 22 and Semmelweis utca 19 ⓦ www.choxolat.hu. Perhaps the best place in the city for chocolate gourmands, selling home-made chocolate as well as imported products (all made with a minimum of sugar) and fabulous hot chocolate – ask for the extra-thick variety, which will warm you up on a winter's day. You can sit at the tables inside, or outside in summer in the courtyard. Sat open till 2pm, closed Sun.

Centrál Kávéház V, Károlyi Mihály utca 9. In its heyday, the decades around World War I, this large coffee house was a popular venue in Budapest's literary scene, and after many years as a dowdy university club, it has now been restored to its former grandeur. Serves a wide range of food throughout the day, from cheap favourites such as creamed spinach to more expensive dishes.

Fröhlich VII, Dob utca 22. Kosher patisserie a 5min walk from the Dohány utca synagogue, and a great people-watching place. Specialities include the best *flódni* (apple, walnut and poppy-seed cake) in the city. Mon–Thurs

9am–6pm, Fri 7.30am–3pm, Sun 10am–4pm; closed Sat & Jewish holidays.

Gerbeaud V, Vörösmarty tér 7. A Budapest institution with a gilded salon and terrace, and good service; always packed with tourists.

Király VII, Király utca 19. Small patisserie with a few tables, serving excellent pastries, cakes and ice cream.

Lukács VI, Andrássy út 70. One of the city's old coffee houses, this was beautifully restored by the bank with which it now shares the building. However, prices have shot up, sadly ending its status as a popular locals' haunt.

Mai Manó VI, Nagymező utca 20. Small, friendly, smoky café that spills out onto the street from underneath the Mai Manó Photography Museum. Serves sandwiches, croissants and good coffees.

Muvész VI, Andrássy út 29. There's an air of faded grandeur in this coffee house that's more notable for its decor – chandeliers and gilt – than for its rather standard cakes. In summer the inside room gets very stuffy and smoky, with no a/c. Still, the presence of elderly ladies in fur hats bears witness to the venue's success in retaining a loyal clientele over the years.

Múzeum Cukrászda VIII, Múzeum körút 10. Friendly hangout near the National Museum that is usually packed with students. Fresh pastries arrive early in the morning. Open daily 24hr.

New York VII, Erzsébet körút 9-11. This coffee house was a popular haunt of writers in the early

1900s. Recently restored as part of the *Boscolo* hotel, it has lost none of its magnificence, but high prices mean it has struggled to win back its place among today's impoverished intelligentsia.

🎿 **Szalai** V, Balassi Bálint utca 4. Old-style cake shop, one of the few remaining in Budapest, serving very good cakes, and with a few tables beneath its large gilt-framed mirrors for those who want to eat in. May–Oct closed Tues, Nov–April closed Mon.

Buda

Ági Rétes II, Retek utca 19. *Rétes* all baked on the cosy premises of this patisserie a few metres from the Fény utca market by Moszkva tér. For such a minute place – there is just one table – the range of strudels is impressive: down a coffee as you try the plum (*szilva*), cheese (*túrós*) cherry (*meggyes*) or poppyseed (*mákos*) varieties. Mon–Fri 10am–6pm, Sat 10am–2pm.

Angelika I, Batthyány tér 7. Atmospheric old coffee house in a former convent – even the funky refit with new furniture, staff and loud music can't totally destroy the place, though you are less likely to get old ladies meeting for their regular coffees these days. Also has a lively terrace.

Artigiana Gelati XII, Csaba utca 8. Exotic flavours of the best quality ice cream in town, a couple of minutes up the road from Moszkva tér. Closed Mon.

Cziniel III, Nánási út 55. Large, popular café north of the Roman ruins at Aquincum, with excellent ice creams and chestnut purée. With its own play area,

it's a good place to bring children, and it's also handy if you've been on the riverbank enjoying the bars and restaurants on the Római-part or want to head further out from Aquincum (take bus #34 from the ruins).

Daubner III, Szépvölgyi út 29. It is a trek to get to this patisserie in Óbuda, and it has no tables, but the place is always crowded, especially at weekends, when people will patiently queue up for its delicious cakes, such as the plum slipper (*szilvás papucs*) or pumpkin-seed scone (*tökmagos pogácsa*). The family sold the whole business off recently – recipes and all. It remains to be seen if standards fall. Closed Mon.

Rétes Büfé XII, Normafa. This hut at the top of the Buda Hills by the old tree where Bellini's aria was sung (see p.117) is a place of pilgrimage for families, walkers and (in winter) skiers who flock to the hills. You can expect to queue for the excellent *rétes* on fine days. The *Rétes Kert* across the road is run by the same crowd.

Ruszwurm I, Szentháromság tér 7. Near the Mátyás Church in the Várhegy, this diminutive Baroque coffee house can be so packed that it's almost impossible to get a seat in summer. Delicious cakes and ices.

Tranzit Art Café XI, Kosztolányi Dezső tér. The listed 1960s bus station at the side of the square has been turned into a delightful no-smoking café, while in summer the long concrete shelter where the buses once drew up is a very relaxed scene. One of the few cafés with baby-changing facilities.

Sandwich bars, self-service restaurants and fast-food diners

Budapest has taken to fast food in a big way, and you'll have little trouble finding a *McDonald's*, *Pizza Hut*, *Subway* or *Burger King* if you want one. For a quick bite in a less commercial setting, the Chinese stand-up joints and Turkish kebab outlets all over town are cheap, though you may wonder what goes into some of the food. The recent economic hardships have encouraged a revival of cheap local eateries, and if you want to eat like the average Hungarian, look out for a *önkiszolgáló étterem* (self-service restaurant), a *főzelék* establishment (serving dishes of creamed vegetables, *főzelék*, which taste much better than they sound), or another Hungarian peculiarity, the *étkezde* – a small lunchtime diner where customers sit at shared tables and eat hearty home-cooked food. All the places listed below are in Pest, except for the Retek utca branch of Duran Sandwich Bar.

Bombay Express VI, Andrássy út 44. Pop into this self-service Indian place two blocks from the Oktogon for vegetable samosa, dahl, chicken tikka masala, lamb Hyderabad or spicy kebabs, to eat in or take out.

Duran Sandwich Bar V, Október 6 utca 15 & XII, Retek utca 18. A sandwich and coffee chain – filling a surprising gap in Budapest. The artistic open sandwiches (180–250Ft) of caviar, puréed paprika, smoked beef, pickled herring and suchlike really zap the taste buds. Both branches open Mon–Fri 8am–5.30pm, Sat 9am–1pm.

Falafel VI, Paulay Ede utca 53. See map, p.74. Despite its long-standing popularity, Budapest's foremost falafel joint hasn't changed its working formula or expanded to glossy new premises. You just pay your money and stuff your pitta breads as full as you can. Seating upstairs. Mon–Fri 10am–8pm, Sat 10am–6pm.

Hummus Bar VII, Kertész utca 39 and V, Alkotmány utca 20. See map, p.74. Two small outlets of this new chain serving very good falafel, hummus and salad combinations. Seating in the gallery at both outlets.

Kádár Étkezde VII, Klauzál tér 10. See map, p.74. Diner with delicious home cooking; traditional Budapest Jewish food (non-kosher) on Friday. Mon–Sat 11.30am–3.30pm; closed mid-July to mid-Aug.

Kis Mama Konyhája IX, Lonyay utca 7. See map, p.74. Self-service lunchtime joint near the Great Market Hall, offering decent and very cheap food – mostly Hungarian, but there's also pasta and pizza. Mains from 600Ft. Mon–Fri 10am–6pm, Sat 10am–3pm.

Marie Kristensen Sandwich Bar IX, Ráday utca 7. The Danish flavour the name implies is hard to spot – this is just a decent, regular sandwich bar just off Kálvin tér. Closed Sun.

Sahara VIII, József körút 82. See map, p.67. Close to the Corvin cinema at Ferenc körút metro station, this bright place serves the freshest, tastiest Turkish/Middle Eastern food in the city, eaten at shared tables. Takeaway service available. No smoking downstairs – you can smoke shishas upstairs. No alcohol.

Vapiano V, Bécsi utca 5. See map, p.74. Fast food Italian-style near Deák tér in central Pest. Excellent pastas and salads made with fresh ingredients before your eyes. You are given a card as your enter, and you go up to the pizza, pasta, salad or dessert counter to order; your purchases are recorded on your card and you pay as you leave. Pasta and pizzas 1200–2000Ft.

Restaurants

The biggest change in the city's **culinary scene** has been the appearance of a number of very good restaurants offering high-quality food and the best in Hungarian wine. Places such as *Klassz* and *Café Kör* are hardly cheap even by Western standards, but are extremely popular regardless and always packed. There has also been a welcome diversification in recent years, with many new places offering Chinese and Japanese food, mainly to wealthy tourists and nouveau-riche natives. Restaurants with Hungarian Gypsy bands tend to be touristy, but do have a certain distinctive charm. It is wise to **reserve** a table if you're determined to eat somewhere in particular, though you can usually find an alternative within a couple of blocks.

We've included phone numbers where booking is advisable, though of course not all staff will speak English. While more and more restaurants have introduced no-smoking sections, **smoking** is generally accepted (though a total ban in restaurants is expected soon). Many of the places listed here take **credit cards** – a surprising exception being the excellent *Café Kör*.

A final **note of caution**: waiters in Budapest are known to make "mistakes" with your bill, and foreign visitors are especially easy targets for overcharging. Other more common tactics include offering expensive "specials of the day", overcharging or demanding exorbitant amounts for the wine. Don't be shy about querying the total, and avoid the seedier tourist joints in the Belváros.

Pest

The busy streets of **Pest** have perhaps the best restaurants in the city, but also the most tacky rip-offs too, particularly within the Nagykörút. Most of the following are easily accessible from downtown Pest, though you should reserve a table to avoid a wasted journey.

Within the Nagykörút

The places below appear on the map on p.74.

🏃 **Alföldi** V, Kecskeméti utca 4 ☎1/267-0224. Traditional cheap eaterie in the centre up from Kálvin tér that has changed little in almost forty years – with the same crumpled table cloths, grumpy service and *pogácsa* (savoury scone). It is heavy Hungarian food from the plains (the Alföld) – big bean and goulash soups, all very cheap.

Belcanto VI, Dalszínház utca 8 ☎1/269-2786. Right across from the Opera House, this is a smart place where the waiters periodically burst into song, making for a lively atmosphere. It serves good international food, but with mains starting at 5000Ft, this isn't a cheap evening out.

🏃 **Bock Bisztró** VII, Erzsébet körút 43-49 ☎1/321-0340. A great place to eat, both classy and relaxed, with friendly staff and delicious, reasonably priced food (mains 2800–4400Ft), and children's portions at 70 percent of the full price. Meat takes pride of place here, in true Hungarian fashion, but there are also modern takes on classic dishes: the Esterházy chicken and smoked duck breast are both recommended. Located within the *Grand Corinthia* hotel, the *Bock* takes its name from one of Hungary's top vintners, József Bock, and its stock includes many labels that you won't find elsewhere in the city. Many wines can be ordered by the glass. Booking essential. Unobtrusive live guitar or accordion music in the evenings. Closed Sun.

Bouchon VI, Zichy Jenő utca 33 ☎1/1/353-4094. Pleasant restaurant set up by former *Café Kör* staff. Matching the *Kör* would be a challenge, but the friendly manager runs a cheerful place serving traditional Hungarian fare. Mains from 2300Ft, and you can order a wide selection of wines by the glass. Small portions are available at 70 percent of the full price. Closed Sun.

🏃 **Café Kör** V, Sas utca 17 ☎1/311-0053. Buzzy place near the Basilica, with a very relaxed feel and English-speaking staff. Its wines and grilled meats are excellent, as are the salads, and the specials of the day (displayed on a board) are recommended – the roasted pike-perch in garlic is always a favourite. Main courses 2000–4000Ft. Booking essential. The only downside to the intimacy of the place is that smoking is allowed throughout. No credit cards. Closed Sun.

Carmel VII, Kazinczy utca 31 ☎1/322-1834. Long-established Jewish restaurant that turned glatt kosher in 2008. The food has improved recently and the decor has become classier with a/c. In August and September there are klezmer-style concerts on Thursdays from 8pm (2000Ft). Open till 4pm on Fri, closed Sat.

Csarnok V, Hold utca 11 ☎1/269-4906. Good, down-to-earth Hungarian restaurant that used to serve the workers at the market a few doors along; the clientele is now more upmarket, but its unpretentious feel has been preserved. Specialities are mutton, lamb and bone-marrow dishes from 1400Ft upwards, and there are also traditional dishes such as *pacal* (tripe). Closed weekends.

Eklektika VI, Nagymező utca 30 ☎1/266-1226. Laid-back café-restaurant with a youngish clientele and a strong arty feel, with changing displays by local artists on the walls. It's open all day, serving buffet breakfast, an all-you-can-eat lunch, and great suppers at a very reasonable price – mains from 1800Ft.

Fausto's Osteria VII, Dohány utca 5 ☎1/269-6806. This excellent and elegant Italian restaurant was originally opened by master chef Fausto DiVora. Even though he has moved to his new, more upmarket *Fausto's* off Andrássy út, the service and cooking remain outstanding. Mains start at 2600Ft, but the three-course chef's menu is just 2800Ft. Both restaurants closed Sun.

Fészek VII, Kertész utca 36 ☎1/322-6043. Housed in an artists' club on the corner of Dob utca, this has a wonderful arcaded courtyard under the shade of a huge chestnut tree in the summer, and it is worth visiting for the setting alone. Shame the food on the huge menu does not achieve the same standards. In winter the restaurant moves into the sparse but elegant inside room, and the menu is much smaller. Main courses from 1600Ft.

🏃 **Fülemüle** VIII Kőfaragó utca 5 ☎1/266-7947. Popular and relaxed restaurant a few minutes' walk from Rákóczi út, serving dishes typical of middle-class secular Jewish Budapest: *sólet* (beans), goose soup with matzo dumplings, and duck leg with cabbage and "broken" potato. Prices are reasonable, with mains from 2600Ft.

Gerlóczy V, Gerlóczy utca 1 ☎235-0953. This atmospheric corner café on quiet Károly Kammermayer tér, not far from the busy Károly körút, gets packed at lunchtime with office staff popping in for a quick lunch. The food is adequate bistro fare.

Govinda V, Vigyázó Ferenc utca 4 ☎1/473-1310. Hare Krishna vegetarian restaurant serving good, inexpensive set meals (1800Ft for a large plate), accompanied by the whiff of soporific incense. Closed Sun.

🏃 **Il Terzo Cerchio** VII, Dohány utca 40 ☎1/354-0788. The Third Circle of Dante's hell was full of gluttons, and this Florentine-run pizzeria has its share. It's popular with Italian visitors, which must be a good sign, and serves up good food at reasonable prices: pastas and pizzas from 1600Ft.

Károlyi V, Károlyi Mihály utca 16 ☎1/328-0240. It's the courtyard setting in the heart of the city, inside the gates of the Petőfi Museum and backing onto the Károlyi garden behind, that makes this place so special. The interior is also pleasant, and even nicer when the piano player takes his breaks. The food is good-sized portions of trad Hungarian fare. Mains 1700–3500Ft.

Két Szerecsen VI, Nagymező utca 14 ☎1/343 1984. Buzzy place just off Andrássy út, good for coffee and breakfast but also for supper. Excellent starters, including a very good aubergine spread on toast, among its tapas dishes. Mains start at 1900Ft and include the interesting breast of duck in a red wine chocolate sauce with mashed potato (2700Ft). It offers a starter and main course, plus half a bottle of wine for 7500Ft, but the wine list is small and surprisingly expensive. Open till 1am.

Klassz VI, Andrássy út 41 ☎1/413 1545. This strikingly decorated restaurant-cum-wine bar is one of the best places in Budapest – *klassz* means "super", which describes it well. Since it's small, popular and does not take reservations, you'll need to get there early to be sure of a table. Its wines include top Hungarian vintages, most of which are available by the glass, and the staff can advise on what goes well with what. The duck in a honey sauce is delicious (2400Ft), and there's also *mangalica* – a Hungarian breed of hairy pig that's very in vogue on Budapest menus, but may be a touch fatty for some tastes. Closes 6pm Sun.

Kőleves VII, Dob utca 26 ☎1/322-1011. The latest incarnation of this restaurant on the corner of Kazinczy utca has a relaxed, art-house vibe but slow service. Mains cost 1500–3700Ft and include veal and chicken dishes (stuffed with olives, goat's cheese etc), and smoked Turkey leg with *sólet* (Jewish baked beans). The menu of the day is 900Ft.

Krizia VI, Mozsár utca 12 ☎1/331-8711. Small and elegant Italian restaurant not far from the Opera House serving fabulous food, with mains from 2600Ft, and good three-course menus for just 2600–2600Ft. The owner makes his own salami and jams. Closed Sun.

Lou Lou V, Vigyázó Ferenc utca 4 ☎1/312-4505. One of the top places in the city – although recent staff changes may undermine its standing. The select French-influenced menu is strong on duck, liver and fish, accompanied by top Hungarian wines, and presentation is excellent, as is the service. Non-smoking section. Mains from 4700Ft, lunch menus 4900Ft. Closed Sat lunch and Sun.

M VII, Kertész utca 48 ☎1/322-3108. Small, wood-panelled place, near the Music Academy and spread over two floors, with a boho atmosphere, slow service and pleasant enough food. The menu includes lots of salads and chicken dishes; a starter, main course and wine will cost about 3700Ft.

Menza VI, Liszt Ferenc tér 2 ☎1/413-1482. Good, moderately priced establishment with stylish retro decor, and retro Hungarian dishes, too, such as *hagymás rostélyos* (braised steak piled high with onions; 1890Ft), and *kolozsvári töltött káposzta* (stuffed cabbage; 1490Ft) that evoke nostalgic memories among the locals. There's a two-course lunch menu for 890Ft. It's on popular drinking square Liszt Ferenc tér, however, and some of the area's loud swagger seems to have rubbed off.

Múzeum VIII, Múzeum körút 12 ☎1/267-0375. This grand nineteenth-century restaurant, with ceiling frescoes and Zsolnay tiles, is under new management, who can hopefully give its old-school approach a modern twist without losing the high standards in the kitchen. Part of the restaurant has been turned back into a coffee house, serving lighter fare and sandwiches. Mains from 2700Ft, Sat lunch menu 3300Ft.

Pomo D'Oro V, Arany János utca 9 ☎1/302-6473. A large, rustic Italian restaurant at the river end of this street, where the interior is split into many different levels, giving it a cosy feel. The woodburning oven turns out excellent pizzas from 1400Ft, while mains start at 1900Ft. A wide range of Italian wines, and some Hungarian too, though all are quite pricey. They serve a small portion – *kisadag* – for children and will provide pencils and paper on request. The deli next door also has seating and serves pasta dishes from 1300Ft.

Rézkakas V, Veres Pálné utca 3 ☎1/318-0038. The smart "Golden Cockerel" (as the name translates) is one of the best places to eat in traditional Hungarian style, with an excellent Gypsy band playing away in the corner. Popular with foreign visitors, so expect to pay from 3000Ft up to 7000Ft for a main course.

Soul Café IX, Ráday utca 11–13 ☎1/217-6986. One of the better places to eat on Ráday, offering European fusion cooking – Hungarian, French, Italian and a *soupçon* of North African – and a good selection of Hungarian wines (try the Tüske Pince rosé). Day menu 980Ft, business menu 1980Ft. Open till 1am.

Trattoria IX, Ráday utca 16 ☎1/215-2888. Another reliable option on Ráday, serving tasty pizza, pasta and antipasto with gusto. Tables outdoors, a/c inside and free wi-fi.

Trattoria Toscana V, Belgrád rakpart 13 ☎1/327-0045. On the Danube riverfront near Szabadság Bridge, this is a favourite spot for authentic Italian cuisine at reasonable prices, in appealing faux-Tuscan surroundings. The atmosphere is relaxed despite the smart business clientele. A clown entertains the kids on Sundays from September to June. Mains from 2400Ft.

Via Luna V, Nagysándor József utca 1 ☏1/312-8058. Popular Italian-style restaurant – its name referring to the neighbouring Hold (moon) utca – close to Arany János utca metro station. Pizzas (from 1400Ft) and good, filling salads.

Beyond the Nagykörút
For locations, see map on p.67.

🏃 **Bagolyvár** XIV, Állatkerti körút 2 ☏1/468-3110. Sister to the *Gundel* (see p.67), but offering traditional Hungarian family-style cooking at far lower prices. Housed in an intriguing Károly Kós-style building, it aims to recreate the atmosphere of the interwar middle-class home, both in its menu and its service (all the staff are women – reflecting the quaint idea that in those days all women stayed at home). It's an excellent introduction to Hungarian cooking. Mains 2000–3300Ft, with a three-course menu at 3000Ft.

Chez Daniel VI, Szív utca 32 ☏1/302-4039. Fresh ingredients, including fish, are a plus at this pricey French restaurant run by idiosyncratic master chef Daniel Labrosse. In summer things move out into the atmospheric courtyard. Booking recommended.

Firkász XIII, Tátra utca 18 ☏1/450-1118. Done up like a journalists' haunt from the turn of the last century, *Firkász* serves decent traditional Hungarian food, with creamed veg stews and the like at reasonable prices – mains from 2000Ft.

Gundel XIV, Állatkerti körút 2 ☏1/321-3550. Budapest's most famous restaurant offers plush

surroundings and an expensive – but good – menu (mains from 5700Ft). The all-you-can-eat Sunday brunch (11.30am–3pm; 5800Ft) is the cheapest way of getting a taste. Smart dress is required, though ties aren't compulsory for brunch. Booking essential. At the side of the building, the *1984 Wine Bar* (Mon–Sat 5–11pm) offers a cheaper taste of *Gundel* cuisine, to accompany a good selection of vintages.

Kispozsonyi XIII, Pozsonyi út 18. Atmospheric (and smoky) local joint with filling Hungarian dishes; its popularity means you may have to wait for a table. The small terrace affords an escape from the fumes in the summer. Mains 1000–1800Ft.

Lanzhou VIII, Luther utca 1b ☏1/314-1080. Popular with the local Chinese community – always a good sign – the *Lanzhou* is excellent value with a large menu of Chinese specialities, such as spicy tripe, at very reasonable prices.

Okay Italia XIII, Szent István körút 20. A relaxed, lively restaurant that's an old favourite with expats and locals alike, serving up very good pasta and pizza at reasonable prices.

Olimpia VII, Alpar utca 5 ☏1/321-2805. Small place by the Garay tér market hall with nothing Greek about it except the decor. There is no menu, just a choice of three- to six-course meals for up to 6000Ft, served up in a quirky, personable manner. The dishes are small but the combinations are fascinating and delicious, while wines are spectacular, though not cheap. Booking absolutely essential.

Taj Mahal VI, Szondi utca 40 ☏1/301-0447. One of the best places for Indian food in the city, a smart restaurant where all the chefs are from Delhi. Has food from all regions – the dosai are especially good. Closed Mon.

Buda
Despite the plethora of tourist traps in Várhegy, **Buda** offers some excellent possibilities. There is no typical style of Buda restaurant: they range from stylish eateries to small friendly locals. The **"historic" restaurants** in Várhegy tend to charge exorbitant prices for mediocre food – the *Rivalda* is the exception, and is the only one included in the list below. Further out, in Óbuda, you'll find a quirkier selection of restaurants – but it's worth booking before you make the journey.

Várhegy, central Buda and the Tabán
Arcade XII, Kiss János altábornagy utca 38 ☏1/225-1969. See map, p.67. Upmarket place, with a low-key modern interior and a small terrace, serving excellent international cuisine with a strong French influence. There's also a range of good Hungarian wines. A meal will set you back 9000Ft a head with half a bottle of wine, unless you go for more expensive corks such as the Gere Kopár.

Café Pierrot I, Fortuna utca 14 ☏1/375-6971. See map, p.100. A rare elegant hangout in the Communist era, *Pierrot* remains one of the better places in the Castle area today. It serves good, well-presented food, though the prices are steep by local standards and the easy-listening piano music can get a bit much. Salads from 2800Ft, mains from 3500Ft.

Carne di Hall II, Bem rakpart 20 ☏1/210-8137. See map, p.100. Under the same management as

Lou Lou in Pest (see p.125), and serving food that's just as good, even if the pun in the name (a reference to Carnegie Hall) doesn't quite work. Service is leisurely. Delicious steaks and chocolate torte. Mains 2500–4500Ft.

Csalogány 26 I, Csalogány utca 26 ☎ 1/210-7892. See map, p.100. Another fine bistro down the hill towards the river from Moszkva tér that has avoided the temptation to go for showiness and high prices. You may have to wait for your meal, as the exacting chef oversees everything in a very small kitchen. Mains from 2800Ft, lunchtime menu 1200Ft for two courses, 1400Ft for three. Booking essential. Mon–Fri noon–3pm & 7pm–midnight, Sat 7pm–midnight.

Gusto's II Frankel Leó utca ☎ 1/316-3970. See map, p.67. Near the Buda side of Margit Bridge, this charming little bar serves light meals (and very good tiramisu) at moderate prices – main dishes start at 1500Ft. Booking essential. Closed Sat evening & Sun.

Horgásztanya I, Fő utca 27 ☎ 1/489-0236, See map, p.100. An enjoyable fish restaurant that has resisted the forces of modernization, with decor that has remained unchanged for many years, and a regular clientele. Some of the best fish soups in the city are served in generous portions from 900Ft; mains start at 1900Ft.

Márkus Vendéglő II, Lövőház utca 17 ☎ 1/212-3153. See map, p.67. Close to Moszkva tér, this is a great no-frills option after a long walk in the Buda Hills. Large portions of traditional Hungarian dishes, including an excellent *Jókai bableves* (a filling, smoky bean soup) and various stuffed turkey dishes. Prices are still pretty reasonable, with soup, main course and glass of wine at 4100Ft. Menus in English are available.

Rivalda I, Színház utca 5–9 ☎ 1/489-0236. See map, p.100. Unlike so many other places on Castle Hill, the *Rivalda* attracts a loyal local clientele. Prices are fairly steep, but in return you get cooking of a high standard (the chicken with mustard maple syrup and the chocolate gateau are especially recommended) and wacky, theatrically

inspired decor. Mains from 3400Ft, and two- or three-course lunch menus at 4000Ft.

Tabáni Terasz I, Apród utca 10 ☎ 1/201-1086. See map, p.100. An excellent setting, with the summer terrace offering views up to the Buda Palace, and a cosy interior in winter, too. Large portions, with refreshing variations on traditional dishes, such as duck steak grilled with honey and smoked salt at 3100Ft.

Óbuda

Kéhli III, Mókus utca 22 ☎ 1/368-0613. See map, p.67. One hundred years ago this was the favourite haunt of one of Hungary's great gourmands, the turn-of-the-century writer Gyula Krúdy, and today the *Kéhli* still serves the dishes he loved, such as beef soup served with bone marrow on garlic toast (a starter, for 2000Ft). Set in one of the few old buildings in Óbuda to survive the 1960s planning blitz, it's a big place and does attract large groups, but there are plenty of local regulars, too. Most main courses are 3000–4000Ft, and portions are generous; you eat your fill to the accompaniment of a lively Hungarian Gypsy band (from 8pm).

Kerék III, Bécsi út 103 ☎ 1/250-4261. See map, p.67. There is an unchanging feel about the "Wheel", a small place just near the amphitheatre in southern Óbuda. It serves traditional Hungarian food, such as *bableves füstölt csülökkel* (bean soup with smoked pork knuckle; 750Ft) and *vasi pecsenye* (pork marinated in garlic and milk; 1400Ft) at very reasonable prices. No haute cuisine here, just locals out for a meal. *Srámli* (accordion) music is provided by a couple of old musicians (Mon–Sat from 6pm), and there's outside seating in summer.

Kisbuda Gyöngye III, Kenyeres utca 34 ☎ 1/368-6402. See map, p.67. Excellent Hungarian food in the elegant surroundings of the "Pearl of Little Buda", which is filled with furniture typical of a well-to-do, *fin-de-siècle* Budapest home. Piano music and small courtyard at the back. Booking essential. Mains 2300–4000Ft.

Bars and clubs

It's hard to draw a firm line between places to eat and places to **drink** in Budapest, since some patisseries double as cocktail bars, and restaurants as beer halls (or vice versa), while the provision of live music or pool tables blurs the distinction between drinking spots and clubs.

Budapest's nightlife scene is small – spend a few evenings drinking and clubbing and you'll be spotting familiar faces. The scene centres on two main areas in Pest: **Liszt Ferenc tér** (the place to see and be seen; and where most of the larger bars have big screens for football); and semi-pedestrianized **Ráday utca**, running down from Kálvin tér, which, with its innumerable cafés and terraces, styles itself

"Budapest's Soho". There's also another concentration of bars in the VII and VIII districts that take over the courtyard and surrounding rooms in condemned buildings. These *kert* or "garden" bars have become an established feature: some move to new sites each year, but others have settled in one address. Finally, there are the outdoor bars, mainly on Margit-sziget and around the river.

The majority of **wine bars** are nothing like their counterparts in the West, being mainly working men's watering holes offering such humble snacks as *zsíros kenyér* (bread and pork dripping with onion and paprika). Conversely, **beer halls** (*söröző*) are often quite upmarket, striving to resemble an English pub or a German *bierkeller*, and serving full meals. And then there are the bohemian *kert* bars: these may have live music or DJs, table football (*csocsó*), film screenings and other attractions, and serve whatever people are drinking, as well as *pálinka*, the powerful Hungarian schnapps – places such as *Szimplakert* that have managed to survive in spite of local protests at the noise levels. Enduringly popular places such as *West Balkán* move from ruin to ruin but retain their name – a look in the listings magazines (see p.59) will usually reveal their new location should they move. Of the **outdoor summer bars**, you'll find several at the southern end of Margit-sziget, while *Zöld Pardon* is down near Petőfi híd – many of them have dancefloors, and charge a small entry fee.

The **club** scene is especially varied in the summer, when it expands into several large outdoor venues, and there are also one-off events held in the old Turkish baths or sites further out of town (advertised via promotional posters at bus stops). **DJs** to look out for include Sterbinszky and Kühl, the more alternative Naga and Mango, and anything with the Tilos Rádió stamp on it. Expect to pay 500–4000Ft to get into a club, and be warned that it's worth keeping on the right side of the bouncers, who don't play around here.

Most places open around lunchtime and stay open until after midnight, unless otherwise stated, though bars in residential areas have to close their terraces at 10pm. There is a good network of night buses (see p.62) that can help you make your way home, taxis are easy to flag down, and the streets are generally safe. See p.123 for warnings about **rip-offs** in restaurants, which apply equally to bars. Most bars do not take **credit cards**. Bear in mind that Budapest's bars are very **smoky** – the average Hungarian adult gets through more than 3000 cigarettes a year, and most of them seem to be smoked in late-night bars. Hungary is expected to follow the EU line on smoking bans in the near future, but the government is dithering over when this will happen.

Pest

Downtown

For locations, see map on p.74.

Castro Bistro VII, Madách tér 3. This smoky bar with a misleadingly Cuban name is very close to Deák tér. Good music, beer and Serbian food attract a mixed crowd of Hungarians and foreigners. Free wi-fi. Mon–Thurs 10am–midnight, Fri 10am–1am, Sat noon–1am, Sun 2pm–midnight.

Ellátó VII, Klauzál tér 2. Set up in 2007 and an instant success, its dilapidated look of bare bricks and old paintwork give it a relaxed feel. The kitchen serves up decent retro dishes, with a strong Serbian flavour. Mon–Wed noon–2am, Thurs–Fri noon–4am, Sat–Sun 5pm–4am.

Giero VI, Paulay Ede utca 58. Run by a Roma family, who also provide the music. There are just three tables, as a third of the space is given over to the musicians – who play for themselves, their friends, or customers if the band likes them. In summer the *Giero* sometimes turns into a jazz bar.

Gül Baba Szeráj VI, Paulay Ede utca 55. Furnished with Turkish kelims, cushions and lamps, with shishas, wine-tasting nights with food (3500Ft) and muted reggae music, this is a nice place to chill out and talk.

Katapult VII, Dohány utca 1. Small, popular and very red bar opposite the big synagogue. Mon–Sat 10am–2am, Sun 2pm–midnight.

Kuplung VI, Király utca 46. A surprisingly large bar down a narrow alleyway in what was once a police stable and later a moped repair shop (the name means "clutch"). Has table football and, in its highly soundproofed side-room, regular live music and DJs. Daily till 4am.

Mélypont V, Magyar utca 23. A retro basement bar with a strong flavour of 1970s Hungary, "Rock Bottom" is full of memorabilia that won't mean much to the average non-Hungarian. Popular with a youngish crowd, and has table football. Mon–Fri 4pm–1am, Sat 6pm–1am, Sun 6pm–midnight.

Morrison's VI, Révay utca 25 @ www.morrisons .hu. A long-established dance bar that's very popular with students who clearly like its heaving, sweaty atmosphere. The opening of an offshoot, *Morrison's II*, at V, Honvéd utca 40, has hardly helped to alleviate the crush. Entry 500Ft after 9pm. Mon–Sat 7pm–4am.

Old Man's Music Pub VII, Akácfa utca 13 @ www .oldmans.hu. Large, popular joint near Blaha Lujza tér, with live local bands every day from 9–11pm. Daily 3pm–dawn.

Paris-Texas IX, Ráday utca 22. Stylish bar with pool tables and a good atmosphere. Daily noon–3am.

Piaf VI, Nagymező utca 25. This old favourite is basically a small ground-floor bar and cellar frequented by the odd Hungarian film star and lots of wannabes, with occasional jazz or rock live sets. Entry 1000Ft. Daily 10pm–6am.

Sark VII, Klauzál tér 14. Small, heaving bar, decorated with massive murals. DJs and good live music (world/klezmer/Roma) downstairs from September to May. From June to September much of the action moves to the Sark kert at the southern tip of Margit-sziget – see p.74. Daily noon–3am.

Sirály VI, Király utca 50 @ www.siraly .co.hu. The "Seagull" bar is located in one of those condemned buildings that could at any time be closed down, part of an arty cultural centre which seems to rev up the bohemian, lefty feel. Regular jazz and theatre downstairs. Daily 10am–midnight.

Sixtus VII, Nagy Diófa utca 26. The "Sistine Chapel" has long been a smoky favourite with sections of the expat community, but has a good local following, too. It's a cosy place, with just two rooms. Mon–Fri 5pm–2am, Sat 8am–2am.

Spoon V, on the river by the *Inter-Continental hotel* @ www.spooncafe.hu. Set in a boat on the Danube in a great setting, looking across to the Lanchíd and the Buda Palace; the men's toilets have grandstand views of the Royal Palace. There's also a restaurant, which is good but expensive. Daily noon–2am.

Szimplakert VII, Kazinczy utca 14 @ www.szimpla .hu. One of the oldest *kert* bars, spilling over from room to room and with good music, regular film showings (600Ft) in the garden and free wi-fi access (noon–7pm). It has become a standard stop for stag parties, and the main courtyard is packed and noisy at night from mid-May onwards, though it makes a delightful and quiet refuge by day.

Several bars (one for cocktails) and bicycle storage. Daily noon–midnight.

Szóda VII, Wesselényi utca 18 @ www.szoda.com. Busy bar with a retro look behind the main synagogue, with pleasantly laid-back music from the DJs and inexpensive drinks; it also serves food and has free wi-fi access. Mon–Fri 9am–midnight, Sat & Sun 2pm–midnight or later.

Around the Nagykörút

Corvintető VIII, Blaha Lujza tér 1–2 @ www .corvinteto.hu. See map, p.67. Inspired rooftop bar above the old Corvin department store on this busy square, this is a popular venture that will stay open until the building is redeveloped, some time in the next couple of years. You take a lift on the left-hand side of the building – on the way up the lift attendant offers shots of Unicum, the medicinal national drink. Live music or DJs from 9pm, entry 1000Ft or so when music starts. Daily 6pm–5am.

Csiga VIII, Vásár tér 2. See map, p.67. By the Rákóczi tér market hall, this friendly, smoky corner bar is popular with locals and expats. Good food and occasional live music. Mon–Sat 11am–1am.

Jelen VIII, Márkus Emilia utca 2–4. See map, p.67. Another in a succession of great, friendly bars run by Dutch resident Hans, with high ceilings and good music; gets packed as the evening progresses. Live music on Thursdays, funk DJs on Fridays, and good *pálinka* and food. It's in the far right-hand corner of the same former department store as *Corvintető* (see p.67). Thurs–Sat 4pm–4am, Sun–Wed 4pm–2am.

Kiadó VI, Jókai tér 3. See map, p.74. This popular new bar is across Andrássy út from the places around Liszt Ferenc tér, but feels as though it's in another city – much more laid-back than its neighbours, with few pretensions. The ground-floor rooms are open all day from 10am, breakfast and snacks are served during the day; the other door to the right leads downstairs to a cosy bar with sofas, open from 5pm. Both upstairs and downstairs are divided into smaller intimate sections, giving the place a friendly feel. Open daily till 1am.

Moyo VI, Liszt Ferenc tér 10. See map, p.74. One of the smaller bars on the north side of this popular partying square that distinguishes itself from its bigger rivals by its friendly staff and good food. Outside seating, too. Daily 11am–midnight.

Pótkulcs VI, Csengery utca 65b @ www .potkulcs.hu. See map, p.67. Through the small metal door in the wall at no. 65/b, you'll find yourself in a shaded yard, with the bar straight ahead, and a room with sofas and table football off to the left. The "Spare Key" is a laid-back place that attracts a good range of visitors, and the music is excellent too, ranging from klezmer and Roma bands to underground, folk and jazz. Gets very smoky in winter, but has outside seating when the weather's warmer. Mon–Wed & Sun 5pm–1.30am, Thurs–Sat 5pm–2.30am.

Tokaji Borozó I, Falk Miksa utca 32. See map, p.67. Lively, smoky old-style cellar wine bar serving wines from the Tokaj region in northeast Hungary – at 100Ft for a small glass this is not top-end stuff – as well as snacks such as *lepcsánka* (potato pancakes) and *zsíros kenyér*. Mon–Fri noon–9pm.

Trafó Bar Tangó IX, Liliom utca 41 ⓦwww.trafo .hu. See map, p.67. The cellar bar at the vibrant Trafó arts centre has live music and DJs, and gets very crowded. Daily 6pm–4am.

Trocadero Café V, Szent István körút 15. See map, p.67. Excellent Latin music and dancing at this club just up from Nyugati Station. Entry fee varies. Daily 9pm–5am.

Vian VI, Liszt Ferenc tér 11. See map, p.74. One of the least pretentious bars on this posiest of squares, with pleasant staff, a relaxed atmosphere and good food. Free wi-fi access. Daily 9am–midnight.

Buda

Bambi I, Frankel Leó utca 2–4. See map, p.67. One of the few surviving Socialist-Realist bars, with stern waitresses and red plastic-covered seats. It serves breakfast, omelettes, snack lunches, cakes and alcohol all day long. Mon–Fri 7am–9pm, Sat & Sun 9am–8pm.

Kecskeméti Borozó II, Széna tér. See map, p.100. By Moszkva tér, on the corner of Retek utca, this is a crowded, sweaty and smoky stand-up wine bar. A notice on the wall reads "We do not serve drunks", but that would rule out most of the people inside. However, it does serve that staple of Hungarian bar fare, *zsíros kenyér*. Mon–Sat 9am–11pm.

Lánchíd Söröző I, Fő utca 4. See map, p.100. Atmospheric little bar, handily placed at the Buda end of the Chain Bridge. It's a quiet place in daytime, frequented by tourists and the odd regular, but in the evening Robi, the manager, brings in concert DVDs – he loves his music, as the photos of him with BB King and others on the walls testify. Excellent toasted sandwiches. Daily 10am–midnight.

Libella XI, Budafóki út 7. See map, p.67. Friendly unmarked spot near the *Gellért Hotel*. Popular with the student crowd from the nearby Technical University for its bar snacks, chess and draughts. Mon–Fri 8am–1am, Sat noon–1am, Sun 4pm–1am.

Móri Borozó I, Fiáth János utca 16. See map, p.100. Large, cheap neighbourhood venue just up from Moszkva tér, unchanged in more than twenty years. Electronic darts in the room at the far end, and trad Hungarian snacks such as *zsíros kenyér*. June–Aug daily 4–11pm; Sept–May Mon–Sat 2–11pm, Sun 2–9pm.

Platán I, Döbrentei tér. See map, p.67. Popular meeting place near the river, under the plane trees at the foot of the Tabán, with outdoor tables. Serves sandwiches and has wi-fi access. Daily till 10pm.

Outdoor venues

Cha-Cha-Cha Terasz XIII, Athletics Club, Margit-sziget. See map, p.67. The best of the Margit-sziget bars, at the southern end of the island: turning off Margit híd it is the second bar along on the left. This buzzy place is the summer venue of an established bar on Bajcsy-Zsilinszky út, and has 1970s and 1980s music (Hungarian and Western) for dancing and retro/Indie videos (or sports TV) on the big screen, but though it opens mid-May, it doesn't really come alive till mid-June. Late May–Sept daily 6pm–2am.

Római-part III, Rómaifürdő. This is not one bar, but a whole string of open-air bars and cheap eateries lining the riverbank north of Óbuda; the food is mainly of the deep-fried meat and fish with chips variety. Take the HÉV train from Batthyány tér to Rómaifürdő and it's a 10min walk down to the river. Daily noon–10pm.

Sark kert XIII, Margit-sziget. See map, p.67. Another summer island bar: walking up from Margit híd you pass *Cha-Cha-Cha* and it is on the right. Can feel like an unfinished campsite at a Red Sea resort: it is fairly basic in its seating and facilities, but it is a lively place once the crowds arrive. Has occasional live music. Late May–Sept daily 6pm–2am.

Zöld Pardon XI, Goldmann György tér ⓦwww .zp.hu. Camden Lock by the Danube: a large, heaving club near the Petőfi bridgehead, where you can dance to drum'n'bass, deep house and jungle. With an average age of 16 (lots of 14-year-olds), the clientele are all about texting and posing. Live music at 9pm, six bars (one cocktails-only). Bring some 100Ft coins to get through the turnstiles.

Gay Budapest

Budapest's **gay scene** has taken wing in recent years, with new, overtly gay clubs replacing the old, covert meeting places.

Most of the bars listed on below levy an **entry fee** or set a minimum consumption level – being gay in Budapest is an expensive privilege. Some venues give you a card when you enter, on which all your drinks are written down; you pay for your drinks and the entry fee as you leave. Be warned that if you lose the card, you'll have to pay a lot of money. You can find listings for places and events in English in the gay freebie monthly *Na Végre*, found at most gay venues.

Aside from the bars and clubs, the **Turkish baths** are a popular meeting place. Gay activity in the public steam baths was dealt a blow by a TV report in early 2005 showing video footage of gay encounters, taken secretly in the Király baths. Swimming costumes are at present compulsory at the Király and the baths are patrolled, so that action is not as widespread as it once was, but there's still more here than at the other public steam baths. The sun terrace at the Palatinus strand and the roof terrace at the Széchenyi remain popular gay meeting places. Note that increased entry fees mean that you see fewer young local men and more tourists in the baths.

The Budapest gay scene is very male-dominated. There is a **lesbian** group, Ösztrosokk, that meets at Tűzoltó utca 22 on the last Saturday of every month (7pm–4am; entry 500–600Ft; ⓦwww.osztrosokk.femfatal.hu), but otherwise perhaps the best spot for women is *Eklektika*, a laid-back lesbian-run café/restaurant (see p.124). Another **restaurant** with a particularly gay clientele is *Club 93* (V, Vas utca 2; 11am–midnight), a cheap pizzeria near Astoria that is popular after 8pm.

Bars and clubs

Action V, Magyar utca 42 ⓦwww.action.gay.hu. See map, p.74. Near Kálvin tér in Pest, this is a hardcore gay bar, full of young men looking for one-night stands. The entrance is tricky to find – it's 15m along from the big "A" sign on the door. Dark room, video room and live shows on Friday (700Ft entry). Minimum consumption 1600Ft. Daily 9pm–5am.

Capella V, Belgrád rakpart 23 ⓦwww.capellacafe .hu. See map, p.74. Drag queens and lots of kitsch, with decor as outrageous as the acts, on the Pest riverbank. It's become a well-known haunt, and prices are highish. Popular with straights, though more gays come on Wednesdays. Drag shows start at midnight and 1am. Entry 500Ft Wed & Thurs,

1500Ft Fri & Sat, up to 3500Ft on special occasions. Daily 10pm–5am.

CoXx (formerly Chaos) V, Dohány utca 38 ⓦwww .coxx.hu. See map, p.74. The most cultured of the gay bars, this men-only venue in Pest is a friendly place to meet. The ground floor is a gallery and internet café; downstairs is a dancefloor, video rooms and numerous other spaces. Minimum consumption 1000Ft. Daily 9pm–4am.

Le Café M V, Nagysándor József utca 3 ⓦwww .lecafem.com. See map, p.74. The former *Mystery Bar* is a small, friendly place near the Arany József utca metro in Pest, for talking rather than dancing (there's no disco), and it's a good place to start or end the evening. Internet café too, with wi-fi. Free entry. Mon–Fri 4pm–4am, Sat & Sun 6pm–4am.

Entertainment

The range of **entertainment** available in Budapest includes everything from clubbing and folk dancing to opera-going and jazz. There are several sources of listings information in English, details of which appear on p.59. A number of festivals and events which occur annually are described in the box on p.132.

Live music: rock and pop

Budapest attracts every Hungarian band worth its amplifiers and a growing roll call of international stars, appearances by whom are well publicized in the media. Posters around town – particularly around Deák tér, Ferenciek tere and the Astoria underpass – publicize concerts by local bands. Concert ticket prices range from 1000Ft for local bands up to as much as 15,000Ft for stadium gigs by international superstars. Apart from the venues detailed below, bands appear at the places listed on pp.133–135; at

Festivals and events: the Budapest year

The two highlights of Budapest's cultural calendar are the **Spring Festival** (ⓦwww .btf.hu) in late March and the **Autumn Festival** (ⓦwww.bof.hu) held sometime between late September and late October. Both offer music, ballet and drama, including star acts from abroad.

The ten-day **Budapest Film Festival** is usually in February, while the first major national holiday of the year is on **March 15**, when Budapest decks itself out in flags and cockades in honour of the 1848 Revolution, and there are patriotic gatherings at the Petőfi statue and the National Museum. **Easter** is marked by church services and outbreaks of *locsolkodás* (splashing) – when men and boys visit their female friends to spray them with cologne and receive a painted egg or pocket money in return. The fall of Communism has put paid to grandiose parades on April 4 and May 1, but **May Day** remains a national holiday, with a big party in the Városliget organized by the trade unions. In early June Vörösmarty tér and Szent Istvan tér are packed with bookstalls for the very popular **Book Week** (Könyvhét), and there is music and dancing, too.

Two festivals in mid-June are **Athe Sam Roma Arts Festival** (ⓦwww.godorklub .hu), an international event in the Gödör Klub in central Pest that showcases Roma music, art, theatre and film; and the **Bridge Festival** (Hídünnep; ⓦwww .budapestbridge.hu) which commemorates the building of the Lánchíd in the 1840s and marks the start of **Summer on the Chain Bridge**, a two-month long festival that sees the Lánchíd closed to cars each weekend until the middle of August to make way for music, food and craft stalls and jugglers and dancers. Each weekend has a different theme, from theatre to world music or jazz. In late June or early July **Gay Pride Budapest** is the largest event in the gay calendar, a four-day festival culminating in a march along Andrássy út to the Városliget.

Two big summer events are the **Sziget Festival**, one of the largest open-air rock and pop gatherings in Europe, held on an island north of the city in early August, and the **Hungarian Grand Prix**, usually held in mid-August. **St Stephen's Day** (Aug 20), honouring the founder of the Hungarian state, occasions day-long

the vast Puskás Ferenc Stadion, the smaller Kisstadion or the Papp László Sportaréna (all near Stadionok metro station). A number of bars also have live music, such as Jelen, Kuplung, Pótkulcs, Sark and Simplakert (see p.129). The biggest venue of all is the Óbudai (or Hajógyári) sziget north of Margit-sziget, which hosts the week-long **Sziget festival** (ⓦwww.sziget.hu/fesztival), one of the big European music events, in mid-August.

A38 XI, Pázmány Péter sétány ☏1/464-3940, ⓦwww.a38.hu. Housed on a boat that was reputedly given to Hungary in return for writing off the Ukrainian debt and is moored on the Buda side of the river, just below Petőfi híd, it has a separate admission charge (500Ft) for each of its three decks, where top international and Hungarian performers play rock, jazz, folk and world music.
Millenáris Park II, Fény utca 20–22 ☏1/336-4000, ⓦwww.millenaris.hu. The Fogadó concert hall here regularly hosts good rock, folk and jazz concerts and festivals, some featuring international acts. In summer, concerts are held on the park's outdoor stages.
Palace of Arts (Művészetek palotája) IX, Komor Marcell utca 1 ☏1/555-3000, ⓦwww.mupa.hu. This substantial complex on the riverbank in

southern Pest has a top-of-the-range concert hall, theatre and museum, and as the shop window for the capital's culture scene, it sees a superb range of concerts, attracting top international classical, jazz and world music orchestras and acts.
Petőfi Csarnok XIV, Zichy Mihály út 14 ☏1/363-3730, ⓦwww.petoficsarnok.hu. On the edge of the Városliget, this big hall is often used by local and international rock and jazz groups, as well as hosting weekend flea markets and occasional craft fairs.
Trafó IX, Liliom utca 41 ☏1/215 1600, ⓦwww .trafo.hu. A dynamic contemporary arts centre in a former transformer station, it pulls full houses with concerts and theatre and dance performances, by Hungarian and foreign artistes. Good bar downstairs.

celebrations at the Basilica (see p.80), a craft fair and folk dancing at different venues in the Vár and a spectacular display of fireworks at 9pm from barges in the river between the Erzsébet and Margit bridges – check at Tourinform for the precise location so that you can get the best vantage point. Up to one million people gather on the river bank, and the traffic jam that follows the display is equally mind-blowing. If you want to eat out that night, you should book a place well in advance, as all the restaurants are packed. At the end of the month the **Jewish Summer Festival** (Ⓦ www.jewishfestival.hu) attracts an international range of classical, jazz and klezmer music, films and exhibitions.

September heralds the start of the grape harvest, marked in Budapest by the annual **Wine Festival** (Ⓦ www.winefestival.hu). The country's top producers set out their wares on the terrace of the Royal Palace in the Castle district. There is also a Harvest parade through the streets on the hill with folk music and dancing. In October there are two national anniversaries: the **Anniversary of the Arad Martyrs** on October 6 marks the shooting of the thirteen Hungarian generals in 1849 in Arad (Nagyvárad) in present-day Romania, when the 1848 Revolution was crushed by the Austrians with Russian help. Wreaths are laid at the Eternal Flame (see p.82). And then October 23 is a national holiday **commemorating the 1956 Uprising**: ceremonies take place in Kossuth tér, by the nearby Nagy Imre statue, and at Nagy's grave in the New Public Cemetery. Bear in mind that 1956 has left a divided inheritance and tempers can flare.

On **All Saints' Day (Mindenszentek napja)**, November 1, cemeteries around the city stay open late and candles are lit in memory of departed souls, making for an incredible sight as darkness falls.

On **December 6**, children hang up Christmas boots for "little Jesus" to fill, and people prepare for the Christmas Eve feast of jellied carp or turkey. Festivities build up towards **New Year's Eve**, when revellers gather on the Nagykörút, engaging in noisy battles with toy trumpets at the junction with Rákóczi út.

Live music: jazz

When it comes to **jazz** (or *dzsessz*, as it sometimes becomes in Hungarian), don't be fooled by the small number of regular venues in Budapest. The country boasts some brilliant jazz musicians, such as György Vukán, György Szabados, Béla Szakcsi Lakatos and the award-winning pianist Kálmán Oláh. But a new phenomenon is Roma jazz: players in their early twenties or even late teens who are taking the jazz world by storm. Those in the know rate Gábor Bolla as one of the finest tenor saxophone players not just in the city but in Europe, while the pianist Dezső Oláh, the violinist Lajos Sárközi and the Pecek Lajos Trio are also rising names.

One jazz club to look out for is the Harmonia Jazz Workshop (Harmónia Jazz Műhely), which is looking for a new home and may hold sessions at the Budapest Jazz Club (VIII, Múzeum utca 7, by the National Museum) and elsewhere.

Benczúr House (Benczúr Ház) VI, Benczúr utca 27 ☏ 1/321-7334, Ⓦ www.benczurhaz.hu. Mainstream jazz venue in a very grand nineteenth-century villa off the top of Andrássy út that today houses the Post Office Cultural Centre.

Columbus Jazz Club V, Vigadó tér ☏ 1/266-9013, Ⓦ www.majazz.hu. Jazz venue on a boat moored in central Pest that hosts top Hungarian as well as international players.

Gödör Klub V, Erzsébet tér ☏ 06-20/201-3868, Ⓦ www.godorklub.hu. Underground venue at the bottom of the steps in the middle of the square – this was once a huge hole (*gödör* in Hungarian) dug for the new National Theatre, but construction was abandoned after a change of government. Nicknamed the National Hole as years of vacillation followed, it was finally turned into a park and a music venue. It's not a very intimate space but it has a very good range of concerts – jazz, folk, alternative Hungarian pop and Roma acts.

Jazz Garden V, Veres Pálné utca 44A ☎1/266-7364, ⓦwww.jazzgarden.hu. Cellar jazz bar and restaurant. Performers include Hungarian stars Béla Szakcsi Lakatos and Aladár Pege, as well as local resident American blues guitarist Bruce Lewis. Daily except Tues 6pm–2am.

Sirály VI, Király utca 50 ⓦwww.siraly.co.hu. Regular jazz and theatre downstairs in this bohemian place, a very deluxe squat.

Take Five VI, Paulay Ede utca 2 ☎06-30/986-8856, ⓦwww.take5.hu. One of the best venues in the city, a largish cellar club below the Vista travel agency just off Deák tér that gets many of the top performers on its nightly programme. Most performers do two sets, starting at 9pm.

Folk music and táncház

Hungarian **folk music** and **dancing** underwent a revival in the 1970s, as a form of rebellion against the Communist state that frowned on anything it deemed "nationalist". Enthusiasts started "dance houses" or **táncház** modelled on traditional Hungarian village barn dances, drawing inspiration from Hungarian communities in Transylvania, regarded as pure wellsprings of Magyar culture. The movement still exists today, though it has lost the edge of its early years, and has been extended to other cultures – you'll also see adverts for Greek (*görög*), Roma and other dance houses. Visitors are welcome to attend the gatherings (350–800Ft admission; see ⓦwww.tanchaz.hu for more) and learn the steps. There are two dance houses especially for children, where language is no barrier and parents join in. Bear in mind that many dance houses close for the summer months.

Concerts of Hungarian folk music by the likes of Muzsikás, Téka, Tükrös, Ökrös, Csík and Kalamajka take place regularly, while there are also performances by groups such as Vujicsics, inspired by South Slav music from Serbia, Croatia and Bulgaria. Two singers to look out for on the circuit are Beáta Pálya, whose repertoire draws on her Hungarian and Roma roots as well as other cultures, and Ági Szalóki, who captures the traditional female folk sound – she accompanies bands such as the Ökrös Ensemble as well as performing solo. There has been a sudden growth in **Roma** groups, such as Romano Drom, the Szilvási Folk Band and Parno Graszt, while the old Jewish musical traditions are continued by *klezmer* performers such as Di Naye Kapelye, who are far closer to the original spirit than the ubiquitous easy-listening Budapest Klezmer Band. An entertaining blend of the two styles is the Fellegini Klezmer Gypsy band, led by Balázs Fellegi. Apart from the venues listed below, performances take place and in bars such as *Pótkulcs* (see p.129) and *Sirály* (see p.129).

Tickets

Tickets for most big music and theatre events are available from several outlets in the city – the most accessible ones are listed below. Note that there's often a small handling fee slapped onto ticket prices for major international shows.

Broadway ticket office XIII, Hollán Ernő utca 10 ☎1/340-4040. Mon–Fri 11am–6pm.

Cultur-Comfort VI, Paulay Ede utca 31 ☎1/322-0000, ⓦwww.cultur-comfort.hu. Near the Opera and next door to the Hotel Pest. Mon–Fri 9am–6pm.

Rózsavölgyi Record Shop V, Szervita tér 5, near Deák tér. Mon–Fri 10am–6pm, Sat 10am–3pm.

Thália VI, Nagymező utca 19, next door to the Operetta Theatre ☎1/428-0791. Mon–Fri 10am–6pm, Sat 10am–4pm.

TicketExpress VI, Andrássy út 18 ☎06/30-303-0999, ⓦwww.tex.hu. A few doors down from the Opera House. Mon–Fri 10am–6.30pm, Sat 10am–3pm.

A38 See p.132. This floating venue attracts top international and Hungarian folk and world music performers.

Aranytíz Cultural Centre V, Arany János utca 10, Ⓦwww.aranytiz.hu. The Kalamajka ensemble plays here to a packed dancefloor on Saturday nights from late September through to early June, with dance teaching from 7pm; the children's session begins at 5pm. As the evening rolls on, a jamming session often develops with other bands joining in.

Fonó Music Hall (Fonó Budai Zeneház) XI, Sztregova utca 3 Ⓣ1/206-5300, Ⓦwww.fono.hu. The Fonó is a lively international folk and world music venue, 2km south of Móricz Zsigmond körtér – four stops from there on tram #18 or #47. Every Wednesday evening, there's a dance house led by Téka, Méta or Tükrös.

Gödör Klub See p.133. It's always worth seeing what's on at this club underneath Erzsébet tér, with its mix of live Hungarian folk, jazz and Roma – it is one of the best venues for Hungarian Roma acts such as Romano Drom, who play here every month. In June the club hosts a big international Roma arts festival.

Millenáris Park See p.132. The folk band Muzsikás and the top local ethno-jazz group, the Dresch Quartet, are among the Hungarian bands regularly performing here, but they also have international stars in all genres of music.

Muzsikás Children's Dance House TEMI Fővarosi Művelődési Háza, XI, Fehérvári út 47 Ⓦwww.muzsikas.hu. Members of the Muzsikás folk band – if they are not away on tour – play while two dancers take children through some basic steps. Most Tuesdays at 5.30pm Sept–May (300Ft for children, 600Ft for adults). The venue is two stops beyond Móricz Zsigmond körtér on trams #18 and #47.

Opera, ballet and classical music

You can enjoy **opera** and **ballet** in Budapest at a very reasonable price, even treating yourself to several glasses of (Hungarian) champagne in the bar during the interval. Most opera productions are in Hungarian, a custom introduced by Gustav Mahler when he was director of the Opera House. The main venue is the Opera House, which has its own box office (inside the main doors or, if they are closed, round on the left-hand side of the building in Dalszinház utca; Mon–Sat 11am–5pm, Sun 4–7pm). Performances are also held at the nearby Thália Theatre, while the other big opera venue, the Modernist Erkel Theatre in Köztársaság tér, is undergoing restoration and may be open in time for its centenary in 2011.

The city excels in its variety of **classical music** performances. The pick of the larger **ensembles** is the Budapest Festival Orchestra, conducted by Iván Fischer (Ⓦwww.bfz.hu), and the National Philharmonic under Zoltán Kocsis (Ⓦwww.hunphilharmonic.org.hu). Fischer established his orchestra as the first privately funded ensemble in the country and his radical approach has won accolades all around the world. Kócsis made his name as a brilliant pianist but as a conductor has forged distinction out of an ordinary ensemble. Look out also for performances by three excellent **chamber ensembles**: the Liszt Ferenc Chamber Orchestra, the Budapest Strings (*Budapesti Vőnosók*) and the Weiner Száz Orchestra; and Budapest's leading period Baroque group, the Orfeo Orchestra under György Vashegyi.

Budapest is equally well supplied with **soloists**. You'll be lucky to catch the Hungarian pianist András Schiff (now based in Britain), but other internationally recognized pianists who regularly perform here include Tamás Vasary, Péter Frankl, Desző Ránki and Gábor Csalog. The cellist Miklós Perényi is an old hand on the classical circuit, while of the younger generation the names to look out for are the violinists Barnabás Kelemen and József Lendvai, the cellist László Fenyő and the brilliant pianist Gergely Bogányi.

One genre that has long appealed to the Hungarian spirit is **operetta**, with Hungarians making a major contribution to the turn-of-the-twentieth-century Viennese tradition through composers such as Ferenc Lehár and Imre Kálmán. Lehár's *The Merry Widow* and Kálmán's *The Csárdás Princess* still draw the crowds with their combination of grand tunes, extravagant staging and romantic comedy in the suitably over-the-top Operetta Theatre.

Besides the key venues listed below, a few places of worship regularly host concerts, among them the **Kálvín tér church** (see p.95); the **Lutheran Church** on Deák tér (see p.78; the programme includes free performances of Bach before Easter, details of which are posted by the church entrance); and the **Dohány utca synagogue** (see p.91). The **Mátyás Church** on Várhegy (see p.101) stages choral or organ recitals on Fridays and Saturdays between June and September (from 8pm), and less frequently the rest of the year.

The opera, theatre and concert halls take a **summer break** at the end of May, reopening in mid-September; there is a summer season of concerts at open-air venues, including the outdoor stage on Margit-sziget (see p.119), the **Dominican Yard** of the *Hilton* hotel (see p.70) in the Castle District, and the **Vajdahunyad Castle** in the Városliget (see p.89), though the music they offer is fairly mainstream.

A comprehensive listing of classical music events can be found at Ⓦ www .koncertkalendarium.hu, and in the free monthly *Koncert Kalendárium*, available from ticket offices or in listings magazines (see p.59).

Bartók Memorial House (Bartók Emlékház) II, Csalán utca 29 ☎ 1/394-2100, Ⓦ www .bartokmuseum.hu. Concerts – not just of the music of Bartók – are held in the villa where the composer used to live. Tickets are either included in the entry fee or go up to a modest 2000Ft.

Budapest Operetta Theatre (Budapesti Operettszínház) VI, Nagymezo utca 17 ☎ 1/312–4866, Ⓦ www.operett.hu. The magnificently refurbished home of Hungarian operetta, where you can enjoy works by Lehár and Kálmán, as well as modern musicals.

Music Academy (Zeneakadémia) VI, Liszt Ferenc tér 8 ☎ 1/342-0179. Founded by Ferenc Liszt in 1875, it hosts nightly concerts and recitals in the magnificent gold-covered Nagyterem (Great Hall) or the smaller Kisterem. The music is excellent and the place has a real buzz.

National Concert Hall (Bartók Béla Nemzeti Hangversenyterem) in the Palace of Arts (see p.99). This concert hall was designed by a top international architect and has superb acoustics. It attracts top international performers, not just in the classical arena.

Old Music Academy (Régi Zeneakadémia) VI, Vörösmarty utca 35. Performances by young musicians every Saturday morning, in the concert hall of the Liszt Memorial Museum.

Opera House (Magyar Állami Operaház) VI, Andrássy út 22 Ⓦ www.opera.hu. Budapest's grandest venue, with gilded frescoes and three-tonne chandeliers (dress tends towards smart), though plagued by a lack of money. You can still get cheap seats – tickets start at 800Ft, though they go up to 17,000Ft for the best seats in the best shows.

Thália Theatre (Thália Színház) VI, Nagymező 22 ☎ 1/331-0500, Ⓦ www.thalia.hu. On Budapest's "Broadway", the Thália hosts operas and musicals, as well as theatre and dance.

Theatre

Mainstream Hungarian **theatre** is in the doldrums at present, and there is little to tempt the visitor in its melodramatic and unsubtle productions in an incomprehensible language. The newly constructed **National Theatre** (Nemzeti Színház), IX, Bajor Gizi park 1 (☎ 1/476-6800, Ⓦ www.nemzetiszinhaz.hu) is aimed at reviving Hungary's proud traditions, but it has had a troubled birth and less dramatic impact than first hoped. Of the established theatres, the **New Theatre** (Új Színház), VI, Paulay Ede utca 35 (☎ 1/351-1406, Ⓦ www.szinhaz.hu/ujszinhaz) offers reliably solid performances, while locals dress up in their finest for the beautiful **Vígszínház**, XIII, Szent István krt 14 (☎ 1/329 2340, Ⓦ www.vigszinhaz.hu). It is also worth looking out for performances by the provincial theatre company from the town of **Kaposvár**, in southwest Hungary, or by Hungarian companies from outside the borders, such as from Cluj, Romania.

Alternative theatre tends to be more interesting – and since music and dance play a greater part here, language can be less of a barrier. One Hungarian group that has received considerable critical acclaim abroad is **Krétakör**, which was a big hit at the 2005 Edinburgh Festival with its interpretation of Chekhov's *The Seagull*, by the young director Árpád Schilling. Other names to look out for are **László Hudi**, **Frenák Pál** and **Péter Halász**, who have all spent time with foreign ensembles, bringing fresh new ideas back to Hungary. Two promising names in dance are **Réka Szabó**, who runs the Tünet (Symptom) group, and **Krisztián Gergye**. And finally, Hungary has a strong **puppet** tradition and is served by two **puppet theatres** (*bábszínház*): **Kolibri Theatre**, VI, Jókai tér 10 (☎1/311-0870), and the **Budapest Puppet Theatre**, VI, Andrássy út 69 (🖳www.budapest-babszinhaz.hu). Both do shows for children, but the latter also puts on performances aimed at adults – masked grotesqueries or renditions of Bartók's *The Wooden Prince* and *The Miraculous Mandarin*. Alternative theatre venues include the **MU Színház**, XI, Körösy József utca 17 (☎1/466-4627, 🖳www.mu.hu); the **Sirály**, a bohemian cultural centre at VII, Király utca 50 (☎06-20/248-2261, 🖳www.siraly.co.hu); the **Szkéné Színház**, XI, Muegyetem rakpart 3 (☎1/463-2451, 🖳www.szkene.hu) in the main building of the Technical University near the Gellért Hotel; and **Trafó** (see p.98). Dynamic contemporary arts centre that has theatre performances by Krétakör and other groups, as well as many good international companies.

Cinema

Hollywood blockbusters and Euro soft-porn films dominate Budapest's mainstream cinemas, though the city has a chain of art-house cinemas specializing in the latest releases and obscure European films – *angol* indicates a British film, *lengyel* Polish, *német* German, *olasz* Italian, and *orosz* Russian.

The main **film festivals** are the Hungarian Film Festival (🖳www.szemle.film.hu), a parade of the year's new films in February (tickets from the Corvin Film Palace), and the Titanic International Film Festival (🖳www.titanicfilmfest.hu) in April, an alternative festival of Hungarian and foreign films that has been going for more than fifteen years.

Budapest has some of the most beautiful movie houses around. It is worth checking out the Moorish interior of the **Uránia National Film Theatre** (Uránia Nemzeti Filmszínház; VIII, Rákóczi út 21, 🖳www.urania-nf.hu) – as a showcase for Hungarian film – and the coffered ceiling of the turn-of-the-twentieth-century

Hungary on film

Hungarians have an impressive record in film, and many of the Hollywood greats were **Hungarian émigrés** – Michael Curtiz, Sir Alex Korda, George Cukor, and actors Béla Lugosi, Tony Curtis and Leslie Howard to name but a few. In the Communist years Hungarian film continued to make waves, with Miklós Jancsó, Károly Makk, István Szabó, Márta Mészáros and others making films that managed to say much about the oppressive regime in spite of its restrictions. Now the main restriction on film makers is chronic underfunding, but what the Hungarian film industry lacks in money it makes up for in ideas.

Established directors to look out for are **Peter Gothár**, with his absurd humour and love of the fantastic (*Time Stands Still, Let Me Hang Vaska*), **Ildikó Enyedi** (*My Twentieth Century* and *Simon the Magician*), **Béla Tarr** (*Werckmeister Harmonies* and the epic eight-hour *Satan Tango*) and **János Szász**, whose film *The Witman Boys* won the award for best international film at Cannes in 1997. Other younger stars are Kornél Mundruczó, Szabolcs Hajdú, Ferenc Török and Nimród Antal, whose first film, the black comedy *Kontroll*, was a big hit abroad; as well as György Pálfi, whose *Hukkle* similarly won international acclaim. Two new names making feature films are Szabolcs Tolnai, whose film *Sand Glass* about the writer Danilo Kis won widespread praise; and Péter Fazakas, whose first feature film, *Para*, was released in 2008.

Puskin, at V, Kossuth Lajos 18 (Ⓦ www.artmozi.hu), while the **Cirko-gejzir**, V, Balassi Bálint utca 15–17, is an alternative joint complete with Chinese tea before showings. A host of multiplex cinemas has now also appeared in the city, including the **Corvin Budapest Film Palace** (Corvin Filmpalota; VIII, Corvin köz 1, Ⓦ www.corvin.hu), and every shopping mall has one. Cinema **listings** appear in the *mozi* section of the free Hungarian weekly *Pesti Est*. The times of shows are cryptically abbreviated: *n8* or *1/4 8* – short for *negyed 8* – means 7.15; *f8* or *1/2 8* (*fél 8*) means 7.30; and *h8* or *3/4 8* (*háromnegyed 8*) means 7.45pm. "*Mb.*" indicates the film is dubbed – as many are – and *fel.* or *feliratos* means that it has Hungarian subtitles.

Cinema-going is cheap, with tickets costing from 800Ft in the smaller cinemas, 1400Ft or more in the multiplexes. In the summer some of the outdoor bars, such as the *Szimplakert* (see p.129), show films a couple of times a week; there are also summer outdoor and drive-in cinemas on the edge of town – for more details of these contact Tourinform (see p.58).

Sports

Apart from popular spectator sports such as soccer, horse-racing, and the Grand Prix, the city offers a range of **sports facilities** for participators. **Swimming** is very popular in Hungary, and Budapest has plenty of pools, such as the Hajós Alfréd Pool in the southern part of Margit-sziget (see p.119) and the Császár Komjádi Pool (see p.115) – both have an indoor and an all-season outdoor pool. In summer you can find big outdoor pools at the Palatinus strand, surrounded by grass and fried-food stalls, on the Margit-sziget, at Csillaghegy, III, Pusztakúti utca 3 (Szentendre HÉV to Csillaghegy), and at Rómaifürdő, a water park with three big slides, a family slide and sauna, III, Rozgonyi Piroska utca 2 (Szentendre HÉV to Rómaifürdő) – all three are open daily in the summer (May–Sept) from 9am to 7pm. The thermal baths – including the Rudas, the Lukács and the Gellért – also have swimming pools.

Tennis can be played all year round at the Városmajor Tennis Academy in Városmajor Park, near Moszkva tér (Ⓣ 1/202–5337); and at the *Thermal Hotel Helia* in Angyalföld, XIII, Kárpát utca 62 (Ⓣ 1/452-5800) – racquets are available for rent at both; while **squash** enthusiasts should head for either City Squash Club, II, Marcibányi tér 13 (Ⓣ 1/336-0408, Ⓦ www.squashtech.hu), or Top Squash Club, on the fourth floor of the nearby Mammut Mall I (Ⓣ 1/345-8193) – both near Moszkva tér.

If it is the gym you need, most of the larger hotels have **fitness centres** open to non-residents. When it snows, you can **ski** at Normafa in the Buda Hills (see p.117). Equipment can be rented from Suli Sí by the entrance of the Császár Komjádi pool at II, Árpád Fejedelem utca 8 (Ⓣ 1/212-0330), or Bikebase at VI, Podmaniczky utca 19 (daily 9am–7pm; Ⓣ 1/269-5983, Ⓦ www.bikebase.hu). Skates can be rented at the **ice rink** in the Városliget between November and March – the rink turns into a rowing lake in summer, where you can rent boats, though for the more adventurous there is canoeing on the Danube: the Béke Boathouse, a ten-minute walk from the Rómaifürdő HÉV station (or take bus #34 to the door from the Árpád híd station) at III, Rómaipart 51–53 (Ⓣ 1/388-9303), rents out canoes and kayaks. If the Palvölgyi and Szemlőhegyi **caves** on p.118 are too easy for you, then Caving under Budapest (Ⓣ 06-20/928-4969, Ⓦ www.barlangaszat.hu) leads more demanding two- to three-hour tours from the Pálvölgyi cave – you do need to be fit and fairly agile, as you'll be climbing on walls and squeezing through passageways, and you are given helmets, headlights and overalls.

Football

Hungary's great footballing days are long past – the golden team of the 1950s that beat England 6–3 with stars such as Ferenc Puskás and József Bozsik is a world away from today's national squad, struggling to qualify for big tournaments. The club scene is also in deep crisis, with teams floundering in a financial desert.

While **international matches** are held at the Puskás Ferenc Stadium – generally filling just a third of its 76,000 seats – club football revolves around the turf of three **premier league teams**.

Ferencváros (aka FTC or Fradi), based at IX, Üllői út 129, near the Népliget metro (Ⓦ www.ftc.hu), is the biggest club in the country and almost a national institution; its supporters, dressed in the club's colours of green and white, are the loudest presence at international matches too. The club has long had right-wing ties: this was the fascists' team before the war, and in recent years it has attracted a strong skinhead – and anti-Semitic – element. Fradi has struggled in recent seasons, and financial difficulties have now relegated the club to the second division. It's in the process of being bought by businessman Kevin McCabe, who also owns the British club Sheffield United.

One of Fradi's big rivals is **MTK**, VIII, Salgótarján utca 12–14 (tram #37 from Blaha Lujza tér; Ⓦ www.mtkhungaria.hu). "Em-tay-kah" – as it is popularly known – has traditionally had strong support among the Jewish community, and unlike its neighbour it is still a major contender in the top division. MTK's ground was the setting for scenes in the film *Escape to Victory*. The other is **Újpest**, IV, Megyeri út 13, four stops on bus #30 from Újpest Központ metro station (Ⓦ www.ujpestfc.hu). Formerly the police's team, Újpest's purple strip is another regular contender for the Hungarian championship. Its 13,000 all-seater stadium was completed in 2001.

See the daily paper *Nemzeti Sport* for details of fixtures. The **season** runs from late July to late November and late February to mid-June. Most matches are played on Saturday afternoons, with tickets costing 800–3000Ft.

Horse-racing

Horse-racing was introduced from England by Count Széchenyi in 1827 and flourished until 1949, when flat racing (*galopp*) was banned by the Communists. For many years punters could only enjoy trotting races, but in the mid-1980s flat racing resumed at **Kincsem Park**, X, Albertirsai út 2–6 (Pillangó utca on the red metro, and then either walk or catch #100 bus). **Flat racing** takes place here on Sundays from spring to autumn; **trotting** – *ügető*, where the horse is harnessed to a light carriage – is all year round, mostly on Saturdays. Races are advertised in *Fortuna* magazine. Both types have a devoted and excitable following, which makes attending the races entertaining; the atmosphere at the tracks is informal, but photographing the racegoers is frowned upon, since many attend unbeknownst to their spouses or employers.

Betting operates on a tote system, where your returns are affected by how the odds stood at the close of betting. The different types of bet comprise *tét*, placing money on the winner; *hely*, on a horse coming in the first three; and the popular *befutó*, a bet on two horses to come in either first and second or first and third. Winnings are paid out about fifteen minutes after the end of the race.

The Hungarian Grand Prix

The **Hungarian Grand Prix** takes place in summer – usually mid-August – at the purpose-built Formula One racing track, the **Hungaroring**, at **Mogyoród**, 20km northeast of Budapest. The event was first held in 1986, but every year financial uncertainties surrounding the event spark rumours concerning its future. Assuming it's going ahead as normal, you can get details from Tourinform, any listings magazine or the website ⓦ www.hungaroring.hu.

Tickets are available from Ostermann Forma-1, V, Apáczai Csere János utca 11, third floor (ⓣ1/266-2040), online at the address above; or from booths in Ferenciek tér. Prices range from €35–90 for the first day to €100–290 for the final day, and €110–400 for a three-day pass – the price being partly determined by the location, and whether you book in advance or (risking disappointment) on the day. You can reach the track by special buses from the Árpád híd bus station; trains from Keleti Station to Fót, and then a bus from there; or by HÉV train from Örs vezér tere to the Szilasliget stop, which is 1800m northeast of Gate C.

Children's Budapest

The city offers a healthy range of activities for kids, from state-of-the-art playgrounds to roller-skating parks, with concessions on most entry tickets for under-14s. Don't expect anything especially high-tech, however, as a lack of cash dogs the facilities, but many of the city's playgrounds have been refurbished in recent years, and plenty of places have activities specifically for children, from the **Palace of Arts**, which has events most weekends, to restaurants such as *Trattoria Toscana*, which has a clown to entertain children at weekends.

From Klauzál tér's scaled-down assault course to the folksy wooden seesaws and swings erected on Széchenyi-hegy, there are children's **playgrounds** all over Budapest – the best are in the **Millenarium Park** (see p.115) and the **Zoo** (p.89). Improvements to the Zoo have made it a great place to visit; kids can feed the camels and giraffes, tickle the rhinos, and stroke the goats, sheep and farm animals. The Zoo's new attraction is the **Zoo Funhouse** (ⓦ www.jatekmester.hu), a brilliant indoor playcentre for babies and children aged up to 10 – there's also the chance to be taken by the zookeepers to see the animals being fed. Nearby is **Városliget** (p.89) with its mock castle and lake – allowing skating or rowing according to the season – as well as the **Transport Museum** with its old trains, the **fairground** and the **circus**.

Budapest's **public transport** – where children under 6 travel free – will keep children happily entertained. **Trams** are an endless source of fun, the best ride being along the embankment in tram #2. Across the water, the **Sikló** (see p.110) is a great experience, rising up above the rooftops from the Lánchíd to the Royal Palace. A popular way for families to spend an afternoon in the Buda Hills is to go on the "**railway circuit**" – the Cogwheel Railway, the Children's Railway and the chairlift (see p.117), but the best place for young train buffs is the **Hungarian Railway History Park**, where kids can clamber over all kinds of locomotives and even get to drive a steam train (p.84). In the summer you can also travel on **steam trains** that run from Nyugati Station.

On the edge of town in southern Buda you can get close to the sharks, feed the stingray and experience the rainforests in the huge aquarium-terrarium at the **Tropicarium** (see p.114), while some of the city's best outdoor fun is to be had up in the Buda Hills at **Challengeland**, at Csillebérc (see p.118), where children aged 3–12 can go on ropewalks and swing from tree to tree. Another popular destination is the **Görzenál Skatepark** at III, Árpád fejedelem útja (ⓣ1/250-4800; Szentendre HÉV to Timár utca), where you can rollerblade, skateboard and cycle on ramps and jumps to your heart's content.

Thanks to Budapest's geology there's entertainment underground too: the Hospital in the Rock and the **Buda Castle** Labyrinth (p.105 & 000) on Várhegy or, further out, the natural beauty of the caves in the Buda Hills (see p.118).

▲ Budapest Zoo

Two other museums that merit a mention are the **Natural History Museum** (see p.98), which is full of colour and activity, with interactive games and lots to look at, plenty of it at child height; and the **Palace of Miracles** (see p.115), a great interactive playhouse that is a hands-on science museum, and has good explanations in English.

Budapest has a strong tradition in **puppetry** (see p.137), or if you want to learn some folk dancing there are two dance houses especially for children (see p.135).

Finally the **Summer on the Chain Bridge** festival, every weekend from mid-June to mid-August on the Lánchíd, has regular events aimed at children (see p.132).

Shopping

Budapest's range of **shops** has expanded massively in recent years, as big international names such as Mango and Benetton have appeared in its streets, and more especially in its range of new malls. Most shops are **open** Monday to Friday 10am–6pm, and Saturday until 1pm, with most foodstores open from 8am to 6pm or 7pm. Recently some shops in the centre of the city have begun to stay open later on Saturdays. The big shopping malls all have longer opening hours, till around 8pm every day except Sunday, when they close at 6pm. You can usually find a 24-hour – *non-stop* – shop serving alcohol, cigarettes and some food in the centre of town, though in the residential parts of Buda they may be harder to find.

The main **shopping areas** are located to the south of Vörösmarty tér in central Pest, in particular in and around pedestrianized Váci utca, which has the biggest concentration of glamorous and expensive shops, as well as branches of popular Western stores including H&M, Mango, Springfield, Esprit and Zara. The nearby Deák Ferenc utca has been jazzed up as "Fashion Street" and attracted names such as Sisley, Tommy Hilfiger and Benetton. The main streets radiating out from the centre – Bajcsy-Zsilinszky út, Andrássy út and Rákóczi út – are other major shopping focuses, as are the Nagykörút (especially between Margit híd and Blaha

Lujza tér) and the Kiskörút. Shops in the Várhegy are almost exclusively given over to providing foreign tourists with folksy souvenirs such as embroidered tablecloths, Hussar pots and fancy bottles of Tokaj wine.

Modern **shopping malls**, combining major shopping centres with entertainment facilities under one roof, have now spread right across the city. Three of the closest to the centre are Mammut (ⓦwww.mammut.hu) by Moszkva tér, Mom Park (ⓦwww.mompark.hu), XII, Alkotás utca 53, above Déli Station, and Westend (ⓦwww.westend.hu), by Nyugati Station.

Budapest has two main **flea markets**: Petőfi Csarnok (Sat & Sun 7am–2pm; see p.89) in the Városliget, which has expanded fast; and the more expensive but potentially very rewarding Ecseri piac at XIX, Nagykőrösi utca 156 (Mon–Fri 7am–4pm, Sat 7am–noon; take bus #54 from Boráros tér at the Pest end of Petőfi híd), where Saturday is the biggest day and sellers are aware of the money to be made from rich foreign tourists, but where there are also bargains to be found, either early on a Saturday or at closing time.

The most popular **souvenirs** to bring home are wine, porcelain, foodstuffs (such as paprika, salami and goose liver) and CDs. Budapest's **Antiques Row** is Falk Miksa utca, at the Pest end of Margit Bridge. For foodstuffs, head for the **market halls**, such as the spectacular Great Market Hall (Nagycsarnok) in Pest, and the Fény utca market behind the Mammut malls near Moszkva tér in Buda. There is a burgeoning organic market (*bio-piac*) at XII, Csörsz utca 18, behind the Mom Park mall, where you'll find the most brightly coloured paprika in town.

The emergence of a thriving **wine industry** is reflected in the number of new wine shops in the city. The Budapest Wine Society at I, Batthyány utca 59, near Moszkva tér, has a good selection and the English-speaking staff know their wines (Mon–Fri 10am–8pm, Sat 10am–6pm, ⓦwww.bortarsasag.hu). **In Vino Veritas** at VII, Dohány utca 58–62, close to Blaha Lujza tér, has an excellent range of wines. For something a little stronger try the Magyar Pálinka Háza VIII, Rákóczi út 17, which sells Hungarian schnapps in a surprising range of flavours.

One of the best places for **porcelain** is Haas & Czjzek, at VI, Bajcsy-Zsilinszky út 23, opposite the Arany János metro station, which stocks pieces by all the main producers.

For **music**, the Rózsavölgyi store at V, Szervita tér 5, has an excellent selection of classical music, with pop and folk downstairs, plus sheet music; the CD Bar at Krúdy Gyula utca 6 (Mon–Fri 10am–8pm, Sat 10am–4pm, ⓦwww.cd-bar.hu) is strong on classical music; while the staff at Wave, VI, Révay utca 4 off the bottom of Bajcsy-Zsilinszky út are well informed on underground and Hungarian folk. MesterPorta at I, Corvin tér 7 near Batthyány tér is strong on folk music – you can also get your own hurdy-gurdy here. The more impersonal MCD at V, Sütő utca 2 is a CD megastore off Deák tér with a wide selection of all kinds of music.

The best selection of secondhand classical records and CDs is at Concerto Records, VII, Dob utca 31 (Mon–Fri noon–7pm, Sun noon–4pm), and for secondhand rock and blues records and CDs try Lemez Dokk, VIII, Horánszky utca 27 and Rockin' Box at VI, Paulay Ede utca 8 (both Mon–Fri noon–6pm).

If you're looking for **English-language books**, Bestsellers at V, Október 6 utca 11 has a very good all-round selection; Libri at V, Váci utca 22 is a foreign-language specialist store; Írók Boltja at VI, Andrássy út 45 – the "Writers' Bookshop"–has a wide range of Hungary-related books at the back; the CEU bookshop at V, Zrinyi utca 12 has a good selection of Hungarian literature in English; and up on Várhegy is Litea at I, Hess András tér 4. For secondhand books, there is The Red Bus bookstore at V, Semmelweis utca 14; upstairs at Alexandra at VII, Károly körút 3 (open daily till 10pm); or Treehugger Dan at VI, Csengery utca 48 (ⓦwww.treehugger.hu), which is packed with secondhand books and has a gay and lesbian section.

Clothes and footwear have not always been a great attraction in Hungary, but there are some shops making waves: Tisza shoes is the best known, at VII, Károly körút 1. Otherwise, Budapest is strong on quirky designers such as Manier at V, Nyáry Pál utca 4 (Ⓦ www.manier.hu) and Vasseva, at VI, Paulay Ede utca 67 (Ⓦ www.vasseva.com).

Listings

Airlines Air France, VIII, Rákóczi út 1–3 Ⓣ 1/483-8800; British Airways/Qantas, Ferihegy airport desk Ⓣ 1/777-4747; KLM, VIII, Rákóczi út 1–3 Ⓣ 1/373-7737; Lufthansa, Ferihegy airport desk Ⓣ 1/411-9900; Malév, XIII, Váci út 26 Ⓣ 1/235-3222.

Airport information Flight arrivals and departures available on Ⓣ 1/296-7000 or from Ⓦ www.bud.hu.

Banks and exchange Cash dispensers can be found across the city. The best places for changing money are the larger banks such as the Magyar Külkereskedelmí Bank at V, Türr István utca 9, by the top of Váci utca; the exchange offices around Vörösmarty tér and Váci utca tend to give poor rates.

Car rental Avis V, Szervita tér 8, by the petrol station under the multistorey car park Ⓣ 1/318-4240, Ⓦ www.avis.hu; Budget *Hotel Mercure Buda*, I, Krisztina körút 41–43 Ⓣ 1/214-0420, Ⓦ www.budget.hu; Europcar V, Erzsébet tér 9–10 Ⓣ 1/505-4400, Ⓦ www.europcar.hu; Hertz V, Váci utca 19–21 Ⓣ 1/296-0999, Ⓦ www.hertz.hu. All these companies have offices at the airport.

Embassies Australia, XII, Királyhágó tér 8–9 Ⓣ 1/457-9777, Ⓦ www.ausembbp.hu; Canada, XII, Budakeszi út 32 Ⓣ 1/392-3360, Ⓦ www.kanada.hu; France, VI, Lendvay utca 27 Ⓣ 1/374-1100, Ⓦ www.ambafrance-hu.org; Germany, I, Úri utca 64 Ⓣ 1/488-3500, Ⓦ www.deutschebotschaft-budapest.hu; Ireland, V, Szabadság tér 7, Bank Center, seventh floor Ⓣ 1/301-4960; UK, V, Harmincad utca 6 Ⓣ 1/266-2888, Ⓦ www.britishembassy.hu; US, V, Szabadság tér 12 Ⓣ 1/475-4400, Ⓦ www.usembassy.hu.

Hospitals and dentistry There is 24hr medical help at V, Semmelweis utca 14/b (entrance on Gerlóczy utca) (Ⓣ 1/311-6816), near Astoria; and at weekends at II, Ganz utca 13–15 (Ⓣ 1/202-1370). A 24hr private clinic with English-speaking personnel is the American FirstMed Center at I, Hattyú utca 14, near Moszkva tér (Ⓣ 1/224-9090, Ⓦ www.firstmedcenters.com); the IMS (International Medical Services) offers medical care 8am–8pm weekdays at XIII, Váci út 184 near the Gyöngyösi út station on the blue metro in northern Pest (Ⓣ 1/329-8423; Mon–Fri 7.30am–8pm) and during evenings and weekends at III, Vihar utca 29

in Óbuda (Ⓣ 1/388-8257, Ⓦ www.imskft.hu). SOS Dental Service, VI, Király utca 14 (Ⓣ 1/267-9602) is a round-the-clock private English-speaking dentist – one of many dentists in the street.

International buses and trains Bookings are required on all international train routes. Buy your tickets 24–36 hours in advance at one of the railway stations or ring Ⓣ 1/371-9449 or 06-40/494-949. Hungarian Railways (MÁV) has its online booking service and timetables at Ⓦ elvira.mav-start.hu/. The Vienna-bound *Wiener Waltzer* often runs late, so reserve sleepers in Budapest. Also bring drinks, as the buffet staff overcharge shamelessly. International bus services depart from Népliget bus station, where you can buy tickets (Mon–Fri 6am–6pm, till 9pm mid-June to mid-Sept, Sat–Sun 6am–4pm).

Internet access Wi-fi access is widely available in many hotels and cafés – you can find hot spots in the city on the website Ⓦ www.hotspotter.hu/en/ – and internet cafés are relatively easy to find in the centre.

Laundry Irisz Szalon, V, Városház utca 3–5 (Mon–Fri 7am–7pm), is one of the few self-service launderettes left in the city; or you can get washing done in the small Laundromat Mosómata near the Basilica at Ó utca 24–26 (Mon–Fri 9am–7pm, Sat–Sun 10am–4pm), where a wash and dry costs 1,600Ft.

Lost property For items left on public transport go to the BKV office at VII, Akácfa utca 18 (Mon–Fri 8am–5pm). Lost or stolen passports should be reported to the police station in the district where they were lost.

Pharmacies Details of each district's 24hr pharmacy are posted in every pharmacy's window. Central 24hr pharmacies include those at XII, Alkotás utca 2, opposite Déli Station, and at VI, Teréz körút 41, near Oktogon. For herbal remedies try Herbária, V, Vamház körút 4 or II, Margít körút 42.

Photocopying Copy General at V, Kalman Imre utca 22, just off Bajcsy-Zsilinszky ut, is open 24 hours.

Post offices There are several post offices (*posta*) with longer opening hours: the main one at V, Petőfi Sándor utca 13 (Mon–Fri 8am–8pm, Sat 8am–2pm); the one by Keleti Station at VIII, Baross tér 11c (Mon–Fri 7am–9pm, Sat 8am–2pm); the one by Nyugati Station at VI, Teréz körút 51 (Mon–Fri 7am–8pm, Sat 8am–6pm); the one in the Mammut Mall by Moszkva tér (Mon–Fri 8am–8pm, Sat 9am–2pm); inside Tesco at XIV, Pillangó utca 15 near the Pillangó utca stop on the red metro (daily 24hr).

Religious services in English Anglican: Sun 10.30am, VII, Almássy utca 6 ☎06-23/452-023; Baptist: Sun 10.30am, International Baptist Church, II, Törökvész út 48–54 (Móricz Zsigmond Gimnázium) ☎1/319-8525; Roman Catholic: Sat 5pm, Pesti Jézus Szíve Templom, VIII, Mária utca 25 ☎1/318-3479.

Travel details

Trains

Where only InterCity are given, there are also slightly slower express services to the same destination.

Batthyány tér (HÉV) to: Pomáz (every 10–15min; 30min); Szentendre (every 10–20min; 40min).

Déli Station to: Balatonfüred (every 1–2hr; 2hr 30min–3hr 30min); Balatonszentgyörgy (every 1–2hr; from 3hr); Dombóvár (7 InterCity daily; 2hr); Pécs (6 InterCity daily; 2hr 50min); Siófok (hourly June–Sept, otherwise 8 daily; from 1hr 45min); Székesfehérvár (every 20–30min; from 1hr); Szekszárd (6 daily; from 3hr 10min); Tapolca (every 1–2hr; 4–5hr); Veszprém (7 daily; 2hr); Zalaegerszeg (5 daily; 4hr).

Keleti Station to: Békéscsaba (hourly; 2hr 30min); Eger (hourly; 2hr); Győr (hourly; 1hr 30min–2hr); Kaposvár (6 daily; 3hr); Komárom (every two hours – and hourly from Déli Station; 1hr 10min–1hr 25min); Miskolc (InterCity hourly; 2hr); Sárospatak and Sátoraljaújhely (hourly; 3hr 30min–4hr); Sopron (4 InterCity daily; from 2hr 30min); Szekszárd (5 daily; from 2hr 30min); Szombathely (4 InterCity daily; 2hr 50min); Tata (every 2hr– and hourly from Déli Station; 1hr).

Nyugati Station to: Debrecen (InterCity hourly; 2hr 30min); Esztergom (every 40min–1hr; 1hr 30min); Kecskemét (hourly; 1hr 20min); Nyíregyháza (InterCity hourly; 3hr); Szeged (InterCity hourly; 2hr 30min); Szob (hourly; 1hr); Szolnok (hourly – and also from Keleti; from 1hr 15min); Vác (every 30min; from 25min); Vácrátót (twice an hour; 40min–1hr 10min).

Buses

Árpád híd to: the Danube Bend: Balassagyarmat (7 daily; 2hr); Esztergom (2 daily and Mon–Fri every 40min – also 3 daily from Széna tér, next to Moszkva tér; from 1hr 20min); Pilisszántó (hourly on weekdays; 45min); Pilisvörösvár (every 20min on weekdays – also from Széna tér; from 30min); Vác (hourly; 40min).

Népliget to: Lake Balaton, Transdanubia and the Great Plain: Baja (8 daily; from 3hr 20min); Balatonfüred (5 daily; 2hr–2hr 40min); Békéscsaba (2 daily; 4hr); Dunaújváros (hourly; 1hr 20min); Győr (every 2hr; 1hr 50min); Herend (5 daily; from 2hr 10min); Harkány (2 daily; 4hr 30min); Hévíz (4 daily; from 2hr 50min); Kalocsa (9 daily; from 2hr 30min); Kaposvár (3 daily; from 3hr); Kecskemét (hourly; from 1hr 20min); Keszthely (5 daily; from 2hr 30min); Kiskunfélegyháza (10 daily; 2hr); Mohács (3 daily; from 3hr 30min); Nagyvázsony (2 daily; 3hr); Pécs (5 daily; 4hr); Siklós (1 daily; 4hr 50min); Siófok (7 daily; 1hr 35min–2hr 10min); Sopron (2 daily; 3hr 50min); Sümeg (4 daily; from 3hr 20min); Szeged (6 daily; 2–3hr); Székesfehérvár (every 15–45min; 1hr 15min); Szekszárd (hourly; 3hr); Szombathely (2 daily; from 3hr 30min); Velence (6 daily; 1hr); Veszprém (every 30min–1hr; 2hr); Zalaegerszeg (5 daily; from 3hr); Zirc (4 daily; from 2hr 40min).

Stadion to: northern Hungary: Aggtelek (4 daily, with one transfer; 5hr); Eger (hourly; 2hr); Gödöllő (every 1hr–1hr 30min; 45min); Gyöngyös (every 30min; from 1hr 15min); Mátraháza (6 daily; 2hr); Miskolc (5 daily, changing at Eger; 4hr); Salgótarján (every 1hr–1hr 30min; from 1hr 45min).

Hydrofoils and ferries

These operate from May to September, as weather permits, with more running June to August.

Belgrád rakpart international landing stage: Hydrofoils to Vienna (April–Oct 1 daily; 6hr to Bratislava).

Vigadó tér pier: boats to Esztergom (1 daily at weekends and some other days; 5hr 30min); Szentendre (2 daily; 1hr 25min); Vác (1 daily; 2hr 15min); Visegrád (2 daily at weekends and some other days; 3hr 30min). Hydrofoils (1–2 at weekends) to Esztergom (1hr 30min), Vác (40min); Visegrád (1hr).

Bathing matters

They say drill anywhere in Hungary and you'll find a thermal spring – a boast that's not too far off the mark. Throughout the country, countless hot springs and wells lurk beneath the relatively thin surface of the Carpathian basin, providing a plentiful supply of superheated, mineral-rich water for the country's numerous baths. From the magnificent Turkish-style bath houses of Budapest, to Europe's largest outdoor thermal bath at Hévíz, or any number of other spas and wellness centres, taking a dip in one of these wonderfully restful affairs is an experience not to be missed.

Chess players, Széchenyi baths ▲

Gellért baths ▼

Turkish domes, Király baths ▼

Origins of bathing

The first springs were discovered some two thousand years ago in the Roman town of **Aquincum** (meaning "abundant water") in north Budapest, but it wasn't until the **Turkish** occupation of the sixteenth and seventeenth centuries that a bathing culture really developed. The end of the nineteenth century witnessed the discovery of more springs – and the construction of more baths – and today Hungary boasts over eighty towns and settlements accommodating more than 120 baths, many in historic buildings and impressive sights in their own right. Swimming aside, the thermal waters – with **temperatures** ranging from around 30°C anywhere up to a scorching 75°C – boast a gamut of medicinal properties and are reputed to cure myriad ailments, including rheumatic and arthritic complaints, respiratory, skin and even gynecological problems. Many baths are an important **social** hub too, whilst in some you can enjoy the somewhat surreal spectacle of people playing chess on floating boards while immersed chest high in steaming water.

Budapest's bath houses

With some 30,000 cubic metres of mineral water gushing from over 100 springs, **Budapest** fully deserves its reputation as a major spa city – indeed some of Europe's grandest bath houses are to be found in the capital. The earliest remains of baths here date back to the Bronze Age, and a succession of invaders have since capitalized on the benefits of the local waters. The oldest surviving structures are the Turkish baths on the Buda side of the river; built in the late sixteenth century, the **Király** and the **Rudas** baths have preserved their original layout, with a central bathing pool surrounded by smaller pools below old Turkish cupolas. In the late nineteenth century, as a fashion for spas swept across Europe, Budapest's spas were dressed up in a new magnificence, as typified by the splendid neo-Baroque **Széchenyi** baths in the Városliget and the Art Nouveau **Gellért** baths inside the hotel of the same name. During the Communist era, the baths were as popular as ever – a place to meet and gossip in the murky mists – but they suffered prolonged neglect. In recent years, however, major investments have seen the buildings restored and their facilities upgraded with new features such as whirlpools – Budapest's baths are now far more salubrious.

▲ Outdoor pool, Széchenyi baths

▼ Hévíz

Countryside bathing

Beyond the capital, there are very few towns or settlements that do not possess some sort of thermal bathing facility, be it an open-air pool, spa resort, wellness centre or Aquapark. The best-known is **Hévíz**, reputedly the world's second-largest thermal lake, where, even in winter, the temperature never drops below 30°C; bobbing on the steaming water in rented rubber tubes is *the* thing to do, while mud from the bottom of the lake is used to treat a wide range of locomotive disorders. Around two-thirds of the country's thermal springs are located on the Great Plain, the largest group of them being at the **Hungarospa** in Hajdúszoboszló, a huge complex of pools and steam rooms, which also incorporates Hungary's largest water park – there's more splashing and sliding at two new Aquaparks in **Nyiregháza** and **Debrecen**. The Northern Uplands has its fair share of thermal waters too,

Budapest bath house ▲

Architectural detail, Széchenyi baths ▼

including a unique thermal water cave in **Miskolc-Tapolca**, the highlight of which is a "pounding shower", recommended for those with circulation problems. Elsewhere in the Uplands region, the **Salt Hill** baths near Eger are so-named after the thick crystallized bank of salt deposits which have formed around the pools; this five-star complex now comprises some seventeen pools plus an array of saunas, cabins and baths. Over to the west in Transdanubia, the small spa town of **Harkány**, south of Pécs, houses the region's premier baths, renowned for its sulphuric-rich hot mud baths and also featuring an enormous *strand* for kicking back on.

Bathing etiquette

Taking to the waters can be a confusing business, particularly in the more traditional bath houses; a standard ticket gets you into the pools as well as the sauna and steam rooms, while supplementary tickets will buy you a **massage** or a **soak** in a private tub or mud bath. You'll often have the choice of **changing** in a communal room (*öltöző*) and using a locker (*sezkrény*), or a slightly more expensive cubicle (*kabin*), though either way you will be given a *kötény* – a small loincloth for men and apron for women – which offers a vestige of cover. Once changed, the attendant will lock your cabin and give you a tag (or key) which you tie to your costume or the strings on your *kötény* – in some pools, bathing caps (*uszósapka*) are compulsory and, like swimsuits, these can be rented from the ticket office. Some baths impose strict limits on the length of your stay, while several of the big baths offer a small refund if you stay less than four hours – the shorter the stay the higher the refund.

The Danube Bend

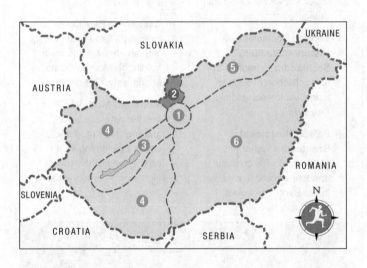

CHAPTER 2 # Highlights

✱ **Ferry ride along the Danube**
A leisurely cruise along the river is the most enjoyable way to reach the historic Danube towns. See p.148

✱ **Margit Kovács Museum, Szentendre** Unique and entertaining collection of sculptures and reliefs from the nation's favourite ceramicist. See p.153

✱ **Serbian Ecclesiastical History Collection, Szentendre** Extraordinarily rich collection of Serbian icons, vestments and relics. See p.153

✱ **Palapa Restaurant, Szentendre** Top-notch Mexican food, a colourful atmosphere and live music in the Bend's grooviest restaurant. See p.155

✱ **Hungarian Open-Air Museum** The best of Hungary's open-air museums, with a fantastic cross section of dwellings from around the country. See p.155

✱ **Visegrád Hills** Good hiking and superb panoramas of the sweeping Danube Bend. See p.163

✱ **Esztergom Basilica** Hungary's largest cathedral, with an atmospheric crypt holding the tomb of Cardinal Mindszenty. See p.166

✱ **Memento Mori, Vác** This enlightening exhibition, starring three mummies, sheds fascinating light on the lives of the town's eighteenth-century citizens. See p.174

▲ Cruising on the Danube

The Danube Bend

To escape Budapest's humid summers, many people flock north of the city to the **Danube Bend** (Dunakanyar), one of the grandest stretches of the river, outdone only by the Kazan Gorge in Romania. Entering the Carpathian Basin, the Danube widens dramatically, only to be forced by hills and mountains through a narrow, twisting valley, almost a U-turn – the "Bend" – before dividing for the length of Szentendre Sziget (Szentendre Island) and flowing into Budapest. The **historic towns** of Szentendre, Esztergom and Visegrád on the west bank could each easily detain you for a day, as could hiking in the Pilis mountains, while the quieter east side has many attractions too, boasting the sedate town of Vác, the gardens of Vácrátót and the charms of Nagymaros and Zebegény, as well as the neighbouring Börzsöny highlands, with further walking opportunities.

The west bank

The natural defence presented by the broad river and the hilly western bank has long attracted the inhabitants of this region to build their castles here. The Romans built a camp to keep the barbarians at bay, unwittingly staking out the sites of the future castles of the Magyar kings, who, a thousand years later, had to repel the Mongols arriving from the east. **Esztergom**, the scene for the Hungarians' official conversion to Christianity in the tenth century, served as the royal seat for three hundred years, after which the kings moved their base downriver to the citadel of **Visegrád**. With the expulsion of the Turks in the seventeenth century, the fertility and beauty of the landscape became the main attractions. Baroque **Szentendre** was established in the eighteenth century when Serbs fleeing up the Danube from the Turks settled here – later, in the 1920s, it became an important artists' colony. The **Pilis range** of mountains, filling the countryside between the three towns, makes for excellent hiking.

Its proximity to Budapest makes Szentendre the logical place to start your trip, the easiest way to get here being via the HÉV train which departs every twenty to thirty minutes from Batthyány tér (see p.109; 1100Ft return). From Szentendre there are frequent **bus** services to Visegrád, which then continue westward to

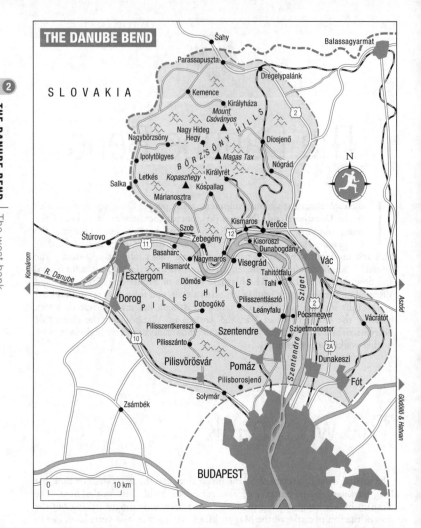

THE DANUBE BEND

SLOVAKIA

Šahy
Balassagyarmat
Parassapuszta
Drégelypalánk
Kemence
Királyháza
Mount
Csóványos
Nagy Hideg
Nagybörzsöny   Hegy
Diósjenő
BÖRZSÖNY HILLS
Ipolytölgyes   Magas Tax
Nógrád
Salka   Letkés   Kopaszhegy   Királyrét
Márianosztra   Kóspallag
Kismaros   Verőce
Szob
Štúrovo   Zebegény   Kisoroszi
Basaharc   Nagymaros   Dunabogdány   Vác
Pilismarót   Visegrád
Esztergom   Dömös   Tahitótfalu
PILIS HILLS   Tahi
Dorog   Dobogókő   Pilisszentlászló
Pilisszentkereszt   Leányfalu   Pócsmegyer   Vácrátót
Pilisszántó   Szentendre   Szigetmonostor
Pilisvörösvár   Pomáz   Dunakeszi
Pilisborosjenő   Fót
Zsámbék   Solymár

BUDAPEST

0   10 km

R. Danube   Komárom   Aszód   Gödöllő & Hatvan

Esztergom. Both these towns are also accessible direct from Budapest: hourly buses from the Árpád híd terminus follow an anticlockwise route around the Bend – although Esztergom can be reached more directly by the less scenic clockwise route that goes via Dorog; this is also the route taken by **trains** to Esztergom from the capital's Nyugati station. Train access is otherwise limited in the Bend: you can catch a train to Visegrád only by going up the east bank to Nagymaros via Vác and taking the ferry across the river, but there is no onward train to Esztergom. In summer you can take the more leisurely option of travelling by **ferry** (ⓦwww .mahartpassnave.hu) from Budapest's Vigadó tér pier to Visegrád and Esztergom via Vác, as well as Szentendre.

The Danube

The Danube is the second-longest river in Europe after the Volga, flowing 2857km from the Black Forest to the Black Sea. Between the confluence of the Bereg and Briach streams at Donaueschingen and its shifting delta on the Black Sea, the Danube is fed by over three hundred tributaries from a catchment area of 816,000 square kilometres, and has nine nations along its banks. Known as the Donau in Germany and Austria, it becomes the Dunaj in Slovakia and then the Duna in Hungary before taking a course through Croatia, Serbia and Bulgaria as the Dunav, Romania as the Dunarea and the Ukraine as the Dunay, forming the frontier for much of the way. Used by armies and tribes since antiquity, this "dustless highway" deeply impressed the German poet Hölderlin who saw it as an allegory for the mythical voyage of the ancient German forefathers to the Black Sea, and for Hercules' journey from Greece to the land of the Hyperboreans. Attila Jószef described it as "cloudy, wise and great", its waters from many lands as intermingled as the peoples of the Carpathian Basin. While the Danube's strategic value ended after World War II, economic and environmental concerns came to the fore in the 1980s, when the governments of Hungary, Austria and Czechoslovakia began to realize a plan to dam the river between Gabçikovo and Nagymaros, though the controversial project was eventually shelved.

Szentendre and around

With its fabulous Baroque heart, **SZENTENDRE** (St Andrew), 19km north of Budapest, is the Bend's siren draw. Called "the Montmartre of the Danube" by Claudio Magris (see p.452), it remains a delightful maze of houses painted in autumnal colours, with secretive gardens and lanes winding up to hilltop churches. The town's location on the lower slopes of the Pilis range is not only beautiful, but ensures that Szentendre enjoys more hours of sunlight than anywhere else in Hungary, making it a perfect spot for an artists' colony.

Before the artists moved in, Szentendre's character had been formed by waves of refugees from **Serbia**. The first influx followed the catastrophic Serb defeat at Kosovo in 1389, which foreshadowed the Turkish occupation of Hungary in the sixteenth century, when Szentendre fell into ruin. After Hungary had been liberated, the Turkish recapture of Belgrade in 1690 precipitated the flight of 30,000 Serbs and Bosnians led by Patriarch Arsenije Carnojevič, 6000 of whom settled in Szentendre, which became the seat of the Serbian Orthodox Church in exile. Prospering through trade, they replaced their wooden churches with stone ones and built handsome town houses. However, as Habsburg toleration waned and phylloxera (vine-blight) and floods ruined the local economy, they began to trickle back to Serbia, so that by 1890 less than a quarter of the population was Serb. Today, only a few dozen families of Serbian descent remain.

In the 1920s, thanks to its proximity to Budapest and the excellent light conditions, Szentendre became a working artists' colony, and today its links with art are as strong as ever, with some two hundred artists working here and the town's countless museums and galleries vying for the attention of the peak-season tourist crowds. Although the town can get swamped in summer, it's still possible to escape the tourists and enjoy the quieter side of the place.

A good time to visit is for Szentendre's **summer festival** (Szentendrei Nyár), which runs from late June to late August and encompasses jazz and folk music evenings, organ concerts, dancing and theatrical performances; it culminates with a pop concert and fireworks on August 20. On the preceding day, a **Serbian festival** with *kolo* (circle) dancing takes place at the Preobrazenska Church.

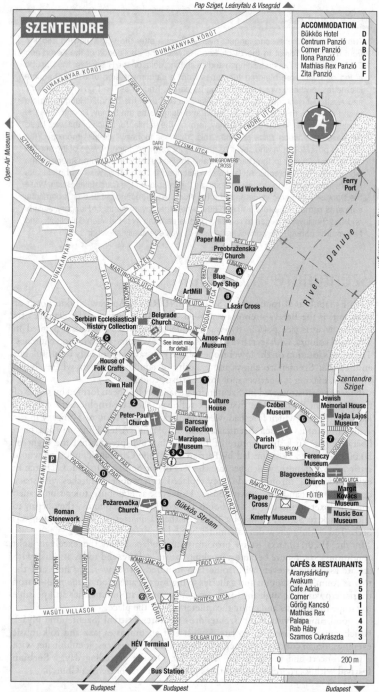

SZENTENDRE

ACCOMMODATION
Bükkös Hotel	D
Centrum Panzió	A
Corner Panzió	B
Ilona Panzió	C
Mathias Rex Panzió	E
Zita Panzió	F

N

Open-Air Museum ◀

Visegrád and Esztergom ▶

Ferry Port

River Danube

DUNAKANYAR KÖRÚT
EGRES UTCA
MANDULA UTCA
ADY ENDRE UTCA
DUNAKORZÓ
SZTARAVODAI ÚT
MEHÉSZ UTCA
HOLD UTCA
DARU PIAC
DEZSMA UTCA
BOGDÁNYI UTCA
ISKOLA UTCA
ANGYAL UTCA
DUNAKANYAR KÖRÚT
MARTINOVICS UTCA
ÁRZEN UTCA
FÜLÖP DEÁK
RÁKÓCZI UTCA
RÉV UTCA
SISA UTCA
MALOM UTCA
DUMTSA JENŐ UTCA

VINEGROWERS' CROSS
Old Workshop
Paper Mill
Preobraženska Church
Blue Dye Shop
ArtMill
Lázár Cross

SZENT ISTVÁN
CERI UTCA
Serbian Ecclesiastical History Collection
Belgrade Church
GOZSDU U.
Ámos-Anna Museum

House of Folk Crafts
Town Hall
See inset map for detail

Szentendre Sziget

Peter-Paul Church
Culture House
PETER-PÁL UTCA
Barcsay Collection
Marzipan Museum
① ③④ ℹ️ ②
TATION UTCA
DUMTSA JENŐ UTCA

DUNAKORZÓ

INSET MAP (detail):
Czóbel Museum
Jewish Memorial House
ALKOTMÁNY UTCA
Vajda Lajos Museum
HUNYADI UTCA
BOGDÁNYI UTCA
Parish Church
TEMPLOM TÉR
Ferenczy Museum
Blagovesténška Church
RÁKÓCZI UTCA
GÖRÖG UTCA
Plague Cross
✉️
FŐ TÉR
Margit Kovács Museum
Music Box Museum
Kmetty Museum
⑥ ⑦ ⑤

P
PAPRIKABÍRÓ UTCA
BÜKKÖS PART
Roman Stonework
Požarevačka Church
Bükkös Stream
KOSSUTH UTCA
PETŐFI UTCA
KOVÁCS UTCA
ⒹⒺⒻ
RÓMAI SÁNC KÖZ
DUNAKANYAR KÖRÚT
FÜRDŐ UTCA
KERTÉSZ UTCA
ATTILA UTCA
ORTORONY UTCA
NAGY LAJOS
ÁRADI UTCA
VASÚTI VILLASOR
@
✉️
KOSSUTH UTCA
BOLGÁR UTCA

HÉV Terminal
Bus Station

CAFÉS & RESTAURANTS
Aranysárkány	7
Avakum	6
Cafe Adria	5
Corner	B
Görög Kancsó	1
Mathias Rex	E
Palapa	4
Rab Ráby	2
Szamos Cukrászda	3

0   200 m

Arrival and information

Szentendre's **bus and train (HÉV) stations** are next door to one another on
Dunakanyar körút, from where it's a ten-minute walk to the town centre. There
are two docks for **Danube ferries**: one for the boat to Szentendre Sziget
(Szentendre Island), located 100m north of the *Centrum Panzió* on Dunakorzó
(March–Oct hourly; 200Ft); the other, 500m further north, for services between
Budapest and Esztergom (see p.144).

For **information** on the town and the Danube Bend, the busy but helpful
Tourinform office is at Dumsta Jenő utca 22 (June–Aug Mon–Fri 9am–6pm, Sat
& Sun 10am–6pm; Sept–May Mon–Fri 9.30am–4.30pm, Sat & Sun 10am–2pm;
T 26/317-965, E szentendre@tourinform.hu). Szentendre's main **post office** is at
Kossuth ucta 23–25 (Mon–Fri 8am–7pm, Sat 8am–noon), with another at
Rákóczi utca 15 (Mon–Fri 8am–4pm). There is a currency exchange machine on
Fő tér. **Internet access** is available at Silver Blue, across from the post office on
Dunakanyar körút (daily 10am–8pm).

Accommodation

There is no agency to help you find private rooms in Szentendre, but Tourinform
has a comprehensive list of accommodation (it does not book rooms) and there
are plenty of *Zimmer frei* signs advertising vacancies. There's **camping** at
Pap Sziget (T 26/310-697, W www.pap-sziget.hu; May–Sept), located on the
small island of the same name (Priest's Island) about 1.5km north of the centre; it
also has two- to four-person chalets by the river (❹), a pension (❷) and restaurant.
The camping fee includes use of the swimming pool on the island. To get there
take any bus heading towards Visegrád or Esztergom and get off at the Pap Sziget
stop, by the *Danubius Hotel*.

Bükkös Hotel Bükkös part 16 T 26/312-021,
F 310-782. The best thing about this place is its
idyllic location by a stream lined with weeping
willows; the rooms are comfortable enough, if a
touch old-fashioned and careworn. Reasonable
value. ❺

Centrum Panzió Dunakorzó T 26/302-500,
W www.hotelcentrum.hu. One of the best options in
town, a warm and welcoming pension with eight
good-sized, peach-coloured rooms, some of which
overlook the Danube. ❺

Corner Panzió Dunakorzó 4 T 26/301-524,
E cornerpanzio@yahoo.com. Just a few paces
down from the *Centrum*, this small riverside
pension has six modern and compact rooms
with lots of fresh-smelling wood. The adjoining
restaurant is good fun too (see p.155). ❺

Ilona Panzió Rákóczi utca 11 T & F 26/313-
599. Ideally located pension, tucked away a

couple of minutes' walk from the centre
of town. Rooms are on the small side, but are
lovely and peaceful and there's a breakfast
terrace. ❹

Mathias Rex Panzió Kossuth utca 16
T 26/505-570, W www.mathiasrexhotel.hu.
The pick of the town's accommodation, this
classy, modern pension has large, coolly furnished
rooms with big beds, and brilliant-white
bathrooms. There's also a fabulous cellar
restaurant (see p.155). ❻

Zita Panzió Őrtorony utca 16 T 26/313-886,
E info@zitapanzio.hu. Close to the stations and
very cheap, this modest, family-run place
possesses six rooms (some with three or four
beds), and without shower, but all with TVs.
Breakfast is included but there's also use of a
communal kitchen. ❸

The Town

Most of Szentendre's tourist attractions are centred on, or within close proximity
to, the main square, Fő tér, thus easily explored by foot. On your way in from the
stations, you can make a short detour to examine a hoard of **Roman stonework**
(Romái Kótár castrum; March–Oct Mon–Fri 9am–4pm) on Dunakanyar körút.
Its opening times are unreliable, however, and you may have to look at the stones

from behind the wire fence. The eroded lintels and sarcophagi belonged to Ulcisia Castra, a military town named after the Eravisci, an Illyrian–Celtic tribe subdued by the Romans during the first century AD.

Kossuth utca to Fő tér

A five-minute walk up Kossuth utca, just before the Bükkos stream, you'll encounter the first evidence of a Serbian presence – the **Požarevačka Church**. Typical of the churches in Szentendre, this was built in the late eighteenth century to replace an older wooden church, although its Byzantine-style iconostasis, dating from 1742, was inherited rather than specially commissioned. The church is usually closed, except for Sunday services. Beyond the stream, Dumtsa Jenő utca continues past the Tourinform office, on the corner, and the **Marzipan Museum and Pastry Shop** at no. 12 (Marcipán Múzeum és Cukrászda; daily 10am–6pm; 400Ft), whose weird and wonderful marzipan creations include Disney characters, busts of famous Hungarians, and a large-scale model of the Hungarian parliament building – you can even watch the women working on their next creation. A few paces further up at no. 10 is the **Barcsay Collection** (Barcsay Gyüjtemény; Tues–Sun: March–Oct 9am–5pm; Nov–Feb 10am–4pm; 500Ft), a museum housing drawings and paintings by Jenő Barcsay (1900–88), who was born in Transylvania but lived and worked in Szentendre from 1929. His dark prewar canvases – mainly landscapes such as *Transylvanian Hills* and *Szentendre Streets* – give way to more abstract works after the war, avoiding the strictures of the regime. His later works included wall-length mosaics, tapestries and anatomical drawings, these last confirming his skill as a draughtsman.

A little further on, the road is crossed by Péter-Pál utca where a left turn brings you to the **Peter–Paul Church**, a yellow and white Baroque church built in 1708. Its original furnishings were taken back to Serbia after World War I, and the church is now Roman Catholic. Organ recitals take place at the church regularly; ask at Tourinform for details.

Around Fő tér

Swarming with buskers and tourists during summertime, Szentendre's main square, **Fő tér**, is a place either to savour or avoid. At the centre of the square stands the Plague Cross, its triangular marble base decorated with icons, which was erected by the merchants' guild after Szentendre escaped infection in 1763. From here, diverging streets and alleys lead to an assortment of galleries and museums around the square, as well as to the many tourist shops, especially down Bogdányi utca.

The **Kmetty Museum** (Kmetty János Múzeum; Tues–Sun: March–Oct 9am–5pm; Nov–Feb 10am–4pm; 500Ft), immediately on your left if entering the square from Dumtsa Jenő utca, contains some delightful watercolours by János Kmetty (1889–1975), and, downstairs, his blue, Cubist paintings from a later period. To the right as you enter the square, and accessed via the shop at no. 1, is the charming little **Music Box Museum** (Muszikáló Múzeum; Sat & Sun 10am–5pm; 600Ft), a private collection of eighteenth- and nineteenth-century musical pieces – gramophones, boxes, clocks and toys – though the most outstanding exhibit is a working orchestrion dating from 1900.

On the north side of the square is the Church of the Annunciation, or **Blagovestenška Church** (April–Oct Tues–Sun 10am–5pm, Nov–March Fri–Sun 10am–5pm; 250Ft), the most accessible of the Orthodox churches in the town. Painted by Mihailo Zivkoviç (1776–1824) of Buda in the early eighteenth century, the church's icons evoke all the richness and tragedy of Serbian history. The building itself is thought to have been designed by András Mayerhoffer in the 1750s, on the site of an earlier wooden church dating from the time of the Serbian migration in 1690. Look out for the tomb of a Greek merchant of Macedonian origin to the left of the entrance, and the Rococo windows and gate facing Görög utca (Greek Street).

Just behind the church, at Vastagh György utca 1, is by far the most popular of the town's galleries, the **Margit Kovács Museum** (Kovács Margit Múzeum; daily 9am–5pm; 700Ft). This is a wonderful collection that never fails to delight, the themes of legends, dreams, religion, love and motherhood giving Kovács' graceful sculptures and reliefs universal appeal. Her expressive statues with their big eyes aren't particularly well known abroad, but in Hungary Kovács (1902–77) is duly honoured as the nation's greatest ceramicist and sculptor.

Back on the main square, next door to the church, a portal carved with emblems of science and learning provides the entrance to a former Serbian school, now the **Ferenczy Museum** (Ferenczy Múzeum; Tues–Sun: March–Oct 10am–6pm; Nov–Feb 9am–5pm; 500Ft). Károly Ferenczy (1862–1917) pioneered Impressionism and *plein air* painting in Hungary, while his eldest son Valér (1885–1954) swung towards Expressionism. His younger children, daughter Nóemi (1890–1957) and son Béni (1890–1967), branched out into tapestries and sculpture respectively, and there are plenty of examples from each of the artists.

Several of the square's buildings (nos. 8, 17, 19 & 22) are old Baroque **trading houses** with their dates and trades engraved above the gates. The former Pálffy House (no. 17) bears the sign of the merchants' guild, combining the patriarchal cross of Orthodoxy with an anchor and a number four to symbolize Danube trade and the percentage of profit deemed appropriate by the guild.

A short walk out of the top western end of the square brings you into Rákóczi utca with the Baroque **Town Hall** on your left, which hosts summer concerts in its courtyard, while opposite at Rákóczi utca 1 is the **House of Folk Crafts** (Népmüvészetek Háza; Tues–Sun: March–Oct 9am–5pm; Dec–Feb 10am–4pm; 500Ft), in an old bellhouse, with small temporary displays on blacksmithing and wine-making.

Templom tér and around

From Fő tér or Rákóczi utca, you can ascend an alley of steps to gain a lovely view of Szentendre's rooftops and gardens from **Templom tér**, where **craft stalls** plying their wares are regularly set up under the acacia trees to help finance the restoration of the Catholic **parish church**. Of medieval origin, with Romanesque and Gothic features, it was rebuilt in the Baroque style after falling derelict in Turkish times; the frescoes in its sanctuary were collectively painted by the artists' colony. Across the square, the **Czóbel Museum** (Czóbel Múzeum; Tues–Sun: March–Oct 10am–6pm; Nov–Feb 10am–4pm; 500Ft) exhibits paintings of brooding nudes by Béla Czóbel (1883–1976) and his wife Mária Modok (1896–1971), whose fierce brush strokes challenged the Neoclassical trend of the Horthy era.

A minute's walk north of Templom tér, the burgundy spire of the Orthodox episcopal cathedral, **Belgrade Church** (contact the Serbian museum if you wish to visit – see below), rises above a walled garden off Alkotmány utca – the entrance to the grounds is from the corner of Alkotmány utca and Pátriárka utca. Built during the late eighteenth century, it has a lavishly ornamented interior with icons, painted by Vasilije Ostoic, depicting scenes from the New Testament and saints of the Orthodox Church. There are many old tombstones in the churchyard with Cyrillic inscriptions. If the church is closed, ask over at the **Serbian Ecclesiastical History Collection** in the episcopal palace (Szerb Egyháztörténeti Gyüjtemény; Tues–Sun: May–Sept 10am–6pm; Oct–April 10am–4pm; 500Ft), whose outstanding hoard of icons, vestments and reliquaries comes from churches in Hungary that fell empty after the Serbs returned to the Balkans and the last remaining parishioners died out. The museum also houses various relics from Serbia including a pair of wedding crowns donated by the Karadjordjević dynasty in 1867. If you fancy attending a service you can do so at 6pm on Saturdays and 10am on Sundays during the summer and at 5pm on Saturdays and 10am and 4pm on Sundays during the winter.

From the Belgrade Church you can follow Alkotmány utca back down towards the main square. Just before you get there, you pass two more museums hiding in Hunyadi utca on your left. The **Vajda Lajos Museum** at no. 1 (Lajos Vajda Múzeum; Tues–Sun: March–Oct 10am–6pm; Nov–Feb 10am–4pm; 500Ft) commemorates the work of a Szentendre painter who died in the Holocaust. Vajda's early work reveals Cubist and constructivist influences, while his later charcoal works seem to foretell the approaching torment. Although the museum is housed in a wealthy bourgeois villa, the artist himself was poor – as you can see from the materials he worked with. Downstairs is an excellent display of works by artists of the "European School", including Bálint Endre and Jenő Barcsay. This group formed after the war but was quickly stopped by the Communists. On the other side of Hunyadi utca, a few steps further along, is the **Szántó Jewish Memorial House and Synagogue** (Szántó Emlékház és Zsinagóga; April–Oct Tues–Sun 10am–4pm; donations accepted), set up by the grandson of a Holocaust victim, Lajos Szántó, who lived in the town. Most of Szentendre's Jewish community, which never numbered more than 250, were deported and killed during the Holocaust. The documents and relics are few, but they make a moving display.

Bogdányi utca

Heading northeast from Fő tér, Bogdányi utca is packed with stalls, attended by shop assistants dressed up in folk gear. The **Wine Museum** at no. 10 (Bormúzeum; daily 10am–10pm; 200Ft, plus 2200Ft for wine tasting) is really there to lure people into the *Labirintus* restaurant, but otherwise does a fair job of describing Hungary's wine-making regions using maps, wine-bottle labels and other artefacts. Next door at no. 10b a painterly couple is commemorated by the **Ámos-Anna Museum** (Tues–Sun: March–Oct 10am–6pm; Nov–Feb 10am–4pm; 500Ft); the museum contains works from the last years of Imre Ámos's life, including *Self Portrait with Angel* from 1938 and the disturbing Apocalypse series of 1944, the year he died in a Jewish labour camp. Downstairs, his wife Margit Anna's works are split into two periods: the warm, mellow pictures from before the Holocaust to the right of the entrance, and to the left the uncomfortably bright, sometimes grotesque images that she produced after the war.

A little further along, Bogdányi utca opens onto a square at the far corner of which stands the **Lázár Cross**, a small iron cross that's easy to miss behind the parked cars that fill the square. It honours King Lázár of Serbia, whom the Turks beheaded after the battle of Kosovo in revenge for the death of Sultan Murad. His body was brought here by the Serbs and buried in a wooden church. When the relic was taken back to Serbia in 1774, the place was marked by a cross in his memory.

Beyond the square, and the welter of tourist shops and stalls, is the **ArtMill** (Müvészetmalom; daily 10am–6pm; 1000Ft), a contemporary art centre constructed out of the remnants of an old sawmill. Realized with considerable local government support, this impressive exhibition hall holds a varied collection of paintings by local artists, plus a smattering of international ones, and also serves as the focus for community-based art projects and events. A few steps on at no. 36, the **Kovács Blue Dye Shop** (daily 9am–6pm) showcases a traditional style of folk dyeing: everything – pillow cases, skirts, oven cloths, you name it – is blue, and there's a small display to show how it is done.

The **Preobraženska Church**, a few steps further along Bogdányi utca, was erected by the tanners' guild in 1741–76, and its *embonpoint* enhanced by a Louis XVI gate the following century. Though its lavish iconostasis merits a look, the church is chiefly notable for its role in the Serbian festival on August 19, when it hosts the Blessing of the Grapes ceremony (recalling Szentendre's former role as a wine-producing centre). This is followed by a traditional procession round the church and further celebrations in the town square and elsewhere. At the far end of Bogdányi utca, five minutes' walk further on, is another cross, the **Vinegrowers' Cross**, raised by a local guild and fittingly wreathed in grapevines.

Eating and drinking

Many of Szentendre's **restaurants** tend to be tourist-oriented, particularly those on or around Fő tér which are crowded with tour groups during the summer; there are, though, more agreeable alternatives away from the main square, with an unusually good selection of ethnic restaurants to choose from.

Likewise, there are some choice **drinking** options on the fringes of the centre, and during warmer weather a string of cafés along Dunakorzó open up their terraces. *Café Adria* at Kossuth utca 4 is a lovely Greek-themed café by the Bükkös stream, featuring a colourful, playful interior with square wooden tables and cushioned, pew-style seating, and in the summer there's a small outdoor terrace; while *Avakum*, a cool cellar café near the Belgrade Church at Alkotmány utca 14, is a good place to escape the heat and enjoy a refreshing cup of tea or glass of wine. For good coffee and sumptuous cakes, take a break at the bright and breezy *Szamos Cukrászda*, Dumtsa Jenő utca 14.

Restaurants

Aranysárkány Alkotmány utca 1a. A popular tourist haunt, the "Golden Dragon", a minute's walk up from Főtér, is a smart, upscale Hungarian restaurant with a/c – useful as it's got an open kitchen. A good option is the tourist menu which, for 3000Ft, gets you a fairly substantial three-course meal.

Corner Dunakorzó 4. Enjoyable and informal Serbian restaurant with typically meaty and filling dishes such as *pljeskavica* and *čevapi*, lamb and beef burgers and meatballs served in thick soft pittas.

Görög Kancsó Görög utca 1. One of several restaurants down by the river, this is a stylish establishment serving predominantly Greek dishes (and wines). There's plenty to keep veggies happy too, with tasty *spanakopita* (cheese and spinach pie) and *dolmades* (vine leaves stuffed with various fillings).

Mathias Rex Kossuth utca 16. Cool, good-looking cellar restaurant in the pension of the same name, with a slightly more imaginative menu than most places in town, such as trout with walnut and crispy goose with apple; excellent meat platters too. Closed Mon.

Palapa Dumsta Jenő utca 14a. Brilliant Mexican restaurant/bar that's got it all; a vibrant and colourfully decorated interior, terrific dishes and snappy service. Add to this regular live music in the courtyard and some fine cocktails and you've got the most enjoyable place to eat in town.

Rab Ráby Kucsera utca 1a. Housed in an eighteenth-century smithy just across from the Peter-Paul Church, this atmospheric old restaurant is similar to the *Aranysárkány* but more traditionally Hungarian in style and a touch cheaper.

Hungarian Open-Air Museum

The **Hungarian Open-Air Museum** (Szabadtéri Néprajzi Múzeum; March–Oct Tues–Sun 9am–5pm; 1200Ft, 1600Ft on festival days; ⓦ www.skanzen.hu) on Sztaravodai út, 4km to the west of town, is easily the most enjoyable local attraction. Hungary's largest open-air museum of rural architecture (termed a *skanzen*, after the first such museum, founded in a Stockholm suburb in 1891), it will eventually include "samples" from nine different regions of the country – seven have been finished so far – and the remains of a Roman villa. The museum is accessible by **buses** running roughly every hour from the bus terminal; get off when you see the spires in a field to the right; the entrance is 100m off the road. You can get an excellent **book** on the contents of the museum, which guides you round building by building, and has maps both of the layout of the museum and of the villages. Each building also has its warden, who can explain everything in great detail, though usually only in Hungarian.

Downhill to the right from the entrance is a composite village from the **Upper Tisza** region in northeast Hungary, culled from isolated settlements in the Erdőhát. The guide points out the finer distinctions between the various humble peasant dwellings scattered among the barns and woven pigsties. As you walk towards the church, the houses move up the social scale, as even the fences show, going from rough wickerwork to a smart plank fence. The first house, a poor cottage from Kispalad, has mud floors, which the warden sprinkles in the traditional way to stop the dust rising, and a rough thatch. Further down is a house with wooden roof tiles and wooden floors. Rural carpenters produced highly skilled work, examples of which are the circular "dry mill" from Vámosoroszi, the wooden bell-tower from Nemesborzova, and the carving inside the Greek Catholic church from Mándok (on a hilltop beyond).

As you walk up past the Calvinist graveyard, where the grave markers from four villages include the striking boat-shaped markers from Szatmárcseke in eastern Hungary, signs point you to the remains of the third-century Roman village, and on to the **Western Transdanubia** section. The thatched houses from the Orség region are often constructed of wood and covered in adobe. The school from the village of Kondorfa has its old benches with slates for writing on, a towel and basin for washing, and behind the door the children's little home-spun bags. The teacher's living quarters are at the other end of the building, separated by a kitchen with an apron chimney, where the smoke goes out of a hole in the roof. At one end of the L-shaped house from Szentegyörgyvölgy dating from the nineteenth century, a small hen ladder runs up to the roof for the poultry, and in the open end of the attic you can see large woven straw baskets for storing grain. By contrast, the next section, originating from the ethnic German communities of the Kisalföld (Little Plain) in **Northwest Transdanubia**, seems far more regimented. Neatly aligned and whitewashed, the houses are filled with knick-knacks and embroidered samplers bearing homilies like "When the Hausfrau is capable, the clocks keep good time". The next region is **The Great Hungarian Plain**, featuring a house from Süsköd which has a beautiful facade on the street and a visitors' room or "clean room" laid out for Christmas celebrations with a Nativity crib and a church-shaped box. In the fields of the Great Plain region stands a windmill from Dusnok, built in 1888 and with its sails still operating.

Located near the hilly part of the museum to the north is the **Bakony and Balaton–Uplands** section. The constructions here are some of the most interesting in the museum, with several communal buildings on display including a fire station, a working watermill and a Catholic church. The four neatly aligned stone dwelling houses reflect the varying financial standings of those living in the region during the early twentieth century. The two newest sections are **Southern Transdanubia**, whose dwellings are mostly either timber-framed, thatched wooden structures, or houses of sturdier construction built with solid stone walls (typically those near the Danube); and the **Upland Market Town**, represented here by the local traditions of stone-built architecture, such as the dwelling with a panelled stove and kitchen with central oven, and downstairs, a press house with a wooden ceiling.

Demonstrations of folk dancing and traditional crafts such as weaving, pottery and basket-making take place at the museum most Sundays as well as on public holidays, but check on the museum website or at the Tourinform office in town for precise dates of events. Local **festivals** are also celebrated here, such as the wine festival in mid-September, when folkloric programmes and grape-pressing take place. The huge *Jászárokszállás* **restaurant** (daily 10am–10pm) inside the museum serves up dishes and wines from the various regions. Shops outside the museum entrance sell snacks and ice creams as well as local crafts, including beautiful handmade paper from the Vincze paper mill.

Szentendre Sziget

Across the water from Szentendre is the sparsely populated **Szentendre Sziget** (Szentendre Island), stretching from below Szentendre up almost to Visegrád. Its open expanses have escaped the holiday-home development seen on the road north of Szentendre, and the villages here give you the feeling that time has passed them by. Access to the island is poor, with only one bridge connecting it to the mainland at **Tahitótfalu**, 10km north of Szentendre. Buses run from the Budapest Árpád híd bus terminal to Tahitótfalu, and ferries from each main settlement on the bank go across to the island. There's also one car ferry connecting Vác on the east bank with the road to Tahitótfalu (see p.172).

The island makes excellent terrain for horseriding, and one of its best **riding** schools is Bodor Major, near the ferry terminal to Vác on the eastern side of the island (2500Ft for 50min, 3000Ft for 1hr cross-country; ☎26/585-020, @info @bodormajor.hu); in summer it also puts on horse shows. It's also got a smart little pension, the *Lipiscai* (⑤), on site. Better still, towards the southern tip of the island in the settlement of **Szigetmonostor**, there's the *Rosinante Fogadó* (☎26/722-000, @www.rosinante.hu; ⑦), a delightful, country-style inn with elegantly furnished rooms, spa facilities and an à la carte restaurant – it's a ten-minute walk from the ferry dock for passenger boats arriving from Szentendre (see p.151).

One of the more curious local events, and one which befits an island covered in strawberry fields, is the **Eperfesztival** (Strawberry Festival), which takes place during the first weekend of June. Staged on the mainland by the bridge, the festival involves various shows and concerts, the highlights being a monumental tug-of-war across the bridge between the two communities and a competition to see who has, amongst other things, the biggest, smallest and fattest strawberries.

Visegrád and around

When the hillsides start to plunge and the river twists, keep your eyes fixed on the mountains to the west for a first glimpse of the citadel and ramparts of **VISEGRÁD**, 23km north of Szentendre. The citadel is almost as it appeared to János Thuroczy in 1488, who described its "upper walls stretching to the clouds floating in the sky, and the lower bastions reaching down as far as the river". At that time, courtly life in Visegrád, the royal seat, was nearing its apogee, and the palace of King Mátyás and Queen Beatrice was famed throughout Europe. The papal legate Cardinal Castelli described it as a "paradiso terrestri", seemingly unperturbed by the presence of Vlad the Impaler, who resided here under duress between 1462 and 1475.

Tucked in between the hills and the river as the Danube flows north, Visegrád is a compact town, with most local activity centred around the ferry and the

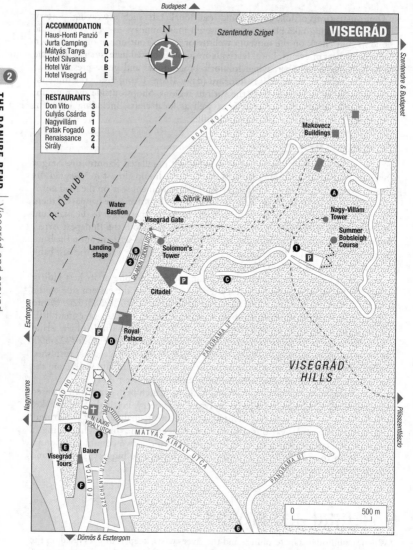

church. The three main **historical sites** all lie north of the centre: the Royal Palace and Solomon's Tower down near the river, and the citadel perching on top of the hill above. All the river sites are within easy walking distance, but unless you've got your own wheels, the climb up to the citadel (there's no public transport) is fairly taxing. While here, you can also visit the surrounding **Visegrád Hills**, boasting gorgeous views, and providing an unexpected but appropriate setting for several works by the visionary architect Imre Makovecz (see box, p.163). Though the ruins can be visited on a flying visit, the hills require a full day and a fair amount of walking, with the option of longer hikes or pony-trekking.

Arrival and information

Boats from Budapest and Esztergom land at Visegrád just below Solomon's Tower, little more than fifteen minutes' walk north of the centre. Ferries to and from Nagymaros dock to the south of town opposite the *Sirály* restaurant. **Buses** make two stops in Visegrád – there is no bus station here – by the ferry and boat stations. You can also travel by **train** from Nyugati Station to Nagymaros-Visegrád on the Szob line, and then catch one of the hourly ferries across to Visegrád.

With no Tourinform here, you'll have to rely on Visegrád Tours, located in the reception of the *Hotel Visegrád* (see below), for **information**, though they're next to useless. The **post office** is at Fő utca 77 (Mon–Fri 8am–4pm).

Accommodation

Visegrád has just about the right amount of accommodation for a town of its size and most of its **hotels** are pretty good value. In addition, Bauer, Fő utca 46 (daily 9am–5pm; ☏26/397-127, ✉travel@bauerreisen.hu), can help in finding private **rooms** (❷). You'll also see plenty of *Zimmer frei* signs along Fő utca and Széchenyi utca.

The nearest place to **camp** is at *Kék Duna Camping* (☏26/398-102; May–Sept), located within the extensive grounds of the *Haus-Honti Panzió* (see below). Not so easy to reach is *Jurta Camping* near Mogyoró-hegy (Hazelnut Hill; ☏26/398-217; May–Sept), though it's in a lovely rural setting and there are some fine views.

Haus-Honti Panzió Fő utca 66 ☏26/398-120, ⓦhttp//:ohm.hotelhonti.hu. Good-value, family-run place comprising older but perfectly adequate rooms in the pension overlooking a stream, and larger, airy rooms with balconied terraces in a newer, hotel-style building facing the Danube. Triples available in both. ❺–❻

Mátyás Tanya Fő utca 47 ☏26/398-309. Along from the Royal Palace, this mid-range option is set down in a restful location by the river with large gardens and spacious, if uninspiring, rooms furnished with dark wood. ❹

Hotel Silvanus Fekete-hegy ☏26/398-311, ⓦwww.hotelsilvanus.hu. If it's a bit of seclusion you're after, this upmarket hotel just beyond the citadel is just the ticket; first-rate rooms, most with splendid views of the Danube, alongside comprehensive wellness and sporting facilities. ❽

Hotel Vár Fő utca 9 ☏26/397-522, ✉varhotelvisegrad@axelero.hu. Formerly a hunting lodge, this handsome riverfront hotel has large, warm rooms, with some nice touches such as colourful floor rugs and wood-framed pictures of old Visegrád on the walls. ❺

Hotel Visegrád Rév utca 15 ☏26/398-160, ⓦwww.hotelvisegrad.hu. Thoroughly modern outfit near the riverfront with polished, burgundy and brown coloured rooms, all with wi-fi – some rooms face the Danube, some the castle. ❼

The ruins of Visegrád

The layout of the **ruins of Visegrád** (whose Slavic name means "High Castle") dates back to the thirteenth century, when Béla IV began fortifying the north against a recurrence of the Mongol invasion. Its most prominent features are the citadel on the hill and Solomon's Tower near the riverside below, part of the fortification that forms a gate over the road that you pass through arriving from Budapest. The Royal Palace itself is inconspicuously sited, further inland and 500m south of Solomon's Tower. As Visegrád fell into dereliction after the Turkish occupation, mud washing down from the hillsides gradually buried the palace entirely, and later generations doubted its very existence. In 1934, however, the archeologist János Schulek made a breakthrough. While at a New Year's Eve party, after he had been in Visegrád for some time hunting for the lost palace without success, the wine ran out and Schulek was sent to get some more from the neighbours. An old woman told him to go down to the wine cellar, and there he found clues in the stones that convinced him the palace was here, later unearthing one of the palace vaults.

The Royal Palace

Now largely excavated and partially reconstructed, the **Royal Palace**, ten minutes' walk from the centre at Fő utca 27–29 (Királyi palota; Tues–Sun 9am–5pm; 1100Ft), spreads over four levels or terraces. Originally founded in 1323 by the Angevin king Charles Robert, the palace was expanded by subsequent kings, the largest development occurring in the reign of Mátyás Corvinus.

Walking up from the entrance, you pass the *kőtár* (lapidarium) on your left, with its collection of excavated stones from Roman to medieval times, before arriving at the palace proper. Here you enter the **cour d'honneur**, which was constructed

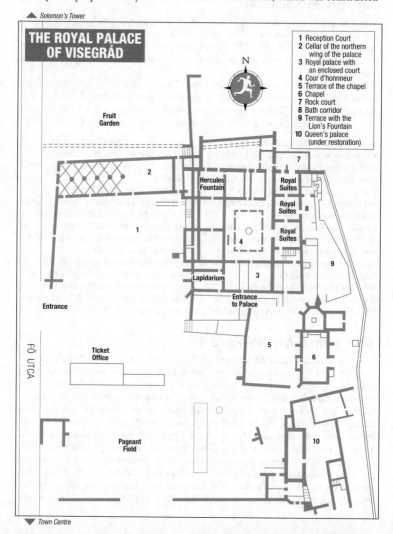

▲ Solomon's Tower

THE ROYAL PALACE OF VISEGRÁD

N

1 Reception Court
2 Cellar of the northern wing of the palace
3 Royal palace with an enclosed court
4 Cour d'honnneur
5 Terrace of the chapel
6 Chapel
7 Rock court
8 Bath corridor
9 Terrace with the Lion's Fountain
10 Queen's palace (under restoration)

Fruit Garden

2

Hercules Fountain

Royal Suites

Royal Suites

Royal Suites

7

8

9

1

4

Lapidarium

3

Entrance to Palace

Entrance

FŐ UTCA

Ticket Office

5

6

Pageant Field

10

▼ Town Centre

for Charles's successor, Louis, and provided the basis for subsequent building by Sigismund and, later, Mátyás Corvinus. Much work on this inner courtyard has been completed in recent years, with pristine reconstructions of the pilastered **Renaissance loggia**, the cloistered walks and the surrounding rooms, which now contain a voluminous display of exhibits, mainly ceramic vessels, weaponry and glazed stove tiles. One room holds the red marble **Hercules Fountain** which would spout wine during important events; although far from complete, a good proportion of the original parts, including the foundation, were discovered and subsequently pieced together, hence it now stands like an impossible jigsaw.

Legend has it that Mátyás was eventually poisoned by his wife Beatrice, who wanted to rule on her own. The chalice containing the fatal potion may well have passed between the **royal suites** that once stood beneath an overhang on the third terrace, separated by a magnificent **chapel**. Now also renovated, the royal suites remain mostly bare, save for some superb-looking dark green ceramic tile stoves. Reportedly, the finest sight at this time was the garden on the fourth terrace, embellished by the **Lion Fountain**. A perfect copy of the original (carved by Ernő Szakál) bears Mátyás's raven crest and piles of sleepy-looking lions, although, unlike the original, it's not fed by the gutters and pipes that channelled water down from the citadel. The original pieces are displayed in Solomon's Tower. From this elevated position there are lovely views down to the palace's fragrant **fruit garden**.

Back across towards the entrance is the **wine cellar**, where the Hungarian, Czech and Polish kings signed the closing document at the Visegrád Congress of 1335. Called to discuss the growing Habsburg threat, they failed to agree on any concrete steps, but nevertheless managed to consume 10,000 litres of wine and vast amounts of food in the process. In February 1991, Visegrád played host to another less extravagant summit, when the prime ministers of Hungary, Poland and Czechoslovakia met here to put together a joint strategy for trade and EC membership in the post-Communist era. Again the setting for signing the final document was the cellar, and again the results were limited – although it did mean that a display of stonework from the age of King Mátyás was put together so that the cellar would not be totally empty. Work has begun on creating an entrance at ground level into the cellar, but this is taking some time to realize.

Each year, usually the second weekend in July, the grounds play host to the **International Palace Games**, a series of rousing medieval pageants with jousting and archery tournaments intended to re-create the splendour of Visegrád's Renaissance heyday; in addition there are crafts workshops and lots of eating and drinking. For more information contact Tourinform in Szentendre (see p.151).

Solomon's Tower

Five minutes' walk north along Fő utca, just after it rejoins the main highway, you can take a right onto Salamon torony utca, which climbs up through the gate of the old castle fortifications to reach **Solomon's Tower** (May–Sept Tues–Sun 9am–5pm; 650Ft), a mighty hexagonal keep, buttressed on two sides by unsightly concrete slabs, and named after an eleventh-century Hungarian king. The **Mátyás Museum** on the ground and first floor of the tower exhibits finds from the palace, including the white Anjou Fountain of the Angevins; the original pieces of the Lion fountain, together with a reconstruction of the child Hercules struggling with the hydra; and the red marble *Visegrád Madonna*, a Renaissance masterpiece that shows many similarities to the works of Tomaso Fiamberti nearby. The next two floors present the history of Visegrád up to the Turkish occupation. It's worth climbing to the top for the view of the lines of fortification running down from the citadel on both sides, meeting at the Water Bastion by the

▲ Visegrád citadel

river. However, neither this, nor the **ruined Roman fort** to the north, atop Sibrik Hill, is worth a special detour, so you might want to save your energy for the climb to Visegrád's citadel.

The citadel

Dramatically sited on a crag directly above Solomon's Tower and commanding a superb view of Nagymaros and the Börzsöny mountains on the east bank, Visegrád's thirteenth-century **citadel** (Fellegvár; daily mid-March to mid-Oct 10am–6pm; rest of year 10am–4pm; closed when it snows, as the battlements are too slippery; 1500Ft) served as a repository for the Hungarian crown jewels until they were stolen by a treacherous maid of honour in the fifteenth century. Following the last major rebuilding work later that same century, the castle was occupied by the Turks, then the Habsburgs, before falling into decay. Its restoration began in the late nineteenth century, after an eager local priest brought the government's attention to the dire state of the place, and work still continues slowly. Its condition before the work began in 1870 is shown inside in a photograph in the **exhibition** on the history of the castle, which includes a hologram of the crown and drawings of how the castle looked at different periods. Elsewhere, there's a ridiculous waxworks display of various characters frolicking at a medieval banquet and, in the innermost courtyard, an exhibition on hunting and fishing and a stash of ferocious-looking weaponry. As lame as these displays are, it's worth paying the expensive entrance fee for what are some of the finest views of the Danube anywhere along its stretch.

You can reach the citadel from the centre of town via the "Calvary" **footpath** (signposted *Fellegvár* and marked by a red cross on the way), heading up to the left off Nagy Lajos Király utca, 50m behind the church. It takes its name from the calvary of reliefs that you follow on your way up. Alternatively, you can start from Solomon's Tower and walk through the top gate and uphill, looking out for signs up to the right after ten to fifteen minutes. Both routes involve around forty minutes of steep walking; the latter track is slightly tougher. Alternatively, if you have your own wheels, you can take the scenic Panorama Route up to the citadel.

The Visegrád Hills

Thickly wooded and crisscrossed with paths, the **Visegrád Hills** are a popular rambling spot. From the car park near the citadel, it's a 500-metre walk up the main road to another car park; from here you can follow a signposted path off to the left, which leads to the **Nagy-Villám observation tower** (kilátó; 10am–5pm: April–Oct daily; Nov–March Sat & Sun; 100Ft). Sited at the highest point on the Danube Bend, it offers wonderful panoramas of Szentendre Sziget and the Bend and, on a clear day, views as far as Slovakia. You can also hike from here over into the Pilis range (see p.170). The *Nagyvillám* (closed Nov–Feb) on the way up is a good spot to stop for a moderately priced meal with fine views. You can also visit the collection of wooden buildings designed by **Imre Makovecz** at Mogyoró-hegy (Hazelnut Hill), 1km north of the observation tower (see box below). Back down by the car park is the **Summer Bobsleigh Course** (Nyári Bob), where you can race down a one-kilometre run (350Ft for one run, 1800Ft for six; daily: April–Oct 9/10am–6/7pm; Nov–March 11am–4pm; ☎26/397-397), except on rainy days when the brakes are rendered ineffective.

If you feel like **hiking**, you could try the twelve-kilometre trail marked with blue stripes running from the tower, via Paprét (Priest's Meadow), to Pilisszentlászló, which takes two to three hours. Although Visegrád itself has nowhere to swim, there is a salubrious terraced strand and natural warm-water **pool** 4km away at Lepence, at the Pilisszentlászló turn-off towards Dömös. A series of pools has been cut into the hillside overlooking the Danube, making it one of the most spectacular open-air pool complexes in Hungary – it is, however, currently closed pending construction of a spa hotel.

Eating and drinking

Visegrád has a healthy stock of **restaurants**, and whilst some are inclined towards large tourist groups, there are some decent possibilities elsewhere. With

---

Imre Makovecz at Visegrád

Imre Makovecz was a promising architect in the Kádár years, but was branded a troublemaker for his outspoken nationalism, banned from teaching, and "exiled" to the Visegrád forestry department in 1977. During this time he made many of the wooden buildings which can be seen at Mogyoró-hegy in Visegrád. Over the next decade he refined his ideas, acquiring a group of student followers for whom he held summer schools. Employing cheap, low-technology methods in a way he branded as specifically Magyar, he taught his students how to construct temporary buildings using raw materials such as branches and twigs. The Cultural House near Jurta Camping in Visegrád is an excellent example, with a turfed roof and a light homely interior that has worn well.

Now one of the most influential architects in Hungary, Makovecz's buildings can be found all over the country. They include the community centres in Sárospatak, Zalaszentlászló and Szigetvár, churches at Paks and Siófok, and the oesophagus-like crypt of the Farkasréti cemetery in Budapest. Makovecz also designed the much admired Hungarian Pavilion at the 1992 Expo in Seville, with its seven towers representing the seven Magyar tribes. He has won a considerable amount of praise abroad, with strong support from Prince Charles, for whom his anti-modernist, back-to-nature style has a strong appeal. However, his generous use of wood does not appeal to all environmentalists, and his dabbling in right-wing politics turns his whole idea of a return to the "real" Hungarian style of building, once a righteous tool against the old regime, into something less appealing.

nowhere really specific to **drink**, most consumption tends to take place in these same restaurants.

Restaurants

Don Vito Fő utca 83. By far the town's most enjoyable eatery, this stylish pizzeria, featuring three brightly decorated rooms (the no-smoking one has lovely squishy brown seating) and a long wooden bar, offers fabulous stone-baked pizzas. It's also the best place in town to drink and there's live music at weekends during the summer.

Gulyás Csárda Nagy Lajos király utca 4. The "Goulash Inn" is a fairly low-key restaurant located just up from the church, but it's a well-established place and serves all the Hungarian standards at very reasonable prices.

Patak Fogadó Mátyás király utca 92. Pleasantly isolated about 1.5km north of town on the road to

the citadel, and with a lovely terrace overlooking a stream, the *Patak* offers a varied menu, with hunter's stew and roast venison alongside fish and pasta dishes.

Renaissance Fő utca 11. Top tack here in this seriously touristy, but fun, restaurant, where you can feast on suckling pig or roast deer while wearing a cardboard crown, and be serenaded by a pantalooned man with a lute.

Sirály Rév utca 15. Attached to the *Hotel Visegrád*, this sprawling, rather clinical place is essentially geared up for large groups, but the food – there's a standard and à la carte menu – is a mix of both Hungarian and international specialities.

Esztergom

Beautifully situated in a crook of the Danube facing Slovakia, **ESZTERGOM**, 25km on from Visegrád, is dominated by its basilica, whose dome is visible for miles around. The site is richly symbolic, since it was here that Prince Géza and his son Vajk (the future king and saint Stephen) brought Hungary into the fold of Roman Catholic (not Orthodox) Christendom, in the nation's first cathedral. Even after the court moved to Buda following the Mongol invasion, Esztergom remained the **centre of Catholicism** until the Turkish conquest, when the clergy dispersed to safer towns and it became an Ottoman stronghold, besieged by Christian armies. While the town recovered in the eighteenth century, it wasn't until the 1820s that it became the Primal See again, following a nationwide campaign. As part of the *ancien régime*, the Church was ruthlessly persecuted during the Rákosi era (though the basilica was well maintained, allegedly because the wife of the Soviet leader Khrushchev liked it). From the 1960s onwards, however, the Communists settled for a *modus vivendi*, hoping to enlist the Church's help with social problems and to harness the patriotic spirit of the faithful. The avowedly Christian government elected in 1990 did its best to restore Church property and influence, and, while this process slowed down after the Communists returned to power, their concordat with the Vatican in 1997 eased fears of it going into reverse.

Esztergom combines historic monuments and small-town charm in just the right doses, with a summer festival as an inducement to linger. The town's layout is easily grasped and most of the pensions and restaurants are within walking distance of the centre.

Arrival and information

If you arrive by bus from Visegrád, it's best to get off near Basilica Hill or in the centre rather than travelling on to the bus station on Simor János utca, where services from Budapest terminate. From the train station, 1km further south, buses #1 and #5 run into the centre. Ferries from Budapest tie up on the Danube embankment of Prímás Sziget, fifteen minutes' walk from the centre. **Slovakia** is only just across the Mária Valéria Bridge; you can walk or drive there and back quite easily, but remember to carry your passport with you.

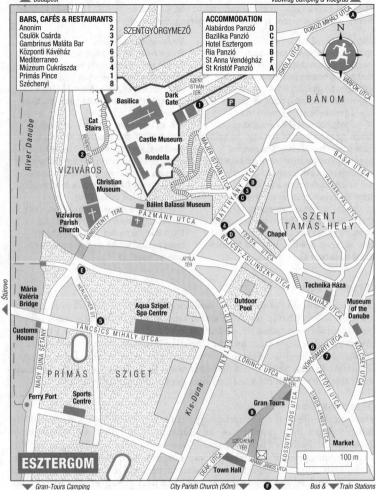

BARS, CAFÉS & RESTAURANTS
Anonim	2
Csulök Csárda	3
Gambrinus Maláta Bar	7
Központi Kávéház	6
Mediterraneo	5
Múzeum Cukrászda	4
Primás Pince	1
Széchenyi	8

ACCOMMODATION
Alabárdos Panzió	D
Bazilika Panzió	C
Hotel Esztergom	E
Ria Panzió	B
St Anna Vendégház	F
St Kristóf Panzió	A

The only source of **information**, albeit limited, is the Gran Tours agency at Széchenyi tér 25 (Mon–Fri 8am–5pm, Sat 9am–noon; ☏33/502-001, ✉grantours @freemail.hu), who can also arrange private rooms and concert bookings. The **post office** is at Arany János utca 2 (Mon–Fri 8am–7pm, Sat 8am–noon).

Accommodation

During July and August, the cheapest option is a college **dorm bed** (❶), bookable through Gran Tours (see above), who can also organize **private rooms** (❶–❷). Of the two **campsites**, *Gran-Tours Camping*, 500m south of the Mária Valéria Bridge on Prímás Sziget (☏33/402-513, ✉fortanex@t-online.hu; pension ❸, 4-person chalets ❹; May–Sept), has better facilities (including a pool, tennis courts and restaurant) and is far more conveniently located than *Vadvirág Camping*, 3km along the road to Visegrád near the tail end of the #6 bus route (℡33/312-234; May–Sept), with grassy tent space and two-person chalets (❶).

Alabárdos Panzió Bajcsy-Zsilinszky utca 49 ℡33/312-640, ⓦwww.alabardospanzio.hu. Attractive, Mediterranean-style villa on an alley off the main road, midway between the upper and lower town, with rooms (all with wi-fi) in two adjacent buildings, each one priced according to size and view. ❹–❺

🏃 **Bazilika Panzió** Batthyány utca 7 ℡33/520-685, ⓦwww.bazilika.eu. Just around the corner from the *Alabárdos*, this fabulous place is more boutique hotel than pension; gorgeous rooms painted in cream and beige tones beautifully offset with splashes of burgundy. Sauna and jacuzzi included in the price. ❼

Hotel Esztergom Helischer utca, Prímás Sziget ℡33/412-555, ⓦwww.hotel-esztergom.hu. Despite its faceless 1970s concrete exterior, this pleasantly located hotel has a reasonable mix of older and newer rooms, the latter with balconies facing the Danube. ❼

Ria Panzió Batthyány utca 11–13 ℡33/313-115, ⓦwww.riapanzio.com. Just along from the *Bazilika*, this is a comfortable, welcoming pension with spotless, lime-green rooms in two buildings, one of which is wheelchair accessible. There's also secure parking, a pocket-sized garden and bikes for rent. ❻

St Anna Vendégház Erzsébet Királyne utja 2 ℡33/404-050, ⒺSztanna@vnet.hu. Delightful guesthouse about 800m south of the centre (just beyond Hősök tere), with a selection of cosy rooms (unusually, with tea-making facilities) positioned around a pretty, flower-filled inner courtyard. ❺

St Kristóf Panzió Dobozi Mihály utca 11 ℡33/414-153, ⓦwww.szentkristofpanzio.com. Good-quality pension on the Visegrád road, 10min from the basilica, with spacious, a/c rooms and apartments, a lovely garden and a good restaurant. ❺

The Town

The main focal point of the town is **Basilica Hill**, whose landscaped slope appears on maps as Szent István tér. After seeing the basilica and the castle remains here, you'll probably want some refreshment before heading downhill to the **Víziváros**, where art buffs can get stuck into the **Christian Museum** and others will be drawn to the shady *korzó*, a weeping-willow-lined promenade beside the Kis-Duna, separating **Prímás Sziget** from the lower town. In the **lower town**, the emphasis is on enjoyment, with cafés and bars, and an outdoor thermal pool.

The basilica

Built on the site of the first cathedral in Hungary, where Vajk was crowned as King Stephen by a papal envoy on Christmas Day, 1000 AD, Esztergom's Neoclassical **basilica** (Bazilika; daily 7am–6pm; free) is the largest in the country, measuring 118m in length and 47m in width, and capped by a dome 100m high. Representing a thousand years of faith and statehood, it was begun by Pál Kühneland and János Packh in 1822, and finally completed by József Hild in 1869, thirteen years after its consecration, once the dome was in place. Liszt's *Gran Mass* was composed for the occasion (*Gran* being the German name for Esztergom). In 1991, the church hosted two events symbolizing its triumph over Communism: the reburial of the exiled Cardinal Mindszenty and the first papal visit to Hungary.

The exterior of the basilica is unadorned except for the primates' coats of arms flanking the great bronze doors that are only used on special occasions. Its nave is on a massive scale, clad in marble, gilding and mosaics, while its main altarpiece was painted by the Venetian Michelangelo Grigoletti, based on Titian's *Assumption* in the Frari Church in Venice. The basilica's most impressive architectural feature stands to the left of the entrance, the lavish red and white marble **Bakócz Chapel**, whose Florentine altar was salvaged by Archbishop Tamás Bakócz (1442–1521) from the original church. To the right lies the **treasury** (kincstár; daily: March–Oct 9am–4.30pm; Nov & Dec 10am–3.30pm;

600Ft), an overpowering collection of bejewelled croziers, chalices, vestments and papal souvenirs – the most prized exhibit here is the thirteenth-century oath cross, traditionally used for the coronation of Hungarian kings.

Towards the nave are two stairways, the first leading to a **crypt** (krypta; daily 9am–5pm; 200Ft), which is like a set from a Dracula film, with seventeen-metre-thick walls to support the enormous weight of the basilica, and giant stone women flanking the stairway down to gloomy vaults full of entombed prelates. Though several other mausolea look more arresting, it is the **tomb of Cardinal Mindszenty** (see box below) that transfixes Hungarians. The other stairway ascends for over three hundred steps to the stiflingly hot interior of the **cupola** (kupola; May–Oct daily 9am–5pm; 300Ft), though any discomfort is forgotten the moment you step outside and see the magnificent **view** of Esztergom, with the Slovak town of Štúrovo across the water.

The Castle Museum and around

On slightly higher ground, a few paces from the basilica, are the red-roofed, reconstructed remains of the palace founded by Prince Géza in the tenth century, now presented as the **Castle Museum** (Vár Múzeum; Tues–Sun: April–Oct 10am–6pm; Nov–March 10am–4pm; 800Ft). A royal seat for almost three hundred years, it was here that Béla III entertained Philip of France and Frederick Barbarossa on their way to the Third Crusade. After Buda became the capital, Hungary's primates lived here, and the Renaissance prelate János Vitéz made it a centre of humanist culture, where Queen Beatrice spent her widowhood. Although the palace was sacked by the Turks in 1543 and twice besieged before they were evicted in 1683, enough survived to be excavated by Leopold Antal in the 1930s – indeed, it is more impressive than the remains of Buda's royal palace.

Traces of the frescoes that once covered every wall in the palace can be seen in the vaulted living-hall from Béla III's reign (1172–96), whence a narrow stairway ascends to the study of Archbishop Vitéz – known as the **Hall of Virtues** after its allegorical murals of *Intelligence*, *Moderation*, *Strength* and *Justice*. Beyond lies the **royal chapel**, whose Gothic rose window and Romanesque arches were executed by craftsmen brought over by Béla's two French wives; its frescoes of saints and the Tree of Life reflect his Byzantine upbringing. A spiral staircase leads to the palace rooftop, offering a panoramic view of Esztergom and the river, and a fresh perspective on the basilica.

The return of Cardinal Mindszenty

When the much travelled body of Cardinal József Mindszenty was finally laid to rest with state honours in May 1991, it was a vindication of his uncompromising heroism – and the Vatican realpolitik that Mindszenty despised. As a conservative and monarchist, he had stubbornly opposed the postwar Communist takeover, warning that "cruel hands are reaching out to seize hold of our children, claws belonging to people who have nothing but evil to teach them". Arrested in 1948, tortured for 39 days and nights, and sentenced to life imprisonment for treason, Mindszenty was freed during the Uprising and took refuge in the US Embassy, where he remained for the next fifteen years, an exile in the heart of Budapest.

When the Vatican struck a deal with the Kádár regime in 1971, Mindszenty had to be pushed into resigning his position and going to Austria, where he died in 1975. Although his will stated that his body should not return home until "the red star of Moscow had fallen from Hungarian skies", his reburial occurred some weeks before the last Soviet soldier left, in preparation for the pope's visit in August of that year. Nowadays the Vatican proclaims his greatness, without any hint of apology for its past actions.

Held within another of the castle's brick vaulted rooms is a **lapidarium**, showcasing some superb stone monuments and fragments garnered from the original palace as well as other churches that stood on the hill at one stage or another; mullion windows and vaulted ribs stand alongside late Gothic and Renaissance keystones and capitals, and pieces of red marble gravestones, which were particularly fashionable in the fourteenth and fifteenth centuries.

During June and July, **plays** and **dances** are staged in the **Rondella** bastion, whose exit is guarded by a giant statue of a warrior. As you descend the hillside, notice the monumental **Dark Gate**: a tunnel built in the 1820s as a short cut between church buildings on either side of the hill and later exploited by the Soviet army, which maintained a base there until 1989. The former primate's wine cellars, next door, have been converted into the *Prímás Pince* restaurant (see opposite).

The Víziváros and Prímás Sziget

Leading down from the ramparts of the basilica, the **Cat Stairs** (Macskalépcső) are cut into the side of the hill and it's an unrelenting, but breathtaking, climb down to the **Víziváros** (Watertown), a small district of Baroque churches and seminaries where practising choirs are audible along the streets. Turning left at the bottom of the steps brings you to Mindszenty tér and the Primate's Palace at no. 2, which now houses the **Christian Museum** (Keresztény Múzeum; Wed–Sun: May–Oct 10am–6pm; Nov–April 11am–3pm; 750Ft), Hungary's richest hoard of religious art. Here you can feast your eyes on the largest collection of Italian prints outside Italy, Renaissance paintings and wood carvings by German and Austrian masters, fourteenth-century icons from Venice, and the unique "Lord's Coffin of Garam-szentbenedek" – a wheeled, gilded structure used in Easter Week processions, from around 1480. The museum's wide-ranging collection also includes some sprawling tapestries, a stash of decorative artwork, and Orthodox icons from Russia and Serbia. Next door to the museum stands the Italianate Baroque **Víziváros Parish Church**.

Turning into Pázmány utca, you come to the **Bálint Balassi Museum** at no. 13 (Tues–Sun 9am–5pm; 200Ft), which mounts temporary historical exhibitions rather than dwelling on the romantic poet Bálint Balassi (1554–94), who died trying to recapture Esztergom from the Turks. This half-crazed philanderer was famous for sexually assaulting women and then dedicating verses to them – behaviour that resulted in him being beaten unconscious on several occasions.

Back down by the parish church, you can cross a bridge onto **Prímás Sziget** (Primate's Island), a popular tourist spot with a campsite, restaurants, spa centre (see opposite) and other sporting facilities. A little way south of the landing stage for ferries to Štúrovo is the reconstructed **Mária Valéria bridge** that connects the two towns. Blown up by retreating Germans at the end of World War II, the bridge was left neglected until, after years of wrangling and protracted negotiations between Hungarian and Slovakian ministers, an intergovernmental agreement to rebuild the bridge was finally signed in 1999.

The lower town and Szent Tamás-hegy

While Rákóczi tér, with its supermarkets and banks, is the de facto centre of the **lower town**, its most attractive feature is the **Kis-Duna sétány**, a riverside walk lined with weeping willows and villas, popular with promenaders. Inland, civic pride is manifest in the brightly painted public buildings on the main square, **Széchenyi tér**, none more so than the town hall, distinguished by Rococo windows that once belonged to Prince Rákóczi's general, János Bottyán, whose statue stands nearby. The old part of town extends as far south as the **City Parish Church**, built on the site of a medieval monastery where Béla IV and Queen Mária Lascaris were buried. To the right of its gateway is a plaque showing the level of the flood of 1832.

The taming of the river is one of the themes of the **Museum of the Danube** at Kölcsey utca 2 (Duna Múzeum; Mon & Wed–Sun: May–Oct 10am–6pm; Nov–April 10am–4pm; 500Ft). Count Széchenyi was the prime mover of the plan to curb flooding and improve navigation on the Danube, using the labour of thousands of Hungarian navvies and technology imported from England – including the steam-dredger *Vidra*, a model of which can be seen. Very much an educational facility, there's plenty to keep kids entertained, including touch screens, a large walk-on flood protection map and a water play area.

To end with an overview of the lower town, walk up Imaház utca past a flamboyant, Moorish-style edifice that was once Esztergom's synagogue and is now a science and technology house, or **Technika Háza**. Shortly afterwards you'll find a flight of steps leading to **Szent Tamás-hegy** (St Thomas's Hill), a rocky outcrop named after the English martyr Thomas à Becket. A **chapel** was built here in his honour by Margaret Capet, whose English father-in-law, Henry II, prompted Thomas's assassination by raging "Who will rid me of this turbulent priest?" Even after her husband died and Margaret married Béla III of Hungary, her conscience would not let her forget the saint. The existing chapel (postdating the Turkish occupation) is fronted by a trio of life-size statues representing Golgotha.

Eating and drinking

Esztergom has a reasonable selection of **restaurants**, with solid Hungarian fare dominating the menus. If you're catering for yourself, there's a daily outdoor **market** on Simor János utca. The best of the **pavement cafés** are in the vicinity of Rákóczi tér, particularly the *Központi Kávéház*, on the square itself, and the colourful *Múzeum Cukrászda*, on Bajcsy-Zsilinszky utca next to the *Alabárdos Panzió*, both of which have a tempting selection of cakes. The most vibrant night-time venue is the *Gambrinus Maláta Bar* at Vörösmarty utca 3 (Mon–Thurs & Sun 1pm–1am, Fri & Sat till 2am), an intimate tangle of varnished branches with dance music on the jukebox.

Anonim Berényi utca 4. Housed in an old town house opposite the Cat Stairs, this is a fairly old-fashioned, low-key place, but it's very welcoming and the Hungarian food is top drawer.

Csulök Csárda Batthyány utca 9. True to its name, the popular "Knuckle Inn" offers the full gamut of dishes (roasted lamb knuckle, knuckle of ham pancake, bean soup with knuckle), alongside poultry, game and fish – with dining in the cosy brick cellar or on the outdoor terrace.

Mediterraneo Helischer utca 2. Just a stone's throw from the Mária Valéria Bridge, this good-looking restaurant is right on the mark with its varied and appealing menu featuring the likes of butterfish fillet, roast duck and creamy noodles.

Primás Pince Szent István tér 4. Heavily frequented by busloads of tourists, the cavernous bowels of the former primate's wine cellars – all brick-vaulted ceilings, thick pillars and neat rows of tables laid out like a school dining room – are an enjoyable place to tuck into solid national grub.

Széchenyi Széchenyi tér 16. Nicely situated on the main square, this is the most agreeable of the lower town's restaurants, a friendly, stylish place serving delicacies such as fish skewers, boiled trotters and goose with cabbage, in addition to cheap noodle dishes.

Entertainment

Summer is the time for **concerts** in Esztergom, with an annual programme of choral and organ music in the basilica and the Víziváros parish church, plus an internationally oriented **Guitar Festival** during the first half of August in odd-numbered years (Ⓦwww.guitarfestival.hu); further details of both can be obtained from Gran Tours (see p.165). There are plenty of opportunities to **swim** here, either at the Aqua Sziget indoor **spa centre** (Mon–Fri & Sun 10am–8pm, Sat 10am–9pm; 2650Ft for a day ticket) on Prímás Sziget, or the **outdoor pool** with saunas and steam rooms (May–Sept daily 6am–7pm; Oct–April Tues–Sat 6am–7pm,

Sun 8am–4pm; 600Ft), between Kis-Duna sétány and Bajcsy-Zsilinszky utca. Elsewhere, you can work up a sweat in the sports centre (daily 8am–10pm) or on the tennis courts near *Gran-Tours Camping*.

The Pilis range and around

Whether you describe them as mountains or hills, the **Pilis range** (Pilis hegység), behind the west bank, offers lots of scope for **hiking** amidst lovely scenery. The beech and oak woods on these limestone slopes are most beautiful in the autumn, but there's a possibility of sighting red deer or wild boar at any time of year. Ruined monasteries and lodges attest to the hermits of the Order of St Paul and the royal hunting parties who frequented the hills in medieval times.

Pilisvörösvár and Pillisszántó are directly accessible by bus from Árpád híd terminal in Budapest, as is Pomáz, from where buses go on to Pilisszentkereszt and on up to Dobogókő. Buses to Pomáz frequently make the short trip from Szentendre. There are no direct buses from Esztergom. You can also catch the **HÉV train** to Pomáz (near Szentendre) from Budapest's Batthány tér, or you can hike up from the Nagy-Villám Tower at Visegrád. If you're planning any walking, buy a **map** of the Pilis in Budapest or the Danube Bend towns, which shows the paths (*turistaút/földút*), caves (*barlang*), and rain shelters (*esőház*) throughout the highlands.

Pomáz

POMÁZ, on the HÉV line between Budapest and Szentendre, is an excellent place from which to step off into the Pilis, with regular buses leaving from the HÉV station, on the eastern edge of town, to Dobogókő, 18km northwest of Pomáz. Before doing so, though, it's worth exploring the town, most of which is fairly recent, though the Roman sarcophagus outside the town hall on the main street indicates that people have been living and dying here for quite some time. Serbian immigrants fleeing from the Turks arrived in the late seventeenth century, and by the nineteenth century there was a flourishing German community here too.

The first point of interest you come to as you walk up to the town from the HÉV station is the **ethnographical collection** of folk costumes and embroidery (Magyar Néprajzi Gyűjtemény; Tues & Thurs 1–5pm, Sat & Sun 10am–6pm; 400Ft), behind the colourful Transylvanian gate at József Attila utca 28b. It was put together by private collector János Hamar and covers four regions of Hungarian-speaking communities; every spare centimetre of furniture here is covered with decoration. The **Community History Collection** at Kossuth Lajos utca 48 (Község Történeti Gyűjtemény; mid-April to mid-Oct daily 10am–6pm; 200Ft), a ten-minute walk up the road just past Hősök tere, on the left of the main road, offers something more local. It re-creates homes in Pomáz belonging to the Serbian and German communities, and includes a very nice enamel stove which also served as a boiler, with a tap on one side to let out the hot water. The Swabian community, originally from Germany, was mostly deported back there after World War II, and links with the deported families have only been officially re-established over the last decade or so.

Pomáz's Serb community has been shrinking steadily during the last century, although you can still hear old ladies chatting to each other in Serbian on street corners, and the town is proud of its traditional Serbian dance group which has won prizes in Belgrade. Ten minutes further up Kossuth Lajos utca, at Szabadság tér, is a **Plague Cross** erected in 1792. Five minutes' walk up to the right along the suitably named Szerb utca stands the **church of St George**, which holds Masses for the small community at 10am on the second and fourth Sundays of the month. Your best chance to look around the church is to go in just before the service starts. The church's main **annual celebration** is the feast of its patron saint on May 6. The square behind the church, Vujicsics tér, takes its name from the Serbian composer Tihamer Vujicsics (1929–75), who was born in the street beyond; a plaque on Plébánia utca marks the spot. The **Vujicsics Ensemble**, which preserves his memory, started in Pomáz in 1974 (it's now based in Szentendre) and is now one of Hungary's foremost folk ensembles, performing both nationally and internationally on a regular basis (see p.459).

(see p.459).

If you wish to stop over, there's the *Kara Hotel* at Beniczky utca 63 (☎26/325-355, ⓦ www.karahotel.hu; ❸), ten minutes' walk up the main road past the Plague Cross, which has simple clean rooms (including several triples), while its cordial cellar restaurant, the *Rákospince*, is the best place to **eat** in town. All buses from the HÉV terminal pass by here.

Dobogókő and Dömös

Standing in the shadow of 756-metre-high Pilis-tető, **DOBOGÓKŐ** has been a hiking centre since the late nineteenth century, when one of Hungary's first hostels was established here, and is still the best base for walking in the Pilis. The most popular way to see the area is to take the bus up to the resort, and then to walk down the Rám precipice – a four- to five-hour hike that's not advisable in wet weather – to Dömös, which offers fabulous views down to the river.

The hostel building at Dobogókő, just up through the trees from where the buses turn round, is now home to the small **Museum of Rambling and Nature Tourism** (Thurs, Sat & Sun 9am–2pm; 200Ft). Exhibits include old photos of the area, showing that there was hardly a tree around the village a hundred years ago, and some old equipment, including skis with a strip of seal fur on the bottom to prevent the ski from slipping downhill. Behind the museum is an observation point which affords lovely views of Szob and Zebegény on the other side of the Danube.

The *Eötvös Loránd Tourist House* (☎26/347-534; dorm beds 1500–3000Ft), next to the museum, offers the cheapest **accommodation** around, whilst, with permission, tents can be pitched on the grassy area in front of the house. Campers can use the *Tourist House*'s bathroom and restaurant, which serves strudels and other snacks during the week, and lunch at weekends from noon to around 6pm. Just down from here is the *Hotel Nimród* (☎26/547-003, ⓔ nimrodhotel@t-online.hu; ❻), a fairly average place swamped in heavy brown decor, although boasting a couple of pools, sauna and solarium. There's another possibility on the main road leading up to Dobogókő, about 1km from the top of the hill, where the *Platán Panzió* (☎26/347-680, ⓔ platanpanzio@t-online.hu; ❹) has bright, wood-furnished rooms and an attractive restaurant.

Aside from the hotels, for **food** there is the *Ízek Háza*, opposite the *Hotel Nimród*, or the *Bohém Tanya* by the car park at the bus terminus, both serving solid Hungarian fare; or for a filling bean goulash or toasted sandwiches head 300m down past the *Hotel Nimród* to the *Zsindelyes Csárda*, a wooden construction by Imre Makovecz, which also houses the engine house of the ski lift. At busy times of year you may also find some steaming stew cooking over a fire, or an impromptu grill set up on the ends of the trails, at the edges of the bus terminus.

Walking up to Dobogókő from the river, the best starting point is **DÖMÖS**, 7km west of Visegrád, where buses between Visegrád and Esztergom stop off. Inconspicuous wooden signposts near the stream in the centre of the village indicate the start of trails into the hills, where raspberries abound in early summer. Follow the Malom tributary for 2.5km and you'll reach a path that forks right for the Rám precipice (3hr) and Dobogókő (4–5hr), and left for the Vadálló Rocks (3hr) beneath the towering "Pulpit Seat" – a 641-metre crag that only the experienced should attempt to climb.

The east bank

Compared to its western counterpart, the Danube Bend's **east bank** has fewer monuments and, consequently, fewer visitors. **Vác**, the only sizeable town, has a monopoly on historic architecture, styling itself the "city of churches". Not far from the town is the beautiful botanical garden at **Vácrátót**, while further north you can view some of the finest scenery in the Danube Bend at **Zebegény** and **Nagymaros**, which, like other settlements beneath the **Börzsöny range**, mark the start of trails into the highlands.

Starting **from Budapest**, you can reach anywhere along the east bank within an hour or two by train from Nyugati Station, or by bus from the Árpád híd terminal. The slower alternative is to catch a boat from Budapest's Vigadó tér pier to Vác (2hr 30min), or on to Nagymaros and Zebegény. There are also regular ferries from the west bank.

Vác and around

The town of **VÁC**, 40km north of Budapest, has a worldlier past than its sleepy atmosphere suggests, allowing you to enjoy its architectural heritage in relative peace. Its bishops traditionally showed a flair for self-promotion, like the cardinals of Esztergom, endowing monuments and colleges. Under Turkish occupation (1544–1686), Vác assumed an oriental character, with seven mosques and a public *hammam*, while during the Reform Era it was linked to Budapest by Hungary's first rail line (the second continued to Bratislava). In 1849 two battles were fought at Vác, the first a victory for the town over the Austrian army, followed a few months later by a defeat in July 1849 when the town was captured; the battles are commemorated by a bright green **obelisk** by the main road from Budapest, shortly before you enter the town. More recently Vác became notorious for its prison, which has one of the toughest regimes in the country and was used to incarcerate leftists under Admiral Horthy and "counter-revolutionaries" under Communism. Though Vác's legacy of sights certainly justifies a visit, it's not worth staying unless you're planning to visit Vácrátót (see p.176) or Zebegény (see p.177), or are coming especially for the annual festival at the end of July (see p.175).

Arrival and information

From the **train station**, at the northern end of Széchenyi utca, it's a ten-minute walk down to Március 15 tér, while the **bus station**, on Szent István tér, is a few minutes closer to the main square. Disembarking at the landing stage for **ferries** from Budapest, you can see the prison and triumphal arch to the north; head south along the promenade and the town centre is on the left, up Eszterházy utca as you reach the wharf for **ferries to Szentendre Sziget** (hourly; 400Ft for passengers, 1400Ft for a car; last ferry leaves around 9pm). From the ferry you can walk across the island to Tahitótfalu (4km), or take the waiting bus.

The super-helpful Tourinform, at Március 15 tér 17 (July & Aug Mon–Fri 9am–7pm, Sat & Sun 10am–6pm; rest of year Mon–Fri 9am–5pm, Sat 10am–noon; ☎27/316-160, ⓦwww.tourinformvac.hu), has all the **information** you need, both on the town and other attractions along the east bank. The **post office**

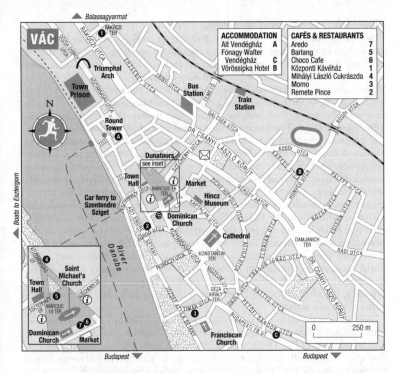

is at Posta park 2 (Mon–Fri 8am–7pm, Sat 8am–noon) and there's **internet** access at Matrix, Rév Köz 2 (daily 9am–10pm, Fri & Sat 9am–midnight).

Accommodation

For a reasonably large town, Vác has surprisingly little **accommodation**, so you might wish to opt for a private room (②), bookable through Dunatours at Széchenyi utca 14 (Mon–Fri 8am–4pm, Sat 8am–noon; ☎27/310-950, ✉info @dunatours.com). The only hotel in town is the *Vörössipka*, a ten-minute walk east of Március 15 tér at Honvéd utca 14 (☎27/501-055, ⊛www .vorossipkahotel.hu; ⑥–⑦), which has slick, heavily wood-furnished rooms, all with wi-fi, each priced according to size and whether they're street facing (which are quite noisy) or not. Otherwise, two very comfortable and extremely friendly places are the four-room *Alt Vendégház*, Tabán utca 25 (☎27/316-860, ✉altvendeghaz@invitel.hu; ④), and the *Fónagy Walter Vendégház* at Budapest fő út 36, ten minutes south of the main square (☎27/310-682, ✉fonwal @freemail.hu; ④), with its own wine cellar and leafy courtyard restaurant where you can taste and buy Hungarian wines.

The Town

The heart of town is Március 15 tér, a beautiful, wide open square containing numerous buildings of architectural interest and a fascinating museum. From here narrow streets and steps on one side lead down to the river, ferries and the riverside promenade, with the prison and Triumphal Arch to the north, while to the south stands the town's enormous cathedral.

Március 15 tér and around

One of the most eye-catching squares in the entire country, **Március 15 tér** is a perfect triangular wedge framed by a handsome melange of sunny, pastel-coloured Baroque and Rococo buildings. At its heart are the recently excavated ruins of **St Michael's Church** (Szent Mihály temploma), which had developed piecemeal since its thirteenth-century origins. What you see now – foundation walls, sections of nave and parts of a crypt – dates mainly from the eighteenth century; the crypt itself can be visited in summer (May–Sept Tues–Sun 10am–5pm; 300Ft). The Baroque style evolved into a fine art here, as evinced by the gorgeous decor of the **Dominican church** (Fehérek temploma) – also known as the White Friar's Church – on the south side of the square. During renovation work in 1994, the church crypt was rediscovered, unearthing some remarkable finds, not least 262 corpses (166 of which were positively identified) which had been preserved in a state of mummification owing to the crypt's microclimatic conditions. Three of the mummified corpses (a male, female and infant) – dating from the eighteenth century – are now on display in a chilly medieval cellar located opposite the church at no. 19, otherwise known as the **Memento Mori Museum** (Tues–Sun 10am–6pm; 1000Ft); also retrieved from the bodies were an immaculately preserved assortment of clothes and other burial accessories (including crucifixes, which were traditionally placed in the hands of the deceased), alongside their colourfully painted wooden coffins – typically, the adult coffin would be painted brown or dark blue, and the child's coffin green and white.

Elsewhere on the square, at no. 6 stands the original Bishop's Palace, converted into Hungary's first Institute for the Deaf and Dumb in 1802. It was Bishop Kristóf Migazzi (1714–1803) who erected Vác's cathedral (see below) and the Baroque **Town Hall** across the square, its gable adorned with two prostrate females bearing the coats of arms of Hungary and of Migazzi himself. During his years as Bishop of Vác (1762–86), this ambitious prelate was the moving force behind the town's eighteenth-century revival, impressing Empress Maria Theresa sufficiently to make him Archbishop of Vienna.

There's a colourful and lively **market** (Mon–Sat 8am–2pm) selling flowers, fruit and vegetables in the side street behind the Dominican church, and further down, at Káptalan utca 16, the **Hincz Museum** (Tues–Sun: April–Oct 10am–6pm; Nov–March 10am–4pm; 500Ft) gives a brief overview of the town's history, including some excellent photos. You will also find works by the local artist who gives his name to the museum upstairs on one side of the entrance, and temporary displays on the other side.

The cathedral

A short walk further down Káptalan utca brings you to the back of Vác's **cathedral** (Székesegyház; March–Nov Mon–Sat 10am–noon & 1.30–6pm, Sun 7.30am–7pm) on Konstantin tér. Chiefly impressive for its gigantic Corinthian columns, Migazzi's church is a temple to self-esteem more than anything else. Its Neoclassical design by Isidore Canevale was considered revolutionary in the 1770s, the style not becoming generally accepted in Hungary until the following century. Migazzi himself took umbrage at one of the frescoes by Franz Anton Maulbertsch, and ordered *The Meeting of Mary and Elizabeth*, above the altar, to be bricked over. His motives for this are unknown, but one theory is that it was because Mary was depicted as being pregnant. The fresco was only discovered during restoration work in 1944. From the cathedral you can head along Múzeum utca to Géza király tér, the centre of Vác in medieval times, where there's a Baroque **Franciscan church** with a magnificent organ, pulpits and altars.

Along the waterfront to the prison

From the Franciscan church you can follow the road down to the **riverside promenade**, József Attila sétány, where the townsfolk of Vác walk on summer weekends and evenings. The northern stretch of the promenade, named after Liszt, runs past the **Round Tower**, the only remnant of Vác's medieval fortifications. Beyond the dock for ferries to Budapest and Esztergom rises the forbidding hulk of the town's **prison**. Ironically, the building was originally an academy for noble youths, founded by Maria Theresa. Turned into a barracks in 1784 – you can still see part of the older building peering awkwardly above the blank white walls of the prison – it began its penal career a century later, achieving infamy during the Horthy era, when two Communists died here after being beaten for going on hunger strike to protest against maltreatment. Later, victims of the Stalinist period were imprisoned here, but in October 1956 a mass escape occurred. Thrown into panic by reports from Budapest where their colleagues were being "hunted down like animals, hung on trees, or just beaten to death by passers-by", the ÁVO guards donned civilian clothing and mounted guns on the rooftop, fomenting rumours of the Uprising among prisoners whose hopes had been raised by snatches of patriotic songs overheard from the streets. A glimpse of national flags with the Soviet emblem cut from the centre provided the spark: a guard was overpowered, locks were shot off, and the prisoners burst free. Edith Bone was an inmate at the time, an English journalist who had been accused of spying and imprisoned for fifteen years in 1949. Robert Maxwell was also imprisoned here during World War II, accused of spying, then using his original name of Ludvik Hoch.

The **Triumphal Arch** (kőkapu) flanking the prison was another venture by Migazzi and his architect Canevale, occasioned by Maria Theresa's visit in 1764. Migazzi initially planned theatrical facades to hide the town's dismal housing (perhaps inspired by Potemkin's fake villages in Russia, created around the same time), but settled for the Neoclassical arch, from which Habsburg heads grimace a stony welcome.

Eating, drinking and entertainment

Whereas the medieval traveller Nicolaus Kleeman found Vác's innkeepers "the quintessence of innkeeperish incivility", modern visitors should find things have improved. The town's best **restaurant** is the ⚔ *Remete Pince*, at Fürdő utca 16, an elegant brick-vaulted cellar with candle-topped tables and wrought-iron chairs, while the flower-bedecked terrace is lovely in warmer weather. On Március 15 tér, *Aredo* is a contemporary restaurant whose varied meat dishes (filet mignon, saddle of lamb, venison stew in red wine) are superb – the two-course set lunch (700Ft) is very good value; and, in a cellar down some steps in the very centre of the square, the *Barlang* is a neon-lit place with red leather seating serving pizza. Down by the river, at Tímár utca 9, is *Momo*, where you can dine on baked and grilled fish on one of the restaurant's three levels of terracing.

You'll find few, if any, lively **drinking** spots in town, but do check out the exquisite *Choco Café* (open till 8pm), next to the *Aredo* restaurant, where you can mull over a long menu of chocolate drinks in every conceivable flavour, such as almond, cinnamon, and orange and nutmeg; and the *Mihályi László Cukrászda*, a tiny, salon-like place at Köztársaság út 21 (open till 6pm) with a toothsome selection of the most perfectly formed cakes.

Vác's major annual **festival** is the three-day Váci Világi Vigalom (literally, the Vác Secular Entertainment, though why secular no one seems able to say) at the end of July, which includes folk, rock and pop music and exhibitions, and takes place on Március 15 tér and down by the river.

Vácrátót

VÁCRÁTÓT, 35km from the centre of Budapest in the hinterland of Vác, has one of Hungary's best-known **botanical gardens** (Botanikus kert; daily: April–Oct 8am–6pm; Nov–March 8am–4pm; 700Ft; ⓦwww.botkert.hu). Founded in the 1870s by Count Vigyázó, it was subsequently bequeathed by him to the Hungarian Academy of Sciences. Complete with waterfalls and mock ruins, the garden contains thousands of different trees and shrubs from around the world, covering 2.3 square kilometres and taking a good two hours to walk round. On some Saturday evenings in the summer, concerts are held on the lawns in front of the former manor house, with a backdrop of tall copper beeches on one side and a lake on the other. Tickets (around 2000Ft) are available from Tourinform in Vác (see p.172)

Motorists can reach Vácrátót from Budapest by turning east off Route 2, north of Sződliget (about 5km before Vác). Although the village is accessible by **train** from Nyugati Station in Budapest, the station is 3km away from the gardens and connecting coaches can be unreliable. Hourly **buses** from the northern end of the blue metro (Újpest) in Budapest and from Vác stop directly outside the gardens.

Nagymaros and Zebegény

The north bank of the Danube gradually becomes steeper as you head towards two settlements, **Nagymaros** and **Zebegény**, both of which merit attention for their atmosphere and as starting points for reaching the Börzsöny hills.

Nagymaros

Twenty kilometres west from Vác along the bank of the Danube, **NAGYMAROS**, the home of nobles in the age of royal Visegrád, is a quietly prosperous village with an air of faded grandeur. The village lies across the river from Visegrád, with a superb view of the latter's citadel: "Visegrád has the castle, but Nagymaros has the view", as the locals have always boasted.

The railway line cuts the village firmly in two; above the line, whitewashed houses straggle up the hillside, while below is the main road, and beyond that the river and **ferry** to Visegrád (passengers 400Ft, cars 800Ft). From the Nagymaros-Visegrád **train station**, duck under the bridge and walk past the *Mátyás Király Restaurant* to the main road, Váci utca; 100m to the right is the leafy main square, Fő tér, itself bisected by Váci utca. At the bottom half of Fő tér, in a renovated building near the river, is an **exhibition** (Sat & Sun noon–6pm; 500Ft) honouring the renowned Hungarian explorer and biologist, Kálmán Kittenburger (1881–1958). Born in Léva (in present-day Slovakia), Kittenburger repeatedly visited Africa where he amassed thousands of items including many new animal species. Although a handful of items are on show here – including, somewhat bizarrely, an elephant's foot that has been forged into a small drinks holder – most of the exhibits are personal effects, such as rifles, chests, boots and walking sticks.

At the top of Fő tér, on the other side of the rail line, is a **Gothic church**, parts of which date back to 1509 – although it's usually closed, take a look at the fine stone portal presaging the nave, and the rib-vaulted ceiling with frescoes. After 1500m, the path divides at a car park – one fork heads south to Hegyes-tető, where you can enjoy a **panoramic view of the Bend**, while the other heads up into **the Börzsöny**, towards Törökmez, a five-kilometre walk away along a footpath marked with red signs.

If you're looking to stay over, the *Szent István Fogadó*, 300m south of the ferry dock at Váci utca 36 (☎27/594-090, ✉info@szentistvanfogado.hu; ❺), is a smart eight-room guesthouse with fresh, air-conditioned rooms. Otherwise, you'll likely find some private **accommodation** by wandering the streets in search of *Zimmer frei* signs, or you can head up through the beech woods to the unassuming but picturesquely located *Törökmező Hostel* (☎27/350-063; dorm bed 2000Ft). Although it looks rather undistinguished from the outside, the red-brick *Maros* **restaurant**, right next to the ferry dock, has good Hungarian food and pizzas, and terrific river views from its terrace.

Zebegény

At **ZEBEGÉNY**, 5km further along the bank of the river, where the Danube turns south, the excellent light and the magnificent view of the Bend have lured painters for years. Most of this exceptionally pretty village lies to the east of the rail tracks. From Route 12 you pass under the train station and immediately come to the distinctive **Catholic Church** (1908–14), the only one in Hungary to be built in the National Romantic style, an amalgam of Art Nouveau and folk art, designed by Károly Kós. Inside, frescoes by Aladár Körösfői Kriesch depict Emperor Constantine's vision of finding the Holy Cross in Jerusalem with his mother, St Helena. Five minutes' walk behind the church over the stream and down to the right brings you to one of Zebegény's curiosities, the so-called **Sailing History Museum** at Szőnyi utca 9 (Hajózástörténeti Múzeum; April–Oct daily 9am–6pm; 600Ft), housing the bizarre private collection of Captain Vince Farkas, who has sailed the world and amassed some nifty carved figureheads in the process (though how tigers and totem poles fit in is a puzzle). Following Szőnyi utca for another ten minutes brings you to Bartóky utca, where, at no. 7, you'll find the **István Szőnyi memorial house** (Szőnyi István Emlékmúzeum; Jan–Oct Tues–Sun 10am–4pm; 400Ft), home of the eponymous artist for much of his life. Szőnyi (1894–1960) initially honed his artistic skills under the tutelage of Károly Ferenczy (see p.153) in Budapest, before settling in Zebegény where he worked on graphics, etchings and oil paintings. Each summer, the house hosts an international **art school**.

▲ Catholic Church, Zebegény

There's a good sprinkling of **accommodation** here; crossing the bridge behind the church, take a left along Kossuth utca for ten minutes, then another left, to reach the *Malomkerék Vendégház* at Malom utca 21 (☎27/373-010; ❸–❹), which has well-kept rooms and a couple of equally pleasant apartments; it also acts as the **information office** for the village, in addition to having bicycles and canoes available for rent. Twenty minutes' walk further on, turn right at the end of the village to get to the *Almáskert Panzió* at Almáskert utca 13 (☎27/373-037; ❷), whose timber-balconied rooms overlook a neat lawn. Around 1km to the south of the village, on the main road to Vác at Dózsa György út 26, is the *Kenderes Hotel* (☎27/373-444, ✉kendereshotel@invitel.hu; ❹) which, though a little tired, is decent enough and has rooms overlooking the Danube. Both the *Almáskert* and *Kenderes* have decent **restaurants**, the latter serving some Balkan and Transylvanian dishes.

The Börzsöny range

The **Börzsöny range**, squeezed between the Danube and Slovakia, sees few visitors despite its scattering of hostels and forest footpaths, and its abundance of rabbits, pheasants and deer is watched only by circling eagles. It's feasible to camp rough here, though most of the places covered below offer some form of accommodation. Would-be walkers should buy Cartographia's *Börzsöny-hegység* map of the hills (available at the Tourinform office in Vác or from map shops), which shows paths and the location of hostels (*túristaház*).

Mount Csóványos (939m) is the highest peak in the Börzsöny, and also the most challenging. Hikers usually approach it from the direction of **DIÓSJENŐ**, a sleepy mountain village that's accessible by bus or train from Vác. Diósjenő's **campsite** (☎35/364-134; May–Sept), at Petőfi Sándor utca 61, lies just over 1km from the village and 2km from the train halt. Close by, at no. 73, is the *Play Panzió* (☎35/364-466, ✉info@play-panzio.hu; ❸), with simple, bright rooms, and there's a pizzeria here too.

An alternative route into the mountains begins at Kismaros, 12km up the Danube from Vác. From here **narrow-gauge trains** trundle to **KIRÁLYRÉT** (April–Oct 5 daily; Nov–March 4 daily Sat & Sun only; 55min), with connecting trains to and from Budapest from the main-line station across the road. Close to the station is the *Fővárosi Önkormányzat Üdülője*, a hostel with cheap beds (☎27/375-033; dorm bed 2500Ft), and you can eat cheaply at the local restaurant. Supposedly once the hunting ground of Beatrice and Mátyás, this "Royal Meadow" has paths going in several directions. One trail, marked in green, goes across to the village of Nógrád with its ruined castle, 5km from Diósjenő on the Diósjenő–Vác railway line. Another, marked in red, leads to the Magas-Tax peak about ninety minutes' walk away, with another cheap hostel, the *Magas Tax Turistaház* (☎60/346-150; dorm bed 2500Ft). The path goes on to the "Big Cold" peak, **Nagy Hideg Hegy**, which has excellent views, and branches out to Mount Csóványos and the villages of Nagybörzsöny and Kóspallag; use the *Börzsöny-hegység* map to guide you.

Nagybörzsöny, Kóspallag and Márianosztra

From Nagy Hideg Hegy, a trail marked by blue squares leads westwards to **NAGYBÖRZSÖNY**. You can also get here by bus from Szob and make this your starting point for walking east. A wealthy town during the Middle Ages, Nagybörzsöny declined with the depletion of its copper, gold and iron mines in

The main claim to fame of Szob, the last town on the Hungarian north bank of the river, is as the border crossing for trains to Slovakia. Crossing into Slovakia by road is either unnecessarily long or overcomplicated depending on how you choose to do it: you can either take the ferry from Szob across the Danube to Basaharc, travel 12km up the road to Esztergom, and there catch another ferry back across to Slovakia; or you drive 30km north to Parassapuszta on the Ipoly River, which demarcates the frontier. The neighbouring village of Drégelypalánk, 7km away, is on the Vác–Diósjen–Balassagyarmat train line (trains roughly every 2hr). The crossing at Letkés/Salka can be used only by Hungarians and Slovakians.

the eighteenth century, and is now a mere logging village with an overdose of churches – four in all. The walled thirteenth-century Romanesque **Church of St Stephen**, on the left as you enter the village, was left stranded as the cemetery chapel when the village moved closer to the mines in the fifteenth century. If you are walking from the centre of the village, stop in at Petőfi utca 17 en route to ask for the gigantic church key, as the church is normally closed. Just across the road from the house is the Gothic **Miners' Church**, some of whose features have survived later alterations; again, if the church is closed, ask at Petőfi utca 17. Just below the church, an exhibition of folk costumes, home furnishings and mining accessories can be found at the **Mining Museum** at Petőfi utca 19 (Tues–Sun 10am–4pm; 200Ft), with explanations in Hungarian and German only, but you get the general feel anyway. Just up from the main square, where the bus terminus is located, you will find the village's still-working, nineteenth-century **watermill** (vizimalom; Tues–Sun 10am–4pm; 100Ft). For **accommodation**, there are basic doubles (shared bathrooms) at the *Butella Vendégház* (☎27/378-035; ❷), just above the main road near the Romanesque church; or a ten-minute walk along the track past the wine bar leads down to the *Nagybörzsöny Község Vendégház*, by a fishing lake – a rather out-of-the-way site where you can get a room (☎27/377-450; ❷). Otherwise it is worth asking in the village about private rooms.

The other trail from Nagy Hideg Hegy (marked with a blue horizontal line) runs south down to **KÓSPALLAG**, another prosaic village, notable only as a place to catch **buses** to Vác (6 daily; last bus at 3pm). However, pursuing the path onwards, things improve beyond the Vác–Szob road junction below the village, where the path wanders through beech woods to a lovely open meadow graced with a solitary tree and the first view of the Danube. Cutting southwest across the meadow puts you back on the path to the *Törökmező Hostel* (see p.177). The path divides by the exercise camp in the woods, and heading west along the path marked with green signs you come down to Zebegény (5km). Alternatively, you can head on another 4km along the blue path, past the hostel, to a car park at the junction of paths to Hegyes-tető (Hilly Peak) and Nagybörzsöny.

If you take the road from Kóspallag to Szob, you come to **MÁRIANOSZTRA**, a place of pilgrimage 9km from Szob and served by hourly buses. These **pilgrimages** take place on the second Sunday in May, and on the Sundays preceding August 15 and September 14. The Baroque church in the centre of the village (now in the courtyard at the entrance of a men's prison) dates from 1360, and retains some original fragments. One curiosity is the copy of the *Black Czestochowa Madonna*, the original of which was taken to Poland in 1382 by Hungarian monks sent to found the monastery there. An hour's walk north from the village takes you to **Kopasz hegy** (Bald Hill), which affords some of the best views in the region.

Travel details

Trains

Esztergom to: Budapest (hourly; 1hr 30min); Komárom (4 daily; 1hr 30min).

Vác to: Balassagyarmat (10 daily; 2hr 10min); Budapest (every 30min; 45min); Diósjenő (12 daily; 50min); Nagymaros (every 30min–1hr; 20min).

Vácrátót to: Aszód (5 daily; 30min); Budapest (hourly; 1hr 10min); Vác (hourly; 15min).

Buses

Esztergom to: Budapest via the Bend (every 30–40min; 1hr 15min) or via Dorog (every 30min; 1hr); Komárom (5 daily; 1hr 30min); Szentendre (hourly; 1hr 30min); Visegrád (hourly; 40min).

Pomáz to: Dobogókő (Mon–Fri every 30min–1hr, Sat & Sun hourly; 40min).

Szentendre to: Budapest (every 30min–1hr; 30min); Esztergom (hourly; 1hr 30min); Pomáz (every 20–30min; 10min); Visegrád (hourly; 40min).

Szob to: Nagybörzsöny (hourly; 35min).

Vác to: Balassagyarmat (hourly; 1hr); Budapest (every 30min–1hr; 30min); Diósjenő (Mon–Fri 8 daily, Sat 2 daily; 1hr); Kóspallag (Mon–Fri 6 daily, Sat & Sun 2 daily; 90min); Vácrátót (Mon–Fri hourly, Sat & Sun 2 daily; 45min); Nagymaros (hourly; 30min).

Visegrád to: Budapest (every 30min–1hr; 1hr); Dömös (hourly; 15min); Esztergom (hourly; 40min).

Ferries

The following ferries operate April to September.
Basaharc to: Szob (hourly; 10min).

Esztergom to: Budapest (1 daily; 4hr 30min); Štúrovo, Slovakia (hourly; 10min); Szentendre (2 daily; 1hr 25min); Vác (1 daily; 2hr 30min); Visegrád (1–2 daily; 1hr 25min).

Kismaros to: Kisoroszi (every 30min–1hr 30min; 10min).

Leányfalu to: Pócsmegyer (every 30min–1hr; 10min).

Nagymaros to: Visegrád (hourly; 10min).

Pilismarót to: Zebegény (hourly; 10min).

Szob to: Basaharc (hourly; 10min).

Tahitótfalu to: Vác (hourly; 10min).

Vác to: Budapest (1 daily; 1hr 20min); Esztergom (1 daily; 2hr 30min); Tahitótfalu (hourly; 10min).

Visegrád to: Budapest (1 daily; 3hr 30min); Esztergom (1–2 daily; 1hr 45min); Kisoroszi (2 daily; 20min); Nagymaros (hourly; 10min); Vác (1 daily; 45min); Zebegény (1–2 daily; 50min).

Riverboats

Unless otherwise stated, the following riverboats operate a daily service June through August, with a Saturday and Sunday service in May and September.

Esztergom to: Budapest (4hr); Vác (2hr 15min); Visegrád (1hr 30min).

Szentendre to: Budapest (May–Sept Mon–Fri 1 daily, Sat & Sun 2 daily, April & Oct Sat & Sun 1 daily; 1hr 30min–2hr); Visegrád (May–Aug 1 daily, April & Sept–Oct Sat & Sun 1 daily; 2hr).

Vác to: Budapest (1hr 45min); Esztergom (2hr 15min); Visegrád (45min).

Visegrád to: Budapest (2hr 30min); Esztergom (2hr); Szentendre (May–Aug 1 daily, April & Sept–Oct Sat & Sun 1 daily; 1hr 30min); Vác (45min).

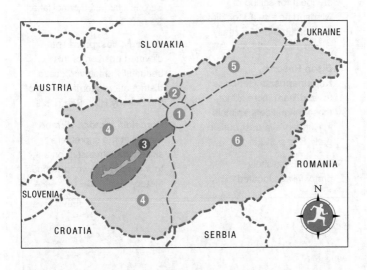

3

Lake Balaton and the Bakony

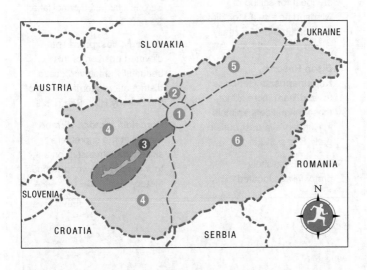

CHAPTER 3 # Highlights

* **Bory's Castle, Székesfehérvár** Take a wander around this marvellously eccentric mid-twentieth-century suburban folly. See p.192

* **Watersports on Lake Balaton** The clean, shallow waters of Lake Balaton are ideal for sailing or windsurfing – head for Siófok, Balatonfüred or Keszthely. See p.195, p.205 & p.216

* **Bison Reserve, Kápolnapuszta** Get close to, and learn more about, these magnificent animals in Hungary's largest buffalo park. See p.202

* **Tihany** Exquisitely pretty village located in Hungary's first national park. See p.209

* **Model Railway Museum, Keszthely** Just one of several highly engaging museums in Balaton's most charming lakeside town. See p.220

* **Thermal lake, Hévíz** Wallow in temperatures of 30°C in Europe's largest thermal lake. See p.222

* **Várhegy, Veszprém** The elevated position of this beautifully preserved castle district affords terrific views of the Bakony Hills. See p.229

* **Porcelain factory, Herend** Marvel at the supremely skilled craftsmanship on a tour around the world-famous factory. See p.233

▲ Taking the plunge at Lake Balaton

Lake Balaton
and the Bakony

Lake Balaton, affectionately known to Hungarians as "Balcsi", is the nation's substitute for a coastline. Millions of people come here every summer to enjoy the lake's remarkably clean, milky green waters, which, with an average depth of only 3m, are warm enough to swim in from May to October. Though few would subscribe to the old romantic view of Balaton as the "Hungarian sea", it is still the largest freshwater lake in Europe – nearly 80km long and varying in width from 14km to a mere 1.5km at the point where the lake is almost cut in two by the Tihany peninsula – and all that remains of the ancient Pannonian Sea that once covered the region.

Though its **history** is hardly writ large, the region was first settled in the Iron Age, and has been a wine-growing centre since Roman times. During the sixteenth century, it formed the front line between Turkish and Habsburg-ruled Hungary, with an Ottoman fleet based at Siófok and an Austrian one at Balatonfüred. Spas and villas began to appear from 1765 onwards, but catered largely to the wealthy until the Communists began promoting holidays for the masses after World War II. During the 1960s, footloose youths started flocking here, and in the 1970s and 1980s there was a boom in private holiday homes and room-letting, fuelled by an influx of tourists from Germany and Austria. Today, visitors from these two countries still provide the bulk of tourists, although an increasing number of other foreigners are beginning to discover some of the undoubted charms of the lake, thanks in part due to the recent opening of the country's second civilian airport, Sármellék, near Keszthely. If visiting, it's best to do so outside July and August as this is the time when the natives descend upon the lake in their masses.

Balaton's low-lying **southern shore** is largely characterized by a continuous chain of fairly indistinguishable resorts, though it does boast brash and bustling **Siófok**, indisputably the lake's number-one party town, as well as some terrific wine regions a little further south. By contrast, waterfront development on the **northern shore** has been limited by reed beds and cooler, deeper water, and the attractions, such as the beautiful **Tihany peninsula**, elegant **Balatonfüred**, and the wine-producing **Badacsony Hills**, are of a less hedonistic bent, instead offering splendid scenery and sightseeing. The compact western end is perhaps the most appealing part of the lake, providing the setting for the delightful university town of **Keszthely**, the world's second-largest thermal lake at nearby **Hévíz** and

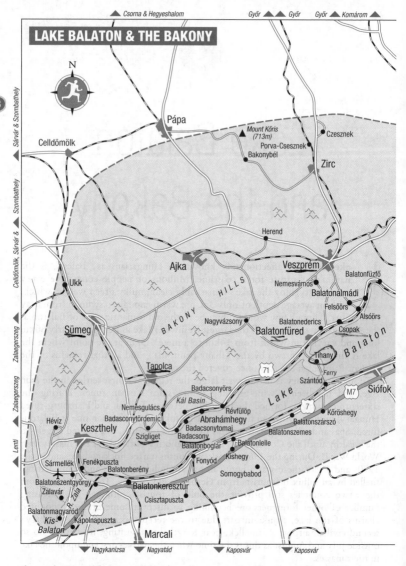

LAKE BALATON & THE BAKONY

the reedy **Kis-Balaton** nature reserve, home to a bison reserve and a superb venue for bird-watching.

Midway between Budapest and Balaton lies **Lake Velence**, a miniature version of Balaton, beyond which is **Székesfehérvár**, well worth a visit for its romantic Belváros (Inner Town) and "Bory's Castle". The thickly wooded **Bakony** region to the north of Balaton is dotted with picturesque villages and ruined castles, and is the setting for the historic towns of **Veszprém**, **Sümeg** and **Tapolca**, plus the world-famous porcelain factory at **Herend**.

Lake Balaton is easily accessible from Budapest and Transdanubia. **Trains** from Budapest's Déli Station run to all the main resorts, with daily InterCity services

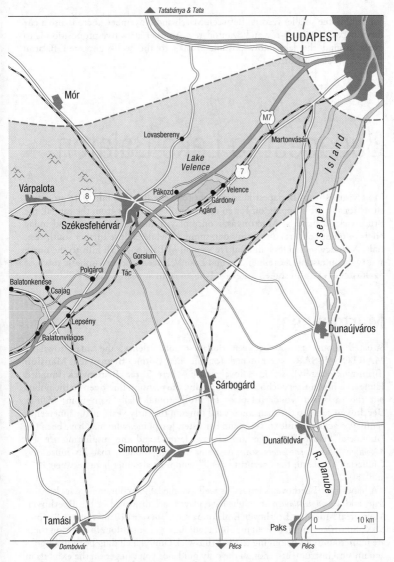

providing the fastest access to Keszthely (2hr 30min) via the southern shore. **Buses** to Székesfehérvár, Veszprém and Balaton leave from the Népliget depot. If you're driving to Balaton, the M7, which passes the north shore of Lake Velence then down along the southern shore of Balaton towards the Croatian border, is the quickest road; to get to the northern shore, turn off the M7 onto Route 71 for Balatonfüred.

A great way to see – and get around – the lake is by ferry. From mid-April to October, **passenger ferries** run from Siófok to Balatonfüred and Tihany on the opposite bank, and between Fonyód and Badascony and Keszthely. During July and August, a number of other services shuttle back and forth across the lake connecting the smaller resorts. Between March and November, there is also a **car ferry** between Tihany-rév and Szántód-rév. Another attractive proposition is to **cycle** around the lake, now possible thanks to the well-signposted Balaton cycleway (Balaton Kőrűt).

Budapest to Lake Balaton

Most visitors from Budapest head straight for Lake Balaton, but there are a few attractions worth stopping off for en route. Just half an hour from the capital, the Brunswick Mansion at **Martonvásár** once played host to Beethoven and today holds outdoor concerts of his music in summer, while, a little further southwest, **Lake Velence** resembles a diminutive version of Balaton, with hills to the north and two contrasting shorelines. Beyond Lake Velence is the atmospheric town of **Székesfehérvár**, and some impressive Roman ruins at nearby **Tác**.

Martonvásár

Situated about halfway between Budapest and Velence, the small town of **MARTONVÁSÁR** is renowned for the neo-Gothic **Brunswick Mansion** (Brunszvik Kastély), set in a lovely park where **Teréz Brunswick** founded Hungary's first nursery school in 1828; sadly, the mansion isn't open to the public but the park is a wonderful place to stroll around (daily 8am–6pm; 500Ft). **Beethoven** came to the mansion several times in the early years of the nineteenth century, teaching music to Teréz and her sister, Josephine, who may have been the "immortal beloved" of Beethoven's love letters, and the inspiration for his *Moonlight* and *Appassionata* sonatas. Some reckon, though, that his muse was Giulietta Guicciardi, the "beautiful devil" whom he also met here between 1800 and 1806.

A handful of Beethoven's letters, as well as a medallion containing a lock of his hair, and a *hammerklavier* he might have played, are displayed in the **Beethoven Memorial Museum** (Beethoven Emlékmúzeum; Tues–Fri 10am–noon & 2–4pm, Sat & Sun 10am–noon & 2–6pm; 500Ft) adjoining the mansion. In addition there are numerous items belonging to the Brunswick family, including portraits, books and musical instruments, though the only guidance you can get on the exhibits in English is a small leaflet sold at the ticket desk (50Ft). Housed in a small hut to the left of the mansion, the **Nursery Museum** (Óvodamúzeum; mid-March to Oct Tues–Fri 10am–2pm, Sat & Sun 11am–5pm; Nov to mid-March same hours but closes 3pm Sat & Sun; 350Ft) offers a cramped display of artefacts, including a row of enamel potties set in a wooden bench, and photos from the past 150 years illustrating Hungary's pioneering role in nursery education.

A more compelling reason to come to the mansion is for the **summer evening concerts**, held on an island in the middle of the park beneath a great bower of beech and sycamore. Armed with mosquito repellent and a couple of bottles from the bar-buffet, you can listen to the music as the sun sets through the trees. Tickets

(2000–3000Ft) are available from the booth at the park entrance, or from the Central Box Office.

Arriving by **train**, it's a ten-minute walk down Brunszvik utca to the park entrance, while **buses** drop you off at the post office by the traffic lights, from where it's a two-minute walk. Should you wish to **stay**, there are a couple of places on Budai út, the main road towards Budapest (turn left at the traffic lights up from the park): the very simple *Macska Pension* at no. 21 (①22/460-127; ❸), and the smart *Hotel Marton*, 450m further up at no. 83 (①22/460-342, ⓔinfo @hotelmarton.hu; ❺). The only **restaurant** here is *Postakocsi* at Fehérvári utca 1, on the corner of Dósza György út, leading up to the park.

Lake Velence

It's hard not to smile when told that Velence, 50km from Budapest and just 15km from Székesfehérvár, is the Hungarian name for Venice, though the town probably came by the name because Italian craftsmen working in Székesfehérvár lived here in the Middle Ages, rather than from any more romantic similarities. Today, the 26 square kilometres of **Lake Velence** (Velencei-tó) serves as a lesser Balaton, though its resort aspect is balanced by a strong wildlife presence. Reeds cover up to a half of the lake's surface, helping to maintain the quality of the water, and the western end is a nesting ground for some 30,000 **birds**, which migrate here in spring. According to legend, three sisters, who turned themselves into herons to escape the Turks, return home here every year. The lake itself is dotted with several resorts, with **Velence** to the east, and the conjoined settlements of **Agárd** and **Gárdony** on the southern shore, the most important destinations. The northern shore, meanwhile, contains more in the way of cultural and natural attractions.

Arrival and information

Arriving at the **southern shore**, orientation couldn't be easier: wherever you get off the **train**, simply head for the lake. The **northern shore** is accessible by hourly **buses** from Székesfehérvár or by **ferry** from Agárd (May to mid-June & Sept to mid-Oct Sat & Sun every 1hr 30min; mid-June to Aug daily hourly; 500Ft one way), which docks at the small peninsula, Szúnyog Sziget (Mosquito Island), near Pákozd.

Information can be obtained from three Tourinform offices on the lake; in Gárdony, at Szabadság utca 16 (mid-June to mid-Sept Mon–Fri 9am–6pm, Sat & Sun 10am–5pm; mid-Sept to mid-June Mon–Fri 9am–4pm; ①22/570-078, ⓔgardony@tourinform.hu), located across the road from the *Ponty* restaurant by the group of small apartment blocks; in Velence, at Halász utca 37 (same times; ①22/507-030, ⓔvelence@tourinform.hu); and at Pákozd (see p.189).

Accommodation

Like Balaton, Lake Velence closes down from October to April and is very busy the rest of the year, so it's worth booking accommodation in advance rather than just turning up. **Apartments**, **cottages** (❸–❹) and **private rooms** (❷) are bookable through Sol Tours in Gárdony, at Szabadság utca 12 (May–Sept Mon–Sat 9am–6pm; Oct–April Mon–Fri 9am–5pm; ①22/570-158, ⓦwww.soltours.hu) – they've also got an office in Velence at Ország utca 25 (April to mid-Oct Mon–Fri 9am–5pm, Sat 9am–1pm; ①22/470-497) – or you can rent direct from householders (look for *Zimmer frei* signs), although they may not be any cheaper than the rest of the accommodation on offer.

There are numerous **campsites** (all mid-April to mid-Oct), spread between the three resorts, the largest being *Panoráma Camping*, a lovely lakeside site on Kemping utca (☎22/472-043, Ⓦwww.campingpanorama.hu; chalets ❷) on the eastern shore, roughly 2km from Velence station; facilities include tennis courts, a minigolf course, water-bikes and restaurants. In Agárd, try *Park Strand Camping*, another large, well-equipped site located some 500m west of the train station at Chernel István út 56 (☎22/370-308), or the smaller *Termál Camping* (☎22/579-230), which also has a pension (❸) and is down by the resort's thermal baths on Határ utca (see below); guests qualify for reduced admission prices to the baths.

Hotel Helios Tópart utca 34 ☎22/589-330, Ⓦwww.hoteljuventus.hu. Just ten minutes' walk from Velence station and very near the lake, this pleasant small hotel has comfortable en-suite rooms plus its own pool. There's a free beach opposite, but you can use the *strand* and facilities of the nearby *Hotel Juventus*, run by the same people. May–Sept. ❻

Hotel Juventus Kis köz 6 ☎22/589-330, Ⓦwww .hoteljuventus.hu. Peaceful, unprepossessing lakeside hotel 5min on from the *Helios*, with smart, colourful and comfortable rooms; pool, sauna and tennis courts alongside its own bit of beach. ❻

Kis Szárcsa Vendégház Kazinczy utca 19 ☎22/579-979, Ⓦwww.kisszarcsa.hu. Super five-room guesthouse in a residential area down towards the thermal baths in Agárd, hence only really practical if you have your own transport; all rooms have TV, radio, DVD players and wi-fi. ❻

Touring Hotel Tópart utca 1 ☎22/370-019, Ⓦwww.touring.uw.hu. Small and friendly lakeside hotel a 10min walk west of Agárd station, beside the pier, with clean if somewhat dated rooms. Bikes, canoes and water-bikes can be rented here. May–Sept. ❺

The lake

The **southern and eastern shores** of the lake are one continuous strip of holiday homes and campsites, along an enclosed, mainly grassy, *strand*. If it weren't for the individually named train stations, **Velence**, **Gárdony** and **Agárd**, you'd never realize that there were three separate settlements along the shore. The **beaches** alternate between ones where you have to pay for a swim and the dubious privilege of using the changing rooms, and *szabad strand*, free ones with fewer facilities, such as the *strand* a few minutes' walk north of Velence train station in front of the *Hotel Helios*. **Watersport** facilities are widely available along this stretch of the lake, and it's an ideal spot to learn windsurfing as the water is only 1–2m deep, warming up to an acceptable 22–26°C over summer – the best place to start is the **water sports school** in Agárd, at Topárt utca 17 (☎22/370-052). In winter, the lake often freezes solid and ice-skating becomes the favoured sport. For something less energetic, you can always head for the **thermal baths** (Gyógy és Termálfürdő) in Agárd, 1km or so south of the lake at the end of Határ utca (daily 8am–9pm; 1700Ft, 1300Ft after 6pm).

The most interesting of the lake's sights are located on the less built-up **northern shore**, close to the peninsula where ferries dock (Szúnyog Sziget). A fifteen-minute walk along the road, then turning right up through the grassy path, brings you to **Mészeg Hill**, where an obelisk commemorates the Battle of Pákozd on September 29, 1848, the first Hungarian victory of the 1848–49 Revolution – there are some fine views of the lake and its extensive reed beds from this elevated position. In the building close by, there's a small **museum** (March–Oct Tues–Sun 10am–6pm; 600Ft) exhibiting various paraphernalia from the battlefield, as well as some photos of the unveiling of the obelisk in 1951, in addition to a Tourinform office, and a café (both same hours) serving light snacks.

A ten-minute walk downhill brings you to the **Don Chapel**, a memorial to the Hungarian soldiers who died in Russia during World War II, fighting on the side of the Nazis. This canopy-chapel is designed to ease an old wound for

Hungarians, who lost over 100,000 men in Russia, mainly at the River Don, but were unable to mourn them during the Communist era. Just below the chapel is the **Pákozd-Sukoró Arborétum** (April–Oct Tues–Sun 10am–6pm; 300Ft), a rather dreary collection of local trees, plants and rocks. A better reason for heading this way is to climb the wooden lookout tower (*kilátó*), which affords some splendid views of the lake and the Velence hills, some of the oldest in Hungary, formed from magma and granite. There is more geology above the village of **PÁKOZD**, thirty minutes' walk under the motorway and left along the main road. Turning off the main road just past another 1848 monument, it's a stiff walk up the 241-metre-high **Pogány-kő** (Pagan Rock), where several colossal "rocking stones" (*ingókővek*) – blocks of granite polished in the shapes of various animals – sway perceptibly in the wind.

Eating

The best of the lake's **restaurants** are in Agárd, though there's little to distinguish between them; schnitzels and stews are the order of the day, alongside the lake's main fish, *fogas* (pike-perch), which is typically rolled in flour and paprika then fried. The *Gulyás Csárda*, just up from the train station on the main road, Balatoni utca, is the most personable place, with lots of wooden bench seating, chunky tables and peasant-like furnishings spread along the walls. Just across the road, the much larger *Nádas Csárda* does a good job of reeling in the tourists, while the *Csutora*, a fifteen-minute walk west along the same road at no. 131, is of a similar bent but has a slightly more varied menu. In Gárdony, the popular *Ponty*, 100m left along the main road as you exit the station at Szabadság utca 9, has a good selection of fresh fish and salads.

Székesfehérvár and around

Reputedly the site where Árpád pitched camp and founded his dynasty, **SZÉKESFEHÉRVÁR**, 60km southwest of Budapest, was probably the first Hungarian town. Its name (pronounced "**saik**-esh-fehair-var") comes from the white castle (*fehérvár*) founded by Prince Géza, whose son Stephen made it his royal seat (*szék*). As the centre of his efforts to civilize the Magyars, it was named in Latin "Alba Civitas" or "Alba Regia". Since this medieval town was utterly destroyed by the Turks, Székesfehérvár today owes its Belváros to the Habsburgs, and its high-rise suburbs to the final German counterattack in 1945, which levelled almost everywhere else. The town's narrow winding streets, its diverse museums and galleries, and the wonderful suburban folly known as **Bory's Castle**, make it fully deserving of a visit. A particularly good time to be here is for the **Royal Days International Folk Dance Festival**, a week-long jamboree of music and dance taking place in mid-August.

Arrival and information

Székesfehérvár's **train station** is 1km south of the centre; catch any bus heading up Prohászka Ottakár út, which subsequently becomes Várkörút, and get off near the Romkert. The well-run **bus station** is more conveniently located on Piac tér, just a few minutes' walk from the Belváros. The very helpful Tourinform, inside the Hiemer House at Városház tér 1 (mid-May to mid-Sept Mon–Fri 9am–6pm, Sat & Sun 9am–4pm; mid-Sept to mid-May Mon–Fri 9am–5pm; ☏22/537-261, Ⓦwww.tourinform-fejer.hu), has lots of good

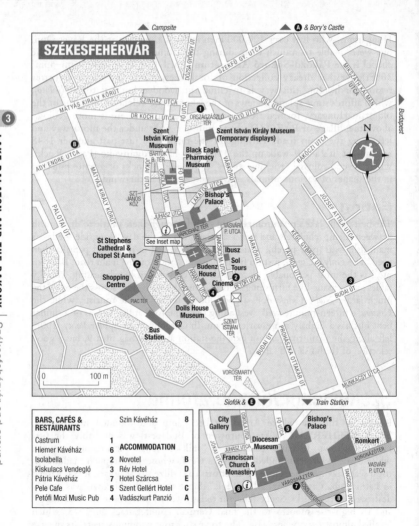

information to hand. The **post office** is on Szent István tér (Mon–Fri 8am–7pm) and there's **internet** access at *Cafe 19*, on the second floor of the bus station building (Mon–Sat 9am–10pm, Sun till 8pm).

Accommodation

Székesfehérvár has a limited but decent stock of **hotels**, all fairly well scattered around town. Alternatively, **private rooms** (❷) can be booked through Sol Tours, Kossuth utca 10 (June–Aug Mon–Fri 9am–6pm, Sat & Sun 9am–5pm; Sept–May Mon–Fri 9am–5pm; ☎22/385-321, Ⓦwww.soltours.hu), while Tourinform can advise on **college** accommodation (❶–❷) over the summer and at weekends throughout the year – most colleges, though, are on the outskirts of town. The *Ifjúsági* **campsite** is at Bregyó köz 1 (☎22/313-433; May–Sept), about fifteen minutes' walk north of the centre (or buses #12 and #14).

Novotel Ady Endre utca 19–21 ☎22/534-300, ⒲www.novotel-szekesfehervar.hu. Efficient, business-like chain hotel featuring all the requisite four-star comforts, including pristine rooms with a/c, internet, and tea-making facilities. Excellent buffet breakfast. ➑

Rév Hotel József Attila utca 42 ☎22/327-015, ⒻF327-061. This *üdülőház* (workers' hotel), 500m east of the centre, has ten rooms, all extremely basic and with washbasin only, available throughout the year. ➋

Hotel Szárcsa Szárcsa utca 1 ☎22/325-700, ⒲www.szarcsa.hu. Despite its unsightly location 1.5km south of town, this is easily the classiest place going; the rooms, coloured in deep greens and reds, come with gorgeous, wood-carved antique and period furnishings, and there's also an outdoor pool, steam bath and jacuzzi. ➑

Szent Gellért Hotel Mátyás király körút 1 ☎22/510-810, Ⓔszentgellert@axelero.hu. Bright hotel in a cracking location near the bus station and Belváros, containing a good mix of doubles and triple rooms, as well as dorms sleeping up to six. Dorm beds ➋, doubles ➎

Vadászkurt Panzió Berényi út 1 ☎22/507-514, ⒲www.jagerhorn.hu. Welcoming pension a short way north of the centre, containing good-sized rooms with lots of stripped pine, each with a kitchenette. Bus #26A from the bus station and #32 from the train station. ➎

The Town

The majority of Székesfehérvár's sights are within the immediate vicinity of the handsomely preserved **Belváros**, which occupies approximately the same area as the great castle once did. The one exception is **Bory's Castle**, though this is easily reached by bus.

Városház tér

Városház tér, the gorgeous, elongated main square, recalls Székesfehérvár's revival under Maria Theresa, with its Baroque town hall, Franciscan church and Zopf-style **Bishop's Palace** (Puspöki palota), built with stones from the ruined cathedral by Bishop Milassin, whose coat of arms appears on the gable. Opposite stands the eighteenth-century **Franciscan church and monastery**, on the corner of which is Megyessy's fine relief of warring Turks and Hungarians; the monastery houses the **Diocesan museum** (Egyházmegyei Múzeum; Mon–Sat 10am–6pm, Sun 2–6pm; 1000Ft), featuring a glittering array of reliquaries, cups and ciboria, sculptures and altar pieces, and a room dedicated to Ottokár Prohászka, the town's bishop from 1905 until his death in 1927; extolled as a theological modernist, Prohászka was no less renowned for his frequent anti-Semitic tirades.

A short walk east of the square, along pedestrianized Koronázó tér, brings you to the **Romkert** (Középkori Romkert; April–Oct Tues–Sun 9am–5pm; 600Ft), or "Garden of Ruins", which holds the excavated **foundations of the cathedral** where King Stephen was buried. Designed for him by Italian architects in an attempt to rival St Mark's in Venice, it hosted the coronations of 38 Hungarian kings. After the town fell to the Turks in 1543, the cathedral was plundered of its gold and jewels, and then blown up. In the mausoleum next to the entrance is a richly carved Roman sarcophagus found in 1803 and believed to hold the remains of King Stephen, minus his right hand which resides in St Stephen's Basilica in Budapest (see p.80). Unless you want to see the sarcophagus, you may as well save the entrance fee by viewing most of the ruins from Koronázó tér.

North of Városház tér

Running off to the north of Városház tér, **Fő utca** is so perfectly preserved that you expect to see crinoline-clad ladies emerging from the **Black Eagle Pharmaceutical Museum** at no. 5 (Fekete Sas Patika Múzeum; Tues–Sun 10am–6pm; 400Ft). The eighteenth-century pharmacy operated right up until 1971, and there remains much to see, not least the original Baroque wood-carved fixtures and fittings – made in the local Jesuit workshop in 1758 – and displays on traditional remedies, though the showpiece items are a splendid horseshoe-shaped Empire-style table complete with glass cabinets, and a medicine press.

Next to the Baroque church of St John across the street (also founded by the Jesuits) is the permanent collection of the **Szent István Király Museum** (Tues–Sun: May–Sept 10am–4pm; Oct–April 10am–2pm; 600Ft), a lively exhibition on local history featuring a superb collection of archeological finds and domestic treasures from the Neolithic period through to the time of Turkish rule. Especially notable is the hoard of Celtic goods, including pottery, urns and jewellery, and a stone dedication block featuring a relief of Mithras, the sun god, ritually slaying the bull. The museum also puts on temporary shows of contemporary Hungarian art at Országzászló tér 3, at the top of Fő utca (Tues–Sun 2–4pm; 260Ft).

Around the back of St John's Church, at Oskola utca 10, is the **City Gallery** (Városi Képtár; Tues–Sun: April–Oct 10am–6pm; Nov–March 9am–5pm; 800Ft), which has a brilliant display of nineteenth- and twentieth-century Hungarian art. The Deák Collection, which was bequeathed to the city by a local collector, is housed in three interconnecting medieval houses, with a labyrinth of small rooms exhibiting works by top Hungarian artists, such as Victor Vasarely, Rippl-Rónai, Jenő Barcsay and József Egry, whose typically warm Balaton scenes, *Greeting* and *Lake Balaton Region with a House*, are the highlights here. In the same block is a collection of sculptures by Erzsébet Schaár (same hours as the gallery; 400Ft); ask the people at the main desk to direct you to them.

South of Városház tér

More of the historic architecture is clustered south of Városház tér. Walking south down Arany János utca, you'll pass the hulking **St Stephen's Cathedral** (Szent István székesegyház), a much rebuilt Baroque edifice that dates back to the thirteenth century – crane your neck to view the impressive, oversized stone statues of Stephen, László and Imre. Standing in the cathedral's shadow is the **Chapel of St Anna**, the only remnant of medieval Székesfehérvár spared by the Turks, who put it to use as a mosque – notice the Koranic inscriptions and arabesque murals.

Continuing south along Arany János utca, you'll come to the fanciful Zopf-style **Budenz House** at no. 12 (Budenz ház; Tues–Sun: March–April & Oct 10am–2pm; May–Sept 10am–4pm; 500Ft), with a collection of beautiful old furniture and Hungarian art belonging to the Ybl family. The renowned architect Miklós Ybl (1814–91) was born here, and in one of the rooms downstairs you can see his drawing cabinet and photos of buildings he designed, including the Budapest Opera House (see p.85). The house itself is over two hundred years old and named after its former owner Budenz József, a researcher of Finno-Ugrian languages and founder of Hungarian comparative linguistics. Further down the street, a left turn takes you into **Petőfi utca**; a **plaque** on the wall of the cinema marks the house where the ubiquitous Sándor Petőfi lived for a couple of months at the end of 1842 as a travelling actor – it's now a popular jazz music club (see opposite). Close by, at Megyeház utca 17, the **Dolls' House Museum** (Fehérvári Babaház; March–Oct Tues–Sun 9am–5pm; 600Ft) features an exquisite collection of eighteenth-century dolls' houses and porcelain dolls, while, for the boys, there's a small assemblage of model toys.

Bory's Castle

The town's most popular, and curious, sight is **Bory's Castle** (Bory Vár; March–Nov daily 9am–5pm; 600Ft), situated out in the eastern suburbs at Máriavölgy utca 54, beyond the microchip and TV factories. An extraordinary and wildly eclectic structure combining features of Scottish, Romanesque and Gothic architecture, it was built between 1923 and 1959 in an ordinary suburban street by a group of students directed by the architect and sculptor **Jenő Bory** (1879–1959). Originally just a small cottage with a vineyard, Bory gradually enlarged the premises so as to include a gallery, loggia and a large courtyard spotted with numerous columns and towers. The castle's rooms (only open Sat & Sun 10am–noon & 3–5pm) are stuffed with paintings of Ilona Komocsin, Bory's wife, while the colourful gardens are filled with statues of Hungarian kings and other eminent characters. Although the overall effect of Ilona's multiple images is slightly morbid, the castle is a marvellous place to wander around and explore. **Buses** #26 and #26A from the bus station, and #32 from the train station, run regularly to the castle.

Eating and drinking

The town is not exactly blessed with an abundance of places to eat, though there are several **restaurants** worth investigating. The most interesting is the medieval-themed *Castrum* at Várkör út 3, where you can park yourself on a bench and tuck into stuffed, grilled and roast meat dishes and sup beer from ceramic jars. Elsewhere, the refined *Kiskulacs Vendéglő* at Budai út 26, with its elegant interior and rather more prosaic outdoor dining area, offers moderate to expensive Hungarian food plus an accomplished wine list, while *Isolabella*, in a small courtyard at Kossuth utca 14, is an imaginatively designed place with separate rooms for different cuisines (Mexican, Greek, Hungarian and Italian) and decor to match.

There are several enticing **drinking** possibilities on or around the fringes of Városház tér; for a daytime coffee, choose between the *Pátria Kávéház* at the square's southern end; the large, glass-fronted *Pele Cafe* at its northern end; or the cosy *Hiemer Cafe*, housed in the building of the same name next to Tourinform. The best evening venues, meanwhile, are the *Szín Kávéház* on Vasvári Pál utca (Mon–Sat till 1am, Sun till 10pm), with a terrific terrace overlooking the Romkert, and the groovy *Petőfi Mozi Music Pub*, Arany János utca 22 (Wed–Sat 6pm–2am; ⓦ www.petofimozi.org), where you can expect to hear live jazz at least two or three nights a week.

Tác

Tác, 10km south of Székesfehérvár and 3km off the M7 motorway, is the site of Hungary's largest archeological park; by **train** (6 daily) you'll need to get off at Szabadbattyán station and catch a local bus, or take a **bus** from Székesfehérvár's bus terminal (every 2hr) and alight in the centre of the village at the Soviet war memorial (a rare sight in Hungary now), where signs point towards the **Roman ruins of Gorsium**, twenty minutes' walk away (daily: April–Sept 10am–6pm; Oct–March 10am–4pm; 750Ft including entry to the museum). Gorsium began life as a military camp, but by the beginning of the second century had become the religious centre of Pannonia. Following heavy damage during the third century, Emperor Diocletian founded the city of Herculia over the ruins; it then remained a settlement of sorts until the late sixteenth century when it was finally destroyed by the Turks. Covering two square kilometres, the site has been under excavation since 1958, though to date barely a third has been uncovered. The foundations so far revealed include a palace, a temple, the forum, a theatre and a cemetery, with some well-preserved grave markers lining the paths of the site. It is worth getting a map at the entrance as it is hard to make sense of it otherwise. Carved stonework and other finds are displayed in a **museum** to the right of the entrance (same hours). The ruins host an annual **festival** called the "Floralia" at the end of April, which celebrates the arrival of spring; its highlights are a flower show, craft stalls, Greek plays and gladiatorial combat. Tickets (around 1500Ft) are available from Tourinform in Székesfehérvár (see p.189).

Lake Balaton: the southern shore

The **southern shore** of Lake Balaton is almost entirely built up, with an endless procession of *strand* – the generic term for any kind of bathing place. Hungarians call these **beaches**, though they are in fact grassy sunbathing areas with concrete embankments along the shoreline. While the discerning head for **Balatonvilágos**, the masses plump for **Siófok**, which has no peers when it comes to partying. In **Balatonszárszó** you can even find a touch of history, while the South Balaton wine route covers the region around the villages of **Balatonlelle**, **Balatonboglár** and **Kishegy**, which are also notable for their festivals. Nature only reasserts itself at the western end of the lake, where the River Zala flows through the reeds into the **Kis-Balaton** (Little Balaton) – the location for a bird and bison reserve. All the resorts along the southern shore are accessible by **train** from Budapest or Székesfehérvár.

Balatonvilágos

Approaching the southern shore by train, you'll catch your first glimpse of Balaton at **BALATONVILÁGOS**, a five-kilometre-long village that came into being following the amalgamation of two resorts, Aliga and Világos. Built on wooded cliffs along the shore, the village was once a favoured haunt of Party officials and boats were forbidden to dock in its harbour – even those seeking refuge from a storm. Today it is one of the lushest, least commercialized resorts around the lake, and whilst there's little in the way of genuine excitement here, decent, affordable accommodation abounds – useful if you're struggling to find anything in Siófok. Moreover, unlike many other resorts, it has what can be termed proper **beaches**; near the church on Zrínyi út is a paying beach (700Ft), while the free beach (*szabad strand*) is another 1km or so further on towards Balatonaliga.

Storm warnings

From May to September Balaton is prone to occasional **storms**. Twenty-four storm signalling stations dotted around the lake indicate when storms are approaching, or when the wind is getting up, via a series of yellow flashing lights: thirty flashes per minute indicates winds of 40–60km per hour; sixty flashes per minute means winds of over 60km per hour. In the case of sixty flashes per minute it is forbidden to enter the water and windsurfers or sailors should head for land at once.

The **Tourinform** office is at the eastern end of the resort in Balatonaliga, at Aligai út 1 (June–Aug daily 9am–5pm; Sept–May Mon–Fri 9am–1pm; ☎88/446-034, ⓔbalatonvilagos@tourinform.hu) – alighting at the Balatonaliga train station, walk down the road, turn left, and then left again under the bridge. Most of the **accommodation** is located towards the western end of the village, so alight at Balatonvilágos station and head down the steep road. The extremely pleasant *Napfény Hotel*, at Rákóczi út 12 (☎88/480-632; ❺), is by far the best place to stay, with nine intimate, air-conditioned rooms and a lovely lakeside beer garden. Five hundred metres further on, at no. 33, is the much larger but not quite as agreeable *Dalma Panzió* (☎88/480-883, ⓦwww.dalmapanzio.hu; ❺). There's plenty of dirt-cheap accommodation in several workers' hostels (all around 3000Ft for a dorm bed) along Rákóczi út and Zrínyi út, such as the *Aranyhid üdülő* (☎88/480-616), next door to the *Napfény Hotel*, and the *Kék-Balaton üdülő* at Zrinyi út 3 (☎88/480-827). Just up from the train station in Balatonaliga, the *Hársfa Vendégfogadó* (☎22/480-870; ❹) is a quiet little guesthouse and is just about the best place to eat in the resort.

Siófok

SIÓFOK, 6km down the shore from Balatonvilágos, is the largest, busiest and most vibrant resort on Balaton: crammed with bars and restaurants, it has long been the choice venue for young party-goers and was the first to introduce strip bars and sex clubs to augment the traditional pleasures of boozing, guzzling, sunbathing and dancing. Though its vitality might appeal for a while, you'll probably find that a day or two here will suffice – and finding accommodation can be tough.

Arrival and information

The centrally located **bus** and **train stations** are next to each other on Fő utca, the town's main axis, while **ferries** to and from Balatonfüred on the northern shore dock to the west of Jókai Park, at the mouth of the Sió Canal. **Information** can be obtained from the incredibly busy Tourinform office, currently housed in the water tower (Víztorony) on Szabadság tér, but which is set to move just across the road (June–Aug daily 8am–7pm; Sept–May Mon–Fri 9am–4pm, Sat 9am–noon; ☎84/315-355, ⓦwww.siofok.com). The **post office** (Mon–Fri 8am–7pm, Sat 8am–noon) is opposite the train station at Fő utca 186, and there's **internet access** at Net-Game, Kálmán Imre sétány 11 (daily 10am–7pm).

Accommodation

There's plenty of accommodation to go around in Siófok, though the town gets swamped during July and August, and booking ahead is strongly advised. **Private rooms** (❸–❹) are bookable through Tourinform (see above) and Siótour at Batthyány utca 2/B (June–Aug Mon–Fri 9am–6pm, Sat 9am–2pm; Sept–May Mon–Fri 9am–4pm; ☎84/313-111, ⓦwww.siotour.hu). If the accommodation situation looks bleak then head for Balatonvilágos, just three stops and fifteen minutes away on the train, where there are further options (see opposite).

There are several **campsites** around, the largest and most accessible of which are *Aranypart Camping*, 5km east of the centre (bus #2) at Szent László utca 183–185 (☎84/353-399; chalets ❹; May to mid-Sept), and *Ezüstpart Camping*, 4km west of the centre (bus #1 from the Baross Bridge) at Liszt Ferenc sétány 5 (☎84/350-374;

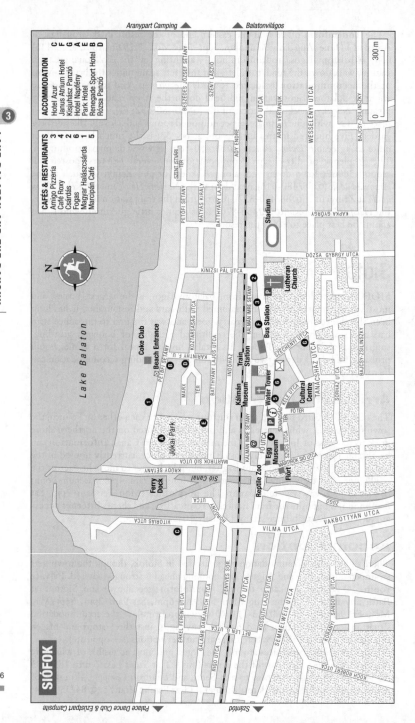

SIÓFOK

Aranypart Camping ▲   ▲ Balatonvilágos

300 m
0

ACCOMMODATION
Hotel Azur   C
Janus Atrium Hotel   F
Kisjuhász Panzió   G
Hotel Napfény   A
Park Hotel   E
Renegade Sport Hotel   B
Rózsa Panzió   D

CAFÉS & RESTAURANTS
Amigo Pizzeria   3
Café Roxy   4
Csárdás   2
Fogas   6
Magyar Halászcsárda   1
Marcipán Café   5

Lake Balaton

N

BESZÉDES JÓZSEF SÉTÁNY
SZENT LÁSZLÓ
FŐ UTCA
ARADI VÉRTANÚK
WESSELÉNYI UTCA
BAJCSY-ZSILINSZKY
SZENT ISTVÁN TÉR
ADY ENDRE
PETŐFI SÉTÁNY
MÁTYÁS KIRÁLY
BATTHYÁNY LAJOS
KINIZSI PÁL UTCA
KÁLMÁN IMRE SÉTÁNY
KAPKA GYÖRGY
DÓZSA GYÖRGY UTCA
Stadium
Lutheran Church
Bus Station
P
KÖZTÁRSASÁG UTCA
KÁRINTHY F U
BATTHYÁNY LAJOS UTCA
INDÓHÁZ
Train Station
SZÉCHENYI UTCA
TANÁCSHÁZ UTCA
SÖRHÁZ UTCA
BAJCSY-ZSILINSZKY UTCA
Coke Club
Beach Entrance
PÉTER SÉTÁNY
MARX TÉR
Kálmán Museum
Water Tower
KELE UTCA
Cultural Centre
FŐ TÉR
SZODASAG UTCA
Jókai Park
KÁLMÁN IMRE SÉTÁNY
KRÚDY SÉTÁNY
MÁRTÍROK SIÓ UTCA
FŐ UTCA
Reptile Zoo
Egg Museum
Fürt
MÁRTÍROK SIÓ UTCA
ZUGÓ
VAKBOTTYÁN UTCA
Ferry Dock
Sió Canal
HORGONY UTCA
VITORLÁS UTCA
VILMA UTCA
ERKEL FERENC UTCA
GALAMB
DAMJANICH UTCA
FÉNYVES SOR
FŐ UTCA
KOSSUTH LAJOS UTCA
SEMMELWEIS UTCA
BÉL TÉN G. UTCA
RIGÓ UTCA
KORÁNYI SÁNDOR UTCA
KOCH RÓBERT UTCA

Palace Dance Club & Ezüstpart Campsite ▲   ▲ Szántód

Szántód ▼

chalets ❸; May–Sept). There are also two decent **hostels** around 2km west of the centre near the Balatonszéplak train station: the *Villa Benjamin Hostel*, at Siófoki utca 9 (☎84/350-704; ❷–❸), has doubles and multi-bed rooms, while the much larger *Touring Hostel* at Cseresznye utca 1/0 (☎84/310-551, Ⓔtouring @siofok-hostel.com; ❷; May–Sept) has doubles with shared bathroom facilities.

Hotel Azur Vitorlás utca 11 ☎84/501-415, ⓦwww.hotelazur.hu. Siófok's premier hotel offers a range of differently sized rooms (smaller ones have shower, larger ones bath and shower), all immaculately turned out and sumptuously furnished. The first-rate wellness centre has a superb indoor pool. ❾

Janus Atrium Hotel Fő utca 93–95 ☎84/312-546, ⓦwww.janushotel.hu. Serene hotel on the busy main road, with smooth, darkly furnished rooms boasting some classy touches; also possesses a gorgeous little basement pool and jacuzzi, and a pleasant atrium-style coffee house. March to mid-Nov. ❽

Kisjuhász Panzió Széchenyi utca 14 ☎84/311-289, Ⓔkisjuhas@axelero.hu. Five minutes south of the rail and bus stations, this cordial pension has spotless a/c rooms with fridge. Triples and quads available too. ❺

Park Hotel Batthyány Lajos utca 7 ☎84/310-539, ⓦwww.parkhotel.hu. Although hardly flush with character, this quiet hotel has decent, pine-furnished rooms with high ceilings, and is idyllically located in Jókai Park. ❻

Renegade Sport Hotel Petőfi sétány 4 ☎84/311-506, ⓦwww.renegadeworld.hu. Characterful hotel whose effortlessly cool rooms, each painted a different pastel colour, are furnished with low-slung wooden beds and wrought-iron lighting; despite its location right on the beachfront, the windows are fully soundproof. ❽

Rózsa Panzió Karinthy Frigyes utca 5 ☎&ⓕ84/310-722. Located between the station and the beach, this is a large, peaceful pension with basic, modernish rooms. Triples, quads and apartments available. May–Sept. ❺

The town and beaches

With its high-rise hotels and packed beaches, there's little trace of Siófok's prewar reputation as a quietly elegant resort, nor much evidence of the town's long history. The canal that the Romans began in 292 AD was later made use of by the Turks, who stationed a fleet of 10,000 men here to confront the Austro-Hungarian fleet across the water at Balatonfüred. A small **gallery** at the top of the 45-metre-high water tower on central Szabadság tér displays photos of Siófok a century ago and offers a view of the town today, though you have to climb over 120 steps to get there (above Tourinform, same hours, see p.195; 400Ft).

Heading west from the water tower, there are a couple of small, rather curious attractions that'll keep you entertained for an hour or so: at Fő utca 156, the **Reptile Zoo** (Hullő Reptil Zoo; daily June–Aug 10am–8pm, May & Sept 9am–6pm; 600Ft) houses a colourful assortment of reptiles and fish; just behind here, at Szűcs utca 4, the small **Egg Museum** (Tojás Múzeum; Tues–Sat 10am–6pm; 400Ft) is essentially a shop; the painting of eggs has long been a popular folk art in Hungary, and the cabinets here hold dozens of these exquisitely patterned eggs (in addition to crystal, china and ceramic ones), variously painted with religious, floral or zoomorphic motifs.

Heading east from the water tower, down Fő utca, you'll soon reach the striking modern **Lutheran Church** (May–Sept daily 9am–noon & 3–7pm; Oct–April Sun only 10am–noon), designed by the visionary architect Imre Makovecz (see box, p.163). It not only embodies his ideas about organic architecture and nationhood, but constitutes a rebuke to the immorality and materialism of Siófok – or at least that's assumed to be the significance of the hollow-eyed face of an old man carved into the wooden facade. The points of the roof are meant to be the shoulders of his sheepskin coat.

Siófok's most famous son is the operatic composer **Imre Kálmán** (1882–1953), who was born near the train station at Kálmán Imre sétány 5. There's a fine bronze statue of Kálmán in a small bandstand in front of the station, and his former home has been turned into a **museum** (Tues–Sat 10am–5pm, Sun 10am–1pm; 300Ft), its small rooms crammed with personal effects – including his piano, bureau and walking stick – as well as photos and programmes from such operettas as *The Gypsy Princess* and *Countess Maritza*, unfortunately without any English explanation. The streets between the train station and the shore are an enjoyable place to wander, with avenues of plane trees screening some magnificent turn-of-the-twentieth-century **villas**, many of them turned into garishly decorated restaurants or pensions.

The lakeside features two main waterfront resort areas: **Aranypart** (Gold Shore) to the east of the Sió Canal, and **Ezüstpart** (Silver Shore) to the west. Though the central stretch of shoreline consists of paying **beaches** (daily mid-May to mid-Sept 7am–7pm; 1000Ft), there are free *strand* 1km further along at both resort areas. Having larger hotels and more nightlife in the vicinity, Aranypart is the livelier and noisier of the two. You can rent **windsurfing** boards and small **sailing** boats at most beaches, while **horseriding** and **pleasure cruises** can be arranged through Siótour (see p.195).

Eating

Restaurants, both traditional Hungarian and more modern establishments, abound in Siófok, the best of them scattered along Fő utca. Petőfi sétány, meanwhile, is littered with snack bars. One terrific **café** is *Marcipán*, on the corner of Fő utca and Kele utca (daily 6am–9pm), where you can indulge in sweet and savoury treats and great coffee.

Amigo Pizzeria Fő utca 99. The pick of the restaurants along this street, this thoroughly modern, very large and very enjoyable place has an outstandingly varied menu including fish, poultry and beef, as well as a "sharpfood" menu (ie very hot) – the pizzas are fantastic too and there's also a decent veggie menu.

Café Roxy Szabadság tér 1. Informal and very popular restaurant-cum-bar offering a choice selection of dishes including pickled salads, mixed grills and stuffed savoury pancakes, in addition to a breakfast menu. It's also a good spot for a daytime coffee or evening glass of wine.

Csárdás Fő utca 105. Seasoned, old-fashioned joint with a reliably solid Hungarian menu, heavy on the pork and beef, but with established favourites such as dumplings, bean soup and Hortobágy pancakes; live Gypsy music in summer.

Fogas Fő utca 184. Little to choose between this and the *Csárdás*, but this large eatery opposite the train station is a touch more colourful, offers more in the way of game food, and has a delightful winter garden.

Magyar Halászcsárda Petőfi sétány 3. The most agreeable of the lakeside restaurants, this large two-floored establishment is just the business if it's the wet stuff you're after; fresh fish plucked straight from the lake then cooked just the way you like it.

Nightlife and entertainment

Indisputably Balaton's number-one party town, Siófok boasts some serious **nightlife**, though it's almost exclusively restricted to the period between June and early September. The main focus is Petőfi sétány, with bars and clubs rammed to bursting along its entire length. The big draw is the *Coke Club*, a self-contained cluster of bars on the main beach, while other popular venues include *Renegade*, owned by the hotel of the same name, and *La Siesta*. The two big-hitters for serious clubbers are the *Palace Dance Club*, 2km west of town at Deák Ferenc utca 2 (ⓦ www.palace.hu), which regularly attracts big-name DJs and is served by a free shuttle bus from the water tower every hour from 9pm; and *Flört* (ⓦ www.flort .hu), a high-energy techno club just off Fő utca at Sió utca 4 – both venues open daily mid-May to mid-September till around 5am and charge around 3000Ft entrance fee. There are also regular **pop and rock concerts** on one of the *strand*

▲ Party time at Siófok

by the hotels in the centre of town – look out for flyers around town or check with Tourinform (see p.195).

Siófok being the birthplace of Imre Kálmán, **operetta** plays a major part here, manifest in the annual **Imre Kálmán Anniversary days** each October, with performances of his works (usually in German) in the **Imre Kálmán Cultural Centre** (Kulturális Központ; box office Tues–Fri noon–8pm, Sat 10am–6pm; tickets 3000–4000Ft) behind the water tower on Fő tér. Throughout the rest of the year, the centre hosts a range of **organ concerts** and **piano recitals**.

The town's two other main annual festivals are the **Siófolk International Folklore Festival**, a five-day event in early July with parades and dancing by troupes from around the world; and in mid-October the three-day **Egg Festival** (**Tojásfesztivál**), which celebrates the spherical wonder with music and dance, and lots of gastronomic happenings including an attempt to create the world's biggest egg dish.

The southern shore to Kis-Balaton

Beyond Siófok the southern shore abounds with smaller resorts, such as **Balaton-szárszó**, which boasts an interesting museum, and the villages of **Balatonlelle** and **Balatonboglár**, which lie at the heart of the region's main wine road. The shore winds up at **Kis-Balaton**, site of a peaceful nature and bison reserve.

Szántód and around

The small village of **SZÁNTÓD**, 11km down from Siófok, is the point of departure for **car ferries** to Tihany-rév (see p.209) on the northern shore (daily: March–May & mid-Sept to Nov every hour, last ferry at 6pm; June to mid-Sept every 40min, last ferry at 10pm; 10min; 1400Ft per car, 500Ft per person & 300Ft per bike). If for some reason you need to **stay** here, try the friendly, hostel-like *Rév Hotel*, five minutes' walk from the ferry at Szent István út 162 (T84/348-245, E revhotel@elender.hu; ❹; May–Sept), or *Rév Camping*, next door (T84/348-859; June–Aug). The nearest **train station** is Szántód-Kőröshegy, some 2km south of the ferry dock near Route 7.

One kilometre back towards Siófok along this route is a cluster of eighteenth- and nineteenth-century farm buildings converted into a "tourist and cultural centre" at **Szántódpuszta** (daily: mid-April to May & Sept to mid-Oct 8am–5pm; June–Aug 8am–6pm; 800Ft). *Puszta* has two meanings: one is the flat plains of eastern Hungary, and the other, of which Szántódpuszta is a good example, is a large farmstead common in western Hungary. This complex of restored thatched buildings includes a **manor house**, built in 1716 and housing a local history exhibition with beautiful old photos, wine cellar (now a restaurant), granary, inn and blacksmith's workshop (that's sometimes in operation), whilst another keeps a small aquarium. The old stables, meanwhile, have been converted into an equestrian centre, with riding available (2500Ft per hr) and horse-shows (2000Ft) staged in summer. You can **stay** at the simple and old-fashioned *Patkó Fogadó* (T84/348-714; ❹; May to mid-Sept), run by the Helikon office at the entrance to the complex.

Balatonszárszó

Five kilometres on from Szántód, the small town of **BALATONSZÁRSZÓ** is one of the lake's oldest, most serene resorts. However, it's perhaps better known as the place where the tragic proletarian poet, **Attila József** (1905–37), took his own life. Dismissed by his literary peers and rejected by both his lover and the Communist Party, he threw himself under a local freight train on December 3, 1937. Attila spent his last days in a pension that's now a **memorial museum** at József Attila utca 7 (April–Oct Tues–Sun 10am–noon & 1–6pm; 500Ft), a couple of streets south of the train station. The museum charts the poet's life in chronological order with an impressive collection of his literary works, photos and personal effects, and concludes with the events of that fateful day, including newspaper cuttings, a piece of track and the crumpled, blood-stained shirt he was wearing when struck by the train; unfortunately all captions are in Hungarian only.

If you're looking to **stay** here then your best bets are the comfortable *Cseri Panzió*, 400m south of the train station at Fő utca 30 (T84/363-221, E cseri @externet.hu; ❹), or the less attractive but perfectly acceptable *Főnix Hotel* (T84/362-961; ❹), 100m west of the station opposite the beach entrance. There's **camping** at *Zöldpont*, an excellent little private site 100m up from the *Cseri Panzió* at Fő utca 40 (T84/363-091; May–Sept).

Balatonlelle, Balatonboglár and around

During the Kádár era, the settlements of Balatonlelle and Balatonboglár were merged into a single entity called Boglárlelle, but since 1991 they have re-established their own identities and also made the most of the revival of the wine industry since then, becoming the main centre of **wine tourism** on the southern shore of the lake. The fifty-kilometre-long strip of land that makes up this, the fifth-largest wine region in the country, yields an equal number of quality red and white wines. For more information check out the South-Balaton Wine Route Association's website, W www.dbb.hu.

Balatonlelle and around

The tidy little resort of **BALATONLELLE** does its bit to attract tourists by staging the lively **Wine Week Festival** during the first week of August, featuring wine and music, and an arts and crafts fair. There's some good **accommodation** here, too, the best of which is the lovely *Viktória Panzió*, some 400m west of the train station at Szent István utca 13 (☎85/554-233, ⓔviktoria@ferry.hu; ❺), which has polished, well-furnished rooms; the *Lelle Park*, 200m east of the station at Köztársaság út 11 (☎85/450-317, ⓦwww.lellepark.com; ❻–❽; May–Sept), which has immaculate air-conditioned apartments, with full kitchen facilities, sleeping two to six people; and, around 1km along from here at no. 31, the bright *Hotel Francoise* (☎85/352-429; ❺). The large and well-equipped *Aranyhíd* campsite is at Köztársaság út 53 (☎85/350-449; mid-May to mid-Sept). Both the *Viktória* and the *Lelle Park* have very good **restaurants**, while the latter also has a smart pub.

Wine lovers should also venture 3km inland to **KISHEGY** (you'll have to walk or take a taxi if you don't have your own transport), where you can taste and buy wine in the **Szent Donatus winery** at Kishegyi utca 42 (Mon–Fri 7.30am–noon & 12.30–6pm, Sat 10am–6pm; ☎85/454-701, ⓦwww.garamvariszolobirtok.hu); expect to pay around 150–200Ft per glass. It's another 2km to the *Szent Donatus Csárda* at the top of the hill (the staff at the winery can direct you), where you can get stuck into solid Hungarian fare and sample more wines while gazing over the lake (May to mid-Sept daily noon–10pm).

Balatonboglár and around

BALATONBOGLÁR, 3km west of Balatonlelle, plays host to several more good festivals, most notably the five-day **Jazz and Wine Festival** at the end of July, and the massive **Grape Gathering Festival** (Boglári Szüreti) from August 18 to 20, which takes place on two stages down by the Platán *strand*, with a big fair and a procession, a competition for the title of Wine Queen, nightly firework displays, and, of course, lots of wine. In neighbouring Várhegy, a spherical **lookout tower** commands a sweeping view from Keszthely to Tihany, while atop Temetődomb (Cemetery Hill), behind the two chapels, there are regular exhibitions by artists from June to August. Another fun time to be here is the last Saturday in July when the **swim across Balaton** takes place; each year several thousand greased-up swimmers set off from **Révfülöp**, 5.2km away on the northern shore, to Balatonboglár in this popular amateur swim-fest.

Arriving at the **train station**, exit left and it's around 800m to Vörösmarty tér in the centre of town. Balatonboglár's **Tourinform** office is a couple of minutes' walk from here at Erzsébet utca 12–14 (June–Aug daily Mon–Sat 9am–7pm; Sept–May Mon–Fri 8am–4pm; ☎85/550-168, ⓔbalatonboglar @tourinform.hu). You can book private **rooms** – and **rent bikes** (1500Ft per day) – through Fredo Tourist, located across the tracks at Tinódi utca 16 (June–Aug daily 8am–8pm, rest of year Mon–Fri 9am–4pm; ☎85/350-288, ⓔfredo @fredotourist.hu). *Vasutas Üdülő*, 1.5km east of the station at Kodály Zoltán utca 45 (☎85/350-634; ❶), has cheap beds, or for something marginally more comfortable, head along to *Família Hotel* at no. 64 (☎84/350-604; ❸; May–Sept). The *Sellő Campsite* (☎85/550-367; April–Sept) is on the west of the landing stage at Kikötő sétány 3.

There are some terrific places in Balatonboglár for **wine-tasting**, and few better than the **Légli winery** at Árpád utca 47 (daily 9am–5pm; ☎85/550-310, ⓦwww.legliotto.hu), whose outstanding whites include Chardonnay (Landord), Sauvignon Blanc and the fabulous Légli 333 (cuvee) – tasting

(2000Ft) typically comprises five or six wines and some nibbles, and although appointments are not necessary, you're best off calling in advance. From Vörösmarty tér, walk to the top of Szabadság utca and it's on the corner of Árpád utca and Attila utca.

During the first weekend of June the small village of **SOMOGYBABOD**, 12km south of Balatonboglár, stages the **Somogybabod Off-Road Festival**, an established event for off-road enthusiasts with lively concerts and huge beer tents complementing the series of races on the reconditioned track; more information can be obtained from Tourinform in Balatonboglár.

Kis-Balaton

At the far end of the lake, reeds obscure the mouth of the River Zala and stretch for many kilometres upstream to **Kis-Balaton** (Little Balaton). This lake once covered forty square kilometres, but was half-drained in the 1950s to provide irrigation for new crop land, and was nearly destroyed by the dumping of pollutants into the Zala during the 1980s. Its rehabilitation was begun in the 1980s, as attempts were made to improve the quality of water in Lake Balaton. The first stage of the process, diverting water back through the reed beds that act as a filter for the lake, has been completed, but there is much debate about how successful this has been, and whether further steps should be taken. It has certainly restored the area as a paradise for birds and bird lovers, with over eighty species of birds found here.

Located on the northeastern edge of the lake, near the village of **Zalavár** is the **Kis-Balaton House** (Kis-Balaton ház; March–Oct Tues–Sun 9am–noon & 1–6pm; 500Ft; ☎83/710-002), which demonstrates the workings of the water system, and has a small exhibition on the lake's flora and fauna. Also within the grounds is a water playground for kids, a café, and a cycle hut where you can rent **bikes** (1000Ft per 2hr, 2000Ft per 5hr). Most of the lake is actually off limits to visitors, but there is designated access around 5km south of Zalavár on **Kányavár Island**, itself reached by a specially reconstructed timber bridge. If you would like to visit some of the lake's closed off areas, you can do so on a guided "Safari" which takes place in June and July (Wed 11am & 2pm, Sat 2pm; 1500Ft), departing from the Kis-Balaton house and lasting around two hours. The easiest way to get to Zalavár is by hourly bus from Keszthely (see p.216).

The settlement of **Kápolnapuszta**, about 20km south of Keszthely, is home to Hungary's largest **Bison Reserve** (Bivalyrezervátum; daily 9am–7pm; 550Ft). Established in 1992 with just sixteen buffalo, the reserve now keeps some 200 of the animals, which account for about a third of Hungary's total stock; prior to World War II there were over 200,000 buffalo in the territory of Hungary. A well marked-out trail – which takes approximately 45 minutes to walk – allows you to get close (but not too close – there's an electric fence) to the animals, while regular information boards do an excellent job of explaining their various habits and activities. The buffalo are herded out to pasture from spring to late autumn, though they can still be visited indoors during the winter. Without your own transport, however, getting here is both tricky and time-consuming: the best way is to take a **bus** from Keszthely to either Balatonmagyaród or Sármellék, from where there are more frequent buses to Balatonmagyaród – from here, though, it's still a good thirty-minute walk to the reserve.

Lake Balaton: the northern shore

The resorts of **Balatonalmádi** and **Balatonfüred** on the **northern shore** of the lake are more genteel than their southern counterparts, with a certain faded elegance, but the crowds of tourists are just as big, while the Tihany peninsula, and in particular the pretty village of **Tihany**, attracts even greater numbers. The shoreline beyond Tihany is dominated by holiday homes and nondescript resorts, although the local vineyards make a few visits to wine cellars a temptation. The biggest wine centre, however, is on the slopes of the **Badacsony Hills**, whose picturesque village, **Badacsony**, draws big crowds throughout the summer. For walkers, there is plenty to explore in the hinterland, including the volcanic shapes around Badacsony Hills. Buses run alongside the shore to the enjoyable university town of **Keszthely**, whilst trains follow the lake for most of its length before turning inland to Tapolca, where you should change for Keszthely.

Balatonalmádi

The first major settlement along the northern shore is **BALATONALMÁDI**, a resort since 1877, which now has a pleasantly faded air, although most visitors to this part of the shore pass straight through, favouring instead the more buoyant resort of Balatonfüred. However, its decent beaches, pleasant lakeside walks and varied cultural programme make it worth stopping off for. The best time to visit is during the **Balatonalmádi Days** at the end of July, a nine-day cultural festival featuring folk dancing, operetta and a big craft fair around the lakeside area. The **grape harvest** celebration in mid-September is a smaller event – a day of wine and music, with a grand procession through the town.

All the sights in the town are church-related. A few minutes' walk west of the main square, Városház tér, the small **Chapel of the Holy Right Hand** (Szent Jobb Kápolna), tacked on to the left side of the Church of Szent Imre, at Óváry Ferenc utca 47, was originally located in the Royal Palace in Buda and housed the holy right hand of St Stephen, which is now in St Stephen's Basilica in Budapest. During the reconstruction of Buda Palace after World War II, the chapel was spared from destruction by Stalinists, and rebuilt at Balatonalmádi in 1957. Peering through the bars of the gate you can see the impressive gold mosaic executed by Károly Lotz in 1896.

Two other unusual churches lie in the older suburb of **Vörösberény**, a thirty-minute slog uphill along Petőfi utca and Veszprémi út (or take one of the regular buses from the bus station). The Baroque **parish church**, built in 1779 for the Jesuits, contains interesting frescoes depicting the order's founder, St Ignatius, as well as some contemporary figures; you can get the key from the *plébánia*, two houses behind the church. Just uphill stands a fortified thirteenth-century **Calvinist church**, whose shape has undergone many changes over the years; only fragments of frescoes and a couple of windows remain from the original. The key is available from the priest's house (Református Lelkész Hivatal), directly below the church at Veszprémi út 105. On Friday evenings in July and August the church hosts **concerts** of Renaissance and Baroque music – check with Tourinform for details (see below). If you've got time, and some energy, you could walk the **Red Sandstone Path**, a six-kilometre-long, circular trail which takes in the **Óvári lookout tower** in the forest to the north of town – you can pick up a guiding leaflet from Tourinform.

Balatonalmádi has a paying **beach** (May–Sept daily 8.30am–7pm; 500Ft) by Városház tér in the centre of town, and a free beach (*szabad strand*) half an hour's walk west at Káptalanfüred.

Practicalities

The **bus** and **train** stations are situated at the top and bottom of the main square, Városház tér, respectively, while in July and August **boats** from Balatonfüred and Tihany arrive at the pier, ten minutes' walk east of the main square through the lakeside park. Tourinform, between the stations on Városház tér (mid-June to mid-Sept Mon–Fri 9am–7pm, Sat & Sun 9am–5pm; mid-Sept to mid-June Mon–Fri 8.30am–4.30pm; ☎88/594-081, ✉balatonalmadi@tourinform.hu), has lots of **information** to hand. Although it can't arrange private rooms, Balatontourist, 200m up from Városház tér at Petőfi utca 6 (May–Sept Mon–Sat 8.30am–6pm, Sun 9am–noon; Oct–April Mon–Fri 8.30am–4pm; ☎88/584-106, ✉balmadi @balatontouristutazas.hu), does have a good selection of **flats** (❸–❺), sleeping between two and ten people. The **post office** is at Petőfi utca 19 (Mon–Fri 8am–4pm, Sat 9am–noon).

Unlike many resorts on the northern shore, Balatonalmádi has few appealing possibilities when it comes to **accommodation**. The standout option is the classy *Ramada Hotel*, 300m east of Városház tér at Bajcsy-Zsilinszky utca 14 (☎88/620-620, ⊛www.ramadabalaton.hu; ❾), whose impeccably turned out rooms have superb lake views. Otherwise, there's the mellow, five-room *Hotel Viktória*, a five-minute walk further along at no. 42 (☎88/438-940, ✉viktoria @viktoriahotel.hu; ❹), which also has a sauna, solarium and terraced restaurant. The cheapest option around is the *Pedagógus Üdülő* (Teacher's Holiday Home) at Dózsa György utca 13 (☎88/438-518; ❶; May–Sept), just behind the Church of St Imre, offering basic rooms with basins and shared bathrooms. The best of the town's several **campsites** is the large *Yacht Camping* (☎88/584-101, ✉yacht@balatontourist.hu; bungalows ❹; May to mid-Sept), some 600m to the right of the train station and across the tracks at Véghely utca 16 – the site boasts excellent amenities, including a minimarket, creche and sports facilities, and has direct access to the lake.

The town's two outstanding **restaurants** are down by the ferry pier on Véghely Dezső út. The stylish *Kikötő*, at no. 5, is part of the Almadi Yacht Club but isn't as haughty as you might expect, and boasts a decent international menu featuring Argentinian steak; and a few paces across the park, at no. 1, is the *Liget Kávéház*, a slightly more reserved place in a Baroque building with period furnishings, serving a limited but high-quality range of Hungarian meals and coffees.

Csopak

The dispersed village of **CSOPAK**, 9km down Route 71 towards Balatonfüred, has made a name for itself in recent years for its **wine**, and this is the main reason for visiting – whites predominate here, of which the best known is Olaszrizling. Csopak's main annual event is the **Wine Days Festival** (*Borhét*), which takes place in the third week of August and, aside from wine, entails lots of singing and dancing down by the waterfront at the entrance to the *strand*. Otherwise, there are numerous **cellars** around the old village, and many houses advertise dens where you can pop in to taste – and buy – the local hock. One of the best in the village is the Varga Borház (daily 8am–7pm), located in the large factory-like building at Füredi utca 3, a fifteen-minute walk north of the village just off Route 71. Smaller cellars, where you can also eat as you taste the wines, include the Linczy Pince at Berekháti utca 34, a few minutes' walk up from the train station (May–Oct daily 5–11pm), and the Söptei Pince at Istenfia utca 5, 200m down from the Varga Borház and then twenty minutes' walk west along Füredi utca (May–Oct daily 11am–11pm).

Practicalities

Arriving by train, walk up the main street, Kossuth utca, to the old village, or, to get to the *strand* and the resort area, walk across Route 71 and then along Fürdő utca; the ferry is a couple of minutes' walk beyond. There's a small, seasonal, **information** office (June–Aug daily 8am–8pm) at the train station, while 200m along Kossuth utca, in a beautifully restored manor house at no. 16, the headquarters of the **Balaton Uplands National Park** (daily 9am–5pm; Ⓦwww .bfnpi.hu) has some good materials on the various sights along the lake's northern shore, plus some excellent maps of the park itself if you fancy some walking – it also rents **bikes**.

Located within the park grounds is the lovely *Park Villa* (Ⓣ87/555-260, Ⓔbfnp@bfnp.kvvm.hu; ❸; May–Sept), another restored building with modern, sunny rooms but no extras. There's further **accommodation** down near the waterfront, namely the *Ifjúsági Üdülő*, a large, hostel-like complex a few minutes' walk east of the *strand* at Sport utca 9 (Ⓣ87/446-505; dorm bed 2500Ft, doubles ❷–❸; May–Sept; no IYHF discounts in July & Aug), which has basic rooms with showers; and the *Hotel Piroska* next door at nos. 5–7 (Ⓣ87/446-461; ❹; mid-May to mid-Sept) which, though outwardly unappealing, has perfectly fine rooms with balconies overlooking the gardens.

There are some good places to **eat** here; two places within the village, both with outside seating and serving traditional Hungarian cuisine, are the *Dobó Restaurant* at the top of Kossuth utca (no. 103), and the *Malom Csárda* in an old watermill ten minutes' walk up at Veszprémi út 3, on the main road. For something quite different, and just that little bit spicier, check out the *El Paso* steakhouse down towards the lake at Fürdő utca 24.

Balatonfüred

Seventeenth-century chronicles tell of pilgrims descending on **BALATON-FÜRED** to "camp in scattered tents" and benefit from the mineral springs. Some 30,000 people come here every year for treatment at the springs, mingling with hordes of tourists, giving this popular Balaton resort a distinctive, sedate air. Füred, as it is often called, is split into two, with the older centre a couple of kilometres away from the lake; here you'll find shops, churches and a market along its Baroque main street, Kossuth utca. Most visitors head for the resort area beside Balaton, whose centrepiece is the leafy Gyógy tér, with its sanatorium, springs and slicked-up nineteenth-century facades, leading down to a tree-lined lakeside promenade. On either side are beaches and a mix of modern hotels and antebellum villas.

Arrival and information

The **bus** and **train stations** are conveniently located next door to each other on Castricum tér – midway between the old town and the lakeside resort, both of which are within comfortable walking distance. Alternatively, bus #1 takes a roundabout route to the embankment before heading west along Széchenyi utca. **Ferries** from Siófok and Tihany dock at the pier at the western end of the promenade.

The **Tourinform** office is inside the Kisfaludy House at Kisfaludy utca 1 (July–Aug Mon–Sat 9am–7pm, Sun 10am–6pm; June & Sept Mon–Fri 9am–5pm, Sat 9am–1pm; Oct–May Mon–Fri 9am–4pm; ☎87/580-480, ⓦ www.balatonfured .hu); there's also a summer-only office (same times), 2km west of the centre at Széchenyi utca 47, by the *Füred* campsite.

The **post office** is at Zsigmond utca 14 (Mon–Fri 8am–4pm), and there's **internet access** at Net Espresso, Horváth Mihály utca 3 (Mon–Fri 8am–10pm, Sat & Sun 10am–10pm), and CyberClub, Kőztársaság utca 6 (daily 11am–8pm).

Accommodation

The town has a reasonable stock of good-value **accommodation** but it's advisable to book ahead, and essential in the period from the last weekend in July to August 20. During July and August budget accommodation (around 2500Ft for a dorm bed) can be found at the *Széchenyi Ferenc Kollégium* on Hősök tér, up in the main town (☎87/342-641), and the *Lóczy Diákotthon Kollégium*, just a short way north of the stations at Bartok Bela utca 4 (☎87/343-428). Twenty minutes' walk west of the promenade (bus #1 or #1B or any Tihany bus), at Széchenyi utca 24, lies the huge *Füred* **campsite** (☎87/580-241, ℮cfured@balatontourist.hu; mid-April to mid-Oct), offering a swimming pool, tennis, watersports and bungalows (②–④) on the lakefront.

Hotel Annabella Deák Ferenc utca 25 ☎87/889-431, ⓦwww.danubiushotels.com/annabella. The town's major package-tourist hotel, complete with tidy, if slightly tired, rooms all with balcony and some with views over to the lake. It also has indoor and outdoor pools and an enormous beer garden. April–Oct. ⑤–⑥

🏃 **Anna Grand Hotel** Gyógy tér 1 ☎87/580-315, ⓦwww.annagrandhotel.hu. This wonderfully restored building now houses one of the lake's most opulent hotels; from the cool marble lobby to the immaculate high-ceilinged rooms decorated in smooth, understated beige tones, the *Anna* simply oozes class. ⑨

Hotel Blaha Lujza Blaha Lujza utca 4 ☎87/581-210, ⓦwww.hotelblaha.hu. Formerly the summer home of the nineteenth-century actress and singer Lujza Blaha, this handsome Neoclassical building has smartish rooms, some of which are quite small, so it's worth paying the minimal extra for

the larger ones; also sports a sauna, solarium, fitness centre and an accomplished restaurant (see p.209). ⑥

Korona Panzió Vörösmarty utca 4 ☎87/343-278, ⓦwww.koronapanzio.hu. Decent, family-run pension with neatly furnished rooms, some with balcony, just 5min from the train and bus stations and 10min from the waterfront. Good value. ⑤

Hotel Silver Resort Zákonyi Ferenc 4 ☎87/583-000, ⓦwww.silverresort.hu. Superbly located down by the marina, this inconspicuous low-rise runs the *Anna Grand* close with its impeccable, orange and brown coloured rooms, most of which have fabulous lakeside views. ⑧

Hotel Vasutas Erkel Ferenc utca 1 ☎87/342-492, ℮hotelvasutas@t-online.hu. Despite possessing zero atmosphere, this is one of the more agreeable workers' hotels, with spartan but very clean rooms (superior ones have a/c) in a peaceful spot 150m north of the lake. ⑤–⑥

The lakeside

Walking around Balatonfüred's resort area makes you feel like an extra in Resnais' film, *Last Summer in Marienbad*, and you almost expect to come across tubercular countesses and impoverished artists. Despite the crowds and a few high-rise hotels, this once elegant spa has managed to retain most of its old Central European charm. The tone is set by the elegant tree-lined promenade that runs east from the pier,

The Anna Ball and other events

The big event in Füred's calendar is the **Anna Ball** on the last Saturday of July. Magnate Zsigmond Horváth held the first ball on Anna's Day, July 26, 1825, in honour of his granddaughter Anna, and since the collapse of Communism this traditional social occasion has gained in stature. Crowds gather around Gyógy tér to watch the ball-goers, before they retire to the *Anna Grand Hotel* for the main ball. The following day the beauty queen elected at the ball is paraded around town in a horse-drawn carriage.

Besides the sailing competitions on the lake, Füred has two other regular events in August. On the second weekend of the month, keen **swimmers** set off on the 3.6km to Tihany – a challenge that usually attracts in excess of four thousand participants. The same weekend sees the start of the three-week Wine Festival (Borhetek), with stalls set up along the promenade, where you can taste local vintages. There are also concerts during summer in the Calvinist church on Kossuth utca in the main town (the whitewashed church rather than the red sandstone one at the top of Ady utca).

where you can admire the view across to the Tihany promontory and the far side of the lake. The promenade is named Tagore sétány after the Bengali poet Rabindranath Tagore who came here in 1926 and planted a tree near the pier in gratitude for his cure. Indira and Rajiv Gandhi and a host of other Indian figures have followed suit, as have various Nobel prize-winners and the odd Soviet cosmonaut.

A few minutes up from the middle of the promenade, you come to the aptly named **Gyógy tér** (Health Square). Its columned, pagoda-like **Kossuth Well** gushes carbonated water, while other springs feed the sanatorium and cardiac hospital on the northern and eastern sides of the square. Excavations suggest that the Romans were the first to exploit the springs, using the waters to treat stomach ailments and, when mixed with goats' milk whey, as a cure for lung diseases. The hospital's **mineral baths** are reserved for patients only. On the western side of the square stand two former trade union holiday homes; the beautifully renovated *Anna Grand Hotel* (see p.207), and, similarly tarted up, the eighteenth-century **Horváth House**, one of the first inns in a land where innkeeping developed late, patronized by writers and politicians during the Reform era – a sanatorium for uranium miners during Communist times, it now accommodates luxury apartments.

Running westwards between the two is Blaha Lujza utca, named after the "Nation's Nightingale", who spent her summers here in a **villa** at no. 4 (now the *Hotel Blaha Lujza*) and had her tea at the *Kedves Cukrászda* across the road (see opposite). Just past the hotel at the junction with Jókai utca stands the mid-nineteenth-century **Round Church**, modelled on the Pantheon in Rome. Across the road, the **Jókai Memorial House** (May–Sept Tues–Sun 10am–6pm; 600Ft) was built by the nineteenth-century novelist Mór Jókai, whose novels are often compared to those of Dickens; Queen Victoria is said to have been among his fans. He came to Balatonfüred at the age of 37, half expecting to die from a lung infection, and built the villa as a refuge; he didn't die, however, until the ripe old age of 84. The museum preserves Jókai's furniture, a selection of his paintings, sketches and books, and a handful of personal effects.

Eating and drinking

Decent eating possibilities are woefully thin on the ground in Balatonfüred; most of the lakeside **restaurants** are fairly samey – big, open-terraced places knocking up grilled meat and fish dishes for the masses, such as the *Borcsa* and

---

Balatonfüred activities

With wooded hills on one side and water on the other, Füred offers plentiful opportunities for recreation. Balatonfüred's two main **beaches** (both mid-June to mid-Sept daily 9am–6pm; 750Ft) are located at the eastern end of Tagore sétány: the Eszterházy and, fifteen minutes' walk further east, the Kisfaludy. The Városi strand on Széchenyi utca west of the centre by the *Hotel Marina* is best for **swimming** (though not for kids, as it drops away quickly). **Pedaloes** and **windsurfing** boards are available at every *strand* and yachts can be rented from Opticonsor at Köztársaság utca 1 (☎87/341-188), Lisa Hajó at Füred Camping (☎06-30/9373-044) and the Fekete Péter School at Zákonyi utca 8 (☎06-30/9378-519), which also offers **sailing** lessons. You can rent **bicycles** (350Ft per hr, 2500Ft per day) from Tempo 21, near the stations at Ady Endre utca 52, or Bike Extrem, a little further up at no. 20. **Tennis courts** (2000Ft per hr) can be found at various locations, including the tennis centre next to the *Hotel Margareta* at Széchenyi utca 27 and at the Kiserdő Park in the centre of town. Tourinform can help arrange **horseriding** at the riding school in the Koloska Valley, a few kilometres outside town (☎87/340-280).

Stefánia Vitorlás Étterem at either end of Tagore sétány. Away from the lakeside, the restaurant in the *Hotel Blaha Lujza* is just about the most appealing place in town, with some attractive dishes such as pheasant, deer and veal in paprika. A short walk up the road, at Zsigmond utca 1, the *Arany Csillag* is a refined little pizzeria offering some two dozen types of pizza, including stuffed ones, alongside fresh pasta and crisp salads.

By way of contrast there are several super **cafés** dotted around, best of which is the effortlessly cool *Karolina*, near the *Silva Resort* at Zákonyi sétány 4 – with soft lighting, fabulous furniture, and unbeatable coffee and cakes; the neighbouring *Arany Mokka* is a similarly classy affair. Elsewhere there's Lujza Blaha's favourite coffeeshop, the elegant *Kedves Cukrászda* at Blaha Lujza utca 7, and local favourite *Bergmann*, at the top of Zsigmond utca, whose cakes are a match for any in town. For a more vigorous bout of **drinking**, pop into the *Macho Pub*, a Mexican-themed haunt behind the train station at Vasút utca 4 (daily 8pm till late).

Tihany peninsula

A rocky finger of land that was declared Hungary's first national park in 1952, the **Tihany peninsula**, 7km west of Balatonfüred, is historically associated with the Benedictine order and a castle (no longer in existence) that withstood 150 years of Turkish hostility. As one of the most beautiful regions of Balaton, Tihany gets swamped with visitors over summer, rivalling Szentendre as the most touristy place in Hungary, with folksy stalls lining the streets and parking as expensive as in Budapest. Nevertheless, it's easy to escape the crowds by hiking into the interior.

The lakeshore road from Balatonfüred passes along the eastern side of the peninsula, through Diós (where Avar graves have been discovered) and Gödrös, entering **Tihany village** above the inner harbour (Belső Kikötő), where ferries from Balatonfüred and Siófok arrive. At the tip of the peninsula, 2km on, lies **Tihany-rév**, where car ferries cross to Szántód. Next to the ferry is the expensive *Club Tihany* resort complex. Besides the paying **beaches** by *Club Tihany* and the Tihany docks, there are free *strand* along the reedier shores between Gödrös and Diós, and south of Sajkod on the other side of the peninsula.

Arrival and information

Tihany is connected to Balatonfüred by hourly **buses**, which stop in the village by András tér below the abbey church. The peninsula is also connected by bus with Badacsony to the west. **Ferries** from Balatonfüred and Siófok (mid-April to Oct) arrive at the inner harbour, while from March to November the car ferry from Tihany-rév goes across to Szántód on the southern shore (see p.199). Regular buses link the ferries with the upper village, or, alternatively, you could jump on the naff **tourist train** that stops below the abbey (June–Sept 9.30am–8.30pm, every 30min; 500Ft).

Information is available from Tourinform, located down from the abbey at Kossuth utca 20 (mid-April to mid-June Mon–Fri 9am–5pm, Sat 10am–4pm; mid-June to mid-Sept Mon–Fri 9am–7pm, Sat & Sun 10am–6pm; mid-Sept to mid-April Mon–Fri 10am–4pm; ☎87/538-104, ⓦwww.tihany.hu). **Internet access** is available at Postaköz 1 (daily 10am–8pm), just behind the **post office** (Mon–Fri 8am–4pm). If you'd like to explore some of the inland areas but don't fancy walking, **bicycle rental** is available at Kossuth utca 32 (May–Sept 10am–6pm; 2000Ft for half-day, 3000Ft for day).

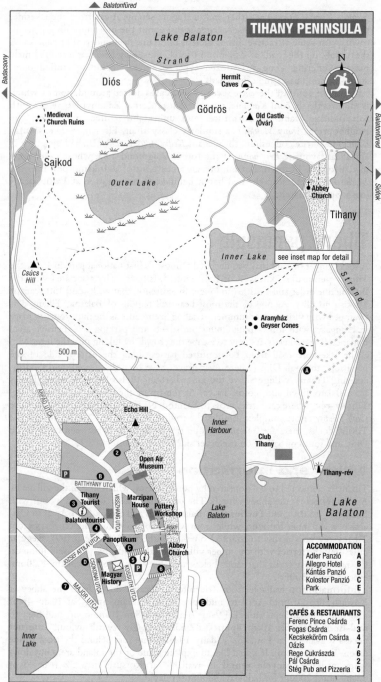

▲ Balatonfüred

TIHANY PENINSULA

Lake Balaton

Strand

Diós

Hermit Caves

Gödrös

▲ Old Castle (Óvár)

● Medieval Church Ruins

Sajkod

Outer Lake

† Abbey Church

Tihany

Inner Lake

see inset map for detail

▲ Csúcs Hill

● Aranyház
● Geyser Cones

❶
Ⓐ

0 ——— 500 m

Echo Hill ▲

Inner Harbour

❷
Open Air Museum

P
Ⓑ
BATTHYÁNY UTCA

Marzipan House

Club Tihany

Tihany Tourist
❸ ⓘ
Balatontourist
❹

Pottery Workshop

Lake Balaton

Panoptikum
Ⓒ
❺
Ⓓ
Abbey Church †

⚓ Tihany-rév

Magyar History
P
❻

❼
Ⓔ

Ⓐ ÁRPÁD UTCA
VISSZHANG UTCA
JÓZSEF ATTILA UTCA
CSOKONAI UTCA
KOSSUTH UTCA
MAJOR UTCA

Lake Balaton

Inner Lake

ACCOMMODATION
Adler Panzió	A
Allegro Hotel	B
Kántás Panzió	D
Kolostor Panzió	C
Park	E

CAFÉS & RESTAURANTS
Ferenc Pince Csárda	1
Fogas Csárda	3
Kecskeköröm Csárda	4
Oázis	7
Rege Cukrászda	6
Pál Csárda	2
Stég Pub and Pizzeria	5

▼ Szántód

N

③

LAKE BALATON AND THE BAKONY |

Accommodation

There is a reasonable, if largely dull, choice of **accommodation** in the village, with prices not as high as you might expect here. There's also a good stock of **private rooms** (❷–❸) and **apartments** (❹), bookable through Tihany Tourist at Kossuth utca 11 (daily: April–June & Sept–Oct 9am–5pm; July & Aug 9am–8pm; ☎ 87/448-481, ⓦ www.tihanytourist.hu), or Balatontourist at Kossuth utca 12 (June–Aug Mon–Sat 8.30am–7pm, Sun 8.30am–1pm; Sept to mid-Oct Mon–Fri 8.30am–4.30pm, Sat 8.30am–1pm; ☎ 87/538-071, ⓔ tihany@balatontourist.hu). Alternatively, if you simply wander the streets you'll see plenty of *Zimmer frei* signs dotted around.

Adler Panzió Felsőkopaszhegyi 1/a ☎ 87/448-755, ⓦ www.adler-tihany.hu. One kilometre south of the upper village, this homely place has large, a/c rooms with showers, some with small balcony, as well as a swimming pool, sauna and restaurant. Mid-March to Oct. ❺

Allegro Hotel Batthyány utca 6 ☎ 87/448-456, ⓦ www.allegrohotel.hu. This delightful, boutique-style establishment is the most agreeable place in the village, offering attractive, good-sized, a/c rooms, in addition to a neat little swimming pool and garden terrace. Mid-March to Oct. ❽

Kántás Panzió Csokonai utca 49 ☎ 87/538-065, ⓦ www.kantas-panzio-tihany.hu. Ordinary but restful, friendly, and very reasonably priced, six-room pension just down behind the post office. ❹

Kolostor Panzió Kossuth Lajos utca 14 ☎ 87/448-408. Located above a restaurant, this somewhat gloomy place has sombre, old-fashioned rooms decked out in lots of wood panelling, but it's central and cheap. ❹

Park Fürdőtelepi utca 1 ☎ 87/448-611, ⓦ www.hotelfured.hu. Tihany's principal hotel is the *Park*, on the east side of the peninsula. The hotel's two wings comprise the *Kastély* (Castle), a grand mansion confiscated by the Communist Party as its summer house, which has moderately impressive rooms, and the *Park* itself, a marginally cheaper, more modern building next door. Mid-April to mid-Oct. ❻–❼

Tihany village and around

In contrast with Tihany-rév, **TIHANY** village, on the top of the hill halfway along the eastern side of the peninsula, is a traditional-looking place, full of old houses built of grey basalt tufa, with thatched roofs and porticoed terraces, their windows and doors outlined in white.

In days gone by, the village was dominated by a Benedictine abbey overlooking Balaton, established in 1055 at the request of Andrew I and founded, true to the biblical injunction, upon a rocky promontory; it was later transformed into a fortress, and eventually demolished in the seventeenth century. Andrew's body lies in the crypt of the **abbey church** – the only one of the Árpád line to remain in the place where he was buried. The building itself is Baroque, the original having succumbed to the ravages of wars and time. Inside are virtuoso eighteenth-century **woodcarvings** by Sebestyén Stulhoff, who lived and worked in the abbey for 25 years after his fiancée died (her features are preserved in the face of an angel to the right of the altar), and grandiose **frescoes** by Károly Lotz, Székely and Deák-Ebner. The church (daily: May–Sept 9am–6pm; Oct–April 10am–3pm; 500Ft) provides a magnificent setting for **organ concerts** over summer – contact Tourinform for programme details (see p.209). The abbey's foundation deed, held at Pannonhalma Monastery in Transdanubia (see p.252), is the earliest document to include Hungarian words among the Latin.

From the church, it's a few minutes' walk down Pisky sétány, a parapet overlooking the waterfront, to a small **Open-Air Museum** (Szabadtéri Múzeum; May–Oct Tues–Sun 10am–6pm; 360Ft) exhibiting two well-preserved houses. The peasant house, with a beautiful entrance way, was built in the early nineteenth century and inhabited up until 1960; note the cross on the chimney, a common feature in this region. Behind this is an old Fishermen's Guild House, its mud-brick walls clad in thin stone to give an impression of wealth. Inside are the old boats the fishermen used, and a "wooden dog" sledge for fishing on ice. In the traditional way, the mud floor of the veranda is washed with mud daily to deal with the dirt and cracks. Folk dancing performances are held on the open-air stage most Sunday evenings throughout July and August at 6pm.

Behind the museum at Batthyány utca 26 is a **pottery house** (Fazekasház; daily: May–Sept 9am–7pm, Oct–April till 4pm), where earthenware made from the red clay of the area and glazed in bright greens and blues is made and sold. Opposite, at no. 17, the seductively titled **Marzipan House** (Marcipán Ház; daily 10am–6pm; 400Ft) contains one room of marzipan-moulded Disney characters (and, somewhat bizarrely, models of Naomi Campbell and Karl Lagerfeld), while the other is brimming with a tempting assortment of marzipan, chocolates and confectionery. Continuing along the lakeside walk for another five minutes, you come to the scenic vantage point of **Echo Hill**. An echo can theoretically be produced by standing on a short concrete pedestal and projecting your voice onto the wall of the abbey church. Legend goes that the echo is the voice of a princess, drowned in the lake by the King of the Water following her refusal to fall in love with his son. By taking a well-marked path onwards, you can circumambulate the **Óvár** (Old Castle), a volcanic outcrop riddled with cells carved by Russian Orthodox monks in the eleventh to fourteenth centuries, whence hot springs gush forth.

Back down in the village, on Kossuth utca, there are two more attractions, though, quite frankly, you're best off saving your money: at no. 35, the **Panoptikum** (daily 10am–6pm; 1200Ft) features some rather dubious waxworks figures, mostly great Hungarian historical figures, but also some pirates, though where Sir Francis Drake and Sir Walter Raleigh fit in here is anyone's guess; while, just around the corner, behind the post office on Posta-koz, **Magyar História** (daily 10am–6pm, show times hourly; 1000Ft) is a 45-minute audiovisual spectacle chronicling four thousand years of Hungarian history.

Inland walks

A trek inland will allow you to escape the crowds and enjoy the beauty of the peninsula, whose geology and microclimate have produced an unusual flora and fauna. The **Inner Lake** (Belső-tó), whose sunlit surface is visible from the abbey church, fills a volcanic crater 25m above the level of Balaton. From its southern bank, you can follow a path for a couple of kilometres through vineyards, orchards and lavender fields to the **Aranyház geyser cones** – rock funnels forced open by hot springs.

The northerly **Outer Lake** (Külső-tó) was drained for pasture in 1809, but started to be refilled in 1975. Its reed beds are harvested by hand over winter in the traditional manner, and provide a sanctuary for mallards, gadwalls and other **birds**. On the western side of the peninsula, a lookout tower atop **Csúcs Hill** (232m) offers a **panoramic view** of Balaton. The trail, marked in red, is a ninety-minute round-trip from Tihany village.

Eating

While **bars** and snack stalls cluster round the dock at Tihany-rév, **restaurants** are concentrated in the village, with some less expensive, less frequented wine cellars and restaurants in the streets around the Inner Lake. Homestyle Hungarian cuisine with frills is the rule in Tihany, and you'll be paying over the odds in most restaurants – note that the majority of them are seasonal. For **coffee and cakes** head for the *Rege Cukrászda*, in the little courtyard just up from Tourinform – there are glorious views of the lake from the outdoor terrace; or *Café 2 You*, a frantic little place at the junction of Batthyány utca and Visszhang utca.

Ference Pince Csárda Cserhegy 9. This secluded, sprightly restaurant and wine cellar 1km south of the village is well worth the trek for its grilled and roast meat dishes and local wines – you'll see the sign pinpointing its location 200m up a dusty track. April–Oct.

Fogas Csárda Kossuth utca 9. Great fish (grilled pike-perch, catfish, roast trout) is the order of the day in this perky little place on the main street, pleasantly cluttered with peasant-style decor and suitably attired waiters. March to mid-Nov.

Kecskeköröm Csárda Kossuth utca 19. This restaurant has a solid reputation, with game an established favourite, while its sloping terrace with

wooden tables and benches gives it a relaxed, casual feel. April–Oct.

Oázis Major utca 47. Down towards the inner lake away from the crowded centre, this welcoming place offers wholesome Hungarian meals in a convivial atmosphere, though the highlight is the bright, flower-filled garden. April–Oct.

Pál Csárda Visszhang utca 19. Very popular place with a pretty, vine-shaded courtyard and a highly creditable regular menu, in addition to a different set menu each day. March–Oct.

Stég Pub and Pizzeria Kossuth utca 18. The least touristy eatery in the village, this informal gaff offers oven-baked pizzas and salads, and is also the best place for a beer. Open til 1am.

The Badacsony

A hulk of volcanic rock with four villages at its feet, backed by dead volcanoes ranged across the Tapolca basin, **the Badacsony** is one of Balaton's most striking features. When the land that was to become Hungary first surfaced, molten magma erupted from the sea bed and cooled into a great semicircle of **basalt columns**, 210m high, which form Badacsony's southeastern face. The rich volcanic soil of the lower slopes has supported **vineyards** since the Age of Migrations, when the Avars buried grape seeds with their dead to ensure that the afterlife wouldn't be lacking in wine. Nowadays, the harvest consists of Zöldszilváni, Szürkebarát (Pinot Gris), Olaszrizling and Kéknyelő (Blue Stem); the last variety is exclusive to the region. The **wine harvest festival** in the village of Badacsony during the second week in September is a time of street processions, folk dancing and music – and of course lots of wine to be drunk. Out of season, Badacsony is just about the most desolate place around the lake.

Arrival and information

Although trains and buses also call at the other villages – Badacsonytomaj, Badacsonylábdihegy and Badacsonytördemic – Badacsony proper is where everyone gets off, with ferries arriving from Balatonboglár, Fonyód and Szigliget. Badacsony's **train station** is right in the centre of the village, just up from the **ferry** pier, while **buses** stop on the main street, Park utca. Beyond Badacsony the train line veers northwards up to Tapolca in the Bakony, so it's easier to continue along the shore by **bus**, changing at Balatonederics if necessary.

Maps and **information** are available from Tourinform, 100m north of the train station at Park utca 14 (mid-June to Aug daily 9am–7pm; May to mid-June daily 9am–5pm; April & Sept Mon–Fri 9am–3pm; ☎87/431-046, ℮badacsonytomaj @tourinform.hu), and the **post office** is close by at no. 3 (Mon–Fri 8am–4pm).

Accommodation

Given the popularity of the place, **accommodation** in Badacsony is scarce, though nearby Badacsonytomaj (2km east on the road to Balatonfüred) has further options, and there's a brilliant hostel in Révülöp, further east along the lake. Moreover, there is a reasonable stock of **private rooms** (➋–➌) bookable through Miditourist, at Egry sétány 3 (daily: July & Aug 8am–8pm; May, June & Sept to mid-Oct 9am–6pm; ☎87/431-117, ⓦ www.miditourist.hu) and Park utca 53 (June–Sept daily 8am–8pm; Oct–May Mon–Sat 9am–4pm; ☎87/431-028). Badacsony's **campsite** is on the shore, fifteen minutes' walk west of the ferry pier (☎87/531-041; mid-May to Sept), while, 1km or so beyond Badacsonytomaj, in Badacsonyörs, is the larger *Balaton Camping* (☎87/571-031; May to mid-Sept).

Badacsony Hostel Római út 1, Badacsonytomaj ☎ & ⓕ 87/471-057. Five minutes up from the station, this friendly hostel offers accommodation in functional but clean two- to five-bedded rooms with shared bathrooms. April–Oct. Dorm bed ➊

Borbarátok Panzió Római út 88, Badacsonytomaj ☎ 87/471-500, ⓦ www.borbaratok.hu. The "Wine Friends" pension has six lovely rooms a 15min walk along from *Badacsony Hostel*, with tidy, colourful rooms, and which also makes its own wine (see opposite). April–Oct. ➎

Hullám Hostel Füredi út 6 ☎ 87/463-089, ⓦ www.balatonhostel.hu. Not in Badacsony itself, but around 8km east of the village in Révülöp, this super, and extremely welcoming, hostel is one of the country's best; super clean three-, four- and six-bed dorms, as well as en-suite singles and

doubles; internet, laundry and bike rental all available. Prominently sited, it's a 5min walk from the station along the main road (exit left). ➋–➍

Hotel Neptun Római út 170 ☎ 87/431-293, ⓦ www.borbaratok.hu. Just up the road from Tourinform, this sister hotel to the *Borbarátok* incorporates both a neat and colourful pension and a clean, bright hostel with shared bathrooms and a large communal area. April–Oct. Hostel doubles ➋, pension ➎

Hotel Volán Római út 168 ☎ 87/431-013, ⓔ info @vhotel.hu. Neo-Baroque heap with a 1980s annexe possessing purely functional rooms – note that the actual hotel entrance is on Egry sétány, just along from Miditourist. April–Oct. ➎

Badacsony village and around

In high summer **BADACSONY** village is absolutely packed, and however you get here, you'll arrive in the midst of a mass of stalls selling folksy crafts, wine and fried fish. Just over the level crossing at Egry sétány 12, the **Egry József Museum** (Egry József Emlékmúzeum; May–Sept Tues–Sun 10am–6pm; 450Ft) exhibits the works of local lad József Egry (1883–1951), one of Hungary's foremost painters. Born into a poor family, Egry worked as a locksmith and roofer before winning a scholarship to the Academy of Fine Arts. He moved to Balaton after World War I, thus beginning a thirty-year love affair with the lake, as evinced by an exquisite series of paintings, which capture the changing light and moods of the lake beautifully. This wonderful collection also features some interesting family and self-portraits, as well as some of his sketches and photographs.

From May until October you can take one of the **jeep–taxis** (600Ft per person), which leave from in front of the Tourinform office on Park utca and whizz you, at alarmingly high speeds, 3km uphill through the vineyards to the charming **Róza Szegedy House** (Szegedy Róza Ház; May–Sept Tues–Sun 10am–6pm; 400Ft). Róza Szegedy met her future husband, poet Sándor Kisfaludy (see p.226), on the slopes of the Badacsony in 1795, and when they married five years later they used her Badacsony house as a summer home; its views proved to be an inspiration to his poetry. As well as a selection of his literature, the museum contains some of her old furniture, including an ornate card table and her bed. The former wine-press room now houses a cool little wine bar (same times as museum), where you can sample and buy a selection of local wines.

From the museum you can follow a path up to the **Rose Rock** (Rózsakő), where it's said that if a man and woman sit upon it with their backs to Balaton and think about each other, they'll be married by the end of the year. The trail continues through the beechwoods to the **Kisfaludy lookout tower** (437m), about an hour's walk from the museum, and on another twenty minutes to the **Stone Gate** (Kőkapu), two massive basalt towers flanking a precipitous drop. For **longer hikes** into the hills further north, offering an escape from the crowds, it's a good idea to buy a 1:80,000-scale map of the region from one of the tourist offices. A four-kilometre walk northwest from the Stone Gate will bring you to **Gulács-hegy**, a perfectly conical hill (393m) near the Nemesgulács halt for trains en route to Tapolca. The **Szent György-hegy** (415m), on the far side of the tracks, boasts some impressive basalt **organ pipes** and the region's finest vineyards, where Szürkebarát is produced. A few kilometres to the east, the 375-metre-high **Csobánc-hegy** is crowned by a **ruined castle**; this hike will probably take the best part of a day and leave you closer to Tapolca than Balaton. Don't be alarmed if you hear bangs in the fields around you: it's just the local way of scaring birds off the grape crop.

Three kilometres northeast of Badacsony, near the settlement of **BADAC-SONYÖRS**, signposts point up the hill to the **Folly Aborétum** (April–Oct Tues–Sun 9am–6pm; 350Ft), a stiff twenty-minute climb that rewards visitors with excellent views and a small park offering a peaceful contrast to Balaton. This private collection of cedars, cypresses and pines from all over the world was started by one doctor Gyula Folly in 1905, and takes about an hour to walk around.

Eating and drinking

The best of the **restaurants** hereabouts – and the only one open year round – is the *Borbarátok* (in the pension of the same name – see opposite) where, in addition to the comely restaurant, you can also dine in either the cellar, gallery or sunny garden; the food is upscale Hungarian but also features some Transylvanian dishes, while the home-cultivated wine is first-rate, with tastings also possible (around 1500Ft for five wines). A remote spot, but with tremendous views, is the *Kisfaludy Ház* just up from the Róza Szegedy House, which offers excellent Hungarian food and live Gypsy music on summer evenings. In Badacsony itself, the *Hárksert Vendéglő*, in the *Hotel Neptun*, offers a more standard Hungarian menu, but is a pleasant antidote to the *Halászkert* at Park utca 5 – the definitive tourist restaurant, with pricey food, waiters touting at the entrance and musicians eagerly plucking away with a beady eye on your forint. These last three restaurants are open between April and October only. In addition, during the summer there are stacks of **snack** and **wine stalls** in between the train station and Park utca.

Szigliget

After the crowded Badacsony, the lush **Szigliget peninsula** is a marked contrast. Both the main road and the train line go inland of the picturesque village of **SZIGLIGET**, 5km west of Badacsony, giving it a pleasant secluded feel. Though the peninsula has been built up with holiday homes, these are mainly privately owned, and accommodation is almost entirely in private houses. Earlier inhabitants of the region included a people known as the Lads, who occupied this area when the Magyars entered the region in the tenth century.

The centre of the village, which lies on the west of the peninsula at the top of Kossuth utca, is dominated by a former Esterházy mansion (closed to the public), now a holiday resort for the Writers' Union, and the ruins of **Szigliget Castle** (Szigligeti vár; March–Oct daily 9am–6pm; 450Ft), a twenty-minute signposted walk uphill. Originally commissioned in 1260 by Pannonhalma Monastery in the wake of the Mongol invasion, the present remains date from the sixteenth century. During the Turkish occupation, the Hungarian fleet moored at Szigliget under the protection of the castle, but in the seventeenth century lightning struck the castle and burnt it down. Although there remains a fair bit to see – including several of the towers, a section of the living quarters and part of the former stables – the main reason for visiting is to take in the superlative views of the lake and the Bakony Hills. Just below the castle is the *Vár Vendéglő* and the *Várkávézo*, the former a touristy, but decent enough, restaurant, the latter a pleasing little coffee house. A little further down, at Kossuth utca 3, is the **Esterházy Wine Cellar** (Eszterházi Pince; daily: June–Sept noon–10pm, Oct–May noon–4pm; ☎87/461-044), which offers tours of its enormous eighteenth-century cellars, whilst you can also purchase wine from the shop here. During the summer they also stage folklore programmes, comprising music, dance and food (July & Aug Mon, Wed & Fri 6pm; 5000Ft), and though these are generally the preserve of big tour groups, you could always try and see if there are places available. Heading down Kossuth utca for 2km you come to the **strand**, which is slightly quieter than your average Balaton beach (May–Sept daily 9am–6pm; 400Ft); boats from Keszthely and Badacsony arrive at the port 500m further on. Just before the turning for Badacsonytördemic, another couple of kilometres on, are the remains of a twelfth-century **church** with a restored octagonal tower.

Access to the village is by **bus** running between Tapolca and the train station at Badacsonytördemic (10 daily), serving all points around the peninsula. If you wish to stay here, pretty much your only option is to hunt down a **private room**, many of which are advertised along Kossuth utca.

Keszthely and around

A tradition of freethinking that dates back to the eighteenth century gives **KESZTHELY** a sense of superiority over other resorts, and its university ensures that life isn't wholly taken over by tourism. Perched at the far western tip of the lake, and the hub of several ferry, bus and train routes, the town gracefully absorbs thousands of visitors during peak season and yet manages not to look bleak and abandoned the rest of the year. With the Belváros and Festetics Palace to admire, and a thermal lake awaiting bathers at nearby **Hévíz**, Keszthely is one of the most appealing and enjoyable towns on Balaton. It's also the best place from which to approach the attractions at Kis-Balaton (see p.202).

Arrival and information

Arriving at Fly Balaton **airport**, around 12km southwest of town near the village of Sármellék, the easiest and cheapest way into Keszthely (or Hévíz) is by using the BusExpress service (☎83/318-063, ⓦwww.busexpress.hu), which offers door-to-door transfers for around 1500Ft – you must book in advance if travelling to the airport; a taxi will cost around 2000Ft. The **train** and **bus stations**, with services to Budapest, the Bakony and major towns in Transdanubia, are further south, at the bottom end of Mártírok útja, but most buses entering town drop passengers on downtown Fő tér, sparing them a 600-metre trudge along Kossuth utca, Keszthely's main axis. Arriving by **ferry** near the main *strand*, you can walk up Erzsébet királyné útja to the centre in less than fifteen minutes.

Information can be obtained from Tourinform at Kossuth utca 28 (mid-June to Aug daily 9am–7pm; Sept to mid-June Mon–Fri 9am–5pm, Sat 9am–noon;

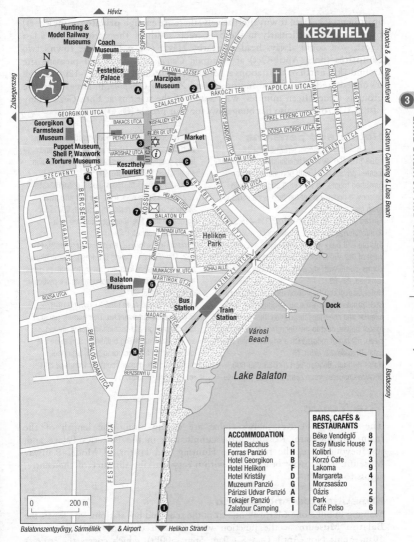

Hunting & Model Railway Museums	
Coach Museum	
Festetics Palace	**A**
Marzipan Museum	
Georgikon Farmstead Museum	**B**
Puppet Museum, Shell P, Waxwork & Torture Museums	
Keszthely Tourist	
Helikon Park	
Balaton Museum	
Bus Station	
Train Station	
Dock	
Városi Beach	
Lake Balaton	

Héviz

Tapolca & ► Balatonfüred

Castrum Camping & Libas Beach

Badacsony

Zalaegerszeg

N

0   200 m

Balatonszentgyörgy, Sármellék ▼ & Airport   ▼ Helikon Strand

ACCOMMODATION

Hotel Bacchus	C
Forras Panzió	H
Hotel Georgikon	B
Hotel Helikon	F
Hotel Kristály	D
Muzeum Panzió	G
Párizsi Udvar Panzió	A
Tokajer Panzió	E
Zalatour Camping	I

BARS, CAFÉS & RESTAURANTS

Béke Vendéglő	8
Easy Music House	7
Kolibri	7
Korzó Cafe	3
Lakoma	9
Margareta	4
Morzsasázo	1
Oázis	2
Park	5
Café Pelso	6

☎83/314-144, Ⓦwww.keszthely.hu). The main **post office** is at no. 44 (Mon–Fri 8am–6pm, Sat 8am–noon), while there's **internet access** available at the *Stones Cyber-Cafe*, at Kisfaludy utca 17.

Accommodation

There is no shortage of **accommodation** in Keszthely and even during July and August you should be able to find something. Dormitory beds (July & Aug; 2500Ft) are available at the *Vajda Hostel*, Gagarin utca 2 (☎83/311-361), and the *VSZK Kollégium*, just up from the stations on Mártírok útja (☎83/515-300). Keszthely Tours, at Kossuth utca 25 (Mon–Fri 9am–6pm, Sat 9am–1pm; ☎83/314-287, Ⓦwww.keszthelytourist.hu), have a good selection of affordable apartments (④–⑤) in town; alternatively, there are enough **private rooms** (②–③) to go around, particularly in the backstreets south of the station or, as a last resort, you could always head to nearby Hévíz (see p.222). The town's two **campsites** (both April–Oct) are *Castrum Camping*, a clean and pleasant site around 1km north of the stations at Móra Ferenc utca 48 (℡83/312-120), though it's aimed predominantly at motorists; and *Zalatour Camping*, in large, attractive grounds some fifteen minutes' walk south of the stations at Entz Gezá sétány (℡83/312-782) – it also has bungalows for four people (②–③).

Hotels and pensions

Hotel Bacchus Erzsébet királyné utca 18 ℡83/510-450, ⓦwww.bacchushotel.hu. Centrally located private hotel, with perfunctory, pine-furnished rooms, all with wi-fi and some with balcony. It boasts one of the best restaurants in town (see p.221). ⑥

Forras Panzió Római út 1 ℡83/311-418, ⓔinfo@forraspanzio.hu. Brute ugly it may be, but this big and busy hostel-style place, a few blocks west of the stations, has clean, variously sized dorms, some with showers, some with shared facilities. ②–③

Hotel Georgikon Georgikon utca 20 ℡83/312-363, ⓔmoor@georgikon.hu. Despite its grubby exterior and cheerless disposition, this renovated manor house, next to the Georgikon Museum, has clean, utilitarian rooms with a small kitchen area in each. Breakfast is extra. ④

Hotel Helikon Balaton-part 5 ℡83/889-600, ⓦwww.danubiusgroup.com. Lakeside high-rise with smoothly furnished, good-sized rooms, most with fantastic views; there's a sauna, pool and tennis courts, and a causeway leading to its own small island just offshore. ⑦

Múzeum Panzió Múzeum utca 3 ℡&ⓕ83/313-182. Just a 5min walk from the bus and train stations, on a leafy residential street, this is an agreeable little five-room pension run by a hospitable proprietor. ④

Párizsi Udvar Panzió Kastély utca 5 ℡83/311-202. The "Parisian Court" is a fresh, good-looking pension in a plum location just by the palace gates; the three-bed rooms and apartments are particularly good value. ④

Tokajer Panzió Apát utca 21 ℡83/319-875, ⓦwww.pensiontokajer.hu. This homely pension has charmingly old-fashioned rooms spread across three adjoining buildings, and there are lots of extras too, including pool, whirlpool, exercise room, games room for kids, and bike rental. April–Oct. ⑤

The Town

The majority of Keszthely's sights are strung along the length of the main thoroughfare, Kossuth utca, culminating in the Festetics Palace and, just beyond here, the rather fine Hunting and Historical Model Railway Museum. The town's beaches are within easy walking distance of the centre, across to the east.

Kossuth utca and around

Walking uphill along Mártírok útja from the train and bus stations, you'll pass the **Balaton Museum** at the junction with Kossuth utca (May–Oct Tues–Sun 10am–6pm; Nov–April Tues–Sat 9am–5pm; 500Ft), which covers the region's history and wildlife, with artefacts dating back to the first century AD, when road-building Romans disrupted the lifestyle of local Celtic tribes. Mock-up displays of fishing and thatching scenes are used to illustrate the life of the lakeside population. Heading on up Kossuth utca for ten minutes brings you to **Fő tér**, a strangely shaped square in the middle of which stands the **Trinity Statue**, erected in 1770. On the eastern side of the square, the much-remodelled **Church of Our Lady of the Hungarians** was originally constructed in the fourteenth century, and was at one point rebuilt as a fortress to repel the Turks, before becoming the property of György Festetics (see opposite) in 1799. Further reconstruction in the late nineteenth century included the addition of the neo-Gothic tower, and the church still retains a Gothic rose window above its portal.

North of Fő tér is the pedestrianized section of Kossuth utca, a colourful, bustling thoroughfare given over to cafés, buskers and strollers. Just beyond the Tourinform office, a plaque on the right, at Kossuth utca 22, marks the **birthplace of Karl Goldmark**. Born in 1830, the son of a poor Jewish cantor who enrolled him in Sopron's school of music, Goldmark went on to study at the Vienna Conservatory. Almost shot as a rebel for giving concerts in Győr during the 1848 Revolution, he survived to compose *Merlin*, *Zrínyi* and *The Queen of Sheba*. In the courtyard through the archway is the newly restored **synagogue**, dating from 1852, though unfortunately it's not possible to enter. A black **obelisk** nearby commemorates the 829 Jews who were deported from here in 1944.

Further along Kossuth utca, take a left down Bakacs utca where you'll find a quartet of attractions (all daily: June–Sept 9am–6pm; Oct–May 10am–5pm; 300Ft each). The first one you come to is the **Waxwork Museum** (Panoptikum), featuring life-size models of legendary and eminent Hungarians such as King Stephen, Árpád and Petőfi; it's made all the more enjoyable thanks to the English captions explaining each person's role in Hungarian society. Just around the corner is the **Shell Parliament** (Csiga Parlament), an extraordinary seven-metre-long, 2.5-metre-high reconstruction of the Budapest Parliament building – extraordinary in the sense that it took one indefatigable woman, Ilona Miskei, fourteen years of her life to piece together 4.5 million Pannon sea-snail shells to get the finished result. The building next door houses the delightful **Folk Costume Puppet Museum** (Népi Babamúzeum), a vast collection of exquisite porcelain dolls dressed up in folk costumes representing the multifarious regions of Hungary. Upstairs, don't miss the superb assemblage of beautifully carved, wooden model churches and gates, which are typically found in the Erdőhát region in northeastern Hungary. Fourthly, there's the **Torture Museum** (Kínzó Múzeum), a rather comical collection of waxwork figures in various states of mutilation and dismemberment.

Ten minutes' walk north, beyond the end of Kossuth utca and 200m down from the palace gates at Katona József utca 19, the **Marzipan Museum and Pastry Shop** (March–Dec Tues–Sun 10am–6pm; 160Ft) is well worth a stop, not only to view the exquisitely made marzipan works, but also to sample one of the many tempting marzipan desserts.

The Festetics Palace

The imposing neo-Baroque **Festetics Palace** (Festetics kastély) assumed its present form in 1887, and with one hundred halls and rooms, some eighteen of which can be visited, it is one of the largest, and most expensive to visit, in Hungary (June Tues–Sun 9am–5pm; July & Aug daily 9am–6pm; Sept–May Tues–Sun 10am–5pm; 1700Ft or 2000Ft if combined with the Coach Museum). The Festetics family is chiefly remembered for Count György, founder of Keszthely's agricultural university, the Georgikon, in 1797. During the early nineteenth century, the palace's salons attracted the leading lights of Magyar literature and became Hungary's first public forum for criticism. More recently, there was a national scandal in 1989 when it was discovered that a porn version of the life of spy Mata Hari had been filmed here while school parties were touring other parts of the palace.

The highlights of the palace are a gilt, mirrored **ballroom** and the **Helikon Library**, a masterpiece of joinery by János Kerbl, built in 1801 and containing over 90,000 books in diverse languages, the oldest of which – *Chronica Hungarorum* – dates back to 1488. Chinese vases and tiled stoves jostle for space with portraits of the family racehorses and dachshunds (whose pedigrees are proudly noted), and the pelts and heads of tigers, bears and other animals shot by Count Windishgrätz.

▲ The Festetics Palace

Wine buffs might care to check out the palace's **wine museum** (600Ft), essentially a collection of many of the country's finest wines, reposed within the original sixteenth-century cellars – a better reason to visit is for a tasting session, available by prior appointment (2500Ft; ☎30/267-2188).

Housed in the immaculately renovated former stables at the rear of the palace is the quite splendid **Coach Museum** (Hintómúzeum; same times; 800Ft or 2000Ft if combined with the palace), which proudly displays an assortment of eighteenth- and nineteenth-century carriages – principally parade and hunting coaches, though the oldest one here is a Hungarian bride coach from 1770.

The Hunting and Historical Model Railway Museum, and Georgikon

Occupying a former military warehouse west of the palace on Pal utca are the **Hunting and Historical Model Railway Museums** (Vadászati és Modellvasút-kíállítás; same times as Festetics Palace; 800Ft each or 1200Ft for both). The former features an impressive collection of hunting trophies from the 1930s, in addition to a brightly presented natural history section, with a wide variety of stuffed animals, all themed by continent. Up on the top floor, and emphatically not to be missed (for kids and adults alike), is one of Europe's largest model railways; some 40m long, this fantastic creation replicates, in extraordinary detail, the original Vienna to Trieste line, including the famous Semmering mountain railway in southern Austria.

Ten minutes' walk south of the museum, at Bercsényi utca 67, is the **Georgikon**, the first college of its kind in Europe when it was established in 1797. Students attending the three-year course lived and worked together in a cluster of white-washed buildings, some of which have been converted into the **Farmstead Museum** (Majormúzeum; May–Oct Tues–Sun 10am–5pm; 500Ft). Sheltered here is an impressive and voluminous gathering of dairy and viticultural equipment, cartwrights' and blacksmiths' tools, as well as old Ford tractors and two enormous steam ploughs manufactured by the British company John Fowler in 1912. The Georgikon was the forerunner of today's **Agricultural University**, a green and daffodil-yellow pile halfway along Széchenyi utca.

Eating, drinking and entertainment

Keszthely's **restaurant** scene is steady rather than spectacular, and if you're here for any length of time you'll probably find yourself visiting the same places. Rather dispiritingly, **nightlife** largely revolves around a string of tacky, neon-lit clubs and strip bars scattered around town.

Restaurants

Two appealing **self-service** places are *Oázis*, at Rákóczi tér 3 (Mon–Sat 11am–4pm), a vegetarian joint which has a different menu for each day of the week, as well as a decent salad bar, and the more wide-ranging *Morzasázó*, 200m further down the road at no. 12 (Mon–Fri 11am–7pm, Sat & Sun 11am–4pm).

Bacchus Erzsébet királyné utca 18. The *Bacchus* hotel's handsome cellar restaurant features chunky tables and chairs culled from old bits of wine press, upturned ceramic lamps and other wine artefacts; the food, meanwhile, is an upscale take on familiar Hungarian dishes (hot stews, steaks on a platter) but also features plenty to keep veggies content (corn pie, egg dumplings, potato pancakes); first-rate wine too.

Béke Vendéglő Kossuth utca 50. Awkwardly pitched somewhere between bar and restaurant, this modern eatery offers reasonable homestyle Hungarian food, as well as a good choice of beers and wines.

Lakoma Balaton utca 9. A restful, understated place with an intriguing and wildly eclectic menu, offering dishes like kangaroo steak, stuffed snails, and, for the more adventurous, stew of cock's balls. Happy, smiley service to accompany your food.

Margaréta Bercsényi út 60. The locals' favourite, this bustling place might not look much, with its tightly packed ranks of plain wooden tables and thick bench seating, but its food – grilled pork and beef, stews, fish, savoury pancakes – and busy atmosphere make it the best value-for-money place in town.

Park Vörösmarty utca 1a. A distinctly modest and old-fashioned affair, where you can get stuck in to big plates of hearty Hungarian fare whilst a cimbalom player taps away in the background.

Cafés and bars

The most agreeable of the many **cafés** along Kossuth utca is the warm *Korzó Café* at no. 7, which has super cakes too, while *Café Pelso*, a smart, two-tiered wood and glass building on Fő tér, also has top-notch coffee – during the summer the top terrace opens up and it becomes a really vibrant place (May–Sept till midnight; Oct–April till 9pm).

Most **drinking** venues are, predictably enough, student focused and include the *Easy Music House* across from the post office at Kossuth Lajos utca 79, which has live dance and Latin music, and the *Kolibri* next door – both are similarly rowdy and stay open till the small hours. For something a little more sophisticated, there's **wine-tasting** to be had in the beautiful eighteenth-century cellars of the *Bacchus* hotel (2500Ft for six wines plus snacks, see above), or the cellars of the Festetics Palace (see opposite).

Festivals and beaches

Keszthely has a rich festival tradition, the highlight being the week-long **Balaton Festival** each May. One of the largest festivals on Balaton, it brings pop and classical concerts, theatre programmes and art exhibitions to venues across town, including the lakeside, the palace, the Balaton Museum and the pedestrian stretch of Kossuth utca. In May of even-numbered years, the **Helikon Festival of Chamber and Orchestral Music**, a celebration featuring young musicians, takes place in the palace. Another regular event is the five-day **Wine Festival**, starting at the end of July/beginning of August, with folk music, dance performances and a plethora of stalls selling wine and offering tastings along the avenue just south of the *Helikon* hotel near the lake. The **Theatre Festival**, featuring plays by Shake-speare, is performed on an open-air stage in the palace grounds at the end of July/beginning of August. The palace is also the setting for frequent **philharmonic concerts** throughout July and August, while there are **organ recitals** at the Lutheran church. The summer months are further enlivened by rock, folk and jazz **concerts** on Fő tér, and buskers and jugglers along Kossuth utca.

Keszthely has three **beaches** (all May–Sept daily 8am–7/8pm). The main town beach is the clean and pleasant Városi *strand* (800Ft), located near the ferry dock and with its own quay; to the northeast of Városi, at the end of Lóczy Lajos utca, is the Libás *strand* (500Ft), while to the south, near the *Zalatour* campsite, there's the Helikon *strand* (500Ft); which also has a giant water chute. You can rent **pedaloes** (1000Ft per hr) and **windsurfing** gear (800Ft per hr, 2500Ft per day) at all three beaches.

Hévíz

HÉVÍZ, 8km northeast of Keszthely, boasts the second-largest **thermal lake** (Gyógy-tó) in the world after Lake Tarawera in New Zealand. The temperature rarely drops below 30°C even during winter, when steam billows from the lake and its thermal stream, and Indian waterlilies flourish on its surface. The lake is replenished by up to eighty million litres of warm water a day gushing up from springs 1km underground, and is completely flushed out every couple of days.

Exploited since medieval times for curative purposes as well as for tanning leather, the lake was salubriously channelled into a bathhouse by Count György Festetics in 1795. By the end of the nineteenth century, Hévíz had become a grand **resort**, briefly favoured by crown princes and magnates like those other great spas of the Habsburg empire, Karlsbad and the Baths of Hercules. They'd be hard-pressed to recognize it today, with high-rise hotels, tacky bars and a raft of souvenir stalls setting the tone.

Although the wooden terraces and catwalks surrounding the **baths** (*tófürdő*; daily: July–Aug 8am–7.30pm; March–May & Sept–Nov 8.30am–5.30pm; Dec–Feb 9am–4.30pm; 3700Ft per day, 2900Ft for 5hr, 2100Ft for 3hr; ⓦwww.spaheviz.hu) have a vaguely *fin-de-siècle* appearance, the general ambience is modern, with people sipping beer or reading newspapers while bobbing on the lake in rented inner tubes. Prolonged immersion isn't recommended on account of the slightly radioactive water (the lake is not suitable for under-12s), though mud from the lake is used to treat locomotive disorders. The busiest months are May and September, when the water is at its optimum temperature for bathing. You can rent all the necessaries here, including cubicles (1200Ft), towels (900Ft) and rubber rings (500Ft).

A small **museum** (Tues–Sat 10am–6pm; 300Ft), inside the cinema building at Rákóczi utca 9, relays the history of the baths through old images and photos, whilst also paying tribute to the pioneering work of doctors Károly Moll, inventor of the weight bath, and Vilmos Schulhof, one of the leading exponents in the field of baneology.

Practicalities

The **bus station** is on Deák tér, opposite the baths, from where it's a short walk to the well-equipped **Tourinform** office at Rákóczi utca 2 (July & Aug Mon–Fri 9am–6pm, Sat & Sun 10am–7pm; Oct–April Mon–Fri 9am–5pm, Sat 10am–4pm; ☎83/540-131). Just up the road at no. 8, Zalathermal (May–Sept Mon–Sat 9am–6pm, Sun 9am–5pm; Oct–April Mon–Fri 9am–5pm, Sat 9am–1pm; ☎83/341-048, ⓔinfo@zalatourheviz.hu) has a decent selection of private rooms (**❷**), though Kossuth and Zrínyi utcas are both teeming with *Zimmer frei* signs anyway. At the southern end of the lake, the four-star *Castrum Gyógycamping* (☎83/343-198, ✉heviz@castrum.eu) has tidy plots for tents and trailers and a neat little guesthouse (**❹**).

With half-hourly buses from Fő tér in Keszthely, there's no need to linger in Hévíz, but, should you decide to stay, the town is bursting with **accommodation**, including several cheapish options: best-value is the very homely *Astoria Panzió*, close to the baths at Rákóczi utca 11 (☎83/340-393, ⓦwww.astoriapanzio .hu; **❹**), with a mix of small and large air-conditioned rooms; while at Petőfi utca 18 (the street parallel), the *Hotel Alba* (☎83/343-123, ✉hotel.alba@freemail .hu; **❸**) is dated but extremely cheap.

Two more good-value hotels lie just across the road from each other on Széchenyi utca: at no. 21, the friendly and tidy *Napfény* (☎83/340-642, ✉napf .hot@t-online.hu; **❹**) also rents out bikes, and at no. 23, the *Pannon* (☎83/340-482, ⓦwww.pannonhotelheviz.hu; **❹**) features small, colourful rooms. If you want to go more upmarket, try the *Beta Hotel Park* at Petőfi utca 26 (☎83/ 341-190, ⓦwww.danubiusgroup.com; **❼**), an elegant thirty-room hotel housed in two villas linked by a walkway; its facilities include sauna, jacuzzi and fitness centre.

Hévíz's few **restaurants** are fairly tourist-oriented. The two best places, both combining standard Hungarian and fish dishes, are somewhat inconveniently located fifteen minutes' walk southwest of the centre on Tavirózsa utca, the street north of Kossuth utca; although there's little to choose between the *Tavirózsa* at no. 4 and the *Magyar Csárda* at no. 1, the former is a touch more polished and has a better vegetarian range. Of those down by the baths, the *Rózsakert* on Rákóczi utca, offering lots of grilled meats, is about the best there is. Take coffee at the funky *Macchiato* **café**, Széchenyi utca 7.

The Bakony

The Bakony range cuts a swathe across central Transdanubia, as if scooped from the ground to provide space for the lake and piled as a natural embankment behind the lowlier Balaton highlands. Abundant vineyards testify to the richness of the volcanic soil, and mineheads to the mineral wealth beneath it. With dense woods and narrow ravines, the Bakony was the Hungarian equivalent of Sherwood Forest during the centuries of warfare and turmoil, and the setting for a dozen castles, the finest of which stand at **Sümeg** and **Nagyvázsony**. The regional capital, **Veszprém**, boasts a wealth of historic architecture and serves as a base for trips to **Herend**, location of the world-famous porcelain factory, while **Tapolca** is currently enjoying a revival, belying its old reputation as a dour mining centre.

Access to the western end of the Bakony is from Tapolca, where **buses** and **trains** go to Sümeg. Buses also run from Tapolca here via Nagyvázsony and Nemesvámos towards Veszprém, the main transport hub, from where buses serve all the Bakony villages and towns, as well as the major Route 8 to Herend.

Tapolca

Ten kilometres inland from Balaton, the charming small town of **TAPOLCA** was a relatively unimportant village until the 1960s, when it became the capital of Hungary's mining industry. Today, it offers several interesting tourist attractions, as well as serving as something of a transport hub, with regular buses and trains from Keszthely, including *nosztálgia* **steam trains** in July and August, and services to and from Balatonfüred.

The town's biggest draw is the **Cave Lake** (Tavasbarlang; July & Aug daily 9am–7pm, mid-March to June & Sept–Oct daily 10am–5pm; Nov to mid-March Sat only 10am–4pm; 1000Ft includes boat rental), a ten-minute walk east of the main square, Fő ter, on Kisfaludy utca. Discovered in 1902 during a well-digging, the cave was the first in Hungary to be opened to the public, in 1913, with electrical lighting installed a few years later. Used as an air-raid shelter during World War II, the cave was subsequently robbed of its water by mining, and so was closed down as a visitor attraction, only to reopen in 1990. Today around 250m of the main passage can be explored, 70m by foot, the rest by boat. The temperature of the cave is around 18°C, so there's no need for extra layers of clothing.

Just behind Fő tér to the south is the wonderfully serene and picturesque **Mill Lake** (Malom-tó), fed by thermal springs and bisected by a low footbridge and the *Hotel Gabriella*, housed in an eighteenth-century watermill – the mill wheel, with its slowly turning blades, still hangs precariously outside. A delightful strolling spot, the smaller, narrower lake (Kis-tó) is fringed by weeping willows whilst the larger lake (Nagy-tó) is encircled by softly coloured buildings and a couple of cafés. On summer Sunday evenings at 8pm, the pontoon on the larger lake stages free **classical concerts**. In the group of buildings behind the hotel, signs point you to an old school housing the **School Museum** (Iskola or Városi Múzeum; June–Aug Tues–Sun 10am–5pm; Sept–May Tues–Fri 10am–4pm; 500Ft). Reconstructed in 1813, it operated as a school until 1884, after which time it became the residence of the local choir-master; inside you can view a rather unexciting assemblage of books, desks and school uniforms among other accessories from a hundred years ago, and the teacher's bedroom next door. Across the lake from the hotel, the **Szent Antal Wine Museum** (Bormúzeum; May–Sept Sat & Sun 9am–9pm; 450Ft) houses an exhibition on the history of Balaton wines; tastings are included in the entry price and you can buy a selection of wines from the region.

Practicalities

While the **train station** is 1.5km southwest of the town centre, served by regular buses or a fifteen-minute walk along Dózsa György utca, the **bus station** is on Deák Ferenc utca, a minute's walk from Fő tér. **Information** can be obtained from Tourinform at Fő tér 17 (mid-June to mid-Sept Mon–Fri 9am–6pm, Sat & Sun 9am–5pm; mid-Sept to mid-June Mon–Fri 9am–4pm; ☎87/510-777, Ⓦwww.tapolca.hu). The **post office** is at Deák Ferenc utca 19 (Mon–Fri 8am–6pm, Sat 8am–noon).

If you fancy stopping overnight, there is plentiful **accommodation** in town, the plushest place being the immaculate four-star *Hotel Pelion*, 400m north of the Cave Lake at Kőztársaság 10 (☎87/513-100, Ⓦwww.hunguesthotels.hu; ❾) – its facilities include indoor and outdoor thermal pools, tennis and squash courts, and, somewhat uniquely, a medicinal grotto. Right next to the Cave Lake, at Kisfaludy utca 1, sits the *Szent György Panzió* (☎87/413-809, Ⓔgardos2@t-online.hu; ❹), a fine, mustard-coloured building with boxy but bright rooms. Although they're nothing particularly special, all rooms in the *Hotel Gabriella*, at Batsányi tér 7 (☎87/511-070, Ⓦwww.hotelgabriella.hu; ❹–❺), have terrific views overlooking the Mill Lake; while some

100m east of here at Arany János utca 14, there is the *Varjú Fogadó* (☎87/510-522, Ⓦwww.varjufogado.hu; ❹), whose modern, spacious and colourful rooms, and spotless bathrooms, make it the best deal of the lot. For a **private room** (❷) head to Balatontourist, just off Fő tér at Arany János utca 2 (Mon–Fri 9am–4pm, Sat 9–11.30am; ☎87/510-131, Ⓔtapolca@balatontouristutazas.hu).

Both the *Szent György Panzió* and *Hotel Gabriella* have the best **restaurants** in town; the former, a gorgeously decorated place with enticing chef's specials, is marginally more superior, though the latter does have a fabulous terrace overlooking the lake. For coffee, cakes and ices head to the *Dream Team Café* on the corner of Fő tér and Kossuth utca.

Sümeg

SÜMEG, 14km north of Tapolca, has always drawn crowds of tourists, thanks to its dramatic-looking castle dating from the eighteenth century, when Sümeg was the seat of the bishops of Veszprém. All of Sümeg's sights are located less than a couple of minutes' walk from Kossuth Lajos utca, the town's main thoroughfare.

Arrival, information and accommodation

Arriving in Sümeg by **train**, head along Darnay Kálmán utca, which segues into Lukonich Gábor utca, before turning left at the stone church and onto Kossuth Lajos utca; the **bus** station is on Flórián tér, at the southern end of Kossuth Lajos utca. There's **information** at the small Tourinform office at Kossuth utca 15 (mid-June to mid-Sept Mon–Fri 9am–6pm, Sat & Sun 9am–5pm; mid-Sept to mid-June Mon–Fri 9am–4pm; ☎87/550-276, Ⓔsumeg@tourinform.hu), whilst Balatontourist in the adjoining office (Mon–Fri 8.30am–4pm, Sat 8.30am–noon; ☎87/550-259, Ⓔsumeg@balatontouristutazas.hu) can arrange **private accommodation** (❷).

There's no shortage of **hotels** in town, with pride of place going to *Hotel Kapitány* at Tóth Tivadar utca 19, round the far side of the Várhegy (☎87/550-166, Ⓦwww.hotelkapitany.hu; ❻–❾); it has two sections, the rooms in the newer, modern wing are super smart, while those in the older, original wing are gloomy and careworn – note that the price of these does not include use of the hotel's extensive wellness facilities, while, for both wings, you'll pay extra for the (admittedly great) views up to the castle. In the centre, at Kossuth Lajos utca 13, the utilitarian *Kisfaludy* hotel (☎&Ⓕ87/352-128; ❹) also has rooms sleeping four to six people. Up past the Franciscan church, at Vak Bottyán utca 2, is the *Hotel Vár* (☎87/352-352, Ⓔhotelvar@axelero.hu; ❺; mid-March to mid-Nov), an outwardly unappealing, chunky stone-walled building, which conceals big, colourful and modern wood-furnished rooms, including some triples and quads. Cheapest of all is the basic student accommodation at Vároldal utca 5, above the Bishop's Stables near the castle (☎87/550-087; dorm bed 3000Ft, doubles ❷), although only the most fanatical equine-lover is likely to be enticed by the horsey smells.

The Town

Baroque mansions line Deák utca, which leads down from Kossuth Lajos utca to the **Church of the Ascension** (March–Sept Mon–Sat 9am–noon & 1–6pm, Sun 1–6pm; Oct–Feb Mon–Sat 9am–noon & 1–3pm, Sun 1–6pm); if it's shut, ask for the key at the *plébánia*, across the road at Biró Marton utca 3. Outwardly unprepossessing, the church contains magnificent **frescoes** by Maulbertsch, who, with a team of assistants, managed to cover the whole interior within eighteen months, mostly in biblical scenes. Exceptions are the rear wall, which depicts his patron, Bishop Biró (1696–1762), and the wall facing the choir, which shows the churches Biró sponsored in Sümeg and Zalaegerszeg. In the former, the man kneeling before the bishop has Maulbertsch's features, as does the shepherd in the Adoration scene.

Retracing your steps to cross Kossuth utca you come to Kisfaludy tér. To the left is the **Town Museum** (Városi Múzeum; May–Sept Tues–Sun 10am–6pm; Oct–April Mon–Fri 8am–4pm; 400Ft), whose oddly jumbled collection includes local archeological finds, some ecclesiastical artwork, and exhibits pertaining to the local pottery industry, which was one of the foremost guilds in the region during the late nineteenth century. Most of the space here, however, is given over to furniture and other objects belonging to Sándor Kisfaludy (1772–1844), the romantic poet of Balaton who was born in this house. Poetry aside, Kisfaludy was one of the leading figures of the Hungarian language reform movement, and was also instrumental in establishing *Auróra*, Hungary's first literary journal.

Up from the square behind the trees stands the crumbling, overgrown **Bishop's Palace** (Püspöki Palota; May–Sept Wed–Sun 10am–6pm; Oct–April Mon–Fri 8am–4pm; 400Ft), commissioned by Márton Biró, the Bishop of Veszprém, in the mid-eighteenth century. Although the palace is still being painstakingly renovated, you can at present view the old oval chapel, replete with beautiful ceiling frescoes and also featuring a fine high altar complete with sculptures of King Stephen's sons, Imre and László; it's also possible to visit the wine cellar, part of which is now an excellent wine bar and shop (Mon–Fri 11am–4.30pm), although proper tasting sessions are reserved for groups only. On the right side of the square is the second-oldest building in town after the castle, the **Franciscan Church and monastery**, originally dating from the seventeenth century, though the present church owes more to alterations the following century. The church hosts special celebrations on September 13, when the miraculous statue of the Virgin draws crowds of believers.

Heading up Vak Bottyán utca to the right of the church, a five-minute walk brings you to the former **Bishop's Stables** (Váristálló), where some forty horses are still kept today; the **riding school** (Capári Lovasiskola) here offers an excellent programme, including lessons for beginners, trots around the yard and cross-country rides (2500–3500Ft). You can also just wander around the stables to view the horses or take a look at the small Hussar exhibition tucked away in a corner of the stable office (daily 9am–6pm; free). Just beyond the stables is a cluster of souvenir stalls that leads up from Route 84 to the entrance of the castle.

Sümeg Castle

The most impressive sight in town is **Sümeg Castle** (Sümeg vár; daily: May–Oct 9am–7pm; Nov–April 9am–4pm weather permitting; 1000Ft), one of the best-preserved fortifications in Hungary and worth visiting for its tremendous views alone. Dominating Sümeg from a conical limestone massif, a unique Cretaceous outcropping among the basalt of the Bakony, the castle was built during the thirteenth century as a defence against marauding Mongols. It was reinforced several times over the next few hundred years, proving impregnable to the Turks, but eventually falling to the Habsburgs in 1713. Beyond the remains of the castle chapel – albeit now with a wooden roof – and a modest exhibition of weaponry, there's precious little to see, but the views really are quite superb. It's a reasonably steep ten-minute climb up to the castle, but if this is beyond you, take one of the **minitaxis** which leave from the top of Vároldal utca, where the path to the castle begins (April–Oct; 400Ft, 700Ft return).

Down below the castle, a specially constructed arena (Várjátékok) – designed to evoke an authentic medieval atmosphere with its wooden bench seating, striped canopies and colourful battle standards – has been created; from late June through August, it hosts a full and lively programme of jousting and other martial games (details from Tourinform).

Eating and drinking

Eating choices in town are thin on the ground: by far the most enjoyable **restaurant** is the medieval-styled *King Saint László* in the *Hotel Kapitány*, and while the menu isn't particularly extensive, the food is top drawer, with beef and game dominant. Elsewhere, other half-decent **restaurants** include the *Kisfaludy*, inside the hotel of the same name, which knocks up cheap Hungarian food, and *Scotti*, opposite the Kisfaludy Museum, providing the full gamut from pizzas and spaghetti to steak and fish. Otherwise, there's the *Vár Csárda* up by the castle, though it's a rather hollow place aimed squarely at tourists.

Nagyvázsony and Nemesvámos

NAGYVÁZSONY, a sleepy market town 20km from Tapolca (and also accessible by bus from Balatonfüred), harbours **Kinizsi Castle** (April–Oct Tues–Sun 9am–5pm; 500Ft), given by King Mátyás to Pál Kinizsi, a local miller who made good as a commander. Formidably strong, he is said to have wielded a dead Turk as a bludgeon and danced a triumphal jig while holding three Turks, one of them between his teeth. During the sixteenth century, this was one of the border fortresses between Turkish and Habsburg-ruled Hungary. It is now a ruin, except for the pale thirty-metre-high stone keep housing an exhibition of weapons and fetters, and the inevitable waxworks display of people being tortured, while the chapel across the way contains Kinizsi's red marble sarcophagus. Throughout July and August, **jousting** displays are held within the castle grounds, in addition to classical concerts.

If you wish to **stay**, the very cordial *Malomkő Panzió* on the high street, Kinizsi utca 47–49 (T88/264-165, Wwww.malomko.hu; ❹), offers bright rooms, a covered pool and a terrific little restaurant, or, a shade closer to the castle, you'll find the *Vázsonykő Panzió* at Sörház utca 2 (T80/264-344, F264-707; ❸; mid-April to Nov), where you can also get good Hungarian home cooking and wine.

Approaching Veszprém, you can't miss the roadside *Betyár Csárda* (mid-April to mid-Oct daily noon–midnight), an eighteenth-century **inn**, 600m before the village of **NEMESVÁMOS**. If you ignore the odd modern fixture and today's clientele, it's possible to imagine it as it once must have been: servants hurrying from the tap-room with its huge casks to the cellar, where swineherds, wayfarers and outlaws caroused, seated upon sections of tree trunk. Poor though most were, Bakony folk were proud of their masterless lives among the oak forests, esteeming the *kondás*, with his herd of pigs, and the highwaymen who robbed rich merchants. These highwaymen called themselves *szegénylegények* ("poor lads"), and the most audacious, Jóska Savanyú, claimed the tavern as his home. Although the food and atmosphere are undeniably enjoyable, it's all rather hammed up for the tourists, with kitsch folklore programmes at 6pm each day throughout July and August.

Another 300m past the inn, a right turn brings you to the village of Nemesvámos itself, 2km beyond which are the **ruins of a Roman villa** (Római Kövi Villagazdaság; May–Sept Tues–Sun 10am–6pm; 600Ft). Its reconstructed frescoes and mosaics convey an impression of the lifestyle of wealthy Roman colonists in the early centuries of the Christian era.

Veszprém

VESZPRÉM, 15km northwest of Lake Balaton, spreads over five hills cobbled together by a maze of streets that twist up towards its old quarter on a precipitous crag overlooking the Bakony Hills. Like Székesfehérvár, it became an episcopal see in the reign of Prince Géza, who was converted to Christianity in 975. It was here in 997 that King Stephen crushed a pagan rebellion with the help of knights sent by Henry of Bavaria, father of his queen, Gizella. During medieval times, Veszprém was the seat of the queen's household and the site of her coronation – hence its title the "Queen's Town". Utterly devastated during the sixteenth century and rebuilt after 1711, its castle district (Várhegy) and downtown parks are now juxtaposed with apartment buildings, a technical university and chemical factories. Considering its proximity to the lake, Veszprém makes a good base for visiting the Balaton resorts without having to stay there, and is also good for excursions to Nagyvázsony, Nemesvámos and Herend.

Arrival and information

Arriving at the **train station** 2km out to the north, catch bus #2 or #4 to the tall tower block near downtown Szabadság tér (built by the Communists so that the view

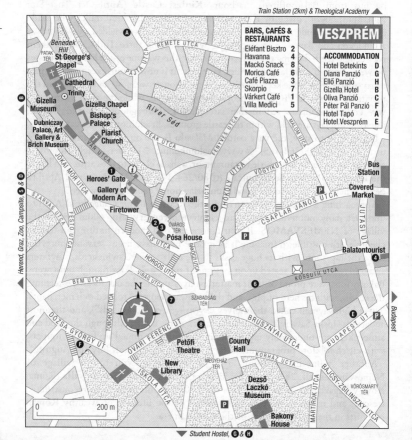

of the town would not be dominated by the castle and cathedral); the **bus station** is more conveniently situated five minutes' walk northeast of the town centre on Piac tér. From Szabadság tér, you can head north towards the Várhegy or strike out into the lower town. **Drivers** coming in from the west cross the 150-metre-long Valley Bridge over the River Séd, glimpsing the Várhegy en route to the centre.

Information is available from Tourinform, by the Heroes' Gate at Vár utca 4 (June–Aug Mon–Fri 9am–6pm, Sat & Sun 10am–4pm; May & Sept Mon–Fri 9am–5pm, Sat & Sun 10am–4pm; Oct–April Mon–Fri 9am–5pm; ☎88/404-548, ⊛www.veszpreminfo.hu); between June and August it also organizes a free two-hour city walking tour – check with the office for days and times. The **post office** is on Kossuth utca (Mon–Fri 8am–7pm, Sat 8am–noon).

Accommodation

The town is blessed with numerous very fine **hotels** and **pensions**, but if you're looking for something a little cheaper, Balatontourist, at Kossuth utca 25 (Mon–Fri 8.30am–5pm; ☎88/544-488, ⓔveszprem@balatontouristutazas.hu), has plenty of private **rooms** (❷). In July and August there is cheap accommodation in the student hostel at Egyetem utca 12, beyond Veszprém University, 1km south of the centre (☎88/429-811; bus #2Y, #4, #8 or #14Y; dorm bed 2500Ft), and at the Theological Academy (Hittudomány Akadémia; ☎88/426-116; dorm bed 2500Ft) at Jutási út 11, which is easier to reach, being twenty minutes' walk up the main road from the bus station – buses into town pass it. The tiny *Erdei* **campsite**, out by the zoo at Kittenberger Kálmán utca 14 (☎88/326-751; mid-April to mid-Oct), also has a motel attached (❷).

Hotel Betekints Veszprémvölgyi utca 4 ☎88/579-280, ⊛www.betekints.hu. Classy hotel down in the Fejes Valley northwest of town, featuring all the requisite comforts of a four-star: big, plush rooms with large beds, chairs and sofa, and immaculate bathrooms. Price includes use of pool, sauna and fitness suite. ❽

Diana Panzió József Attila utca 30 ☎88/421-061, ⓔinfo@panziodiana.hu. Quiet ten-room pension with large, though slightly dowdy, rooms and a good restaurant in an attractive villa on the road towards Tapolca (bus #4 from the train station or town centre). ❹

Éllő Panzió József Attila utca 25 ☎88/420-097, ⊛www.ellopanzio.hu. Opposite the *Diana*, this smart, secure villa has fancily furnished, richly hued rooms with spectacularly clean bathrooms. Three wheelchair-accessible rooms too. ❺

🎿 **Gizella Hotel** Jókai Mór utca 48 ☎88/579-490, ⊛www.hotelgizella.hu. Characterful hotel in a beautifully restored eighteenth-century building just below Castle Hill; many of the original details, including the Baroque ceilings and wooden beams, have been retained and the rooms sparkle

with character – the best value-for-money hotel in town. ❼

🎿 **Oliva Panzió** Buhim utca 14–16 ☎88/403-875, ⊛www.oliva.hu. Marvellous pension in the heart of the old centre offering eleven cool, olive-green, dark-wood-furnished rooms with a/c, mini-bar and wi-fi, plus one of the best restaurants in town (see p.232). ❼

Péter Pál Panzió Dózsa György út 3 ☎88/328-091, ⊛http://peterpal.hu. Engaging little pension with bright, somewhat small, rooms in the main part, and larger, quirkier rooms in a renovated annexe, a couple displaying the original bare-brick walls. ❹

Hotel Tapó Pajta utca 19 ☎88/591-450, ⊛www .tapo.hu. Located on the bank of the River Séd with views across to the castle district, this stylish place has smooth, designer-furnished rooms and a first-class restaurant to boot (see p.232). ❺

Hotel Veszprém Budapest út 6 ☎88/424-677, ⊛www.hotelveszprem.hu. Ignore the grim exterior and depressing reception – the rooms in this 1970s low-rise are perfectly reasonable; those at the back overlooking Kossuth utca are considerably quieter. ❹

The Town

The **Várhegy** (Castle District) is the heart of Veszprém, a spiny, cobbled thoroughfare that harbours the town's most worthwhile museums and galleries, and its most important ecclesiastical architecture. Beyond here, handsome

Óváros tér is a lovely place to stroll around, while the remaining attractions are dispersed between the somewhat more prosaic **lower town** area, and over to the **west**, near the impressive viaduct.

Óváros tér

The castle district is presaged by **Óváros tér**, a handsome, tree-laden cobbled plaza overlooked by Art Nouveau buildings on one side and Baroque and Rococo edifices on the other. Most are painted in pinks, blues and the shade known as "Maria Theresa yellow" – the colour scheme the empress ordained for public buildings throughout the Habsburg Empire. The most prominent of these is the Baroque **Town Hall** (Városháza), originally built as the home of the Kaposvári family, and, opposite, at no. 3, the custard-coloured **Pósa House** (Pósaház), which features a striking pediment with a crown, and cherubs playfully holding a garland. Initially the residence of the Cistercian order of Zirc, the house was then passed over to local bookseller and printer, Endre Pósa. Over on the opposite, eastern, side of the square, the **Kinizsi House** is the most flamboyant example of Secessionist architecture in the area, its facade spotted with bright green and yellow mouldings.

The castle district

From Óváros tér, the path leads up to the **Várhegy** (Castle District), accessed via the **Heroes' Gate**, a neo-Romanesque portal erected in 1936 to commemorate the dead of World War I. In the courtyard to the left of the gate the 48-metre-high Baroque **Firetower** (Tűztorony; April–Oct daily 10am–6pm; 300Ft) offers exceptional views of Veszprém's rooftops and the Bakony hills, while a traditional recruiting tune is played every hour on the hour by a carillon in the dome. Housed in a renovated building in the same courtyard is the **Gallery of Modern Art** (Vass Gyűjtemény; May–Oct daily 10am–6pm; Nov–April Tues–Sun 10am–5pm; 500Ft), an enjoyable and smartly presented little exhibition of mostly abstract works.

Continue for five minutes along Vár utca, past well-preserved eighteenth-century buildings, and you'll come to a **Piarist Church and Monastery** (Piarista templom; May to mid-Oct Tues–Sun 10am–5pm), now used for temporary exhibitions, whose facade bears three Greek letters encapsulating the Piarist credo "Mary, Mother, God". Across the street, at no. 29, stands the recently renovated **Dubniczay Palace**, a handsome Baroque edifice built in 1751 according to the designs of Canon Istvan Dubniczay. Today the palace accommodates two fabulous museums: occupying the greater part of the building is the **Carl László Collection** (Tues–Sun 10am–5pm; 800Ft), an eclectic sweep of modern art acquired by the eponymous medic and playwright; beautifully presented, the collection comprises lithographics, prints, collages and mixed fabric compositions, in addition to a smattering of industrial and pop art.

Located to the rear of the palace, in the room originally used as a barn but which also incorporates part of the old castle walls, is the **Brick Collection of the Hungarian Construction Industry Museum** (same times; 300Ft), which is actually a whole lot more interesting than it sounds; this Tegularium is a fascinating assemblage of variously sized, shaped and coloured stamped bricks, including many marked with royal or religious motifs, coats of arms, or imprinted with the names of brick-factory owners – during the early twentieth century there were more than half a dozen brick factories in the region, the last one closing down in 1960.

Immediately beyond the palace, the street broadens out into the main square, **Szentháromság tér** (Trinity Square), in the centre of which is the **Trinity Statue**, erected in 1750 on the orders of Bishop Márton Padányi Biró. The square's single most impressive, and dominant, building is the **Bishop's Palace** (Püspöki Palota; May to mid-Oct Tues–Sun 10am–5pm; 500Ft), a typically massive Baroque pile by Jakab Fellner, with the distinction of having had the first flush toilets in Hungary, installed in the late eighteenth century. It's possible to view some half a dozen of the palace's rooms, the most impressive of which is the Dining Hall, by virtue of its ceiling frescoes depicting the four seasons, and the wall paintings of Veszprém and Sümeg castles as they probably once were. During the palace's construction, workmen unearthed a vaulted chamber believed to be part of Queen Gizella's palace, which stood on the site until the fourteenth century. Dubbed the **Gizella Chapel** (Gizella-kápolna; May to mid-Oct Tues–Sun 10am–5pm; 200Ft), this tiny space contains Byzantine-style frescoes of the Apostles from the thirteenth century. Across the square, at no. 35, you can view the **Gizella Museum** (Gizella királyné Múzeum; same times; 400Ft), which keeps a small but rich collection of eighteenth- and nineteenth-century ecclesiastical objects, such as votive statues, chasubles, vestments and paintings.

Behind the Trinity Statue looms the **St Michael Cathedral**, whose interior is every bit as austere as its exterior. Having been razed and resurrected half a dozen times since the eleventh century, its current neo-Romanesque incarnation, dating from 1907–10, has only a Gothic crypt to show for its origins – its most prominent tomb is that of Bishop Biró himself. However, a glass dome behind the cathedral shelters the excavated remains of **St George's Chapel** (Szent György kápolna; May to mid-Oct Tues–Sun 10am–5pm; 200Ft; access from Vár utca), where Stephen's son Imre is said to have taken an oath of celibacy. His canonization, like that of Stephen and the latter-day King László, cemented the Árpáds' adherence to Catholicism and gave the Hungarians their own saints with whom to identify. Statues of Stephen and Gizella duly watch over the parapet at the far end of Vár utca, while a flight of steps round the far side of the cathedral leads down to **Benedek Hill**, the spur which commands a fine panoramic view of the Séd Valley and the Bakony Hills.

The lower town

Returning to Óváros tér, head down Rákóczi utca, and at the lights in Szabadság tér turn right onto Óvári Ferenc út to find the Art Nouveau **Petőfi Theatre** (Petőfi Színház), built in 1908. The first large building in Hungary to be constructed from reinforced concrete, it boasts a circular stained-glass window entitled *The Magic of Folk Art*, whose symbolic figures represent the attachment of Hungarians to their land. Its designer, Sándor Nagy, was one of the Gödöllő Pre-Raphaelites; another of his designs, *The Hunting of the Magic Deer*, a depiction of a Magyar myth, decorates the rear of the building. The interior is no less impressive, and, if you can, it's well worth trying to catch a performance here (see p.232).

A five-minute walk past the Eclectic-style **County Hall** brings you to the **Dezső Laczkó Museum**, behind the trees at Erzsébet sétány 1 (Tues–Sun: April–Sept 10am–6pm; Oct–March noon–4pm; 650Ft), which features an array of local history exhibits from all periods, including Bronze Age pottery and Roman mosaics unearthed in the villa at Balácapuszta (see p.227), regional folk costumes, and material on the Bakony's highwaymen. Standing somewhat incongruously next door is the **Bakony House** (May–Sept Tues–Sun 10am–6pm; entry on the same ticket), a 1930s clone of a traditional homestead, filled with peasant artefacts.

West of town

Two more sights lurk to the west of the castle district, either side of the impressive, fifty-metre-high **St Stephen's viaduct**. About ten minutes' walk along Jókai Mór utca, below the castle, is an antique **watermill** – one of many that once lined the banks of the Séd – and, passing under the viaduct, on Kittenburger Kálmán utca, is the **Kittenberger Zoo** (daily: May–Sept 9am–6pm; April & Oct 9am–5pm; Nov–March 9am–3pm; 1300Ft), named after the eponymous nineteenth-century zoologist (see p.176); one of Hungary's more respectable zoos, the well-kept enclosures harbour an impressive collection of animals, including Sri Lankan leopards, Sumatran tigers and Iberian wolves, while a specially designed African savannah keeps a variety of species native to that continent.

Eating

The best **restaurants** in town are generally those in the hotels and pensions, but that is certainly no bad thing here – indeed you'll find few better ones anywhere in the region. For a quick snack, head to the popular *Mackó Snack*, Megyeház tér 2, where you can grab burgers and salads. The covered **market** (Mon–Fri 6am–6pm, Sat 6am–2pm), next to the bus station, is a good place to pick up bread, fruit and dairy products.

Café Piazza Óváros tér 4. Cosy, engaging little place in which to enjoy light meals of pizza, pasta, soups and salads – good breakfast options too.

Elefánt Bisztro Óváros tér 6. A few steps along from *Cafe Piazza*, this relaxing bistro is very similar, though the menu is slightly more limited and a touch more expensive.

Oliva Buhim utca 14–16. The restaurant in the *Oliva* pension, with its eclectic menu (including Thai wok dishes) and wine list, mellow decor and Mediterranean-style grill garden, is the most satisfying place to eat in town – moreover, there's live jazz at weekends in the summer.

Tapó Pajta utca 19. Stylish place in the hotel of the same name, which leans heavily towards game dishes, a theme continued by the animal heads on the walls and the wooden/fur seating. Pop into the adjoining *Safari Bar* afterwards for a drink.

Várkert Vár utca 17. Housed within a handsome brick-vaulted cellar, this restaurant-cum-café/club up in the castle district is just the spot for an informal bite to eat, with lamb, duck, goose, and rooster's testicles amongst the items on its varied menu.

Villa Medici Kittenburger Kálmán utca 1. Located 1km northwest of town out in the Fejes Valley, inside the hotel of the same name, this very posh and fantastically pricey restaurant offers international fare of the highest order. No less impressive, but a touch cheaper, is the *Nosztálgia* restaurant immediately next door, which sticks to Hungarian cuisine.

Drinking and entertainment

The town is surprisingly devoid of commendable **cafés**, but one worth trying is *Marica*, at Kossuth utca 5, where you can take a cappuccino whilst sitting on a raised wooden deck terrace admiring the concrete surrounds. Similarly, there are few obvious **drinking** venues around, but your best bet is the happy *Várkert Cafe and Club* (see above), where you can catch DJs and live bands (all different genres) most weekends. Otherwise, there's the faux-Irish *Skorpió Bar* at Virág utca 1, or the *Havanna Cocktail Bar* at Kossuth utca 25, which, in addition to its repertoire of fancy cocktails, has a tastefully designed gaming room out back – all the above are open until at least 1 or 2am at weekends.

   Theatre in Veszprém is enormously popular, with performances at the Petőfi Színház usually selling out fast; tickets can be purchased at the box office inside the theatre (Mon–Thurs 8am–4pm, Fri 8am–3pm; ☎88/424-235; 2500–3000Ft). One of the largest events in the Veszprém calendar is the **Gizella Days Arts Festival** (Gizella Napok), held every year in the second week of May in honour of István's wife. To mark the occasion, a series of concerts, exhibitions and dance events is held in the castle district and in the cultural centre at Dózsa György utca 2.

Herend and around

Twelve kilometres west of Veszprém, **HEREND**'s famous **porcelain factory** makes for an enjoyable side-trip or an interesting stopover en route to Pápa or Szombathely, in Transdanubia. A pottery was founded in the village by Vince Stingl in 1826, and in 1851 Herend porcelain gained international renown when Queen Victoria ordered a chinoiserie dinner service at the Great Exhibition. Other famous buyers have included Tsar Alexander II, Kaiser Wilhelm I, the Shah of Iran and the British royal family. The factory remains one of the largest porcelain manufacturers in the world, exporting over 75 percent of its products – mainly to Japan and America – and employing some 1600 people, all of whom must attend a three-year training school before beginning in the factory.

A five-minute walk from the **bus** station, at Kossuth Lajos utca 140, is the visitor complex, the highlight of which is the **mini-factory** (mid-April to mid-Oct daily 9.30am–5pm; mid-Oct to mid-April Tues–Sat 9.30am–4pm; 1800Ft, includes entrance to museum; Ⓦ www.porcelanium.com), where you can see how porcelain is made; the fascinating forty-minute tour starts with a short film on the history of Herend porcelain before you are whisked around the various stages of production, observing plaster mould-makers, clay basket-weavers, glazers and painters all demonstrating their supreme, and highly individual, skills. Your guide will be keen to point out that, for all the technological advances, every single piece made here is still done by hand.

The visitor centre's well-presented **museum** (mid-April to mid-Oct daily 9am–4.30pm; mid-Oct to mid-April Tues–Sat 9am–3.30pm), just across the courtyard, displays a vast number of hand-painted dinner services, vases and statuettes; although many pieces are rather over the top and just a little too fanciful, it is nevertheless an impressive collection – in particular, look out for the ornamental wine canteen with pierced walls from 1867 and a Chinese Imari Plate from the 1850s.

Adjacent to the factory is the hugely elegant, and very expensive, *Apicus* **restaurant** (mid-April to mid-Oct Tues–Sat noon–6pm) and **coffee house** (mid-April to mid-Oct daily 9am–6pm; mid-Oct to mid-April Tues–Sat 9am–5pm); coffee is served, naturally enough, from the finest Herend porcelain cups. Each summer the centre puts on a number of open-air programmes with brass-band music, folk dancing, plays and the like.

After Herend the scenery deteriorates around Ajka, but 6km beyond Devecser (where the rail line turns northwards towards Celldömölk) there's a great view of the Bakony from a lookout tower near **Sómlóvásárhely**.

Travel details

Trains

Balatonfüred to: Budapest (every 1–2hr; 2hr 15min–3hr); Székesfehérvár (every 1–2hr; 1hr 15min–1hr 30min); Tapolca (every 1–2hr; 50min–1hr 20min).

Balatonszentgyörgy to: Keszthely (hourly; 15min); Nagykanizsa (every 1–2hr; 40–50min).

Keszthely to: Balatonszentgyörgy (hourly; 15min); Budapest (3 daily; 3hr 30min); Tapolca (hourly; 30min).

Siófok to: Budapest (hourly June–Sept, otherwise 8 daily; 1hr 45min); Székesfehérvár (hourly; 40–50min).

Székesfehérvár to: Balatonfüred (every 1–2hr; 1hr 15min–1hr 30min); Budapest (every 1hr–1hr 30min;

1hr–1hr 15min); Komárom (5 daily; 1hr 30min);
Siófok (hourly; 40–50min); Szombathely (6 daily; 2hr
30min); Veszprém (hourly; 40min–1hr).
Tapolca to: Balatonfüred (every 1–2hr; 50min–1hr
20min); Celldömölk (8 daily; 1hr–1hr 20min);
Keszthely (hourly; 30min); Sümeg (every 1hr
30min–2hr; 25min).
Veszprém to: Budapest (6 daily; 1hr 45min–2hr
15min); Győr (4 daily; 2hr 15min); Székesfehérvár
(hourly; 40min–1hr); Szombathely (10 daily; 1hr
45min–2hr 30min).

Buses

Badacsony to: Keszthely (8 daily; 1hr).
Balatonalmádi to: Balatonfüred (10 daily; 25min);
Budapest (4 daily; 2hr); Csopak (8 daily; 15min);
Veszprém (every 30–40min; 25min).
Balatonfüred to: Balatonalmádi (10 daily; 25min);
Budapest (5 daily; 2hr 15min); Győr (5 daily; 2hr);
Nagyvázsony (3 daily; 45min); Sopron (2 daily; 4hr);
Székesfehérvár (7 daily; 1hr 15min); Tapolca
(4 daily except Sun; 1hr 30min); Tihany (hourly;
30min); Veszprém (every 30min–1hr 30min; 30min).
Hévíz to: Keszthely (every 30min; 15min);
Zalaegerszeg (every 45min; 45min).
Keszthely to: Badacsony (9 daily; 1hr); Balaton-
magyaród (Mon–Fri 2 daily; 40min); Budapest
(6 daily; 3hr 45min); Hévíz (every 30min; 15min);
Pécs (3 daily; 3hr 45min); Sármellék (Mon–Fri
every 1hr–1hr 30min; Sat & Sun 8 daily; 30min);
Sopron (2 daily; 3hr); Sümeg (every 40–60min;
1hr); Tapolca (hourly; 40min); Zalaegerszeg (every
45min–1hr; 1hr); Zalavár (Mon–Fri every 1hr–1hr
30min; Sat & Sun 8 daily; 40min).
Siófok to: Budapest (4 daily; 1hr 45min–2hr
15min); Pécs (4 daily; 2hr 30min); Szekszárd
(5 daily; 1hr 45min); Veszprém (6 daily; 1hr 30min).
Sümeg to: Győr (5 daily; 2hr 15min); Keszthely
(9 daily; 45min); Pápa (6 daily; 1hr 20min); Sárvár
(Mon–Fri 5 daily, Sat & Sun 3 daily; 1hr 15min);
Sopron (3 daily; 2hr 15min); Tapolca (Mon–Fri
hourly, Sat & Sun 5 daily; 35min).
Székesfehérvár to: Balatonfüred (7 daily; 1hr
15min); Budapest (every 30–45min; 1hr);
Dunaújváros (10 daily; 1hr); Győr (6 daily; 1hr
40min); Kalocsa (2 daily; 3hr); Martonvásár (7–10
daily; 40min); Pákozd (hourly; 20min); Pécs
(2 daily; 4hr); Siófok (5 daily; 1hr); Szekszárd
(6 daily; 2hr); Tác (7 daily; 30min); Velence (8–10
daily; 40min); Veszprém (every 30min–1hr; 1hr).
Tapolca to: Balatonfüred (2 daily except Sun; 1hr
30min); Keszthely (hourly; 40min); Nagyvázsony
(12 daily; 45min); Sümeg (Mon–Fri hourly, Sat &
Sun 6 daily; 30min); Szigliget (Mon–Fri 10 daily,
Sat & Sun 6 daily; 25min); Veszprém (Mon–Fri
every 45min–1hr, Sat & Sun 8 daily; 1hr).

Tihany to: Balatonfüred (hourly; 30min); Veszprém
(4 daily; 45min).
Veszprém to: Balatonfüred (every 1hr–1hr 30min;
30min); Budapest (every 45–90min; 2hr 15min);
Győr (8 daily; 2hr); Herend (every 30–40min;
30min); Nagyvázsony (7 daily; 25min);
Nemesvámos (hourly; 25min); Siófok (8 daily;
1hr 30min); Székesfehérvár (every 45min–1hr
30min; 1hr); Tapolca (hourly; 1hr); Zirc (every
30–40min; 45min).

Ferries

Badacsony to: Balatonboglár (July–Aug 4 daily;
1hr); Balatonföldvár (July–Aug 1 daily; 2hr 45min);
Fonyód (mid-April to May & Sept–Oct 6 daily; June
8 daily; July–Aug 9 daily; 25min); Keszthely (July–
Aug 4 daily; 2hr); Siófok (June–Aug 1 daily; 4hr
30min); Szigliget (July–Aug 4 daily; 30min); Tihany
(June–Aug 2 daily; 3hr).
Balatonboglár to: Badacsony (July–Aug 4 daily;
45min); Révfülöp (June 4 daily; July–Aug 6 daily;
25min).
Balatonföldvár to: Balatonfüred (July–Aug 1 daily;
1hr); Tihany (June 4 daily; July–Aug 5 daily; 30min).
Balatonfüred to: Balatonalmádi (July–Aug 2 daily;
1hr 30min); Balatonföldvár (July–Aug 1 daily; 1hr);
Siófok (mid-April to May & Sept–Oct 4 daily; June
8 daily; July–Aug 9 daily; 1hr); Tihany (mid-April to
May & Sept–Oct 3 daily; June 7 daily; July–Aug
9 daily; 20min).
Fonyód to: Badacsony (mid-April to May &
Sept–Oct 5 daily; June 8 daily; July–Aug 9 daily;
25min); Keszthely (1 daily; 3hr).
Keszthely to: Badacsony (July–Aug 4 daily; 2hr);
Szigliget (July–Aug 4 daily; 1hr 30min).
Révfülöp to: Balatonboglár (June 4 daily; July–Aug
6 daily; 25min).
Siófok to: Badacsony (July–Aug 2 daily; 4hr
30min); Balatonfüred (mid-April to May & Sept–Oct
4 daily; June 7 daily; July–Aug 8 daily; 50min);
Tihany (mid-April to May & Sept–Oct 3 daily; June
7 daily; July–Aug 8 daily; 1hr 20min).
Szántódrév to: Tihany-rév (March–Nov every
40–60min; 10min).
Szigliget to: Badacsony (July–Aug 5 daily; 25min);
Keszthely (July–Aug 4 daily; 1hr 30min).
Tihany to: Badacsony (July–Aug 2 daily; 3hr);
Balatonalmádi (July–Aug 2 daily; 2hr);
Balatonföldvár (July–Aug 5 daily; 35min);
Balatonfüred (mid-April to May & Sept–Oct 3 daily;
June 8 daily; July–Aug 10 daily; 30min); Siófok
(mid-April to May & Sept–Oct 3 daily;
June–Aug 7 daily; 1hr 15min).
Tihany-rév to: Szántódrév (March–Nov every
40min–1hr; 10min).

Transdanubia

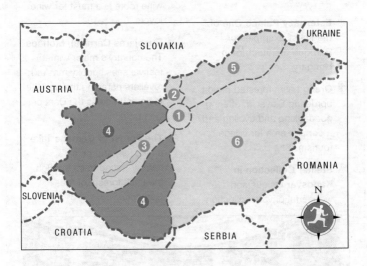

CHAPTER 4 # Highlights

✳ **Pannonhalma Monastery**
Hungary's most impressive
monastery is also a
UNESCO World Heritage
Site. See p.252

✳ **Sopron** Atmospheric
town featuring a gorgeous
Belváros stuffed with
Baroque buildings.
See p.258

✳ **Esterházy Palace** One of
the finest examples of
Baroque architecture in
Hungary. See p.268

✳ **Őrség** Lush, forested region
bordering Slovenia, offering
good hiking and cycling and
a popular area for village
tourism. See p.283

✳ **Steiner Collection in
Kaposvár** Unique and
wonderful private collection

of cast-iron objects and
ornaments. See p.291

✳ **Pécs** One of Hungary's most
vibrant cities, with sights
galore and the eclectic Pécs
Weeks festival of arts and
food. See p.294

✳ **Villány-Siklós wine road**
Hungary's most established
wine route is a must for wine
lovers. See p.304

✳ **Busójárás Carnival, Mohács**
The country's major winter
festival sees spooky masked
revellers parading through the
town and across the Danube.
See p.308

✳ **The Forest of Gemenc** Take
a hike (or jump on a
narrow-gauge train) through
the thick forests of the
Gemenc. See p.312

▲ The library at Pannonhalma Monastery

Transdanubia

A vast area encompassing the western half of the country, **Transdanubia** – the Dunántúl – is a region of considerable charm and variety, and one which, perhaps more than any other region in Hungary, is a patchwork land, an ethnic and social hybrid. Enclosed to the north and the east by the River Danube, its valleys, hills, forests and mud flats have been a melting pot since Roman times, when the region was known as Pannonia. Settled since then by Magyars, Serbs, Croats, Germans and Slovaks, it has been torn asunder and occupied by the Turks and the Habsburgs, and only within the last 150 years has it emerged from a state of near-feudalism.

Stark testament to these centuries of warfare are the castles which stand at the core of every main town. Around each weathered *vár* (castle) sprawls a Belváros, with rambling streets and squares overlooked by florid Baroque and the odd Gothic or Renaissance building. In the predominantly flat region of northern Transdanubia – bordering Slovakia to the north – the small lakeside town of **Tata** and the larger, more ebullient city of **Győr** both provide fine examples of this genre, whilst close by is the superb **Pannonhalma Monastery**.

In contrast, western Transdanubia, which neighbours Austria and Slovenia, has a far more varied topography, with the idyllic **Őrség hills** great for rambling, cycling and other leisurely pursuits. Though **Szombathely** has the most to show for its Roman origins, with its Temple of Isis and other ruins, the must-see towns in this region are **Sopron**, with its cobbled streets and beautifully distinct Belváros, and delightfully sleepy **Kőszeg**.

Cosseted by the rolling **Mecsek Hills**, the dashing city of **Pécs**, boasting a Turkish mosque and minaret, is the highlight of southern Transdanubia – a relatively flat tract of land sandwiched between Lake Balaton in the north and Croatia to the south. In the southernmost reaches, almost scraping the Croatian border, the **Villány-Siklós** wine road has some of the lushest vineyards in the country, and there are more excellent wine-tasting opportunities at **Szekszárd**, close to the **Forest of Gemenc** on the way back to Budapest.

While many towns host spring or summer **festivals**, the most interesting events take place in southern Transdanubia, such as the masked Busójárás Carnival at **Mohács**, seven weeks before Easter, and the Pécs Weeks of Art and Gastronomy in June and July. During summer, **concerts** are also held in two unique settings – the **Esterházy Palace** at **Fertőd** and the rock chambers of **Fertőrákos**, both close to Sopron. At the monthly **market** in Pécs, you'll sense the peasant roots underlying many Transdanubian towns, whose sprawling *lakótelep* (apartment buildings) house recent immigrants from the countryside.

Transport links between the region's towns and cities are excellent. Express trains from Budapest run regularly to the major centres, and there are also plenty of buses and trains to and from Lake Balaton.

Northern Transdanubia

Most of **Northern Transdanubia** consists of the **Kisfölд** (Little Plain), a fertile but rather monotonous landscape that focuses your attention on the region's towns. Heading west from Budapest, it's possible to go via **Zsámbék**, with its splendid ruined church, but otherwise the main routes lead to **Tata**, a delightful small town nestled around a large lake, with a medieval castle cocooned amid Baroque and Neoclassical buildings. By far the largest and liveliest city in the region is **Győr**, which also makes a good base for excursions to **Pannonhalma**, Hungary's most impressive monastery, and the wetlands of the **Szigetköz** with their abundant birdlife. If heading south towards Balaton, the appealing small town of **Pápa** is worth a brief stop. All the towns en route are served by frequent trains from Budapest's Déli or Keleti stations, and can also be reached by bus from Népliget Station.

Zsámbék

Now a peaceful village 30km west of Budapest, **ZSÁMBÉK** was an important cross-roads in early medieval times, dominated from 1258 by the hilltop church constructed by the Premonstratensian order. Marking the start of the transition from Roman-esque to Gothic style, it is a key part of Hungary's architectural heritage, and, although partially demolished by an earthquake in 1763, still immensely impressive.

Buses still stop at the crossroads of Szent István tér and Akadémia utca, just north of which you'll see the church ruins and the equally hulking early Baroque castle of the Zichy family, now a Catholic teaching college. Facing the castle is the Török-kút park, named after a sixteenth-century Turkish well. You'll pass some nice old wine cellars on the way up to the **church** (Romtemplom; April–Oct Tues–Sun 9am–5pm; Nov–March Fri–Sun 9am–4pm; 450Ft), where the two towers still stand, with the remains of a rose window between them, plus one nave wall and the outline of the cloister; in addition, a large cellar contains a few carved stones and photos of the ruins as they were in 1889, the year they were restored; unusually, red brick was used in the restoration to show clearly what was not authentic.

On the other side of the village, at Magyar utca 18, the **Lamp Museum** (Lámpa Múzeum; Tues–Sun 9am–5pm, April–Oct to 6pm; 300Ft) is an unusual private collection of 1200 railway and other lamps, all crammed into a lovely traditional village house with peacocks strutting around the lawn.

The village is known for its **Zsámbéki Szombatok** or Zsámbék Cultural Saturdays (weekly in June and July), with a varied programme of plays, concerts, exhibitions and children's events, next to the church. In summer the Zsámbéki Nyári Színház (Zsámbék open-air theatre) stages plays at a former rocket base about 2km north of the village (off the Szomor road).

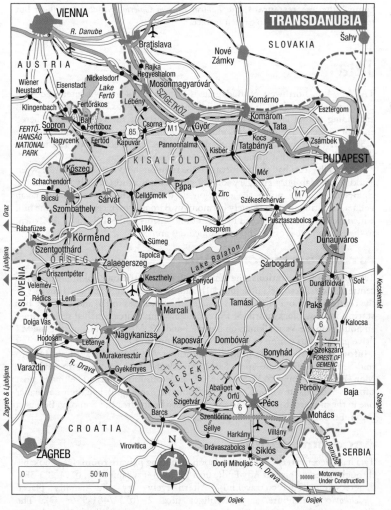

Practicalities

Zsámbék is reached by frequent **bus** from Széna tér in Budapest, leaving four times an hour (two direct and two via Perbál) on weekdays, and at least hourly at weekends. The village is 9km north of **Bicske**, on the main railway line from Budapest to Győr and Vienna, with buses running at least hourly from the train station.

Should you wish to **stay** overnight, the *Hegyalja Vendéglő* is a simple restaurant with rooms (☎23/342-107; ❷), on the road up to the church, at Corvin János utca 1. Otherwise, there are various riding stables around Zsámbék offering accommodation, or you could stay in Bicske at the *Central Café Panzió* (☎22/565-133; ❷) or the *Hotel Báder* (☎22/350-090; ❹) on Highway 1 on the eastern edge of town, where there's also camping. The best place to eat in Zsámbék is at the

Lamp Museum's **restaurant**, the *Lampás Étterem Galéria*, which has a short but tempting menu and a nice garden terrace.

Tata

TATA, 74km northwest of Budapest, is a small lakeside town interlaced with canals and streams, at its most charming on misty mornings, when its castle, mills and riding school appear as wraiths on the shores of the central lake. There's enough to see in a leisurely day, plus horseriding, fishing and swimming for the more active. In winter there's ice-skating, plus the spectacle of the tens of thousands of geese that spend the colder months on the lake.

Historically, Tata had the misfortune to be right on the war-torn border between Turkish and Habsburg Hungary for 150 years. It was almost wholly rebuilt in the eighteenth century under the direction of the Moravian-born architect Jakab Fellner, resulting in an extremely harmonious Baroque town centre up on the hill, which has been left untouched by later developments in the Tóváros (Lake Town) to the east, where most of the tourist facilities are.

Arrival and information

Tata has two **train stations**: the main (Vasútállomás) station, 1.5km north of the centre just off Bacsó Béla utca (bus #1); and the Tóvároskert Station, 1km east of the centre, where only local trains stop (reached by buses to Baj and #5). The **bus station** is a few blocks north of the castle on Május 1 utca, reached several times an hour from the Vasútállomás on buses #1 and #2. Motorists coming off the M7 drive past the bus station to the top of Ady Endre utca.

Information is available from Tourinform at Ady Endre utca 9 (mid-June to mid-Sept Mon–Fri 9am–6pm, Sat & Sun 9am–5pm; mid-Sept to mid-June Mon–Fri 8am–4pm; ☎34/586-046, ✉tata@tourinform.hu). The main **post office** is in the old town on Kossuth tér (Mon–Fri 8am–7pm), and there's a smaller one in the modern district on the corner of Ady Endre utca and Somogyi Béla utca (Mon–Fri 8am–4pm).

Accommodation

Tata has a decent array of accommodation, including **private rooms** (❷), bookable through Gerecse Travel at Ady Endre utca 13 (Mon–Fri 8am–5pm; ☎34/483-384, ✉gerecsetravel@gerecsetravel.hu). Alternatively, try the handily placed *Nedeljkovic* guesthouse at Hattyúliget utca 2 (☎34/481-936; ❷). The *Fényes-Fürdő* **campsite**, which also has chalets and a motel (both ❸), is by the thermal baths, where bus #3 terminates (☎34/481-208, ☏www.fenyesfurdo.hu; May to mid-Sept/pool all year). Down by the lake, at Fáklya utca 2, *Öreg-Tó Kemping* (☎34/383-496, ☏www.tatacamping.hu; April–Oct) also has chalets (❶) plus tent space, while next door at Fáklya utca 4, the optimistically named *Öreg-Tó Club Hotel* (☎34/487-960, ☏www.oregtohotel.hu; dorm bed 1800Ft) is a Hostelling International affiliate offering basic hostel accommodation all year.

Arnold Hotel Erzsébet királyné tér 8 ☎34/588-028, ☏www.hotels.hu/arnold. In a peaceful spot behind the *Hotel Kristály*, this is a pretty classy place, with ultramodern rooms, and a stylish restaurant. ❺
Berta-Malom Panzió Mikovényi út 60 ☎34/587-146, ☏www.bertacentrum.hu.

Housed in a Baroque mill straddling a stream, this lively place incorporates a steakhouse and sports club (both open to 10pm) as well as attractive rooms. ❺
Kalóz Fregatt Hotel Almási út 2 ☎34/382-382, ☏www.hotels.hu/kaloz. Smack in the town centre,

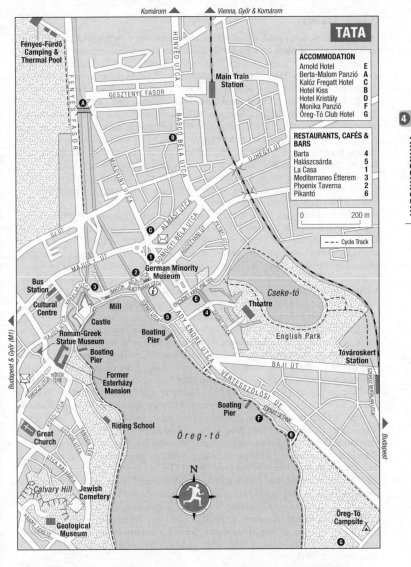

Komárom ▲ ▲ Vienna, Győr & Komárom

TATA

ACCOMMODATION
Arnold Hotel   E
Berta-Malom Panzió   A
Kalóz Fregatt Hotel   C
Hotel Kiss   B
Hotel Kristály   D
Monika Panzió   F
Öreg-Tó Club Hotel   G

RESTAURANTS, CAFÉS & BARS
Barta   4
Halászcsárda   5
La Casa   1
Mediterraneo Étterem   3
Phoenix Taverna   2
Pikantó   6

0   200 m

--- Cycle Track

Fényes-Fürdő Camping & Thermal Pool

Main Train Station

GESZTENYE FASOR

HONVÉD UTCA

BASCÓ BÉLA UTCA

ÚJHEGYI ÚT

MIKOVINY UTCA

ALMÁSI UTCA

SOMOGYI BÉLA UTCA

ÁGOSTYÁNI ÚT

FELBEI UTCA

German Minority Museum

Bus Station

Cultural Centre

Mill

Castle

Roman-Greek Statue Museum

Boating Pier

Former Esterházy Mansion

Riding School

Great Church

Calvary Hill

Jewish Cemetery

Geological Museum

ADY ENDRE UTCA

ERZSÉBET KIRÁLYNÉ TÉR

Cseke-tó

Theatre

English Park

Tóvároskert Station

BAJI ÚT

VÉRTESSZŐLŐSI ÚT

Boating Pier

TÓPART SÉTÁNY

Öreg-tó

N

Öreg-Tó Campsite

Budapest & Győr (M1)

Budapest

HŐSÖK TERE

KOSSUTH UTCA

EÖTVÖS TÉR

TANODA TÉR

UTCA KÁLVÁRIA

ARANY FEKETE

---

this colourful building houses five cramped and dreary rooms, though its pub is worth a visit (see p.243). ⑤
Hotel Kiss Bacsó Béla utca 54 ☏ 34/586-888, ⓦ www.hotelkiss.hu. This unmistakable pink building, between the train station and the centre, has 47 magnificently furnished, a/c rooms, all with internet access. Stunning indoor pool, sauna, solarium and whirlpool. ⑧
Hotel Kristály Ady Endre utca 22 ☏ 34/383-577, ⓦ www.hktata.hu. This late eighteenth-century

building on the noisy main road now boasts two wings; the older one has huge, but rather staid, doubles and singles with showers or baths, while the newer building has infinitely smarter rooms. ⑥
Monika Panzió Tópart sétány ☏ 34/383-208, ⓦ www.hotels.hu/monikapanzio. Large and very dull rooms, though the pleasant lakeside setting compensates somewhat. ⑤

The Town

All Tata's attractions are located within close proximity to the **Old Lake** (Öreg-tó), with the best place to start being the stumpy eighteenth-century clocktower at the west end of Somogyi utca. Across the main drag, Ady Endre utca, is the **German Minority Museum** at Alkotmány utca 1 (Német Nemzetiségi Néprajzi Múzeum; April-Oct Tues–Sun 10am–6pm; Nov–March Wed–Fri 10am–2pm, Sat & Sun 10am–4pm; 300Ft). Swabians, Bavarians and other German settlers have long inhabited Transdanubia, and Tata (like Székesfehérvár and Pécs) was almost entirely German-speaking for many centuries. In keeping with their ethic, the folk costumes are less flamboyant than Magyar attire. The museum is housed in the former Nepomucenus Mill, built in 1758 and straddling a weir. A hundred metres further east, at Bartók Béla utca 3, is the **Cifra Mill** (Cifra-malom), dating back to 1587. Tata is famed for its eighteen water mills, mostly Baroque; however, the town's bountiful springs dried up in the 1960s due to mining in the nearby hills, and are only now beginning to recover.

Just beyond here lies Tata's moated fourteenth-century **castle** (Öregvár; always open; free). Once the hunting lodge of King Sigismund, it was badly damaged by both the Turks and the Habsburgs, and only one of the original corner towers remains; nevertheless its grounds are always popular with courting couples and passers-by. Its residential "keep" was reconstructed in 1897 for a visit by Franz Josef II, and now contains a museum of Roman miniatures and faïence by the eighteenth-century local craftsman Domokos Kuny (Kuny Domokos Múzeum; mid-April to mid-Oct Tues–Sun 10am–6pm; mid-Oct to mid-April Wed–Fri 10am–2pm, Sat & Sun 10am–4pm; 750Ft).

From the castle a path leads through the park to an impressive, decrepit pile built in the 1760s as an **Esterházy Mansion** (May–Sept Wed–Sun 10am–6pm; 300Ft), where the Habsburg King Francis took refuge from Napoleon in 1809 and later signed the Schönbrunn peace treaty. After years of use as a psychiatric hospital, a handful of the mansion's rooms are now open for tours. From here you can wander up to Hősök tere and the Baroque old town, laid out by Fellner. Down to the right, Tata's former synagogue now houses the **Greek-Roman Statue Exhibition** (Görög-Római Szobormásolatok Kiállítása; April–Sept Tues–Sun 10am–6pm; Oct–March by appointment; 300Ft; ☎34/381-251), containing life-sized plaster casts of the Elgin Marbles, Hercules and Laocoön.

The climax to Fellner's endeavours occurs further along on Kossuth tér, where his statue stands in front of the twin-spired **Great Church** designed by himself and József Grossman, but which wasn't completed until seven years after Fellner's death in 1780. A crag behind the church is named **Calvary Hill** (Kálvária-domb) and has a crucifixion monument, to which a more secular age has added an outdoor **Geological Museum** (Szabadtéri Geológiai Múzeum; April–Oct Tues–Fri 10am–4pm, Sat & Sun 10am–5pm; 300Ft), a **nature reserve** and a **lookout tower** offering fine views of the town and into Slovakia (May–Aug Tues–Sun 9am–5pm; 300Ft).

East of busy Ady Endre utca, peace returns as you turn off by the *Hotel Kristály* into Hattyúliget utca, leading to the 500-acre **English Park** (Angol Kert) surrounding the **Small Lake** (Cseke-tó). Laid out in the 1780s in the naturalistic English style, the park contains a fake ruined church cobbled together from Roman and Benedictine stonework, and an outdoor **theatre** and **swimming pool**, added in the twentieth century. The palm house at the park's entrance has been transformed into a conference centre and restaurant, while Hungary's Olympic team has its main training facility along the park's southern edge.

Activity seekers will also find plenty to do in Tata. On the western shore of the Old Lake, at Fekete utca 2, is a grandiose **Riding School** (Lovasiskola; daily 9am–noon

& 2–6pm; ☎30/2422-233), modelled on the Spanish Riding School in Vienna, which has been going for over a century; it offers lessons (900–1500Ft for 1hr), cross-country riding through the woods (1200Ft), and carriage rides (3600Ft). Tourinform can supply details on **angling** in the lakes out towards the **thermal pool** (May–Sept 9am–7pm; 900Ft) at Fényes-Fürdő on Fényes Fasor, reached by bus #3. Rowing **boats** (*csónak*) and pedal boats (*vízibicikli*) can be rented on the eastern side of the Old Lake, from a spot 500m south of the *Monika Panzió*.

Eating, drinking and entertainment

The classiest **restaurants** in town are *La Casa* at Országgyűlés tér 3, with a richly diverse menu of fish, sometimes including barbecued crabs and grilled swordfish, and the *Pikantó*, down by the lake at Tópart sétány 13, which has a similarly Mediterranean flavour in addition to some sophisticated Hungarian specials such as paprika-spiced pancakes; this should not be confused with the slightly more downmarket *Pikant* alongside. Aside from these, the *Phoenix Taverna* at Bartók Béla utca 1 might not look like much from the outside, but it's the most intimate place around and serves reassuringly solid Hungarian food, whilst further along towards the castle, the *Mediterraneo Étterem* at Váralja utca 20 does a fair job of preparing authentic Mediterranean dishes using the freshest vegetables, fruits and spices. The lakeside *Halászcsárda*, at Tópart sétány 10 (closed Mon), should satisfy even the most demanding of seafood connoisseurs with its array of freshly caught fish.

For **drinking**, just about the liveliest place is the *Kalóz Fregatt Pub*, attached to the hotel of the same name (see p.241), a breezy, pirate-themed place knocking up jugs of beer, cocktails and a varied live music programme at weekends. A gem of a coffee house is the very ornate *Barta*, by the entrance to the English Park at Sport utca 1, which serves fine coffees in its best china.

Tata's main annual happening is the **Water-Music-Flower Festival** on the last weekend of June, featuring concerts and dancing, a flower show, and a craft fair in the castle grounds.

Komárom and around

KOMÁROM, 18km northwest of Tata, is the main crossing between Hungary and Slovakia, linked by 500-metre-long road and rail bridges to Komárno, across the Danube. The two towns formed a single municipality until 1920 and ethnic Magyars still predominate on the Slovak side, where streets and shops are signposted in both languages. Though neither town has much to offer in the way of sights, the easy crossing and good **connections to Bratislava** from Komárno make this a useful stepping stone en route to the Slovak capital.

The confluence of the Danube and the Váh has been a fortified crossing point since Roman times, reaching its apotheosis in the nineteenth century with the building of three Habsburg fortresses. The most accessible of these is the **Monostori Fortress** (Monostori Erőd; March–Oct Tues–Sun 9am–5pm; 1050Ft; ⓦ www.fort-monostor.hu), 1km west of the train station, which can lay fair claim to being one of the largest fort complexes in Central Europe. Covering 32 square kilometres and containing 4km of underground passages, Monostori was built following the 1848–49 Hungarian Revolution, and was also one of the most technologically advanced fortresses of its day, with a complex system of bastions, trenches and gun shelters. Later it served as a training base for the Hungarian army, and, during World War II, as a transportation camp and prison, before Soviet troops moved in. Following their departure in 1990 the fort underwent a major restoration programme, reopening as a public monument in 1998. The decently presented **museum** inside the fortress relates the history of the three forts on the Danube's south bank and the two on the north bank, together with a bakery museum and lots of Warsaw Pact military hardware.

The star-shaped (as its name implies) **Csillag Fortress** (Csillagerőd; May–Oct Sat & Sun noon–2pm; 300Ft), east of the centre on Bem utca, was built between 1871 and 1877 on the site of a fort erected in 1586 to control the confluence of the Váh with the Danube; nowadays it serves as a storage depot and there is little for visitors to see. At the same time, the far less impressive **Igmánd Fortress** (Igmándi Erőd; March–Oct Tues–Sun 9am–5pm; 300Ft) was constructed 2km south of the centre down Igmándi út. It contains little more than a museum displaying Roman stoneworks, but if you're keen to visit, take a left down Térffy Gyula and follow the path to the right. For a more relaxing time, head to the **thermal baths** at Táncsics utca 34, fifteen minutes' walk from the station, which is open all year (daily 9am–8pm; 1050Ft; ⓦwww .komthermal.hu).

Practicalities

From the station, right by the Danube, it's a couple of minutes' walk east to the bridge across to Slovakia, with the **Tourinform** office just south on the main road at Igmándi út 2 (Mon–Fri 9am–5pm, Sat & Sun 9am–1pm; ⓣ34/540-590, ⓔkomarom@tourinform.hu). There's plenty of **accommodation** in town, starting with the most convenient, the *Vasmacska Panzió* just south of the bridge at Erzsébet tér 2 (ⓣ34/341-342, ⓦwww.vasmacskapanzio.hu; ❸), a functional new place which also has apartments and a decent restaurant. Most of the other options are near the baths to the east on Táncsics utca; best is the colourful and welcoming *Forrás Hotel* at no. 34 (ⓣ34/540-177, ⓦwww.hotelforras.hu; ❻), while the less exciting *Thermal Hotel* at no. 38 (ⓣ34/342-447, ⓦwww.komturist.hu/thermal .html; ❺) has a mix of dingy older rooms and perfectly acceptable newer ones. The marginally better *Juno Hotel* is across the road at Bem utca 5 (ⓣ34/340-568, ⓦwww.junohotel.hu; ❺). There are **campsites** attached to both hotels, plus the *Solaris*, at Táncsics utca 36 (ⓣ34/344-777), which has apartments with shared showers (❸); all three sites are open year-round. Rates at all these hotels and campsites include admission to the baths. The best **restaurants** are in the *Juno Hotel* and the *Bogáncs Étterem* beside the *Thermal* hotel at Bem utca 36, although there's little to choose between their Hungarian menus. *Riviera Snack and Drink* at Táncsics utca 34 is a breezy place serving both hot sandwiches and fuller meals (with a decent vegetarian choice), and it also has a bar.

Into Slovakia: Komárno

It takes a couple of minutes to walk from Komárom train station to the bridge into Slovakia. There are now no longer any passport checks, but if you don't fancy walking across there are four buses a day from Komárom train station to Komárno, and four trains (taking just nine minutes). From Komárno (also known to Hungarians as Rév-Komárom), there are regular trains to **Bratislava**, 95km away. If you're **entering Hungary**, trains run at least hourly from Komárom to Budapest, Tata and Győr, and there are fairly frequent buses to Esztergom (for the Danube Bend).

At Palatinova ulica 13, the small **Museum of the Danube** (Podunajské Múzeum; Tues–Sun 9am–5pm; free) covers the city's history up to 1848, and also houses an art gallery. Next door is a small **Orthodox Church** (Pravoslávny kostol) built in the early eighteenth century by Serbian refugees who had fled from the Turks.

Also part of the museum is the **Zichy Palace** (Zichyho palac; same hours) at Námesti generála Klapku 9, which covers local history from 1848 to 1945 and also pays tribute to two local sons, **Franz Lehár** and **Mór Jókai**. The former, the composer of *The Merry Widow*, was born here in 1870 and initially followed in his father's footsteps as bandmaster with the local garrison, while Jókai was a prolific writer of sentimental novels. You'll need Slovak or Hungarian to appreciate the displays. Komárno's **bus and train stations** are 2km northwest of the main street, Záhradnícka Slovanská, where the **tourist office** at Zupná 5 (Mon–Fri 9am–5pm; ☎00421/35/7730-063, ✉tik@komarno.sk) can arrange **accommodation** in one of the town's hotels or pensions.

Győr and around

The industrial city of **GYŐR** (pronounced "dyur"), 40km east of Komárom, harbours a waterfront Belváros stuffed with Baroque mansions and churches, where streets bustle and restaurants vie for custom. With so much to enjoy around the centre, you can easily forget the high-rise apartments and factories that form the rest of Győr, whose Rába Engineering Works, producing trucks and rolling stock, is one of the country's most successful industries. The city also makes an excellent base for excursions to Pannonhalma Monastery (see p.252) and the Szigetköz wetlands (see p.255).

Győr's **history** owes much to its location at the confluence of the Rába and Rábca rivers with the Mosoni-Duna branch of the Danube, in the centre of the Kisalföld. The place was named Arrabona by the Romans, after a local Celtic tribe whom they subjugated, while its current name derives from *gyürü*, the Avar word for a circular fortress. During the Turkish occupation of Hungary, Győr's castle was a Habsburg stronghold and the town was known as Raab (after the Rába River). After its military role diminished, Győr gained industrial muscle and a different kind of clout. In the 1956 Uprising, its city hall was occupied by a radical Provisional National Council that pressed the Nagy government to get Soviet troops out and to quit the Warsaw Pact immediately.

Arrival and information

Győr's **bus and train stations** are on the southern edge of the centre, behind the very grand wedding-cake-like city hall, only ten minutes' walk from the Belváros along Baross Gábor utca and across Szent István út – a veritable wind tunnel of an avenue that separates the new and old towns.

Tourinform, housed in a glass pavilion at Árpád utca 32, on the corner of Baross utca (June to mid-Sept Mon–Fri 8am–8pm, Sat & Sun 9am–6pm; mid-Sept to May Mon–Fri 9am–5pm, Sat 9am–1pm; ☎96/311-771, ⊛www.gyor.hu), can supply **information**, as well as book accommodation and change money. The main **post office** is opposite the theatre at Bajcsy-Zsilinszky út 46 (Mon–Fri 8am–6pm), although the one by the train station has longer opening hours (Mon–Fri 8am–7pm, Sat 8am–noon), as does that at the Interspar hypermarket, just east of the centre on the Budapest road, Budai utca (Mon–Fri 8am–8pm, Sat 7.20am–3pm, Sun 9.20am–2pm). **Internet access** is available at *Internet Sarok*, Liszt Ferenc utca 20 (Mon–Fri 10am–9pm, Sat 10am–10pm, Sun 1–9pm; 600Ft for 1hr), though the entrance is actually on Pálffy utca; and at *Nemszingli Café & Net*, Apaca utca 10 (Mon–Thurs 8.30am–10pm, Fri 8.30am–midnight, Sat 10am–midnight).

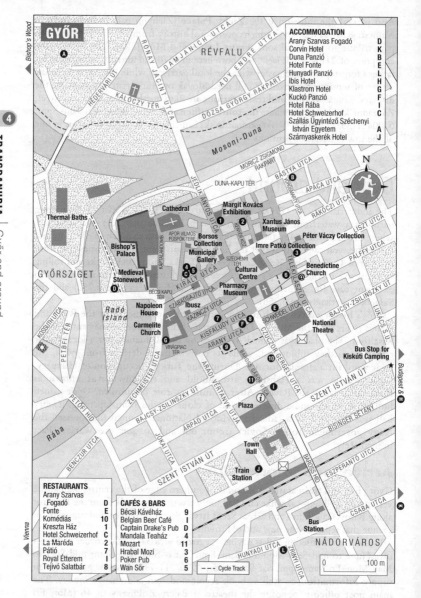

GYŐR

ACCOMMODATION
Arany Szarvas Fogadó — D
Corvin Hotel — K
Duna Panzió — B
Hotel Fonte — E
Hunyadi Panzió — L
Ibis Hotel — H
Klastrom Hotel — G
Kuckó Panzió — F
Hotel Rába — I
Hotel Schweizerhof — C
Szállás Ügyintéző Széchenyi
  István Egyetem — A
Szárnyaskerék Hotel — J

RESTAURANTS
Arany Szarvas
  Fogadó — D
Fonte — E
Komédiás — 10
Kreszta Ház — C
Hotel Schweizerhof — 2
La Maréda — 2
Pátió — 7
Royal Étterem — I
Tejivó Salatbár — 8

CAFÉS & BARS
Bécsi Kávéház — 9
Belgian Beer Café — I
Captain Drake's Pub — D
Mandala Teaház — 4
Mozart — 11
Hrabal Mozi — 3
Poker Pub — 6
Wan Sör — 5

- - - Cycle Track

0 _____ 100 m

Accommodation

Győr is bursting with good-value **hotels** and pensions, many of them tucked away amongst the narrow streets and squares of the old town. For **private rooms** (②–③), head to Ibusz at Kazinczy utca 3 (Mon–Fri 8am–5pm, Sat 9am–noon; ☎96/311-700, ✉gyor@ibusz.hu). The cheapest option is a student residence, notably the *Szállás Ügyintéző Széchenyi István Egyetem* (István Széchenyi University

Student Hostel), at Egyetem tér 3, door K4, room 106 (℡ 96/503-447 or German 613-551), across the bridge in Révfalu (bus #11), which usually has a few rooms (●) year-round, though they go fast – book through Tourinform. All the **campsites** listed below are some distance from the town centre.

Hotels and pensions

Arany Szarvas Fogadó Radó sétány 1 ℡ 96/517-452, ⓦ www.aranyszarvas-gyor.hu. Nautically themed pension brilliantly located on Radó Island; delightful pine-furnished rooms with mini-bar, internet access and small balcony, plus gym and sauna. ❹

Corvin Hotel Corvin utca 17 ℡ 96/515-490, ⓦ www.corvinhotel.hu. Modern hotel and pension (a block to the north) with well-equipped rooms 400m east of the bus station. Very good value. ❹

Duna Panzió Vörösmarty utca 5 ℡ & ⓕ 96/329-084, ⓦ www.hotelspaar.hu. Appealing sky-blue pension on a quiet road east of Duna-kapu tér, with antique furniture in some rooms. ❹

Hotel Fonte Kisfaludy utca 38 ℡ 96/513-810, ⓦ www.hotelfonte.hu. Named after the well discovered during construction, this gorgeous hotel has fantastically comfortable rooms with great beds, safe and internet access, plus the classiest restaurant in town (see p.250). ❻

Hunyadi Panzió Hunyadi utca 10 ℡ 96/329-162, ⓦ www.hotels.hu/hunyadi. Quality pension with bright, exuberantly coloured rooms in a good location just behind the bus station. Good little bar serving meals downstairs too. ❹

Ibis Hotel Szent István út 10B ℡ 96/509-700, ⓦ www.ibis.hu. A modern block with a/c and accessible rooms, this is reliably as good as every Ibis hotel worldwide. ❺

Klastrom Hotel Zechmeister utca 1, off Bécsi kapu tér ℡ 96/516-910, ⓦ www.klastrom.hu. Occupying the eighteenth-century priory behind the Carmelite Church, this is far less impressive than you'd expect from this fine building (apart from the conference room in the Baroque library). ❻

Kuckó Panzió Arany János utca 33 ℡ 96/316-260, ⓦ www.kuckopanzio.hu. Agreeable seven-room pension in a lovely old townhouse, above a nice café in the heart of the Belváros. Note that the stairs are very steep. ❹

Hotel Rába Árpád utca 34 ℡ 96/889-400, ⓦ www.danubiusgroup.com/raba. Comfortable and thoroughly modern hotel with big, airy rooms just a stone's throw from the Belváros. ❻

Hotel Schweizerhof Sarkantyú köz 11 ℡ 96/512-358, ⓦ www.schweizerhof.hu. Along with the *Fonte*, this is the finest hotel in town: a lobby on each floor and individually styled, designer-furnished rooms with a/c and internet access. ❼

Szárnyaskerék Hotel Révai Miklós utca 5 ℡ 96/314-629, ⓕ 317-844. The "Winged Wheel Hotel", named after the symbol of the State Railways, occupies the old hostel building across from the train station. Spartan rooms with and without bathroom. ❷–❸

Campsites

Kiskúti Camping Kiskútliget ℡ 96/318-986, ⓦ www.eszallas.hu/kiskuti. Large site 3km east of the centre, beyond the stadium, with a motel and chalets (both ❷). Take bus #8 from Szent István út, opposite Lukács Sándor utca. Open all year.

Napsugár Külső Veszprémi út 19 ℡ 96/411-042. Situated 5km south of the centre; take the Kismegyer bus from the bus station. Can be noisy, as it's near a (minor) railway line. May to mid-Oct.

Pihenő 10-es Fő út ℡ 96/316-461, ⓦ www.piheno.hu. By the old main road to Budapest, 5km east of the centre, with chalets (❸). Take bus #11 towards Szentiván from the bus station. Open all year.

The Town

Almost everything of interest in Győr lies within the **Belváros**, a web of streets and alleys stretching from Széchenyi tér to Káptalandomb, near the confluence of the Rába and Mosoni-Duna. Protected by preservation orders and traffic restrictions, it is a pleasure to wander around. Heading up pedestrianized Baross Gábor utca from the train station, antique side streets beckon on your left, narrow and shadowy with overhanging timbered houses – the perfect setting for a conspiracy. Indeed, Communists met secretly during the Horthy years at no. 15 on Sarló köz, a cobbled alley forking off Kazinczy utca.

Turning off Baross Gábor utca down Kazinczy utca, you come out into **Bécsi kapu tér** (Vienna Gate Square), overlooking the River Rába, which reputedly escaped flooding in the eighteenth century thanks to a miracle-working statue of

▲ Győr street

Mary of the Foam occupying a chapel beside the former **Carmelite Church**. Entering the church (built in the 1720s) through a portal whose inscription proclaims "I worked zealously for the Lord of Hosts", you'll find a richly decorated high altar and other furnishings carved by Franz Richter, a lay brother in the order. Behind the church stands the erstwhile monastery, later used as a refugee centre and military prison and now housing the *Klastrom Hotel*.

On the eastern side of the square are two **mansions** with finely wrought ironwork. The Zichy Palace at no. 13, built in 1778–82, has a balconied Zopf-style facade bearing the coat of arms of the Ott family, who owned it at a later date. Next door, at no. 12, stands the Altabek House, with two corner oriel windows dating from the sixteenth century, and a Baroque portico. Just around the corner, at Király utca 4, is the so-called **Napoleon House**, where the emperor stayed during a visit in 1809; the Municipal Art Gallery puts on temporary exhibitions here (Tues–Sun 10am–6pm; 900Ft).

From Bécsi kapu tér you can carry on uphill to the surviving bastions of Győr's sixteenth-century **castle**, housing the Lapidarium, underground casements full of Roman and medieval stonework (April–Oct Tues–Sun 10am–6pm; 300Ft). The castle successfully resisted the Turks for decades – unlike the town, which was frequently devastated.

Káptalandomb and the waterfront

Káptalandomb (Chapter Hill) has been crowned by a **cathedral** (daily 8am–noon & 2–6pm; free) ever since King Stephen made Győr an episcopal see in the first decade of the eleventh century, so the existing building incorporates Romanesque, Gothic and Baroque features. Just inside the entrance on the north side, the Gothic Hederváry Chapel contains a **reliquary bust of St László**, who ruled from 1077 to 1095 and was later canonized. Sensitively moulded and richly enamelled, it is a superb example of the goldsmith's art from the workshop of the Kolozsvári brothers. Also here is the tomb of Bishop Vilmos Apor, who was shot by Soviet soldiers on March 29, 1945 whilst trying to protect women and girls seeking refuge in the cellar of the Bishop's Palace (see opposite), and died a few days later;

he was beatified in 1997. The frescoes inside the cathedral were painted by Franz Anton Maulbertsch, who decorated numerous Hungarian churches in the eighteenth century, while the Bishop's throne was a gift from Empress Maria Theresa.

The building behind the cathedral, at Apor Vilmos püspök tere 2, houses the **Miklós Borsos Collection** (Borsos Miklós Állandó Kiállítás; Tues–Sun 10am–6pm; 750Ft), a marvellous assemblage of sculptural art by the self-taught artist who designed the Kilometre Zero monument in Budapest. Borsos (1906–90) worked in a range of media, producing a prolific number of sculptures – mostly female nudes, torsos and mythological figures – in addition to statuettes and copper discs with reliefs of eminent Hungarian and European composers, artists and writers. On the other side of the cathedral lies the **Bishop's Palace** (Püspökvár), a much remodelled edifice whose oldest section dates from the thirteenth century. Although the palace is not open to the public, a section of the old cellars has been cleverly converted into a small **museum** (Apor Kiállítás; March–Oct Tues–Sat 10am–4pm; 750Ft), with exhibitions on Győr during World War II and the city's wartime bishop, **Vilmos Apor** (see opposite). Bullet holes in the ceiling of the first room show where Apor was gunned down. Guided tours (hourly, Tues–Sun 10am–4pm) are in Hungarian, though it's possible to arrange an English guide if you call a day or two ahead (☎96/525-090 or mobile 20/312-8735).

From here you can walk down Káptalandomb, past the Zopf-style Provost House at no. 15, to reach **Duna-kapu tér**, a waterfront square alongside which Danube grain ships once moored, and where food **markets** are still held on Wednesdays and Saturdays. Notice the iron weathercock on top of the well – an allusion to the one that the Turks fixed above the town's gate, boasting that they would not leave Győr until it crowed.

Around Széchenyi tér

Heading up Jedlik Ányos utca from Duna-kapu tér, you'll find the **Ark of the Covenant** (Frigyláda emlékmű), a splendid Baroque monument erected by Emperor Karl III in 1731 by way of apology for his soldiers who knocked the monstrance from a priest's hands during a Corpus Christi procession. Across the road, on the corner of Káposztás köz (Cabbage Alley), the upstairs rooms of the medieval-style Kreszta House holds the **Margit Kovács Collection** (Tues–Sun 10am–6pm; 450Ft), featuring ceramic pieces by the Győr-born artist. Whilst the work on display is not as enlightening as the museum of her work in Szentendre (see p.153), it is still a delight and worth viewing for its highly distinctive vases, figurines and reliefs.

On the other side of the road, Kenyér köz (Bread Alley) and Szappanos köz (Soap Alley) lead to **Széchenyi tér**, traditionally the main square, overlooked by eye-like attic windows from the steep roofs of surrounding buildings. Notice the **Iron Stump House** at no. 4, so-called after a wooden beam into which travelling journeymen hammered nails to mark their sojourn. It now contains the stimulating **Imre Patkó Collection** (Patkó Imre Gyűtemény; Tues–Sun 10am–6pm; 300Ft), which, in addition to housing a number of objects from Africa and Oceania rounded up by the art historian Imre Patkó, has an impressive display of twentieth-century Hungarian and Western European paintings. Next door a fine mansion (built in 1740) houses the **Xantus János Museum** (Tues–Sun 10am–6pm; 600Ft), named after a locally educated nineteenth-century archeologist who emigrated to America and later travelled in China. The free English-language leaflet describes the varied and fascinating artefacts relating to local history, while the collections of tiled stoves and Hungarian stamps need no explanation.

On the south side of the square, beyond an ornate **Marian Column** erected in 1686 to commemorate the recapture of Buda from the Turks, stands the Benedictine **Church of St Ignatius**, designed by the Italian Baccio del Bianco in the 1630s. A painting in the sanctuary by the Viennese artist Paul Troger depicts the saint's apotheosis. Beside the adjacent monastery is the **Pharmacy Museum** (Mon–Fri 7.30am–4pm; free), a beautifully furnished seventeenth-century apothecary's that's still in use. North of the square, at Nefelejcs köz 3, an ex-hospice with two minuscule Renaissance-style yards contains the fabulous **Péter Váczy Collection** (Tues–Sun 10am–6pm; 450Ft) of fifteenth- to eighteenth-century Hungarian and European sculpture, paintings and furniture – look out for the English chair that magically converts into a mini-stepladder. The fine old pink-peach Esterházy palace at Király utca 17 houses the **Municipal Gallery of Art** (Városi Művészeti Múzeum; Tues–Sun 10am–6pm; 900Ft), which houses the Radnai Collection, a permanent exhibition of paintings and drawings by eminent Hungarian artists such as Egry, Kmetty and Barcsay, plus temporary exhibitions by Hungarian and international contemporary artists.

Across the river

Should you want a change of scenery, walk across the bridge over the Mosoni-Duna to the leafy **Révfalu** (Ferry Village) district, where a fifteen-minute walk will bring you to the **Bishop's Wood** (Püspök-erdő), a large park with deer and other fauna. Alternatively, you can cross the Rába via a small island linked by bridge to Bécsi kapu tér and the **Győrsziget** district. On the far side, on Fürdő tér, is the newly renovated **thermal baths complex** (Mon–Thurs & Sun 9am–8.30pm, Fri & Sat 9am–9pm; 2400Ft per day, 1950Ft for 3hr, 1050Ft after 6pm; Ⓦwww .gyortermal.hu), which features both indoor and outdoor baths, as well as an indoor **swimming pool** with chutes and slides (1050Ft). Down Kossuth utca, at no. 5, stands the recently restored former **synagogue**, a domed construction built in 1870 to the designs of Károly Benkő. Now owned by the university, it's used for concerts, particularly during the Mediawave festival (see opposite), and houses the splendid János Vasilescu Collection of postwar Hungarian art (Vasilescu János Gyűjtemény; Wed–Sun 10am–6pm; 450Ft), notably works by Lili Ország, Victor Vasarely and László Moholy-Nagy.

Eating, drinking and entertainment

There's no shortage of good **restaurants** to choose from in Győr, and there are enough drinking spots for a good evening out.

Restaurants

Arany Szarvas Fogadó Radó sétány 1. The hotel's restaurant offers a Hungarian menu including carp and duck, either in the nautically themed pub or on the terrace facing the town's fortifications and cathedral.
Fonte Schweidel utca 17. The restaurant in the *Hotel Fonte* is wonderfully lit and supremely sumptuous, with first-class international food and a marvellous wine list. Expensive.
Komédiás Czuczor Gergely utca 30. Understatedly cool cellar restaurant with an attractive menu of moderately priced fish, game, grilled meats and stews, and good vegetarian options; plus a courtyard taverna. Closed Sun.

Kreszta Ház Jedlik Ányos utca 3. Tasty, wholesome and extremely generous portions of stock Hungarian dishes, in convivial surrounds.
La Maréda Apáca utca 4. Pretty posh, featuring some impressive dishes such as hot smoked salmon, roast lamb and guinea fowl, plus a bistro (from 8am) that's good for salads, sandwiches and hot breakfasts.
Pátió Sarló köz 7. Overly glitzy place above the *cukrászda* of the same name, offering a fairly exotic menu including cream soups, stuffed pheasant, deer steak and catfish in paprika and sour cream.
Royal Étterem Árpád utca 34. Despite its somewhat sterile location inside the *Hotel Rába*, the food here is excellent, as are the (expensive) Belgian beers.

Hotel Schweizerhof Bécsi kapu tér 9. Across the way from the main hotel, its restaurant is one of the classiest in town, with restrained decor and fine cooking; there's also the less formal *Bacchus* wine cellar. Mon–Sat 6pm–midnight (depends on the number of guests).

Tejivó Salatbár Kisfaludy utca 30. Hectic, canteen-style place with salads and pastas priced by weight – perfect for a breezy snack stop. Mon–Fri 8am–5pm, Sat 8am–1pm.

Bars and cafés

There are several places in town to enjoy a sit-down and a drink, whether alcoholic or caffeine-based.

Bécsi Kávéház In the courtyard at Arany János utca 18–20. Also known as the *Wiener Kaffeehaus*, this is a long-established favourite for coffee and cakes.
Belgian Beer Café in the *Hotel Raba*, Árpád utca 34. Unsurprisingly, a good place to drink fine (if pricey) Belgian beers.
Captain Drake's Pub Radó sétány 1. A saloony place inside the *Arany Szarvas Fogadó* (see opposite) and also on its riverside terrace facing the town's fortifications and cathedral.
Hrabal Mozi Teleki utca 21. The coolest hangout in town which, in addition to films and gigs (see below), hosts lots of alternative happenings.

Mandala Teaház Sarkantyú köz 7. This beautifully scented haven behind the *Hotel Schweizerhof* is a great place to kick back over a pot of tea.
Mozart Baross Gábor utca 30. A classic coffee house.
Pátió Cukrászda Sarló köz 7. Above the restaurant (see opposite), there's good coffee as well as an eye-popping selection of cakes.
Poker Pub Liszt Ferenc 8. An enjoyable cellar bar. Closed Mon.
Wan Sör Király utca 9. Smoky little boozer down a tiny alley with head-thumpingly loud music and a youngish crowd.

Entertainment and festivals

Culturally, Győr has plenty to offer. In particular it's worth looking out for performances by the **Győr Ballet Company**, which achieved international renown under its founder Iván Márko, formerly the lead dancer of Maurice Béjart's Twentieth Century Ballet Company. Although Márko has moved on, the locals still cherish it, and performances at the **National Theatre** frequently sell out; the building, on the corner of Bajcsy-Zsilinszky utca and Czuczor Gergely utca, is easily identifed by its Op-Art mosaics by Victor Vasarely. Tickets (900–2400Ft) can be obtained from the designated ballet box office in the theatre (Tues–Fri 10am–noon & 3–5pm, Sat & Sun 1hr before performances). Tickets for the **Philharmonic Orchestra**, which mostly plays at the Richter Hall at Aradi Vértanűk utca 16, can be obtained at Kisfaludy utca 25 (Mon–Thurs 8am–4pm, Fri 8am–2pm).

The *Hrabal Mozi* at Teleki utca 21 puts on art films and world music events (☏96/550-850, ⓦwww.hrabalmozi.hu). There are also gigs at the *V2 Music Club* on Mórics Zsigmond rakpart, and films at *Cinema City Győr Plaza* at Vasvári Pál utca 1, south of the centre opposite the hospital.

The **Bartók Cultural Centre** at Czuczor Gergely utca 17 is a regular venue for foreign **films**, exhibitions and concerts, especially during the **Mediawave festival** in late April/early May – one to two weeks of avant-garde film, theatre and music (ⓦwww.mediawavefestival.hu). The **Győr Summer Days** (Gyori Nyár; ⓦwww .fesztivalirodagyor.hu) from mid-June to mid-July is a larger festival of music, theatre and dance at various venues throughout town, including Széchenyi tér, the Synagogue and Radó Island. Finally, the **Baroque Nostalgia Art Festival**, (ⓦwww.barokk.hu), featuring guitar music, theatrical performances and a Bach concert, takes place during the first two weeks of October at several venues including the Zichy Palace. Tourinform can tell you more about all the city's festivals and events.

Pannonhalma Monastery

Twenty kilometres southeast of Győr, the low-lying Kisalföld meets a spur of the Bakony, a glorious setting for the fortress-like **Pannonhalma Monastery** or, in full, the Arch-abbey of St Martin on the Sacred Mount of Pannonhalma (282m). According to the medieval chronicler known as Anonymous, it was here that Árpád was "uplifted by the beauty of Pannonia" after the Magyar conquest, and Prince Géza invited the **Benedictine Order** to found an abbey in 996. The Order helped Géza's son Stephen weld the pagan Magyar tribes into a Christian state, and remained influential until its suppression in 1787 by Emperor Josef II. His successor re-established the Benedictine order in 1802 on condition they committed themselves to pedagogy as well as prayer. Today some 320 boys live and study in the school here, with around fifty monks resident at the monastery.

The monastery manifests a variety of styles, the postwar school buildings contrasting with the Baroque exterior of the **basilica** and a Neoclassical **tower**. The late-Romanesque/early-Gothic church is the third on this site, having been rebuilt first in 1137 after a fire and then by Abbot Oros (1207–43), who later gave King Béla IV 220kg of silver to help him rebuild the country after the Mongol invasion. Although it was subsequently enlarged and tinkered with, the Gothic elements have been faithfully retained, most notably the high, simple vault. The interior furnishings, however, are mostly mid-nineteenth century, remodelled by Ferenc Stornó after the Turks plundered the originals. Notice, too, the marble sepulchres of two abbots and a princess. From the church you pass through an exquisitely carved Gothic portal (though the door is nineteenth century) and into the **cloisters**, dating from the early thirteenth century and rebuilt in 1486. Near the doorway is a fourteenth-century fresco, discovered by accident in the early 1990s, whilst on the wall by the doorway are some sixteenth-century graffiti – "Hic fuit", which translates as nothing more spectacular than "I Was Here".

Although Pannonhalma's most sacred treasures are displayed on only a couple of days around August 20, its medieval codices and ancient books are permanently on show in the magnificent Empire-style **library**. The 400,000-volume collection (around 120,000 of which are on display) includes the foundation deed of Tihany Abbey, dating from 1055 and the earliest known document to include Hungarian words (55 of them) amongst the customary Latin. Entering the library, you'll see copies of this and of Pannonhalma's charter, granted in 1002. The monastery's **art gallery** (March–Nov) displays a portrait of King Stephen and paintings by Italian, Dutch and German artists of the sixteenth and seventeenth centuries, plus works marking the monastery's millennium in 1996 – an apt time for UNESCO to add it to its World Heritage List. A ten-minute walk away is the monastery's modern **wine cellar**, where you can taste a selection of wine harvested on the surrounding slopes (1950Ft). Another profitable sideline is the selling of **lavender** (*levendula*) oil from the fields surrounding the monastery. It's advertised as a remedy for depression, insect bites and moths in clothes, and sold in the village shops and at the visitor centre.

Visitors are only admitted on **guided tours**, starting at the new, and very ugly, visitor centre 200m north of the monastery. After a fifteen-minute film, visitors are escorted along a modern walkway to the monastery where the tour proper begins. Tours in English run at 11.20am and 1.20pm (Tues–Sun; June–Sept daily, also at 3.20pm; 3000Ft); or there are more frequent ones in Hungarian, with English text (May daily 9am–4pm, hourly; June–Sept daily 9am–5pm, hourly; mid-March to April & Oct to mid-Nov Tues–Sun 9am–4pm, hourly; mid-Nov to mid-March Tues–Sun 10am–3pm, hourly except midday; 2100Ft). Churchgoers have a choice of three **Masses** on Sunday: in Hungarian at 9am and 11.30am, and one with Gregorian chant at 10am. **Organ recitals** (1800Ft) are given six times a year (including Aug 20, Sept 16, Oct 23 & Dec 26; all at 3.30pm), drawing crowds of music lovers; book at least a week in advance through the Tricollis office (see below).

Practicalities

Pannonhalma can be reached from Győr by any bus or train heading for Veszprém (or vice versa). The train station is 2km west of the village on Petőfi utca, whilst buses pass through the village centre, several a day (check in Győr before leaving) continuing right up to the monastery which is otherwise a steep ten-minute walk up Váralja (following yellow-stripe hiking marks). The 10am bus from Győr is ideal for the 11.20am tour and a leisurely return. **Information** is available from Tourinform in the cultural centre, halfway to the station at Petőfi utca 25 (mid-June to mid-Sept Mon–Fri 9am–6pm, Sat & Sun 9am–5pm; May to mid-June & mid-Sept to Oct daily 10am–4pm; Nov–April Mon–Fri 10am–noon & 1–4pm; ☎96/471-733, ✉pannonhalma@tourinform.hu), or Tricollis in the visitor centre (open same times as monastery; ☎96/570-191, Ⓦwww.bences.hu).

While neither office can arrange private **accommodation**, both can give a few addresses. Otherwise, there are three places to stay in town: the most comfortable is the *Hotel Pannon* at Hunyadi utca 7b (☎96/470-041, Ⓦwww .hotelpannon.hu; ❹), with the alternatives being the smaller *Familia Panzió* at Béke utca 61, 600m off Petőfi utca (☎96/470-192; ❸), and the extraordinarily bland *Pax Hotel* at Dózsa György utca 2, just off Petőfi utca (☎96/470-006, Ⓦwww.hotels.hu/paxhotel_pannonhalma; ❹). The *Panorama* campsite (☎96/471-240; May–Sept) is beautifully sited on the hillside at Fenyvesalja utca 4a, 300m south of the village centre off Lestár utca.

Of the several **restaurants** in the village, the best is that of the *Hotel Pannon*, which is surprisingly accomplished. The *Szent Márton*, across the car park from the visitor centre, is fine, although mainly frequented by coach parties. Finally, the *Borpince* on Szabadság tér has wine-tasting and also serves up hot and cold plates.

Pápa

Forty-five kilometres south of Győr, down towards the Bakony Hills, the small town of **PÁPA** grew up in the Middle Ages as a milling village, with 26 mills along the Tapolca stream. Its golden age was in the eighteenth century, when the Esterházy family encouraged German settlers. It missed out on the nineteenth-century industrialization drive, thus preserving its elegant Baroque centre, though during the Communist era the Tapolca suffered the same fate as many other streams and springs in the region, being destroyed by pollution and mining. Today the town is best known for its Calvinist College, founded in 1531 and one of the few religious schools to remain in church hands during Communist times, whose illustrious alumni include the national poet Sándor Petőfi and the novelist Mór Jókai. The town is also known as the birthplace of Ferenc Gyurcsány, Hungary's prime minister since 2004.

Dominating the main square is the Catholic **Church of St Stephen**, built by Jakab Fellner and József Grossman in 1774–86, with frescoes by the Austrian painter Franz Anton Maulbertsch from the life of the saint (not the Hungarian king but the original martyr). The largest church in Pannonia, it was commissioned by Bishop Károly Esterházy, who from 1783 had the same team build the U-shaped **Esterházy Mansion** behind the church on the ruins of the old castle. The finest Baroque parts of the mansion (including a local history museum) have been closed for some years now and there are few signs that the profoundly slow restoration work is anywhere near completion. The castle's chapel has been well restored and is now the reading room of the town's library. Instead, you could stroll through the **Várkert**, an extensive English garden (ie an unkempt park with lots of trees) behind the mansion, which is a favourite spot with the locals.

The first Calvinist place of worship, used from 1531 to 1752, is a humble building on Ruszek kőz, the alley leading from the bus station to the Catholic church. The square in front of the church and Fő utca, leading south, are both lined with fine Baroque buildings. At Fő utca 6, the **Calvinist History and Art Museum** (Református Egyháztörténeti és Egyázművészeti Múzeum; May–Oct Tues–Sun 9am–5pm; 300Ft), housed in the former chapel, has temporary exhibitions downstairs and a few pieces of peasant-style painted church furniture from the eighteenth and nineteenth centuries upstairs. When the chapel was built in 1783, Catholic restrictions required that it should not face onto the street, and should have no tower. Not until 1931–34 did the congregation build a proper church, just down the road on Március 15 tér.

Across the road from the Calvinist church, at no. 12, is the delightful **Blue Dyers' Museum** (Kékfestő Múzeum; April–Oct Tues–Sun 9am–5pm; Nov–March Tues–Sat 9am–4pm; 450Ft), one of the largest of its kind in Central Europe. Blue dyeing was a method of colouring cotton popular among the German communities of western Hungary; it declined after the postwar deportation of Germans and was an endangered craft by the 1960s (when the museum opened), but is now back in fashion with Hungarians. The museum fronts a workshop run by the Kluge family from 1783 until 1957, where the original vats and drying attic can still be inspected and demonstrations are held; you can also buy blue-dyed items here.

From the rear of the Calvinist church you can return along pedestrianized **Kossuth utca**, full of turn-of-the-twentieth-century shops and buildings. Turning left down Petőfi Sándor utca, you'll find the house where Petőfi lived in 1841–42 while attending the school right next door at no. 13; this was in use from 1797 to 1895, when it was replaced by the grand pile on Március 15 tér. Further down on the left at no. 24 is an empty **synagogue**, a beautiful but battered relic of a community that barely survived the Holocaust.

Practicalities

Arriving by bus, you'll be dropped two minutes' walk east of the centre on Szabadság utca, while the train station is ten to fifteen minutes' walk north of the centre. All the sights in town are concentrated on Főutca and the parallel Kossuth utca, leading south under an archway from Fő tér. **Information** is available at the small Tourinform office at Kossuth utca 18 (June–Aug daily 9am–5pm; Sept–May Mon–Fri 9am–5pm, Sat 9am–noon; ☎89/311-535, Ⓔ papa@tourinform.hu), and **private rooms** (❷) can be booked through Ibusz at Fő utca 4 (Mon–Fri 8.30am–4.30pm, Sat 8.30am–noon; ☎89/323-936, Ⓔ ntours@globonet.hu;). Two excellent places to **stay** are the *Caesar Panzió* at Kossuth utca 32 (☎89/320-320, Ⓦ www.caesarpanzio.hu; ❸), a cracking little pension whose cool, air-conditioned rooms incorporate some neat touches; and the *Arany Griff Hotel*, in the Baroque row facing the Catholic church at Fő tér 15 (☎89/312-000, Ⓦ www.hotelaranygriff.hu; ❹), with pastel-furnished rooms and more than ample space, including a little entrance hall and gleaming bathrooms. If these are both full, there's the small and grubby *Főnix Panzió* at Jókai utca 4, just past the Blue Dyers' Museum (☎89/324-361, Ⓦ www .fonixpanzio.try.hu; ❷). The *Termál Camping*, at Várkort út 7, beyond the bus station at the hot baths (☎89/320-735, Ⓦ www.termalcamping.hu), is the only five-star **campsite** in Hungary, with features such as a minimarket and bike rental.

The *Arany Griff* also has the best **restaurant** in town, serving Hungarian specialities, as well as a funky café spilling out onto the pavement at the front. The *Vadásztanya*, at Rákóczi út 21, leading west from Kossuth utca, also has Hungarian food in more modest surrounds. At Kossuth utca 8 the *Esti Kornél Kávéház* is a fairly traditional café, next to the *James Joyce Irish Pub*.

The **post office** is at Kossuth utca 27 (Mon–Fri 8am–6pm, Sat 8am–noon), facing an **internet** joint at no. 30 (Mon–Fri 8am–5pm, Sat 8am–noon). In mid-June, the town hosts the **United Toys Festival**, a series of classical and rock concerts, exhibitions and children's activities, most of which take place in the Várkert. There's also the four-day **Somló wine festival** at the end of August.

The Szigetköz

Twenty kilometres from Győr, you can turn south off the highway to **LÉBÉNY**, but it's only recommended for fans of ecclesiastical architecture, since the village's sole attraction is a thirteenth-century **Benedictine Church** that once came under the jurisdiction of Pannonhalma. Together with the church in Ják (see p.280), this is touted as one of the oldest and finest examples of Romanesque architecture in Hungary, though it was actually restored to its original style after receiving a Baroque face-lift from the Jesuits in the mid-seventeeth century. One or two buses an hour run from Győr to Lébény, most continuing to Mosonmagyaróvár.

To the north of the highway, however, lies the **Szigetköz** or "island region", bounded by the meandering Mosoni-Duna and the "old" or main branch of the Danube. This picturesque wetland abounds in rare flora, **birdlife** and fish, making it something of a paradise for hikers and naturalists alike. Unfortunately, the **Gabcikovo hydroelectric barrage** has reduced water levels sharply, thus badly affecting the ecology and wildlife of the region. If you want to explore the area on horseback, there are lots of **riding** stables; one of the best, awarded the five horseshoe grade, is the Szelle Lovasudvar at Sérfenyő utca 99, in **DUNASZIGET**, 10km northeast of Mosonmagyaróvár (☎96/233-515 evenings or mobile 20/935-3223, ⓦwww.szellelovasudvar.hu), which organizes a number of riding tours around the region. The minor road across the Szigetköz, running between Győr and Mosonmagyaróvár, is part of the international Danube **cycle route** and there's plenty of **accommodation** along the way. In **MECSÉR**, 3km off the road, is the *Dunaparti Panzió* at Ady Endre utca 45 (☎96/213-386, ⓦwww.dunaparti.hu; ❸), which also rents out **kayaks**, while a good place to eat is *Pusztacsárda 1804* (Thurs & Fri 6–11pm, Sat & Sun noon–11pm), an enormous thatched barn of a place 2km south of the village near route 1. In **HÉDERVÁR**, about 5km north of Mecsér, you can try the *Kék Apartman* at Kossuth utca 13 (☎96/215-430, ⓦwww .kek-apartman.hu; ❸), which rents out **bikes**, or, if you've got the money, the 300-year-old *Kastely Hotel* at Fő út 47 (☎96/213-433, ⓦwww.hedervar.hu; ❾), which also has a very posh restaurant and a botanic garden. Close by, in **LIPÓT**, there's the *Holt-Duna Camping* at Holt-Duna út 1 (☎96/555-513; May–Sept); the *Sari Vendégház*, near the hot baths at Rákóczi utca 18 (☎96/720-620, ⓦwww .sarivendeghaz.hu; ❷); and the modern *Wellness Orchidea* spa hotel at Rákóczi utca 42 (☎96/674-042, ⓦwww.orchideahotel.hu; ❻). Up near the Slovak border in **DUNAKILITI** the *Princess Palace Hotel* at Kossuth utca 117 (☎96/671-071; ⓦwww.princesspalace.hu; ❾) is a brand-new French-style château complete with golf course; and the *Szigetköz Wellness Hotel* (☎96/671-470, ⓦwww.szigetkozhotel .hu; ❼) is a new health resort. There's also the *Vizpart Camping* (☎96/224-579) in Dunakiliti. Fishing enthusiasts can obtain **angling licences** from Tourinform in Mosonmagyaróvár (see p.257).

Mosonmagyaróvár and around

MOSONMAGYARÓVÁR, 39km northwest of Győr, is a fusion of two settlements near the confluence of the Mosoni-Duna branch of the Danube and the Lajta River. While **Moson** is utterly prosaic, dominated by Highway 1, running through its middle, **Magyaróvár** – where you'll find the restaurants and hotels – is a pleasant, fairly touristy, old town with a picturesque castle and bridges. Both are visibly prosperous, thanks in the main to all the Austrians who come here to shop or for inexpensive medical care – there are well over one hundred dentists in town. The best time to visit is late autumn, when the crowds have thinned and the first pressing of grapes takes place at local **vineyards**.

The chief attraction is **Óvár Castle** (usually open; free) at the north end of the town (follow the signposts for Bratislava). Founded in the thirteenth century to guard the western gateway to Hungary, it gave the town its medieval name, Porta Hungarica. Much remodelled over the years, since 1818 it has housed an Agricultural Institute, now a faculty of the University of Western Hungary; the small main building contains small exhibitions on the fauna of the Hanság region and on the poet Nikolaus Lenau, a student here in 1822–23 (Mon–Fri 9am–noon & 1–2pm; free). You can also see a chapel built in 1712 as a plague memorial, and the Secession-style university buildings, dating from 1912, and go up onto the gatehouse battlements.

The cobbled streets running down through the town are worth exploring, even if they have been strongly kitschified for the crowds of Austrian tourists. The **church of St Gotthard**, rebuilt in 1777 in Baroque style, shelters the remains of Archduke Frederick Habsburg, supreme commander of the Austro-Hungarian armies in World War I. From here it's a short step west to Fő utca, the main road running round the west side of the old town of Magyaróvár, where the **Cselley Ház** at no. 19 is one of the town's oldest buildings, dating in part from the fourteenth century. It's notable for its stone-framed windows, wrought-iron window grilles, and its panelled ceilings on the first floor. It houses the **Gyurkovich Collection of Famous Hungarian Paintings** (Gyurkovich Gyűtemény; Tues–Sun: May–Sept 10am–6pm; Oct–April 10am–2pm; 600Ft), donated by an art-loving doctor and including works by some of the big names in Hungarian art such as Mihály Munkácsy. There's a Roman sarcophagus in front of the building and similar stonework in the basement. Following Fő út on down for ten minutes to the junction with Kossuth utca, you come to the **Hanság Museum** at Szent István Királyút 1 (Hansági Múzeum; Tues–Sun: May–Sept 10am–6pm; Oct–April 2–6pm; 600Ft), with its Neoclassical porticos, which is one of the oldest provincial collections in Hungary. There are some worthy exhibits on show, such as Roman and Celtic grave goods, Hussars' uniforms, furniture from a peasant household, and documents pertaining to the

Into Slovakia and Austria

Mosonmagyaróvár is the last stop before two major border crossings. **Rajka**, 19km north, handles traffic bound for the Slovak capital of Bratislava, 15km away, while **Hegyeshalom** is the main road and rail crossing into Austria, from where it's 45km to Vienna. While the latter used to be famous for its queues of Ladas and Trabants carrying families of Hungarians to the hypermarkets on the Austrian side, passport controls have now been abolished and traffic now moves quickly in both directions. Although there is no longer any need for trains to stop at Hegyeshalom for passport checks or to change locomotives, they still halt to switch drivers, although this will ultimately end when the same modern signalling system is installed in both countries. Trains from Vienna to Budapest do not call at Mosonmagyaróvár, but there's a direct train every two hours from Vienna's Sudbahnhof as far as Győr.

events of October 26, 1956, when one hundred demonstrators were shot dead by secret police in front of the town's barracks. The town's **thermal baths** are in Magyaróvár at Kolbai utca 10 (daily 8am–7pm; 1200Ft).

Practicalities

The **bus** and **train stations** are located in the south of Moson on Hild tér; buses #1, #2, #5 and #6 run along Szent István Király út, past **Tourinform** at Kápolna tér 16 (mid-June to mid-Sept Mon–Fri 9am–6pm, Sat & Sun 9am–5pm; mid-Sept to mid-June Mon–Fri 9am–4pm; ☎96/206-304, ⓦwww.mosonmagyarovar.hu), and then into Magyaróvár, 1.5km further on.

Most of the town's **hotels** are located in Magyaróvár, the best being the *Hotel Thermal*, part of the thermal baths complex at Kolbai utca 10 (☎96/206-871, ⓦwww.thermal-movar.hu; ❼), which has bikes for rent; and the *Solaris Hotel*, in a quiet, leafy road at Lucsony utca 19 (☎96/215-300, ⓦwww.hotels.hu/solaris; ❹). There are private rooms to let nearby on Kigyó utca. In Moson the best place is the hospitable *Hotel Corvina*, 500m north of Tourinform at Mosonyi Mihály utca 2 (☎96/218-131, ⓦwww.corvinahotel.hu; ❹), which has bright, airy rooms; there's also the *Motel NET.T* at Kölcsey út 4 (☎96/576-796, ⓔmotelnett@axelero.hu; ❸), just northwest of the station on Highway 86, which is simple but adequate, with a 24-hour restaurant. There's **camping** space at the *Termál Hotel Aqua* at Kigyó utca 1 (☎96/579-168, ⓦwww.tha.hu), and at the crowded *Kis-Duna* site, 2.5km east from the train station at Gabona rakpart 6 (☎96/216-443, ⓦwww.hotels.hu/kis_duna; May–Oct), which also has a motel (❷). Those with transport may prefer *Vizpart Camping* (see p.255) in Dunakiliti, 12km north near the Danube.

Of the several brazenly tourist-oriented **restaurants** spilling out onto Magyar utca in Magyaróvár, the *Magyaros Vendéglő* at no. 3 is the best. Just south at Szent Laszló tér 4, the *Borclub Étterem és Vinotéka* has a pleasant terrace and serves a good range of Hungarian wines by the glass.

Western Transdanubia

Western Transdanubia, part of the region bordering Austria and Slovenia, has a sub-Alpine topography and climate, ideal for wine growing and outdoor pursuits. Its Baroque towns and historic castles evince centuries of Habsburg influence and doughty resistance against the Turks, and the region's proximity to Austria has given it a wealthier and more developed status than any other part of Hungary. The beautiful town of **Sopron**, with its magnificent Belváros, makes an ideal place to start, with several enjoyable attractions nearby: the Esterházy Palace at **Fertőd**, the Széchenyi Mansion at **Nagycenk** and the **Fertő-Hanság National Park** – excellent cycling country. Heading south, **Kőszeg** is one of the prettiest towns in Hungary, whilst larger **Szombathely** has plenty to show for its Roman past. It is also a good base from which to explore the castle at **Sárvár** or the picturesque **Őrség region**, where village tourism is thriving.

The following north–south itinerary is possible by public transport, since Sopron is easily accessible by express trains and buses from Budapest, Győr or Vienna, whereas other places are easier to reach using local services. Starting from Balaton, however, it's easier to work your way north via Szombathely or **Zalaegerszeg** (in which case, you should backtrack through the following sections).

Sopron

With its 115 monuments and 240 listed buildings, **SOPRON**, tucked away in the far northwestern corner of the country, 79km west of Győr, can justly claim to be "the most historic town in Hungary", as well as one of the most attractive. Never having been ravaged by Mongols or Turks, the inner town retains its medieval layout, with a melange of Gothic and Baroque that rivals the Várhegy in Budapest – but with even fewer cars on the streets. Founded as Roman Scarbantia, it was a walled town by the early fourth century and became a major stage on the Amber Road, the trade route from the Baltic to the Adriatic. Wine has been made here since the twelfth century, although red varieties took over only in the nineteenth century, introduced by German-speaking settlers who would only take payment from Napoleon's soldiers in the safer blue notes, hence the name Kékfrankos or French Blue for the main local grape.

Sopron is also the base for excursions to the Esterházy Palace and the vintage steam train at Nagycenk amongst others. Its proximity to Vienna means that Austrians have long come here to shop, eat out and get their teeth fixed – there are *Zahnartz* (dentist) signs everywhere in Ödenburg, as they call Sopron. While the local economy benefits, visitors will find that prices are almost at Budapest levels and accommodation can be in short supply in the high season. Be warned that some museums are closed from October until March.

Franz Liszt is seen to a certain extent as a local boy, although his birthplace in Raiding is now across the border in Austria; his first public concert, at the age of 9, was given in the casino, where the Liszt Cultural Centre now stands.

Arrival and information

From Sopron's **train station**, it's just 500m up Mátyás király utca to Széchenyi tér, on the southern edge of the Belváros. International tickets, for the hourly GySEV trains leaving to Vienna, are sold next to the taxi desk in the main hall. Arriving by **bus**, it's five minutes' walk along Lackner Kristóf utca to Ógabona tér, on the northwest side of the Várkerület that surrounds the Belváros. Many buses towards Fertőd, Nagycenk, Szombathely and Sárvár also stop at Csengery utca 52, near the train station, while those arriving in Sopron drop passengers off across the road.

Information is provided by Tourinform, inside the Liszt Cultural Centre at Liszt utca 1 (mid-June to mid-Sept Mon–Fri 9am–7pm, Sat & Sun 9am–6pm; mid-Sept to mid-June Mon–Fri 9am–5pm, Sat & Sun 9am–3pm; ☏99/517-560, ⊚www .tourinform.sopron.hu). If you're in the mood to visit several museums in one day then purchase a **museum pass** (*felonőtteknek*; 2400Ft), available from the Firewatch Tower, which allows entry into all museums. The **post office** is at Széchenyi tér 7–10 (Mon–Fri 8am–7pm, Sat 8am–noon) and there's **internet access** at *Szintézis Sopron*, Balfi utca 3 (Mon–Fri 7.30am–9.30pm, Sat 9am–9.30pm), and the *Teaház es Kávézó*, Széchenyi tér 16 (Mon–Fri 9am–10pm, Sat & Sun 10am–10pm).

Accommodation

There's a decent choice of **accommodation** in town, though you should book ahead in summer. During July and August **dormitory beds** are available at the *Középiskolai Fiu Kollégium* at Erzsébet utca 9 (☏99/311-260) and the *Hetvényi Leány Kollégium* at Mátyás király utca 21 (☏99/320-211), both just down from

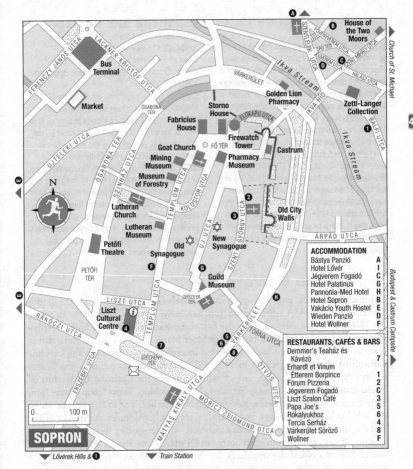

SOPRON

Lövérek Hills & ① ▼   ▼ **Train Station**

Széchenyi tér, or at the *Nyugati–Magyarországi Egyetem* at Ady Endre utca 5 and also at Baross utca 4 (☎99/518-194, ⓔsekoll@sek.nyme.hu), ten minutes' walk southwest of the centre.

Hotels and pensions

Bástya Panzió Patak utca 40 ☎99/325-325, ⓦwww.bastya-panzio.hu. Large pension with neat, compact rooms and shiny clean bathrooms, just west of Sas tér – from the bus station go straight up Patak utca. **⑤**

Jégverem Fogadó Jégverem utca 1 ☎99/510-113, ⓦwww.jegverem.hu. Just uphill from the Belváros, this converted eighteenth-century inn is named after the old ice pit in the middle of its restaurant (see p.263). Very popular, with just five rooms, so essential to reserve. **④**

Hotel Lővér Várisi utca 4 ☎99/888-400, ⓦwww .danubiushotels.com/lover. Peaceful, secluded hotel

on the fringes of the Lővérek Hills, a 20min walk from the city centre (bus #1 or #2). Well-appointed rooms and good facilities, including a pool and tennis courts. **⑥**

Hotel Palatinus Uj utca 23 ☎99/523-816, ⓦwww.palatinussopron.com. A fine and very central new hotel, although the rooms are surprisingly bland. **④**

Pannonia-Med Hotel Várkerület 75 ☎99/312-180, ⓦwww.pannoniahotel.com. A lovely old building with a splendid foyer, wrought-iron balconies and comfortable rooms with fluffed-up pillows and fancy towels. A Best Western but you wouldn't know it. Underground car park, pool, sauna and gymnasium are just some of the facilities. ❼–❽

Hotel Sopron Fövényverem utca 7 ☎99/512-261, ⓦwww.hotelsopron.hu. Up on Koronázó-domb (Coronation Hill) just north of the Belváros, with a mix of very ordinary 1970s rooms and newer, more stylish ones, some with terrific views of the old town. Facilities include sauna, solarium, tennis courts and parking. ❼–❽

Wieden Panzió Sas tér 13 ☎99/523-222, ⓦwww.wieden.hu. Across from the *Jégverem*, this pension has various sized, but rather staid, doubles. ❹

Hotel Wollner Templom utca 20 ☎99/524-400, ⓦwww.wollner.hu. In a 300-year-old building in the heart of the Belváros, this outstanding hotel oozes class. Gorgeous rooms come with minibar, oak bureaus and large, handsome beds, and the hotel also boasts a beautiful inner courtyard and hanging garden, and a superb restaurant and wine cellar (see p.263). ❼

Campsite and hostels

Brennbergi Youth Hostel Brennbergi utca ☎99/313-116, ⓦwww.tabor.sopron.hu. Open all year; 4km west of the city centre (bus #3 or #10 from the bus station). Dorm beds 1950Ft.

Castrum Balfi Gyógykemping Fürdő sor 59, Balfi ☎99/339-124, ⓔcastrum.sopron-balf@t-online .hu. Currently the closest campsite to Sopron, 8km east on the way to the Esterházy palace at Fertőd, this is open all year and also has rooms. ❷

Vakácio Youth Hostel Ady Endre utca 31 ☎99/338-502, ⓦwww.vakacio.info. On the corner of Lövér utca, about 15min from Tourinform or the train station (bus #10 from the bus station or #10Y from the train station). A clean but functional backpackers' hostel, with rooms ranging from twins (avoid the tiny no. 4 right behind reception) to 8/9-person bunk rooms. Microwave and fridge available. Dorm beds 3600Ft.

Around the Belváros

Compact and easily explored on foot, the **Belváros** holds most of the sights. Templom utca provides a direct route from Széchenyi tér to the heart of the Belváros, but you should take a detour along the first turning to the right, to admire **Orsolya tér**, in the centre of which is the now defunct Maria Fountain (Mária Kút), dating from 1780. This romantic-looking cobbled square takes its name from the Ursuline **Church of the Virgin**, rebuilt in 1864 and sandwiched between two neo-Gothic edifices dripping with loggias, one of which contains the **Catholic Collection of Ecclesiastical Art** (Katolikus Gyűjtemény; May–Oct Mon, Thurs & Sun 10am–4pm; 300Ft), consisting of vestments, goldsmithery and the like. The square was the site of the Salt Market in olden days, and animals were butchered under the arcades of the building at no. 5. Today, this houses a museum, with temporary displays only.

From Orsolya tér you can head north up **Új utca** (New Street), which is actually one of Sopron's oldest thoroughfares. Its chunky cobblestoned pavements follow a gentle curve of arched dwellings painted in red, yellow and pink, with a view of the Firewatch Tower beyond. During the Middle Ages it was called Zsidó (Jewish) utca and housed a flourishing mercantile community, until they were accused of conspiring with the Turks and expelled in 1526, only returning to Sopron in the nineteenth century. At no. 22, a tiny medieval **synagogue** (Ó-Zsinagóga; May–Oct Tues–Sun 10am–6pm; 750Ft) stands diagonally opposite a slightly newer one, at no. 11, now hidden by a Baroque facade. At the end of the street you emerge onto Fő tér.

Fő tér

The focal point of **Fő tér** is the cherubim-covered **Holy Trinity Statue**, which local Protestants took as an affront when it was erected in 1700 by Cardinal Kollonich, who threatened: "First I will make the Hungarians slaves, then I will make them beggars, and then I will make them Catholics." Behind it stands the triple-aisled **Goat Church** (Kecsketemplom; Mon–Sat 8am–6pm, summer 7am–9pm), built for the Franciscans in about 1280, where three monarchs were later crowned and seven parliaments were convened. Its curious name stems from the legend that the church's construction was financed by a goatherd whose flock unearthed a cache of loot – in gratitude for which an angel embraces a goat on a pillar. Although there are some Baroque features, it remains one of the outstanding examples of Hungarian Gothic architecture.

Before crossing the square to visit the mansions on its northern side, check out the **Pharmacy Museum** at no. 2 (Patikamúzeum; Tues–Sun: April–Sept 10am–6pm; Oct–March 10am–2pm; 450Ft), which preserves the seventeenth-century Angel apothecary's shop. Though remodelled since then, its Biedermeier-style walnut furnishings and artefacts from the Dark Ages of pharmacology certainly deserve a look.

Directly opposite the church stands the **Fabricius House** at no. 6, which unites a Baroque mansion on Roman foundations with a fifteenth-century patrician's house. It contains three small museums (all Tues–Sun: April–Sept 10am–6pm; Oct–March 10am–2pm; 900Ft each): the Archeological Museum (Régészeti Gyűjtemény és Kiállítás) displays finds from the Amber Road, notably the Iron Age Sun Disk and the 1200-year-old Cunpald Goblet, and is also noted for its "whispering gallery"; the Bourgeois Home (Polgári Lakások) shows the changes in interior design and furnishing between the seventeenth and eighteenth centuries; and the Lapidarium in the Gothic cellar includes three large Roman statues unearthed during the construction of the town hall. Next door at no. 7 is the **Lackner House**, named after the seventeenth-century mayor who bequeathed it to Sopron; his motto "Fiat Voluntas Tua" ("Thy will be done") appears on the facade.

The Renaissance **Storno House** (Storno Gyűjtemény) at no. 8 has the finest pedigree, however. King Mátyás stayed here in 1482–83, as did Franz Liszt in 1840 and 1881. It is still owned by descendants of Ferenc Storno, painter, architect and master chimney sweep, who restored Pannonhalma and other medieval churches during the nineteenth century. The family's private collection of furniture, Liszt memorabilia and Roman, Celtic and Avar relics is displayed in an enjoyably eccentric **museum** on the second floor (Tues–Sun: April–Sept 10am–6pm; Oct–March 10am–2pm; 1200Ft).

The Firewatch Tower

North of Fő tér rises Sopron's symbol, the **Firewatch Tower** (Tűztorony; April–Oct Tues–Sun 10am–6pm, May–Aug till 8pm; early May to mid-Sept also open Mon; 900Ft), set atop the town wall built by the Romans, who established Scarbantia here during the first century AD. As its name suggests, the tower was erected after a great blaze in 1676 for fire-watchers, who also blew trumpets to signal the hours. Above a square thirteenth-century base rises a seventeenth-century cylinder with a Baroque balcony, offering a stunning **view** of Fő tér and the Belváros.

Abutting the south side of the tower is the **Gate of Loyalty**, built in honour of the townfolk's decision to reject the offer of Austrian citizenship in 1921. The motif shows Hungaria surrounded by kneeling citizens, and Sopron's coat of arms, which henceforth included the title "Civitas Fidelissima" ("the most loyal citizenry"). Walking through the gate and under the Firewatch Tower, you'll emerge onto **Előkapu** (Outer Gate) utca, where the houses are staggered for defensive purposes, and "errant burghers" and "gossiping, nagging" wives were once pinioned in stocks for the righteous to pelt with rotten food. The **Várfal** promenade (Mon–Fri 9am–8pm, Sat & Sun 9am–6pm) is a passage that leads off to the left beside the city walls, dodging around the back of houses and emerging on the ring road outside the walls.

At the end of Előkapu you can cross Várkerület to examine the colourfully tiled facade of the **Golden Lion Pharmacy** at no. 29, or head to the right along the boulevard to view a bastion of the **medieval town walls**. Alternatively, cut through to the east side of the Town Hall to see the remains of the **Castrum**, where the medieval city walls were built (after becoming a free royal town in 1277) on the remains of the Roman town walls; some Roman foundations are visible plus a stretch of street leading to the second-century Forum, under the present city hall.

Templom utca

Templom utca, a picturesque street of Baroque facades, heads south from Fő tér. Standing just around the corner from the Goat Church on Fő tér is the square's finest sight, a fourteenth-century **chapterhouse** (Káptalanterem; May–Oct daily 10am–noon & 2–5pm, with tours on the hour Mon–Fri; free) behind the Baroque facade of no. 1, whose Gothic pillars and vaults are decorated with images of the seven deadly sins and the symbols of the Evangelists.

On the opposite side of the road, at nos. 2–4, a Baroque mansion built by the Esterházy family now houses two museums of fairly specialized interest. The **Central Museum of Mining** (Központi Bányászati Múzeum; Tues–Sun: April–Oct 10am–6pm; Nov–March 10am–4pm; 600Ft) has some curious artefacts from the Brennberg pits in Sopron's western suburbs, the oldest coal mines in Hungary. The adjacent door leads to the **Museum of Forestry** (Erdészeti Gyűjtemény; daily except Wed; May–Oct 1–6pm; Nov–April 10am–1pm; 300Ft), although you'd have to be a real die-hard to appreciate the vast collection of tools and instruments. The mansion is also notable as Haydn often stayed here, while in 1840 Liszt slept next door at no. 6.

At no. 19 a building erected around 1400 and remodelled in the 1760s contains the **Lutheran History Museum** (Országos Evangélikus Múzeum; mid-April to mid-Oct Wed–Fri 2–5pm, Sat & Sun 10.30am–1pm & 2–5pm; 150Ft), which explains how all the Evangelical churches were confiscated in 1674, obliging Lutherans to worship at home until the authorities relented. The adjacent **Lutheran Church** dates from 1782, but only acquired its tall neo-Romanesque bell-tower eighty years later, due to restrictions on the faith decreed by Emperor Josef II. On the other side, the profusely ornamented Töpler House at no. 22 is named after a physician who devoted his life to fighting epidemics, while the courtyard of no. 15 contains a neo-Renaissance loggia.

Beyond the Belváros

While the Belváros is spectacular, there is more to see as you move out of the centre, with art and architecture to the north, a folly to the west, and beautiful countryside to the south.

Ikva híd, crossing a narrow stream which used to flood noxiously in the nineteenth century, points towards some more sights. Off to the right at Balfi utca 11 is the private **Zettl-Langer Collection** (April–Oct Tues–Sun 10am–noon; Nov–Jan & March Fri–Sun 10am–noon; 450Ft) of porcelain, earthenware and weaponry, assembled by nineteenth-century businessman and sometime painter Gusztáv Zettl. His descendants still live here and will give you a guided tour through the collection.

A five-minute walk up Dorfmeister and Szent Mihály utca from Ikva híd takes you past the **House of the Two Moors** (so-called after the statues flanking its gate) on your left at Szent Mihály utca 9, to the Gothic **Church of St Michael** further uphill, whose gargoyles leer over a decaying thirteenth-century Chapel of St Jacob. Nearby stand the tombstones of Soviet soldiers killed liberating Sopron from the Arrow Cross puppet government, which massacred hundreds of hostages before fleeing in April 1945 with the Coronation Regalia (which was handed over to the US Army for safekeeping and held in Fort Knox until Jimmy Carter returned it to Hungary in 1978).

The Fool's Castle

In the southwestern garden suburbs, 3km from the centre, at Csalogány köz 28, lurks a bizarre **"Fool's Castle"** (Taródi-vár; 300Ft), built by local eccentric Istvan Taród in the 1950s. The castle's cold, dark rooms are crammed with a ramshackle assortment of paintings, furniture and other curios, including a couple of rusting motorbikes, while up on the roof you can view the crumbling stone turrets and pillars, and the not-so-distant Lővérek Hills. Whilst it can't compare to the extravagant Bory Castle in Székesfehérvár (see p.192), it's nonetheless an oddly enjoyable place to wander around. It's still inhabited by Taród's descendants, and though there are no set opening hours, you can usually gain admission whenever someone's at home. To get here, take bus #1 from Széchenyi tér, which drops you near the covered pool (Fedett Uzsoda) in the Lővér suburb, walk 50m back, turn left up Fegyves Sor, another left up Harsfa Sor, and then follow the road round.

The Lővérek Hills and the Burgenland

A kilometre or so further south of the castle are the sub-Alpine **Lővérek Hills**, a standing invitation to hikers. Bus #1 or #2 will drop you at the *Hotel Lővér* near the start of the path up to the **Károly lookout tower** (Károlymagaslati Kilátó; daily: May–Aug 9am–8pm; April, Sept & Oct 9am–7pm; March 9am–5pm; Nov–Feb 9am–4pm; 300Ft), which offers marvellous views of the surrounding countryside. Several **hiking trails** continue through the rolling forests to the west, and it's even possible to hike into Austria. Both sides of the border are inhabited by bilingual folk engaged in viticulture, following the division of the **Burgenland** region between Hungary and Austria (which got the lion's share) after the collapse of the Habsburg empire – an amicable partition, it seems, since nobody complains about it today.

Eating and drinking

Given the town's popularity, the range of places to **eat** and **drink** is somewhat disappointing, though wine buffs can choose from several good cellars.

Restaurants

Erhardt et Vinum Étterem Borpince Balfi utca 10. An attractive new restaurant in a Baroque house with tasteful modern lighting, plus a winebar in the courtyard; Hungarian cuisine, with game and vegetarian dishes.

Fórum Pizzeria Szent György utca 3. Enjoyable pizzeria also offering spaghetti, lasagne, Mexican dishes and a salad bar. Despite the waiters being overworked, the service is excellent.

Jégverem Fogadó Jégverem utca 1. Mammoth portions of fine homestyle cooking in this popular, frenetic restaurant inside the pension of the same name, and in the courtyard. The menu is adventurous, but service is slow and with an open kitchen it can get a bit stuffy.

Rókalyukhoz Várkerület 112. A fairly prodigious pizza menu awaits at this informal restaurant/pub.

Head downstairs for a more intimate dining experience.

Tercia Serház Liszt Ferenc utca 1. Large, modern and pleasantly informal basement restaurant under the Cultural Centre, offering a very reasonably priced and colourful menu, including stews, dumplings, lamb, fish, and, for the more adventurous, baked brain.

Várkerület Söröző Várkerület 83. Fairly basic place opposite the *Rókalyukhoz*, serving Hungarian cuisine and grilled meats, with a buzzing bar and beer garden at the rear.

Wollner Templom utca 20. You're guaranteed an exquisite dining experience in the *Hotel Wollner*'s distinguished restaurant. Expensive – but first-class – helpings of Hungarian and international cuisine.

Cafés, bars and cellars

The two best **cafés** in town are the *Liszt Szalon Café* (and chocolate shop), a classy, relaxing place with a lovely courtyard in the heart of the Belváros at Szent György utca 12, and the cosy *Demmer's Teaház és Kávézó* at Széchenyi tér 16, offering a complete range of teas alongside some delicious strudels and roulades. The sociable *Hungariá Kaveház* in the Liszt Cultural Centre has the best summer terrace.

Drinkers in search of the fine local Soproni beer should head for *Rókalyukhoz* (see p.263) or the Western-themed *Papa Joe's*, a few paces along at Várkerület 108. Hearty red Kékfrankos and white, apple-flavoured Tramini can be sampled in **wine cellars** such as the *Cezár Pince* at Hátsókapu utca 2, which boasts vintage oak butts and leather-aproned waiters and also serves meat platters; or the less refined *Gyógygödör Borozó* at Fő tér 4. There's also good wine tasting to be had in the more formal surrounds of the *Hotel Wollner's* cellar (see p.263).

Festivals

Sopron is at its liveliest during the **Spring Days** (late March) and **Festival Weeks** (mid-June to mid-July), when all manner of concerts and plays are staged at the Petőfi Theatre on Petőfi tér, the Liszt Cultural Centre on Széchenyi tér, and many other venues in the region. You can get details from Tourinform and tickets from the festival office, in the same building (Tues–Fri 9am–5pm, Sat 9am–noon; ☎99/511-730, ⓦwww.prokultura.hu). In mid-October the town hosts a festival to celebrate the **Grape Harvest**, with wine tasting, folk dancing and music.

Around Sopron

There are several attractions around Sopron worth visiting. East of town is the lovely **Fertő-Hanság National Park**, to the north of which is **Fertőrákos**, whose old quarry is a splendid venue for summertime concerts. Travelling eastwards will bring you to the village of **Nagycenk**, with its own stately home and a popular steam railway, and then to the magnificent, but slowly decaying, **Esterházy Palace** in Fertőd. There are buses every thirty to sixty minutes (every 1hr 30min–2hr to Lake Fertő) to the following places from the bus station in Sopron. Trains are less frequent and call at rather less convenient stations at Nagycenk and Fertőd, but may be useful for onward connections.

The Fertő-Hanság National Park

Fifteen kilometres east of Sopron lies the **Fertő-Hanság National Park**, a once extensive swampland that has gradually been drained and brought under cultivation since the eighteenth century. Prone to thick fogs, the area is traditionally associated with tales of elves and water sprites, and with the dynastic seats of the Esterházy and Széchenyi families at Fertőd and Nagycenk. The most obvious feature on the map is the shallow, reedy expanse of **Lake Fertő**, known to Hungarians as Fertő-to and to Austrians as the Neusiedler See, which was out of bounds under Communism to prevent escapes. This allowed **wildlife**, especially birds, to flourish, and the area is now being developed as a nature reserve and resort, noted for its wild beauty; it was added to Unesco's World Heritage List in 2001. The lake makes especially good **cycling** country, having a 110-kilometre-long cycle track all the way around it (35km of which is in Hungary), with campsites en route and *Zimmer frei* signs in most of the villages. This route heads north via Fertőrákos (see opposite) and enters Austria by a cycle/pedestrians-only border crossing (April–Oct daily 6am–10pm). Heading east, this also forms a route from Sopron to Fertőd, which is highly recommended; it's just a short detour into Sarród (just west of Fertőd) to see the informative displays at the National Park headquarters at Rév-Kócsagvár 4.

Fertőrákos Quarry

On the fringes of the park, 8km north of Sopron (past the country's biggest and highest-security prison), the village of **FERTŐRÁKOS** translates as "infectious slough", due to the fetid lake that once lapped at its edges. Nowadays the waters are healthy and the village (*Kroisbach* in German) is clean and welcoming. Limestone has been hewn since Roman times from the episcopal **quarry** (Kőfejtő; daily: March–April 8am–5pm; May–Sept 8am–7pm; Oct 8am–5pm; Nov, Dec & Feb 8am–4pm; 375Ft) at the top of the main road, Fő utca, that runs down through the village. Vienna's St Stephen's Cathedral and Ringstrasse were built with stone from Fertőrákos, where quarrying only ceased in 1945. The result is a Cyclopean labyrinth of gigantic chambers and oddly skewed pillars, resembling the mythical cities imagined by H.P. Lovecraft; animal and plant fossils attest that the land was once submerged beneath a prehistoric sea.

To the right as you enter, a path leads up to a monument to the Paneuropean picnic (see box below) and loops around the quarry to a viewpoint from where you can head for the exit (and restaurant) or go back and down into the caves, which are a bit chilly but not at all smelly. It would make sense to combine your visit to the quarry with one of the **concerts** staged in the Cave Theatre, carved out in 1970 and holding some 750 people. The majority of concerts take place during the Sopron Festival Weeks (tickets available from the Sopron festival office – see opposite).

Everything in the village is situated on the very long Fő utca – buses stop outside the quarry and elsewhere along this main street. A five-minute walk downhill from the quarry brings you to the **Mineral Museum** at no. 99 (Ásványmúzeum; April–Oct Tues–Sun 9am–5pm; June–Aug to 7pm; Nov–March call ☎99/355-286; 370Ft), exhibiting all manner of rocks and stones hewn from the quarry and elsewhere in Hungary. In front of the town hall at no. 139 is the only sixteenth-century pillory still in place in the country, followed by the former **Bishop's Palace** (Püspöki kastély; guided visits May–Oct daily except Tues 10am–6pm;

The Paneuropean picnic

In November 1988 the Hungarian Communist Party's lacklustre leadership was swept aside by the new generation of reformers. The process of removing the electronic alarm system along the Hungarian-Austrian border began in May 1989, and on June 27 the Austrian and Hungarian Foreign Ministers symbolically cut the "Iron Curtain". However, Hungary was still bound by the Warsaw Pact to prevent East Germans in particular from reaching the West.

Activists in Hungary came up with the idea of a demonstration in the form of a **picnic**, with groups meeting on either side of the border fence. Then permission was given for a border crossing north of Sopron, closed since 1948, to be reopened for three hours on the afternoon of August 19, to allow a Hungarian delegation to walk to the Austrian village of St Margarethen (Szentmargitbánya) and be received by the mayor and accompanying oompah band.

In the event, between 10,000 and 20,000 people turned up, and before the delegation – delayed by an overrunning press conference – could reach the border, several hundred East Germans, who had been issued with West German passports in Budapest, rushed across. Over the next few days many more fled to the West, before the Hungarian guards stopped the exodus; nevertheless, on September 11 the border was permanently opened to East German citizens and the collapse of the DDR, and of the Berlin Wall, became inevitable. Clearly the picnic itself did not bring this about, but it's still seen as a highly symbolic event, and is commemorated on August 19 every year.

Nov–April Sat & Sun 10am–3pm; 370Ft) at no. 153, which dates back in parts to the Middle Ages, although its current Baroque appearance is due to three bishops of Győr (Sopron being at the time a Lutheran city) who rebuilt it between the mid-seventeenth and the mid-eighteenth centuries – their crests are placed above the central three first-floor windows. Restoration is under way, and there are plans to create a local history museum here; for now, the cellar and some first-floor rooms are open, and the caretaker is a very engaging multilingual guide. The highlight is the chapel, used as a store for agricultural chemicals for four decades but still in remarkably good shape; there are fine frescoes here and elsewhere, including the *Seven Arts* and the *Rest on the Flight into Egypt*.

Boat trips on the lake are offered by Fert-Tavi Hajózási, at Hajókikötő 1 in Fertőrákos (mid-April to mid-Oct; ☎99/355-165, ✉seffer@freemail.hu) and by Drescher Hajózási at Kitaibel Pál utca 32A in Sopron (April–Oct; ☎99/355-361, ✉csefan@axelero.hu). Cycle and canoe tours, in search of flora and fauna, can be arranged through Na-Túra at Fő utca 91 (☎99/355-718, ⓦwww .na-tura.hu).

There's stacks of **accommodation** in the village, including dozens of households advertising private rooms. The best of the guesthouses are the flower-decked *Szentesi Panzió* at Fő utca 66 (☎99/355-238, ⓦwww .szentesipanzio.hu; ❸); the cosy *Horváth Ház Panzió* (☎99/355-368, ⓦwww .horvathhazpanzio.hu; ❸), in an old peasant dwelling at Fő utca 194; and the four-room *Várfal Panzió*, further down the road at no. 222 (☎99/355-115, ⓦwww.varfal-schlosser.hu; ❸), with neat little rooms and charming hospitality; this is also the home of the Fertőrákos Hospitality Association, which organizes a village festival on July 18 (ⓦwww.fertorakos-vendegvaro .hu), and a World Heritage List infopoint. The *Ráspi* **restaurant** at Fő utca 78 is renowned for its Hungarian dishes and wine, whilst the interior, with its thick wooden beams and benches, and candle-topped tables, is a delight – the owners also rent out **bikes** (150Ft per hr, 900Ft per day).

To the north of the village, just short of the pedestrian- and cycle-only border crossing, is the **Cave of Mithras** (Mithras-barlang; May–Aug Tues–Sun 9am–5pm; 900Ft), where Roman soldiers worshipped the Persian Sun God. This was believed to have been destroyed in World War I but has been carefully reconstructed, with a Baroque-style shelter over the mouth of a cave in which a mural portrays Mithras killing the bull, symbol of darkness and evil.

The Széchenyi Mansion and Railway

One of the region's major feudal seats lies on the southern fringe of Fertő-Hanság National Park in the village of **NAGYCENK** (pronounced Nodge-senk). Frequent buses from Sopron can drop you at the **Széchenyi Mansion** (Széchenyi Emlék-múzeum) 800m northeast of the village on Route 85 (the Győr road); there are almost as many buses on Route 84 (the Sárvár road) which will drop you in the village, from where it's a ten-minute walk to the mansion.

Trains on the Sopron-Szombathely line stop on the west side of the village; follow the road for ten minutes, to the square in front of the church, where you should turn left and then right on Vám utca, from where the mansion is signposted. As the family home of Count Széchenyi, "the greatest Hungarian" (see box opposite), it has never been allowed to fall into ruin, and was declared a museum in 1973. The first part of the museum (Tues–Sun: mid-March to Oct 10am–6pm; Nov to mid-March 10am–2pm; 1050Ft) includes portraits, personal effects and furniture from his household – the first in Hungary to be lit by gas lamps and to have flush toilets – and details his many achievements. There's useful guidance in the form of a button on the wall of each room which, when pressed, gives a short spiel about the contents – though it can get rather chaotic when several people are all vying to hear one of the six different languages available. Upstairs, the museum proceeds to document the development of Hungarian industry since Széchenyi's day, with Hungarian and German texts and particular emphasis on transportation and communications.

Adjoining the mansion is a 200-year-old **Stud Farm** (Tues–Sun 10am–5pm; 300Ft), which houses an exhibition of carriages, saddles and other equipment – or you can just wander around the yard and admire the magnificent horses. Széchenyi and his brother both saw horsebreeding, and English-style racing, as crucial for the improvement of Hungarian agriculture and transport, and both established studs. If you'd rather go for a walk, head north through the mansion's front garden and across Route 85 to find a lovely (if heavily pollarded) **avenue of limes**, planted in the mid-eighteenth century, that's now a nature conservation area. At the far end of the three-kilometre-long avenue are the remains of a Gothic cell once inhabited by the "Nagycenk Hermit", whom the Széchenyis employed to pump the church organ on Sundays, and the tomb of István Széchenyi's son Béla, himself a noted biologist and traveller.

Also north of the highway, just to the left of the avenue, is a shining example of Hungary's heritage industry – the **Széchenyi Railway**. This outdoor museum of **vintage steam trains** (Múzeum Vasút) is always open, but comes alive every weekend from early April to early October, when hundred-year-old engines run five times a day along a narrow-gauge line (specially built in the 1970s), past fields full of stooks of drying reeds, to terminate at Fertőboz, 4km away on the Győr-Sopron railway, though some turn back earlier. Tickets (600Ft) can only be bought on site, so you'll just have to turn up and hope for the best. Bicycles are carried for an additional 150Ft each way.

Count Széchenyi

Count István Széchenyi (1791–1860) was the outstanding figure of Hungary's Reform Era. As a young aide-de-camp who had fought at Győr and Leipzig he cut a dash at the Congress of Vienna and did the rounds of stately homes across Europe. The "odious Zoltán Karpathy" of Bernard Shaw's *Pygmalion* (and the musical *My Fair Lady*) was based on his exploits in England, where he steeplechased hell for leather, but still found time to examine factories and steam trains. Back in Hungary, he pondered solutions to his homeland's backwardness and donated a year's income from his estates to establish the Hungarian Academy of Sciences. He published *Hitel* (Credit), a hard-headed critique of the nation's feudal society in 1830, and was appointed by the government to develop Hungary's transport infrastructure, regulating the rivers (giving a 25-percent increase in cultivable land), introducing steamships on the Danube and Lake Balaton, and working to link the Baltic to the Mediterranean by rail via Budapest.

Though politically conservative, Széchenyi was obsessed with **modernization**. A passionate convert to steam power after riding on the Liverpool & Manchester Railway, he invited Britons to Hungary to build rail lines and Budapest's Chain Bridge. He also promoted horsebreeding and silk-making, and initiated the taming of the River Tisza and the blasting of a road through the Iron Gates of the Danube. Although previously opposed to Kossuth, in 1848 he lost his fear of revolution and took the transport portfolio in Hungary's first independent government.

Alas, his achievements were rewarded by a melancholy end. The failure of the 1848 Revolution triggered a nervous breakdown, and, although Széchenyi resumed writing after his health improved, harassment by the political police led him to commit suicide. His funeral became a patriotic demonstration and a protest against despotism.

Where the road to the station leaves the **village** stands the neo-Romanesque **Church of St Stephen**, designed by Ybl in 1864. Its portal bears the Széchenyi motto "If God is with us, who can be against us?" In the cemetery across the road from the church stands the **Széchenyi Mausoleum** (May–Oct Tues–Sun 10am–6pm; 300Ft), with a chapel decorated by István Dorfmeister, and a crypt including the graves of István Széchenyi and his wife.

The best **place to stay** is naturally the grand *Kastély Hotel* (T 99/360-061, W www.szechenyikastelyszallo.hu; ⑥) in the mansion's west wing; its restaurant is also excellent. In the village, the *Classic Étterem & Panzió*, by the main bus stop at Soproni út 2 (T 99/360-345, W www.classicnagycenk.hu; ④), has attractive modern rooms and a restaurant with a long menu including game and vegetarian dishes, plus a nice wine list. The *Vakacio Guest Hostel* at Rákóczi utca 9 (T 99/338-502, W www.vakacio-vendeghazak.hu; 3600Ft each), a block west of Route 84 north of the centre, is a branch of the Vakacio hostel in Sopron, with rooms for between two and nine people, and a guest kitchen. In addition, **private rooms** (❷) are advertised widely around the village.

Fertőd and the Esterházy Palace

The village of **FERTŐD**, some 15km beyond Nagycenk and 25km east of Sopron, began life as an appendage to the palace and was known as "Esterháza" until the family decamped in 1945. As you enter the village, postwar housing gives way to stately public buildings endowed by the Esterházys, presaging the palace at the eastern end – which is impossible to miss so long as you stay on the main street.

The Esterházy Palace

Built on malarial swampland drained by hundreds of serfs, the **Esterházy Palace** was intended to rival Versailles and remove any arriviste stigma from the dynasty (see box opposite). Gala balls and concerts, hunting parties and masquerades were held here even before it was completed in 1776, continuing without a let-up until the death of Prince Miklós "the Ostentatious" in 1790. Neglected by his successor, who moved his court (and orchestra) back to Eisenstadt, the palace was left to decay. From 1900 Duke Miklós IV began to refurbish the house, while his wife did the same for the gardens, which more or less survived the Communist period as an experimental fruit farm. However, the mansion's picture gallery, puppet theatre and Chinese pavilions disappeared, while its salons became storerooms and stables. Restoration only began in earnest in 1958, and is still unfinished due to the prodigious cost.

Ornate Rococo wrought-iron gates lead into a vast horseshoe courtyard where hussars once pranced to the music of Joseph Haydn, Esterházy's resident maestro. The U-shaped wings and ceremonial stairway sweep up to a three-storey Baroque facade. **Guided tours** (every 40min; mid-March to Oct Tues–Sun 10am–6pm; Nov to mid-March Fri–Sun 10am–4pm; 1800Ft) cover 23 of the 126 rooms in the palace, whose faded splendour still speaks of its one-time magnificence. Tours are only in Hungarian, but you'll be given a leaflet in English or another language of your choice. The highlights of the ground floor are the panelled and gilded **Sala Terrena** and several blue-and-white **chinoiserie salons**, their walls painted by fairly mediocre artists – unlike J.I. Mildorfer's superb fresco on the ceiling of the **Banqueting Hall** upstairs, which is so contrived that Apollo's chariot seems to be careering towards you across the sky whatever angle you view it from. There are more Mildorfer frescoes in the tiny oval chapel restored in 2001.

The Esterházy family

Originally of the minor nobility, the **Esterházy family** began its rise thanks to **Miklós I** (1583–1645), who married two rich widows and sided with the Habsburgs against Transylvania during the Counter-Reformation, for which he was rewarded with the title of count. His son Paul was content to make his mark by publishing a songbook, *Harmonia Celestis*; but **Miklós II** "the Ostentatious" (1714–90) celebrated his inheritance of 600,000 acres and a dukedom by commissioning the Fertőd palace in 1762. Boasting "anything the Kaiser can do, I can do better!", he spent 40,000 gulden a year on pomp and entertainment. After his death the family moved to Eisenstadt, in present-day Austria, and became gradually less important in Hungary, until under the Communists they were expropriated and "un-personed". Today, one descendant drives trams in Vienna, while two others (from a separate branch of the family) are respected figures back home: the writer **Péter Esterházy** and his cousin, **Marton Esterházy**, once centre forward for the national football team. Internationally, however, the best-known bearer of the family name is **Joe Esterhasz**, the Hollywood scriptwriter of *Basic Instinct* and *Showgirls*.

The family is remembered above all for patronizing many **great musicians**, most notably Joseph Haydn, who worked at Fertőd from 1761 to 1790 and claimed the isolation, so far from Vienna, "forced [him] to become original". Franz Schubert spent the summers of 1818 and 1824 as music tutor with a minor branch of the family in Zseliz (now in Slovakia). Franz Liszt's father was steward on the Esterházy estates and in 1805–08 played cello in the orchestra at Eisenstadt, directed on one occasion by Beethoven for the premiere of his *Mass in C*, while the son's stellar career was made possible by Count Michael Esterházy and four other aristocrats funding his studies in Vienna.

An adjacent room houses a **Haydn exhibition**, although this mainly consists of photocopied manuscripts and (identical) portraits. As the deputy *Kapellmeister* from 1761, and *Kapellmeister* proper from 1766, Haydn directed the palace orchestra, opera house and marionette theatre until 1790. **Concerts** are held here at weekends between late May and mid-September; tickets (6000Ft) can be purchased from the palace (☎99/537-640). The tour over, you can wander around the **French Gardens** or parterre at the back, with its "goosefoot" of three vistas through the forest to the south, and the English Garden on the west side of the mansion, although these can be visited free of charge anyway.

Practicalities

The nearest **train station** is at Fertőszéplak-Fertőd, a thirty-minute walk from the mansion (turn right as you exit the station and follow Fő utca through the village of Fertőd), but this only sees six trains a day in each direction, on a branch line to Pamhagen and Neusiedl am See in Austria. To get here you will in any case have to change at Fertőszentmiklós station, on the main line to Győr, which has a more frequent service and could be ideal if you wanted to bring a bike and cycle back to Sopron (turn left from the station then head left/north up the road to the centre of Fertőd, or turn right at the end of the village and then left into the park). Far more convenient are **buses**, which run several times an hour from Sopron's bus station, picking up near the train station at Csengery utca 52, and continue, largely parallel to the lakeshore and the international cycle route, via **Balf**, where there are hot springs, rooms and a campsite (see p.260), to the palace gates.

From mid-June to the end of August **Tourinform** opens an office opposite the gates at Haydn utca 2 (Mon–Sat 9am–5pm; ☎99/537-140, ✉fertoaj@tourinform.hu). There's **accommodation** in new luxury apartments in the palace (☎99/537-649,

@hotel@mag.hu; ⑨) and several possibilities in the village, including the very pleasant 🏠 *Újvári Panzió* (☎99/537-097, ⓦwww.hotels.hu/ujvari_fertod; ❸), a modern suburban house at Kossuth utca 57a, about 500m from the palace and 130m down the road to Sarród (where the Fertő-Hanság National Park has its thatched headquarters), whose genial host makes his own wine and will ensure that you have a most enjoyable stay. There's also the *Kata Vendégház* at Mikes Kelemen utca 2 (☎99/370-857, ⓦwww.hotels.hu/kata_fertod; ❸), which has large rooms and shared bathrooms plus use of the kitchen and living room; this is 1km south off Vasút sor, the road to Fertőszentmiklós train station. A third option is the *Dori Hotel*, a bizarre, wooden structure 250m from the palace at Pomogyi utca 1, on the road north to the border (☎99/370-838, ⓦwww.dorihotel.hu; ❹); it also has a campsite (mid-April to mid-Oct), chalets (❸–❺) sleeping up to seven, and a restaurant with a good vegetarian choice.

The *Kastélykert* and *Gránátos* **restaurants** are sited across the main road from the palace in its former guardhouses and serve stock Hungarian meals. You can grab a simple snack at the *Joco Ételbár*, Fő utca 24, and coffee and pastries at the *Elit Kávéház*, Fő utca 1. For really good local food, however, it's worth travelling 3km west towards Sopron, to the village of **Fertőszéplak**, where you'll find the *Polgármester Vendéglő* up behind the church at Széchenyi utca 39; the village is known for its row of five peasant-Baroque model houses just east of the church, built by the Széchenyi family for its tenants.

Kőszeg and around

Nestled amidst the sub-Alpine hills along the Austrian border, the small town of **KŐSZEG**, 50km south of Sopron, cherishes its status as the "Hungarian Thermopylae", for its heroic resistance to the Turks, and a town centre which can justifiably claim to be one of the prettiest in Hungary. While its castle recalls the medieval Magyar heroism that saved Vienna from the Turks, its Baroque houses and *bürgerlich* ambience reflect centuries of Austrian and German influence, when Kőszeg was known as Güns. Despite a summer blitzkrieg of tourists that briefly arouses excitement and avarice, this is basically a sleepy, old-fashioned town where people still leave cartons of raspberries and blackberries outside their houses and trust you to leave money for them.

Arrival and information

On **arrival** at Kőszeg's bus station on Liszt Ferenc utca, walk 150m up Kossuth utca to the Várkör, a horseshoe-shaped road that follows the course of the fifteenth-century town walls; most things of interest lie within this area. Arriving at the train station 1.5km to the south of town, take a bus to the junction of Fő tér and the Várkör.

The **Tourinform** office at Jurisics tér 7 (mid-April to mid-Oct Mon–Fri 8am–6pm, Sat 9am–1pm; mid-Oct to mid-April Mon–Fri 8am–5pm; ☎94/563-120, ⓦwww.koszeg.hu) also doubles up as the Írottkő Natúrpark Information Centre (ⓦwww.naturpark.hu), and so can provide information on both the town and the outlying regions, including suggested walks – it also has **bikes** for rent (1800Ft per day). All four of Kőszeg's museums are covered by a **day ticket** (*napibérlet*; 600Ft), available from the General's House by the entrance to the Heroes' Tower. The **post office** is opposite the church at Várkör 65 (Mon–Fri 8am–4pm, Sat 8–11am).

Gyöngyvirág Campsite

RESTAURANTS
Bécsikapu Söröző	3
Cukrászada	E
Ibrahim Kávézó	7
Kék Huszár	1
Kulacs Vendéglő	5
Oinoteka-Borárium	4
Pizzeria da Rocco	8
Poncichter Weinstube	2
Portré Panzió	B
Taverna Florian	9
Teeház Fehér Tigris	6

ACCOMMODATION
Hotel Aranysárkány	F
Arany Strucc Hotel	E
Hotel Írottkő	C
Jurisics Miklós Gymnázium	A
Kóbor Macska	D
Portré Panzió	B

KŐSZEG

Train Station & F

Accommodation

There's ample **accommodation** in Kőszeg, all of it very affordable. Beds are available all year at the *Jurisics Miklós Gymnázium* at Szent Imre herceg utca 9 (☎94/361-404, ✉jmg@jurisich-koszeg.sulinet.hu; dorm bed 2400Ft) – follow the *Turistaszallo* signs to the modern wing on the south side of the school's hilltop main building. Although it doesn't offer private rooms, Savaria Tourist at Várkör 69 (Mon–Fri 8am–4pm, Sat 8am–noon; ☎94/563-048, ✉tourist.koszeg@vivadsl.hu) does have three-bed apartments (③) in town. Rooms are also available (in association with the Nature Park) at the Pont Vendégház (Craft Gallery; ☎94/563-224, ⓦwww.pontvendeghaz.hu; ③) diagonally opposite Tourinform at Tábláház utca 1. The small and neat *Gyöngyvirág* **campsite**, in a suburban garden at Bajcsy-Zsilinszky utca 6, also has rooms in its adjoining pension (☎94/360-454, ⓦwww.gyongyviragpanzio.hu; ②).

Hotel Aranysárkány Rákóczi Ferenc utca 120 ☎94/362-296, ⓦwww.clubhotel-aranysarkany .hu. Agreeable, and cheap, pension-type place near the train station with neat, pine-furnished rooms. ③

Arany Strucc Hotel Várkör 124 ☎94/360-323, ⓦwww.aranystrucc.hu. One of the oldest hotels in Hungary, first recorded in the 1590s, "The Golden Ostrich" is a characterful place with fairly simple

double rooms with showers; the bigger rooms have minibar. ④

Hotel Írottkő Fő tér 4 ☎94/360-373, ⓦwww .hotelirottko.hu. An ugly block on the main square, with tatty, musty-smelling rooms with either bath or shower. Triples are good value. ⑤

Kóbor Macska Várkör 100 ☎94/362-273, ⓦhttp:// kobormacska.hu. The eighteenth-century "Stray Cat Inn" occupies a splendid spot just to the west of the inner town; large rooms with showers literally *in* the bedroom and shared toilets. Breakfast extra. ❸ **Portré Panzió** Fő tér 7 ☎94/363-170, ⓦwww .portre.com. Stylish pension on the main square,

with sunny yellow-and-blue rooms, subtly furnished with wooden desks and chairs, and smart rugs. ❹

The Town

The focal point of the town, and hub of most of the activity, is **Fő tér**, whose main landmark is the run-down **Church of the Sacred Heart**, built in 1894; it's reminiscent of an oversized space rocket, but the fancifully patterned interior is worth a peek, as is the plague column in front, raised in 1713. To the west of Fő tér, Városház utca leads up to the 27-metre-high **Heroes' Tower** (Hősök tornya; Tues–Sun 10am–5pm; 300Ft). Erected to mark the four-hundredth anniversary of the siege of Kőszeg, this fake medieval portal was one of several commemorative gates raised in the 1920s and 1930s, when Hungary was gripped by nostalgia for bygone glories and resentment towards the Successor States. The entrance to the tower is via the Baroque **General's House** at Jurisics tér 6 (Tábornok Ház; Tues–Sun 10am–5pm; 450Ft), containing several rooms of exhibits on bookbinding, carpentry and other historic guilds and crafts.

Beyond the archway lies **Jurisics tér**, an engaging cobbled square whose antique buildings are watched over by two churches and a limestone Trinity statue, raised in 1739. The most eye-catching facades are those of the seventeenth-century **Town Hall** at no. 8 (embellished with oval portraits of the Hungarian coat of arms, the Virgin and Child and St Stephen) and the so-called **Lada House** at no. 12, whose interesting features include heraldic figures, angels' heads, and a niche with a statue of St Imre. Across the square, at no. 7, is a beautifully sgraffitoed building (now a

▲ Church of the Sacred Heart, Kőszeg

pizzeria), where the pillory stood in medieval times, and, further along at no. 11, is the **Golden Unicorn Pharmacy Museum** (Patikamúzeum; March–Nov Tues–Sun 10am–5pm; 450Ft), which preserves an eighteenth-century apothecary's. The superb oak and chestnut furnishings were removed from the Jesuit Cloister in 1773 following the dissolution of the order, and brought to the pharmacy a few years later when it was opened – you can have a look, too, at the upstairs drying area, where the raw materials were cleaned, chopped and stored.

Past Jurisics tér's fountain, the Baroque **Church of St Imre** was built in 1615–40 for the Hungarian Calvinist congregation after German Lutherans took over the adjacent church of St James; since 1673 it has been Catholic. Immediately to its north, the tatty exterior of the **Church of St James** belies its handsome interior; an early Gothic hall church with fine but faded frescoes at the east end of the south aisle, dating back to 1407, the year the church was completed. The tomb of Miklós Jurisics (see p.274) is in the crypt, and there's a Renaissance memorial to his children on the north wall.

Facing the churches, Chernel utca is lined with some fine houses, notably a very cool Secession house at no. 18 (on the corner of Várkör) which houses temporary art shows. Just north of the two churches, the sixteenth-century Gombossy House at Rajnis utca 3 houses the new **Postal Museum** (Postamúzeum; summer daily except Tues 10am–6pm; winter Wed 2–6pm, Thurs 11am–6pm, Fri & Sat 10am–4pm, Sun 11am–4pm; 300Ft), which displays stamps and historic postcards of Kőszeg.

Rajnis utca leads north to Várkör, where you'll find a former **synagogue** at no. 38, which can only be viewed from the street. Built in 1859, the redbrick complex resembles an outlying bastion, having two crenellated towers with slit windows, and originally included a *yeshiva* and a ritual bath. Its dereliction is a sad reminder of the provincial Jewish communities that never recovered from the Holocaust, for – unlike the Budapest ghetto – their extermination was scheduled for the summer of 1944, when Eichmann's death-machine still ran at full throttle. Oddly, a **Lutheran bell-tower** stands next to the synagogue. When the barn-like Lutheran church behind it was built in 1783, József II had decreed that non-Catholic churches could not have bell-towers or steeples; this bell-tower was only built in 1930, but at double the usual height, as if to compensate.

From Várkör you can head up Hunyadi utca to the west for ten minutes, passing a number of fortress-like villas, to the **Chernel Arboretum** of sub-Alpine trees (Chernel-Kert; Mon–Thurs 9am–3pm, Fri till 1pm, although the gate may well be open at other times); towards the rear of the gardens is a one-roomed museum dedicated to the works of local ornithologist István Chernel (same times; 300Ft). Just beyond, by the car park, is the István Bechtold Nature Conservation Visitor Centre (Bechtold István Természetvédelmi Látogatóközpont-belépőjegy; May–Oct Tues–Sun 10am–5pm; Nov–April Tues–Fri 10am–4pm; 900Ft; ⓦwww .buboscinege.hu), a modern circular building packed with displays on the Írottkő Nature Park (see p.274). Heading the same distance in the opposite direction you'll come to the outdoor **swimming pool**, across the river: follow Kiss János utca eastwards from Várkör then go to the right – a signpost in Fő tér points towards the *strand*. Otherwise, head back the other way to the castle.

The Castle

The Turks swore that **Kőszeg Castle** was "built at the foot of a mountain difficult to climb; its walls wider than the whole world, its bastions higher than the fish of the Zodiac in heaven, and so strong that it defies description". Since the castle is actually quite small, with not a mountain in sight, the hyperbole is probably explained by its heroic defence during the month-long **siege of 1532**, when the Grand Vizier Ibrahim and eighty thousand Turks were resisted by four hundred soldiers under Captain Miklós Jurisics (actually a Croatian called Nikola Jurisich). After nineteen assaults the Sultan abandoned campaigning until the following year, by which time Vienna was properly defended. Little did they know that the defenders were on the point of surrendering. Today's visitors won't find anything dramatic when they cross the grassy moat into an ugly yard made worse by postwar additions, although the **Town Museum** (Városi Múzeum; Tues–Sun 10am–5pm; 600Ft), in the east wing of the castle, has a reasonable display of military relics and furniture owned by town officers, as well as two rooms on viticulture, including the "Grape Book" – a log book which has documented, largely in the form of sketches, local wine making since 1740 and is still updated every year on St George's Day. In summer the castle really comes to life with the staging of **medieval games** in the moat and concerts in the yard (see below).

Eating, drinking and entertainment

The best **restaurants** in town are the *Taverna Florian* at Várkör 59, a smart cellar serving Mediterranean cuisine (Tues–Sat 5–10pm, summer and weekends also 11.30am–2.30pm), and the one in the *Portré Panzió* (see p.272), which sports a garden terrace and pavement café. Near the *Florian*, at Várkör 55, *Pizzeria da Rocco* has some drab rooms but a nice bar, often with live music, and a great garden by the castle walls. Two humbler places are the *Kulacs Vendéglő* at Várkör 12, which is also good for a lighter snack, and the *Kék Huszár* at Várkör 62 (behind the castle on Károly Róbert tér), which has an agreeable straw-roofed beer garden.

The pace of life here dictates that **drinking** options are few and far between. Aside from the bar at the *Portré*, you could try the *Bécsikapu Söröző*, opposite St James' Church at Rajnis utca 5, or the beer garden at the back of the *Kék Huszár*. If you enjoy quaffing wine in medieval surroundings, the vaulted ceiling and high Gothic windows of the *Poncichter Weinstube* at Rajnis utca 10 provide an ideal setting. For a more contemporary feel, try the *Oinoteka-Borárium* at Rajnis utca 1 (Wed & Thurs 11am–6pm, Fri & Sat 10am–7pm, Sun 10am–4pm).

The best coffee, strudel and ices are to be had at the *Ibrahim Kávézó*, a few paces along from the *Portré Panzió* at Fő tér 17, whose long, narrow and Oriental-styled interior leads to a lovely terrace area. There's coffee, hot chocolate, cakes and pastries at Soproni Zoltán's lovely old-fashioned shop at Rákóczi utca 4 (Mon–Fri 5am–noon & 12.30–4pm, Sat 5am–noon). The *Cukrászada* of the *Arany Strucc Hotel* at Várkör 124 is a delight, like a bourgeois sitting room with lovely deep armchairs, serving coffee and alcoholic drinks. The *Teeház Fehér Tigris* at Fő tér 28 is a very civilized venue for supping tea.

Wine lovers are well catered for in Kőszeg, with the **Grape Festival** on April 24 celebrated with events such as wine contests, concerts and folklore programmes, and a **Wine Festival** on the last weekend of September featuring a carnival, brass band and horse shows. The **Summer Festival** takes place in July and August, with theatre and opera in the castle yard.

The Írottkő Nature Park

Up against the border, immediately west of Kőszeg, the **Írottkő Nature Park**, established in 1997, is one of the dividends of the ending of the Cold War, with what was once a militarized border zone now a popular and well-managed recreation area. Information is available from the Írottkő Natúrpark Information Centre in Kőszeg's Tourinform office (see p.270), as well as at Savaria Tourist (see p.271).

While there are reasonably long hikes on the Hungarian side, it's also possible to continue into Austria (the Írottkő border crossing is open April–Oct 7am–8pm, Nov–March 8am–4pm). The new Alpannonia hiking route leads in six days from Kőszeg to Semmering (on the Vienna-Graz railway), its main route marked with a white swirl on red signs, and feeders with a white swirl on yellow.

The park's easiest hike is along the well-signposted trail through the hills to the **Óház lookout tower**, 5km west at an altitude of 609m. Built in 1996, this was named Óház or Old House due to its medieval foundations; set out along Temetö utca (south of the arboretum) past the run-down Jewish cemetery behind a row of cypresses at the corner of Park utca. From the Óház tower you can head back into town past the Seven Springs (Hétforrás), a spring with seven waterspouts commemorating the chiefs of the seven Magyar tribes, and the steps, lined with Stations of the Cross, up to the Calvary church. At the bottom of the hill you can turn left to reach a boating lake, or bear right for town, passing the Szálasi shelter in the hillside where **St Stephen's Crown** was hidden from bombing from December 1944 to March 1945, before being smuggled out of Hungary.

Alternatively, continue about 6km further southwest to the 884-metre **Írottkő tower**, on the Austrian border; this was built, in a similar castle-like style to the Óház tower, in 1913. Its name (Geschriebenstein in German) means Written Stone, due to an inscribed slab about 40m from the tower; again, there are remains of an Árpád-era fortress here.

Cak, Velem, Bozsok and Horvátszidány

If you want to explore further afield, there are four attractive villages in the Kőszeg-Hegyalja region, south of town. There's a signed cycle route, or buses bound for Velem or Bozsok can drop you off in pretty **CÁK**, 6km south of Kőszeg, with a protected row of old thatched wine and fruit cellars at Petőfi utca 19 (Szabadtéri Múzeum, key at Petőfi utca 36; mid-April to Oct Tues–Sun 10am–noon & 2–6pm; 300Ft), actually little more than wattle-and-daub hovels with straw hats on. You can stay at the *Pincesor Vendégház*, Petőfi utca 37 (☎94/361-036, ⍟www.falusi.hu/cakivendeghaz; ❷), or camp at *Cáki Sátorverőhely*, Petőfi utca 31 (☎94/363-371; May 15–Sept 30). The *Csikó Csárda*, at Fő utca 56, near the bus stop at the entrance to the village, is a good place for lunch, and if you want to continue you can pick up the walking trails, marked with a yellow stripe, to the neighbouring villages of Bozsok and Velem, and to the Írottkő tower.

VELEM, 4km further down the road, is famous for its handicrafts and on August 20 each year holds the **Craftsmen's Feast** at the Creative House, where the traditional crafts and trades of the village are celebrated, along with wine drinking and other folklore programmes. At the entrance to the village is the sprawling **Millennium Memorial Park** (Millenniumi Emlékpark), a somewhat kitsch assemblage of mini attractions – including a doll museum and waxworks exhibition – built in 2001 to commemorate the millennium. You'll also find a large, rustically styled restaurant here. A couple of kilometres east, on the edge of Kőszegszardahely, there's a fine two-wheel **watermill** (May–Oct Tues–Sun 9.30am–5pm).

Accommodation is available at the *Boróka Villa* at Kossuth utca 8 (☎94/936-0036, ⍟www.boroka-villa.hu; ❺), while the *Kern Vendégház* at Rákóczi utca 56 (☎94/363-612, ⍟www.kern.inf.hu) is affiliated to Hostelling International, with beds from 2400Ft for members. In addition village tourism is flourishing here and you'll find many houses advertising rooms for the night.

Five kilometres further southwest is **BOZSOK**, basically a one-street village with a largely seventeenth-century manor house set in a lovely park at Rákóczi utca 1.

It now serves as the bland *Sibrik Castle Hotel* (Sibrik Kastélyszálló; ☎&ⓕ94/360-960; ❹), while, in the same grounds, the Dobrádi Riding School offers **riding lessons** and trips in the region (daily: April–Oct 9am–noon & 2–6pm; Nov–March 10am–noon & 2–5pm; ☎94/363-342). A cheaper option is the *Szilvia Panzió* at Rákóczi utca 120 (☎94/361-009, ⓦwww.hegyimenok.fw.hu; ❷), with **camping** alongside (*Napsugár Nyaraló*, Rákóczi utca 119; ☎94/310-694; mid-March to mid-Nov); otherwise, many houses along this street offer rooms. For **refreshments** head to the *Aranypatak* at Rákóczi utca 29, or the *Imperial Pub*, 500m further along the road at no. 101.

The village of **HORVÁTSZIDÁNY**, 6km east of Kőszeg at the junction of the bus routes to Sárvár and Sopron, is also known as Hrvatski Židan or Croatian Zsidány, due to Croatian colonists being invited to settle after the 1532 siege; there's an Exhibition of Ethnic Croatians at Fő utca 6 (Mon–Fri 8am–4pm; weekends by appointment), featuring costumes and other handicrafts.

Szombathely and around

Commerce has been the lifeblood of **SZOMBATHELY** ("Saturday market") ever since the town was founded by Emperor Claudius in 43 AD to control trade on the Amber Road from the Baltic to the Adriatic. Savaria, as it was then called, soon became the capital of Pannonia Superior, and a significant city in the Roman Empire. It was here that Septimus Severus was proclaimed emperor in 193 AD and Saint Martin of Tours was born in 317. Under Frankish rule in the eighth century, the town, known as Steinamanger, prospered through trade with Germany. Nowadays, it is Austrians who boost the economy, flooding in for shopping, hairdos or medical treatment in the town they've nicknamed "the discount store".

From a tourist's standpoint, the chief attractions are the outdoor **Village Museum** (Skanzen) and **Roman ruins**, and a **Belváros** stuffed with Baroque and Neoclassical architecture. Szombathely is also the base for a side-trip to the beautiful Romanesque church at **Ják** and, further out, the spa and castle at **Sárvár**, home of the infamous "Blood Countess" Erzsébét Báthori. If you're here at **Easter** time, there are colourful religious processions in Szombathely and other towns in the region.

Arrival and information

Arriving at the attractive **train station**, walk west along Széll Kálmán utca – 100m to the left of the station as you exit – to get to the centre (just under 1km), or catch a #2, #3, #5, #7, #7Y, #10 or #11 bus to Mártírok tere, close to Fő tér. The intercity **bus station** is next to the Romkert, just ten minutes' walk west of Fő tér, reached by bus #5 from the train station.

The Tourinform office is located on the southwestern corner of Fő tér at Kossuth utca 1–3 (Mon–Fri 9am–5pm; ☎94/514-451, ⓔszombathely @tourinform.hu). Train information and tickets are available from MÁV Tours at Király utca 8 (Mon–Fri 8.30am–4.30pm). The **post office** is at Kossuth utca 18 (Mon–Fri 8am–6pm, Sat 8am–noon) and there's **internet access** at the *Paparazzi Club* at Fő tér 36 (Mon–Wed 7.45am–10pm, Fri & Sat 7.45am–1am, Sun 2–10pm) and at Hollán Ernő utca 12.

Accommodation

The cheapest **accommodation** is in one of the three centrally located colleges, with beds in shared (❶) and private rooms (❷–❸) available all year through Ibusz at Fő tér 44 (Mon–Fri 8am–5pm, Sat 8am–noon; ☎94/314-141,

4

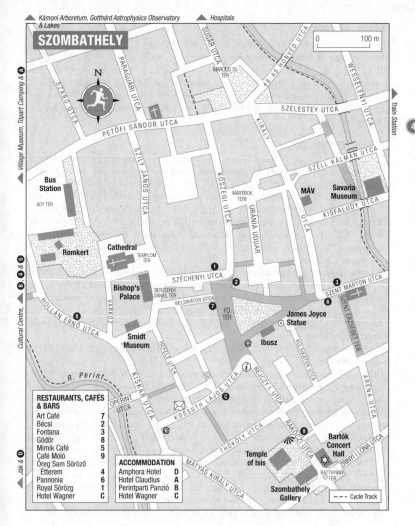

SZOMBATHELY

0   100 m

N

PARAGUARI UTCA

SZABÓ UTCA

SUGÁR UTCA

MÁRCIUS 15 TÉR

48-AS HONVÉD UTCA

WESSELÉNYI UTCA

Train Station

SZELESTEY UTCA

PETŐFI SÁNDOR UTCA

SZILY JÁNOS UTCA

KIRÁLY UTCA

SZÉLL KÁLMÁN UTCA

KISFALUDY UTCA

KŐSZEGI UTCA

URÁNIA UDVAR

**Bus
Station**
ADY TÉR

MÁRTÍROK TERE

MÁV

**Savaria
Museum**

Romkert

Cathedral
TEMPLOM TÉR

**Bishop's
Palace**
BERZSENYI DÁNIEL TÉR

SZÉCHENYI UTCA

BELSIKÁTOR UTCA

❶
❷
❼
FŐ TÉR

❸
❻

SZENT MÁRTON UTCA

SZENT ERZSÉBET TÉR

**James Joyce
Statue**

**Smidt
Museum**

HEFELE UTCA

VÁRKÖZ

HOLLÁN ERNŐ UTCA

❽

R. Perint

KISKAR UTCA

OPERINT UTCA

KOSSUTH LAJOS UTCA

BEJCZY L UTCA

KISSIKÁTOR UTCA

@   **Ibusz**

ⓘ

C

@

RESTAURANTS, CAFÉS & BARS
Art Café	7
Bécsi	2
Fontana	3
Gödör	8
Mimik Café	9
Café Mólo	
Öreg Sam Söröző Étterem	4
Pannonia	6
Royal Sörözg	1
Hotel Wagner	C

ACCOMMODATION
Amphora Hotel	D
Hotel Claudius	A
Perintparti Panzió	B
Hotel Wagner	C

THÖKÖLY UTCA

MÁTYÁS KIRÁLY UTCA

RÁKÓCZI UTCA

ZRÍNYI ILONA UTCA

ARÉNA UTCA

❾

**Temple
of Isis**

**Bartók
Concert
Hall**

BATTHYÁNY TÉR

**Szombathely
Gallery**

--- Cycle Track

Village Museum, Tópart Camping & ❹

Cultural Centre, ❺ ❹ & ❽

Ják & ❻

Ⓔ szombathely@ibusz.hu). *Tópart* **camping**, by the Anglers' Lake 2km west of town at Kenderesi utca 14 (☎ 94/509-039; May–Sept), has chalets sleeping two to three (❷) or four to five (❹); it's a ten-minute walk down Gagarin utca, north of the *Hotel Claudius*, or take bus #2C from the centre.

Amphora Hotel Dósza György utca 9 ☎ 94/512-712, ⓦ www.amphorahotel.hu. Elegant little hotel a 10min walk west of Fő tér across the river, with ultramodern, immaculate, a/c rooms, as well as the *Görög (Greek) Pizzéria*. ❼

Hotel Claudius Bartók Béla krt. 39 ☎ 94/313-760, ⓦ www.claudiushotel.hu. A 1970s block next to the baths, now decently renovated. ❻

Perintparti Panzió Kunos Endre utca 3 ☎ 94/339-265. Unfussy five-room place just 300m west of the bus station, across the river. Good value. ❹

Hotel Wagner Kossuth Lajos utca 15 ☎ 94/322-208, ⓦ www.hotelwagner.hu. This small, compact hotel has class stamped all over it; beautifully styled, a/c rooms with lush green carpets, desks with table lamps, and safes. ❼

The Town

There's little to see on the vast main square, Fő ter (more of a triangle really), other than a **statue of James Joyce** coming through the wall just east of Ibusz at Fő tér 40/41 (Leopold Bloom, protagonist of his *Ulysses*, came from Szombathely, and conveniently a family called Blum was identified as living at this address in the mid-nineteenth century). Therefore you're best off making a beeline for the cathedral and the Romkert to the west, and conserve some enthusiasm for the Village Museum.

West of Fő tér

The city's most interesting sights lie to the west of Fő tér around Berzsenyi Dániel tér. Szombathely's **cathedral**, a few paces north on Templom tér, postdates the great fire that ravaged the town in 1716, which explains why it is Neoclassical rather than Baroque or Gothic. The bishopric was only founded in 1777, and the huge cathedral was finished twenty years later. Unfortunately, its exuberant frescoes by Maulbertsch were destroyed by US bombing in the last months of World War II, and painstaking structural restoration has stopped short of re-creating his work. A glass-fronted coffin in the south aisle contains the grisly remains of a mitred saint.

To the right of the cathedral lies the impressive **Romkert** or Roman Garden (April–Nov Tues–Sat 9am–5pm; 450Ft), comprising the remnants of the public baths, potters' workshops, a customs house and some fine segments of mosaic floor from Roman Savaria. Recent research suggests this was the site of either the Basilica of St Quirinus, the largest church in Pannonia, or, more likely, the Roman Governor's Palace.

On the other side of the cathedral is the **Bishop's Palace**, completed in 1783, its facade crowned by statues of Prudence, Justice, Fortitude and Temperance. Although it's not possible to visit the palace, you can view the **Sala Terrena** (May–Sept Tues–Fri 9.30am–3.30pm, Sat 9.30–11.30am; 300Ft) on the right-hand side of the building, which features frescoes of ancient Savaria by Dorfmeister, as well as Roman stoneworks and some glittering ecclesiastical treasures. Next door to the palace, the intriguing **Smidt Museum** (Tues–Sun 10am–5pm; 600Ft) represents the fruits of a lifelong obsession. As a boy, Lajos Smidt (1903–75) scoured battlefields for souvenirs and collected advertisements and newspapers, diversifying into furniture and pictures as an adult. The destruction of many items during World War II only spurred him to redouble his efforts during retirement and, finally, he founded this museum (now run by the city) to house his extraordinary collection. Highlights include huge Celtic swords, Austro-Hungarian uniforms, the dancing slippers of Széchenyi's wife, and clocks galore, as well as the tiny electric tram outside.

South and east of Fő tér

Another relic of ancient Savaria only came to light in 1955, when construction work along Rákóczi utca, five minutes' walk south of Fő tér, uncovered the **Iseum** or Temple of Isis, dating from the second century AD, one of only three such temples extant in Europe. It still looks like a bombsite, with just a few columns standing, and it's not possible to visit the ruins up close, but there's a good view from the balcony leading to the **Szombathely Gallery** (Szombathelyi Képtár; Tues–Sun 10am–5pm, till 7pm Wed; 750Ft), which hosts temporary art shows, an exhaustive display of modern Hungarian art, and a stylish contemporary textile collection. You may have to ask for the lights to be turned on in the permanent collection (Allándo Kiállítás), but it's well worth it, with a great range of mostly abstract or avant-garde works from the 1920s onwards.

Across the road from the gallery stands Szombathely's former **synagogue**, a lovely neo-Byzantine pile built in 1881 and now home to the **Bartók Concert Hall** and music college. Sadly, all that now remains of the town's Jewish presence is a plaque recording that "4228 of our Jewish brothers and sisters were deported from this place to Auschwitz on 4 July, 1944".

A five-minute walk to the northeast of Fő tér, at Kisfaludy utca 9, is the **Savaria Museum** (mid-April to mid-Oct Tues–Thurs 10am–5pm, Fri 10am–7pm, Sat & Sun 10am–4pm; mid-Oct to mid-April Tues, Thurs & Fri 10am–5pm, Wed 10am–8pm, Sat 9am–2pm; 600Ft), which presents Szombathely's history largely in the form of archeological and ethnographical displays, and couldn't be duller if it tried.

Beyond the Belváros

Szombathely's northern suburbs harbour two more attractions which can be reached by bus #1 from Petőfi utca. The **Kámoni Arboretum** (April to mid-Oct Mon–Fri 8am–6pm, Sat & Sun 9am–6pm; mid-Oct to March daily 8am–4pm; 300Ft) contains 2500 different kinds of trees, shrubs and flowers, with an especially varied assortment of roses, while just up the road is the grandly named **Gotthárd Astrophysics Observatory** (Csillag Vizsgáló; Mon–Fri 9am–4pm; 300Ft), with an interesting exhibition on cosmology.

Northwest of the centre lie the **Rowing Lake** (Csónakázótó) and the **Anglers' Lake** (Horgásztó), two smallish ponds where locals fish and go boating near an outdoor **thermal bath** (Fedett Uszoda Termálfürdő; Mon 2–9.30pm, Tues–Fri 6am–9.30pm, Sat & Sun 9am–6pm; 1200Ft). Bus #27 (twice an hour) takes you to both lakes and to the **Village Museum** (Skanzen; April–Oct Tues–Sun 9am–5pm; 750Ft) at Árpád utca 30, beyond the Anglers' Lake. Eighteenth- and nineteenth-century farmsteads are reconstructed here, culled from 27 villages in the Őrség region, and furnished with all the necessities and knick-knacks, making an architectural progression from log cabins to timber-framed wattle-and-daub dwellings. Every other month there are demonstrations of traditional folk crafts and dances of the region.

The green-belt district south of the lakes includes a small **game park** (Vadasz-kert) with deer, pheasants and other wildlife – nothing to get too excited about, but a nice place for a picnic. The park is situated on Víztorony utca; take bus #7 to Jókai utca and walk past the water tower, continuing for ten minutes.

Eating and drinking

Szombathely has a handful of terrific **restaurants** and some good cafés.

Art Café Fő tér 10. This elegant café is by far the most popular in town.

Café Mólo Rákóczi utca 5. North of the music college, this stylish, modern café-restaurant serves pizza, salads, vegetarian and other main dishes.

Fontana Savaria tér 1D. A cool café-restaurant.

Gödör Hollán Ernő utca 10–12. Sister restaurant to the *Jégverem* in Sopron (see p.263), this is a huge and immensely enjoyable cellar restaurant, serving roisteringly hearty meals. Closes 3pm Sun.

Hotel Wagner Kossuth Lajos utca 15. The hotel's beautifully appointed dining area is the setting for Hungarian cuisine of great distinction, including an above-average vegetarian menu. Closes 4pm Sun.

Mimik Café Ady Endre tér 5. In the Cultural Hall, this is a delightfully retro 1950s-style coffee-bar,

serving little more than drinks and hot dogs. Closed Sun.

Öreg Sam Söröző Étterem Gagarin 14 ⓦwww .oregsam.hu. Just west of the centre, this beerhall/ restaurant has a beautifully kept garden and terrace in addition to the wood-panelled main room, and serves filling Hungarian and German meals and beers. Closed Sun.

Pannonia Fő tér 29. With its thick wooden beams, bench seating and soothing lighting, this is an ideal venue for exceptional dishes of game, poultry and fish, as well as pizza. There's also a small wine shop.

Royal Söröző On the north side of Fő tér. A pavement café that also serves draught beer and meals; also the *Bécsi*, opposite.

Festivals

The town stages several major cultural events, the most important of which are the **Spring Days** in late March, the **International Dance Festival** in June, and, biggest and best of all, the **Savaria Historical Carnival** (Történelmi Karnéval; ⓦwww .savariakarneval.hu) at the end of August, featuring Roman games, medieval theatre, music and food, and a final, spectacular torch-lit procession. There is a strong musical tradition in Szombathely, home to an orchestra, the **Savaria Symphony**, and an early music ensemble, the Capella Savaria. The international **Bartók Festival** in mid-July is another highlight, with a two-week series of seminars and concerts. At other times of the year, check out what's happening at the Bartók Concert Hall, the hideous 1960s **Cultural Centre** on Március 15 tér, or the cultural hall on Ady Endre tér, west of the bus station.

Ják

With hourly buses (some continuing to Körmend) from Szombathely to the village of **JÁK**, 16km southwest, and trains stopping nearby at Ják-Balogunyom, you can easily visit Hungary's most outstanding **Romanesque abbey church** (daily: April–Oct 8am–6pm; Nov–March 10am–2pm; 300Ft), which is far more impressive than the scaled-down replica in Budapest's Városliget. The church sits on a hilltop overlooking the feudal domain of Márton Nagy, who founded it in 1214 and personally checked that his serfs attended Sunday services, whipping any who failed to do so. The church was built in two stages and completed in 1256, with some Gothic elements; facing it is the circular chapel of St James (Szent Jakab Kapelle), completed in 1260, which is used by the village and left open.

The church is similar in plan to its ruined contemporary at Lébény (see p.255), and likewise influenced by the Scottish Benedictine church in Regensburg, the point from which Norman architecture spread into Central Europe. It was restored in the 1890s by Frigyes Schulek, the architect of the Fishermen's Bastion in Budapest, who added the stumpy spires atop Ják's towers. The church's most striking feature is the magnificent **portal** on the western facade, where Christ and his apostles surmount a Norman zigzag arch composed of six orders and many sub-orders. Inside, the barely visible **frescoes**, and the exquisite medieval **altarpieces** in the north and south aisles, can be viewed by depositing a 100Ft coin in the slot. By the car park on the south side of the church is a shop where you should pay your entry fee and can ask to see the former **abbot's residence**, which displays a handful of locally excavated artefacts. Although there's no real reason to stay here, there is the *Jaki Turistaház* (☎94/321-436; ❷), just below the church on the main road, as well as several *Zimmer frei* signs around the village.

Sárvár

SÁRVÁR, on the River Rába 25km east of Szombathely, from where trains and buses run hourly, is the most recently developed **spa centre** in Hungary, following the discovery of hot springs over 25 years ago. The spas were developed to attract hard currency from German and Austrian tourists and still do a roaring trade, but aside from wallowing and quaffing, the town's only real attraction is the fortress that gives Sárvár its name – **"Mud Castle"**.

Arrival and information

The **train station** is 800m to the north of town on Selyemgyár utca – take bus #1 or #1V, or it's a ten-minute walk along Hunyadi János utca and Batthyány utca towards the castle; the **bus station** is 300m west along Batthyány utca, just beyond the fire station with a pair of nineteenth-century handpumps in front. **Tourinform** is located opposite the castle entrance at Várkerület 33 (July & Aug Mon–Fri 9am–5pm, Sat 9am–1pm, rest of year Mon–Fri 9am–4pm; ☎95/520-178, Ⓔsarvar@tourinform.hu), with the main **post office** next door at no. 32 (Mon–Fri 8am–6pm, Sat 9am–noon).

Accommodation

Thanks mainly to the baths, there's loads of accommodation in town and even in August you shouldn't have a problem. **Private rooms** (❷) are available through Savaria Tourist, next to Tourinform (May–Sept Mon–Fri 8am–5pm, Sat 8am–noon; Oct–April Mon–Fri 8.30am–4.30pm; ☎95/320-578, Ⓔsavariatourist .sarvar@enternet.hu), or look for *Zimmer frei* signs on Feket utca, for instance. There's tent-space at the year-round *Sárvár* **campsite** behind the baths at Vadkert utca 1 (☎95/326-502, Ⓔinfo@sarvarfurdo.hu), which has chalets sleeping two (❸); the site can be reached by taking bus #1Y to the end of the line.

Hotel Arborétum Medgyessy Ferenc utca 20 ☎95/520-630, Ⓦwww.hotelarboretum.hu. Tucked away on a quiet residential street behind the arboretum, this great-value place has cool, ultra-modern rooms. ❻

Hotel Bassiana Várkerület 29-2 ☎95/521-300, Ⓦwww.hotelbassiana.hu. A stylish new four-star place on the east side of the castle park. ❻

Danubius Health Spa Resort Rákóczi út 1 ☎95/888-400, Ⓦwww.danubiushotels.com/sarvar. Supremely comfortable place with indoor and outdoor thermal pools, sauna, gym and curative facilities; service is good but somewhat impersonal. ❽

Platán Hotel Hunyadi János utca 23 ☎95/326-484, Ⓦwww.platanhotel.hu. Between the train station and the centre, this delightful small hotel has generously sized rooms

with pristine bathrooms, designer beds and minibar; also has a great café and restaurant (see p.282). ❻

Szieszta Panzió Rákóczi út 57a ☎95/320-456, Ⓦwww.sziesztapanzio.try.hu. Facing the baths, this place has lounge-type rooms with sofa and small balcony; included in the price is use of the two pools (one indoors, one with sliding roof) and whirlpool – a water-lover's paradise. ❹

Tinódi Panzió Hunyadi János utca 11 ☎95/320-225, Ⓦwww.tinodifogado.hu. 200m up from the *Platán*, this place has minimal but colourful rooms, with small beds and small bathrooms. ❹

Wolf Panzió Rákóczi út 11 ☎95/321-499, Ⓦwww.wolfhotel.hu. Big, blue-furnished rooms with more than ample cupboard space, TV and fridge. The same owners run the slightly smarter *Wolf Hotel* (❺) across the road at Alkotmány utca 4 (☎95/320-460). ❹

The Town

Though the term "Mud Castle" might have been appropriate until the fourteenth century, it hardly applies to **Sárvár Castle** today, which stands in the heart of the town encircled by the Várkerület. Reached by a long low brick bridge across the surrounding moat, it's busy with locals wheeling bikes through to reach the town's library. Modified by many owners over the centuries, its pentagonal layout and palatial interior are owed to the **Nádasdy family**, particularly Tamás Nádasdy, who hired Italian architects and made this a centre of Renaissance humanism. It was here that the first Hungarian translation of the New Testament was printed in 1541. The **Festival Hall** is decorated with Dorfmeister frescoes of biblical episodes, allegories of art and science, and murals (dating from 1653) depicting the "Black Knight" Ferenc Nádasdy, Tamás's son, routing the Turks. Ferenc was also a humanist, and patron of Sebestyén Lantos Tinódi, the poet who exhorted his countrymen to resist the Turks. The **Ferenc Nádasdy Museum** (Nádasdy Ferenc Múzeum; Tues–Sun 9am–5pm; 600Ft), inside the castle, displays a voluminous array of weapons, uniforms and memorabilia associated with Tamás and Ferenc, but barely a reference to the latter's wife, the infamous Countess Báthori (see box, p.282).

The former castle gardens across the Várkerület to the east are now a large **arboretum** (daily: April to mid-Oct 9am–7pm; mid-Oct to March 9am–5pm;

300Ft), which has been a protected reserve since 1952, though its oldest trees date from the eighteenth century. Now, these extensive gardens feature black pines, ash and yew trees, as well as a beautiful collection of azaleas and magnolias. From here it's nearly 1km along Rákóczi utca to the **thermal baths** (Mon–Thurs & Sun, 9am–8pm, Fri & Sat 9am–9pm; 2400Ft, after 5pm 1500Ft, after 8pm 900Ft) at Vadkert utca 1. The renovated complex includes three indoor pools and several outdoor pools (May–Sept), a sauna centre (naked; 1800Ft), and numerous special treatment facilities. For something a little more animated, the owners of the *Vadkert Fogadó*, just behind the baths on Vadkert utca, run a **riding school** (daily 8am–4pm; 1800Ft per hour; ☎95/320-045) and also have **tennis courts** for use.

Eating, drinking and entertainment

There's a definite shortage of really good **restaurants** in town. The best one is the *Várkapu*, just west of the castle at Várkerület 5 (daily 8.30am–10pm), whose varied menu includes pizza, fish, rabbit, duck and that most rare of meats in Hungary, lamb; you can dine in its refined interior or on the stylish outdoor terrace. Otherwise, the restaurants in the *Platán Hotel* and *Tinódi Panzió* are worth trying, the former offering some game dishes and the latter serving Hungarian food and pizza. The *Platán* also has the best **café** in town, while the *Tercia konditorei*, in the baths complex, has some delicious pastries. For more serious drinking, with English beer on tap (plus 20 teas, including maté and red bush), head to *Club 63* at Batthyány utca 63. The *Café Mirage* at Rákóczi utca is a very stylish café-*konditorei*,

---

Countess Erzsébet Báthori

Countess Erzsébet Báthori has gone down in history as *Die Blutgräfin* (The Blood Countess), who tortured to death over six hundred women and girls, sometimes biting chunks of flesh from their necks and breasts – the origin of legends that she bathed in the blood of virgins to keep her own skin white and translucent. Yet there's a strong case that the accusations arose from a conspiracy against her by the Palatine of Hungary, **Count Thurzó**, and her own son-in-law, Miklós Zrínyi, grandson of the hero of Szigetvár.

Born in 1560, the offspring of two branches of the Báthori family (whose intermarriage might explain several cases of lunacy in the dynasty), Erzsébet was married at the age of 15 to Ferenc Nádasdy and assumed responsibility for their vast estates, which she inherited upon his death in 1604. To the chagrin of her sons-in-law and the Palatine, she refused to surrender any of them. Worse still from a Habsburg standpoint, the election of her nephew, "Crazy" Gábor Báthori, as Prince of Transylvania raised the prospect of a Báthori alliance that would upset the balance of power and border defences on which Habsburg rule depended.

In December 1610 Thurzó raided her residence at Čachtice, and claimed to have caught her literally red-handed. Under torture, her associates testified to scores of **secret burials** at Sárvár, Čachtice and elsewhere, and the Countess was immediately walled up in a room at Čachtice, where she died in 1614. Although Thurzó amassed nearly three hundred depositions, no trial was ever held, as the death of Gábor Báthori reduced her political significance to the point that it served nobody's interests to besmirch the Nádasdy and Báthori names.

While there's little doubt that there was a **conspiracy** against the Countess, it's hard to believe that she was totally innocent. There were accusations of her cruelty at Sárvár even before her widowhood, and the theory that the tortures were actually medical treatments doesn't explain the most atrocious cases. Probably the best one can say is that she was a victim of double standards in an era when brutality was rife and the power of nobles unbridled.

also serving pizza and fine Slovak Zlaty Bazant beer; it also has rooms (☎30/456-0276, ⓦwww.galeriapanzio.hu; ❸).

Sárvár's key event is the **International Folklore Festival**, celebrated in mid-August in the castle's courtyard, and in the same vein, but only in even-numbered years, there are the so-called **History Days**, with concerts, traditional dancing and singing. The **International Summer Meeting of Electro-Acoustic Music** at the end of July features open rehearsals and free concerts.

The Őrség

The forested **Őrség region**, some 30km south of Szombathely, has guarded Hungary's southwestern marches since the time of the Árpáds. Dotted with hilltop watchtowers and isolated hamlets, every man here was sworn to arms in lieu of paying tax. The people became used to their freedom and refused to be bound into serfdom by the Batthyány family, whose seat was at nearby Körmend. Moist winds from the Mediterranean make this the rainiest, greenest part of Hungary, while the heavy clay soil allows no form of agriculture except raising cattle, but provides ample raw material for the local pottery industry. Until well into the twentieth century, when the Őrség declined as villagers migrated to Zalaegerszeg, houses were constructed of wood plastered with clay. Today, the region's soft landscapes and folksy architecture are a powerful draw and village tourism is flourishing, with many homes offering a bed and food.

There are several approaches, depending on your starting point, although your best bet is to take one of the ten or so daily buses from **Körmend** to **Őriszentpéter**, perhaps the nicest of the villages. Alternatively, you could take a train (eight daily) from Zalaegerszeg via Zalalövő to Őriszentpéter. Given the limited bus services and quiet roads, **cycling** is an ideal way of getting around. Bikes can be rented at several villages, but it's wise to bring waterproof clothing for the inevitable drizzles.

Őriszentpéter

ŐRISZENTPÉTER is the obvious base for exploring the region, a straggling village made up of groups of houses (*szer*), built on nine separate ridges to escape flooding, each with one road bearing the same name – Városszer, Szikaszer, etc – and numbered round in a circle. During the last weekend of June the village hosts the **Őrség Fair**, with folk music, dancing and handicrafts. Buses run to Szentgotthárd, Körmend and Zalalövő from the bus station just to the right from the central roundabout facing the *Centrum Panzió*; there's also a new train station 1km south of the centre, up the track on the east side of the *Centrum Panzió*. It also boasts the best tourist facilities in the Őrség, including a tourist **information** office at Városszer 55, 1.4km west, near the Romanesque church (Mon–Fri: April–Sept 9am–noon & 1–4pm; Oct–March 10am–4pm; ☎94/548-023, ⓦwww.orsegnet.hu), whose helpful staff can advise on **private accommodation** in the whole region. To the rear is the headquarters of the Őrség National Park (☎94/548-034, ⓦhttp://onp.nemzetipark.gov.hu), with information panels (in Hungarian) outside and a short educational path in the woods.

Rooms are advertised all along Városszer and Kovácsszer. Alternatively, the ⚸ *Centrum Panzió* at Városszer 17 (☎&ⓕ94/350-319; ❸), by the village's central roundabout, has simple, cool rooms with TV and bathroom, not to mention a bowling alley with a 1950s-rocket-scientist control desk. To the rear, at Városszer

16, the *Horvárth Kert Panzió* (☎94/548-053; ❹) is quiet and welcoming. You can get decent **meals** at the *Bognár Étterem*, 600m up the hill from the bus station at Kovácsszer 96, including the local speciality *dödölle* (fried potato and onion dumplings served with soured cream). You can **rent bikes** at Varósszer 69 (☎70/378-5761) and Városszer 116 (☎94/428-989; 1500Ft a day), and **horseriding** can be arranged at Szikaszer 18. There's a **post office** at the central roundabout (Mon–Fri 8am–4pm).

Beside the road to Szalafő, 2km west of the centre of the village, stands a beautiful thirteenth-century **Romanesque church** with a finely carved portal and traces of frescoes inside, which can only be properly seen by attending Sunday Mass (8.30am; not the first Sun of the month), or taking the external stairs (daily 10am–2pm; obtain the key from the priest next door) to the choir loft, where there's a decent view of the interior and information in French, German and Hungarian. A hedge marks the line of the sixteenth-century defensive walls, with a moat outside.

Szalafő

The village of **SZALAFŐ**, 6km up the road from Őriszentpéter, likewise consists of small separate settlements on adjacent ridges, with a church and bar at the hub of the radiating roads. From here it's 3km to Pityerszer, a mini **Village Museum** (mid-April to Oct Tues–Sun 10am–5pm; 300Ft) of heavy-timbered houses typical of the region, which gives a good idea of life as it was five or six decades ago. Notice the little hen ladders that run up the sides of the houses. Tickets are sold at the *büfé* across the road from the museum, where you can also get refreshments. There are buses (Mon–Fri 4 daily, Sat & Sun 2 daily) from Körmend and Őriszentpéter to Szalafő-felső, the terminus, and you'll find the museum a further kilometre's walk in the same direction.

If you happen to be here on **May 1**, look out for **dancing** around the tall, slender may tree. The origins of this ritual have long been lost, but many pine trees in the Őrség region are stripped of their lower branches as teenaged boys shin up to retrieve bottles of champagne suspended from the higher branches. Some even plant may trees in their girlfriends' gardens in the middle of the night.

Lots of houses advertise **rooms** for rent; try the *Csörgő Vendégház* at Csörgőszer 20 (☎94/428-623; ❷), run by the same people who run the bar in the centre of the village. They can also direct you to several houses selling delicious goat's and cow's cheese (*sajt*) and milk (*tej*). The *Hubertus Vendégház*, by the entrance to the village at Alsószer 20, serves hot **meals**.

Other villages in the region

Seven kilometres east of Őriszentpéter at **PANKASZ**, you can stop to admire the rustic **wooden bell-tower**; follow signs off the main road to the *Posta* for 200m. **Bikes** and **rooms** can be rented at **HEGYHÁTSZENTJAKAB**, 3km

Into Slovenia

Hungary has two **road crossings into Slovenia**. Most traffic heads to the Rédics/Dolga Vas crossing, 30km south on Route 75, running down from Keszthely. The Hodoş/Salovci crossing is quieter; the turn-off is midway between Őriszentpéter and Magyarszombatfa. A **railway** has recently been constructed, from Zalalövő to Murska Sobota via the Hodoş crossing, although this currently carries only one international train a day in each direction.

further north, off the road between Zalalövő and Pankasz (but served by buses to Őriszentpéter), where you will find the comfortable *Trófea Panzió* (⊤94/426-230; ❺) and a popular swimming **lake**, the Vadása-tó.

More appealing, though, are two villages along a minor road south of Őriszentpéter. In the hills along the Slovenian border, 12km away, the tiny village of **MAGYARS-ZOMBATFA**, with just three hundred residents, preserves the old tradition of **Habán pottery**, sold through the local Potters' House (Fazekasház). The road continues 6km southeast to **VELEMÉR**, also known for its ceramics, whose single-aisled Romanesque **church** contains beautiful frescoes from 1377. To view them, ask for the key at the house signposted *Templomkulcs*. The church lies across the fields, hidden in the trees, about 500m from the main road. There are nine daily buses (four at weekends) to Velemér from Őriszentpéter via Magyarszombatfa.

Zalaegerszeg

As capital of Zala county, **ZALAEGERSZEG**, just 37km west of Keszthely, is itself familiarly known as Zala; it began to metamorphose after the discovery of oil in 1937, and is now the most industrialized town in southwestern Hungary, with a population of 70,000. Despite the futuristic television tower featured on

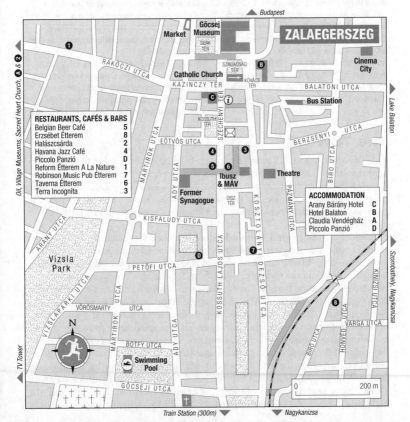

tourist brochures and the bleak downtown area of housing estates and landscaped plazas, Zala hasn't totally forgotten its past: vestiges of folk culture from the surrounding region are preserved in two museums and an annual festival.

Arrival and information

The **bus station** is on Balatoni út, a few minutes east of the main thoroughfare, Széchenyi tér, while the **train station** is a fifteen-minute walk south (reached by buses #1, #7, #10 or #11). **Information** and maps can be had at Tourinform, at Széchenyi tér 4 (June–Aug Mon–Fri 9am–6pm, Sat 9am–4pm; Sept–May Mon–Fri 9am–5pm; ☎92/316-160, ✉zalaegerszeg@tourinform.hu). Zala's main **post office** is at Berzsenyi Dániel utca 6A (Mon–Fri 8am–7pm, Sat 8am–noon). You can get online at the *Procomp Internet Kávézó*, on Iskola utca at the rear of the *Arany Bárany Hotel*.

Accommodation

The town's sleeping options are not especially exciting, though you'll have little trouble finding something. The cheapest accommodation is a **private room** (②), available through Ibusz at Európa tér 6 (Mon–Fri 8.30am–noon & 12.30–4pm; ☎92/511-880, ✉zalaegerszeg@ibusz.hu).

Arany Bárány Hotel Széchenyi tér 1 ☎92/550-040, ⊕www.aranybarany.hu. The "Golden Lamb", in a fine old building in the centre, has smooth, decently furnished rooms in a modern wing, some with shower, some with bath. ❼

Hotel Balaton Balatoni út 2a ☎92/550-870, ⊕www.balatonhotel.hu. Hideous modern block, but it's central and has a spa, and the peachy/pink rooms, each with balcony, are actually quite fine. ❼

Claudia Vendégház Körmendi út 16 ☎92/596-738, ⊕www.hotels.hu/claudia. Ordinary, but clean, seven-room pension, 1km beyond the Oil and Village museums. Discounts for stays of more than one night. ②–③

Piccolo Panzió Petőfi Sándor utca 16 ☎92/510-055, ⊕www.piccolo.hu. Eight-room family pension with cosy rooms, each with small bathroom and minibar; the garden restaurant is a good place to eat. Booking essential. ③

The Town

Zala's north–south axis, Kossuth utca, is pretty drab until it reaches several squares at the northern end, more like wide streets than plazas, where Baroque and Art Nouveau buildings offer a touch of colour and an idea of how Zala looked before postwar planning changed its appearance. It's somehow appropriate that the town's most famous sons exemplify the Hungarian genius for making the best of an adverse situation.

The sculptor **Zsigmond Kisfaludi Strobl** enjoyed early success with busts of British royals and Hungarian aristocrats, and then switched to producing glorified workers (and the Liberation Monument in Budapest) under Communism, earning himself medals and the nickname "Step from Side to Side". You can chuckle over his oeuvre, including busts of George Bernard Shaw (who declared it "better than the original") and Somerset Maugham, at the Art Nouveau **Göcsej Museum** at Batthyány utca 2 (Tues–Sat 10am–5pm, in summer also Sun till 4pm; 300Ft), which also features a colourful display of archeological finds from the region, including earthenware, jewellery and mosaics. The city centre is dominated by the Neoclassical Roman Catholic church immediately to the south on Szabadság tér; completed in 1760, the fine frescoes of Mary Magdalene are by the Austrian Johann Cimbal. To the west, Deák tér bears a statue of local politician **Ferenc Deák**, who negotiated the historic Compromise between Hungary and the Habsburg Empire in 1867 that created the Dual Monarchy. Behind the County

Hall (built in 1730–32), on the north side of the square, is a lively **market** selling Göcsej cheese and other local produce. A few hundred metres to the west along Rákóczi utca, facing the big InterSpar supermarket, the **Sacred Heart church**, a perfect pastiche of the Baroque style, was built in 1926–27 by the future **Cardinal Mindszenty**, at that time still the parish priest Jószef Pehm; leader of the Hungarian church from 1945 to 1975, he was ultra-conservative but stood up bravely for the Church and the people against Fascist and Communist domination. Imprisoned for six months by the Fascists, he was then tortured and jailed for life by the Communist regime; he was released during the 1956 revolution, before fleeing to the US embassy and spending seventeen years there before being allowed to go into exile in Vienna.

Heading south, it's five minutes' walk to Zala's former **synagogue** (Tues–Fri 10am–6pm, Sat 2–6pm), an unmistakeable, lilac-painted edifice at Ady Endre utca 14. As it's now a concert hall and gallery, it's possible to view the Eclectic-style interior, designed by József Stern in 1903, though marred by lurid stained-glass windows and a massive organ, installed in the 1960s. Six kilometres to the west of town is the **TV Tower**, reached by hourly bus from the bus station; its viewing platform, complete with bar, affords fine views of the Göcsej Hills (daily 10am–8pm; 300Ft).

The open-air museums

Zala's main attractions are three outdoor museums (April–Sept Tues–Sun 10am–4pm; 375Ft each), clustered together 2km northwest of the centre (bus #1, #1Y or #8Y). Coming by train from Zalalövő, you can get off at Zalaegerszeg-Ola station; the railway is being rebuilt and a cycleway will soon run along the old trackbed most of the way west to Zalalövő. Giant pumps, drills and other hardware dominate the **Oil Industry Museum** (Olajipari Múzeum), which examines the industry's history in Hungary. Unfortunately, exploratory drilling in the 1950s and 1960s discovered far more hot springs than oil, and the most promising field was found to straddle the Romanian border, so domestic production amounts to a fraction of Hungary's requirements.

Next door, the **Göcsej Village Museum** (Göcseji Falumúzeum) is the oldest of the *skanzen* in Hungary, and whilst it can't compare with the one in Szentendre (see p.155), it does hold nearly fifty original constructions. These include a watermill, a smithy, and several beautifully carved and painted gables, but the majority are dwellings from the late nineteenth century, complete with furniture and artefacts characteristic of the surrounding **Göcsej region**. Traditionally, this was so poor and squalid that no one would admit to being a part of it, and enquirers were always hastily assured that its boundaries began a few kilometres on, in the next village. The third, and smallest, of the museums is the **Finno-Ugrian Ethnographical Park**, still being developed but currently comprising around half a dozen pine-log cabins typical of those once inhabited by the Finno-Ugric peoples.

Eating and entertainment

The town has several decent **eating** options. Local **entertainment** consists of whatever's on at the cultural centre on Kisfaludy utca. The *Filmcentrum* at Széchenyi tér 4 shows art films, while *Cinema City*, in the Zala Plaza shopping centre northeast of the centre, screens blockbusters. For nightlife, there's only the wonderfully 1970s nightclub and the 24-hour casino both in the *Arany Bárány Hotel*. The major festival in town each year is the **Egerszeg Days**, a five-day event with concerts and folklore programmes held during the second week of May.

Belgian Beer Café Kossuth Lajos utca 5. With a pleasant rear terrace, this offers inventive meat-heavy dishes as well as delicious if pricey Belgian beer.

Erzsébet Étterem Bersenyi utca 13. If you don't mind the odd train rumbling by, this offers a good-value Hungarian menu.

Halászcsárda Rákóczi utca 47. Out towards the Village Museum, this is an excellent fish restaurant.

Havana Jazz Café On the alley behind the *Belgian Beer Café*, this has rather less raucous music, although the drinks are much the same. Mon–Thurs 11am–11pm, Fri 11am–midnight, Sat 6pm–midnight, Sun 6–10pm.

Piccolo Panzió Petőfi Sándor utca 16. This pension (see p.286) also has a pleasant garden restaurant, either for a meal or a drink.

Reform Étterem A La Nature Rákóczi 29. A health-food shop and café serving salads, veggie/tofu burgers and felafel. Mon–Thurs 8am–5pm, Fri 8am–3pm.

Robinson Music Pub Étterem Petőfi utca 24. A pub that also serves pizza and has wi-fi and occasional live bands.

Taverna Étterem Kossuth Lajos tér 2/Európa tér. Decent Hungarian grub served amid rustic wooden furniture and raw wool seat covers.

Terra Incognita Kosztolányi utca 5. Upstairs in the round building at the corner of Berszenyi utca, this is a very stylish restaurant and coffee house with a rooftop terrace (on top of a car park, but none the worse for that).

Southern Transdanubia

Bordered to the south by Croatia and to the north by Balaton, **Southern Transdanubia** is less built-up and more rural than the other Transdanubian regions and also, bar a couple of isolated hilly areas, much flatter, and, not surprisingly, largely agricultural. The outstanding draw is **Pécs**, the region's attractive capital, whose many museums, fabulous nightlife and festivals can easily detain you for a few days. The hilly region south of Pécs should also appeal, particularly to wine lovers, with the marvellous **Villány–Siklós wine road** yielding some superlative reds, whilst just west of Pécs is **Szigetvár**, renowned for its castle and Turkish ruins. Although the **Völgység**, the valley region between Lake Balaton and the **Mecsek Hills**, is pretty to drive through, none of the towns is really worth stopping for. Travelling from Balaton by train, however, you could take in the sights of **Kaposvár** while changing trains. Express trains from Budapest to Pécs usually run via Dombóvár, while intercity buses are routed through **Szekszárd**, the most appealing small town in the region, within reach of the lovely **Forest of Gemenc**, part of the Duna-Drava National Park. In stark contrast, the steel town of **Dunaújváros** will undoubtedly appeal to devotees of 1950s Socialist-Realist aesthetics.

Kaposvár and around

Capital of Somogy county, the industrial town of **KAPOSVÁR**, just 53km south of Lake Balaton, lies between the hilly slopes of the Zselic region and the valley of the River Kapos. The town is blessed with a fabulous stock of museums and, with an elegant centre stuffed with numerous Art Nouveau and Neoclassical buildings, it's well worth a visit. Apart from being famous for its theatre and as the birthplace of József Rippl-Rónai, father of Hungarian Art Nouveau, Kaposvár is a stepping stone for walks in the **Zselic nature conservation area**. With frequent direct trains to Fonyód, there's easy access to Lake Balaton.

Arrival and information

Kaposvár's **stations** are close to each other, with local buses next to the train station on Budai Nagy Antal utca and long-distance services across the road on Petőfi Sándor tér. The centre of town, essentially the east–west axis of Fő utca, is a couple of blocks to the north. Here, you can get **information** from the helpful Tourinform office at no. 8 (mid-June to mid-Sept Mon–Fri 9am–6pm, Sat 9am–5pm, Sun 9am–2pm; mid-Sept to mid-June Mon–Fri 9am–5pm, Sat 9am–2pm; ☎82/512-921, ⓦwww.tourinformkaposvar.hu). There's one free **internet** terminal here, plus others at *X-Café*, Teleki utca 8 (actually on Varósház utca; Mon–Fri 9am–6pm, Sat 9am–1pm) and *InterCafé*, Dosza György utca 18 (Mon–Fri 7.30am–8pm). The **post office** is at Bajcsy-Zsilinszky utca 15 (Mon–Fri 8am–7pm, Sat 8am–noon).

Accommodation

There's a good choice of accommodation in town. Ibusz, at Széchenyi tér 8 (Mon–Fri 8am–5pm, Sat 8am–noon; ☎82/512-300, ⓔkaposvar@ibusz.hu), can arrange a room in one of the centrally located colleges, notably the *Kaposvári Képzési Központ Kollegium* at Szent Imre utca 14B (☎82/527-720, ⓔszallas@etk .pte.hu; ❹), or **private rooms** (❷) in the town and in the villages of the Zselic Hills; and Siotour, in the *Csokonai Fogadó Panzió* at Fő utca 1 (Mon–Fri 8am–4.30pm; ☎82/320-537), can also arrange private accommodation in town. The nearest reliably open **campsite** is *Kaland Park*, 12km southwest, beyond Szenna, at Fő utca 28 in Patca (☎82/484-023, ⓦwww.kalandpark.hu).

Csokonai Fogadó Panzió Fő utca 1 ☎82/312-011, ⓕ316-716. In the renovated eighteenth-century Dorottya Ház on the main street, but rather run-down. Rooms come with or without shower, although the ubiquitous brown decor is a bit wearing. Breakfast not included. ❷–❸

Diófa Panzió József Attila utca 24 ☎82/422-504, ⓦwww.diofapanzio.hu. Up the hill from Kossuth tér, this cheap pension has rooms with TV, phone and minibar but is ultimately rather bland. ❸

Hotel Dorottya Széchenyi tér 8 ☎82/418-055, ⓦwww.hoteldorottya.hu. Kaposvár's most characterful hotel, built in the nineteenth century, retains many of its original features, including a nice old lift and thick wooden beams in most of the rooms. ❺

Fogadó a Bárányhoz Városház utca 4 ☎82/527-600, ⓦhttp://fogadoabaranyhoz.internettudakozo .hu. A new hotel, restaurant and café run by

catering students, right in the centre of town; there are seven a/c rooms – good if with smallish bathrooms – a lift, disabled rooms and free internet. ❸

Hotel Kapos Ady Endre utca 2 ☎82/316-022, ⓦwww.kaposhotel.hu. From the outside this seems less than promising, but the variously sized rooms are reasonably modern, spacious and well equipped. Also has a coffee house. ❹

Pálma Panzió Széchenyi tér 6 ☎&ⓕ82/420-227. Small, private pension just up from the *Dorottya*, with standard rooms and bathrooms. ❸

Tenisz Club Panzió Iszák utca 37 ☎82/411-832 or 20/969-0640, ⓔsamflo@hu.inter.net. West of the stations and across the river, this good-value place has satisfying cucumber green-and-black coloured rooms, all neatly furnished and some with balcony; there's a restaurant-bar. ❸

The Town

Most of Kaposvár's attractions are located along or just off the pretty, pedestrianized main street, Fő utca, and around Kossuth tér, the main square, dominated by the Neoclassical church of Our Lady of the Assumption, built in 1885–86. At Fő utca 12, the **Vaszary Art Gallery** (Vaszary Képtár; Mon–Fri 9am–5pm, Sat 9am–noon; 1500Ft) hosts temporary shows plus a permanent exhibition on the Kaspovár-born photographer Juan Gyenes (Gyenes János; 1912–95), who made his name in Spain with Dalí and his circle. Other galleries showing often excellent temporary art shows can be found in the County Hall (Csokonai köz 3; Mon–Fri

8am–4pm), the City Cultural Centre (Csokonai utca 1; daily 10am–8pm) and the County Cultural Centre (Somssich utca 18; Mon–Fri 8am–4pm).

At Fő utca 10, the former town hall, opened in 1832, houses the **Somogy County Museum** (Somogy Megyei Múzeum; Tues–Sun: April–Oct 10am–4pm; Nov–March 10am–3pm; 375Ft), which contains the usual mix of local ethnographic and historical material. It's best to head straight to the top floor and the gallery of contemporary art, where you'll find works by prominent Hungarians such as Egry, Kmetty and Vaszvary (see opposite). The museum is also known as the Rippl-Rónai Museum – not for the artist Jószef Rippl-Ronai (born on this street at no. 19 above the Golden Lion Pharmacy) but for his lesser-known brother, Ödön, who donated his entire collection to the city. Indeed, the gallery doesn't contain any of Jószef's paintings; instead, you'll find these at the **Rippl-Rónai Villa** on Fodor József utca, in the suburb of Rómahegy (Rome Hill), 3km southeast of the centre (Emlekmúzeum; Tues–Sun: April–Oct 10am–6pm; Nov–March 10am–4pm; 300Ft); take bus #15 from the bus station. Born in 1861, Rippl-Rónai first studied in Munich and then under the academic painter Munkácsy before refining his own style in Paris, influenced by Postimpressionism and Art Nouveau. His return home in 1902 marked the end of his "black period", when some of his best-known works such as *Lady with a Black Veil* were produced, and the start of a "sunlit" one reflecting "the colours that surround me in my new house and garden". In his later years he abandoned oils and turned to crayon. The villa contains pictures from each phase, plus furniture, glassware and ceramics.

A couple of minutes' walk north of Kossuth tér past the *Hotel Kapos* is the **Somogy Sports Museum** at Kontrássy utca 3 (Somogyi Sportmúzeum; Tues, Thurs & Fri 10am–5pm, Sun 9am–1pm; 300Ft), stuffed with memorabilia from every sport imaginable; naturally enough, the displays of trophies, photographs and sporting equipment focus on Hungarian sporting achievement, and a fair chunk of the museum is given over to Olympic mementoes, including uniforms for the opening ceremonies. Five minutes up the road, at Zarda utca 9, the **Vaszvary Memorial House** (Tues–Sun: Oct–March 10am–4pm; April–Sept 10am–6pm; free) has been converted into a lovely little gallery featuring paintings and sketches by János Vaszvary, born in this house in 1867. Down in the cellar at Fő utca 31 is the **Terrárium** (Mon–Fri 10am–5pm, Sat 10am–noon, Sun 2–5pm; 450Ft), housing a collection of rare and exotic reptiles such as the Madagascar boa and Cuvier dwarf caiman.

One attraction not to be missed is the fabulous **Steiner Collection**, five minutes' walk east of Rákóczi tér at Gróf Apponyi utca 29 (Steiner Gyűjtemény; Mon–Fri 5–8pm, Sat & Sun 10am–7pm or by appointment, call ☏82/311-327; free), a private collection of cast-iron articles and ornaments from the nineteenth century. The owner, József Steiner, started his unique collection in 1989 after purchasing an old iron stove, which inspired him to search for ever more unusual cast-iron objects. The collection now consists of an entire cellar of stoves and baths, a garden full of cast-iron grave markers and a house crammed with everything from kitchen utensils, table clocks and lamps, to chandeliers and a bust of Lajos Kossuth from 1848.

Eating and drinking

Kaposvár has a handful of pretty good **restaurants**, the best being the *Corner House Restaurant and Pub* at Bajcsy-Zsilinszky utca 2, a thoroughly modern outfit offering superb meat dishes including boar, deer and rabbit. Further along the same street at no. 54, *El Gecco* is a colourful, cosy Mexican place also serving up steaks and grills, and, if you don't mind dreadful kitsch, the film-themed *Mozivilág* at Dózsa György utca 3 has a particularly good steak menu. Simpler snacks are available at *Beluga*, a tiny pizzeria and grill café at Noszlopy utca 10, and *Ham-Piz*, at Bajcsy-Zsilinszky utca 13, serving pizzas, burgers, roasted meats and salads. *Szicilia*, above the *Beluga* at Noszlopy utca 6, serves pizza and the like plus daily specials.

A delightful, out-of-the-way **coffee shop** is the *Múzsa Kávéház* at Szent Imre utca 21 – a serene, old-style place also serving teas, beers and cocktails. In summer, cafés and bars spill out onto the pedestrianized stretch of Fő utca, but for more tub-thumping entertainment year-round, head to *Central Park* at Szent Imre 29, a stereotypical **disco** with a glitzy bar which really cranks it up at the weekend.

Entertainment

Kaposvár's distinctive **Csiky Gergely Theatre**, on Rákóczi tér, is one of the best in Hungary and has gained kudos abroad with its staging of Bulgakov's *The Master and Margarita*; tickets are available from the ticket office (Színház Jegypéntzár), alongside Tourinform at Fő utca 8 (Mon–Fri 9am–5pm, Sat 9am–2pm). To celebrate Mihály Csokonai's comic literary epic *Dorottya*, the first Saturday of February each year is given over to the **Dorottya Napok Fesztival** (Dorothy Day Festival), a day of carnival festivities and folk games along Fő utca. The day concludes with a mass ball at the *Hotel Dorottya* on Széchenyi tér, which is where most of the action in the book takes place. Especially during the town's **Spring Festival** (Tavaszi Fesztíval; mid-March to mid-April), there are concerts in the **Liszt Concert Hall** at Kossuth utca 21. There's also a **cinema** on the corner of Noszlopy utca and Városház utca.

Those with children, or just tired of hot weather, should head for the **hot baths** just southeast of the train station at Csík Ferenc sétány 1 (Virágfürdő; Tues–Sun 9am–7pm; 2550Ft; open-air pool daily in summer 9am–8pm; 900Ft), with 25- and 50-metre pools and a spa bath plus the new Adventure Baths, with slides, waterfalls, water curtains, and even a piranha chamber.

The Zselic region

Nature lovers will enjoy **walking in the Zselic region** south of Kaposvár, with its water meadows, woods and rolling hills. Maps (*A Zselic*; 1:60,000) are available from Tourinform and bookshops in Kaposvár, showing marked trails; you can follow one from the village of **SZENNA**, 8km southwest (buses from stand 9 of Kaposvár's bus terminal). Opposite the village's main bus stop, at Rákóczi utca 2, is one of Hungary's smallest **skanzen** (Szabadtéri Néprajzi Gyűjtemény; Tues–Sun: April–Oct 10am–6pm; Nov–March 10am–4pm; 450Ft), just five houses, complete with furnishings and personal belongings, three cellars and a Calvinist church, built in 1785 in a folk-Baroque style with an interesting cassette ceiling, all transplanted from elsewhere in the region. **Village tourism** is thriving here and you'll have little problem finding a **room** (either directly or through Ibusz in Kaposvár). One recommended place is the *Ágnes-Vendégház* at Kossuth utca 1 (☎82/712-273; ❷), which can also provide hot meals upon request.

Szigetvár

SZIGETVÁR, 41km south of Kaposvár through the Mecsek hills, and 33km west of Pécs, rivals Kőszeg for its heroic resistance to the invading Turks. Every Hungarian child is taught the story (see opposite), which is enshrined in poetry and music, and in a colossal painting in the Hungarian National Gallery in Budapest. Although a striking new community centre designed by Imre Makovecz (see box, p.163) has aroused some attention, and the local **thermal baths** are as agreeable as any, it is the **castle** and **relics of the Turkish occupation** that are still the main attractions of this dusty town.

The Town

Szigetvár can easily be explored on foot. From the train station the castle is signposted up Rákóczi utca, but you might prefer to cut across to the right through the adjacent bus station and cross Istyadoffy Miklós utca to the sixteenth-century **Turkish House** at Bástya utca 3 (Török Ház; May–Sept daily 10am–noon & 1–3pm; 300Ft), a simple brick building across the road from the market. Originally a caravanserai, it now displays a modest collection of Turkish artefacts.

Heading a couple of hundred metres back along Szecsődi Máté utca, you'll reach Rákóczi utca at a splendid Secessionist school; turning right, you soon come to **Zrínyi tér**, where what was built as the **Mosque of Ali Pasha** in 1596 was converted in the late eighteenth century into a Baroque church (daily 8am–noon); only the Turkish-style windows betray its origins. The altar painting and a fresco inside the dome of the siege were painted by Dorfmeister in 1788. A block to the east on Horváth Márk tér, the **Franciscan church** was built in 1688 and remodelled in Baroque style in 1731. At this point your eyes will be drawn by the twin towers of Makovecz's **Cultural Centre** at József Attila utca 9, a typically bizarre structure by the eccentric Hungarian architect, resembling an alien spacecraft come to earth. During its construction the town council ran out of money and refused to trim other budgets to fulfil Makovecz's conception of the project, to his outrage, resulting in the auditorium remaining a flexible open space with temporary seating.

Returning to Zrinyi tér and turning right past a snarling lion statue on to Vár utca, it's a straight, 200-metre walk up the road to the castle.

The Castle

As the town's name, Island Castle, suggests, this quadrilateral fortress (Tues–Sun: April & Oct 9am–5pm; May–Sept 9am–6pm; Nov–March 9am–4pm; 600Ft) was once surrounded by lakes and marshes. Under local strong man Bálint Török, it resisted sieges by the Turks in 1541 and 1554, but its finest hour came in 1566, when 2400 soldiers under **Miklós Zrínyi**, governor of Croatia, resisted the onslaught of 100,000 Turks for 33 days. Enraged by the loss of 20,000 troops and the failure of his seventh attempt to march on Vienna, **Sultan Süleyman** died of apoplexy before the siege finally wore down the defenders. Spurning offers of surrender, Zrínyi donned his court dress before leading a final suicidal sally when they could no longer hold out.

Beyond a giant stone thumb, erected to mark the millennium, as well as a plaque in Hungarian and Cyrillic which replaced the ugly Soviet war memorial in 2000, you enter by a gateway through the massive, low red-brick ramparts to the park-like interior, with a small yellow mansion in the middle. Once the summer residence of Count Andrássy, this now holds a **museum** (Vár Zrínyi Miklós Múzeum) in which coloured miniatures of Turkish life are counterpointed by praise for Magyar heroism. Reproductions of engravings of the siege show that Sziget really was a series of islands. Copies of the epic *Szózat* (Appeal) are on display, penned by Zrínyi's grandson, himself a general. A cry for liberty and a call for endurance, this seventeenth-century poem was adapted as a chorale by Kodály in 1956. Its single performance at the Budapest Academy turned into an emotional symbolic protest against the Rákosi regime. Chanting crowds took up the refrain, *Ne Bántsd a Magyart!* ("Let the Magyars alone!"), causing government members to walk out.

The museum is now linked to a **mosque** (Szulejmán Szultán Dzsámija) immediately on its north side; built after the castle's capture, its minaret has been decapitated but the interior survives, complete with ornamental grilles, Koranic inscriptions and frescoes depicting the deaths of Zrínyi and Süleyman (added later by the Hungarians). At no time, however, was the sultan buried here – though his viscera once reposed in another mosque nearby (see below).

The Hungarian-Turkish Friendship Park

One of those ideas that appeal to politicians but leave the public cold, the **Hungarian-Turkish Friendship Park** (Magyar-Török Barátság Emlékpark) was opened in 1994 by Turkey's prime minister, as a token apology and symbol of reconciliation. While a memorial to Süleyman on the spot where his tent once stood (and he presumably expired) was acceptable, local people objected to a larger-than-life statue of the sultan until the Turks commissioned one of Zrínyi, whereupon it was agreed to place them side by side rather than confronting one another.

For the record, Süleyman's heart and innards were buried in a **mosque** built nearby shortly after his death, and taken back to Constantinople when campaigning ceased. After the Turks were finally driven out, the mosque was turned into a church, though its past was acknowledged by a plaque.

The park is 3km north of Szigetvár on the left-hand side of the road to Kaposvár, so it's easily accessible by bus, while the mosque, which is 3km east down a dead-end road, is served only by the eight daily buses to Zsibót (far fewer at weekends).

Practicalities

Szigetvár's **bus** and **train stations** are about 500m down Rákóczi utca from the main square, Zrínyi tér. There's a **tourist office** in the Cultural Centre (Mon–Fri 9am–5pm, Sat 9am–2pm). For comfort, price and location, by far the best place to **stay** is the new and very smart *Szeráj Panzió* at Kossuth tér 3 (☎73/414-145, ⓦwww.szerajpanzio.hu; ❹). The three other places are much of a muchness: the *Kumilla Hotel* at Olay Lajos utca 6, behind the Makovecz building (☎73/510-248, ⓦwww.hotelkumilla.hu; ❹), is just about the best, with a sauna and free use of the **thermal baths** 150m away at Tinódi Sebestyén utca 23 (Gyógy Fürdő; daily 8.30am–7pm daily; 2250Ft, 1500Ft after 2pm, or outdoor pools 1500/1050Ft; sauna, jacuzzi 600Ft/475Ft extra); the *Hotel Oroszlán* at Zrínyi tér 2 (☎73/310-116, Ⓔmexbor@t-online.hu; ❸), whose rooms are better than the grim building and welcome suggest; and *Lenzls Panzió*, at József Attila utca 63 (☎73/413-045, ⓦwww.lenzls.de; ❹), which has fairly cluttered rooms but is otherwise fine. There's hostel accommodation from September to mid-June at the *Zrinyi Miklós Gimnázium és Kollégium*, Szent István Lakótelep 3 (☎73/312-927; dorm bed 1800Ft), and **camping** from May to September at the nearby *Thermal Motel & Camping* (☎73/510-147, Ⓔszviz @szigetviz.hu). There's the better, Dutch-run *Camping Idyll* (☎73/546-612, ⓦwww.campingidyll.hu) off the road to Pécs – head east for 10km then go 3km north to Nagyváty.

The *Szeráj Panzió* also has the best **restaurant** in town (closed Sun), or, beyond the *Lenzl Panzió* on József Attila utca, which offers Bavarian food and beer, there's the *Kisváros*, at no. 81, and the *Flórián*, opposite at no. 58 – both serve stock Hungarian fare. The **post office** is at József Attila utca 27–31 (Mon–Fri 8am–5pm, Sat 8–11am).

Pécs and the Mecsek Hills

After Budapest, **PÉCS** (pronounced "paych"), 65km southeast of Kaposvár, is probably the finest town in Hungary. Its red-and-orange-tiled rooftops nestle against the slopes of the Mecsek Hills, and the sprawling Communist-era housing estates can easily be forgotten once you are inside the old town. Pécs has a reputation for art and culture, boasting many excellent art galleries and museums, some fine examples of Islamic architecture, and the biggest market in western Hungary. Furthermore, it has one of the most diverse festival programmes in the country. As Transdanubia's leading centre of education, its population of 160,000 includes a high proportion of students, giving Pécs a youthful profile. The city is overlooked by the **Mecsek Hills**, where the Turks planted fig trees that still flourish, and where, until recently, uranium was mined.

Though prehistoric settlements existed here, the first town was Sopianae, settled first by the Celts and later by the Romans, who raised it to be the capital of the new province of Pannonia Valeria. Made an episcopal see by King Stephen, the town, known as Quinque Ecclesiae or Fünfkirchen (Five Churches), became a university centre in the Middle Ages. Under Turkish occupation (1543–1686) its character changed radically, its Magyar/German population being replaced by Turks and their Balkan subjects. Devastated during its "liberation", the city slowly recovered, thanks to viticulture and the discovery of coal in the mid-eighteenth century, although both the coal and uranium mines are now closed.

Arrival and information

From the **train station** on Indóház tér, it's not far to the centre, reached by buses #30, #32 and #33. From the **bus station** on Zólyom utca you can walk to Széchenyi tér in ten minutes. Most city buses pass on one side or the other of the Árkád mall, which is effectively the main interchange; tickets cost 300Ft. The motorway from Budapest will open in 2009 or 2010.Pécs's **airport** is 9km south on the Harkány road; cars can be rented from Hertz here (⊕072/526-667; Mon–Fri 8am–5pm, Sat & Sun by arrangement). Mistral Intercity Airport Shuttle (⊕72/570-186, ⓦwww .mistral-minibus.hu) operates minibuses to Pécs, Budapest and Balaton airports.

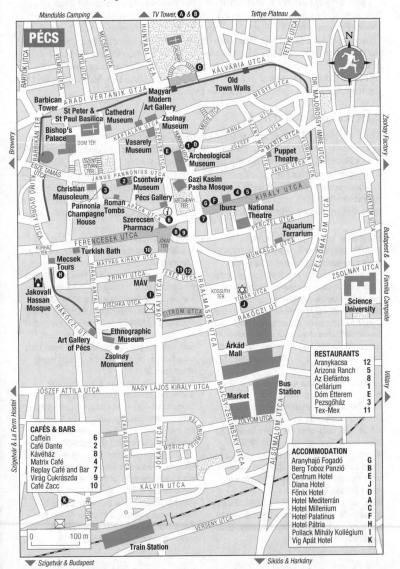

At Széchenyi tér 9 – marked by spectacular Zsolnay tiles – the large and very busy Tourinform office (May to mid-Oct Mon–Fri 8am–5.30pm, mid-June to Sept also Sat 9am–2pm; mid-Oct to April Mon–Fri 8am–4pm; ☎72/213-315, ⊛www.visitpecs.hu) has a staggering amount of **information** to hand, and although it doesn't make bookings it can arm you with a comprehensive list of all accommodation in the region. You can also leave luggage here. There's very cheap **internet access** in the same office (same times). A separate office next door at Széchenyi tér 7 (Mon–Fri 2–6pm, Sat & Sun 10am–8pm) gives out information on Pécs's year as **European Capital of Culture** in 2010.

There are **post offices** at Jókai Mór utca 10 (Mon–Fri 7am–7pm, Sat 8am–noon); just west of the train station (Mon–Fri 8am–7pm, Sat 8am–noon); in the Árkád mall (Mon–Fri 8am–7pm, Sat 8am–3pm); and at Pécs Plaza, Megyeri utca 76 (Mon–Fri 10am–8pm, Sat 10am–7pm, Sun 10am–2pm). The MAV office at the corner of Jókai utca and Zrinyi utca (Mon–Fri 8.30am–5pm) can provide information and make reservations for trains, and sells daily bus passes. With so many museums to choose from you'd do well to invest in a **day ticket** (*napijegy*; 2100Ft), which admits you to the majority of them; these are available from any museum.

Accommodation

There are plentiful **hotels** and **pensions** in town, in addition to stacks of cheap beds in the many college halls of residence (see opposite); some are open at weekends throughout term time, others only in the summer vacation (late June to late Aug). These can be approached directly or booked through Ibusz at Király utca 11 (Mon–Fri 9am–6pm, Sat 9am–1pm; ☎72/212-157, ⓔpecs@ibusz.hu). Ibusz can also book **private rooms** (❷), as can Mecsek Tours at Ferencesek utca 41, around the corner towards the mosque (Mon–Fri 8am–4pm; ☎72/513-306, ⓔutir@mecsektours.hu).

Hotels and pensions

Aranyhajó Fogadó Király utca 3 ☎72/310-263, ⊛www.aranyhajo.hu. In a listed building, the "Golden Ship" claims to be one of Hungary's oldest hotels, and although the rooms are a little dated they retain a certain character. ❺

Berg Toboz Panzió Fenyves sor 5 ☎72/510-555, ⊛www.tobozpanzio.hu. A quiet pension high above the city, with views of the woods and small comfy rooms with minibar and TV. Take bus #34 or #35 from the train station or the Barbakán to the Kikelet stop. ❺

Centrum Hotel Szepesy Ignác utca 4 ☎&ⓕ72/311-707. This ageing hotel has glum, old-fashioned rooms, though its price and location compensate somewhat. You could also try next door at no. 6, which often has beds advertised. ❷

Diana Hotel Timár utca 4a ☎72/328-954, ⊛www.hoteldiana.hu. Sweet, pension-type place opposite the synagogue with appealing a/c rooms with fridge and shower, but avoid those facing noisy Rákócziút. ❺

Főnix Hotel Hunyadi út 2 ☎72/311-680, ⊛www .fonixhotel.hu. Rooms with and without shower in this reasonably modern, if a little colourless, place just off Széchenyi tér. ❺

Hotel Mediterrán Hidegvölgyi utca 1 ☎72/514-119, ⊛www.mediterranhotel.hu. An ex-hostel gone upmarket, with comfortable rooms, and a view of the hills dominated by a quarry; take bus #35 from the train station or the Barbakán to the end of the line, and follow signs downhill for 300m. ❺

Hotel Millennium Kálvária utca 58 ☎72/512-222, ⊛www.hotelmillennium.hu. A modern hotel on the south side of Calvary Hill, just beyond the town walls (with free parking); the rooms are immaculate, while those on the top floor offer splendid views across town. ❼

Hotel Palatinus Király utca 5 ☎72/889-400, ⊛www.danubiusgroup.com/palatinus. Renovated Secession pile right in the centre, with a magnificent lobby but rather ordinary rooms, though some are a/c; there's wi-fi in the business centre. ❼–❽

Hotel Pátria Rákóczi út 3 ☎72/889-500, ⊛www .danubiusgroup.com/patria. Sister hotel of the *Palatinus*, with a mix of older and newer rooms; it's worth paying the extra for the latter, with tea- and coffee-making facilities. ❼

Víg Apát Hotel Mártirok utca 14 ☎72/313-340, ⊛www.vigapathotel.hu. Just 200m west of the train station, this well-run hotel has colourful, refreshing rooms and good service. ❹

Campsites, hostels and colleges

Familia Camping Gyöngyösi utca 6 ⓣ72/327-034. This year-round campsite, in an orchard 2km east of the centre, also has rooms (②). Take bus #2/2A or #21 from Árkád; #31 or #43 from the train station; or #60 from the bus station, as far as the Gyárváros church – from here it's a short walk north, behind the Lidl store (7am–9pm), good for breakfast provisions.

Hunyadi Mátyás Kollégium Széchenyi tér 11 ⓣ72/310-875. A boys' hall of residence run by Cistercian monks. Open all summer and weekends during term time. ❶

JPTE Kollégium Damjanich utca 30 ⓣ72/310-055. University hall of residence with four-bed rooms. Open June–Aug. ❶

Kodály Zoltán Kollégium Kodály Zoltán utca 20A ⓣ72/326-968. College hostel located 500m west of the basilica. Open July & Aug. ❶

Laterum Hotel/Youth Hostel Hajnóczy utca 37 ⓣ72/252-113, ⓦ www.laterum.hu. A decently revamped workers' hostel opposite the Uránváros bus terminal, a few kilometres west on the road to Szigetvár; take bus #2/2A, #4, #24 or #27. Open all year. ❹

Mandulás Camping Ángyán János utca 2 ⓣ72/515-655, ⓕ515-657. Campsite in the woods below the TV tower. Rooms with showers and toilets (②–③). Bus #34 from the train station or the Barbakán stops outside. Open mid-April to mid-Oct.

Pollack Mihály Kollégium Jókai Mór utca 8 ⓣ72/315-846. Brilliantly located college close to the main post office. Open all summer and weekends during term time. ❶

Szántó Kovács János Kollégium Szántó Kovács János utca 1C ⓣ72/251-462, ⓦ www .pannonlargo.hu. The largest college hostel in town, with three- to five-bed rooms with private showers available all year, also two-bed rooms with shared bathrooms in July/Aug; entry from Stadion utca, just off Route 6 to the west. ❶

Around the Belváros

Most of Pécs' sights lie within the historic **Belváros**, encircled by a road marking the extent of the medieval town walls, and centred on Széchenyi tér. Passing Kossuth tér en route to the centre, don't miss one of the city's finest monuments, an elegant **synagogue** built in 1865 (Zsinagóga; May–Sept Mon–Fri & Sun 10am–5pm; 300Ft). Its carved and stuccoed interior is beautiful but haunting, emptied by the murder of over four thousand Jews now listed in a Book of Remembrance – ten times the number living in Pécs today. Thanks to local efforts, state support and contributions from abroad, this was one of the first synagogues in Hungary to be restored, in the 1980s.

Further uphill, as Irgalmasok utcája nears Széchenyi tér, you'll spot the **Zsolnay Fountain** in front of a church to your right; the bulls' heads on the fountain are modelled on a gold drinking vessel from the "Treasure of Attila".

Before entering Széchenyi tér, take a look at pedestrianized **Király utca**, traditionally the *korzó* where townsfolk promenade. Among the buildings worth noting here are the Art Nouveau **Hotel Palatinus**; the **Nendtvich House** at no. 8, with its ceramic ornamentation; the **National Theatre**, surmounted by a statue of Genius; and the **Vasváry House** at no. 19, with its allegorical figurines.

Széchenyi tér

With its art galleries and tourist offices, modern-day **Széchenyi tér** is centuries removed from its Turkish predecessor, a dusty square crowded with "caravans of camels laden with merchandise from India and the Yemen". At its top end stands the Belváros church, with ornate window grilles and scalloped niches that denote its origins as the **Mosque of Gazi Kasim Pasha** (Belvárosi templom; April 15–Oct 15 Mon–Sat 10am–4pm, Sun 11.30am–4pm; Oct 16–April 14 Mon–Sat 10am–noon, Sun 11.30am–2pm; donations acccepted), which the Turks built from the stones of a medieval Gothic church. The dome was painted in 1883 and an extension was added on the north side (with a fine organ) in 1939, but otherwise the mosque is unspoilt, its vaulted interior and Islamic prayer niche (*mihrab*) decorated with Arabic calligraphy.

Behind the mosque on the north side of the square, the **Archeological Museum** (Régészeti Múzeum; May–April Tues–Sun 10am–4pm; Nov–March Tues–Sat 10am–3pm; 450Ft) covers the history of the region from Neolithic times to the Magyar conquest, but pales in comparison to the real Roman tombs a few streets over on Apáca utca (see p.300). Heading down the square, you'll find a selection of contemporary artwork in the **Pécs Gallery** at no. 10 (Mon & Wed–Sat noon–6pm, Sun noon–6pm; 300Ft) – it's worth a quick look in case there's anything remarkable, but with so many art collections in Pécs it pays to be selective.

A few paces further down, just past the Tourinform office at Apáca utca 1, look into the nineteenth-century **Szerecsen Pharmacy** (Múzeumpatika; Mon–Fri 9am–6pm, Sat 9am–1pm; free), whose gorgeous wood-carved furnishings are inlaid with ceramic tiles from the Zsolnay factory, which is where the drinking fountain with the sculpture of the Black Saracen was also made. At this point, you have the option of three routes to the basilica – along Káptalan, Janus Pannonius or Apáca utca – via a clutch of museums.

Káptalan utca

Káptalan utca has no fewer than five museums virtually next to each other. The **Zsolnay Museum** at no. 2 (Zsolnay Kerámia Kiállítás; Tues–Sun: April–Oct Mon–Sat 10am–6pm, closes 4pm Sun; Nov–March 10am–4pm; 900Ft) is a must for its vases, plaques and figurines from the Zsolnay Porcelain Factory, founded in 1853 by Vilmos Zsolnay and the chemist Vince Wartrha, the inventor of the iridescent eosin glaze (see box below). Some pieces are exquisite, others totally kitsch. In the basement are sculptures by Amerigo Tot, whose *Erdély Family* with its clamped grave-posts symbolizes the plight of the ethnic Hungarians of Romania. This is the oldest known dwelling in Pécs, built by 1324, and the niche seats in the gateway date from the fourteenth century. The "Zsolnay Cultural Quarter" is to be the heart of Pécs's offerings as European Capital of Culture in 2010; the museums and gardens of Káptalan utca are to be renovated, with an open-air theatre, and the Zsolnay factory, east of the city centre, will also be refurbished for cultural activities.

Across the road at no. 3, the **Vasarely Museum** (Tues–Sun: May–Oct 10am–6pm, closes 4pm Sun; Nov–April 10am–4pm; 900Ft) exhibits lurid Op-Art canvases by Viktor Vasarely, who was born in this house in 1908, but made his name in Paris and

Zsolnay

The Zsolnay Porcelain Factory was founded in 1853 by Miklós Zsolnay, succeeded by his son Vilmos, who in 1886 introduced the frost-resistant ornamental **pyrogranite tiles** that were widely used by Secession architects such as Miklós Ybl and Ödön Lechner in buildings including the Matthias Church, the Hungarian Parliament, the Museum of Applied Art, the Covered Market, the Geological Institute and the Gellért Baths, all in Budapest, and the **post office** here on Jókai utca. This was followed in 1893 by the distinctively iridescent **eosin glaze**, which became a great favourite of artists such as József Rippl Rónay.

The company was very successful until World War I, when it was converted to producing insulators and then tableware; it was nationalized in 1948, but regained its independence, and the Zsolnay name, in 1982; privately owned since 1991, it is once again very successful, and the factory, east of the city centre at Zsolnay utca 37, is busy again. You can see, and buy, the company's wares at the **Zsolnay Márkábolt shops** at the factory (Mon–Fri 7.30am–3.30pm, Sat 9am–1pm; ☎72/313-636, ⓦwww.zsolnay.hu), and also at Jókai tér 4 (Mon–Fri 9am–5.30pm, Sat 9am–1pm). There are also **tours**, in English or German (Mon–Fri 9am–noon, or by appointment on ☎72/507-652).

New York. In the same building, the **Central Museum of Mining in Mecsek** (Mecseki Bányászati Kiállitások; Tues–Sun: April–Oct 10am–6pm; Nov–March 10am–4pm; 600Ft) includes an underground replica mine. The **Magyar Modern Art Gallery**, next door to the Zsolnay Museum at no. 4 (Modern Magyar Képtár; Tues–Sun: May–Oct 10am–6pm, closes at 4pm Sun; Nov–April 10am–4pm; 600Ft), presents a *tour d'horizon* of Hungarian art since the School of Szentendre (1890–1955), with sections devoted to constructivist evocations of proletarian struggle by Béla Uitz (1887–1972), who lived for fifty years in the Soviet Union, and abstract works by Ferenc Martyn (1899–1986), whose great-grandfather emigrated from Ireland to Hungary by 1804. Outside are striking sculptures by Péter Székely (1923–2001); the separate museums devoted to Martyn and Székely (who both spent their careers in Paris) are now closed. At no. 5 (Tues–Fri: May–Oct 10am–4pm; Nov–April 10am–3pm; 450Ft, tickets from the Magyar Modern Art Gallery) is a curious exhibit by Erzsébet Schaár (1908–75); entitled *Utca* ("Street"), this enormous sculpted piece of work, featuring a series of delineating walls with rigid, haunting figures peering through doors and windows, is widely regarded as her finest work.

The Csontváry Museum

If you only visit one place in Pécs, make it the **Csontváry Museum** at Janus Pannonius utca 11–13 (Tues–Sat 10am–6pm, Sun 10am–4pm; 900Ft). Kosztka Tivadar Csontváry (1853–1919) was born in Slovakia in the same year as Van Gogh, and his artistic career was similarly affected by madness and the pursuit of "the path of the sun". His fascination with Hebrew lore and the Holy Land was expressed in huge canvases – *Baalbek*, *Mary's Well at Nazareth* and *Pilgrimage* – while his hallucinatory vision of nature produced *Tatra*, *Storm on the Great Hortobágy* and *Solitary Cedar*. One of his most poignant pieces of work is *Híd Mostárban* (1903), a gorgeous, richly coloured painting of the elegant Mostar Bridge in Bosnia – destroyed during the Bosnian war in 1993 and since rebuilt. By 1910, his psychosis had well and truly set in, as evinced by the series of schizoid drawings and sketches in the last room.

After his death, these works came close to being sold as canvas, but at the last moment were purchased by an architect. When Picasso later saw an exhibition of Csontváry's work in Paris, he supposedly described him as the "other great painter in our century besides me", and later told Chagall, "There you are, old master, I bet even you could not paint something like this" – though it's hard to believe he wasn't being ironic.

Dóm tér and around

Looming to the north on the large, cobbled main square is the huge, four-towered **St Peter and St Paul Basilica** (Székesegyház; April–Oct Mon–Sat 9am–5pm, Sun 1–5pm; Nov–March Mon–Sat 10am–4pm, Sun 1–4pm; 900Ft, tour 3000Ft), which has been endlessly rebuilt since the first basilica was founded here in the eleventh century. Though an eleventh-century crypt and fourteenth-century side chapels have been incorporated, its present incarnation (1882–91) is neo-Romanesque, replacing a Baroque design by Mihály Pollack. Its lavish blue and gold murals are by Lotz, Székely and other historicist painters of the 1890s.

The neo-Renaissance **Bishop's Palace** (Püspöki Palota; June–Sept Thurs only, 1hr tour 2pm, 3pm & 4pm; 1800Ft) to the west of the square is embellished with a modern statue of Liszt waving from a balcony, which might have amused its former bishops, Janus Pannonius, also a humanist poet, and György Klimó, founder of its library, who told borrowers: "You don't have to pay for anything. Depart enriched. Return more frequently." Around the corner to the south, a circular **barbican tower** punctuates the old town walls, giving access to Klimó György utca. Just off the north-western corner of the basilica, the remains of the **first Hungarian university** (founded in 1367) and its chapel (1355), containing the tomb of Bishop William, the first chancellor of the university, are now being reconstructed. Continuing west from here, you'll exit through the city walls north of the barbican.

At the eastern end of the basilica a modern building houses the **Cathedral Museum** (Dommúzeum; April–Oct daily 10am–5pm; Nov–March Tues–Sat 10am–4pm; 300/380Ft), home to the cathedral's miscellaneous treasures. Beneath Szent István tér, the lower, park-like extension of Dóm tér, and the surrounding buildings, are various ancient burial chambers, now collectively known as the **Sopianae Early Christian Cemetery World Heritage Site** (Tues–Sun: May–Oct 10am–6pm; Nov–April 10am–4pm; ⓦwww.pecsorokseg.hu; 1200/1600Ft). In all there are sixteen chambers and several hundred tombs; just in 2000 a unique octagonal burial chamber was discovered. The fourth-century **Early Christian Mausoleum** (Ókeresztény Mauzoleum), found under the square in 1975 during the demolition of a fountain, is now visible through a reinforced glass floor; it's decorated with frescoes of the Fall, Daniel in the Lions' Den and a scene of Adam and Eve. It also contains a white marble sarcophagus dating from the third century and some skeletal remains. The **Peter-Paul burial chamber**, on the east side of the square, under the steps to the building facing the Bishop's Palace, was discovered in 1782; it's decorated with biblical scenes featuring the eponymous saints. Also hidden away on the eastern side of the square is the so-called **Wine Pitcher Burial Chamber** (Korsos Sirkamra), with its almost complete fresco of a jug – perhaps the Holy Sacrament – hidden in a small niche.

The necropolis of Sopianae lay more or less beneath Apáca utca (Nun Street), southeast from Szent István tér, where several other tombs decorated with scenes of the Gates of Paradise have been excavated in the courtyard of no. 8. After the Romans went home and waves of migrating tribes swept across Hungary, the tombs were used as refuges and modified accordingly. At no. 14 are the remains of an **Early Christian Burial Chapel** (Témetőkápolna Okeresztény), likewise dating from the third or fourth century AD.

Around the periphery

From the barbican tower, just off Dóm tér, you can head uphill and on to Aradi Vértanuk utca to a section of the **old town walls**, a massive crenellated rampart 5500 paces long, buttressed by 87 bastions, that was erected after the Mongol invasion of the thirteenth century. Above the tunnel, 300m along, is a small garden with a small **Calvary Chapel**, offering a fine view south over the Belváros; built in 1812–17, this was one of the earliest Neoclassical round churches in Hungary.

Alternatively, head downhill around the peripheral boulevard – henceforth Rákóczi út – to find the inconspicuous **Jakovali Hassan Mosque** (Jakováli Haszán Dzsámija; April–Sept Wed–Sun 9.30am–5.30pm; 600Ft). Unlike its counterparts at Szigetvár (see p.293) and Eger (see p.339), this sixteenth-century mosque is still intact (though its minaret is closed), bearing traces of friezes and arabesque carving. The attractive *minbar* pulpit and kilims adorning its cool white interior are gifts from the Turkish Ministry of Culture. Around the corner on Ferencesek utca, you can see the ruins of a Turkish bath outside the *Minaret* restaurant.

At Rákóczi út 15, a small **Ethnographic Museum** (Néprajzi Kiállitás; May–Oct Tues–Sat 10am–4pm; Nov–April Mon–Fri 11am–3pm; 450Ft) contains numerous folk costumes, ceramic vases and other household goods from the Baranya region, as well as a great set of masks, such as those worn at Mohács during the Busójárás Carnival. A few doors along at Rákóczi út 11 a beautifully restored town house is home to the **Art Gallery of Pécs** (Városi Képtár Pécs; Tues–Sun 10am–6pm; 600Ft), showing temporary shows and a collection mostly of Hungarian postimpressionists. On the way back to the centre you can see the surprisingly dull

Zsolnay Monument, with an image of the factory's founder gazing benevolently over the junction with Szabadság utca; and the Romantic-style **post office** on Jókai utca, roofed with Zsolnay tiles. After digesting all these fine museums you may wish to turn your gaze to something more relaxing, in which case you should head for the **Aquarium-Terrarium** at Munkácsy utca 31 (daily: May–Sept 9am–6pm; Oct–April 9am–5pm; 1050Ft), whose sticky cellars house a colourful and substantial display of reptiles and fish.

Out of the centre

For a fresh perspective on Pécs, catch bus #33 from Kossuth tér up to the **Tettye plateau**, 2km from the centre, where a ruined sixteenth-century palace, later used as a Dervish monastery, stands in a park. Higher up and a further kilometre away, **Misina Hill** (534m) is crowned by a **TV tower** with an observation platform (TV Torony; daily 9am–7pm; 600Ft), and a café with a retro 1970s ambience, accessible by bus #35 from the train station and the Barbakán; after 5.30pm you'll need a taxi back to town. Should you care to walk back from the plateau, the Niké szobor is a Soviet war memorial just below the Kőbánya bus stop, with fine views and a picnic area amid pine woods, and Havihegyi utca offers a succession of views as it winds around the hillside, with several picturesque backstreets slinking down past the **All Saints' Church**, whose pastor supplements his income by selling poultry.

All kinds of livestock and farming paraphernalia appear at the monthly **Pécs Market**, a huge country fair held 3km southwest of the Belváros on the first Sunday of each month; take bus #3 or #50 from outside the Konzum store on Rákóczi út and ask to be dropped off at the Vásártér market on Megyeri út. On other Sundays, there's a lively flea market on the same site. The main food market by the bus station is open Monday to Friday from 5am to 5pm, and on Saturdays from 5am to 2pm.

Eating and drinking

Pécs is one of the most sociable cities in Hungary, and with its tremendous array of fine **restaurants**, **cafés** and **bars** to choose from, you're almost guaranteed a good night out.

Restaurants

Aranykacsa Teréz utca 4. The upscale "Golden Duck" has goose, duck and turkey as the mainstays of its menu, plus good set menus (including cheaper vegetarian versions). Expensive. Closed Mon & from 3.30pm Sun.

Arizona Ranch Király utca 21. Better than average American steak house, with a super grill garden; the only place to come for a cooked breakfast (until 11am).

Az Elefántos Jókai tér 6. Informally stylish, and reasonably priced, pizzeria restaurant, with a particularly good selection of pasta dishes.

Cellárium Hunyadi út 2. Vast cellar restaurant under the *Főnix Hotel*; the menu – written like a newspaper – takes some digesting, but once

you've got past that, you'll enjoy the food and the atmosphere. Live music at weekends. Closed Sun.

Dóm Étterem Király utca 3. You can choose to eat in the magnificently decorated section to the rear, or the cosy, vaulted section at the front; specialities include terrific fish and venison as well as pizza, and it's the best place in town for vegetarians.

Pezsgőház Szent István tér 12. Easily the classiest outfit in town, this beautifully lit, vaulted cellar offers an international menu of the highest quality, and a fine champagne and wine list. Closes 3pm Sun.

Tex-Mex Teréz utca 10. Decent Mexican just along from the *Aranykacsa*, with the requisite enchiladas, burritos and tacos; it's rather a party-oriented place, with lots of daily deals on cocktails. Tues–Sat 5–11pm.

Cafés, bars and cellars

With stacks of places to **drink** you'll have little problem in tracking down a place to suit you. Two of the most popular places for an evening beverage are the hip *Caffein* at Széchenyi tér 9, and the hectic *Replay Café and Bar* at Király utca 4 – both also offer a decent food menu, although the *Replay* is more burger-oriented. A couple of more low-key, but more characterful, places are the splendidly relaxed *Café Dante*, in the same building as the Csontváry Museum at Janus Pannonius utca 11, which has wi-fi plus live jazz on Friday and Saturday evenings; and *Café Zacc*, at Mátyás Király utca 2, a lovely, contemplative drinking hole offering teas, cocktails and beers.

For location and range of coffees, the classy, relaxing and no-smoking *Kávézó Az Elefántos* restaurant on Jókai tér has no peers, although the *Virág Cukrászda*, on the peaceful Csészényi tér, does offer irresistible cakes. An excellent café offering **internet access**, including wi-fi, is the cool, orange-walled *Matrix Café*, in a courtyard at Király utca 15 (closed Sun morning).

The **Pécs Brewery** (Pécsi Sörfőzde; ⓦwww.pecsisor.hu), just off Rókusalja utca, produces some of Hungary's best beers – Szalonsör, Gilde, Goldfassl and the brown version of Szalon. As the brewery doesn't run tours, the *Rókus* beer cellar at Rókusalja utca 15 or the homely *Kiskorsó* restaurant on the same street at no. 3 are the nearest you can get to the source. One place that does run tours is the **Pannonia Champagne House** (Pannonia Pezsgőhaz; Mon–Sat noon–8pm) at Szent István tér 12, which has been producing sparkling wines since 1859; one-hour cellar tours, including tasting of five wines, are for groups only, but you should be hooked up if you call in advance (☎72/214-490; 1950Ft).

Entertainment and festivals

Pécs's **opera** and **ballet** companies are highly regarded, and tickets (1200–2400Ft) for performances at the National Theatre on Szinház tér, set back from Király utca, can be scarce – ask about cancellations at the box office, on the west side of the theatre, an hour before the show starts (Tues–Fri 10am–7pm, Sat & Sun 1hr before performance). Tickets for the **Pannon Philharmonic Orchestra** can be obtained from the box office just across from the theatre at Király utca 19 (Filharmónia Jegyiroda; ☎72/310-539, ⓦwww.pfz.hu; Mon–Thurs 9am–4pm, Fri 9am–3pm; open on performance days until the beginning of the performance). The Pécs Cultural Centre (Pécsi Kulturális Központ; Mon–Fri 8am–10pm; ☎72/336-622), at Széchenyi tér 1, is a source of information and tickets for cultural events all over the city. Throughout the year there are **concerts** in many of the city's churches, including organ concerts in the basilica. Pécs will be **European Capital of Culture** in 2010, and information is available now at Széchenyi tér 7 (Mon–Fri 2–6pm, Sat & Sun 10am–8pm).

For children (and adults), the Bóbita **puppet theatre** is at Mária utca 18. **Films** are shown at Uránia Mozi, Hungária utca 19; and Cinema City Pécs Plaza, Megyeri utca 76 (ⓦwww.pecsplaza.net).

The highlights of a packed festival programme are the **Spring Festival**, a two-week programme of classical concerts, dance and film from mid- to late March (ⓦwww.pecsitavaszifesztival.hu); and the **Pécs Weeks of Art and Gastronomy** in mid-June and early July, three weeks of joyously eclectic open-air musical, theatrical and literary events – essentially mini-festivals such as the International Romany Music Festival, the International Adult Puppet Festival and Festival of Fine Arts. In addition, many of the town's restaurants have tasting sessions on the main squares. The **Wine–Song Festival** in September incorporates a male-voice choir festival and a wine procession.

The Mecsek Hills

The karstic **Mecsek Hills** north of Pécs offer panoramic views and trails fanning out from the television tower through groves of sweet chestnuts and almond trees.

If you fancy some **hiking**, buy a 1:40,000 map of the hills, available from most bookshops or tourist offices in town. Alternatively, you can catch a bus from the regional terminal (every 1hr–1hr 30min; also picking up at the *Víg Apát Hotel* and the Uránvárós bus terminal) out to Orfű or Abaliget, two popular resorts forty minutes' ride from town, where **accommodation** can be pre-booked through Mecsek Tours in Pécs (see p.296).

The widely dispersed village of **ORFŰ**, 16km northwest of Pécs, features four artificial **lakes** surrounded by sports facilities, restaurants and accommodation, with an antique **mill** (Malommúzeum; Tues–Sun May–Sept 10am–5pm; Oct–April by appointment; Ⓦ www.orfuivizimalom.hu; 600Ft) in the Szolohegy quarter, to the east of Kis-tó, the smallest lake. The complex actually comprises two mills – a horse-driven mill and oil press, and a watermill, both built in the nineteenth century and closed by 1950, and renovated in the 1970s. On the main road nearby, there's a pool and climbing wall at the *Kis-tó Strand & Étterem*. At Széchenyi tér 12, the main square in the Mecsekrákos quarter, at the southeastern corner of the largest lake, Pécsi-tó, there's an open-air folk museum with kilns, dovecotes and beehives, alongside a nice little church with the priest's quarters at the east end. **Information** can be obtained from the small Tourinform office in the town hall block at Széchenyi tér 1 (Mon–Fri 8am–5pm; Ⓣ 72/598-116, Ⓔ orfu@tourinform.hu). There's loads of **accommodation** in Orfű, including private rooms, mostly in Szolohegy, and pensions clustered around Széchenyi tér; three good ones are the very comfortable *Árkádos Panzió*, by the bus stop at no. 4 (Ⓣ 72/598-020, Ⓦ www.arkados.hu; ❹); the similar *Atrium Panzió* at no. 17 (Ⓣ 72/498-288, Ⓔ orfupanzio@t-online.hu; ❹), with sauna, table-tennis, restaurant, bar and an ATM; and the *Molnár Panzió*, at no. 18 (Ⓣ 72/498-363, Ⓦ www.molnarpanzio.hu; ❷). There's also the large *Panoráma* **campsite**, 1km up the west shore of Pécsi-tó at Dollár utca 1 (Ⓣ 72/378-501, Ⓦ www.panoramacamping.hu; May–Oct), with bungalows with baths (❸), and bikes and windsurfing boards for rent. Across the road are swimming pools with waterslides. The best **restaurant** in the resort is the *Muskátli*, at Széchenyi tér 13 (daily 11.30am–10pm). Various **hiking trails** lead northeast through the Mecsek hills to the much larger town of Komló, from where buses head back to Pécs at least every half-hour.

The larger settlement of **ABALIGET**, a few kilometres further west and 18km from Pécs, has an outdoor **thermal pool** and a 640-metre-long **stalactite cave** (Cseppkő barlang; Tues–Sun: April–Sept 9am–6pm; Oct–March 10am–3pm; 900Ft) beside a lake with a newly repaved path around it plus pedaloes and rowing boats. The cave, whose main branch was discovered in 1819, has relatively few stalactites and stalagmites but does have a series of interesting rock formations, due largely to the active brook within and frequent flooding. The cave is inhabited by blind crabs and also in winter by a large colony of greater horseshoe bats, one of three species that can be found in the Western Mecsek region – there's a curious little exhibition on bats, including lots of dead ones, in the **Bat Museum** (Denevér Múzeum; same times; 450Ft), in the chalet just across from the cave. Should you wish to stay, try the *Hotel Abaliget* (Ⓣ 30/994-3790, Ⓔ hotelabaliget@freemail.hu; ❹), by the car park 300m from the cave; the adjacent *Abaliget Barlang* campsite (Ⓣ 72/517-700, Ⓕ 327-928; mid-April to mid-Oct), with a pension (❸), a motel (❷), chalets (❷) and a restaurant; the *Cseppkő Panzió* at Kossuth utca 107A (Ⓣ 72/498-636; ❷) right at the junction to the cave; or one of the other **rooms** for rent on Kossuth utca.

Harkány, Villány and Siklós

The area south of Pécs offers several attractions. Those in search of a therapeutic wallow in yet another thermal bath should visit **Harkány**, but perhaps a greater draw is the thirty-kilometre-long **Villány-Siklós wine road**, Hungary's first wine route. **Siklós**, a short ride east of Harkány and Hungary's southernmost town, is the white-wine centre of the region and also boasts a fabulous fifteenth-century castle. **Villány** is an absolute must for the wine aficionado, with its extensive vineyards and cellars producing some of the country's finest red wines.

Harkány

Twenty-five kilometres south of Pécs, **HARKÁNY**'s main draws are its enormous open-air **thermal baths** (Gyógyfürdő; daily 9am–6pm; 2700Ft, after 2pm 1890Ft) and outdoor **pools** (Strandfürdő; June–Aug daily 9am–10pm; Sept–May Mon–Thurs & Sun 9am–6pm, Fri & Sat 9am–8pm; 1290Ft, after 2pm 900Ft; Ⓦ www.harkanyfurdo.hu), with a section for wallowing in **hot mud**, therapeutically rich in sulphur and fluoride. The open-air *strand* can be entered from Kossuth utca, the main thoroughfare, to the west or Bajcsy-Zsilinszky utca to the east, while the entrance to the indoor spa is on Zsigmond sétány on the south side of the compound, in the middle of town. Aside from this, there's little to visit except a small **market** near the bus station and an early nineteenth-century **Calvinist Church** at Kossuth utca 66.

The **bus station** is at the southern end of Bajcsy-Zsilinszky utca, beyond the baths. **Information** is available from Tourinform in the small cultural house at Kossuth utca 2 (June–Sept Mon–Fri 9am–6pm, Sat & Sun 9am–5pm; Oct–May Mon–Fri 9am–4pm; ☎72/479-624, Ⓔharkany@tourinform.hu), and **private rooms** (❷) can be arranged here or through Mecsek Tours at Bajcsy-Zsilinszky utca 2, by the pools' entrance (May–Sept Mon–Fri 8am–6.30pm, Sat 8.30am–noon; Oct–April Mon–Wed & Fri 8.30am–4.30pm, Thurs 8.30am–6.30pm; ☎72/480-322, Ⓔharkany@mecsektours.hu). Harkány is swarming with **hotels**, the best of

▲ Vineyard, Southern Transdanubia

which are on Kossuth utca, including the very classy *Xavin* at no. 43 (☎72/580-158, 🔘www.xavin.hu; ❺), with its own lovely indoor pool, jacuzzi and sauna, and the smaller but equally fine *Atrium*, 500m further along at no. 10 (☎72/580-880, 🔘www.atriumharkany.hu; ❹). More modestly, there's the *Kokó Panzió,* just off Kossuth utca at Arany János utca 7b (Easter to mid-Nov; ☎72/480-326, 🔘www.kokopanzio@hu; ❸–❹). Of the hotels by the baths, the only one of any real quality is the immaculately modernized Bauhaus-style *Korona* at Bajcsy-Zsilinszky utca 3 (☎72/480-049, 🔘www.harkanyhotelek.hu; ❻). The *Thermal* **campsite**, at the north end of Bajcsy-Zsilinszky utca (☎72/480-117, 🔘www.mecsektours.hu; mid-April to mid-Oct), also has a basic hotel (❷), motel (❶) and four-bed chalets (❸–❹). The excellent **restaurants** in the *Atrium*, *Xavin* and *Korona* hotels aside, there is a string of pizzerias and pubs along Kossuth utca and a good wine shop at no. 44 (Mon–Fri 10am–1pm & 2–6pm, Sat 10am–1pm). Across the main road from the bus station is a small lake lined by restaurants with waterside terraces. The **post office** is opposite the Calvinist church at Kossuth utca 57 (Mon–Fri 8am–4pm).

Siklós

From Harkány frequent buses continue 5km east across the dusty plain (with a parallel cycle track) to **SIKLÓS**, a compact town huddled around a medieval castle – the town's star attraction. It's also a favoured destination for shoppers from **Croatia**, where goods are much more expensive due to high tariffs and VAT; as a result the local market is a cornucopia of goods, and some shops advertise their wares in Croatian.

From the **bus station** on Szent István tér, follow the main street, Felszabadulás utca, past the post office on Flórián tér and on up to Kossuth tér just below the castle, which is located on Vajda János tér. Opposite the bright peach-coloured Baroque town hall on **Kossuth tér**, no. 12 was the **birthplace of George Mikes**, the émigré writer known for his parodies of British life in the 1960s. A couple of steps down the road to the east stands the sixteenth-century **Malkocs Bej Mosque** (Malkocs Bej dzsámija; mid-April to mid-Oct Tues–Sun 9am–noon & 2–6pm; mid-Oct to mid-April Sat & Sun 9am–4pm; 300Ft), recently restored and stuffed with Turkish carpets and other knick-knacks. Behind the houses facing the mosque is a Serbian Orthodox church, a standard-issue ochre Baroque structure, while there's a fifteenth-century Franciscan church near the castle car park, still largely Gothic, with old frescoes in the choir.

Siklós Castle (mid-April to mid-Oct daily 9am–6pm; mid-Oct to mid-April Tues–Sun 9am–4pm; 900Ft) remained in private hands from its foundation in the fifteenth century up until 1943, when it was confiscated by the state. Bastions and rondellas girdle an impressive platform on which now sits a mansion once occupied by the enlightened Casimir Batthyány, who freed his serfs in 1847, the year before serfdom was abolished. His tomb is in the Gothic chapel, located (with no sense of incongruity according to medieval values) within whipping distance of a dungeon filled with instruments of torture. Next to the dungeon, a small **museum** contains cabinets stuffed with gloves, fans and umbrellas, illustrating the period between the late eighteenth and early nineteenth centuries when these manufacturing industries were thriving – indeed, the factories of Pécs were renowned throughout Europe for the quality of their gloves. The museum cellar holds archeological remains and some rather large cannonballs. From the ramparts – where you'll also find a small coffee shop and rose garden – you can enjoy tremendous views of the adjacent Villány Hills. The **Castle Festival** takes place in the last weekend in June, with international brass bands performing in the courtyard as its highlight. You can return to the bus station and town by a gravel path around the rear of the castle and through the outer bailey.

Siklós's Tourinform office is at Felszabadulás utca 3 (Mon–Fri 8am–4pm; ☎72/579-090, ✉siklos@tourinform.hu), just a few steps away from the town's sole **hotel**, the run-down *Központi*, in a nice Secession building at Kossuth Lajos tér 5 (☎72/352-513, ⊛www.kozponti.hu; ❹), which also has a very ordinary **restaurant** and a cellar wine-bar. Hostel accommodation is available all year at the Kanizsai Dorottya Iskola Diákszálló, Iskola utca 25 (☎72/496-219, ✉szallas @kanizsai-iskola@sulinet.hu; ❶).

Alternatively, you can book a local **room** through Tourinform in Harkány (see p.304) or Pécs (see p.296). There's excellent strudel at the oddly named *Hamburger Cukrászda* by the entrance to the market at Felszabadulás utca 22 (daily 6am–6pm).

Villány

Fifteen kilometres east of Siklós, acres of vineyards lap the slopes of Szársomlyó hill (442m), producing red wine under the appellation Villányi. The village of **VILLÁNY** is of Swabian (German) origin, as you might guess from its neatness and uniformity, with pots of geraniums outside all the houses and everything signposted for the benefit of visitors.

Exiting left from the **train station**, walk for ten minutes past the new winery built by Budapest banker Sándor Csányi, who bought the state winery (founded in 1861 by the Teleki family, renowned for their Phylloxera-resistant hybrids). Taking the second turning to the right (following signs for Siklós), you're on the village's main street, Baross Gábor utca, passing almost at once a small Serbian Orthodox church behind which is the Wine Route **information centre** at Deák

The Villány-Siklós wine road

Running along the sunny southern slopes of the Villány Hills, the **Villány-Siklós wine road** was the first wine route to be set up in Hungary, in 1994. Named after the villages of Villány and Siklós, located 13km apart, the thirty-kilometre-long route winds past eleven settlements and vineyards, through one of the largest concentrations of cellars in the country. However, tasting takes place mainly in Villány, where wineries have outlets for tourists.

It is believed that wine making in the region started during Roman times and continued through the Middle Ages. The industry collapsed as the Ottoman Empire swept all before it, leaving many villages abandoned, but production quickly resumed following their retreat. From 1723 German colonists introduced the Kékfrankos grape, followed in the next century by the Tramina, Rizling and Oporto varieties. However, it is only since the end of Communism that the wider world has been alerted to the region's top-quality wines.

Thanks to its favourable geographical location and Mediterranean climate and soil, the region consistently yields a superb range of red and white wines. Generally speaking, white wines emanate from the more westerly district around Siklós, whilst the more famous reds are produced in Villány and surrounding vineyards.

Some local vintners, such as Attila Gere and József Bock (see opposite), are internationally renowned and have recently produced some of the country's most distinctive and finest reds. Villány's hotels and restaurants were among the first in Hungary to be privatized, creating a demand for good local wine. Most recently, an appelation scheme has been introduced, with labels bearing the letters DHC (Districtus Hungaricus Controllatus), in classic and premium categories.

Other tourist initiatives include the extension of the Danube cycle route south from Budapest to Croatia (by 2010) and the linked Three Rivers Cycle Route (Három Folyó Kerékpáros Túraútvonal; ⊛www.kerekparut.com/?q=en), following the Mura, Drava and Danube along the Croatian border from Austria to Mohács.

Ferenc utca 22 (Borút Iroda; Mon–Fri 8am–4pm; ☎72/492-181, ✉iroda@borut
.hu), which can advise on visiting cellars in the region. Just beyond, after the
town hall, bus stops and **post office** (Mon–Fri 8am–4pm), you'll find the **Wine
Museum**, at Bem József utca 8, just off Baross utca (Bormúzeum; Tues–Sun
9am–5pm; free). The local viticultural tradition goes back two thousand years,
though you won't find anything that ancient here; there are photos and photocopied documents on the ground floor, and barrels and equipment in the
200-year-old cellar, with German and English captions.

You can sample local **wine** at cellars on Diófás tér and beyond it on Baross Gábor
utca, and on Batthyány utca – the names to look out for are Gere and Bock (see
box, oppsite), whose wines have an international reputation; both charge around
1050Ft for three wines, 1800Ft for five wines, or 2400Ft for seven wines,
including snacks. Bock's are labelled *Jammertal* (German for "Valley of Lamenta-
tion"), after a battle in 1687 where the Turks were cut down in the Drava bogs.
Wine lovers should also investigate the Polgár, Blum and Tiffán cellars in
Villánykövesd, 2.5km to the right from Villány station.

The *Oportó Panzió* at Baross Gábor utca 33 (☎72/492-582, ⓦwww.oporto
.hu; ⑥) has first-class **rooms** with polished wooden flooring and pretty pictures
gracing the walls. Otherwise, there is the very comfortable, smoke-free *Gere
Panzió* at Diófás tér 4 (☎72/492-195, ⓦwww.gere.hu; ④), which has a lovely
Mediterranean-style garden and the finest **wine cellar** in the village; or the
Bock Panzió at Batthyány utca 15 (☎72/492-919, ⓦwww.bock.hu; ⑥), where
József Bock has his cellar. There are also many houses in the village advertising
beds (*falusi szálláshely*). The best **meals** in the village, featuring Swabian as well
as Hungarian cuisine, are served in these three pensions, and the *Júlia Vendéglő*
at Baross Gábor utca 41, while if you're heading towards Villánykövesd stop off
at the peaceful *Fülemüle Csárda*. In Villánykövesd itself, the tasteful *Hotel
Cabernet* stands by the station at Petőfi utca 29 (☎72/493-200, ⓦwww
.hotelcabernet.hu; ⑥).

Mohács

The small town of **MOHÁCS**, 41km east of Pécs by the River Danube, is a
synonym for defeat. As a consequence of a single **battle** here in 1526, Hungary
was divided and war-torn for 150 years and lost its independence for centuries
thereafter. The state was tottering before Mohács, however: its treasury depleted,
and with an indecisive teenager on the throne. Only when Süleyman "the
Magnificent" was nearing the Drava did the Hungarians muster an army, which
headed south and engaged the Turks without waiting for reinforcements from
Transylvania. The battle (see box, p.308) was an utter disaster for Hungary, with
the king and perhaps twenty thousand other Hungarians killed, including most
of the governing elite, leaving the country unable to organize resistance as the
Turks advanced on Buda.

The battlefield and town

The battle of 1526 occurred 7km south of Mohács, at a site thenceforth known
as Sátorhely (Place of the Tent), which in 1976 was declared a **memorial park**
(Mohácsi Történelmi Emlékpark; April–Oct daily 9am–6pm; Nov–March Sat &
Sun 10am–4pm; 750Ft) to mark the 450th anniversary of the battle. Though
easily reached by Route 56 (buses from Mohács towards Nagynyárád, Majs,
Lippó, Bezedek or Magyarbóly run past), there's little to see but a bunker-like

The battles of Mohács

After the Ottoman Turks captured Belgrade in 1521 and continued to advance towards Budapest and Vienna, Hungary's King Louis II, then just 16, married Mary of Habsburg in a bid to secure Habsburg support in the inevitable war. However, this merely provoked the Turks, who determined to prevent the alliance taking effect. As they advanced, the apathetic Hungarian leaders gathered their armies too slowly and in the wrong places; after retreating north from the Drava they chose to stand and fight, on August 29, 1526, in the unsuitable site of a swampy plain outside Mohács.

Legend has it that an olive tree planted two hundred years earlier by Louis the Great suddenly became barren on that day, while the royal scribe records how the young king gave orders for the care of his hounds before riding out to meet his fate. The initial Turkish assault was repelled and a counterattack had some success before the Magyars broke ranks to loot the fallen, exposing themselves to a crushing counterattack by Turkish janissaries and cavalry, which caused a rout. Louis fled but fell while fording a stream and, due to the weight of his armour, was unable to escape being crushed to death by his horse.

The Sultan Süleyman ordered that the prisoners should be killed: perhaps a thousand Hungarian nobles, bishops and commanders died, and 14,000 or more soldiers in all. Although the Turks entered Buda and sacked it, they did not stay long; however, the city's eventual occupation in 1541 was inevitable from this point, as no one was left to organize resistance. Hungary itself became a battleground, contested by the Turks and Habsburgs for close to two centuries.

The **second battle of Mohács** (in fact another 15km or so to the southwest) in 1687 was part of the slow process by which the by then moribund Ottoman empire was gradually driven back to the southeast. On this occasion a larger Turkish force was defeated by an Austrian army under Charles of Lorraine, and their commander Suleiman Pasha killed. The Turkish army mutinied and Sultan Mehmet V was deposed, leaving the Ottoman empire in paralysis for a year, while the Habsburgs continued to push into the Balkans.

edifice containing maps of each side's deployments and endless texts in Hungarian – bar a wreath-laying ceremony on Mohács Memorial Day (August 29).

In Mohács itself there are some bizarrely misconceived buildings, notably on Széchenyi tér, where the impressively ugly **Votive Church**, built to commemorate the 400th anniversary of the battle, stands near the **town hall**, built at the same time with oriental motifs including the Sultan's calligraphic signature engraved on a window. To the rear of the town hall at Városház utca 1, the **Kanizsai Dorottya Museum** (April–Oct Tues–Sat 10am–5pm, Sun 10am–noon & 2–4pm; Nov–March Tues–Sat 10am–3pm; 300Ft) has little to say on the battle, but does show ceramics, painted furniture and a few carnival masks, in addition to an exhibition on the diverse ethnic groups that repopulated Mohács in the late seventeenth century, with national costumes from the Croatian, Serbian and Slovenian communities. The town's only other sight is the eighteenth-century **Serbian Orthodox Church**, down towards the river at Szerb utca 2, whose magnificent iconostasis was painted by the Hungarian Csóka Mór.

Each spring, exactly seven weeks before Easter, the streets of Mohács come alive with the annual **Busójárás Carnival**. At night the carnival assumes a macabre appearance, with a procession of grotesquely masked figures waving flaming torches, who cross the River Danube – which rolls through the town disconcertingly near street level – in wooden boats to chase away the winter. Originally, it was probably a spring ritual intended to appease the gods, but over time participants also began to practise ritualistic abomination of the Turks to magically draw the sting of reality. Similar carnivals are held in Serbia, Slovenia and Croatia, where many of the revellers at Mohács travel from.

Practicalities

While the **train station** is half an hour's walk north of the centre, the **bus station** is on Rákóczi utca, close to Szabadság utca, the main street running eastwards across Széchenyi tér and on to the Danube ferry landing stage on Szent Mihály tér. From here the **car ferry** (600Ft for a car, plus 150Ft for each passenger, 300Ft for a bike) crosses the river to the residential area of Újmohács (and the Great Plain) every half-hour between 5.20am and 7pm (to 8pm May–Aug), with further crossings at 4am, 5am, 8.30pm, 9.30pm, 10.30pm and 11.50pm all year round. The Duna-Drava National Park has created a 1.5-kilometre study trail on the Újmohács bank, with six information boards; you can also take a boat to the Nagyrét meadow from Mohács (☏30/377-3409). **Information** is available from Tourinform in the town hall at Széchenyi tér 1 (mid-June to mid-Sept Mon–Fri 7.30am–5pm, Sat 10am–3pm; mid-Sept to mid-June Mon–Fri 7.30am–4pm; ☏69/505-515, ✉mohacs@tourinform.hu), while the **post office** is next door (Mon–Fri 8am–5pm, Sat 8–11am). At Szabadság utca 19 a **bike shop** sells parts and undertakes repairs for tourists tackling the Danube cycle route south from Budapest to Croatia and the linked Three Rivers Cycle Route, following the Mura, Drava and Danube along the Croatian border to Austria.

There's a limited choice of **accommodation**, and it's essential to reserve at carnival time. Your best options are two places either side of the landing stage: the bargain-value *Révkapu Panzió* (☏69/322-228, ⓦwww.mohacsvgv.hu; ❸), now with air conditioning and wi-fi; and the excellent new *Hotel Szent János* at Szent Mihály tér 6–7 (☏69/511-010, ⓦwww.hotel-szentjanos.hu; ❻) which has lovely air-conditioned rooms, including disabled facilities, a rooftop restaurant, sauna and solarium; guests have free use of the gym and free internet access. Also fairly new is the *Pannon Hotel*, east of the centre at Dózsa György utca 17 (☏30/500-8285), a pleasant, smallish mid-range place. Smaller places include the *Duna Panzió*, at Felső Dunasor 14 (☏69/302-450, 20/980-5733, ✉vinodent @freemail.hu; ❹), by the Danube a few minutes from the centre; and the *Korona Panzió*, Jókai utca 2 (☏69/311-480; ❹). Alternatively, there's the year-round *Aréna Camping* at Dunaszekcső, 12km north along Route 56 (☏69/335-161, ✉arenacamp@freemail.hu), which has a small menagerie, lovely views of the river, a restaurant, rooms (❷) and bungalows (❷). This is an attractive village where there are also rooms to rent.

For **eating**, you can choose between the *Hotel Szent János*'s Mediterranean-style restaurant, or the *Veli Aga Vendéglő* at Szentháromság utca 7, a block north of the modern monument at the bottom of the pedestrian section of Szabadság utca, whose cuisine has a distinct Serbian and Turkish flavour.

Moving on, there are **buses** to Pécs and Budapest, and to Baja and Kecskemét or Szeged on the Great Plain; the railway is useful only to reach Villány, from where occasional trains cross into Croatia. By road, there is a **border crossing** into Croatia at Udvar, 11km south of town. There are quite a few buses from both Mohács and Szekszárd to Baja, but to get from one to the other you may have to change at **Bátaszék**, on the Dombovár-Baja railway line – arriving at the station, head left/east to the main road from Szekszárd and then south towards the big red church.

Szekszárd and the Forest of Gemenc

The chance to sample red wine produced in vineyards dating from Roman times and to buy inexpensive black pottery makes **SZEKSZÁRD** the prime stopover between Pécs and Budapest. Baroque squares, leafy streets and ancient wine cellars make this an ideal base to explore the wild, marshy **Forest of Gemenc** – while various festivals are held in early June, early August and mid-September.

Arrival and information

Arriving at the bus or train station on Pollack Mihály utca, it's a ten-minute walk up pedestrianized Bajcsy-Zsilinszky utca to the centre, passing the museum and the synagogue. **Information** can be obtained from Tourinform at Béla tér 7 (Mon–Fri 9am–5pm, Sat 9am–2pm; ☎74/511-263, ✉szekszard@tourinform.hu), where you can also book beds in school dorms (see below). The main **post office** is at Széchenyi utca 11 (Mon–Fri 8am–7pm, Sat 8am–noon), and **internet access** is available at *Internet Klub*, Garay tér 12 (Mon–Sat 2–6pm).

Accommodation

The cheapest accommodation is at the *Illyés Gyula Pedagógiai Főiskolai Kollégium* (☎74/528-327, ✉hamarics@igyfk.pte.hu; ❶) ten minutes' walk north of the centre at Mátyás király utca 3; and the *Rósza Kollegium* (❶) at Kadarká utca 29 (bus #9), where Tourinform can usually find a single bed even midweek; or **private rooms** bookable through Ibusz at Szent István tér 3 (Mon–Fri 8am–5pm, Sat 8am–noon; ☎74/319-822, ✉szekszard@ibusz.hu). The best of the few hotels here is the *Zodiaco* at Szent László utca 19, five minutes' walk north of Béla tér (☎74/511-150, ⓦwww.hotelzodiaco.hu; ❻), a bizarre-looking place with minimally but coolly furnished air-conditioned rooms, each named after a star sign or planet. Other accommodation options boil down to the horrible 1970s *Hotel Gemenc*, behind the Wosinsky Museum at Mészáros Lázár utca 4 (☎74/311-722, ⓦwww.hotels.hu/gemenc; ❹), which has small, stuffy rooms; and the *Alisca Hotel* at Kálvária utca 1, up a steep path above Béla tér (☎&☎74/311-242; ❺), which has fine views over town, but little else to commend it. If all else fails, the *Alfa-Megacentrum* (☎74/511-060, 🖷511-061; ❸) offers cheap rooms at Tartsay utca 8, near the Shell garage heading south from the station. There's a **campsite** (April–Oct) 6km east of the town at the Gemenci Kiránduló Központ (Gemenc Leisure Centre; ☎74/312-552, ⓦwww.hotels.hu/gemenc-kirandulo-kozpont), the entrance to the Forest of Gemenc (see p.312); in addition to tent space, there are Finnish-style wooden cabins (❸).

The Town

Szekszárd is centred on the intersection of two main axes: the busy Széchenyi utca, and, crossing it at right angles, the park-like Szent István tér that eventually leads uphill to Béla tér, via cobbled Garay tér. In a neo-Renaissance pile at the eastern end of Szent István tér, the **Wosinsky Museum** (Wosinsky Mór Megyei Múzeum; April–Sept Tues–Sun 10am–6pm; Oct–March Tues–Sat 10am–4pm; 600Ft, free on Sat) has, on its ground floor, a rich, but wearily presented, collection of Roman artefacts and peasants' costumes and, upstairs, much better new displays, with English captions, covering the Christian era to the mid-nineteenth century. Behind the museum, the former **synagogue** (Tues–Sat 9am–5pm; 150Ft) has been beautifully and tastefully restored inside and out. Outside, the Triumphal

Arch is supported by a modern concrete frame. The synagogue is now used as a concert hall and a venue for temporary art exhibitions.

The final uphill stretch beyond Széchenyi utca leads to Béla tér, where porticoed buildings tilt perceptibly around a column marking the plague of 1730. In the centre of the square, the late Baroque Roman Catholic **church**, completed in 1805, is the largest single-nave church in Central Europe. The Neoclassical **Old County Hall**, on the east side of the square, was built in 1828–36 by Mihály Pollack, on the site of a Benedictine abbey founded in 1061 – the foundations (well cased in concrete) are visible in the courtyard, as is a well that spouts wine at festival time. Of the various small museums inside, the best is the **Liszt Memorial Exhibition** (Liszt Emlék kiallitás; April–Sept Tues–Sun 9am–5pm; Oct–March Tues–Sat 9am–3pm; 300Ft), which commemorates Liszt's four visits to Szekszárd, and displays the piano that he played and a few of his scrawls.

At the top end of the square, Babits utca leads towards the **House of Mihály Babits**, across the bridge at no. 13 (Babits Mihály Emlékház; April–Sept Tues–Sun 9am–5pm; Oct–March Tues–Sat 9am–4pm; 450Ft), a homely residence exhibiting photos and manuscripts related to the journal *Nyugat* (West). This avant-garde publication was edited by Babits and included the Village Explorers' exposés of rural life in interwar Hungary, launching the literary careers of Endre Ady and Gyula Illyés. Alas for Attila József, the finest poet of that era, Babits refused to publish his work in *Nyugat*, earning József's eternal hostility. Babits went to his graveside to ask his forgiveness.

Szekszárd's dark, rich "ox-blood" wine (Szekszárdi Vörös) was exported as far afield as Britain and Turkey in the 1700s, and Franz Liszt, Pope Pius IX and Emperor Haile Selassie are all said to have been admirers. Today, wine lovers can visit the numerous surrounding **vineyards**, or several excellent private **vintners** in town such as the Vesztergombi family, which has a shop at Béla tér 7 (Mon–Fri 10am–noon & 1–5pm, Sat 9am–noon) selling Vida and Sárosdi, as well as its own wines, and a cellar on Kadarka utca, uphill behind the square. The Garay Winery (Garay Pince; summer Mon–Fri 9am–6pm, Sat 8am–5pm; winter Mon–Fri 9am–5pm, Sat 9am–2pm; around 1500Ft for tour and tasting), just below the Old County Hall at Béla tér 1, offers wine and cheese tasting in its cellar (used by the Benedictine abbey from the thirteenth century to store wine paid as a tithe). Many other private cellars open their doors during the Alisca Wine Days (Bornapok) at the start of June (see p.312).

Eating, drinking and entertainment

Though Szekszárd's gastronomic efforts are less remarkable than its wine, it does have a fair range of choices. The best **restaurant** is the *Arany Kulacs kisvendéglő* at Nefelejcs köz 1, which has a non-smoking room, a terrace, and a list of premium *pálinkas*. You can also take in a hugely enjoyable meal at the *Szász Söröző*, Garay tér 18, a medieval-themed place with particularly delicious soups and some fantastic vegetarian options – it's equally great for a beer. The *Főispán*, tucked away to the left of the town hall at Béla tér 1, is a more polished restaurant with seductive, overhanging lamps under which you can enjoy fine Hungarian cuisine, while the *Gilde Söröző* at Kossuth Lajos utca 16, just off Szent László utca, has a reasonably varied, if rather beef-heavy, menu (closes 4pm Sun). Cheap, hot lunches can be washed down with good wine at *Papa's Winehouse* (Papa Borozója; Mon–Fri 9am–8pm, Sat 7am–8pm, Sun 9am–6pm), at the bottom of Garay tér at no. 6. For coffee, cakes and ice cream head to the *Belvárosi Kávéház* next to the *Szász Söröző*, with a pleasant terrace looking down the square.

For **entertainment**, check out the theatre in the modern Babits Mihály Művelődézi Ház (Mihály Babits Cultural Centre), and the Panorama Cinema at its rear. German-speakers should check out the Deutsche Bühne (German Theatre; Ⓦ www.deutschebuehne.hu) – in a lovely Art Nouveau buiding at Garay tér 4, it's the country's own German-language theatre and thus a major cultural centre for the community.

The town's two major wine-related events are the **Alisca Wine Days** (Bornapok) at the start of June, with tastings and craft fairs climaxing in a fish-soup making competition by the Danube, and the **Grape and Wine Harvest**, a three-day festival in the third week of September, where visitors are welcome to help pick and press the grapes, and to enjoy the music, wine and song. Another event worth attending is the **folklore festival at Decs** at the beginning of August. Though only 8km south of Szekszárd, this village was traditionally isolated by marshes yet remained *au courant*, as its menfolk worked as bargees, bringing home the latest news and fabrics from Budapest. Their wives wore beribboned silk skirts and cambric blouses with lace inserts, and later acquired a taste for lime green and yellow metallic thread, making their **costumes** as lurid as rave attire. Some can be seen in the Decs Folk-house (*Tájház*) at Kossuth utca 32 (Mon–Fri 8am–5pm).

The Forest of Gemenc

Part of the Duna-Drava National Park (Ⓦ http://ddnp.nemzetipark.gov.hu) since 1996, the **Forest of Gemenc**, east of Szekszárd, is a remnant of the wilderness of woods, reeds and mudland that once covered the Danube's shifting, flood-prone banks. Only at the beginning of the twentieth century was the river tamed and shortened by 60km, thus helping to stem the annual flooding of its backwaters and the Sárköz (Mud Region). However, marshes and ponds remained to provide habitats for boar, wildcats, otters, red deer, ospreys, falcons, white-tailed eagles, black storks and other **wildlife**. Nowadays, the forest is a nature reserve of sorts, although the deer and wild boar are fair game for Western hunters.

The gateway to the forest is the **Gemenc Leisure Centre** (May–Oct daily 9.30–11am & noon–4pm; ☎ 72/312-552) in **Bárányfok**, a popular recreation spot 6km from Szekszárd on the northwestern edge of the forest; to get there, take any bus heading for Keselyűs (4–5 daily). A short walk from the entrance, the **Life in the Floodplain exhibition** (mid-March to late Oct Tues–Sun 10am–5pm; late Oct to mid-March by appointment, call ☎ 30/255-7866; 600Ft) is housed in the larchwood Trophy House, built in 1896 for the Millennium Exhibition in Budapest and later used to house Archduke Franz Ferdinand's hunting trophies. It now houses exhibits on the forest's flora and fauna and displays on the difficulties that the park's inhabitants have traditionally faced, such as in 1956, when a major flood forced the evacuation of some forty settlements and more than five thousand homes were destroyed. Nearby is the *Trófea* restaurant, a typically rustic *csárda* serving predominantly game and fish (daily till 9pm). The Bárányfok study path, with six information boards, takes around an hour, lingering to watch deer, grey herons or great white egrets.

From here the **forest train** runs all year (steam locomotives hauling open carriages from May to October and diesels with heated ones in winter) through the forest to **Pörböly**, 30km to the south on the road and railway between Bátaszék and Baja; there are only three trains a day (leaving Bárányfok at 10.30am, 1.30pm & 3.30pm; Pörböly at 8am, 9.20am & 1.15pm; 750Ft single, 1050Ft return). The Pörböly Ecotourism Centre (☎ 74/491-483, Ⓦ www.gemencrt.hu) consists of a reception building, housing a souvenir shop, buffet and a ticket office for the forest train, and across the track a museum, with displays on ethnography, forestry, red deer and bee-keeping. Paths lead from here to an arboretum and to observation towers, while south of the highway forest paths lead 1km south to the Nyék-Duna backwater, where there's another observation tower. It's also possible to get off the train at Malomtelelő, 8km north of Pörböly, and take a forest path to an observation tower.

It's possible to hike from north to south through the forest, but the only feasible cycle route is on the dyke alongside the Danube; bikes can be rented at the Gemenc Leisure Centre, and the trains will carry them back to your starting point. **Boat trips** set off for the forest's backwaters from the Karoly IV quay, by the Danube bridge (300m from Tesco) in Baja, 10km east of Pörböly (see opposite).

Szekszárd to Budapest

The road and train line between Szekszárd and Budapest pass through unexciting countryside punctuated by three towns that, although not worth a special visit in themselves, might tempt you to a stopover – **Paks**, **Dunaföldvár** and **Dunaújváros**. If not, and you're driving, consider a **scenic detour** along minor roads through the pretty villages of Högyész, Gyonk and Cece, before rejoining the trunk route at Dunaföldvár. In addition to the **bridges over the Danube** at Baja and Dunaföldvar, motorway-standard bridges have recently been built at Szekszárd and Dunaújváros, and a motorway from Pécs, Mohács and Szekszárd to Budapest will open in 2010.

Paks

PAKS, 30km north of Szekszárd, is the site of Hungary's only **nuclear power station**, four Soviet-designed pressurized water reactors which supply up to forty percent of the country's electricity. Bar some anxiety in the aftermath of Chernobyl, the issue of nuclear power has never aroused much public concern in Hungary except among communities living near the site of proposed nuclear waste dumps, and in Paks itself people are quick to point out that the plant, a good 5km south of town, gets good marks from international safety inspectors.

Around 30,000 people a year visit the power station, though most only stop at the Visitor Centre (Mon–Fri 9am–3pm, Sat 9am–1pm), which features a striking statue of several leading scientists – among them Leo Szilárd, John Neumann and Edward Teller – in weighty discussion, an aquarium of Danube fish, displays on local history and nuclear power worldwide, plus interactive exhibits and cameras trained on the reactor hall and control room. There's also a viewing tower and a post office, offering free cards, pens and stamps. Over-16s can also take an hour-long tour (Mon–Fri only; ☎75/508-833, @uzemalatogatas@npp.hu), viewing the reactor hall and control room through glazed galleries, and walking into the turbine hall.

From the main train station south of downtown Paks, bus #1 takes you past the remarkable **Catholic Church**, two blocks west of Tolnai utca on Hősök tere, built by Imre Makovecz (see box, p.163) in 1989. A strikingly organic structure made of wood, its separate bell-tower has three spires topped by a cross, a crescent and a sun sign – which provoked letters to the press condemning the "Satanic forces" behind it, despite Makovecz's claim that they were early Christian symbols. You can get the key to the church at Hősök tere 19.

The remaining sights are on Szent István tér, the main square in the north of town, where a small City Museum (Városi Múzeum; Tues 10am–4pm, Wed–Sun 10am–6pm; 450Ft) displays finds from Roman Lussonium, just north, sundry Bronze Age, Celtic and Magyar artefacts, plus a table used by the statesman Deák. Nearby, the Catholic church has a barn-like neo-Romanesque interior with a cassette roof. Across the road at Szent István tér 4, a grand classical building that was only the third casino in the country when it was built in 1844 is being converted into a hotel; with luck, the Paks Gallery (Páksi Képtár; Tues–Sun 10am–6pm; free), previously housed here, will reappear. Set up by local artist Károly Halász, it showed a stimulating exhibition of contemporary Hungarian works.

If you're arriving by train it's better to get off at the Paks Duna-part station near Szent István tér rather than the main station over 1km south of the centre, where the bus station is located near the Danube at the bottom of Tancsics Mihály utca. Both are connected to the centre by regular buses. Until the Erszébet Szálloda reopens, the only **accommodation** is the well-refurbished Communist-era *Duna Hotel* at Dózsa György út 75 (T 75/310-891, W www .dunahotelpaks.hu; ⑤).

The *Halászcsárda* fish **restaurant** at Dunaföldvár utca 5a, fifteen minutes' walk upriver from the main square, has a terrace with fine views of the river, and a good reputation, the reactors being well downstream.

Dunaföldvár

DUNAFÖLDVÁR, 24km north of Paks, is by far the prettiest and smallest of the three towns en route to Budapest. Arriving by **bus**, it's a minute's walk north to the main square, Béke tér, while the **train station** is 2km southwest of town on Vasút utca. The town's name derives from the sixteenth-century fortress that was hastily erected to guard the Danube after Belgrade fell to Süleyman's army, of which only the keep – known as the **Turkish Tower** – has survived. To reach it, continue north from Béke tér and take Rákóczi utca, the first on the right. The tower now houses a small museum (Vár Múzeum; Tues–Sun 10am–6pm; 300Ft) containing bits and bobs from the twelfth century, and an assortment of items representing various local trades such as blue-dyers and bootmakers. A better reason to visit is for the fantastic views of the Danube below and the puffing chimneys of the Dunaújváros ironworks away in the distance. Across the courtyard, the **Fafaragó Gallery** (same ticket and times) has paintings and handiwork by local artists and a curious small ethnographic collection in which the school section seems to have been taken over by real school projects. After the Turks were finally driven out, the town was repopulated by outsiders, as its Baroque **Serbian Orthodox Church**, just north of Béke tér at Kossuth Lajos utca 7, attests; the small, white church is likely to remain closed for some time whilst its icons undergo restoration in Szentendre. Besides some elegant **Art Nouveau buildings** in the centre, it's possible to inspect **craft workshops** such as that of the blue-dyer (*kékfestő*) Vadász Istvánné (Mon–Fri 8am–4pm), at Duna utca 6, beyond the new approach to the Danube bridge.

Visits can be arranged through Tourinform, opposite the Turkish tower at Rátkai köz 2 (June to mid-Sept Mon–Fri 9am–5pm, Sat 9am–1pm; mid-Sept to May Mon–Fri 9am–5pm; T 75/341-176, E dunafoldvar@tourinform.hu), which can provide other **information** and book **private rooms** (②) if required. Two central, and good-value, pensions close to each other are the *Prajda Panzió*, Kossuth Lajos utca 22 (T 75/342-182), and the *Varró Panzió*, Petőfi utca 20 (T 75/341-810; ②), which has cooking facilities. The Kék-Duna **campsite**, at

Hősök tere 23, on a wonderful grassy spot on the river bank (☏75/541-107, ✉postmaster@camping-gyogyfurdo.axelero.hu), also has rooms in chalets (●). It's open all year, but out of season you should check in at the **thermal baths**, immediately south (daily 8am–4pm; 1050Ft).

For **eating**, the red-and-black rustically styled *Vár Étterem*, up by the Turkish Tower, is worth a visit as much for the views as for the food, while the *Halászcsárda* fish restaurant, between the baths and campsite on Hősök tere, also has resplendent views across the Danube – the Földvári fish soup is highly recommended. The *Centrum Étterem*, on the north side of Béke tér, is a small, friendly eatery with a good choice of salads and pasta plus Transylvanian-style pork dishes. There's good coffee, cakes and ices at the quaint *Marcipán Cukrászda* at Béke tér 3 (daily 9am–6pm).

Dunaújváros

In total contrast, **DUNAÚJVÁROS** (Danube New Town), 20km upriver, is a monument to Stalinist economics, created around a vast ironworks which the Party saw as the lynchpin of its industrialization strategy for the 1950s. The construction of Sztálinváros (as the town was originally called) was trumpeted as a feat by Stakhanovites, though much of the heavy work was performed by peasants and "reformed" prostitutes living under appalling conditions. Yet, at the same time, it embodied a striving for a brighter future for the working classes – a paradox that has assumed a new form today, as this incarnation of the planned economy has weathered the transition to capitalism better than "traditional" industrial towns such as Ózd in northeastern Hungary. In addition, the planted trees are now mature, hiding the worst of the architecture.

The town's appeal lies in its utopian **Bauhaus and Socialist-Realist aesthetic**, though its uniform rows of blocks make orientation difficult. The tall redbrick town hall on Városháza tér serves as the main landmark in the centre, whence Vasmű utca runs south to the Dunaferr Iron Works. Across the road at Városháza tér 4, the former Party headquarters now houses the **Intercisa Museum** (Tues–Sun 2–6pm; 600Ft), which relates the history of this site from Roman times – mainly in the form of urns and grave goods – before leaping to the twentieth century and the Stalinist era. The latter is epitomized by a book of 14,800 signatures presented to Party Secretary Rákosi "demanding" that Sztálinváros be built – although it doesn't go into much detail about the suffering involved. A few minutes' walk east brings you to a **sculpture park** of rusting iron supplied by the works.

The **Institute of Contemporary Art**, just round the corner at Vasmű utca 12 (Kontárs Művészeti Intézet; Tues–Sun 10am–6pm; free), is worth a visit for its temporary exhibitions of Hungarian and foreign works, and also has a pleasant little coffee bar (see p.316). Further along Vasmű utca, Babits utca leads west to **Bartók tér**, featuring a store with mosaics depicting workers and peasants building the town. On the same square, the **Bartók Cultural Centre** combines Neoclassical and Bauhaus motifs, while through the arcade a school of the same era has separate doors for boys and girls, topped by reliefs of idealized children at study. Leading south from the square is Majus 1 utca, one of the first streets to be built in 1950, and a must for lovers of the Bauhaus style. For real fanatics, the tourist office (see p.316) gives out a free leaflet detailing a two-hour walk around the town's many other Socialist monuments.

Continuing along Vasmű utca you'll pass a **statue of a foundry worker** relaxing, which Party officials complained should show the worker working, not resting, and was consequently not erected until 1961. Another twenty minutes' walk, past the football stadium, brings you to the entrance of the **Iron Works**, like something out of a Cecil B. De Mille set, with an abstract relief of joyous workers above a Neoclassical portico. The works cover a huge area, almost as big as the town itself, and employ some eight thousand people, both from the town and the region; buses from the south stop here, before passing the wooded *cordon sanitaire* to the town itself.

Practicalities

There's no sensible walking route from the **train station**, 2km west of town, but buses #16 and #17 run to the centre every fifteen minutes. The **bus terminal**, near the market on Béke tér, is a short enough walk south of the centre; most buses heading north, including to Budapest, pick up at Városháza tér. As you might expect, Dunaújváros is hardly geared up for tourists, though there is a Tourinform office at Vasmű utca 10a (Mon–Thurs 9am–4pm, Fri 8am–3pm; ☎25/500-148, ✉dunaujvaros@tourinform.hu) dispensing **information**. Ibusz, just north of the cinema at Devecseri utca 8 (Mon–Fri 9am–5pm, Sat 8am–noon; ☎25/409-960, ✉dunaujvaros@ibusz.hu), can book private rooms (❷) or beds in the nicely refurbished *Kerpely Antal kollégium* at Dózsa György utca 33 (☎25/551-237, ⓦhttp://kac.duf.hu/hostelkerpely; ❷; July & Aug). **Hotel** options are limited to the quite awful *Dunaferr Hotel* at Építők utca 2, 400m east of the bus station (☎25/381-073, ✉office.hotel@chello.hu; ❹), and, set back behind it, the smart and business-like *Klub Hotel* (☎25/500-477, ⓦwww.klubhotel.hu; ❻). There is also a **campsite** (☎25/310-285; May–Sept), with an open-air bathing area, on a small island 3km north of the centre, accessible by bus #24 or #26.

Dunaújváros has a few reasonably good **eating** options, the best of which are the *Topo Pizzeria and Salad Bar*, behind the cinema at Kőműves utca 5, and *Geronimo*, to the side of the cinema on Ságvári tér, which has juicy steaks and ribs plus some Mexican dishes thrown in for good measure. There's also the *Aranysárkány*, a fairly authentic Chinese place at Vasmű utca 9–11. The *City Café* at Kőműves utca 9, *Corner Kávézó*, Dósza György tér 2, and the *Topo Pizzeria* are the obvious choices for a daytime or evening drink, while the *Művész Fészek Presszó*, at the rear of the Bartók Cultural Centre, has a nice terrace. The Institute of Contemporary Art (see p.315) has a very stylish little coffee bar, and there are other cafés and bars in the student area, west of the centre on Dósza György utca. **Internet access** is available in the bar in the foyer of the *Dunaferr Hotel*.

Travel details

Trains

Fertőboz to: Nagycenk (April–Oct 5 departures Sat & Sun; 30min); Sopron (5 daily; 10min).
Dunaújváros to: Budapest (7 daily; 1hr 20min–2hr).
Győr to: Budapest (2 per hr; 1hr 30min–2hr); Mosonmagyaróvár (hourly; 30min); Pápa (12 daily; 40min–1hr); Sopron (9 daily; 1hr–1hr 30min); Szombathely (2 daily; 1hr 50min); Veszprém (6 daily; 2hr–2hr 30min).
Kaposvár to: Fonyód (10 daily; 1hr 10min–1hr 30min); Pécs (3 daily; 1hr 35min–2hr 15min).
Kőszeg to: Szombathely (every 1hr–1hr 30min; 30min).

Mohács to: Pécs (3 daily; 1hr 30min); Villány (6 daily; 30min).
Nagycenk to: Fertőboz (April–Oct 5 departures Sat & Sun; 30min).
Pécs to: Budapest (every 2hr; 3–4hr); Fonyód (3 daily; 2hr 50min–4hr); Kaposvár (4 daily; 1hr 35min); Mohács (6 daily; 1hr 30min); Szeged (1 daily; 6hr 10min); Szigetvár (10 daily; 30–50min); Szombathely (4 daily; 3hr 30min–7hr); Villány (8 daily; 35min).
Sopron to: Budapest (14 daily; 2hr 30min–3hr 30min); Győr (8 daily; 1hr 20min); Szombathely (12 daily; 1hr 10min).

Szekszárd to: Baja (8 daily 50min–1hr); Budapest (2 daily; 3hr: 12 daily with 1 change at Pusztaszabolcs 2hr 30min–3hr 10min); Szekesfehervar (2 daily; 2hr 30min).

Szombathely to: Budapest (5 daily; 2hr 45min–3hr 30min); Kőszeg (every 1hr–1hr 30min; 30min); Pécs (4 daily; 4hr 30min–7hr); Sárvár (every 40min–1hr; 15–25min); Sopron (6 daily; 1hr 30min); Székesfehérvár (7 daily; 2hr 15min–2hr 45min); Tapolca (4 daily; 1hr 45min–2hr 15min).

Szigetvár to: Pécs (11 daily; 45min); Szombathely (2 daily; 3hr); Nagykanisza (3 daily; 1hr 40min–2hr 30min).

Villány to: Mohács (6 daily; 30min); Pécs (8 daily; 32min).

Zalaegerszeg to: Budapest (3 daily; 3hr 30min); Szombathely (3 daily; 1hr 25min); Zalalövő (10 daily; 35min).

Zalalövő to: Körmend (6 daily; 35min); Őriszentpéter (8 daily; 15min); Zalaegerszeg (10 daily; 35min).

Buses

Dunaföldvár to: Baja (3 daily; 2hr); Budapest (2 per hr; 2hr); Dunaújváros (every 20–40min; 25min); Kecskemét (10 daily; 1hr 10min); Mohács (2 daily; 1hr 30min); Szeged (hourly; 2hr); Szekesfehérvar (hourly; 1hr); Szekszárd (hourly; 50min).

Dunaújváros to: Budapest (2 per hr; 1hr 30min); Dunaföldvár (every 20–40min; 25min); Győr (9 daily; 2hr 30min); Kecskemét (6 daily; 1hr 40min); Pécs (5 daily; 2hr 30min); Szeged (7 daily; 2hr 30min), Székesfehérvár (every 30min–1hr; 1hr).

Győr to: Balatonfüred (10 daily; 2hr); Budapest (hourly; 1hr 15min–2hr); Lébény (hourly; 40min); Pannonhalma Monastery (every 30min–1hr 30min; 30min); Pápa (every 1hr–1hr 30min; 50min); Sopron (every 40min; 1hr 30min); Sümeg (5 daily; 2hr 15min); Székesfehérvár (9 daily; 2hr); Szombathely (7 daily; 2hr 30min); Tata (3 daily; 1hr); Veszprém (7 daily; 2hr); Zalaegerszeg (7 daily; 4hr 30min).

Harkány to: Budapest (2 daily; 4hr 15min); Mohács (15 daily; 1hr 10min); Pécs (every 30–40min; 45min); Siklós (every 20–30min; 15min); Szekszárd (3 daily; 2hr 15min).

Ják to: Körmend (3 daily; 30min); Szombathely (hourly; 25min).

Kaposvár to: Hévíz (2 daily; 2hr 30min); Nagykanisza (8 daily; 1hr 25min); Pécs (every 1hr–1hr 30min; 2hr); Siófok (10 daily; 2hr); Szekszárd (4 daily; 2hr 15min); Szigetvár (5 daily; 45min); Szombathely (4 daily; 3hr 20min); Zalaegerszeg (2 daily; 3hr).

Komárom to: Budapest (3 daily; 2hr); Esztergom (3–5 daily; 1hr 30min); Győr (2–4 daily; 1hr); Sopron (1 daily; 2hr 45min); Tata (7 daily; 1hr).

Kőszeg to: Bozsok (10 daily; 45min); Cák (13 daily; 20min); Sárvár (6 daily; 1hr 10min); Sopron (6 daily; 1hr 15min); Szombathely (every 40min–1hr; 30min); Velem (11 daily; 30min); Zalaegerszeg (2 daily; 1hr 15min).

Mohács to: Baja (12 daily; 1hr 30min); Budapest (4 daily; 4hr); Harkany (15 daily; 1hr 10min); Kecskemét (3 daily; 4hr); Pécs (2 per hr; 1hr); Szeged (10 daily; 4hr); Szekszárd (6 daily; 1hr).

Őriszentpéter to: Körmend (9 daily; 1hr 15min); Szalafő (4 daily; 15min); Velemér (9 daily; 30min); Zalaegerszeg (7 daily; 25min).

Paks to: Baja (2 daily; 1hr 30min); Budapest (hourly; 2hr); Harkány (2 daily; 3hr); Kescskemét (2 daily; 1hr 40min); Pécs (9 daily; 2hr); Szekszárd (every 30min; 40min).

Pécs to: Abaliget (8 daily; 1hr); Baja (hourly; 2hr); Budapest (5 daily; 4hr); Harkány (every 30min–1hr; 45min); Hévíz (2 daily; 4hr 30min); Kaposvár (every 1hr–1hr 30min; 2hr); Keszthely (4 daily; 4hr); Mohács (every 40min–1hr; 1hr 20min); Orfű (every 1hr–1hr 30min; 1hr); Siklós (every 30min–1hr; 1hr); Siófok (7 daily; 3hr); Szeged (every 1–2hr; 4hr); Székesfehérvár (6 daily; 4hr 30min); Szekszárd (every 1–2hr; 1hr 15min); Szigetvár (every 45min–1hr 30min; 1hr); Zalaegerszeg (8 daily; 4hr 15min).

Sárvár to: Győr (3 daily; 2hr); Kőszeg (every 2hr; 70min); Sopron (4 daily; 1hr 15min); Sümeg (2 daily; 1hr); Szombathely (7 daily; 1hr); Veszprém (2 daily; 2hr); Zalaegerszeg (3 daily; 2hr).

Siklós to: Budapest (1 daily; 5hr); Harkány (every 30–45min; 15min); Mohács (11 daily; 1hr 30min); Pécs (every 30–45min; 1hr); Szekszárd (5 daily; 2hr 30min); Szigetvár (4 daily; 2hr) Villány (every 30min–1hr; 30min).

Sopron to: Balatonfüred (2 daily; 4hr); Budapest (4 daily; 3hr 45min); Esztergom (1 daily; 4hr); Fertőd (every 30min–1hr; 35min); Fertőrákos (every 40min–1hr; 30min); Győr (hourly; 2hr); Hévíz (2 daily; 3hr); Keszthely (4 daily; 3hr 15min); Komárom (1 daily; 2hr 45min); Kőszeg (7 daily; 1hr 15min); Nagycenk (every 30–40min; 20min); Nagykanisza (3 daily; 2hr 30min); Pápa (5 daily; 2hr 30min); Sárvár (4 daily; 1hr 15min); Sümeg (3 daily; 2hr 15min); Szombathely (8 daily; 1hr 45min); Zalaegerszeg (3 daily; 3hr).

Szekszárd to: Baja (12 daily; 1hr); Budapest (hourly; 2hr 30min); Kaposvár (every 1–2hr; 3hr); Mohács (7 daily; 1hr); Paks (every 30min; 35min); Pécs (16 daily; 1hr 15min); Siófok (8 daily; 2hr); Szeged (3 daily; 3hr); Székesfehérvár (4 daily; 2hr); Veszprém (2 daily; 3hr 45min).

Szigetvár to: Kaposvár (8 daily; 45min);
Pécs (every 1hr–1hr 30min; 30min–1hr 20min).
Szombathely to: Budapest (4 daily; 3hr 45min–5hr);
Győr (5 daily; 2hr 30min); Ják (hourly; 25min);
Kaposvár (2 daily; 1hr 40min); Keszthely (2 daily; 2hr
30min); Körmend (hourly; 30–55min); Kőszeg (every
40min–1hr; 35min); Pécs (3 daily; 4hr 40min); Sárvár
(every 45min–1hr 30min; 45min); Sopron (5 daily;
1hr 45min); Zalaegerszeg (12 daily; 1hr 10min);
Veszprém (3 daily; 2hr 10min–2hr 45min).
Tata to: Esztergom (hourly; 1hr 30min); Komárom
(20 daily; 1hr).
Zalaegerszeg to: Budapest (8 daily; 4hr 45min);
Győr (9 daily; 4hr 30min); Kaposvár (6 daily; 3hr);
Keszthely (hourly; 1hr); Körmend (8 daily; 1hr);
Őriszentpéter (7 daily; 25min); Pécs (7 daily; 4hr
15min); Sopron (3 daily; 3hr 15min); Sümeg (6 daily;
1hr 10min); Szombathely (14 daily; 1hr 20min).

International trains

Győr to: Vienna (hourly; 1hr 40min).

Pécs to: Vienna (1 daily; 6hr); Beli Monastir
(Croatia) (2 daily; 1hr 15min–1hr 45min); Osijek
(Croatia) (1 daily; 2hr 30min); Sarajevo (Bosnia)
(1 daily; 9hr 30min).
Sopron to: Vienna (hourly; 1hr 15min).
Szombathely to: Graz (Austria) (4 daily; 2hr
40min–3hr 10min).
Villány to: Beli Monastir (Croatia) (3 daily; 40min);
Osijek (Croatia) (1 daily; 1hr 40min); Sarajevo
(Bosnia) (1 daily; 8hr 40min).
Zalalövő to: Ljubljana (Slovenia) (1 daily; 4hr
20min).

International buses

Sopron to: Frankfurt (1 weekly; 14hr); Munich
(2 weekly; 7hr); Stuttgart (2 weekly; 10hr); Vienna
(1 daily Mon–Fri; 2hr); Wiener Neustadt (1 daily;
1hr 15min).
Szombathely to: Vienna (1 weekly; 3hr 30min).

The Northern Uplands

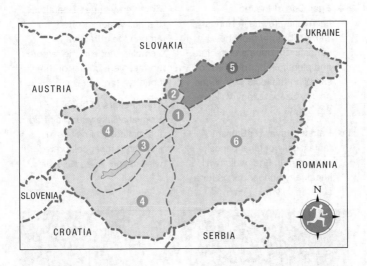

CHAPTER 5

Highlights

5

* **Hollókő** Extraordinary two-street village where traditional customs remain strong. See p.327

* **Narrow-gauge trains** Take a trip on one of the Uplands' delightful narrow-gauge lines. See p.331, p.343, p.345 & p.366

* **Eger** One of the most enchanting towns in Hungary, with a vibrant atmosphere, fantastic Baroque architecture and plentiful opportunities for sampling the local wine in the nearby Szépasszony Valley. See p.335

* **Palacsintavár restaurant** A fantastically original pancake restaurant in Eger which will knock any hunger pangs for a six. See p.340

* **Bükk National Park** Hungary's greenest region is also the best in the country for cycling and hiking. See p.343

* **Aggtelek Stalactite Caves** The largest, and one of the most spectacular, stalactite systems in Europe. See p.352

* **Zemplén villages** Beautiful, tranquil villages dotted around the attractive Zemplén range in the remote northeastern corner of the country. See p.353

* **Wine cellars of Tokaj-Hegyalja** Take your pick from the multitude of cellars in Hungary's most celebrated wine region. See p.356

▲ Narrow-gauge railway, Northern Uplands

The Northern Uplands

Hungary's **Northern Uplands** boast beautiful wooded hills, karstic rock formations, ruined castles and tranquil villages, as well as three major wine-producing regions, offering some of the best wines in the world. With few major centres of population in the region, it makes for an ideal retreat after a few hectic days in Budapest, with opportunities aplenty for hiking, cycling and other relaxing pursuits.

Historically, the Uplands were more important than they are today, both strategically and economically. Most of the fortresses here saw active service against the Turks and the Habsburgs, particularly during the War of Independence (1703–11), led by Ferenc Rákóczi II. In between times, commerce and culture thrived in tandem with highland Slovakia, until the Treaty of Trianon in 1920 severed the links that sustained old market towns like **Balassagyarmat**, while industrialization gave rise to utilitarian towns that did well under Communism but have since become Hungary's "Rust Belt". **Miskolc**, the largest city in the Uplands, is symptomatic of the industrial decline to ravage the region, but it's not without its attractions, and is further redeemed by its proximity to the scenic **Bükk Hills** and the *fin-de-siècle* spa of **Lillafüred**. To the north of Miskolc, the remote Aggtelek National Park, bordering Slovakia, is home to the Upland's greatest natural attraction – the amazing **Aggtelek Stalactite Caves**.

Another appealing aspect of the region is its Jewish heritage, which draws many Jewish-Americans to places like **Sátoraljaújhely**, **Gyöngyös** and **Verpelét** in search of their ancestors. The old synagogues and cemeteries here are even more neglected than the former aristocratic mansions that also languished under Communism, though these are now slowly being restored – most impressively at **Gödöllő**, a short ride away from Budapest. In the Cserhát Hills north of Gödöllő, the outstanding draw is the delightful museum village of **Hollókő**, a UNESCO World Heritage Site. Moving eastwards, beyond the forested **Mátra Hills**, you'll arrive at **Eger**, the most appealing town in the region, if not in Hungary itself, which combines a fabulous castle and Baroque town centre with a viticultural pedigree that's only surpassed by **Tokaj**, a small, sleepy town in the foothills of the **Zemplén Hills**. The Zemplén, in the far northwestern corner of the country, harbour some of Hungary's finest vineyards and prettiest villages, such as **Füzér** and **Boldogkőváralja**, both of which have an impressive **ruined castle**, although the best preserved is at **Sárospatak**, on the eastern lowlands bordering the Great Plain.

The western approaches

Although the westerly Cserhát Hills are accessible by train from Vác on the Danube Bend, the commonest **approaches** are **from Budapest** or the Great Plain. Several trains leave the capital's Keleti Station daily, passing through Hatvan and Füzesabony en route to Miskolc and Szerencs, from where branch lines head further north. Buses from the Stadion terminal run directly to Hollókő and Eger, and the HÉV line makes **Gödöllő** an easy day excursion from the capital. Driving to Eger or Miskolc, the fastest route is via the M3 motorway, which runs close to both towns.

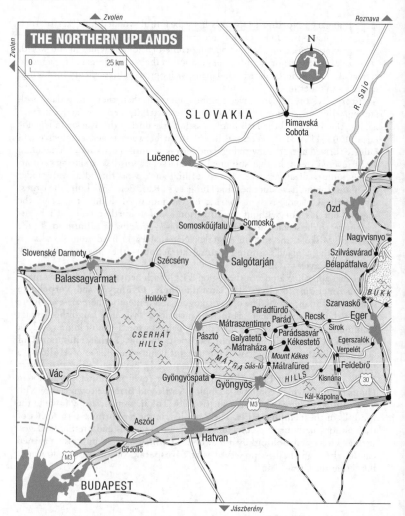

Gödöllő

Only 30km from Budapest, **GÖDÖLLŐ** is readily accessible by HÉV train from the capital's Örs Vezér tere Station (45min) and makes a pleasant stopover for motorists bound for Eger or Miskolc, but as few express trains stop here it's not a convenient place to interrupt a train journey. This small Baroque town used to be a summer residence of the Habsburgs, whose palace rivalled the splendour of the "Hungarian Versailles" at Esterházy (see p.268), while the influence of the early twentieth-century Gödöllő Artists' Colony is still apparent in Hungary, as the town's fine museum attests. Both the palace and the museum are on Szabadság tér, near the junction of the Budapest–Aszód road and Gödöllő's main street, Dózsa György utca.

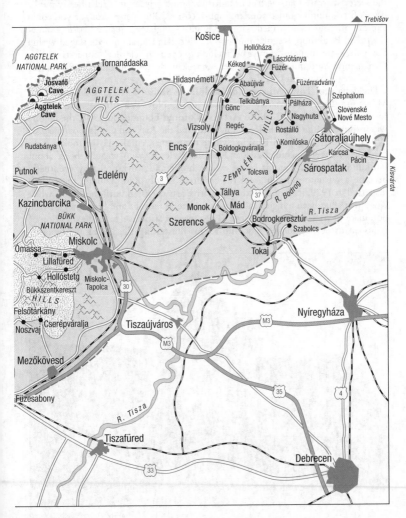

The **Royal Palace** (Királyi Kastély; Tues–Sun: April–Oct 10am–6pm; Nov–March 10am–5pm; last tickets 1hr before closing; 1800Ft) was commissioned by a confidante of Empress Maria Theresa, Count Antal Grassalkovich, and designed by András Mayerhoffer, who introduced the Baroque mansion to Hungary in the 1740s. In the nineteenth century, "Sissy", Emperor Franz Josef's wife, preferred living here to Vienna. However, two world wars took a toll on the palace, which was commandeered as a GHQ first by the "Reds" and then by the "Whites" in 1919–20, and pillaged by both the Nazis and the Red Army in 1944. One wing was later turned into an old people's home, while the rest was left to rot until the 1990s, when the restoration of the palace began. Though this is far from complete, you can visit the state rooms and private apartments used by Franz Josef and Sissy – his decorated in grey and gold, hers draped in her favourite colour, violet – and the secret staircase that she had installed for some privacy in a relentlessly public life. A fifty-minute guided **tour** in English costs 3300Ft per person, or you could explore on your own, armed with the English-language *Guide to Gödöllő*, sold at the palace bookshop. Regular musical and cultural programmes are staged within the palace throughout the year, including open-air classical concerts in the Ornamental Yard during the summer – check with the Tourinform office inside the palace (see opposite) for details.

The delightful **Town Museum of Gödöllő** at Szabadság tér 5 (Gödöllői Városi Múzeum; Tues–Sun March–Oct 10am–6pm; Nov–Feb 10am–4pm; 600Ft) focuses heavily on the **Gödöllő Artists' Colony**. Founded in 1901, the colony was inspired by the English Pre-Raphaelites and the Arts and Crafts movement of William Morris and John Ruskin, whose communal, rural ethos it took a stage further. Members included Aladár Körösfői Kriesch, who wrote a book about Ruskin and Morris, Sándor Nagy, whose home and workshop may eventually become a separate museum, and the architect Károly Kós. Though the colony dispersed in 1920, its stamp on the decorative arts persisted until the 1950s, while Kós's work has been a major influence on Imre Makovecz and his protégés, who dominate today's architectural scene. The museum also has a terrific exhibition of regional history, including mock-up rooms illustrating the life of the Gödöllő

▲ The Royal Palace, Gödöllő

estate, and a room of exhibits from New Guinea donated by the local naturalist and explorer Ferenc Ignácz – there are English captions throughout. For the really keen, there is a **workshop** at Körösfői utca 15–17, where local artists work on and display their projects (enquire at the museum for opening times).

If you have the time and inclination for a stroll, there's a huge **arboretum** on the road to Isaszeg, 3.5km south of the junction (Mon–Fri 8am–4pm, Sat & Sun 8am–6pm; free). Along this road you'll find several stately old trees and buildings, since this whole area on the edge of town used to be part of the palace grounds. If you head 3km down the road towards Aszód, you'll see a Transylvanian-style wooden gateway fronting a **Capuchin Church** that has been a place of pilgrimage ever since workmen dug up an ivory statue of the Virgin in 1759. The Grassalkovich family vault is situated here, and you can also see the grave of Pál Teleki, the wartime prime minister who committed suicide in protest at Hungary's participation in the Nazi invasion of Yugoslavia.

Practicalities

Arriving by HÉV train, get off before the terminal at the Szabadság tér stop, which is bang in the centre of town opposite the palace; the bus station is a couple of minutes' walk east of the HÉV station by the cultural centre. There's excellent **information** from Tourinform inside the palace near the ticket office (same hours as palace; ☎28/415-402, ⓦwww.gkrte.hu), who can also book **private rooms**, although with Budapest so close there's little chance that you'll want, or need, to stay. There are also cheap rooms at the *Szent István Egyetem* (the agricultural university) at Páter Károly utca 1, just east of the main train station (☎28/522-000; ②), or five more expensive ones at the *Galéria Panzió*, Szabadság tér 8 (☎&ⓕ28/418-691; ④). The *Galéria* also has a sublime **restaurant** offering dozens of moderately priced dishes, with exotic choices such as deer stew and shark on the menu. Alternatively, the *Yellow* pub and restaurant at Dózsa György utca 64 is well worth the fifteen-minute walk for its grilled meats or fish and a beer.

The Cserhát Hills

The **Cserhát Hills**, like their loftier neighbours, the Mátra and the Börzsöny, were once continuously forested, with a chain of fortresses guarding the valleys and passes into Slovakia, which formed part of Hungary until 1920. The Treaty of Trianon not only sundered economic ties, but stranded ethnic minorities on both sides of the redrawn border – Magyars in Slovakia, and **the Palóc** in Hungary. The Palóc, though probably of Slovak origin, are noted for their antiquated Hungarian dialect and fantastic costumes that are still worn (with an eye for the tourist trade) at the museum village of **Hollókő**, though you'll learn more about their traditions from the Palóc museum in **Balassagyarmat**.

Elsewhere, you can glimpse the region's feudal past as you pass picturesquely **ruined castles** dotted around the countryside. Taking a closer look inside the Forgách mansion at **Szécsény** gives an insight into the world of the warlords and counts who held sway before industrialization.

Balassagyarmat

After losing its medieval fortress and most of its inhabitants to the Turks, **BALASSAGYARMAT** (pronounced "bolosho-dyarmot"), 90km north of Budapest close to the Slovakian border, was repopulated by Germans, Slovaks and Czechs in the eighteenth century, when its prosperity was reflected in the Baroque edifices along its main street. Today, the town has little to show for its status as the "Palóc capital" except for an imposing nineteenth-century **county hall** on Köztársaság tér, the main square, and the **Palóc Ethnographical Museum** in a grand, eclectic-style building in Palóc Park, a few minutes' walk down Bajcsy-Zsilinszky út (Tues–Sun 10am–4pm; 600Ft). The exhibition covers every aspect of Palóc life from the cradle to the grave, with all kinds of home-made artefacts and a fantastic collection of folk costumes. There are also exhibits celebrating the works of two of Hungary's leading nineteenth-century writers: Imre Madach, whose play *The Tragedy of Man* (written in 1860) is widely held to be Hungary's greatest classical drama, and Kálmán Mikszáth, whose short stories satirized the landed gentry. Another **exhibition** housed in two thatched cottages (Palóc Ház; May–Sept Tues–Sun 10am–4pm; 400Ft) behind the museum presents the traditional Palóc way of life *in situ*. En route to Palóc Park from Köztársaság tér, you'll pass the small **City Gallery** on the corner of Bajcsy-Zsilinszky út (Tues–Sun 9am–5pm; 200Ft), exhibiting work by local artists.

Practicalities

Balassagyarmat's **bus station** lies a block or so north of the central Köztársaság tér, while the **train station** is fifteen minutes' walk south along Kossuth utca. Almost everything else is located on the main Rákóczi fejedelem utca, which runs across Köztársaság tér.

Accommodation is limited to the simple but accomplished *Blues Panzió*, located just off Kossuth utca at Baltik Frigyes utca 3 (☎35/300-189, ⒲www.euroblues .hu; ❺), or the very average *Club Panzió*, a few minutes' walk west at Teleki út 14 (☎35/301-824, ⒺΡanzio@gosser-club-panzio.hu; ❹); there is also a small campsite on the edge of town on the Budapest road, at Kóvári út 13 (☎35/300-965; June–Aug). All the main **eateries** are along Rákóczi fejedelem utca, namely the *Zorba Háza*, a Greek-themed pizzeria in the courtyard at no. 28, and the cheap and pile-it-high Hungarian *Balassa* restaurant at no. 34. For coffee, try the agreeable *Orchidea* café, further down at no. 48.

Szécsény

Just 17km east of Balassagyarmat, the small town of **SZÉCSÉNY** is ennobled by the **Forgách Mansion**, a vivid yellow Baroque pile occupying the site of a medieval fortress that was blown up by the Habsburgs during the War of Independence. As the Forgáchs were previously noted for their Habsburg sympathies, it's ironic that their mansion was the site of the Hungarian Diet's election of Ferenc Rákóczi II as ruling prince and commander-in-chief of the Magyar forces, and the declaration of the union of Hungary and Transylvania in 1705. Today it houses the **Kubinyi Ferenc Museum** (Tues–Sun 10am–4pm; 600Ft), which contains various hunting and local archeology exhibits, in addition to some mocked-up rooms as they would have looked at the end of the nineteenth century; meanwhile, the gatekeeper's lodge holds a collection of religious artefacts collected by Sándor Csoma Körösi, who travelled widely in Asia and compiled the first Tibetan–English dictionary. Down the road, to the right of the mansion, stands a **bastion** from the old fortress (Bástyamúzeum; same hours and price as museum), exhibiting instruments of torture and engravings showing their use, which staff at the museum or at Tourinform will open on request; other remnants of the old **town walls** can be seen in the vicinity.

The mansion is situated on Ady Endre utca, a few minutes' walk from Fő tér, where you'll find an eighteenth-century **Firewatch Tower** (Tűztorony; 200Ft) that has listed three degrees since the town was bombed in 1944. Initially built on the site of a wooden bell-tower to commemorate the passing of the plague, it's not exactly the Leaning Tower of Pisa, but from mid-May to mid-September you can ascend it to enjoy a bird's-eye view of town. The keys can be obtained from the Tourinform office. More intriguingly, you can visit a **Franciscan church and monastery** (Ferences templom & kolostor) on Erzsébet tér, to the west of the Tourinform office on Rákóczi út, which dates back to the Middle Ages. There are guided **tours** of the church and the dining hall, library and monks' cells in the monastery (Tues–Sat 10am, 11am, 2pm, 3pm & 4pm; free), but unless you understand Hungarian, they raise more questions than they answer. You can also enter from the far end of Ady Endre utca, beyond the Forgách mansion.

Practicalities

Buses stop on Király utca, just east of the main square Fő tér, while the **train station** is located 1.5km north of town. Tourinform is at Ady Endre utca 4, just north of Fő tér (Mon–Fri 8am–4.30pm; ⊤&Ⓕ 32/370-777, Ⓔ szecseny@tourinform.hu). In the same building as Tourinform, the *Agro Hotel*, Rákóczi út 90B (⊤&Ⓕ 32/370-382; ❶), has the most basic rooms in town, with bathroom, but book ahead or arrive before 4pm when they close their doors. The alternative is the somewhat lacklustre *Bástya Panzió*, in the attractive servants' quarters of the Forgách Mansion at Ady Endre utca 14 (⊤ 32/372-427, Ⓔ bastyapanzio@profinter.hu; ❹), which has service-able rooms with TV and small bathrooms. The very agreeable *Paradiso* **restaurant**, also in the servants' quarters, serves regional specialities like *tócsni* (potato pancake), while the *Frédi Cukrászda* at Rákóczi út 85 is a good spot for coffee.

Hollókő

From Szécsény there are hourly buses to **HOLLÓKŐ** (Raven Rock), 16km further south, where a ruined fortress overlooks a **museum village** on UNESCO's World Heritage list. Following a fire in 1909, Hollókő's whitewashed Palóc houses were rebuilt in traditional style with broad eaves and carved gables. The old dwellings may now be largely owned by Budapest intellectuals who can better afford the upkeep – their original owners having long since installed themselves in flats on the outskirts – but the village has lost none of its striking appearance.

The traditional Palóc dress is chiefly worn by old ladies attending vespers at Hollókő's wooden-towered **church** – outwardly austere, but decorated inside in vibrant colours and with flowers. Once, each village had its own style of homespun attire: in Őrhalom in the Bőrzsöny Hills, for example, the Hollókő-style cap was transformed into a bonnet by the insertion of a stiff cardboard lining. Fine examples from various localities are displayed in the **Village Museum** at Kossuth utca 82 (Falumúzeum; mid-March to mid-Nov daily 10am–6pm; 250Ft). This Palóc house follows the Magyar peasant custom of having one room where the family lived and slept, and a parlour solely used for storing bedding and entertaining guests, with a jug and basin serving as a bathroom for the whole family. Three wells served the whole village until 1959, when piped water and electricity arrived on the same day.

To delve further into Palóc crafts, visit the **Weaving House** at no. 94 (Szövőház; April–Oct daily 10am–4pm; 200Ft), which contains a workshop and sells local textiles, or the **Táj és a nép** exhibition at no. 99 (Tájház; April–Oct daily 10am–5pm, Nov–March Sat & Sun only; 300Ft), featuring photos of the village over the years. The **Pottery** (Fazekasműhely), at Petőfi utca 7, sells ceramics, gives demonstrations and may even let you have a go at the wheel yourself. Lastly, walk up to the ruined **Hollókő castle** (Vár; April–Oct daily 10am–5.30pm; 600Ft) on the hilltop, which is signposted down past the church (10min), and also accessible by a steeper path through the woods, seldom used by visitors, which you can reach by carrying on down to the edge of the village and turning left uphill. Although the tumbled ramparts and single surviving tower are a far cry from their former glory as the original seat of the Illés family, the views over the village and the lush, green hills are wonderful. The small museum within the castle contains a few unspectacular items, such as cannonballs and tiles, many of which were unearthed during the castle's restoration programme.

Practicalities

There is just one daily **bus** (two at weekends) from Budapest's Stadion terminal to Hollókő, though there are hourly services to Szécsény, plus four a day to Pásztó – the jumping-off point for the Mátra Hills – and Salgótarján. Buses run through the modern part of Hollókő before dropping visitors at the top of Kossuth utca, the main street running down to the church.

Information is available from Kossuth utca 68, which houses both the Foundation for Hollókő (Hollókőért Közalapítvány) and Tourinform (June–Aug Mon–Fri 8am–6pm, Sat & Sun 10am–4pm; Sept–May Mon–Fri 8am–4pm, Sat & Sun 10am–2pm; ☎32/579-011, ⓦwww.holloko.hu), who can reserve **rooms** (❷), or even whole houses (❹), furnished with Palóc wardrobes, embroidered bolsters, and traditional outdoor grills. The main eatery in town (where things close early) is the *Vár* **restaurant** at Kossuth utca 95 (daily 11am–7pm), which has homestyle roasts in suitably cosy surrounds, or there's the *Muskátli* at Kossuth utca 61 (daily 11am–5pm), a coffee shop that also cooks up a few simple dishes.

Hollókőputs on some great **festivals**, and two of the best times to visit are for the **Easter Festival** (Hollókői Húsvéti Fesztivál), when egg-painting and dancing groups form just part of the two-day jollities over the Easter weekend, or on August 20 for the **Castle Tournament** (Hollókői Várjátékok), a day of medieval tournaments and folklore events.

The Mátra Hills

Hungarians make the most of their highlands, and the **Mátra Hills**, where Mount Kékes just tops 1000m, are heavily geared to domestic tourism. Mount Kékes itself is a popular place for winter sports, despite the relatively lacklustre resort facilities at Mátraháza. In the summer, families ramble the paths between picnic sites and beer gardens, unaware of the wild boar and deer that live deeper in the

Hiking in the Mátra and Bükk hills

Taken together, the Mátra and Bükk hills boast over 1000km of walking trails, with hikes to suit all abilities. The **Mátra** range contains the highest peak in Hungary and accompanying panoramic vistas over the surrounding countryside, while the swathes of beech forests that make up the sparsely populated **Bükk** Hills provide unparalleled tranquillity and some marvellous caves.

The most beautiful and diverse hike in the Mátra Hills is the thirty-kilometre **Rákóczi Trail**, which traverses the whole of the range, from Gyöngyös to Parádfürdő. It takes about three days to complete, but you can also do a shortened version covering just the last section in one day. This starts in Páradsasvár, from where the trail passes through beech forests with a halfway resting point at Farkas kút ("Wolf Well"), before crossing the Kis-Hidas-Folyás creek and emerging at Sás-tó; the route then winds up to Matrafüred along the Muzsla Valley. Another hike that affords fantastic views is the nine-kilometre round tour of **Mount Kékes**. Starting from the car park at the top of the mountain, the path heads south towards Sirok before veering left to cross the small creek next to the rocks of Gabi Halála ("Gabi's Death", named after a local woodsman's son who fell to his death here). Pisztrángos-tó makes a peaceful resting point midway, where you can take a drink from the spring or make use of a rain shelter. From here, the trail leads down through the beech groves into Mátraháza and back up the southern ski run to Mount Kékes.

A dramatic but leisurely Bükk Hills trail leads you from Bánkút, at the foot of Mount Bálvány, to Bélapátfalva, an eleven-kilometre marked hike running along the **Bükk Plateau**. The first part of the walk heads south along narrow ravines towards Tar-kő, from which you head west across the plateau. Magnificent cliffs run along its south side affording breathtaking views, before the craggy peaks of Istallós-kő and Vőrős-kő rise up either side of you as you continue westwards. Eventually you make the steep descent into Bélapátfalva where you can explore a Romanesque church which nestles at the foot of the Bélkő rocks.

Getting hold of a hiking **map** is a good idea before you attempt any walk in either range, even though many of the trails are clearly marked on the ground. Maps for the Mátra Hills (*Mátra Turistatérképe*) are available from Tourinform in Gyöngyös, and those for the Bükk Hills (*Bükk Turistatérképe*) can be found at the Tourinform in Eger.

---

thickets of oak and beech. The major settlement here is the town of **Gyöngyös** on the southern rim, while the many villages scattered amongst the hills are principally of interest for their amenities. In any case, it's the hills and forests that are the main attraction.

Gyöngyös

Most visitors approach the Mátra via **GYÖNGYÖS** (pronounced "dyurn-dyursh"), the centre of the Gyöngyös-Visonta **wine** region, where white wine grapes predominate. Gyöngyös itself is a mellow town with enough museums and Baroque monuments to rate an hour or two of sightseeing before pushing on into the hills.

The town's central **Fő tér** is a long, thin square surrounded by Baroque and Art Nouveau buildings, reconstructed after a fire in 1917. On the northeast corner stands **St Bartholomew's Church** (daily 9am–noon), originally Gothic but heavily remodelled in the eighteenth century, when the small building behind it was a music school. Behind the church at Szent Bertalan utca 3, the Baroque **House of the Holy Crown** (Szent Korona-ház) is so named because the Crown of St Stephen was brought here three times for safekeeping between 1806 and 1809. By ringing the bell you can gain admission to a splendid **Ecclesiastical Treasury** (Egyházi Kincstár; Tues–Sun 10am–noon & 2–5pm; 300Ft) of vestments, books and medieval chalices, and view a ceiling fresco that includes a picture of Hungary's last monarch painted in the 1920s, whose final legislative action was to approve the rebuilding of the town after the 1917 fire. The anti-monarchist regime of the time condemned the fresco as illegal, as it depicted a king.

Five minutes' walk east along Kossuth utca brings you to the **Orczy mansion**, a handsome, mint-green Baroque pile named after the eponymous landowning family. Beautifully renovated, it now houses the **Mátra Museum** (Tues–Sun: March–Oct 9am–5pm; Nov–Feb 10am–4pm; 1000Ft) which, aside from exhibits pertaining to the Orczy family, features local archeology and history sections, tableaux on hunting, and a dazzling collection of minerals. By heading south from the museum, past the bus station, and turning right onto Barátok tere, you come to a **Franciscan church** endowed by the Báthori family (see box, p.282), whose coat of arms – three dragon's teeth surrounded by a dragon biting its own tail – appears in the chancel. The Franciscan **Memorial Library** on the first floor (Műemlék Konytára; Tues–Fri 2–4pm, Sat 10am–1pm; free) has a wonderful stock of over 15,000 volumes, including 210 incunabula and five codices, plus other beautiful leather-bound works from European printing houses and exhibitions of illuminated manuscripts.

Before the Holocaust Gyöngyös had a considerable Jewish population, as evinced by the **Great Synagogue** on Vármegye tér, west of Fő tér, a Moorish-Gothic hybrid designed in 1929 by Lipót Baumhorn that once belonged to the Reform community, but now sadly serves as a carpet warehouse. Their Orthodox co-religionists used the older **Memorial Synagogue**, a Neoclassical edifice next door, built in 1816, that nowadays houses a local TV station.

Practicalities

Arriving at the **train station** on Vasút utca, simply follow Kossuth utca past the terminal for the narrow-gauge line, the Orczy Mansion and the main crossroads until you come to central Fő tér. The **bus station** is 100m south of the crossroads, on Koháry út. Tourinform at Fő tér 10 (mid-June to mid-Sept Mon–Fri 9am–5pm, Sat 9am–1pm; mid-Sept to mid-June Mon–Fri 9am–5pm; ☎37/311-155, Ⓔgyongyos@tourinform.hu) can provide **information** on both the town and the Mátra and Bükk hills, with hiking **maps** for sale too. It can also arrange **private rooms** (❷) in Gyöngyös and in the villages of the Mátra hills (see opposite).

The only **hotel** in town is the shiny, but rather characterless, *Hotel Opál*, just east of the bus station at Könyves Kálmán tér 12 (☎37/505-400, Ⓦwww.opalhotel .hu; ❻). Alternatives consist of the very pleasant *Vincellér Panzió*, 400m north of the bus station at Erzsébet királyné utca 22 (☎37/311-691, Ⓦwww.vincellerpanzio .hu; ❺); and cheap and modern hostel-style accommodation in the *Károly Róbert Diákhotel*, north of town along the road to Mátrafüred at Bene út 69 (☎37/518-100, Ⓦwww.krhotel.hu; ❷). The town's one really worthwhile **restaurant** is the fabulously classy *Kékes Étterem*, directly opposite Tourinform on Fő tér, which offers an upscale take on both Hungarian and international dishes; otherwise, there's the *Giardinetto d'Italia*, which has decent pizzas in stylish surroundings, set in a pretty location on Rózsa utca 8, just south of Fő ter. Just around the corner at Zöldfa utca 1, *Goloka* is a super little tea house, while for a beer, there's the grungy *Mephisto Rock Café*, at Kossuth Lajos 16. The **post office** is on Mátyás Király utca (Mon–Fri 8am–7pm, Sat 8am–noon) and **internet** access is available in the library next to Tourinform (Mon–Fri 9am–6pm).

To quit town in style, head for the terminus of the Mátravasút, a **narrow-gauge train line** on Kossuth utca, just beyond the Mátra Museum. One line runs to Mátrafüred, 7km to the north (daily: every 2hr between 8am and 6pm; 400Ft one-way), while the other breaks off after 2km and heads to Lajosháza, 11km away in roughly the same direction (May–Aug Sat & Sun 2 departures at 9.30am & 1.30pm; 400Ft one-way).

The Mátra villages

Though most tourists head straight for Mátrafüred, there are several picturesque **villages** at the foot of the Mátras that are relatively undiscovered, and right in the heart of the **wine country**. With your own transport it's feasible to explore the region thoroughly, but travellers dependent on local buses may have to settle for the village of **GYÖNGYÖSPATA**, 12km west of Gyöngyös. This has a fifteenth-century **Gothic church** with a fine doorway and an imposingly high Baroque "Tree of Jesse" altar (showing the family tree of Jesus), the only one of its kind in Europe. Keys are held in the house just uphill or at the addresses listed on the door. Alternatively, you can follow a minor road for 20km in the direction of Eger to reach **KISNÁNA** and view a **ruined castle** destroyed by Ottomans in the sixteenth century, before carrying on to Verpelét (see p.334). Once a flourishing court, all that remains of the castle are the tower of the inner gate, parts of the wall and a Gothic church tower. There's also a small museum inside the ruins, with a lapidarium (Vármúzeum; Tues–Sun: May–Sept 9am–5pm; Oct–April 10am–4pm; 200Ft).

From Gyöngyös, **buses** run every half-hour or so to Mátrafüred and Mátraháza, and four or five buses a day pass through Parád, Recsk and Sirok on their way to Eger. Recsk and Sirok are also accessible via the branch train line down from **Kál-Kápolna** (the station before Füzesabony on the Budapest–Miskolc line). Anyone intending to visit Sirok or Feldebrő, or go walking in the hills, should buy a large-scale **hiking map** beforehand (*A Mátra turistatérképe* – available from Tourinform in Gyöngyös). Egertourist in Eger (see p.336) and Gyöngyös Tourinform can help find **accommodation** in the villages.

Mátrafüred and Sás-tó

The Mátravasút narrow-gauge train line is the fun way to get from Gyöngyös to **MÁTRAFÜRED**, and takes no longer than the bus, dropping passengers off at the centre of this sloping, popular spa settlement. Although local walks are the main attraction, there is a small **Ethnographical Museum** at Pálosvörösmarti utca 2 (Palóc Néprajzi Magánygyűjtemény; daily 9am–5pm; 300Ft), displaying sumptuous folk headdresses as well as the usual dolls and other folkcraft. Aside from private **rooms**, there's the 1970s-style but perfectly agreeable *Hotel Avar* at Páradi út 24 (☎37/320-131, ⓦwww.avarhotel.hu; ⑥), which has a swimming pool and sauna, or you could try the less expensive *Hegyalja Panzió*, a well-presented former trade-union resort at Béke út 7 (☎37/320-027, ⓔhegyalja .matrafured@t-online.hu; ⑤). For **eating**, there are endless buffets and snack stands in the centre of the village, but if you need something a little more refined you can rely on the restaurant at the *Hegyalja*.

Four kilometres uphill from Mátrafüred, on the bus route between Gyöngyös and Mátraháza, lies **Sás-tó** (Sedge Lake). More of a large pond than a lake, it's a friendly place full of Hungarians boating and fishing amid the usual snack stands. Close by, the vast sprawl of the **Oxygen Adrenaline Park** (June–Aug Mon–Thurs & Sun 9am–7pm, Fri & Sat 8am–9pm; Sept–May Mon–Thurs & Sun 10am–6pm, Fri &

Sat 10am–7pm) offers more than half a dozen different kinds of activity, such as dry bob, zip-lining and quad biking. If you feel like **staying**, *Mátra Sastó Camping* (T 37/374-025, W www.sasto.elpak.hu; mid-April to mid-Oct) is an attractive complex with a motel (③), bungalows (③), and two- and three-bed chalets of varying size (②–④). Heading on, you can easily walk from Sás-tó to Mátraháza along the footpath through the forest, where **wild boars** reputedly lurk.

Mátraháza and Mount Kékes

MÁTRAHÁZA, 9km north of Mátrafüred, is a small village consisting mainly of ex-trade union hostels converted into tourist facilities, plus a few bars, though there are plenty of enjoyable walks in the vicinity. Just outside the village, back down on the road to Mátrafüred, is the chalet-style *Bérc Hotel* (T 37/374-102, E berchotel@t-online.hu; ④), a clean and pleasant place to stay and a great base for hiking; while the friendly *Pagoda Panzió* (T 37/374-023, E postmaster@t-online .hu; ④), set back amongst the trees in the centre of the village, is also well situated. The reliable *Borostyán* restaurant is furnished throughout in wood, and dishes up well-executed traditional food to hungry hikers.

From Mátraháza, you can easily make the quick hourly bus trip to **Mount Kékes**, the highest point (1014m) in the Mátra range. Two **ski runs** (*sípálya*) descend from the summit (you can rent skiing equipment at the slope and the car park during the November–March ski season), which is crowned by a nine-storey telecommunications **tower** offering an impressive view of the highlands (Kilátóto-rony; daily 9am–3.30pm; 350Ft). The simple *Hotel Hegycsúcs* (T 37/567-007, E info@matracentrum.hu; ②) may be only half the height of its neighbouring tower, but its views are still stunning, and it also houses a sauna and gym. There's somewhat more luxurious accommodation around 10km north of here in the mountain hamlet of **Galyatető**, courtesy of the very fine *Hunguest Galya* hotel (T 36/576-576, W www.hunguesthotels.hu; ⑨).

Parádsasvár, Parád and Parádfürdő

Several kilometres east of Galyatető, a group of similarly named villages gathers around Parád, where Count Károlyi tried to set an example to other nobles in 1919 by distributing land to his serfs. **PARÁDSASVÁR** is home to one of the grandest castle hotels in Hungary, the *Kastély Hotel Sasvár* (T 36/444-444, W www .khs.hu; ⑨). Once the hunting seat of the Károlyi and Rákóczi family, the Miklós Ybl-designed Neoclassical pile sits in its own large private parkland, with the most opulent rooms imaginable, a spa, and a selection of excellent restaurants. If that's beyond your wallet, try the lovely *St Hubertus Panzió* (T 36/544-060, W www .hubertuspanzio.hu; ⑥) across the road. The village also boasts a large **glassworks** that has been producing Parád crystal since the 1800s; it's usually open for guided tours, where you can watch the glass-blowers at work, though it has been closed for a couple of years and it's not certain when it will reopen (T 36/364-353). Signposted from the village, 1km up the hill is **Fényes Major Equestrian Farmstead** (Wed–Sun 8am–6pm; 500Ft), which stables the famous **Lippizaner** horses (see box, p.341; horseriding 3000Ft per hr in the yard, 4000Ft in the field, carriage rides 8000Ft per hr; T 36/444-444), as well as keeping a variety of other animals including buffalo and goats.

Three kilometres further east lies **PARÁD**, where, at Sziget utca 10, an old **Palóc House** (Palóc Ház; March–Oct Tues–Sun 9am–5pm; Nov–Feb 10am–2pm; 140Ft), and accompanying pigsty, is fully kitted out with peasant costumes and artefacts, and at Hársfa utca 6, there is an intriguing exhibition of **wood-carving**, signposted *Fafaragó Kiállitása* (Wed–Sun 9am–5pm; 200Ft), by the master craftsman

Joachim Asztalos. His life-size Palóc peasant figures are particularly touching. Inexpensive **accommodation** is available at the well-cared-for *Parádi Kisvendéglo* (☏30/364-831; ❷) at Kossuth utca 234, which has a small garden restaurant serving good home-cooked food. There's a small **information office**, called Paradinform, in the *Tajház* at Kossuth utca 53 (April–Sept Wed–Sun 9am–3pm), where you can pick up info on the region.

In the 1880s, local quarry workers discovered that drinking the shaft water seemed to cure a range of illnesses; today, the popular **thermal spa** of **PARÁDFÜRDŐ** still boasts the sulphurous, fizzy water that is said to mainly benefit digestive complaints. Such are the curative powers of the local water, a **sanitarium**, at Kossuth utca 221, now stands over the village. It holds a unique collection of over 300 mineral waters from 25 countries, which can be viewed and sampled on request. But the village really deserves a visit for its **Coach Museum** at Kossuth utca 217 (Kocsimúzeum; Tues–Sun: April–Sept 9am–5pm; Oct–March 9am–4pm; 500Ft). The splendid collection includes vehicles for state occasions, hunting and gallivanting around in. For the record, the coach, which superseded the cumbersome wagon throughout Europe, was actually invented in the Hungarian village of Kocs, west of Budapest. Some beautiful horses can be seen in adjacent stables, which were designed for the Károlyi family by Miklós Ybl. Standing opposite the sanitarium is the shiny, sprawling *Erzsébet Park* hotel (☏36/444-044, ⊛www.erzsebetparkhotel.hu; ❹), with its full complement of wellness facilities. You'll find two much cheaper **places to stay** along Peres utca, a quiet country lane, which turns left off the main road at the eastern end of the village; namely the *Boróka Mini Hotel* (☏36/364-265; ❹) at no. 18, and the cosier *Izabella Panzió* at no. 43 (☏36/364-221; ❹).

Recsk

Mention **RECSK**, a village 2km east of Parádfürdő, and many older Hungarians will share recollections of terror. During the late 1940s and early 1950s, thousands of the tens of thousands of citizens arrested by the ÁVO were sentenced to labour in the quarries southwest of here. Half-starved and frequently beaten by their jailers, prisoners died of exhaustion or in rockfalls, or more usually while sleeping in muddy pits open to the sky. The operation, modelled on the Soviet Gulag, was highly secretive and few knew what was being carried out until it was eventually closed by Imre Nagy in 1953. **Recsk concentration camp** was effaced by a tree plantation during the Kádár years, and not until 1991 were its victims commemorated. The site, around 5km up from the village near the still working quarry (look for the *Kőbánya* signs), has been turned into a **memorial park** (Recski Nemzeti Emlékpark), though there's little to see beyond a stone monument symbolizing repression, a watchtower, and signs to indicate which buildings once stood there (kitchen, barracks and so on). In the village itself, the **Palóc House** at Kossuth utca (Mon–Fri 8am–noon; free) has typical furnishings to view, as well as some colourful embroidery and textiles.

Sirok, Verpelét, Feldebrő and Egerszalók

The bus from Parádfürdő to Eger stops at **SIROK**, 8km further east of Recsk, and is a great place to visit if you're wild about romantic views. On a mountain top above the village, 1.5km northeast of the train station, there's a ruined thirteenth-century **castle** from which you can admire the mingled peaks of the Mátra, the Bükk and Slovakia. The village itself is also lovely, its old houses nestling among cliffs and crags; some ancient dwellings are carved out of the rock itself – head for Széchenyi utca to see some examples. The village has a **campsite** at Dobó utca 30, at the end of the road towards the castle (☏36/361-558; May–Sept).

Antiquity buffs with their own transport should head 11km south to **VERPELÉT**, where the **Jewish cemetery** on the far side of the village has gravestones from as long ago as 1628, many richly carved or tilting at crazy angles. The cemetery is tended by a Roma Gypsy family living nearby, who can help you climb into the grounds. Alternatively, you can ask for the key from the town hall in the centre of the village (Tues, Thurs & Fri 7.30am–noon & 12.30–4pm). Two hundred metres down from the town hall, at Kossuth utca 60, is the blink-and-you'll-miss-it **Palóc forge-shop** (Kovacsműhely; Tues–Sun 9am–3pm; 50Ft), a diminutive, thatched-roof structure with a little stone chimney where, so legend has it, Hungarian kings have had their horses shod. Ask at the house behind the shop to see its small array of old tools and blacksmith apparel.

Four kilometres further down the road, **FELDEBRŐ** boasts one of the oldest **church crypts** in Hungary, containing twelfth-century frescoes influenced by Byzantine art, and the **grave of King Aba** (1041–44), one of the ephemeral monarchs between the Árpád and Angevin dynasties. Keys for the crypt (Altemplom; daily: June–Sept 8am–6pm; Oct–May till 4pm) are held at Szabadság tér 22, nearby. The local **linden leaf wine** (Debrői hárslevelű) is good for refreshing weary travellers, as you can discover in **wine cellars** such as the one at Árpád út 2, just off the road beside the church.

If you're still feeling weary, then head for **EGERSZALÓK**, 16km from Feldebrő (and just 5km from Eger), home to a stunning **hot spring**, which is worth a look even if you aren't planning a dip, due to its huge crystallized crust of salt deposits that have formed around the pools. Set amongst a thick bank of trees just outside the village, the enormous **Salt Hill Thermal Spa** (Mon–Thurs 10am–6pm, Fri–Sun 10am–8pm; 4000Ft per day, 2500Ft for 3hr) comprises some seventeen pools (indoor and out), in addition to all manner of saunas, cabins and baths. Standing somewhat incongruously in the centre of the village itself, at Széchenyi utca 31, is the *Shiraz Hotel* (T 36/574-500, W www.shiraz.hu; ⑨), a Moroccan-themed establishment featuring beautifully styled rooms and a gorgeous North African bathhouse – non-hotel guests can also use the bath facilities (4800Ft per day).

The Bükk Hills and the Aggtelek National Park

The largest, and most beautiful, of the Uplands' hilly regions is the **Bükk** range, named after the beech trees (*bükk*) that blanket these modest peaks. For those with time to spare, this is fine walking country, while there are also possibilities to participate in more relaxing activities, such as horseriding, boating or riding a narrow-gauge train. The Bükk Hills can easily be reached from either of the region's two major settlements – the gorgeous Baroque town of **Eger**, with its abundance of historical monuments and wine, and the city of **Miskolc**, which conceals a handful of worthwhile attractions underneath its hard-nosed and gritty industrial appearance. Further north, scraping the Slovakian border, the **Aggtelek National Park** contains arguably Hungary's greatest natural wonder, the fabulous **Aggtelek Caves**.

Eger and around

Situated in its own sunny valley between the Mátra and the Bükk, **EGER** is famed for its wine, its minaret, and the heroic legend attached to its castle, which overlooks a florid Baroque town centre. In terms of tourist popularity, this

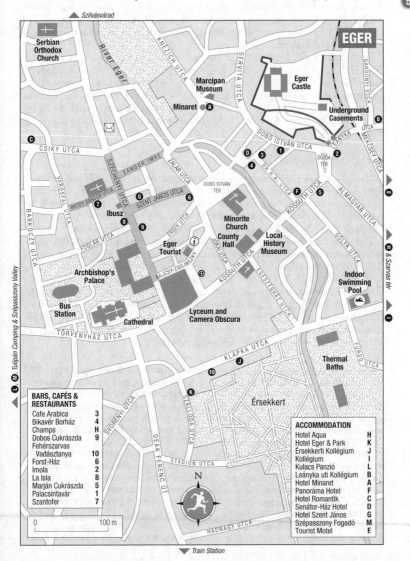

Within the map:

▲ Szilvásvárad

EGER

Serbian Orthodox Church

River Eger

KREZICH UTCA

SERVITA UTCA

GARDONYI UTCA

Marcipan Museum

Minaret ●Ⓐ

Eger Castle

Underground Casements ●Ⓑ

LEÁNYKA UTCA

MÉKSZEY UTCA

Ⓒ CSIKY UTCA

DOBÓ ISTVÁN UTCA

SZÉCHENYI UTCA

SÁNDOR IMRE

ZALAR UTCA

Ⓓ ❸ ❶ ❷

DÓZSA TÉR

DR H.K. UTCA

ALMAGYAR UTCA

❺ Ⓕ

KOSSUTH UTCA

● ▶ & Szarvas tér

GÓLYA UTCA

DOBÓ ISTVÁN TÉR

SZENT JÁNOS UTCA

❼ Ⓖ ❻

BRÓDY SÁNDOR UTCA

VÁROSFAI UTCA

Ibusz ❽

❾

ÉRSEK UTCA

Minorite Church

County Hall

Local History Museum

Eger Tourist ⓘ

FÓGLAR UTCA

JÓKAI UTCA

BARROCZY UTCA

Archbishop's Palace

@

BAJCSY-ZSILINSZKY

KOSSUTH UTCA

EGESZSÉGHÁZ UTCA

Indoor Swimming Pool

● ▶

Bus Station

Cathedral

Lyceum and Camera Obscura

TÖRVÉNYHÁZ UTCA

Ⓜ Tulipán Camping & Szépasszony Valley

FÜRDŐ UTCA

❿

Thermal Baths

KLAPKA UTCA

Ⓙ

SVORÉNYI UTCA

SZÁLLODA UTCA

Ⓚ

Érsekkert

DEÁK FERENC ÚT

STADION UTCA

N

0   100 m

HADNAGY UTCA

▼ Train Station

BARS, CAFÉS & RESTAURANTS

Cafe Arabica	3
Bikavér Borház	4
Champs	H
Dobos Cukrászda	9
Fehérszarvas Vadásztanya	10
Forst-Ház	6
Imola	2
La Isla	8
Marján Cukrászda	5
Palacsintavár	1
Szantofer	7

ACCOMMODATION

Hotel Aqua	H
Hotel Eger & Park	K
Érsekkerti Kollégium	J
Kollégium	I
Kulacs Panzió	L
Leányka uti Kollégium	B
Hotel Minaret	A
Panoráma Hotel	F
Hotel Romantik	C
Senátor-Ház Hotel	D
Hotel Szent János	G
Szépasszony Fogadó	M
Tourist Motel	E

enchanting town is a serious rival to Szentendre and Tihany, and with by far the liveliest atmosphere of anywhere in the Northern Uplands, it is a must on anyone's itinerary.

From Eger, buses and local trains head to various villages bordering the Bükk National Park, notably **Szilvásvárad**, near the **Szalajka Valley** to the north, and **Cserépváralja** to the northeast.

Arrival and information

Travellers arriving at the **bus station**, near the cathedral, can stroll into the centre. Coming from the **train station**, 1.5km south of town on Állomás tér, walk up the road to Deák Ferenc út, catch bus #10, #11 or #12 and get off just before the cathedral. Within the centre of the town, orientation is simple and everything is within walking distance.

The super-helpful Tourinform, at Bajcsy-Zsilinsky út 9 (mid-June to mid-Sept Mon–Fri 9am–7pm, Sat & Sun 9am–4pm; mid-Sept to mid-June Mon–Fri 9am–5pm, Sat 9am–1pm; ☎36/517-715, ✉eger@tourinform.hu), has a wealth of **information** on both the town and activities on offer in the region. The **post office** is at Széchenyi utca 20–22 (Mon–Fri 8am–6pm, Sat 8am–noon) and there's **internet access** at the *Arabesque Netcafe*, Fellnér J utca 1 (Mon–Fri 8am–10pm, Sat 10am–10pm).

Accommodation

Although the town is blessed with a healthy stock of terrific hotels and pensions, Eger is a hugely popular destination, so it's advisable to **book ahead**. Tourinform has a comprehensive list of **private rooms** (❷–❸), but don't do bookings; these are handled by Egertourist next door at Bajcsy-Zsilinszky utca 9 (Mon–Fri 9am–5pm, also July & Aug Sat 9am–noon; ☎36/510-277, ⓦwww.egertourist.hu).

The cheapest option is a bed in one of the town's **student hostels** (*kollégium*), which you can book either direct or through Egertourist – all charge around 1800–2000Ft for a dorm bed. The most central is the *Érsekkerti Kollégium* at Klapka György utca 12 (☎36/413-661, ⓦwww.ektf.hu; July to mid-Sept). Otherwise, there is the *Leányka úti Kollégium*, east of the castle at Leányka utca 6 (☎36/520-430, ⓦwww.uktf.hu; July & Aug), and the *Kollégium* at Pozsonyi utca 4–6 (☎36/424-202; mid-June to Aug). The only **campsite** hereabouts is the year-round *Tulipán Camping*, sited at the entrance to the Szépasszony Valley at Szépasszonyvölgy 71 (☎36/410-580), which also has four-bed chalets (❷).

Hotels and pensions

Hotel Aqua Maklári út 9 ☎36/512-510, ⓦwww.hotelaqua-eger.hu. A very stylish place south of Szarvas tér, with designer-furnished, a/c rooms (all with wi-fi) which have been given some neat touches with bedside rugs, wall pictures and pot plants. Attractive grill terrace and pub, too (see p.341). ❼

Hotel Eger & Park Szálloda utca 1–3 ☎36/413-233, ⓦwww.hotelegerpark.hu. Two conjoined establishments made up of the three-star *Eger*, which has compact, polished rooms, and the much fancier, and pricier, *Park*, whose large rooms ooze class. Reception for both is in the *Eger*. Facilities include a swimming pool, tennis courts, sauna and a bowling alley. ❼–❾

Kulacs Panzió Szépasszonyvölgy ☎36/311-375, ⓦwww.kulacscsarda.hu. Smoothly run and very comfortable place in the heart of the valley, accommodating a handful of cosy, pine-furnished rooms with little balconies. There's also a very good, albeit very touristy, restaurant attached. ❻

Hotel Minaret Knézich Károly utca 4 ☎36/410-233, ⓦwww.hotelminaret.hu. The fine building and great location opposite the minaret promise much, but the darkish rooms come as a bit of a letdown. A small swimming pool in the delightful yard and the jazz club downstairs somewhat make up for it. ❻

Panoráma Hotel Dr Hibay Károly utca 2 ☎36/412-886, ⓦwww.panoramahotels.hu. Ignore the joyless exterior, this restful four-star hotel has spotless, enormous a/c rooms with wi-fi, plus a full complement of wellness facilities. ❽

🏃 **Hotel Romantik** Csiky Sándor utca 26 ☏ 36/310-456, Ⓦ www.romantikhotel.hu. You're sure of a jovial welcome at this compact and perky little hotel a short walk west of the centre, complete with colourful, warm rooms, and a verdant, romantic rock garden. ❼

🏃 **Senátor-ház Hotel** Dobó István tér 11 ☏ 36/320-466, Ⓦ www.senatorhaz.hu. Located in the heart of tourist territory, this eighteenth-century inn is quite delightful, from the wonderfully cluttered reception (a living museum in itself) to the dozen or so characterful, well-equipped rooms. An absolute gem. Reservations essential. ❻

Hotel Szent János Szent János utca 3 ☏ 36/510-350, Ⓦ www.hotelszentjanos.hu. Ultramodern hotel just off Széchenyi utca possessing ten gorgeous pastel-coloured rooms, all with a/c and wi-fi. Fitness and aerobics room and sauna. ❼

Szépasszony Fogadó Szépasszonyvölgy ☏ 36/310-777, Ⓔ szepasszonyfogado@chello.hu. Opposite the *Kulacs Panzió*, this very simple, four-roomed guesthouse is useful for crashing after an evening's drinking. Breakfast not included. ❸

Tourist Motel Mekcsey utca 2–4 ☏ 36/411-101, Ⓔ szallas@tourist-motel.t-online.hu. Just off Szarvas tér, this very simple place has rooms sleeping two to four people. Shared bathrooms and no breakfast, but it's clean and central. ❸

The Town

One of the oldest Magyar settlements in Hungary, Eger was a flourishing Renaissance centre at the time of the Turkish invasion, when it found itself on the front line after the occupation of Buda. To general amazement, its castle withstood the **siege of 1552**, when two thousand soldiers and Eger's **women** (who hurled rocks, hot soup and fat), under the command of **István Dobó**, repulsed a Turkish force six times their number – a victory immortalized in Géza Gárdonyi's novel *Egri Csillagok* (*Eclipse of the Crescent Moon*). During the siege of 1596, however, the castle was held by foreign mercenaries who surrendered after a week, whereupon the Turks sacked Eger, leaving only "blackened walls and buildings razed to the ground" and "the naked bodies of Christians baking in the sun, in some places four yards high".

By the time the Turks were driven out in 1687, Eger had only 3500 inhabitants, including 600 Muslims who subsequently converted to Christianity. Its **revival** in the eighteenth century was directed by the episcopal see, which commissioned much of the Baroque architecture that gives Eger its characteristic appearance. This was largely financed by the local vineyards, whose robust red Egri Bikavér – known abroad as **Bull's Blood** – is still a major money-earner, from both direct sales and the tourism that it generates. Under Communism, local co-ops had little incentive to aim for quality and a lot of fairly rough stuff was produced (which is still on sale), but in recent years, independent producers such as Gál Tibor, Béla Vincze and Vilmos Thummerer have done much to raise standards.

The Cathedral, Lyceum and Serbian Orthodox Church

Eger Cathedral, on Eszterházy tér, occupies a site hallowed since the eleventh century, and looms large above a flight of steps flanked by statues of saints Stephen, László, Peter and Paul, by the Italian sculptor Casagrande. Constructed between 1831 and 1836, this ponderous Neoclassical edifice was architect József Hild's rehearsal for the still larger basilica at Esztergom. Its interior was largely decorated by J.L. Kracker, who spent his last years working in Eger. Particularly impressive is the frescoed cupola, where the City of God arises in triumph as evildoers flee the sword. Between mid-May and mid-October, at around noon, you can hear organ presentations in the basilica. Next to the steps leading up to the cathedral is the entrance to the former **wine cellars** (daily: April–Sept 10am–8pm; Oct–March 10am–5pm; 800Ft), which you can have a look around on 45-minute guided tours (departing on the hour), though in truth there's not a whole lot to see.

Directly opposite the cathedral, the florid, Zopf-style **Lyceum** was founded in the late eighteenth century by two enlightened bishops whose proposal for a university was rejected by Maria Theresa. Now a teacher training college (named after Ho Chi Minh during the Communist era), the building is worth visiting for its **library** (mid-March to mid-Nov Tues–Sun 9am–3.30pm; mid-Nov to mid-March Sat & Sun 9am–1pm, closed Dec 22–Jan; 700Ft), whose beautiful floor and fittings are made of polished oak. There is also a huge trompe l'oeil ceiling fresco of the Council of Trent by Kracker and his son-in-law. The lightning bolt and book in one corner symbolize the Council's decision to establish an Index of forbidden books and suppress all heretical ideas. The library also contains an original letter by Mozart, the only one in the country. While in the building, it's definitely worth checking out the **observatory**, at the top of the tower in the east wing (same hours as the library; 700Ft), where a nineteenth-century **camera obscura** projects a view of the entire town from a bird's-eye perspective.

Close by, at Széchenyi utca 5, stands the **Archbishop's Palace** (Éseki palota), a U-shaped Baroque pile with fancy wrought-iron gates. In the right wing of the palace you'll find the treasury and a history of the bishopric of Eger (Egyházi Gyűtemény; April–Oct Tues–Sat 9am–5pm; Nov–March Mon–Fri 8am–4pm; 400Ft), encompassing numerous items from the eighteenth and nineteenth centuries, such as chalices, reliquaries and robes, including one worn by Maria Theresa when she was crowned queen.

At the far end of Széchenyi utca lies the eighteenth-century **Serbian Orthodox Church** (Rác templom; Tues–Sun 10am–4pm; 400Ft), whose elaborate, gold-braided iconostasis (1789–91) is strikingly similar to the one in the Greek Orthodox Church in Miskolc, and, at 13m high, is just 3m shorter. The former parsonage next to the church now houses a memorial room containing various works of the Serbian poet Mihály Vitkovics and an exhibition of the Hungarian painter and photographer **György Kepes** (May–Oct Thurs–Sun 10am–4pm; Nov–April Mon–Fri 10am–4pm; 400Ft).

Kossuth utca and Dobó István tér

From the Lyceum and Provost House across the way, **Kossuth utca** leads past a Franciscan church, where a mosque stood in Turkish times, and the **County Hall**, whose magnificent gates were wrought by Henrik Fazola – notice the stork with a snake in its beak and a vine in its claws, on the county coat of arms. The same man who designed the gates was also responsible for the prison bars in the old Eger jail at Kossuth utca 9, now a small **history museum** (April–Oct Thurs–Sun: April–Oct 10am–6pm; Nov–March 10am–3pm; 300Ft), displaying artefacts from Eger and Heves county. It also houses a few sporting exhibits but focuses predominantly on the achievements of the local swimming team and water polo club, whose members regularly form the basis of Hungary's repeatedly successful Olympic team. Printed information is available in English detailing the exhibits of each room.

Continuing along Kossuth utca across the bridge, you pass on your right the deserted "Buttler House" that featured in Mikszáth's novel, *A Strange Marriage*, and on your left a synagogue now transformed into a shop. Alternatively, follow Bajcsy-Zsilinszky or Érsek utca into **Dobó István tér**, the starting point for further sightseeing. On the southern side of the square stands the former **Minorite Church**, a twin-towered Baroque edifice completed in 1771, and one of the most stunning in Central Europe. The altarpiece of the Virgin Mary and St Anthony – the church patron – was completed by the ubiquitous Kracker, whilst the Latin inscription above its entrance asserts that "Nothing is Enough for God". The small exhibition of Palóc folk art next door at no. 12 (April–Sept Tues–Sun 9am–5pm; 200Ft) is also worth a visit. More striking, however, are the square's action-packed **statues of warriors** commemorating the siege of 1552, including several women wreaking havoc on Turkish assailants.

A short distance from Dobó István tér, on Knézich utca, stands the town's most obvious relic of the Turkish occupation. Rising some 40m high, and minus its mosque which was demolished in 1841, is the slender, fourteen-sided **minaret** (April–Oct daily 10am–6pm; 200Ft); Eger's most photographed structure, it offers fine views from its balcony, 97 steps up. Just across from the minaret, at Harngöntő utca 4, the **Marcipan Museum** (Kopcsik Marcipania; April–Oct Tues–Sun 10am–6pm; 600Ft) displays more than one hundred creations by local champion confectioner, Lajos Kopcsik – highlights include models of the minaret and an oversized bottle of Bikavér, though the centrepiece is a room whose items are all fashioned entirely in Baroque style.

Eger Castle
With every approach covered by batteries of cannons, you can easily appreciate why **Eger Castle** (daily: March–Oct 9am–5pm; Nov–Feb 10am–4pm; 1200Ft, grounds only 400Ft, discounted admission Mon as exhibitions closed except the underground galleries) was so formidable. Ascending from its lower gate past the Gergely Bastion, the ticket office on your left offers a historical video and English-language cassette for a do-it-yourself tour if you feel so inclined. On entering the inner section of the castle through the Várkoch Bastion, you are also passing underneath the **tomb of Géza Gárdonyi**, on which is inscribed "Only his body lies here".

One of the few Gothic structures left in northeastern Hungary, the **Bishop's Palace** harbours a **museum** containing tapestries, Turkish handicrafts and weaponry. On the ground floor are temporary exhibits and a "**Hall of Heroes**" (Hősök terme), where István Dobó is buried amid a bodyguard of siege heroes carved in best Stakhanovite style. The adjacent **art gallery** boasts several fine Munkácsys and three romantic Transylvanian landscapes by Antal Ligeti.

To the east of this complex lies a jumble of medieval foundations signposted as a "Romkert" – **Garden of Ruins**. Here stood Eger's Gothic cathedral, which was damaged by fire in 1506 and used by the Turks as a gunpowder magazine during the first siege "to spite the Christians". To the south, tour groups gather outside the concrete tunnel entrance to the Kazamata or **underground galleries**, a labyrinth of sloping passages, gun emplacements, deep-cut observation shafts and mysterious chambers.

Out from the centre: the Szépasszony Valley
A pleasant thirty-minute walk west of town is the **Szépasszony Valley** ("Valley of the Beautiful Women"), which is surrounded by dozens of vineyards producing four types of **wine** – Muskotály (Muscatel), Bikavér (the famous Bull's Blood), Leányka (medium dry white with a hint of herbs) and Médoc Noir (rich, dark red and sweet – coating your tongue black). The valley has suffered at the hands of mass tourism, and can be slightly underwhelming if you are expecting lush, cellar-studded countryside (the cellars somewhat resemble a clutch of concrete bunkers), but the compact and friendly neighbourhood is still fun to visit, particularly outside peak season.

Finding the right **wine cellar** is often a matter of luck and taste – some are dank and gloomy, some serve wines of ambrosial quality and others will pour you a trickle of vinegar. That said, the cellars are now much better regulated, with a qualification system in place and bronze plaques denoting those of a certain standard – try Hagymási at no. 19, Juhász at no. 40, and Sike at no. 43. More generally, the cellars down towards the far end of the horseshoe-shaped crescent are fairly lively. Certain cellars also have their own **musicians**, who appear only when tourist numbers have reached critical volume. Most cellars are open daily until at least 8pm, although many do close later depending on custom – expect to pay around 100–150Ft for a glass in most places. Tourinform can also advise you on other good cellars to try. Although there are several very touristy and almost identical **restaurants** in the valley, you're better off ordering some nibbles at one of the cellars, or taking a packed lunch.

Your best bet, if you really don't want to walk, is to arrange before you go for a **taxi** to come and pick you up (try City Taxi; ☏36/555-555; around 1000Ft one-way), or swallow your pride and take the miniature **tourist train** (May–Sept 9am–6pm; 500Ft one-way), which shuttles back and forth between the valley and Dobó István tér.

Eating and drinking

Eger has a fine concentration of first-rate **restaurants** scattered around town. The centre abounds in delightful cafés, too, and whilst genuinely exciting drinking venues may be a little thin on the ground, there are enough decent places to sample the local wines.

Restaurants

Fehérszarvas Vadásztanya Klapka György utca 8. If you don't mind being surrounded by stuffed animals' heads, the "White Deer Hunters' Farm", a glamorous-looking place next to the *Park Hotel*, should satisfy. Extensive and affordable range of game dishes on offer, as well as a nicely priced daily set menu (11am–3.30pm; 800Ft).

Forst-Ház Dobó tér 1. Overlooking the main square, this pleasing and good-looking restaurant boasts a wide-ranging menu, with wild boar stew and joint of rabbit, alongside simpler pasta and mixed grill dishes.

Imola Dózsa tér 4. Just down from the castle on a picturesque little square, the *Imola* is the classiest restaurant in town, sumptuously furnished in smooth wood, with beautiful lighting and crisply laid tables. A modest but inventive menu, with

dishes such as spiced guinea fowl soup, grey cattle stew and grilled goose liver.

Palacsintavár Dobó utca 9, entrance on Fazola Henrick utca. This wonderfully original restaurant offers every pancake imaginable – salty, sweet, vegetarian and many more. In addition to the fine food (if you can't finish your plate, they'll box it up for you), the funky artwork, dim hanging lamps, wicker chairs and amiable staff make this place a must.

Szantofer Bródy Sándor utca 3. Just off Széchenyi utca, this terrific place – accommodating two contrasting rooms, one an atrium-style space with big windows and brown wicker chairs, the other a more traditional interior with stone and wood-panelled walls – serves some of the best Hungarian cuisine in town (pork knuckle, paprika veal stew).

Cafés and bars

Eger has some elegant **patisseries** such as the *Dobos Cukrászda* at Széchenyi utca 6, which has a fabulous, classy hall at the rear (good when the weather gets chilly), and the *Marján Cukrászda* at Kossuth utca 28, famous for its parfaits and cakes iced with marzipan in the style of Palóc and Matyó embroidery. *Café Arabica*, on the corner of Dobó and Hibay Király utcas, is a fine old teahouse with dark wooden tables and stools, and huge bowls of confectionery awaiting the sweet-toothed. An extremely popular hangout in the summer is the café of the *Senátor-ház* hotel, with its sunny little terrace.

Eger's **drinking** venues are somewhat thinner on the ground: *La Isla*, at Foglár utca 2, is a bar/grill-type establishment which just about succeeds in replicating a Cuban feel, while the most authentic pub-type place is *Champs*, at the *Hotel Aqua*, whose enormous grill terrace is a fun place to sup. The *Bikavér Borház*, at Dobó tér 10, is a fabulous spot to try some of the local **wines** – you can either buy by the glass or have a proper tasting session (around 1800Ft for six wines plus nibbles). The alternative, of course, is to head out to the cellars of the Szépasszony Valley (see p.339).

Activities and festivals

The town's **thermal baths** are on Petőfi tér (May–Sept Mon–Fri 6am–8pm, Sat & Sun 8am–7pm; Oct–April daily 10am–6pm; Turkish baths Sat [women] & Sun [men] only; 1200Ft); while just across the road, on Frank Tivadar utca, stands the brilliant, Makovecz-designed indoor **swimming pool** (Mon–Fri 6am–9pm, Sat & Sun 8am–6pm; 850Ft), with its soaring semicircular wooden ceiling. Contact Tourinform if you're interested in **aeroplane tours** over town (May–Aug, weather permitting; 4500Ft per person) or **horseriding** in the Szalajka valleys. A very good riding school is the Mátyus Udvarház Egedhegyi Lipicai Farm at Vécsey völgy 6, 2km northeast of town on the road to Noszvaj, where the saddle-shy can enjoy carriage rides (horseriding 3500Ft per hr; ☏36/517-937, ⓦwww.matyusudvarhaz.hu). You can also get simple accommodation at the stud itself, in the *Mátyus Udvarház* (same telephone; ❷).

The town's cultural traditions are celebrated by a series of immensely enjoyable festivals, chief amongst which is the **Grape Carnival** at the beginning of September, a weekend of predominantly wine-related events, but which also includes folk dancing and a parade of floats. During the last two weeks of March there's the **Spring Festival**, entailing a rich programme of arts, theatre and music; in mid-July, a week of **medieval themed events** takes place on the main square and up in the castle; while, in late August, the **Agria International Folk Dance Meeting** features much consumption of wine alongside a host of fine folk-music concerts. Throughout the summer there are **organ concerts** in the Minorite Church, while folk or rock **concerts** are often held on an open-air stage at the end of the Szépasszony Valley.

Up to Szilvásvárad and the Szalajka Valley

The road and rail line skirt the western foothills of the Bükk as they wiggle northwards towards Putnok. Twelve kilometres out from Eger the scenery is promisingly lush around **SZARVASKŐ** (Stag Rock), a pretty village with the ruins of a thirteenth-century **castle**, a basic **hotel** – the functional *Turistaszálló* at Rózsa utca 8 (☏36/352-085; ❶) – and the *Őko-Park Panzió* at Borsod utca 9

Lippizaner horses

Descended from Spanish, Arabian and Berber stock, **Lippizaner horses** are bred at six European stud farms. The original stud was founded at Lipica in Slovenia in 1580 by the Habsburg archduke Karl, but when Napoleon's troops invaded Italy its horses were brought to Mezőhegyes in southern Hungary for safekeeping. During the wars in former Yugoslavia, a similar rescue mission was carried out by the Austrians. Lippizaner horses are comparatively small in stature – 14.3 to 15.2 hands – with a long back, a short, thick neck and a powerful build. They are usually white or grey. Like their counterparts at the famous Spanish Riding School in Vienna, Szilvásvárad's horses are trained to perform bows, provettes and other manoeuvres that delight dressage cognoscenti.

▲ Lippizaner horses

(☎36/352-201, ⓦwww.oko-park.hu; ⑥), a super little guesthouse with an adjoining campsite occupying a pretty site next to a stream, in the shadow of the rock itself. Six kilometres further on, quarries and an ugly cement factory spoil the view at **BÉLAPÁTFALVA**, where the sole reason to stop is a well-preserved Romanesque **abbey church** (Apátsági templom; mid-March to Oct Tues–Sun 10am–4pm; 300Ft), founded by French Cistercian monks in 1232. Next to the church are the remains of a monastery. To get to the church, follow the signpost off the main road for 2km. If the church is closed, or you wish to have a look outside the seasonal times, contact the information office down in the village at Béla utca 70 (☎36/354-569).

Szilvásvárad

Eight kilometres further north, **SZILVÁSVÁRAD** occupies a dell beside wooded hills rising to the east. Once the private estate of the pro-Fascist Pallaevicini family, and then a workers' resort after 1945, nowadays it is chiefly known as a breeding centre for **Lippizaner horses** (see box, p.341). It's also the site of Hungary's annual **International Coach-Driving Championship**, usually held at the end of July. You don't have to be mad on horses to enjoy the **Horsebreeding Exhibition** at Fenyves utca 4 (Kocsikiállitás; 10am–noon & 2–4pm: June–Aug Mon & Wed–Sun; Sept–May Fri–Sun; 400Ft), which includes a collection of coaches and a stable of beautiful white Lippizaners. The totemic columns in the park around the stud farm are dedicated to the memory of the farm director's beloved mount, Zánka, who died in harness of a heart attack – evoking the time of the Magyar conquest, when favourite horses were buried in graves.

Except during the coach-driving championships, there shouldn't be any problem finding **accommodation**. Just off Egri utca, and at the top of Park utca, is the fantastic ⚜ *La Contessa Kastélyhotel* (☎36/999-033, ⓦwww.lacontessa.hu; ⑨), whose gleaming marble-floored lobby and dazzling white corridors presage sumptuous rooms (some of which have a sauna); the basement spa facilities are first-rate too. Down the hill from *La Contessa*, at Egri utca 2, is the welcoming and relaxing *Szalajka Fogadó* (☎36/564-020, ⓔszalajka.fogado@t-online.hu; ⑤), while another lovely place is the *Kalebas Panzió*, out on the road towards Eger at Egri utca 48 (☎36/355-319; ③), which has views from its neat rooms over a sweet little garden. Close by at Egri út 36, *Hegyi Camping* (☎36/355-207, ⓦwww .hegyicamping.com; May to mid-Oct) has two- to four-bed log cabins (②–③), and there are plenty of private rooms (②) available too – look for the *Zimmer frei* signs. If you fancy exploring the area by **bike**, rentals are organized by Mountain Bike Rental at Szalajka-völgy (900Ft per hr, 2000Ft per day; ☎60/352-695).

The Szalajka Valley

If walking doesn't appeal, it's possible to take the five-kilometre-long narrow-gauge train from Szilvásvárad – the station is south of the village at Szalajka-völgy 6 – into the **Szalajka Valley** (May–Sept 7 daily; April & Oct 4 daily). The valley really begins at Szikla-Forrás, a gushing rock cleft beyond the food stalls and captive **stags** that guard its approaches. Signposted just off the main path is an outdoor **Forestry Museum** (Erdészeti Múzeum; May–Sept Tues–Sun 8.30am–4.30pm; Oct–April daily 8.30am–2pm; 300Ft), exhibiting weathered huts and tools, including an ingenious water-powered forge, once used by the charcoal-burners and foresters of the Bükk. Trout is on every restaurant's menu round here, freshly caught from the streams of the Szalajka Valley.

Higher up, the valley is boxed in by hills, with paths snaking 5km through the woods to the triangular **Istállóskői cave** (*barlang*) and the barefaced **Mount Istállóskő**, which at 959m is the highest in the Bükk range. The second-highest, Bálvány, can be reached by footpath from Istállóskő (8km) or from Nagyvisnyó (9km), the next settlement after Szilvásvárad and on the same branch train line.

The Bükk Hills

Unlike most of the northern hills, the **Bükk** were formed from sedimentary limestone, clay slate and dolomite, and are riddled with sinkholes and caves that were home to the earliest tribes of *homo sapiens*, hunters of mammoths and reindeer. As civilization developed elsewhere, the Bükk declined in importance, except as a source of timber, until the start of the nineteenth century, when Henrik Fazola built a blast furnace in the Garadna Valley, exploiting the iron ore which spurred the industrialization of Miskolc and Ózd. Despite this, almost four hundred square kilometres have been declared a **national park and wildlife refuge**, which can be explored superficially by train and bus, or more thoroughly if you're prepared to do some hiking.

If you are planning to **walk**, a hiking map (*Bükk hegység*) is essential. Since paths are well marked and settlements are rarely more than 15km apart, it's hard to go far astray on foot, but a few **preparations** are advisable (including taking plenty of food and water, as well as some insect repellent). Drinking water (*ivóvíz*) isn't always available, though many of the springs are pure and delicious. To be sure of **accommodation**, make reservations through Egertourist in Eger, or ask for help from Tourinform there (see p.336). If need be, you can also sleep in shelters (*esőház*) dotted around the hills.

The Bükk is particularly lovely in autumn, when its foliage turns bright orange and yellow, contrasting with the silvery tree trunks. Among the mountain flora are violet-blue monkshood which blooms at the end of summer, yellow lady's-slipper, an endangered species in Europe, and the Turk's-cap lily. The undergrowth is

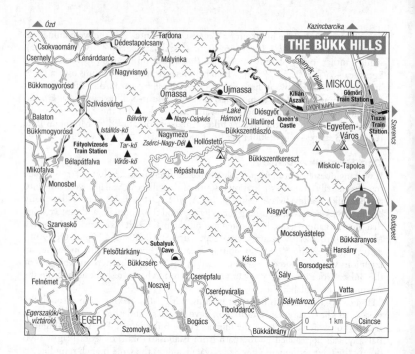

home to badgers, beech martens, ermines and other animals, and you might encounter rock thrushes and other birds in abandoned quarries, or see an imperial eagle cruising overhead. The seldom glimpsed "smooth" snake isn't venomous. In spring, look out for limekilns and charcoal-burners in the forests.

Approaches from Eger

Starting **from Eger**, the most direct approach to the hills is to take a bus, getting off somewhere along the route to Miskolc, or the branch train line up to **Felsőtárkány** – an ideal starting point for walks and a lovely village in its own right, with vine-laden gardens surrounding a small lake. Next to the lake is a **visitor centre** (mid-April to mid-Oct 10am–4pm; ☎36/534-078), where you can pick up materials on the park and view a small natural-history exhibition. The village is also the starting point for the **narrow-gauge railway** up to Stimecz-ház, some 10km distant and a lovely little ride through the forest (May–Sept, departures at 9.30am & 1.30pm, returning at 11.30am & 3.30pm; 350Ft one-way). There's cheap and perfectly adequate **accommodation** in the village at the *Park-Hotel Táltos*, tucked away up the hill at Ifjúság út 1, where you'll also find hostel-style accommodation from May to September (☎36/534-071, Ⓦwww.parkhotel-taltos.fw.hu; ❸, dorm bed 2200Ft), and the *Szikla Fogadó*, Fő utca 313 (☎36/434-604; ❸).

Paths also lead into the Bükk from Bélapátfalva, Szilvásvárad and Nagyvisnyó, north of the range (see p.342), and from villages to the south, accessible by bus from Eger. On the south side, arrowheads and other remains were found in the **Subalyuk Cave**, a Paleolithic dwelling 1km east of **Bükkzsérc** and north of **Cserépfalu**, at the start of one of the footpaths. Further east, "rocking stones" and hollowed-out pillars, used by medieval beekeepers and known as "hive rocks", line the rocky **Felső-szoros ravine** north of **Cserépváralja**.

There's more accommodation 13km northeast of Eger in **Noszvaj**, including a clutch of guesthouses and a Baroque mansion converted into the *De La Motte Kastély Hotel* at Dobó utca 10 (℡36/463-090; ❺–❻), which has rooms in the annexe and more expensive apartments in the main house. The 200-year-old **mansion** can also be visited by non-guests (Tues–Sun 10am–noon & 1–3pm; 400Ft), who can admire the bizarrely decorated rooms with rather kitsch frescoes. Allegedly there were once some voluptuous nudes in the master bedroom, until a new mistress of the house had them painted over.

Approaches from Miskolc

The Bükk can also be visited **from Miskolc** (see p.346), which offers a number of approaches. From Újgyőri Fő tér in the western part of the city (bus #101 from Tiszai Station), a #68 bus will take you to **Bükkszentlászló**. From here you can either walk or hitch via **Bükkszentkereszt**, a small village with a quaint glass-blowing museum, to **Hollóstető**, 6km on, which is on the Miskolc–Eger bus route, though services are infrequent. Bükkszentkereszt offers **private rooms** as well as the *Bükk Fogadó* (℡46/390-165; ❹), while Hollóstető has a **campsite** with **chalets** (℡46/390-183; ❷; May–Sept).

The easiest approach, however, is to aim for **Lillafüred** (see below), a small resort that's accessible by **bus** #5 or #15 (every 30min) from the end stop, Diósgyőr Villamos, in the western part of the city (bus or tram #1 from Tiszai Station), or by **narrow-gauge train** from Miskolc's Kilián Észak terminal (served by bus or tram #1 – alight at the LÁÉV stop, two before the last one). Trains make the delightful thirty-minute trip from Miskolc four times daily year-round with extra trains at the weekend. Both the train, and bus #15, continue via Újmassa to Ómassa, further up the valley.

Lillafüred and its caves

LILLAFÜRED ("Lilla Bath"), 12km west of Miskolc, was named after Lilla, the wife of Count András Bethlen, who established the place as a resort in 1892. Despite its weekend popularity, Lillafüred can still be peaceful and romantic, with its lake and grand hotel set amidst wooded hills. Out of season, the whole place seems rather forgotten.

The village's principal attractions are three **stalactite caves** (*barlang*), two of which can be visited on short guided tours, starting every hour from each cave entrance. The only cave which can't be visited is the **Szeleta Cave**, tucked away above the Miskolc road, and found to contain Ice Age spearheads and tools. The **Anna Cave** (mid-April to mid-Oct daily 10am–3pm; 900Ft), at the bottom of the path that runs down beside the *Palota Hotel*, has a long entrance passage and six chambers linked by stairs formed from limestone. If your appetite for stalactites is still unsatiated, walk 1km up the road towards Eger to find the **Szent István Cave** (daily: mid-April to mid-Oct 9am–5pm; mid-Oct to mid-April 9am–4pm; 900Ft), which is longer and less convoluted, with a "cupola hall" of stalactites, various pools and chambers. Bats can usually be seen roosting above your head.

Two hundred metres beyond this at Erzsébet sétány 33 stands the wooden **house of Ottó Herman** (Fri–Sun 10am–4pm; 400Ft), where the naturalist and ethnographer spent many years trapping and mounting local wildlife until his death in 1914. Stuffed boars, birds and rodents, plus an extraordinary collection of giant beetles, are the main attraction, but you can also see Ottó's top hat and butterfly nets, and a letter from Kossuth. Back down by the *Palota Hotel* is **Lake Hámori**, used for **boating** during the summer and **ice-skating** in winter, while behind the hotel itself is a twenty-metre **waterfall**, supposedly Hungary's highest.

Dominating the resort is the grand *Palota Hotel* at Erzsébet sétány 1 (☎46/331-411, ⓦwww.hunguesthotels.hu; ❻), a nostalgic creation built in 1927 in the style of a medieval hunting lodge; it is, as you might expect, pretty classy, with a fitness centre, pool, sauna and games room – ask for a room with a balcony overlooking the park. Just across from the *Palota*, the *Tőkert Panzió* (☎46/533-560, ⓦwww .tokertpanzio.hu; ❻) offers seven far more modest, but still very agreeable, rooms. Some ten minutes' walk up the hill from here, opposite the Szent István Cave, is the *Ózon Panzió* (☎46/532-594, ⓦwww.ozon-panzio.hu; ❹), whose bright, compact rooms overlook a neat expanse of lawn. All the above have very reasonable **restaurants**, the most glamorous of which is the *Mátyás Terem* in the *Palota Hotel*, although the medieval theme is a touch over the top – note the windows, which represent towns from the former Hungarian territories lost in the Treaty of Trianon. The buzzy, multi-terraced restaurant in the *Tőkert* has idyllic views of the lake, while there's a cluster of snack stands in and around the car park opposite the Szent István Cave.

Újmassa and beyond

Narrow-gauge trains continue from Lillafüred up the Garadna Valley, which cleaves the Bükk plateau. At **ÚJMASSA**, the next stop 4km further west, a **nineteenth-century foundry** and metallurgy museum (mid-April to Oct Tues–Sun 9am–5pm; 300Ft) attests to the work of **Henrik Fazola**, a Bavarian-born Eger locksmith, and his son Frigyes, who first exploited the iron-ore deposits of the Bükk. Nearby are the sooty camps of **charcoal-burners**, who still live for part of the year in the forest.

ÓMASSA, further up the valley, is the last stop on the train and bus routes. From here it's a few hours' walk up a well-marked path to **Mount Bálvány**, southeast of which lies the "Great Meadow" (Nagymező), where wild horses graze. A ski chalet and the summits of **Nagy-Csipkés** (822m) and **Zsérci-Nagy-Dél** (875m) can be reached to the southeast, but more impressive crags lie to the southwest, namely **Tár-kő** (950m) and **Istállós-kő** (959m). The land drops rapidly south of Tár-kő, and water from the plateau descends through sinkholes, bursting forth in a spring at **Vörös-kő** (Red Rock). During winter, when the plateau is covered with snow, the entrances to these **sinkholes** are marked by rising steam.

Miskolc and the Aggtelek Range

The area to the north and east of Bükk National Park is Hungary's "Rust Belt", a region afflicted by the collapse of its heavy industry in the 1990s. **Miskolc**, straddling the transport network, is hard to avoid but holds far more promise than you'd imagine, with a bustling downtown, an impressive castle and "thrashing" cave baths in the nearby resort of Miskolc-Tapolca – plus some tremendous summer festivals to enjoy. The wonderful **Aggtelek Stalactite Caves**, north of Miskolc near the Slovak border, are easily the main draw of the region and the reason why most visitors end up in Miskolc.

Miskolc

Due to the closure of its steel factory and other industries, **MISKOLC** (pronounced "**mish**-koltz"), 61km northeast of Eger and the third-largest city in Hungary, has long suffered from high unemployment and problems with racist attacks on its Roma minority, to which the city council responded at one point by proposing

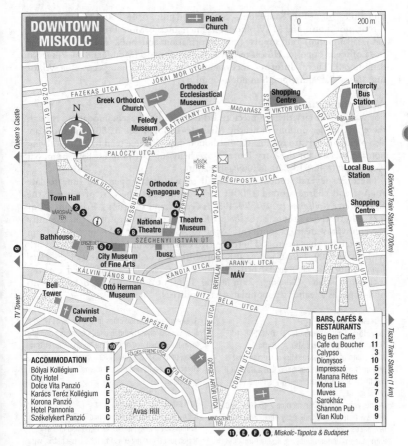

DOWNTOWN MISKOLC

Plank Church

0   200 m

Queen's Castle

DÓZSA GY. UTCA

FAZEKAS UTCA

JÓKAI MÓR UTCA

PETŐFI TÉR

Greek Orthodox Church

Orthodox Ecclesiastical Museum

Feledy Museum

BATTHYÁNY UTCA

MADARÁSZ VIKTOR UTCA

SZENTPÁLI UTCA

Shopping Centre

ADY UTCA

BÚZA TÉR

Intercity Bus Station

DEÁK TÉR

PALÓCZY UTCA

PATAK UTCA

HŐSÖK TERE

DERYNÉ UTCA

KAZINCZY UTCA

RÉGIPOSTA UTCA

Local Bus Station

Gömöri Train Station (700m)

Town Hall

VÁROSHÁZ TÉR

KOSSUTH UTCA

Orthodox Synagogue

❶

National Theatre

ⓐ ❹

Theatre Museum

ⓑ

❺

SZÉCHENYI ISTVÁN ÚT

Shopping Centre

Bathhouse

ERZSÉBET TÉR

❻ ❼

City Museum of Fine Arts

Ibusz

❽

ARANY J. UTCA

KIRÁLY UTCA

TV Tower

KÁLVIN JÁNOS UTCA

KANDIA UTCA

ARANY J. UTCA

MÁV

Bell Tower

Ottó Herman Museum

UITZ

BÉLA UTCA

Tiszai Train Station (1 km)

Calvinist Church

PAPSZER

SZEMERE UTCA

BERTALAN UTCA

BARS, CAFÉS & RESTAURANTS

Big Ben Caffe	1
Cafe du Boucher	11
Calypso	3
Dionysos	10
Impresszó	5
Manana Rétes	2
Mona Lisa	4
Muves	7
Sarokház	6
Shannon Pub	8
Vian Klub	9

❿

ⓒ

FÖLDES FERENC UTCA

ⓓ KIS AVAS

GÖRGEY ARTÚR UTCA

CORVIN UTCA

ACCOMMODATION

Bólyai Kollégium	F
City Hotel	G
Dolce Vita Panzió	A
Karács Teréz Kollégium	E
Korona Panzió	D
Hotel Pannonia	B
Székelykert Panzió	C

Avas Hill

MINDSZENT TÉR

⓫, ⓔ, ⓕ, ⓖ, Miskolc-Tapolca & Budapest

that they all be moved to an outlying housing estate, until dissuaded by a national outcry. However, the city puts a brave face on its woes, at least around the centre, whose oddly appealing main street retains much of its prewar charm, surrounded by relics of the city's Greek and Jewish communities, and nineteenth-century artisans' dwellings with gardens dwarfed by concrete high-rises. Aside from the Queen's Castle and the spa resort of Miskolc-Tapolca, everything of interest is in the city centre.

Arrival and information

The main **points of arrival** are the Tiszai **train station**, 1km east of the centre (tram #1 or #2; bus #1 or #101 for the castle or Majális Park, aiming for Lillafüred or the Bükk Hills), and the intercity **bus station** on Búza tér, from where you can either walk into the centre, or head straight for Miskolc-Tapolca by bus #2 from the adjacent local bus station. Should you arrive at the Gömöri train station instead, walk down to Zsolcai kapu, catch any bus heading west and alight near Ady utca.

There's a wealth of **information** available from Tourinform at Városház tér 13 (mid-June to mid-Sept Mon–Fri 9am–7pm, Sat & Sun 9am–6pm; mid-Sept to mid-June Mon–Fri 9am–5pm, Sat 9am–1pm; ☏46/350-425, ✉miskolc @tourinform.hu). The MÁV office at Szemere utca 1 (Mon–Fri 7.30am–6.30pm, Sat 7.30am–3pm) can supply train information and book tickets, while the **post office** is opposite Hősök tere at Kazinczy utca 16 (Mon–Fri 8am–7pm, Sat 8am–noon). There's **internet access** inside the Plaza shopping centre on Viktor utca (Mon–Sat 9am–9pm, Sun noon–6pm).

Accommodation

For such a large city there is precious little decent hotel accommodation, though there are further options in nearby **Miskolc-Tapolca** (see p.350), and there are also plenty of **private rooms** (➋) – although most of these tend to be in outlying housing estates; for these try Ibusz at Széchenyi út 14 (Mon–Fri 8am–5pm, Sat 9am–1pm; ☏46/518-210, ✉i069@ibusz.hu).

There are several student **hostels**, all of which are open late June to late August and charge around 1800Ft for a dorm bed. The best of these is the *Karács Teréz Kollégium* (☏46/370-495) at Győri kapu 156 (bus #1 or tram #1 or #2). Alternatively, there is the *Bólyai Kollégium* at Egyetem út 17, in the hilly Egyetemváros district south of town (☏46/365-111); take bus #12 from Hősök tere to the last stop. There are two **campsites** in Miskolc-Tapolca, both with chalets (➌): *Éden Camping* at Károly Mihály utca 1, 300m west of the *Hotel Junó* (☏46/368-917; mid-April to mid-Oct), resembles a manicured parking lot; while *Autós Camping*, 2km along Iglói utca (☏46/367-171; May to mid-Sept), is a leafier site popular with motorists.

Miskolc

City Hotel Csabai kapu utca 6 ☏46/555-100, ⓦwww.cityhotelmiskolc.hu. A 15min walk south of the centre, Miskolc's classiest offering has a certain business-like air about it, but the rooms are extremely stylish and very relaxing. ➑

Dolce Vita Panzió Déryné utca 7 ☏46/505-045, ⓦwww.freund.hu. Small, cosy pension just a few paces along from the National Theatre, with modern, though rather sparsely furnished, rooms. ➎

Korona Panzió Kis Avas 18 ☏46/506-882, ✉korona7@axelro.hu. At the foot of the Avas Hill, this rambling old building conceals a mix of older and newer rooms. A reasonable alternative if the *Székelykert* is full (see below). Breakfast not included. ➌–➍

Hotel Pannonia Kossuth utca 2 ☏46/504-980, ⓦwww.hotelpannonia-miskolc.hu. The *Pannonia* is the most central place in town, and though slightly overpriced, it has neat, comfortable rooms, all with a/c and wi-fi. ➑

Székelykert Panzió Földes utca 4 ☏46/411-222, ⓦwww.szekelykertvendeglo.hu. Occupying an old town house just down from the *Korona Panzió*, this small pension has a mix of reasonable, if rather cheerless, single and double rooms, all with TV and bathroom. ➎

Miskolc-Tapolca

Anna Hotel Miskolctapolcai utca 7 ☏46/422-212, ✉info@annahotelmiskolc.hu. Good and cheap option just a few minutes from the cave baths, with warm, sunny rooms. ➍

Bástya Hotel Miskolctapolcai utca 2 ☏46/561-590, ⓦwww.bastyawellnesshotel.hu. Just up from the *Anna Hotel*, this smart hotel has its own comprehensive range of wellness facilities, including indoor and outdoor pools, water massages and jacuzzis. ➑

Zenit Panzió Miskolctapolcai utca 25 ☏46/561-561, ⓦwww.zenitpanzio.hu. Similar in style to the *Anna Hotel*, this fairly decent place possesses large rooms with TV, a/c and internet. Triples and quads available. ➎

The City

The main downtown thoroughfare, **Széchenyi út**, is characterized by an eclectic mix of boutiques and restaurants interspersed with Baroque facades painted pea green and sky blue or in the last stages of decrepitude, which gives the impression of a boom and slump happening simultaneously. Here you'll find the **National Theatre** (Nemzeti Színház), which apart from musicals like *Fiddler on* *the Roof* also stages some good straight drama, and has an alternative theatre run by the ex-rock star Péter Müller. Opened in 1823, it was the first Hungarian-language theatre in the country, fourteen years before Budapest acquired one. Miskolc's thespian tradition is celebrated in the **Theatre Museum**, just around the corner at Déryné utca 3 (Színészmúzeum; Tues–Sun 9am–5pm; 400Ft). Housed in a fine Baroque building across the road from the National Theatre is the **City Museum of Fine Arts** (Tues–Sun: June–Aug 10am–6pm; Sept–May 9am–5pm; 400Ft), an impressive space which is dedicated to showcasing both national and local contemporary artwork, with graphical art, installations and photography particularly prominent. At the far western end of Széchenyi út, a statue of its namesake, Count Széchenyi, appears to be doing a painful form of yoga on **Városház tér**, which looks especially atmospheric with its town hall spotlit at night.

North of Széchenyi út

A century ago, Miskolc was distinguished by its Greek and Jewish communities – the former descended from refugees from the Turks, who fled here during the seventeenth century, and the latter migrating from Sub-Carpathian Ruthenia after it was incorporated within the Austro-Hungarian Empire. Though both are now a shadow of their former size and significance, their places of worship are among the finest monuments in the region.

On the south side of **Hősök tere** is an **Orthodox Synagogue** designed by Ludwig Förster, the architect of the Dohány utca Synagogue in Budapest, whose magnificent but crumbling interior seems painfully empty on major feast days – little over 300 Jews now live in Miskolc, whereas the prewar Jewish population numbered 16,000, of whom 14,000 were sent to the death camps; ask at the office behind the synagogue for the keys. On the far side of the square stands a former **Minorite Church** and monastery, dating from 1729–40.

Heading left onto Deák tér you'll encounter a splendid, newly restored neo-Renaissance pile designed by György Lehóczky in 1927 for the **Forestry Commission** (Erdőigazgatóság), an important institution in this region of wooded hills. Next door stands the **Feledy Museum** (Tues–Sat 9am–5pm; 300Ft), devoted to the work of local artist Gyula Feledy, which reflects his preoccupation with the world of Orthodox Christianity. Greek Orthodox and Uniate religious art from all over Hungary is exhibited in the **Orthodox Ecclesiastical Museum** further along at no. 7 (Orthodox Egyházi Múzeum; Tues–Sat: April–Oct 10am–6pm; Nov–March 9am–5pm; 300Ft) – the undoubted highlight is the splendid collection of icons.

The finest sight in the town is the eighteenth-century **Greek Orthodox Church**, straight down the path from the museum, which contains an extraordinary sixteen-metre **iconostasis**, dating from 1793. The iconostasis incorporates some one hundred icons painted by Greek and Serbian masters and represents revered Orthodox saints and important Orthodox holidays. To the left of this is the *Black Mary of Kazan*, an icon presented by Catherine the Great of Russia, hung with tokens representing prayers for children, health and marriage. There is also a jewelled cross from Mount Áthos, brought by the first Greek settlers. Originally there were about 250 Greek families in Miskolc, who traded in wine and lived around Búza tér, but the quarter was pulled down in the 1960s, and only a handful of families remain from the community.

Further north on the slope above Petőfi tér, the wonderful Gothic-style **Plank Church** (Deszka templom; May–Sept daily 9am–5pm; free) has been completely rebuilt following an arson attack in 1997. There has been a wooden church on this spot since 1698, although it has been torn down and rebuilt several times since. The interior's finely varnished and freshly smelling pine pews are testament to the latest reincarnation. This kind of wooden church is rare in Hungary but common in northern Romania, where architecture of this type, particularly in the northern Maramureş region, reached its zenith in the eighteenth century. The Székely gate at the entrance to the church is typical of the type found in Romania.

Avas Hill

South of Széchenyi út, a once beautiful, but now defunct, domed *fin-de-siècle* **bathhouse** presages the **Ottó Herman Museum** at the foot of Avas Hill (Tues–Sun 10am–4pm; 400Ft), exhibiting a collection of folk costumes, minerals and pottery. The pile of broken mugs is a result of the tradition at wakes of drinking and then smashing your mug. Just uphill stands a Gothic **Calvinist Church** dating from 1560, which features a detached **wooden belfry** (as required by Counter-Reformation ordinances) and Baroque pews decorated with flower motifs, added later.

From here, a maze of paths snakes upwards to the **TV Tower** and observation platform on the summit. The right-hand paths climb through an extraordinary shantytown of miniature villas and rock-hewn **wine cellars**, some up to 50m deep, some of which may be visited. In the summer and early autumn you can roam all over the hill sampling local wine, and even food at some of the bigger cellars. Ten minutes' walk down Mendikás dülő past the TV Tower is a **Jewish Cemetery** with beautifully carved gravestones dating back to the eighteenth century, and memorials to those killed during the war. On weekdays until late afternoon a caretaker will let you in if you ring the bell.

Out of the centre

The oldest building in Miskolc is the **Queen's Castle** (Diósgyőr vár; daily: May–Sept 9am–6pm; Oct–April 10am–4pm; 800Ft), located 7km west of the centre in the suburb of Diósgyőr, beyond the steelworks. Built for King Louis between 1350 and 1375, the castle marked the introduction of the southern Italian type of fortress to Hungary. Though eminently defendable, it served chiefly as a royal holiday home and a residence for dowager queens. Today it is the main site for summer concerts, festivals and events in the city. Blown up in the Rákóczi wars, it has been crudely restored with breeze blocks and poured concrete, but the views from its towers of Miskolc and the Bükk Hills are as splendid as ever. To get there, catch a #1 bus to the *Ady Endre Művelődési Ház* and walk towards the four stone towers poking above the rooftops.

If you feel like a relaxing bath, head out to **MISKOLC-TAPOLCA**, a resort suburb twenty minutes' ride from Búza tér (bus #2). Crammed with holiday homes and school parties, its main attractions are an outdoor **pool** (May–Sept daily 9am–6pm; 1000Ft), complete with rowing boats, water slides, electronic cars and rides; and the **cave baths** (Barlangfürdő; daily: July–Aug 9am–7pm; Sept–June 9am–6pm; 2200Ft, 1000Ft after 4pm), a series of dimly lit warm-water grottoes discovered in the 1920s, culminating in a twelve-metre-high waterfall known as the "pounding shower", which should get your circulation going if nothing else (take bus #2 to the end stop). There's adrenaline of a different kind just across from the baths at the dry **bobsleigh course** (Bobpálya; May–Sept 10am–10pm; Oct–April 10am–6pm; 400Ft for 1 run, 1700Ft for 5 runs).

Eating, drinking and entertainment

Miskolc sports no more than a handful of decent **restaurants** – all fairly well concentrated in the centre – whilst its **nightlife** is reasonably energetic, thanks mainly to the city's large student population.

Restaurants

Café du Boucher Görgey utca 42. Top-quality Belgian restaurant which also happens to be one of the best in town; the pricey but generously portioned food is superb, and the service brisk. The Belgian beers, meanwhile, are a real treat.

Calypso Városház tér 7. Smart, formal-looking restaurant offering an appealing range of dishes, from high-end beef tenderloin, duck and goose, to beef stew and knuckle of pork. In summer, there's a well-shaded wood-decked terrace overlooking the square.

Dionysos Mélyvölgy utca 212. Situated on the slope of the Avas Hill, this delightful Greek restaurant has a rich menu, including fish, lamb and game. Great views from the polished upstairs section. Closed Mon.

Impresszó Széchenyi út 9. Loungey, laid-back kind of place on the main drag, serving Tex-Mex food alongside pastas, salads, bruschettas, hot sandwiches and cooked breakfasts. Good spot for a drink too.

Shannon Pub Széchenyi út 54. Warm, and very welcoming, bistro-style establishment which does a whole lot more than the great draught beers on offer; steaks coated in various sauces are the forte here, in addition to some high-quality Hungarian fare.

Cafés and bars

Two very agreeable **cafés** worth popping into for coffee and cake are *Muves*, a quaint and pleasantly cluttered little spot next to the Museum of Fine Arts, and *Sarokház*, a bit further along at Széchenyi út 2. You can down fancy cocktails, to the background of pumping music, at the groovy *Mona Lisa* next to the Theatre Museum, while *Manana Rétes*, opposite the town hall on Városház tér, attracts a lively, mixed crowd to its weekend DJ sessions. For a beer, head to the cordial *Shannon Pub* (see above), or the relaxing *Big Ben Caffe* at Kossuth utca 8, which also serves hot food. Nightlife of a weightier kind revolves around the *Vian Klub*, a massively popular live music venue at Győri kapu 57. Look out for flyers for Saturday-night raves in the TV Tower, too. In Miskolc-Tapolca over summer, there are regular raves and parties in the *Hotel Junó*, and visiting DJs and groups appear at other venues, as advertised.

Festivals and events

The city's most prestigious event is the **Bartók and International Opera Festival** (Miskolci Nemzetközi Operafesztivál) in mid-June, a week of high-quality concerts starring some of the finest operatic singers in Europe. Each year the works of a different composer are run alongside works of the great Hungarian Béla Bartók. Otherwise, the city is at its liveliest during the **Miskolc Summer Festival** (Miskolci Nyár; June–Aug), when jazz, classical music and opera are performed at the Queen's Castle and in Miskolc-Tapolca. Among its highlights is the **Kaláka Folklore Festival** in mid-July, one of the largest folk gatherings in the region, attended by musicians and dancers from all over Hungary and abroad. The national holiday on **August 20** is marked by equestrian displays and a folk fair in the Queen's Castle. Tickets for operatic, ballet and theatrical performances are available from the National Theatre ticket office at Széchenyi út 23 (Mon–Fri 10am–6pm, Sat 10am–1pm; ☎46/344-862), while for classical concerts head to the Philharmonic ticket office at Kossuth utca 3 (Mon–Thurs 9am–4pm, Fri 9am–3pm; ☎46/315-774).

Aggtelek National Park

A UNESCO World Heritage Site, the **Aggtelek National Park**, bordering Slovakia, comprises an area of 50,000 acres. Like the Bükk, the Aggtelek range displays typical **karstic** features such as gullies, sinkholes and caves, caused by a mixture of water and carbon dioxide dissolving the limestone. The **Baradla caves**, between the villages of Aggtelek and Jósvafő, and the **Béke caves** to the southeast, are the park's real treasures, constituting an amazing subterranean world with Stygian lakes and rivers, waterfalls, countless stalactites and nearly three hundred species of wildlife. Set in remote countryside that's ideal for walking cycling and bird-watching, the caves are deservedly popular with tourists.

Getting to the Aggtelek entails catching an early bus from Budapest, Miskolc or Eger, or travelling later in the day, starting from the industrial town of Ózd, northwest of Miskolc, which has daily services around 8am, noon & 3pm, less frequently at weekends, or Putnok, northeast of Ózd, where there are **buses** to Aggtelek and Jósvafő every ninety minutes. Alternatively, catch one of the six daily (Sunday 1 only) **trains** from Miskolc, which take an hour and drop you at the Jósvafő-Aggtelek station, 10km east of Jósvafő, from where regular buses run to both villages (less frequently on Sundays).

Jósvafő and Aggtelek

Aside from the fortified church with its picturesque cemetery in **JÓSVAFŐ**, and the algae-green lake outside **AGGTELEK**, both villages are fairly unremarkable. Shops are few and social life centres around the church and a few shops. **Information** is available from Tourinform at Baradla oldal 3, by the entrance to the caves in Aggtelek (daily: April–Sept 8am–6pm; Oct–March 8am–4pm; ☏48/503-002, ⓦwww.anp.hu), who can also arrange guided walks and ecotours of the region. There is plenty of **accommodation** in both villages, largely in the form of guest and tourist houses. In Jósvafő, you'll find the decently equipped *Tengerszem Hotel* at Tengerszem oldal 1 (☏48/506-005, ⓔtengerszem_szallo @t-online.hu ❺), tucked away at the end of a lush valley. Accommodation in Aggtelek consists of the *Hotel Cseppkő*, picturesquely situated on a hill by the entrance to the caves at Baradla oldal 2 (☏48/343-075, ⓔhcseppko@freemail .hu, ❹), and the more intimate *Karszt Üdülő* at Deák utca 11 in the village (☏46/382-181; ❸). You might also try the *Baradla Camping* complex right by the cave entrance in Aggtelek (☏48/506-000), which has four-bed chalets studded around the hill above the cave (❷) and a hostel (1800Ft); the camping ground is open between mid-April and mid-October. Both the *Tengerszem* and the *Cseppkő* have **restaurants** and display local bus schedules in their lobbies.

The region is replete with opportunities for leisure activities. Aside from hiking (see opposite), there are **cycling** trails aplenty, including a 51-kilometre circular route heading up towards the Slovakian border and taking in the major villages; you can **rent bikes** in Jósvafő at Fenyves utca 11 (☏48/350-128). There's also **horseriding** available at the Hucul stud in Jósvafő (April–Sept 8am–5pm; Oct–March 8am–3pm; ☏48/350-052; 2000Ft per hr, or 3000Ft for carriage rides; book in advance).

The tourist office or hotels can tell you about the classical music **concerts** that are held in the caves between June and September and at New Year. The main event in the region each year is the **Gömör-Torna Festival**, a week-long affair at the end of July featuring folk and art camps, sporting events, jazz bands and various ensembles from around the country.

Visiting the caves

Both sets of caves are open daily from 9am to 7pm (Oct–March until 4pm), and hourly guided tours leave at 9am, 10am, noon, 1pm, 3pm and 5pm (Oct–March last tour 3pm) from the cave entrances (*bejárat*). The main **Baradla cave passage** twists underground for 22km, and there is a range of **tours** you can take. There are one-hour tours from both ends (2800Ft), or you can do a combined tour (4000Ft). The **Aggtelek** end of the passage is more convoluted and thus more rewarding for shorter tours. No description can do justice to the variety and profusion of **stalactites and stalagmites**, whose nicknames can only hint at the fantastic formations, glittering with calcite crystals or stained ochre by iron oxides. Among them is the world's tallest stalagmite, a full 25m high. In the "Concert Hall", boats sway on the "River Styx", and the guide activates a tape of Bach's *Toccata in D minor* to create a *Phantom of the Opera*-type ambience. **Long tours** (6000Ft) last four hours, take in 4.5km of cave, much of which is unlit, and require some stamina: it's a long time to clamber around dank, muddy caves, however beautiful they are. You need to book in advance for these longer tours (☎48/503-002, ℮ aggtelek@tourinform.hu).

Three-hour guided tours around the **Béke caves** (7000Ft) are also fairly demanding. Although they contain a sanatorium, the underground air being judged beneficial to asthmatics, most of the caves are, in fact, untamed, even unexplored, and as recently as 1973 a new passage was found when cavers penetrated a thirty-metre waterfall. You'll need boots and warm, waterproof clothing, and visitors are issued with helmets.

Excursions in the vicinity

The surrounding countryside is riddled with smaller caves and rock formations, clearly marked on the hiking **map** (*Aggtelek és Jósva főkörnyéke*) sold at the Tourinform office in Aggtelek. This also shows the **border zone** – it's always a good idea to carry your passport when hiking. For those with a car or bike, lots of attractive **villages** are within reach in this part of the highlands, for example **RUDABÁNYA**, where the ten-million-year-old jawbone of *Rudapithecus hungaricus*, an ancient primate, can be seen at the mine where it was excavated. The mine is now closed but there is an exhibition of various mining implements and artefacts in the **Museum of Mining and Minerals** at Petőfi utca 24 (Ásvánbányászafi múzeum; mid-May to mid-Oct Tues–Sun 9am–4pm; 400Ft). There is also a delightful fifteenth-century Gothic church with a painted panelled ceiling, dating from the seventeenth century.

The Zemplén Hills and around

The northeasternmost corner of the Uplands is consumed by the **Zemplén range**, a region largely unspoiled by industry and tourism, and richly textured by nature and history. Its volcanic soil and microclimates provide a favourable environment for diverse wildlife, particularly snakes and birds of prey, while the architecture reflects a tradition of trade and cultural exchange between the Great Plain and the Slovakian highlands. The small town of **Tokaj**, home to Hungary's most famous wine, absorbs most of the region's tourists, surprisingly few of whom make it up to **Sárospatak**, site of the superb Rákóczi castle, or to the smaller **Zemplén villages** such as Füzér and Boldogkőváralja, and the castles that loom over them.

ACCOMMODATION

Millenium Hotel	F
Széchenyi Kollégium	G
Tokaj Hotel	C
Toldi Fogadó	B
Torkolat Panzió	A
Vaskó Panzió	D
Vízisport Turistaház	E

BARS, CAFÉS & RESTAURANTS

Bonchidai Csárda	4
Degenfeld	1
Makk Marci	3
Szent Vince	2

Train Station & **G** ▼

Tokaj

TOKAJ is to Hungary what Champagne is to France, and this small town, 54km east of Miskolc, has become a minor Mecca for wine lovers. Squeezed onto a narrow strip of land between Tokaj Hill and the confluence of the rivers Bodrog and Tisza, its sloping streets and pastel-painted dwellings are rife with wine cellars and nesting storks, overlooked by lush vineyards climbing the hillside towards the "Bald Peak" and the inevitable TV Tower. Though it looks prosperous and laid-back, Tokaj is far from rich, and most people have to work hard to get any kind of living from the vineyards. For those with money to invest, however, there are exciting prospects for exports. In Tokaj, you can sample local wines in the famous Rákóczi cellar, or countless other, humbler places. To see a working winery, take a trip to Tarcal, Mád or Tolcsva in the Tokaj-Hegyalja (see p.357).

Arrival and information

Arriving at the **train station**, south of town on Baross Gábor utca, take your bearings from the large map posted outside before heading down to the main road, Bajcsy-Zsilinszky utca, and into the old centre of Tokaj – a fifteen-minute walk. The main **bus stop** (there is no station here) is on Serház utca, just south of the synagogue. For **information** on wine tours and the Tokaj-Hegyalja villages, drop into Tourinform at Serház utca 1 (June–Sept daily 9am–6pm; Oct–May Mon–Fri 9am–5pm; ☎47/352-259, ✉tokaj@tourinform.hu). The **post office** is at Rákóczi út 24 (Mon–Fri 8am–5pm, Sat 8am–11pm).

Accommodation

Tokaj has a rather average spread of **hotels** and **pensions**, though there is an abundance of **private accommodation**, on which Tourinform can advise, and the streets are awash with *Zimmer frei* signs. Cheap doubles with bathrooms, and quadruples without, can be found at the *Széchenyi Kollégium*, Bajcsy-Zsilinszky utca 15–17 (☎47/352-355; 2000Ft), from late June till late August, and at weekends the rest of the year. The busy and noisy *Vízisport Turistaház* (☎47/352-645, ⓦwww .tokaj-hostel.hu), across the Tisza bridge and immediately to your left by the river, has rooms in a hostel building (1600Ft) as well as a small **campsite**. The much larger *Tiszavirág* campsite (☎47/352-626; April–Oct) lies close by at Horgász utca 11.

Millennium Hotel Bajcsy-Zsilinszky utca 34 ☎47/352-247, ⓦwww.tokajmillennium.hu. Located near the bridge, this unappealing-looking stone building conceals spacious and attractive, albeit slightly plastic-looking, rooms. ⑥

Tokaj Hotel Rákóczi út 5 ☎47/352-344, ⓦwww .hoteltokaj.hu. Another dull building, this large and central hotel, just by the riverfront, has largely uninspiring rooms, but is reasonable value. Breakfast costs extra. ⑦

Toldi Fogadó Hajdú köz 2 ☎47/353-403, ⓦwww .toldifogado.hu. The star turn in town, this very central pension has large and comfortable a/c rooms (with wi-fi) and very obliging staff. Pool, jacuzzi and sauna, and a good restaurant to boot (see below). **⑥**

Torkolat Panzió Vasvári utca 26 ☎47/352-827, ⓦ www.torkolat.uw.hu. In the northern part of the old town, this efficiently run place has nine very homely rooms, each with an individualistic touch. Bikes and canoes are available to guests free of charge. Breakfast costs extra. **④**

Vaskó Panzió Rákóczi út 12 ☎47/352-107, ⓦ www.vaskopanzio.freeweb.hu. Tokaj's cheapest pension, this place is above a bar, so can be a little noisy, but the clean and comfortable rooms are well worth the price. Breakfast costs extra. Check out the little confectionery shop below. **③**

The Town

Wine is omnipresent in Tokaj, with cellars at every step, all kinds of wine-making equipment displayed in shop windows, and barrel staves piled in people's backyards. Rákóczi út, the pedestrianized main street that runs northwards through the centre, has been nicely spruced up, so you can admire its many fine buildings and their Baroque facades at leisure. At no. 54 you'll pass the grand-looking, Zopf-style **Town Hall**, just short of the main square, **Kossuth tér**. To the left of the church on Kossuth tér, you'll find the venerable **Rákóczi cellar**, the most famous in Tokaj and a place of pilgrimage where 20,000 hectolitres of wine repose in 24 cobwebbed, chandelier-lit passages (mid-March to mid-Oct daily 11am–6pm; 2700Ft for tasting of six wines; ☎47/352-408, ⓦ www.rakoczipince.hu). On the outside wall is a plaque commemorating Máté Szepsi Laczkó (1567–1633), a Calvinist minister who invented *Aszú* wine. The cellar now belongs to a foreign firm, but functions much as it previously did. However, you'll get more personal service in smaller **private cellars** in the backstreets above Rákóczi út, such as the excellent Hímesudvar at Bem utca 2, five minutes up from Kossuth tér. Once a hunting lodge owned by the eighteenth-century nobleman János Szapolyai, it now houses the cellars of the Várhelyi family, where you can taste wines and nibble *pogácsa* (savoury pastries); (daily: mid-March to Oct Sun–Thurs 10am–6pm, Fri & Sat 10am–9pm; Nov to mid-March Fri & Sat 10am–6pm; 2500Ft for tasting of six wines; ☎47/352/416, ⓦ www.himesudvar.hu).

Just past Kossuth tér, at Bethlen Gábor utca 7, stands a former Greek house, built in 1790 by the Karáscony family on the back of wealth gained from trading the local wine; this lovely building now accommodates the **Tokaj Museum** (Tues–Sun 10am–4pm; 600Ft), which showcases an excellent local history exhibition, including a re-creation of a drawing room from a Greek wine-trader's house, and Judaica from the former **synagogue** behind the museum on Serház utca – unfortunately, although it's been recently renovated, it's not possible to enter the synagogue. Prewar Tokaj had a large Jewish population, which handled most of the wine trade in conjunction with a smaller number of Greek families – hence the **Jewish cemetery** 6km north along the main road, the keys for which are available from the house just beyond it.

If you fancy a longer walk, follow the road behind Kossuth tér uphill to the summit of Tokaj's 516-metre-high "**Bald Peak**", topped by a TV Tower. The four-kilometre round-trip takes you past dozens of vineyards, each labelled with its owner's name. The TV tower is accessible by road too, but you have to drive round the hill via the village of Tarcal. From the summit you can scan the distant Great Plain and the lush green Tokaj-Hegyalja – the hilly wine-producing region.

Eating, drinking and activities

There's little to get excited about when it comes to **eating** in town, and you may well spend more time in the wine cellars than you initially thought. By far the best option if you do want a meal is *Degenfeld*, Kossuth tér 1, a fantastically classy place whose creative menu includes some great fish dishes. The restaurant in the *Toldi*

5

Tokaji wines derive their character from the special soil, the prolonged sunlight and the wine-making techniques developed here. Heat is trapped by the volcanic loess soil, allowing a delayed **harvest** in October, by which time many of the grapes are overripe and botrytized (attacked by a rot that shrivels them and makes them incredibly sweet). It is these **Aszú grapes** that make the difference between regular *Hárslevelű* (linden leaf) and *Furmint* wine, and the special wines sold in short, stubby bottles under the names *Szamorodni* and *Aszú*, whose qualities depend on the number of hods (*puttony*) of *Aszú* added to 136-litre barrels of ordinary grapes. *Szamorodni* is a word of Polish origin meaning "as it comes". It is typically golden in colour and can be dry or sweet, but never as sweet as *Aszú*. Another crucial factor is the ageing of the wine in cellars encrusted with a black odourless **mould** called *penész*, which interacts with the fermentation process.

Tokaj wine has collected some notable **accolades** since the late Middle Ages. Beethoven and Schubert dedicated songs to it; Louis XVI declared it "the wine of kings, the king of wines"; Goethe, Voltaire, Heine and Browning all praised it; and Sherlock Holmes used it to toast the downfall of von Bork, after troubling Watson to "open the window, for chloroform vapour does not help the palate".

In the Communist era, collective wineries tended to level standards down to the lowest common denominator, but also produced such gems as a 1972 6-*puttonyos*, which has a prize-winning chocolate and almond taste. During the 1990s foreign investors fell over themselves to get involved, resulting in what was known as the **Tokaji Renaissance**. Tokajis from the old days tend to be a richer brown-red in colour due to oxidization, which doesn't occur in the state-of-the-art stainless steel tanks used by foreign wineries. Some like the new style, others prefer the old. You can decide for yourself on **tours and tastings** (expect to pay around 2500–3000Ft for the tasting of six wines) at wineries in the region, of which the following are recommended:

Degenfeld Terézia kert 9, Tarcal ☎47/380-173, ⓦwww.grofdegenfeld.com. Bought by a German sewing-machine magnate for his Hungarian wife, this winery has cellars fronted by a pretty house set among chestnut trees, and an adjoining plush four-star castle hotel (☎47/580-400; ◑).

Disznókő Mezőzombor, outside Tarcal ☎47/569-410, ⓦwww.disznoko.hu. This place's French owners began by scrubbing all the mildew off the cellar walls, to the horror of the locals. The winery was designed by Makovecz (note the circular tractor shed) and has a restaurant and pension attached (same phone).

Hétszőlő Bajcsy-Zsilinszky utca 19, Tokaj ☎47/352-009, ⓦwww.tokaj.com. A Franco-Japanese venture that owns the Rákóczi cellar on the main street and most of the vineyards around town. See p.355 for details.

Megyer-Pajzos in Sárospatak. Now owned by a French company, this famous seventeenth-century cellar is associated with Prince Rákóczi. See p.363 for details.

Oremus Bajcsy-Zsilinszky utca 45, Tolcsva ☎47/384-520. A wise investment by the Spanish, as it was this winery that produced the 1972 6-*puttonyos* mentioned above.

Royal Tokaji Rákóczi út 35, Mád ⓦwww.royal-tokaji.com. Kilometres of old cellars lined with oak barrels and smothered in mould. Owned by a British firm. See opposite for details.

If you would like more information on wineries and cellars in the region contact the Tokaj-Hegyalja Wine Route Association, at Dózsa Gyorgy utca 2 in Tokaj (☎30/456-1556, ⓦwww.tokaji-borut.hu).

Fogadó is also very enjoyable, with a reasonably ambitious Hungarian menu – they've got a pleasant beer garden too. Rather more prosaic options include the touristy *Bonchidai Csárda* at Bajcsy-Zsilinszky utca 21, with its enormous riverside terrace, and *Makk Marci*, a fail-safe pizzeria gaff opposite the post office. If you're looking to drink wine somewhere other than a cellar, head to the classy little *Szent Vince* wine bar at Rákóczi út 42, which also puts on occasional live music.

Activities available in Tokaj include cycling and canoeing, both of which can be arranged through *Vízisport Turistaház* (see p.354). Swimming in the Tisza may be tempting, but is not advised due to the dirtiness of the water and its unpredictable whirlpools. The major festivals in town each year are the **Tokaj Wine Festival** (Tokaj-Hegyaljai Borfesztivál) at the end of May, and the **Grapes Harvest Festival** (Szüreti Napok Tokaj) on the first weekend of October, both of which involve, naturally enough, much consumption of wine.

The Tokaj-Hegyalja

The southern slopes of the Zemplén form the distinctive region known as the **Tokaj-Hegyalja**, which is largely devoted to producing wine. Most of its beautifully sited villages are accessible by bus from Tokaj or Szerencs, a drab little town 18km west of Tokaj (many are also served by the train line from Szerencs to Hidasnémeti), but the paucity of tourist accommodation may oblige you to stick to day-trips – you can stop off at one or two villages a day, depending on schedules.

In **MÁD**, 11km east of Szerencs, it's worth enquiring about **tasting tours** at the British-owned **Royal Tokaji cellars** at Rákóczi utca 35 (T 47/348-601, W www .royal-tokaji.com), in the centre of the village, which is also home to the renowned vintner István Szepsy (allegedly descended from the inventor of *Aszú*), who can be found at Táncsics utca 57 (T 47/348-349). While the train station lies ten minutes' walk down Bányász utca, visitors arriving by bus will pass a folk Baroque-style **synagogue**, built in 1765, whose ornate ceilings are rotting with damp while pigeons desecrate its pews. The talisman-sized key is held at Kossuth út 73, below the former **Rabbi's house** and arcaded **Yeshiva** (religious school), long divided into flats and sunk into disrepair. On the northern edge of Mád lies an old **Jewish Cemetery**, which is also locked; ask around for the key.

▲ Tokaj-Hegyalja vineyard

TÁLLYA, 9km further north, is another wine-producing village with hundreds of barrels maturing in seventeenth-century **cellars** near a former Rákóczi mansion. In the village **church** you can view the font where Lajos Kossuth was baptized, while on the road up to the TV tower, the former synagogue has been turned into an art gallery where exhibitions and **concerts** are held during the Zemplén Days in late August; Tourinform in Sárospatak has details. There's super-smooth accommodation at the gorgeous *Bartfay Udvarhaz*, Rákóczi utca 25 (℡47/598-005, Ⓦwww.bartfayudvarhaz.hu; ❼), in addition to a fine restaurant and wine house, the *Oroszlános Borvendéglő*, next door at no. 23.

MONOK, 10km northwest of Szerencs, was the **birthplace of Kossuth**, whose childhood home at Kossuth utca 18 is now a **museum** (Kossuth emlékek; March–Oct Tues–Sun 9am–5pm; rest of the year by appointment; 400Ft) that casts his career (see box below) in the most favourable light. Monok's other famous son is Miklós Németh, Hungary's Prime Minister during the transition from Communism to democracy in 1989.

Some 30km north of Tokaj and 2km off the road to Sárospatak, the hillside around **TOLCSVA** is honeycombed with 2.5km of cellars full of local **linden leaf wine** (Tolcsvai Hárslevelű). The village is also home to the excellent Spanish-owned **Oremus winery**, which produces some of the finest modern Tokajis (see box, p.356), while you can learn more about the history of the region's wine at the **Wine Museum**, Kossuth utca 32 (Tues–Sun 10am–5pm; 300Ft). Another very good reason for visiting the village is the brilliant ⚜*Ős Kaján* **restaurant** at Kossuth utca 14 (closed Mon); the French-inspired food is terrific, whilst the restaurant itself – deep orange painted walls, thick wood-beamed ceilings and glass tables with cast-iron chairs – looks fantastic. Moreover, there's a lively programme of artistic and musical events going on here throughout the year. If you wish to stay, the *Király Panzió*, at Kossuth utca 61 (℡47/384-555; ❸), is a well-facilitated pension. Tolcsva can be reached by the hourly bus from Tokaj to **KOMLÓSKA**, a pretty little village a few kilometres further uphill. Along the main street, Rákóczi utca, stands a lovely little **regional house** (Ruszin Tájház; Mon–Fri 8am–4pm; 200Ft), a thickly thatched, two-roomed peasant house stuffed with furniture and artefacts;

Lajos Kossuth

Lajos Kossuth was the incarnation of post-Napoleonic bourgeois nationalism. Born into landless gentry in 1802, he began his political career as a lawyer, representing absentee magnates in Parliament. His parliamentary reports, advocating greater liberalism than the Habsburgs would tolerate, were widely influential during the Reform Era. While in jail for sedition, Kossuth taught himself English by reading Shakespeare. Released in 1840, he became editor of the radical *Pesti Hírlap*, was elected to Parliament and took the helm during the 1848 Revolution, whereupon his eloquent idealism tragically fulfilled its latent demagogic chauvinism.

After Serbs, Croats and Romanians rebelled against Magyar rule and the Habsburgs invaded Hungary, the Debrecen Parliament proclaimed a republic with Kossuth as de facto dictator. Having escaped to Turkey after the Hungarians surrendered in August 1849, he toured Britain and America, espousing liberty. So eloquent were his denunciations of Habsburg tyranny that London brewery workers attacked General Haynau, the "Butcher of Vienna", when he visited the city. Karl Marx loathed Kossuth as a bourgeois radical, and tried to undermine his reputation with articles published in the New York *Herald Tribune* and the London *Times*. As a friend of the Italian patriot Mazzini, Kossuth spent his last years in Turin, where he died in 1894.

there's accommodation here at the wonderfully restful *Sólyomvár Panzió*, Rákóczi utca 9 (☏47/538-016; ❹).

The village of **SZABOLCS**, 10km southeast, on the far side of the River Tisza, was once important enough to lend its name to a county in northeastern Hungary. Here you'll find the only surviving earthworks fortress (*földvár*) in Central Europe, dating from the ninth century; the eighteenth-century **Mudrány Mansion** at Petőfi utca 39 (April–Oct Tues–Sun 9am–5pm; rest of year by appointment; 200Ft); and a **Calvinist Church** with fifteenth-century frescoes that was built as a Catholic church in the eleventh century.

The western Zemplén

The western flank of the Zemplén is dotted with **villages** whose remote and sleepy existence today belies their historic significance. Unlike the other parts of Hungary with medieval churches and ruined castles, there's rarely another tourist in sight here, even though the **scenery** everywhere is great. In contrast to the rounded sedimentary hills on the western side of the valley, the volcanically formed Zemplén often resemble truncated cones called *sátor* (tent). If all of this appeals, and you don't mind the lack of bright lights and facilities, the region is well worth exploring.

Though private **transport** is definitely advantageous, most places are accessible by local buses or trains up the Szerencs–Hidasnémeti branch line. The scarcity of **accommodation** could be more of a problem unless you bring a tent, or encounter sympathetic locals. Try to buy a hiking **map** (*Zempléni hegység*) from the Tourinform in Tokaj or Miskolc, which is useful even if you don't intend to go **hiking**. There are two maps: *északi*, covering the northern part, and *déli* the south, showing all the villages mentioned below.

The route described below approximately follows the **Hernád Valley** up towards the river's source in the Slovakian highlands, and the **border crossing** into Slovakia at Tornyosnémeti (by road) and Hidasnémeti (by rail).

Boldogkőváralja and Vizsoly

Best reached by road, since the village lies 2.5km from its train stop, **BOLDOGKŐVÁRALJA** is dominated by a massive **castle** (mid-April to mid-Oct daily 9am–6pm; 250Ft) upon a volcanic mound. Erected in the thirteenth century to discourage a return visit by the Mongols, it commands a spectacular view of the Zemplén Hills, and the surrounding woods are rife with red squirrels. You can **stay** at the sparkling little *Bodóvár Panzió* (☏46/306-062, ⓦ www.bodovar.hu; ❺) at the foot of the road leading up to the castle, which also has modern wellness facilities and a lovely restaurant.

At **VIZSOLY**, 2km from its train station, Korlát-Vizsoly, a thirteenth-century **Calvinist Church** (April–Oct daily 9am–5pm; 300Ft) harbours fantastic frescoes of Jesus's Ascension (leaving his footprints behind) and St George and the dragon, which were only discovered in 1940 after being lost for many centuries. A Latin inscription on the chancel wall reads "If you did not come to pray in this place then leave as you have come." The church also contains an original edition of the **Vizsoly Bible**, the first Hungarian translation of the Bible by Gáspár Károlyi, dean of Gönc, in 1590, which was printed in the house across the road and played a formative role in the development of Hungarian as a written language. In summertime, it's possible to **stay** at the priest's house (*református lelkesz*; known as *Károlyi Gáspár Ifjúsági Tábor*; ☏46/387-187; ❷) at Szent János út 123, where you'll get a warm welcome. There are regular **buses** to Abaújszantó and a daily service to Miskolc and Szikszó.

Gönc and Regéc

Thirteen kilometres further up the valley, amid ravishing countryside, the village of **GÖNC**, accessible by buses from Hidasnémeti as well as by train, was a thriving trade centre in the Middle Ages. It was here that Dean Károlyi was born and translated the Vizsoly Bible, and Sárospatak's Calvinist College took refuge during the Counter-Reformation. Subsequently, the village became famous for making the 136-litre oak **barrels** (*Gönci hordok*) used to store Tokaj wine – sadly no longer made here.

The most tangible relic of this history is the white **Hussite House** at Kossuth utca 85 (Huszita Ház; mid-April to mid-Oct Tues–Sun 10am–6pm; 400Ft), whose Calvinist inhabitants could escape into the maze of cellars beneath the village via a door in the cellar of the house. Notice the Gönc barrel, and the weird bed that pulls out from a table upstairs. If it's shut, the old woman at Rákóczi utca 115, across the stream and off to the right, can let you in; she was born in the Hussite House.

Gönc is very picturesque but facilities are minimal, with nowhere to eat except a cake shop and a single bar, where locals get stuck into *pálinka* at 10am – you can even buy alcohol at the flower shop. However, there is pleasant year-round **accommodation** at Arany János utca 1B at the far end of Kossuth utca (℡46/388-477; ❷), plus the *Turistaszálló*, a school building behind the Hussite House at Károlyi Gáspár utca 33 (℡46/388-052; 1500Ft) over the summer.

Some might enjoy a hard day's **hiking to REGÉC**, along an eight-kilometre ill-marked path skirting the 787-metre-high Gergely-hegy (bring a compass, food and water). Regéc is the site of another **ruined castle**, which is also accessible by two buses a day from Encs, on the Miskolc–Hidasnémeti line, leaving around noon and 2pm.

Telkibánya, Abaújvár and Kéked

Buses from Hidasnémeti to Gönc carry on to **TELKIBÁNYA**, 9km to the east (also served by two buses from Sátoraljaújhely, on the other side of the hills), whose **Mineral Mining Museum** at Múzeum utca 15 (Ipartörténeti Gyűjtemény; mid-April to mid-Oct Tues–Sun 9am–4pm; 300Ft) has a fine collection of Zemplén crystals, pottery and carved heads. The *Gyermektábor* (Children's Camp) at Fürdő utca 17 (℡46/325-766; ❷) offers self-catering **accommodation** during summer, and also out of season if you book ahead, and there are cheap and simple rooms at the *Aranygombos Fogadó*, Múzeum utca 3 (℡46/388-665; ❷).

Buses from Gönc and a limited service (2 daily on weekdays) from Hidasnémeti, 4km away, to Hollóháza (see p.367) can get you to **ABAÚJVÁR**, 9km to the north of Gönc. This pretty village has a picturesque **Calvinist Church** with battered frescoes from 1332; ask for the key on Rákóczi utca, below the church. Another 4km along the way to Hollóháza, buses call at **KÉKED**, which boasts a **fortified manor** (Tues–Sun 10am–4pm; 400Ft) containing rustic knick-knacks and antiques that belonged to the present mayor's grandmother prior to its expropriation in 1947. The manor now houses the *Hotel Melczer*, a posh hotel with an extensive range of facilities (℡46/588-566, ✉keked@t-online.hu; ❻). Otherwise, you can **stay** at the *Kéked Fogadó* at Fürdő utca 13 (℡46/388-077; ❷; May–Sept), near an **outdoor bath** in the forest (May–Aug Tues–Sun 10am–6pm), fed by a cold-water spring.

Sárospatak

Half an hour's train journey from Szerencs, **SÁROSPATAK** ("Muddy Stream") basks on the banks of the River Bodrog – a graceful, serene spot with almost unlimited expanses of green. The town once enjoyed a significant role in Hungarian intellectual life, thanks to its **Calvinist College**: Magyars given to hyperbole used to describe Sárospatak as the "Athens on the Bodrog". In the last twenty years, some fine examples of **Makovecz architecture** have drawn attention to the town, but Sárospatak's main claim to fame is still its historic association with the **Rákóczi family**, whose **castle** is one of the main sights in town.

Arrival and information

The **bus** and **train stations** are located right next to each other at the end of Táncsics Mihály utca, from where it's less than a ten-minute walk into the town centre; head through the park, directly opposite, and then turn right along Rákóczi út. Lots of **information** can be obtained from Tourinform, located towards the castle at Szt. Erzsébet utca 3 (June–Aug daily 10am–6pm; Sept–May Mon–Fri 9am–4pm, Sat 10am–3pm; ☏47/315-316, ✉sarospatak@tourinform .hu), while they've also got **internet access** available. The **post office** is at Rákóczi út 45 (Mon–Fri 8am–6pm, Sat 8am–noon).

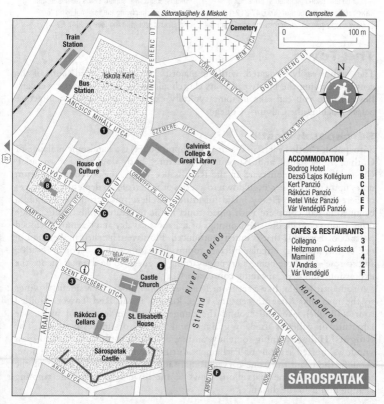

ACCOMMODATION
Bodrog Hotel	D
Dezső Lajos Kollégium	B
Kert Panzió	C
Rákóczi Panzió	A
Retel Vitéz Panzió	E
Vár Vendéglő Panzió	F

CAFÉS & RESTAURANTS
Collegno	3
Heitzmann Cukrászda	1
Maminti	4
V András	2
Vár Vendéglő	F

SÁROSPATAK

Accommodation

The town has a decent stock of centrally located and very affordable **pensions**. In July and August the cheapest beds in town can be found at the efficiently run and very handily located *Dezső Lajos College* at Eötvös út 7 (☎47/312-211; dorm bed 2000Ft). Tourinform can advise on **private rooms** (❷), although they don't make bookings. The two **campsites** are thirty minutes' walk away in Végardó, north of town: *Termál Fürdő Camping* on Határ út (☎47/311-150; April–Sept) is next to the town's thermal baths, while *Tengerszem Camping* at Herczeg utca 2 (☎47/312-744; April–Oct) has bungalows (❷) and good facilities, but charges higher rates all round.

Bodrog Hotel Rákóczi út 58 ☎47/311-744, ⓦwww.hotelbodrog.hu. This utterly soulless mid-rise building doesn't hold out much promise, but the rooms are actually very agreeable – spacious and light with minibar and balcony. In addition it has very modern wellness facilities. ❻

Kert Panzió Rákóczi út 31 ☎47/311-559, ⓦwww.kertpanzio.hu. Midway along the busy main street, behind the big white gate, this small four-room pension has clean, modern rooms. Use of kitchen and sauna included in price. ❹

Rákóczi Panzió Rákóczi út 30 ☎47/312-111, ⓦwww.rakoczipanzio.hu. Across the road from the *Kert Panzió*, this warm and quiet pension has polished rooms, some with jacuzzi showers. Breakfast costs extra. ❺

Retel Vitéz Panzió Attila út 2 ☎47/315-428, ⓔretelvitez@freemail.hu. Pleasantly situated down by the bridge, hence some of the simple, sunny rooms (including triples and quads) overlook the river. Breakfast costs extra. ❸

Vár Vendéglő Panzió Árpád út 35 ☎47/311-370, ⓦwww.varvendeglo.hu. The town's most appealing option, with six serene and immaculately furnished rooms, some with superb views across to the castle – worth paying the minimal extra for. Fabulous restaurant too (see p.364). ❺

The Town

The town is easily navigated, with the majority of sights clustered south of the centre, including the lovely castle, its church and the venerable Rákóczi cellars. Beyond here you can take in some typically exuberant Makovecz architecture before reaching the Calvinist College.

Sárospatak Castle

Sárospatak Castle (Vár; Tues–Sun 10am–6pm; 500Ft) is a handsome mélange of Gothic, Renaissance and Baroque architecture, both doughty and palatial. Grouped around a courtyard in the Renaissance wings, the **Rákóczi Museum** dotes upon the dynasty, even down to a series of watercolours depicting the stages of Ferenc II's exile. Heavy inlaid furniture, jewellery, monstrous stoves, and a banqueting hall complete with piped court music re-create domestic life, while other rooms contain life-size paintings of fearsome cavalry and the moustachioed portrait of Ferenc II that is much reproduced. Plots were hatched by Ferenc I in one of the adjoining circular balcony rooms, beneath a ceiling decorated with a stucco rose – the rose being a cryptic warning to guests to be discreet (hence the expression "sub rosa", meaning conspiratorial).

A romantic loggia, like a set from *Romeo and Juliet*, links the residential wings to the muscular fifteenth-century keep, known as the **Red Tower**. Guided tours (1000Ft) take you around the dungeons and underground wells, the labyrinth of galleries used by gunners and a series of impressive halls. The **Knights' Hall**, remaining somehow austere despite its throne and stained-glass windows, hosted sessions of Parliament during the Independence War – note, though, the beautiful stone-carved Renaissance portals. From the top of the tower there are some marvellous views of the town below and the rippling Zemplén hills in the distance.

The Rákóczi Cellars, St Elisabeth House and Castle Church

Founded in 1531, the **Rákóczi Cellars** (Rákóczi Pince), just outside the castle gates at Szent Erzsébet utca tér 26, are the most impressive in the Zemplén. Hewn out by prisoners from the castle dungeons in the seventeenth century, they are thickly coated in a black *penész*, the "noble mould", whose presence is considered vital to the flavour of local **wine**. The one-kilometre-long cellars consist of three parallel tunnels lined with some one thousand oak barrels through which the wine breathes in humidity exceeding ninety percent. Between the two chilly tasting rooms, there is a famous niche with a bench in it where Ferenc Rákóczi himself used to come and smoke a pipe and plot the overthrow of the Habsburgs. The cellar is now owned by **Megyer-Pajzos**, a French company with a Hungarian name. **Tours and wine-tasting** take place every 45 minutes – book in advance or just show up and wait your turn (daily 10am–6pm; 1800Ft for tasting of six wines; ☎47/311-902, ✉rakoczipince@gmail.com).

A minute's walk away, further up Szent Erzsébet utca, stands **St Elisabeth House** (Szent Erzsébet Ház; Tues–Sat 10am–4pm; 500Ft), allegedly the spot where the eponymous German Catholic saint was born in 1207. Originally built in 1917, the house then functioned as a Roman Catholic school until the early 1990s, when it fell into disrepair, only to be restored in time for the eight-hundredth anniversary of Elisabeth's birth in 2007; it now holds a fine stash of ecclesiatical goodies, including reliquaries, icons and Baroque sculptures.

Adjacent to the house is the **Castle Church** (Vártemplom; Tues–Sun 9am–5pm; 250Ft). Though much remodelled since the fourteenth century, with painted-on rather than genuine vaulting, it remains one of the largest Gothic hall churches in eastern Hungary. Its huge Baroque altar was brought here from the Carmelite church in Buda Castle after their order was banned in 1784. Look out for posters outside advertising **organ recitals**.

The Calvinist College

A short walk north of the centre stands the imposing **Calvinist College** (Mon–Sat 9am–5pm, Sun 9am–1pm; closed Easter, Whitsun & Oct 31; 600Ft).

The Rákóczi family

The Rákóczi family played a major role in Transylvania and Hungary during a turbulent era. Shortly after **György I Rákóczi** acquired Sárospatak Castle in 1616, his Transylvanian estates – and political influence – were augmented by marriage to the immensely wealthy **Zsuzsanna Lorántffy**. In 1630 the nobility elected him Prince of Transylvania, hoping that György would restore the stability enjoyed under Gábor Bethlen – which he did.

Alas, **György II** was as rash as his father was cautious, managing to antagonize both Poland and Vizier Mehmet, whose invasion of Transylvania forced the clan to flee to Habsburg-controlled Hungary in 1658. Here the Counter-Reformation was in full swing, and Magyar landlords and peasants reacted against Habsburg confiscations by sporadically staging ferocious revolts of "dissenters" (*kuruc*). Though the original revolt, led by Imre Thököly, was bloodily crushed, conspirators gathered around György's son **Ferenc I**.

By 1703, the insurgency had become a full-scale **War of Independence**, led by **Ferenc II**, whose irregular cavalry and peasant foot soldiers initially triumphed. By 1711, however, the Magyars were exhausted and divided, abandoned by their half-hearted ally Louis XIV of France, and Ferenc fled abroad as his armies collapsed under the weight of Habsburg power, to die in exile (in Tekirdag, Turkey) in 1735.

Founded in 1531, the college achieved renown under the rectorship (1650–54) of the great Czech humanist **Jan Comenius**, who published several textbooks with the support of György Rákóczi. During the Counter-Reformation, it was forced to move to Gönc, and then to Slovakia, before returning home in 1703. Illustrious graduates include Kossuth, Gárdonyi, the writer Zsigmond Móricz and the language reformer Ferenc Kazinczy. Like the Calvinist College in Debrecen, it has long-standing ties with England and runs an international **summer language school**. Since regaining control in 1990, the church has striven to make the college an educational powerhouse once again. Hour-long **tours** take in the Neoclassical **Great Library** (Nagykönyvtár), to the right of the main entrance, and a **museum** of college history (Iskolamúzeum). The modern building in the courtyard was designed by Makovecz (see box, p.163). Across the road is the leafy **Iskola Kert** (School Garden), full of statues of college alumni.

The Makovecz buildings

Throughout the town centre you can see a succession of buildings by the visionary architect Imre Makovecz, whose association with Sárospatak dates back to 1972, when Makovecz was on the Party's blacklist. His first project for the council was the **department store** on the corner of Rákóczi út and Bartók utca, quite anodyne by Western standards, but far removed from the then prevailing brutalist style. Next came the **House of Culture** on Eötvös utca, whose silvery, insectile facade conceals an amazing wooden auditorium; followed by an **apartment building** on the corner with Rákóczi út, manifesting his passion for asymmetry and organic forms, rooted in a fascination for ancient Celtic and Magyar culture. In the 1990s Makovecz returned to Sárospatak to embellish the Calvinist College and build a delightful **school** on Arany út, just past the castle.

Eating, drinking and entertainment

Two outstanding Hungarian **restaurants** are the stylish *V András* at Béla Király tér 3, a delightfully mellow place with model aeroplanes and airships dangling from the ceiling; and the *Vár Vendéglő*, in the pension of the same name (see p.362), a serene little spot with a fantastic wooden-roofed terrace and some interesting variations on Hungarian dishes. A decent alternative is *Collegno*, opposite Tourinform at Szent Erzsébet utca 22, a welcoming cellar pizzeria with a beer garden out back. Next to the Rákóczi Cellars, *Maminti* is a joy of a teahouse, where you can kick back on squishy floor cushions and sup tea served from sweet little brown ceramic pots. There's a good range of coffee and cakes at the shiny *Heitzmann Cukrászda*, midway between the Calvinist College and the stations at Táncsics Mihály utca 9. There are often various forms of entertainment going on at the cultural house, too.

Tourinform can supply a detailed list of **concerts**, plays and other events happening in town, the most popular of which is the superb **Zémplen Music Days** (Zempléni Művészeti Napok; Ⓦ www.zemplenfestival.hu) in mid-August – a ten-day series of highbrow classical concerts in town and the surrounding villages (tickets can be bought at the National Philharmonic box office in Budapest – see p.135 – or at Tourinform in Sárospatak; 1200–2500Ft). During the last weekend of June a **Jazz and Blues Festival** takes place in the castle gardens. Should you wish to wallow in the **thermal baths**, then head to the recreational complex 2km north of town in Végardó (daily 8am–6pm; 1000Ft, 700Ft after 2pm).

Sátoraljaújhely and around

Easier to reach than it is to pronounce ("**shah**-tor-oll-yah-oowee-hay"), **SÁTORALJAÚJHELY**, 13km northeast from Sárospatak, is the last Zemplén town before the border crossing to Slovenské Nové Mesto in Slovakia. Formerly a thriving county town, it was relegated to a backwater by the Treaty of Trianon and the provincial mergers which made Sárospatak the Zemplén "capital", while its once prosperous Jewish wine-trading community was wiped out in the war. It's a rather downbeat place, and unless you happen to be searching for an ancestor, the reason for coming is to catch buses to the villages around – unless your visit happens to coincide with its **international folk dancing festival** in mid-August.

The Town

From the bus and train stations 1km south of the centre, follow Fasor utca until it joins Kossuth utca, beside the striking red and yellow Reynolds tobacco factory. Across the main road lies a direly neglected **Jewish cemetery**, one of two in Sátoraljaújhely, where Jews amounted to forty percent of the population at the turn of the twentieth century. Further uphill, past a Gothic parish church, one reaches a cluster of Baroque edifices around Kossuth tér. It was from the balcony of the **Town Hall** at no. 5 that Kossuth first demonstrated his talent for oratory, during the Zemplén cholera epidemic and riots of 1830. In the middle of the square stands an almost unrecognizable Soviet war memorial covered with ivy. Off to the right of Kossuth tér, at Dózsa utca 11, is the **Kazinczy Ferenc Museum** (Mon–Sat 8am–4pm; 500Ft), housing a terribly dull local history exhibition.

Some 400m north of Kossuth tér, at Kazinczy út 35, is the much more worthwhile **Prison Museum** (Börtönmúzeum; Tues–Sat 9am–1pm; 500Ft), next door to the town prison, which has functioned as such since 1905. Despite the absence of English captioning, it's an enlightening trawl through the history of the prison (and Hungarian prisons generally), with lots of curious exhibits ranging from governors' outfits and guards' weapons, to prisoners' letters and a collection of ceramic items and other handicrafts made by inmates.

If you fancy some walking, the wild ravines and forested slopes of **Mount Magas** (509m) loom just outside town to the west. These heights saw bitter fighting between Magyars and Slovaks in 1919, and between partisans and Nazis in 1944.

Practicalities

There's plenty of **information** available from Tourinform at Hősök tere 3 (June–Sept Mon–Fri 9am–6pm, Sat & Sun 9am–5pm; Oct–May Mon–Thurs 8am–4.30pm, Fri 8am–1.30pm; ⊕47/321-458, ⒺHYPERLINK satoraljaujhely@tourinform.hu), which also has an extensive list of **private rooms** in the Zemplén. If you want to actually book a room, however, you'll need to head to Ibusz at Kossuth tér 26 (Mon–Fri 9am–5pm; ⊕47/321-757).

The only really decent **hotel** hereabouts is the plush *Hunor*, some 2km west of town near Magas Hill at Torzsás utca 25 (⊕47/521-521, ⓦwww.hotelhunor.hu; ❼), which has fabulously bright and tidy rooms, an indoor pool and bowling alley. Otherwise, in town itself, there's the dowdy *Hotel Henriette*, 50m down from the Kazinczy museum at Vasvári Pál utca 16 (⊕47/323-118, Ⓔhenriettekft@t-online.hu; ❹), while west of Kazinczy út, at Mártírok útja 29, is the marginally better *Csillagfény Panzió* (⊕47/322-619, Ⓔcsillagfenypanzio@t-online.hu; ❹). Hunting down a place to **eat** will yield little joy, with options restricted to the *Halászcsárda* at Kossuth tér 10, one of the least inspiring fish restaurants around (although you may care to try the "Hungover" fish soup); and the *Zempléni Casino* at Kazinczy út 1, which suffices for a pizza. For coffee and cakes the *Sarokház Cukrászda* at Táncsics tér 2 should assuage any sugar pangs. The **post office** is at Kazinczy út 10 (Mon–Fri 8am–4pm, Sat 8–11am).

Around Sátoraljaújhely

In the highlands beyond Sátoraljaújhely there are more villages that are just as lovely as those on the western side of the Zemplén. With a car, you can visit half a dozen of them in a day and not feel cheated if a couple are less appealing than expected. Relying on local buses, you'll have to go for a simpler itinerary and be more selective. You can reach Füzér (2 daily Mon–Sat), Pálháza (10 daily Mon–Fri, 6 daily Sat & Sun), Hollóháza (5 daily Mon–Fri, 5 Sat, 2 Sun), Karcsa and Pácin (8 daily Mon–Fri, 6 daily Sat & Sun) and Telkibánya (1 daily Mon–Fri). **Village tourism** is flourishing in this region, and should you wish to stay there are plenty of houses advertising **rooms** (●). Ibusz in Sátoraljaújhely has information and can make bookings in lodgings in local houses (see p.365). The following itineraries are basically structured around bus routes.

Towards Pálháza and Rostálló

This route can be a long excursion, or even a prelude to hiking over the Zemplén, depending on your inclinations. There are ten buses daily (six at weekends) from Sátoraljaújhely via Széphalom and Füzérradvány to Pálháza, from where you can reach Rostálló in the hills.

At **SZÉPHALOM** ("Beautiful Mill"), 5km from Sátoraljaújhely, the large, well-kept Ferenc Kazinczy memorial park contains the elaborate **mausoleum** of the eponymous writer (Tues–Sun 8am–4pm; 400Ft, which includes entry to the museum – see below). It was largely thanks to Kazinczy (1759–1831) and his associates that Hungarian was restored as a literary language in the nineteenth century rather than succumbing entirely to German, as the Habsburgs would have preferred. A few paces away, the **Museum of Hungarian Language** (same times) celebrates the country's incredibly rich literary heritage, though the absence of English captioning does little to alleviate the understanding of an already very complex language.

If you wish to stay, the *Múzeumkert Panzió*, close to the park at Kazinczy utca 273 (☏47/324-172, ✉muzeumkert@freemail.hu; ❸), has decent rooms (including triples and quads), and also sports a gym, sauna and restaurant.

Six kilometres later, buses stop by an avenue of pines leading to the **Castle Garden** (Kastély Kert) surrounding the **Károlyi manor house** on the edge of **FÜZÉR-RADVÁNY**, whose arboretum of variegated oaks and pines provides a haven for vipers and other wildlife (daily dawn till dusk; free). If the main gates are closed, follow the road round to the left and ask at the lodge. Work continues on converting the manor house into a hotel and museum. In the village there's a youth camp, the *Ifjúsági Tábor*, at Táncsics Mihály utca 14 (☏47/370-657; ●), which lets **rooms** from April to October, or there's the similarly cheap *Nagytanya Fogadó* across the road at Fenyvesalja utca 1 (☏47/370-550; ●) – there is also a small **campsite** here.

Another kilometre or so up the main road lies **PÁLHÁZA**, the place to board the **narrow-gauge train** that runs 9km up to Rostálló. This *erdei vasút* (forest railway) runs three times daily (departing 8.30am, 11.40am & 3.10pm, returning at 9.10am, 12.20pm & 4pm; 45min; 400Ft) between mid-April and mid-October, to coincide with buses for Sátoraljaújhely. Lászlóné Ulicska offers **rooms** with a sauna and a pretty garden at Vörösmarty utca 10, at the eastern end of the village (☏47/370-278, ✉ulicskalaca@freemail.hu; ❸), or there are clean, basic rooms at the *Megálló Turistaház* at Dózsa György utca 160 (☏47/370-121; ●). To really get away from it all, you can stay at the *Kőkapui Vadászkastély* in Pálháza-Kőkapu (☎47/370-032, ⓦwww.kokapu.hu; ❹–❼), an old hunting lodge, 8km from Pálháza, deep in the woods. The best rooms are in the lodge itself, rather than in the annexe, as they overlook the lake. You can rent bikes and boats, and the **restaurant** is quite a hub of activity in the summer months, serving decent post-hike nourishment.

ROSTALLÓ, the train terminus 1km further on, is the starting point for **hikes** in various directions – mostly ambitious ones for which you need proper equipment and a map. A good objective is **István kut** (Stephen's Well), a silver birch wood between Rostalló, Háromhuta and Regéc, noted for its special flora and diverse butterflies.

Füzér, Hollóháza and Lászlótanya

If one excursion is your limit, the village to aim for is **FÜZÉR**, a stopover for buses between Sátoraljaújhely and Hollóháza, only 9km from Pálháza. An idyllic place of vine-swathed cottages, dignified elders and wandering animals, Füzér enjoys an exceptionally temperate climate and maintains its traditional ways less self-consciously than museum villages like Hollókő – though a single old **peasant house** at Szabadság út 11 has been preserved as a *tájház* for visitors to poke around (Tues–Sun 9am–4pm; 200Ft).

The ruined **Perényi Castle** is almost directly overhead, although screened by trees and the precipitous angle of the hill. Erected in case the Mongols should return, it served as a repository for the Hungarian crown from 1301 to 1310, while foreign rivals squabbled over the throne. At a later date it was owned by Countess Báthori, who is said to have murdered several victims here (see box, p.282). From the huge Gothic arches of its ruined chapel there's a magnificent view of the sleepy village below, the blue-green hills along the border and the distant plain beyond – the whole scene enlivened by flocks of swifts swooping and soaring on the powerful thermals. Due to the microclimate, the hillsides abound in **wildlife**, with special flora, vipers, birds of prey and – sometimes – wolves and wildcats. You'll find plenty of houses advertising **rooms**, particularly along Kossuth utca and Árpád utca – just look out for the signs.

The village of **HOLLÓHÁZA**, 5km east of Füzér, is most notable for its **Porcelain Museum** at Károlyi út 11 (Porcelanmúzeum; April–Oct Tues–Sun 9.30am–4.30pm; 600Ft). As well as relating the history of the factory, established in 1831, the museum also documents industrial activity in the region, which began in 1777 with glass production. When the factory shop is closed, an outlet selling seconds is open round the corner (Tues–Sat 10am–4pm). At the top end of the village is a small modern **church**, one wall bearing the stations of the cross by the ceramicist Margit Kovács. There are three clean double **rooms** at the *Éva Panzió* (☎47/305-038; ❷), set up amongst trees just off Szent László utca, the main street running through the village. Also in the centre, at Miki Nándor utca 12, is *Csini Camping* (☎47/305-111; May–Sept), which also has a few double-room apartments (❸). You can enjoy a hearty meal at the *Nagymilic Étterem* at Károlyi utca 46, before pushing on to Lászlótanya, or catching one of the **buses** across the hills to Kéked and Abaújvár (see p.360).

About 6km by road from Hollóháza or a four-kilometre hike from Füzér, the tiny hamlet of **LÁSZLÓTÁNYA** gets its name from the former **hunting lodge** of Count László Károlyi, which stands only 400m from the Slovak border. During the early 1950s, the lodge served as a holiday resort for top Communist officials, notably the then Party leader Mátyás Rákosi, the route being lined by ÁVO guards during his visits. This mock-Tudor folly is currently closed for refurbishment, but it's worth checking with Tourinform in Sátoraljaújhely whether work has finished, as there are plans to reopen it as a hotel. Rákosi slept in the suite at the top of the stairs, if you're curious to know.

Karcsa and Pácin

Heading east from Sátoraljaújhely or Sárospatak (from which there are also buses) brings you to two villages of note, Karcsa and Pácin. On the edge of **KARCSA**, 15km east of Sátoraljaújhely, stands a tenth-century **Romanesque Church** with a Gothic nave and a freestanding belfry. The keys are next door, at the house with the *Belyegzés* sign. In **PÁCIN**, 4km further on, there's a fifteenth- to sixteenth-century **Renaissance manor** exhibiting peasant furniture (May–Sept Tues–Sun 10am–4pm; 400Ft). The kitchen cupboard carries a picture of a woman slaving over the stove, shouting "Hurry up, it's eleven o'clock!" to her husband who sits by the fire.

Travel details

Trains

Balassagyarmat to: Diósjenő and Vác (7 daily; 1hr 15min).

Budapest (Keleti Station) to: Eger (6 daily; 2hr 20min); Miskolc (hourly; 2hr–2hr 30min); Sárospatak and Sátoraljaújhely (6 daily; 3hr 45min–4hr).

Eger to: Budapest (6 daily; 2hr 20min); Füzesabony (every 1hr–1hr 30min; 25min); Szilvásvárad (7 daily; 1hr 5min).

Füzesabony to: Debrecen (every 1hr–1hr 30min; 2hr 10min); Eger (hourly; 20min); Hortobágy (8 daily; 1hr 15min); Tiszafüred (10 daily; 30min).

Miskolc to: Budapest (hourly; 2hr–2hr 30min); Kazincbarcika (every 2hr; 30min); Nyíregyháza (every 1hr–1hr 30min; 2hr); Ózd (every 2hr; 1hr 30min); Putnok (every 2hr; 1hr); Sárospatak (hourly; 1hr 20min); Sátoraljaújhely (7 daily; 1hr 30min); Szerencs (hourly; 30min); Tornanádaska (8 daily; 1hr 40min).

Sárospatak to: Budapest (7 daily; 4hr); Miskolc (8 daily; 1hr 15min–1hr 45min); Sátoraljaújhely (every 1hr–1hr 30min; 10min).

Szerencs to: Mád (9 daily; 10min); Sárospatak (hourly; 1hr); Tállya (9 daily; 20min); Tokaj (hourly; 15–25min).

Buses

Budapest (Népstadion) to: Aggtelek (2 daily; 5hr); Balassagyarmat (every 1–2hr; 2hr 10min); Eger (hourly; 2hr); Gödöllő (every 1hr–1hr 30min; 45min); Gyöngyös (hourly; 1hr 35min); Mátraháza (every 2–3hr; 1hr 50min); Miskolc (1 daily; 4hr 30min).

Aggtelek to: Budapest (1 daily; 5hr); Eger (1 daily; 3hr); Miskolc (1 daily; 2hr).

Balassagyarmat to: Budapest (every 1–2hr; 2hr); Salgótarján (hourly; 1hr); Szécsény (hourly; 1hr).

Eger to: Aggtelek (1 daily; 4hr); Budapest (hourly; 3hr); Debrecen (5 daily; 2hr 45min); Gyöngyös (every 40min–1hr; 1hr 30min); Kecskemét (1 daily; 4hr); Mátraháza (Mon–Fri 8 daily, Sat & Sun 4 daily; 2hr); Miskolc (1 daily; 2hr 30min); Recsk (hourly; 1hr 45min); Sirok (every 40min; 1hr 30min); Szeged (2 daily; 5hr); Szilvásvárad (hourly; 1hr); Szolnok (5 daily; 2hr 30min); Tiszafüred (5 daily; 1hr 15min).

Gyöngyös to: Abádszalók (4 daily; 2hr); Debrecen (2 daily; 4hr 30min); Eger (every 40min–1hr; 1hr 30min); Mátrafüred (every 20–40min; 30min); Mátraháza (every 20–40min; 45min); Miskolc (1 daily; 3hr 15min).

Hollókő to: Szécsény (hourly; 45min).

Mátraháza to: Eger (3 daily; 2hr); Gyöngyös (every 20–40min; 45min); Miskolc (1 daily; 4hr).

Miskolc to: Aggtelek (1 daily; 3hr); Bükkszentkereszt (Mon–Fri hourly, Sat & Sun 8 daily; 1hr); Debrecen (hourly; 2hr); Eger (Mon–Fri every 45min–1hr, Sat & Sun 7 daily; 2hr 30min); Gyöngyös (3 daily; 3hr); Jászberény (2 daily; 3hr); Lillafüred (every 30min; 30min); Mátraháza (2 daily; 4hr); Miskolc-Tapolca (every 10min; 15min); Nyíregyháza (2 daily; 2hr); Ómassa (every 30min; 45min).

Ózd to: Aggtelek (1 daily; 1hr 30min); Debrecen (2 daily; 3hr 45min); Miskolc (2 daily; 3hr 30min).

Sárospatak to: Debrecen (2 daily; 3hr 30min); Sátoraljaújhely (hourly; 20min); Tokaj (2 daily; 1hr 30min).

Sátoraljaújhely to: Debrecen (2 daily; 4hr); Sárospatak (hourly; 20min); Tokaj (2 daily; 2hr).

Szécsény to: Balassagyarmat (every 1hr–1hr 30min; 1hr); Budapest (8 daily; 2hr 15min); Hollókő (hourly; 45min).

Tokaj to: Debrecen (3 daily; 2hr); Sárospatak (2 daily; 1hr 30min).

Food and drink

Combining elements of native and foreign cuisine, Hungary has forged a distinctive culinary tradition, at the forefront of which is the world-renowned goulash, while few Hungarian dishes are complete without a dash of the ubiquitous paprika spice – foodies, meanwhile, will enjoy the country's many colourful gastronomic festivals. The capital's venerable coffee houses are still an institution, while Hungary also boasts a surprisingly strong tradition of wine-making, and a resurgence in the industry in recent years has served to popularize many vintages, not least the famed sweet wines from Tokaj.

Hungarian dishes

Strongly influenced by its Central Asian roots, **Hungarian cuisine** also draws heavily on the culinary traditions of neighbouring or previously occupying peoples such as the Turks, Serbs and Austrians. Hungarian cooking was revolutionized in the late nineteenth century by adventurous restaurateurs who introduced a strong French influence into Budapest's kitchens, marrying eastern flavours with the traditions of the West. For most people, the archetypal Magyar dish is **goulash** (*gulyas*), a thick soup-like stew comprising beef and potatoes, stirred in with onions and peppers, and flavoured with the famous **paprika** (see below) – the typical paprika dish itself consists of meat stewed in the eponymous spice and mixed in a thick sour cream. Not dissimilar is *pörkölt*, a flavoursome ragout of pork, beef or mutton with onions and paprika. Although landlocked, Hungary boasts its own spicy **fish soup** (*halászlé*) – particularly popular in the towns along the Danube and Tisza rivers – while the delicious Balaton pike-perch (*fogas*) features on menus around the lake. Hungarians also do an unusual variation in **soups**, such as chilled sour-cherry (*hideg meggyleves*) and wine (*borleves*). The sweet-toothed, meanwhile, can indulge in stuffed **pancakes** (*palacsinta*) – typically jam, raisins, walnuts or sweet cheese – or *dobostorta*, a heavenly, chocolate-layered **sponge cake** topped with caramel.

Paprika

If there is one foodstuff that is synonymous with Hungarian cuisine, it's **paprika**. Revered as "red gold" (*piros arany*), no one really knows when this member of the *Capsicum* genus was introduced – some theories point to the Age of Migration

Beef goulash ▲

Cake display, Budapest ▼

via the Balkans, while others even credit Christopher Columbus. Its consumption received an important boost during the Napoleonic Wars, when Continental blockades compelled Europeans to find a substitute for pepper. The nineteenth-century preference for milder paprika spurred cross-fertilization experiments, which led to the discovery of capsaicin, produced by the plant in response to drought and sunlight and responsible for its piquancy. Inventions such as the Pálffy roller frame eased the laborious task of chopping and grinding, while the plant's nutritional qualities were investigated by Dr Albert Szent-Györgyi of Szeged University, who won the 1933 Nobel Prize for synthesizing vitamin C (paprika is also rich in vitamin A). In 1994 there was national outrage over the so-called paprika scandal, when it was discovered that powdered paprika was being laced with red lead to look extra ruddy. To protect the public and the reputation of the national condiment, all supplies were withdrawn from shops until the source of the contamination had been identified and fresh, certifiably pure, paprika became available.

▲ Paprika stall, Budapest

▼ Harvesting in Tokaj vineyard

Hungarian wine

Hungarian wines – first introduced by the Romans over two thousand years ago – are a delight, though thus far under-appreciated in the global market. However, it hasn't always been a success story: production ceased completely during Ottoman rule, while decades of low-quality mass output under Communism did little to enhance the reputation of Hungarian vintages. In recent years, however, the industry has been revitalized, with small-scale, family-owned wineries opening up and foreign investors queueing to get a slice of the action. Of Hungary's 22 wine-growing regions, the most celebrated are the **Tokaj-Hegyalja** – whose wines are perhaps the best known abroad, notably the incredibly sweet dessert wine, Aszú – and **Villány-Siklós**, Hungary's first wine road, which consistently yields both fine-quality reds and whites: the Cabernet Sauvignon and Cabernet Franc are particularly treasured. Beyond these two regions, consider sampling the reds of **Szekszárd**, in southern Transdanubia, and the whites of **Lake Balaton**, particularly from around Badascony and Balatonboglár. **Wine cellars** (*borpince*) abound in all these regions and are by far the best places to enjoy a drink, although you could always head to a **wine bar** (*borozo*) instead; most restaurants have a good stock too.

Food festivals

Throughout the year many towns and villages put on **gastronomic events**, with music, dancing and drinking accompanying the local delicacies themselves. The highest-profile foodie happenings are the **Szolnok Goulash Festival**, central to which are hundreds of steaming pots of the stuff, and the rousing **Békéscaba Sausage Festival**, where chefs compete to cultivate their own variation of the spicy local banger. Fish features prominently too, courtesy of the hugely popular **Fish Soup Festival** in Baja, when the town's vast main square is overtaken by a mass of bubbling cauldrons, and the **Tisza Fish Festival** in Szeged, in which both amateur and professional cooks compete to produce the tastiest, most original dishes. More curiously, there's the **Onion Festival** in Makó, the **Horseradish Festival** in the tiny village of Ujleta in the Northern Uplands, and the **Plum Jam Making Festival** in Szatmárcseke, near Nyiregyháza.

Budapest market ▲

Sausage festival ▼

The Great Plain

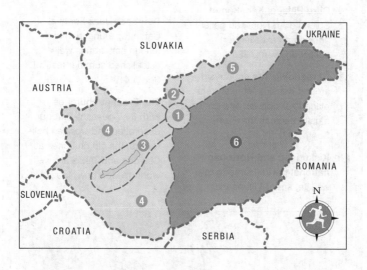

CHAPTER 6   # Highlights

✳ **Wine Tasting, Hajós Pincék**
Take your pick from hundreds
of cellars in this isolated
countryside village. See p.378

✳ **Fish Soup Festival, Baja**
All the fish you could wish
for at this colourful open-
air festival on Baja's main
square. See p.378

✳ **Cifra Palace, Kecskemét**
Splendid Art Nouveau gallery
housing an excellent art
collection. See p.383

✳ **Horseriding** The countryside
around Kecskemét is a great
place to saddle up and go for
a gallop across the Plain.
See p.387

✳ **Kiskunság and Hortobágy
national parks** Home to rare
wildlife, special Hungarian

animal breeds and cowboys
cracking their whips.
See p.388 & p.418

✳ **Great Synagogue, Szeged**
With its magnificent blue-
stained-glass dome and
cavernous interior, this is
the finest of architect Lipót
Baumhorn's synagogues.
See p.393

✳ **Debrecen Jazz Festival**
Catch top Hungarian and
foreign acts at this well-
established summer festival.
See p.417

✳ **The Erdőhát churches**
With their peasant-Baroque
decoration and wooden bell-
towers, the old churches at
Csaroda and Tákos are well
worth the journey. See p.428

▲ Horses at Hortobágy National Park

The Great Plain

C overing half of Hungary, the **Great Plain** (Nagyalföld) is awesome in its flatness. It can be as drab as a farmworker's boots or it can shimmer like the mirages of **Hortobágy National Park**, which, along with **Kiskunság National Park**, preserves the traditional *puszta* landscape – the name used to describe the arid grasslands that once covered almost the entire Plain – and wildlife of the region. In the villages, often with names prefixed by *Nagy-* or *Kis-* (Big or Little), the most characteristic sight is an isolated whitewashed farmstead (*tanya*) with a rustic artesian well, surrounded by flocks of geese and strings of paprika hanging out to dry. Marcell Iványi's short film *The Wind*, which won an award at Cannes in 1996, wonderfully captures the visual and emotional impact of this landscape.

With its often monotonous vistas and widely spaced towns, the Plain is something most people cross as much as visit and, if you're pressed for time, large areas can be skipped with a clear conscience. The Kiskunság National Park aside, the region between the Danube and the Tisza is chiefly notable for the towns of **Szeged** and **Kecskemét**, both flush with some marvellous architecture, though Kecskemét is just ahead when it comes to museums and culture. Of the smaller towns, both **Hódmezővásárhely** and **Gyula**, close to the Romanian border, merit a visit, the latter on account of its fine medieval fortress. Further beyond the River Tisza, the beguiling Hortobágy National Park offers the quintessential *puszta* experience, while **Lake Tisza** is ideal for those seeking more leisurely pursuits. **Debrecen**, Hungary's second-largest town, retains a large student presence and has a high cultural profile, making it a worthwhile place to stop over for a day or two. Heading further east, towards the Ukrainian border, the pace of life slows somewhat with the onset of the **Nyírség** and **Erdőhát** regions, whose gentle rolling landscapes, spotted with pretty little villages and churches with wooden bell-towers, are perfect for visitors keen on experiencing Hungarian rural life.

The Plain has more than its fair share of **festivals**, the best, and most diverse, of which are the Flower Carnival in Debrecen, the equestrian Bridge Fair at Hortobágy, and, for foodies, the wonderful Sausage Festival in **Békéscsaba**, and the Fish Soup Festival in Baja. Meanwhile, the pilgrimages to **Máriapócs** and the tomb of the "miracle rabbi" in **Nagykálló** cast a fascinating light on religious life.

From Budapest, **InterCity trains** are the fastest way of reaching the larger towns of Debrecen and Nyíregyháza to the east and Kecskemét and Szeged to the south. **Buses** from Budapest's Népstadion terminal are the best way of reaching towns such as Kalocsa and Baja, which are awkward or impossible to reach by train. All these services are covered under "Travel Details" at the end of the Budapest chapter.

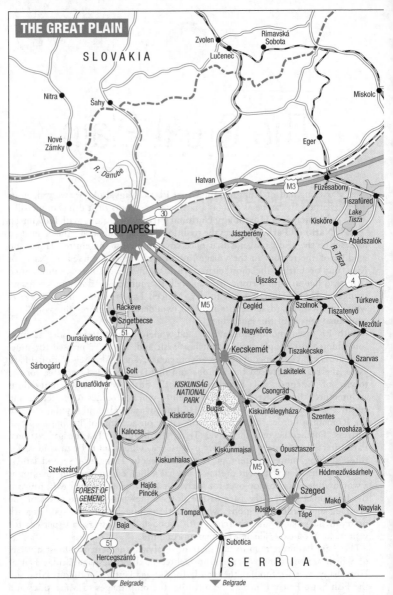

THE GREAT PLAIN

Zvolen
Rimavská
Sobota
Lučenec
SLOVAKIA
Miskolc
Nitra
Šahy
Nové
Zámky
Eger
R. Danube
Hatvan
M3
Füzesabony
Tiszafüred
Lake
Tisza
Kisköre
Budapest
30
Jászberény
Abádszalók
R. Tisza
Újszász
4
M5
Cegléd
Szolnok
Túrkeve
Ráckeve
Tiszatenyő
Szigetbecse
Nagykőrös
Mezőtúr
51
Dunaújváros
Kecskemét
Tiszakécske
Szarvas
Sárbogárd
Lakitelek
Solt
Dunaföldvár
KISKUNSÁG
NATIONAL
PARK
Csongrád
Bugac
Kiskunfélegyháza
Szentes
Kiskőrös
Orosháza
Kalocsa
Kiskunmajsa
Ópusztaszer
Szekszárd
Kiskunhalas
M5
5
Hódmezővásárhely
FOREST OF
GEMENC
Hajós
Pincék
Szeged
Tompa
Makó
Röszke
Nagylak
Tápé
Baja
51
Subotica
Hercegszántó
SERBIA

▼ Belgrade   ▼ Belgrade

For **drivers**, the best route south is the M5, which runs down to Szeged, while the M3 heads east in the direction of Miskolc, and onwards to Nyiregyháza. The best non-toll alternative is Route 30 via Hatvan; Route 4 via Szolnok can be slow with lots of heavy trucks on the road. Although **hitchhiking** is feasible along the trunk routes to Baja, Szeged and Debrecen, it's not worth attempting it elsewhere unless there's no alternative. Conversely, **cyclists** are banned from

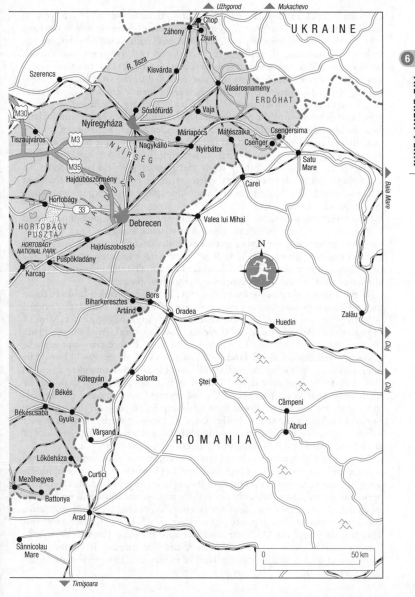

major (single-digit) roads, but should find minor ones delightful. Carts and animals are more common than cars, and wild flowers bloom along the verges.

The Puszta: some history

During medieval times the Plain was thickly forested, with hundreds of villages living off agriculture and livestock-rearing; the mighty **River Tisza**, fed by its tributaries in Transylvania and Maramures, determined all. Each year it flooded, its hundreds of loops merging into a "sea of water in which the trees were sunk to their crowns", enriching the soil with volcanic silt from the uplands and isolating the villages for months on end. However, the Turkish invasion of 1526 unleashed a scourge upon the land: 150 years of nearly unceasing warfare. The peasants who survived fled to the safer *khasse* (tribute-paying) towns like Szeged and Debrecen, leaving their villages to fall into ruin, while vast tracts of forest were felled to build military stockades, or burned simply to deny cover to the partisans (*hajdúk*). Denuded of vegetation, the land became swampy and pestilent with mosquitoes, and later the abode of solitary swineherds, runaway serfs, outlaws (*betyár*) and wolves. People began calling it **the puszta**, meaning "abandoned, deserted, bleak", and something of its character is conveyed by other words and phrases with the same root; for example *pusztít* (to devastate), *pusztul* (to perish, be ruined), and *pusztulj innen* (Clear out of here!). Not surprisingly, most people shunned it, or ventured in solely out of dire necessity.

Yet another transformation began in the nineteenth century, as an unexpected consequence of Count Széchenyi's flood-control work along the Tisza, when soil alkalinity increased the spread of **grassland**. Suitable only for pasturage, in time this became the "Hungarian Wild West", complete with rough-riding *csikósok* (cowboys) and wayside *csárdák* (inns), where lawmen, Gypsies and outlaws shared the same tables, bound not to fight by the custom of the *puszta*.

By the 1920s reality had crushed romance. Irrigation enabled landowners to enclose common pasture for crops, while mechanization denied the evicted sharecroppers and herders even the chance of work on the big estates. Most of Hungary's landless peasants, or **"three million beggars"**, lived on the Plain. True to their promises, the Communists distributed big estates amongst the peasantry and **nationalized land** "for those who till it" in 1947. Two years later, however, following the dictates of Stalinism, the peasants were forced to join state-run cooperative farms. Treated as Socialist serfs, they unanimously dissolved "their" cooperatives in 1956 and reverted to subsistence production, vowing to prevent the landlords from returning. In response to this, the Party pursued a subtler **agricultural policy** from the 1960s onwards, investing in ever larger cooperative and state farms, while allowing peasants to sell the produce of their "household plots" (limited to 1.5 acres).

The coalition government elected after the collapse of Communism in 1989 rejected calls for the return of land to its pre-1947 owners, but as a compromise gave cooperative members the option of leasing or buying the land. But even then, agricultural production was badly hit, as those that became **independent farmers** often lacked the capital for modern equipment. The ongoing economic crisis aside, the largest shadow hanging over agriculture is what will happen now that Hungary has joined the EU: there are widespread fears that this will allow large foreign concerns to buy up the best land, and that meeting EU demands on hygiene and quality will require the kind of money that Hungarian farmers can only dream about.

Between the Danube and the Tisza

Approaching from the direction of Budapest or Transdanubia, your first experience of the Plain will be the region **between the Danube and the Tisza**. Its chief attractions lie along two main routes from Budapest: **Kalocsa** and **Baja**, on the road following the Danube southwards; and **Kecskemét** and **Szeged**, on the trunk road towards Romania. If you're short of time and want to see something of the *puszta* grasslands at **Kiskunság National Park**, the second itinerary has a lot more to offer.

South to Kalocsa and Baja

The route south from Budapest leads eventually to laid-back **Baja**, on the lower reaches of the Danube. On the way you pass **Ráckeve**, close to Budapest – an ideal place to break your journey if you are in a car. If not, it is most easily reached by suburban train from Budapest (HÉV), making a good day-trip from the city. About halfway between Ráckeve and Baja lies the quaint little town of **Kalocsa**, which despite its sleepy atmosphere is actually one of the three archbishoprics in Hungary.

Ráckeve and Szigetbecse

The town of **RÁCKEVE**, 46km south of Budapest, is a diminutive counterpart to Szentendre on the Danube Bend, likewise founded by Serbian (Rác) refugees and rich in Baroque architecture, but far less touristy, despite being easily accessible from Budapest – hourly HÉV trains run from Budapest's Vágóhíd terminal on Soroksári út. Motorists should turn off Route 51 just beyond Kiskunlacháza, and cross the bridge onto Csepel Island, where the town is situated.

Arriving at the HÉV station, it's a pleasant twenty-minute walk along Kossuth utca, the main street running parallel to the Danube, into the centre of town. Along the way, you'll pass the **Savoy Mansion**, a grandiose fusion of Italian and French Baroque with a Neoclassical dome and other nineteenth-century additions. The original building was commissioned by Prince Eugene of Savoy, shortly after his armies drove the Turks from Hungary, and was constructed between 1702 and 1722 according to the designs of J.L. Hildebrandt; it now functions as a hotel (see p.376). Continuing down Kossuth utca, at no. 34 the small **Árpád Museum** (Tues–Sun 10am–6pm; 400Ft) exhibits a bog-standard collection of archeological finds, ethnographic goods and ecclesiastical treasures.

The town's main draw, however, is the magnificent **Serbian Orthodox Church** at Viola utca 1 (Szerb Orthodox Templom; April–Oct Tues–Sat 10am–noon & 2–5pm, Sun 2–5pm; 400Ft), whose blue and white tower, topped by a gilded cross, rises above the rooftops to the west of the town centre. The oldest Orthodox church in Hungary, dating from 1487, it has a Baroque iconostasis – with icons of the apostles and scenes from the life of Christ – and frescoes painted by Teodor Gruntovich between 1765 and 1771, using traces of the original fifteenth-century ones as a guide. The most impressive, and the best-preserved, frescoes are those on the west wall, depicting scenes from the Last Judgement and revered Orthodox saints. The oldest part of the church is the nave, while the narthex and freestanding bell-tower are sixteenth-century additions. Mass is still celebrated on important Orthodox holidays, though the congregation mainly comes from neighbouring villages like Lórév, which have preserved their Serb character.

Ráckeve practicalities

The friendly Tourinform office, in the small cultural centre at Kossuth utca 51 (Mon–Fri 8am–4pm; also mid-June to mid-Sept Sat & Sun 10am–4pm; ☎24/429-747, ⓦwww.tourinform.rackeve.hu), has plenty of **information** to hand. If stopping the night appeals, there are several good **accommodation** possibilities: the fabulously stylish *Kék-Duna Hotel*, at Dömsödi utca 1a (☎24/523-230, ⓦwww.wellnesshotel.hu; ❻), is a cut above anything else in town and also has a beautiful thermal pool in the basement, while the *Savoyai Kastély Hotel* (☎24/485-253, ⓦwww.savoyai.hu; ❻), at Kossuth utca 95, looks great but has rather disappointing rooms. Considerably cheaper, but perfectly fine, is the *Bálványos Panzió*, 500m along from the *Kék-Duna Hotel* at Dömsödi utca 34 (☎24/422-585; ❸), and the *Laguna Panzió*, conveniently sited near the HÉV station at Kossuth utca 108 (☎24/422-939; ❸).

For **eating**, there's first-class international cuisine at the glittering restaurant in the *Kék-Duna Hotel*, while the vaulted cellar restaurant at the *Savoyai* hotel has excellent Hungarian food. Less fancily, there's the *Csöni* at Szent János tér, offering Hungarian standards, or the cosy *Cadran Pizzeria and Pub* by the bridge on Hősök tere.

Szigetbecse

From Ráckeve you can catch a local bus or taxi 4km to the village of **SZIGET-BECSE**, where the renowned Hungarian-born photographer **André Kertész** spent much of his childhood. A small, but very enjoyable, **museum** at Makádi út 40 (May–Sept Sat & Sun 10am–4pm; donations accepted) exhibits over sixty of his early works, ranging from pictures of Szigetbecse to scenes from World War I, including one of troops sitting on a collective latrine. On weekdays throughout the year you can get the key from the mayor's office (polgármesteri hivatal) at Petőfi utca 34, ten minutes' walk away.

Kalocsa

Around 120km south of the capital, **KALOCSA** makes a pleasant and convenient stopover, with regular buses passing through en route to Baja further south. The town is promoted for its flowery **embroidery** and "**painting women**", who made it their business to decorate everything in sight, but is chiefly known as Hungary's "**paprika capital**". If you happen to be here around September 8, when the harvest season officially begins, head out to the surrounding countryside to see the paprika fields transformed into a sea of red.

The Town

Nearly all of Kalocsa's sights are located along Szent István király út, the town's main street running from the bus station through to the cathedral and archbishop's palace at the other end. Starting at the bus station, you can't miss the 22-metre-high **Chronos 8 light tower**, a bequest from the locally born Parisian conceptual sculptor Nicolas Schöffer, some of whose smaller kinetic works are exhibited in the **Nicolas Schöffer Museum** at Szent István király út 76 (Tues–Sun 10am–5pm; 500Ft).

Continuing five minutes up the road, to the pedestrianized stretch of the street, you pass a row of seven small statues commemorating the town's famous archbishops – starting with Asztrik, who brought Pope Sylvester II's gift of a crown to King Stephen in 1000 AD, thereby setting the seal on the deal between the new king and the Christian West. Two hundred metres further along on the left, at no. 25, is the **Viski Károly Museum** (April–Oct Tues–Sun 9am–5pm; 500Ft), which has a dazzling collection of nineteenth-century Magyar, Swabian (*Sváb*) and Slovak (*Tót*) folk costumes. The overstuffed bolsters and quilts on display were mandatory for a bride's dowry. Fifty metres on, across the road at no. 6, the **Paprika Museum** (April–Oct Tues–Sun 9am–5pm; 600Ft) is an exhaustive presentation of the nation's favourite powder (see *food and drink* colour section), with piles of the stuff filling the building with its pungent smell.

Carrying on to the old main square, Szentháromság tér, you'll find Kalocsa's hulking Baroque **Cathedral**, designed by the prolific András Mayerhoffer in the early eighteenth century. Its richly ornamented pink and white interior features a heavily stuccoed ceiling painted with four saints, an ostentatious high altar carved from Carrera marble, and a colourfully attired embalmed bishop. Across the road from the cathedral, at Hunyadi utca 2, is the **Treasury** (Érseki Kincstár; April–Oct Tues–Sun 9am–5pm; 500Ft), which keeps a dazzling assortment of vestments and monstrances, including a beautifully embroidered, eight-centimetre-high reliquary from the sixteenth century. The most important item on display, however, is a twelfth-century processional bronze cross with traces of gold. On the other side of the cathedral, and dating from the same period, is the **Archbishop's Palace** (Érseki Palota; same times and price; Hungarian-only tours begin at noon, 2pm & 4pm; 500Ft), whose grandeur recalls the medieval heyday of Kalocsa's bishopric, when local prelates led armies and advised monarchs. Its 120,000-volume **library** contains medieval illuminated manuscripts, a Bible signed by Luther, and impressive frescoes by Maulbertsch. The library was founded by Archbishop Patachich, who was transferred to Kalocsa from his previous post as a punishment for founding a theatre there, and henceforth stuck to books. His apartments were lodged between his chapel and his library, with a door connecting the two, as can still be seen.

Following Kossuth utca off to the right as far as the hospital, you'll see a signpost for the thatched **Folk Art House** at Tompa utca 5–7 (Népművészetek Háza or Tájház; April–Oct Tues–Sun 10am–4pm; 400Ft). Several of its rooms are decorated with exuberant floral murals, traditionally found in the *tiszta szoba* or "clean room" of peasant households, where guests were entertained. In Kalocsa, almost uniquely, these were painted by groups of women who were respected artisans. Also displayed is a host of Kalocsa embroidery. This has changed considerably over the decades, with embroiderers working entirely in white in the nineteenth century, until blue and red slowly crept into the designs; then, in the 1920s, when the Kalocsa folk dance troupe became more widely known, it was decided to brighten up the costumes so that they would be more startling on stage – hence the present multicoloured, rather twee, designs.

Practicalities

From the **bus station** it's an easy five-minute walk up to Szent István király út to the centre of town, while the **train station** is on Mártírok tere, a fifteen-minute walk along Kossuth utca from the Archbishop's Palace. The **post office** is at Szent István király utca 44 (Mon–Fri 8am–6pm, Sat 8am–noon).

In the absence of a Tourinform office, you can get (limited) **information** from Gold Tours at Szent István király utca 35 (Mon–Fri 8.30am–4.30pm, Sat 8.30am–noon; ☏78/465-347, ✉info@kalocsagoldtours.hu). Comfortably the best **hotel** in town is the beautifully restored 200-year-old *Hotel Kalocsa* on Szentháromság tér (☎78/561-200, ⓦ www.hotelkalocsa.hu; ❼), which has polished rooms and extensive wellness facilities. Alternative options are the effortlessly dull but cheap *Hotel Piros Arany* at Szent István király utca 37 (☎78/462-220; ❸), and the simple, but clean and bright, *Club Hotel* at Szent István király utca 64 (☎78/562-804, ⓔ club502@freemail.hu; ❹).

There are slim pickings when it comes to eating, your best bet being the **restaurant** in the *Hotel Kalocsa*. Otherwise there's the staid but tidy *Klub Étterem* at Szent István király utca 38, and the *Korona*, attached to the Paprika Museum at Szent István király utca 6, not surprisingly offering all manner of paprika-enhanced dishes. For coffee and cake try the neat little *Barokk Kávéház* by the cathedral, and for a beer, *Mozaik*, adjoining the *Hotel Kalocsa*.

Hajós Pincék

Hajós Pincék, 24km southeast of Kalocsa on Route 54 (and 3km beyond the village of Hajós itself), is an extraordinary village: no one actually lives here, the entire settlement being devoted to **wine cellars** – 1260 of them in all. The mainly Swabian population of the surrounding area has been storing and fermenting wine here for centuries, and you can sample it to your heart's content in the cellars along every street. St Orbán's day on May 25 (or the nearest weekend) is when all the vintners come out in force to celebrate the coming harvests with folk dancing and the like. Though there are visitors here all year round, summer is the best time to visit, as you are more likely to find someone in the labyrinth of cellars who will invite you to sample and buy their wine. Although catering mainly to groups, you could also check out the Kovács Wine House (☎78/404-947) at the end of the village on the main road (Route 54), which has wines to taste (1500Ft for six wines) and buy. There are a couple of places to **stay** if you want to hang around: the gaily coloured *Kellermotel* (☎78/504-010; ❹) at the entrance to the village, and the more basic *Judit Panzió*, 200m on from the Kovács Wine House, opposite the petrol station at Borbiró sor 1 (☎78/404-832; ❸), which also has a very ordinary restaurant. There are regular daily **buses** from Kalocsa, and four from Baja on weekdays.

Baja

BAJA, 41km south of Kalocsa on the shady banks of the Sugovica-Danube, is a restful town with an almost Mediterranean climate, whose culinary pride is manifest in its **fish soup** (halászlé) – a rich mix of carp, catfish, pike-perch and paprika that's more like a freshwater bouillabaisse than a soup. This all comes together spectacularly for the **Baja Fish Soup Festival** (Bajai Népünnepély) on the second Saturday in July, when the massive Szentháromság tér is filled with more than 2000 bubbling pots. The river has always been central to the town's life, and in May the feast of St John Nepomuk, the patron saint of fishermen, is celebrated by bringing a statue of the saint down the river in a procession of boats to the centre of town, where you can eat fish soup and taste the local wines. Baja's **Autumn Festival** in September also takes place in the main square – three days of theatre, concerts and more fish soup. At other times the town is a nice place to rest up, but short on sights and excitement.

Arrival, information and accommodation

On arrival at the **bus station** on Csermák Mihály tér, it's a twenty-minute walk along Kossuth Lajos utca and then pedestrianized Eötvös utca to Szentháromság tér – or an extra five minutes if you start from the **train station** on Szegedi út.

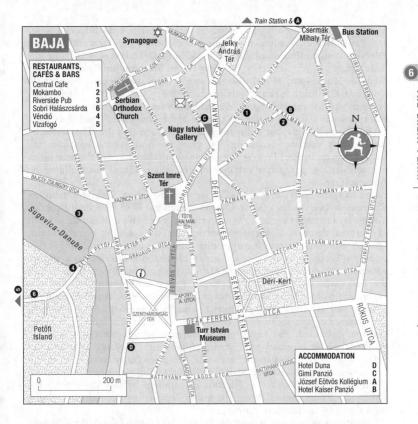

There's limited **information** available from Tourinform at Szentháromság tér 11 (Mon–Fri 8am–5pm; ℡79/420-792, ✉baja@tourinform.hu), while the **post office** is at Oroszlán utca 5 (Mon–Fri 8am–6pm, Sat 8am–noon).

There's cheap **accommodation** ten minutes' walk north from Szentháromság tér at the *József Eötvös College*, Deszkás utca 2 (℡79/324-451; mid-June to Aug), which has dorms (1500Ft) and en-suite doubles (❷); while there are also dorm beds (1300Ft; mid-June to late Aug only) and rooms (❷; all year) at the *Ifjusági Tábor* at Petőfi Island 5 near the bridge (℡79/522-230). *Sugovica Camping* on Petőfi Island (℡79/321-755; May–Sept) is an agreeable site with huts and chalets (❷), and pheasants strutting around at dawn.

The best of the town's **hotels** is the *Hotel Kaiser Panzió* at Tóth Kálmán utca 12 (℡79/520-450, ⓦwww.panziokaiser.hu; ❺), whose smooth, red-coloured rooms are terrific value, as are those in the cracking little *Gimi Panzió*, just behind the Nagy István Gallery at Oroszlán utca 2a (℡79/428-485, ⓦwww.gimicafe .uw.hu; ❸). A third option is the old-fashioned *Hotel Duna* at Szentháromság tér 6 (℡79/323-224, ⓦwww.hotelduna.hu; ❹), which has high, gloomy rooms, though its location compensates somewhat.

The Town

In the heart of town, imposing civic edifices and the massive **Szentháromság tér** – compared rather optimistically in a local leaflet to St Mark's Square in

Venice, but really just a huge cobbled car park – overlook the Sugovica River and Petőfi Island, recalling Baja's importance before the Treaty of Trianon relegated it to a minor border town in 1920. At Deák Ferenc utca 1, off the main square's southeast corner, the **Turr István Museum** (mid-March to Nov Wed–Sat 10am–4pm; 450Ft) is named after a Hungarian general who fought alongside Garibaldi in Italy, just as many Poles and Italians fought with Hungary against the Habsburgs. An exhibition on fishing illustrates the vital role that water and the Danube have played in the city's history, and there's also an excellent ethnographic and natural history section upstairs. The museum's local history display – covering 300 years of local events, including the farcical attempt by Karl IV to regain the Habsburg throne – is in the same block but accessed via a separate entrance on the other side of the building on Roosevelt tér.

Icon buffs should try to visit the late eighteenth-century **Serbian Orthodox Church** on Táncsics utca (Szerb Ortodox templom; Wed 9am–noon; contact Tourinform to view the church at other times), one of two ministering to locals of Serbian descent. Otherwise crudely bare, it contains a magnificent, ten-metre-high iconostasis incorporating some fifty icons representing scenes from the Bible. There is also a German high school catering to a smaller community of Swabians, whom the Habsburgs encouraged to settle here after the Turks were evicted. From the church, a short walk down Telcs Ede utca brings you to Munkácsy Mihály utca and a fabulous Neoclassical **Synagogue** (now serving as a library; Mon–Thurs 1–6pm, Fri 10am–6pm, Sat 8am–noon), with a monument to the town's 5705 victims of Fascism. The building has been sensitively restored, and visitors are welcome to admire what was once the spiritual base of a proud and thriving community. Heading back towards Szentháromság tér, you pass the handsome, pea-green **Nagy István Gallery** on the corner of Arany János utca and Oroszlán utca (mid-March to Nov Wed–Sat 10am–4pm; 450Ft), where a collection of paintings by the Alföld School is displayed – Nagy himself being the group's best-known proponent – along with shows by contemporary artists.

Across the river from the main square lies the green **Petőfi Island** (Petőfi Sziget), where the locals like to go boating, swimming and fishing. It was from here that the last Habsburg emperor was ignominiously deported by a British gunboat, after the failure of his putsch in 1921.

Eating and drinking

The town's three outstanding **restaurants** – all specializing in fish and with terraces overlooking the river – are close to one another on Petőfi Island: down by the bridge, the upmarket *Véndió Étterem* has the most wide-ranging fish menu, though the *Sobri Halászcsárda*, a few minutes' walk further along in a handsome white villa, is renowned for its fish soup – it was founded by the champion *halászlé* chef József "Sobri" Farkas. Completing the trilogy is the sociable *Vizafogó*, occupying a serene little spot ten minutes' walk west on the northwestern corner of the island.

Three popular **cafés** in the vicinity of Vörösmarty tér are *Mokambo*, a cool, cheery place with bright orange walls and squishy chairs opposite the *Hotel Kaiser Panzió*; *Central Café* at Kossuth utca 1, which is also good for tea; and the fun little café-cum-bar in the *Gimi Panzió*. For evening **drinking**, the place to head to is the Halászpart ("Fisherman's Beach"), the river bank opposite the *Véndió*, where a dozen or so cafés and bars do roaring summer trade; the most atmospheric of these is the *Riverside Pub*, which also has **internet access**.

Kecskemét and around

Hungarians associate **KECSKEMÉT** with *barackpálinka* (the local apricot brandy) and the composer Kodály (who was born in what is now the train station), but its cultural significance doesn't end there. Ranking just behind Szeged and Debrecen as a centre of higher education and the arts, Kecskemét rivals both cities in terms of festivals and museums, and surpasses them architecturally. Given this sophistication, you would never imagine that its name derives from the Hungarian word for "goat" (*kecske*).

Besides being one of the most attractive towns on the Plain, Kecskemét is readily **accessible** from Budapest (by train from Nyugati Station or bus from

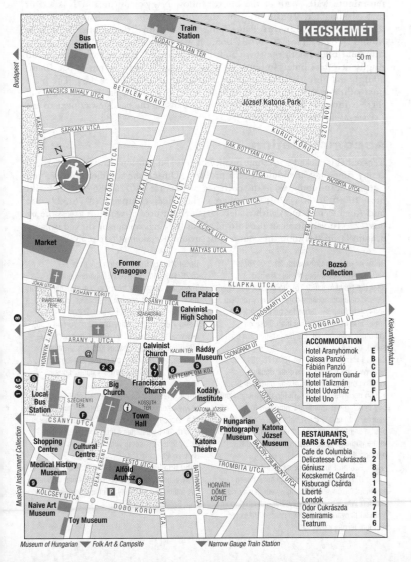

KECSKEMÉT

0   50 m

ACCOMMODATION

Hotel Aranyhomok	E
Caissa Panzió	B
Fábián Panzió	C
Hotel Három Gunár	G
Hotel Talizmán	D
Hotel Udvarház	F
Hotel Uno	A

RESTAURANTS, BARS & CAFÉS

Cafe de Columbia	5
Delicatesse Cukrászda	2
Géniusz	8
Kecskemét Csárda	9
Kisbucagi Csárda	1
Liberté	4
Londok	3
Odor Cukrászda	7
Semiramis	F
Teatrum	6

Népstadion), and there are equally regular services from Szeged (plus less frequent buses from Baja and Cegléd), making it an ideal day excursion from either city, and the prime stopover between them. The town is also a good base for **excursions** to the Kiskunság National Park, with the option of relaxing along the River Tisza, or getting right back to nature by horseriding or renting a farmhouse in the surrounding countryside. There's also the Lakitelek-Tőserdő nature reserve close by, where you can swim or go boating.

Arrival and information

Kecskemét's **bus and train stations** are situated close to each other a ten-minute walk north of the centre; follow Nagykőrösi utca or Rákóczi út to Szabadság tér. Tourinform, on the corner of the town hall on Kossuth tér (June–Aug Mon–Fri 9am–7pm, Sat & Sun 10am–6pm; Sept–May Mon–Fri 8am–5pm; ☎76/481-065, ⓦwww.kecskemet.hu), has stacks of **information** on both the town and the Kiskunság National Park; in July and August it offers ninety-minute sightseeing tours (Wed 5.45pm & Sat 10am; 800Ft), and also has **bikes** to rent (350Ft per hr, 2400Ft per day). The main **post office** is at Kálvin tér 10–12 (Mon–Fri 8am–7pm, Sat 8am–noon), and there is **internet access** at the internet café inside the passageway next to the *Londok café* (daily 10am–10pm).

Accommodation

Kecskemét is packed with some quality **hotels** and pensions, and finding a room at any time of year shouldn't be a problem. During the summer holidays you can get cheap rooms (❷) in the **colleges** at Jókai tér 4 (☎76/486-977) or Izsáki utca 10 (☎76/506-526); and there's the *Autós* **campsite** (☎76/329-398; mid-April to mid-Oct) with chalets (❸) at Sport utca 5, which is accessible by bus #22. Tourinform can also inform about lodgings on one of the old isolated peasant farms (*tanya*) in the countryside around Kecskemét (see p.387).

Hotel Aranyhomok Kossuth tér 3 ☎76/503-730, ⓦwww.hotelaranyhomok. Named after the "golden sands" of the *puszta*, this ugly-looking building actually conceals very modern and comfy rooms – those facing the park are larger and more expensive than those on the other side, though the furnishings are the same. ❻–❽

Caissa Panzió Gyenes tér 18 ☎76/481-685, ⓦwww.caissachessbooks.com. Unusual location on the fifth floor of an apartment block, 10min northwest of Kossuth tér, this friendly and tidy pension has rooms sleeping two to five people, with and without bathroom. Caissa is the patron saint of chess, and the owner, an avid fan of the game, organizes tournaments in the pension. ❷–❹

Fábián Panzió Kápolna utca 14 ☎76/477-677, ⓦwww.panziofabian.hu. It doesn't get any more welcoming than this sweet, family-run pension, which has ten lovely, lilac-coloured rooms (with wi-fi) overlooking a lush garden. Bikes for rent too. Terrific value. ❹

Hotel Három Gunár Batthyány utca 1–7 ☎76/483-611, ⓦwww.hotelharomgunar.hu. Though a bit scruffy from the outside, this central hotel has decent enough, if smallish, rooms (some with a/c) at a fair price. ❻

Hotel Talizmán Kápolna utca 2 ☎76/504-856, ⓦwww.talizmanhotel.hu. Bright, business-like place a short walk west of Kossuth tér, with smooth, immaculately prepared, a/c rooms all with wi-fi. One of the better-value options in town. ❻

Hotel Udvarház Csányi utca 1–3 ☎76/413-912, ⓦwww.hoteluh.hu. Odd location on the first floor of a shopping complex just off Kossuth tér, this is a calm, if characterless, little hotel with smart, nicely lit rooms, some with bath, some with shower. ❻

Hotel Uno Beniczky F utca 4 ☎76/480-046, ⓦwww.hoteluno.hu. Quiet, friendly hotel with neat, tidy rooms in a relatively quiet location just 200m from Szabadság tér. ❻

The Town

Although nothing remains of medieval Kecskemét, its size can be judged from the ring boulevard (körút), which follows the old moat. Unlike most towns in the region, it was spared devastation by the Turks, as the Sultan took a liking to it. Waves of refugees settled here, and Kecskemét became the third-largest town in Hungary, its various religious groups coexisting in harmony. This fortunate history, underpinned by agricultural wealth, explains its air of confidence and the flamboyant, eclectic **architecture**, skilfully integrated with modern buildings by town planner József Kerényi. To enhance its charms, the centre of town consists of two open squares that merge into a single verdant expanse, with traffic diverted several blocks away.

Szabadság tér

The northern end of Szabadság tér is characterized by three strikingly different buildings. Most remarkable is the **Cifra Palace** (Cifra Palota), which resembles a scene from *Hansel and Gretel* on acid, with ceramic mushrooms sprouting from psychedelic tiles above a gingerbread-like facade. Designed by Géza Markus in 1902, this wonderful example of Art Nouveau (termed the "Secessionist style" in Hungary) now houses the **Kecskemét Art Gallery** (Tues–Sun 10am–5pm; 450Ft), whose collection includes work by the Jewish painter István Farkas, who died in Auschwitz. Upstairs is a splendid peacock ballroom with enamel tiles and Art Nouveau motifs that was once a casino. Carry on up the stairs and you'll emerge onto a terrace affording a close-up view of the palace's Art Nouveau chimneys and gables. Originally built to house small shops and flats, the building is one of the architectural gems of Kecskemét, though it has been sadly neglected over the last fifty years. Across the road stands a white, onion-domed former **synagogue** built between 1862 and 1871 in the Moorish style, which was sacked by the Nazis when they deported Kecskemét's Jews in 1944, and transformed in 1970 into a conference centre (Technika és Tudomány Háza), with a hideous interior – there's also a lounge-style café on the ground floor.

▲ Kecskemét

The Transylvanian-Gothic hulk diagonally opposite the Cifra Palace is one of two buildings in Kecskemét in the Art Nouveau style known as **National Romanticism**. Now a **Calvinist high school**, it was built between 1911 and 1913, its steeply pitched roofs and intimidating tower harking back to the vernacular architecture of rural Hungary and Transylvania. Across the road, at Kalvin tér 1, is the **Ráday Museum** (Tues–Sun 10am–6pm; 400Ft), a marvellous collection of seventeenth- and eighteenth-century ecclesiastical art that includes beautifully embroidered communion cloths, baptismal jugs and wine pitchers, and a rustic painted wooden ceiling saved from a church near Lake Balaton just before the whole edifice collapsed. The second part of the museum is a horologists' delight, with two rooms stuffed with clocks, watches and all manner of other nineteenth-century timepieces.

Kossuth tér and around

To the south, across Kossuth tér, is the building that started the whole National Romanticism movement: the **Town Hall**, designed by Ödön Lechner and Gyula Pártos in 1893. Like Lechner's later works in Budapest, it is richly ornamented with Zsolnay tiles inspired by the decorative traditions of Magyar folk art and nomadic Turkic cultures. However, the building itself is a Renaissance-Baroque pastiche, whose lack of "authentic form" was criticized by later National Romanticists such as Károly Kós. Its Grand Hall contains gilded murals by Bertalan Székely, who decorated the interior of the Mátyás Church in Budapest. There are no regular hours for visits, but you can ask at reception (or Tourinform) about access. The bells outside play snatches of Kódaly, Handel, Beethoven, Mozart and Erkel on the hour.

With five churches in the vicinity you can afford to be selective; the three most interesting are on Kossuth tér. Next to the town hall stands the so-called **Big Church** (Nagytemplom; daily: May–Sept 9am–noon & 3–6pm; Oct–April 9am–noon) which is Catholic and Baroque. Designed by Oszwald Gáspár, an eighteenth-century Piarist father, its facade is decorated with reliefs commemorating the Seventh Wilhem Hussars and local heroes of the War of Independence. In the summer months you may be able to climb the church tower, which gives you an excellent view of the city. The **Calvinist Church** was founded in 1683 and enlarged in the 1790s, when its "Red Tower" was added. Its meeting hall contains frescoes similar to those in the town hall. The **Franciscan Church** (Ferences templom) to the east is really the oldest one, but Baroque restoration has obscured its medieval features. Around the corner on Kéttemplom köz (Two Churches Lane) stands the former Franciscan monastery, which now houses the **Kodály Institute** (see box opposite).

Kecskemét's museums

The diversity of Kecskemét's architecture is matched by that of its museums. One not to miss is the **Hungarian Photography Museum** at Katona József tér 12 (Magyar Fotográfiai Múzeum; Wed–Sun 10am–5pm; 400Ft; Ⓦ www.fotomuzeum .hu), one of only two such museums in the country, the other being in Budapest (see p.85). Originally a dance hall, the building was converted into a synagogue in 1918 and sold off by the decimated Jewish community after the last war. Beautifully restored, it retains such original features as the female gallery and the painted ceiling on which Rabbi Loewe's sacred animals appear. The collection itself features rotating exhibitions of the best of Hungarian photography, as well as occasional exhibitions by international photographers. In addition there is a permanent display of vintage cameras and other apparatus. For real photography buffs, it is possible to see the museum's archives, though you should call a day or two in advance.

Zoltán Kodály and József Katona

For a small town, Kecskemét has made a not inconsiderable contribution to national culture, and its Spring Days festival features the work of its two famous sons.

Through his researches into the folk roots of Hungarian music, **Zoltán Kodály** (1882–1967) was inspired to write compositions that eschewed the Baroque and Western strains his colleague Bartók termed "New Style". He also revolutionized the teaching of music, inventing the "Kodály method" that is now applied throughout Hungary and around the world. Kodály's belief that music can only be understood by actively participating in it remains the guiding principle of Kecskemét's **Institute of Music Teaching** (Zenepedagógiai Intézet). Students on the **one-year course** are exhorted to approach music through the human voice, "the most easily accessible instrument for all", and build upon their national folk traditions when teaching children – a task Kodály considered supremely important, claiming "No one is too great to write for the little ones. In fact one has to strive to be great enough." For those who want to know more, there's an exhibition in the institute itself, at Kéttemplom köz 1–3 (daily 10am–6pm; 200Ft).

The town can also boast of **József Katona** (1791–1830), the "father" of Hungarian romantic drama, who was born and died in Kecskemét. His masterpiece, *Bánk Bán* (later made into an opera by Erkel), revolves around the murder of Gertrude, the German-born queen of King Andrew II, by his vassal Bánk. Katona himself expired of a heart attack outside the town hall, the spot now marked by a cloven block. The fallible organ was preserved in a jewelled casket, and his name was bestowed upon Kecskemét's playhouse. Designed by the Viennese architects who built the Vígszínház in Budapest, it is a smaller version of the same and was erected in 1896. During the 1980s, the **Katona Theatre** was directed by film-maker Miklós Jancsó, whose avant-garde productions scandalized many townsfolk. There is now a **museum** (Tues–Sat 10am–2pm; 200Ft) dedicated to the playwright at Katona József utca 5, near the Hungarian Photography Museum, though its literary exhibits lack any explanation in English, and the period furniture isn't actually Katona's own.

Just south of the centre there is a cluster of museums beyond the large modern Erdei Ferenc Cultural Centre. Housed in an old pharmacy at Kölcsey utca 3, the **Medical and Pharmaceutical History Museum** (Orvos és Gyógysz-erészetörténeti Múzeum; May–Oct Tues–Sun 10am–2pm; 200Ft) won't detain you for long, with a collection that consists mostly of old pharmacy bottles, although it does have some fancy old medical instruments and an old weighing chair. More appealing is the nearby **Toy Museum** (Szórakaténusz Játékmúzeum; Tues–Sun: March–Oct 10am–12.30pm & 1–5pm; Nov–Feb 10am–4pm; 450Ft), which occupies an airy wooden building especially designed by Kerényi. It contains a delightful collection of nineteenth- and twentieth-century toys with notes in English, and its helpful English-speaking staff also organize children's workshops. In the run-down house adjacent, the **Naive Art Museum** (Naiv Művészeti Múzeum; mid-March to Oct Tues–Sun 10am–5pm; 300Ft) provides a fascinating insight into the colourful world of the pre-World War I naive artists. This delightful little collection includes wood-carved sculptures of farmers and shepherds, and a series of bright paintings representing indigenous peasant culture.

Fans of Magyar folk art should head 500m south towards the junction of Petőfi utca and the ring boulevard (bus #1, #11 or #22). One block on and to the right, at Serfőző utca 19A, the **Museum of Hungarian Folk Craft** (Népi Iparművészeti Múzeum; Feb to mid-Dec Tues–Sat 10am–5pm; 400Ft) exhibits a wealth of textiles, pottery and embroidery from the 1950s onwards in a seemingly endless succession of rooms. Besides the names of the artists, there is little guidance to the exhibits, and the most striking items – embroidered jackets and waistcoats – are saved for the very last room, if you make it that far.

The extensive **Bozsó Collection** (Bozsó Gyüjtemény; Fri–Sun 10am–6pm; 200Ft) of antique furniture and other artefacts, assembled by a local artist, is housed at Klapka utca 34, 500m east of the Cifra Palace, in a Baroque residence that once belonged to György Klapka, a general in the 1848 Hungarian War of Independence. Finally, just north of Széchenyi tér at Zimay utca 6, is the fascinating **Leskowsky Musical Instrument Collection** (Leskowsky Hangszergyüjtemény; by appointment only, ☎76/486-616; donations accepted), which has more than 1500 instruments from all over the world. Musician Albert Leskowsky takes you on a very personal tour, playing everything from zithers, guitars and washboards to bizarre experimental percussion, giving explanations in excellent English.

Eating, drinking and entertainment

Aside from two or three very good **restaurants**, you'll have your work cut out finding decent places to eat in town. There are some good bakeries in the vicinity of the local bus station, while the large outdoor **market** on Jokai utca (Tues–Sun 6am–noon) packs in lots of fruit, vegetables and local products. **Drinking** possibilities are fairly humdrum too, though there are some agreeable cafés spotted around the centre.

Restaurants

Géniusz Kisfaludy utca 5. Classy, good-looking restaurant offering beautifully presented international food, albeit with a slight French twist; the attractive contemporary decor features soft lemon and navy blue seating, burgundy-coloured walls and mosaic-tiled flooring. Enjoyable place to dine.

🏃 **Kecskemét Csárda** Kőlcsey utca 7. Cosy inn-style place heavy on the peasant decor, with blue-dyed tablecloths, ceramics and strings of paprika hanging from the walls, and suitably attired waiters; the Hungarian food (knuckle of Mangalica is a speciality) is expensive though

genuinely first-rate. Reservations advisable (☎76/488-686).

Kisbucagi Csárda Munkáscy utca 10. Located out in a quarter full of tree-lined older streets, this is a more than passable establishment, serving up dependable Magyar nosh in convivial surrounds.

Liberté Kávéhaz Szabadság tér 2. Understatedly stylish restaurant occupying an elegant old building on the main square, whose creditably varied menu includes some unusual soups (cream of strawberry), pasta dishes, stews and meat-stuffed pancakes.

Drinking

The best daytime **drinking** spots are the popular, diner-style *Londok*, on the corner of Kossuth tér and Széchenyi tér, where you can also grab fast-food snacks, and *Café de Columbia* at Kéttemplomkőz 4. Two super little teahouses are *Teatrum*, a cosy, vaguely arty sort of place with lots of stripped wood a few paces along from *Columbia*, and the tiny *Semiramis*, underneath the *Hotel Udvarház*. If you fancy cake with your coffee, try the *Odor Cukrászda* by the *Liberté Kávéház*, and the *Delicatesse Cukrászda* in an arcade next to *Londok*.

Entertainment

Kecskemét is at its liveliest during the **Spring Festival** in late March, a feast of music and drama coinciding with Spring Festival in Budapest, and the **Hiros Hét**, a week-long local festival in late August featuring street theatre, pageants, wine tasting and craft fairs on Szabadság tér and Petőfi utca. The **Wine and Pálinka Festival** in mid-June, meanwhile, is another excuse to indulge in more wine and the favourite local tipple. The town's key musical event is the bi-annual (even-numbered years)

Kodály Festival, a two-month-long series of concerts in July and August in the Erdei Ferenc Cultural House on Deák Ferenc tér, and other cultural institutions around town. There are other summertime concerts and fairs on Kossuth tér and Szabadság tér, and shows at the **Ciróka Puppet Theatre**, Budai utca 15 (☎76/482-217).

Excursions around Kecskemét

The countryside around Kecskemét is excellent for **horseriding**, with numerous riding schools and stables offering a range of equine-related activities. There are also scores of **farmsteads** that welcome tourists who enjoy riding, walking, fishing or simply relaxing in rural surroundings. Two of the best are the *Somodi Tanya* (☎76/377-095, ⓦwww.somoditanya.hu), 20km west of Kecskemét in **Fulöpháza**, and the *Tanyacsárda* (☎76/356-166, ⓦwww.tanyacsarda.hu) 15km north of Kecskemét in **Lajosmizse**; both offer riding tuition (2800Ft per hr) and carriage rides (same price), and also have restful guesthouse accommodation (both ⑤). If you happen to be in the region on the first Sunday of the month, it's worth visiting the large and lively **animal fair** in Lajosmizse, where you can watch livestock being traded and pick up antiques, clothes and so on.

Kecskemét also makes a good base for **excursions** to the Kiskunság region (see p.388) and the Tisza resorts. Bus #2 from Széchenyi tér can drop you at the Kecskemét KK station on Halasi út, the terminal for narrow-gauge trains to Kiskunság National Park.

Thirty kilometres east of Kecskemét are several low-key **resorts** where you can swim in the Tisza or wander beside it as it meanders through woodlands and meadows. Lakitelek and Tőserdő make for a relaxed excursion from Kecskemét or Kiskunfélegyháza, while Tiszakécske is more of a family holiday centre. **From Kecskemét**, six trains daily stop at Lakitelek en route to Kunszentmárton; to reach Tőserdő you can take the same trains from Kecskemét, alighting at the Szikra station, or catch the bus. **From Kiskunfélegyháza**, the five daily Szolnok trains call at Lakitelek, Tiszakécske and Tőserdő.

The big local attraction is the lovely **Lakitelek–Tőserdő**, a sylvan nature reserve 4km away. Turning off the main road beside the thermal baths (Tősfürdő; May–Aug daily 9am–5pm; 1000Ft), a path runs 1km down to the *Holtág*, a dead branch of the river that's nice for swimming and boating, with cheap **restaurants** and a campsite (mid-May to mid-Sept). Every year on August 20, St Stephen's Day celebrations are held here with concerts and fireworks. Up the road there is **accommodation** at the *Tölgyfa Fogadó* at Napsugár utca 6 (☎76/449-037; ②), and there's another campsite, *Autóscamping*, also with chalets (②), up by the thermal baths (☎76/449-012; May–Aug). The Tőserdő train station is a couple of kilometres south, on the main road.

TISZAKÉCSKE, 8km further north, has more of a tourist industry outside town. Hourly buses run from the train station to the centre, passing by several

Into Romania and Serbia

Besides numerous destinations on the Plain and Eger in the Northern Uplands, the intercity bus station is also the point of departure for **buses to Romania and Serbia**. These are used by ethnic Hungarians returning to Miercurea Ciuc, Oradea, Cluj and Târgu Mures in Romania (designated by their Hungarian names as Csíkszereda, Nagyvárad, Kolozsvár and Marosvásárhely), or Subotica (Szabadka) in the Voivodina region of Serbia. At present, most foreigners are not obliged to have visas for either country if staying less than 90 days. If you do require a visa, however, you should get these in advance, and not attempt to do so at the border.

rooms for rent, before heading to the riverside resort area (Üdülő telep), which has horse-drawn carts and a **children's railway** (May–Sept; 600Ft), **thermal baths** (daily 9am–5pm; 700Ft), and both free and paying **campsites**.

The Kiskunság

The **Kiskunság** region, to the south of Kecskemét, is called "Little Cumania" after the Cumanian (*Kun*) tribes that settled here in the Middle Ages. This sandy tableland was unfit for anything but raising sheep until, in the nineteenth century, it was laboriously transformed by afforestation and soil husbandry to yield grapes and other fruit. While Magyars esteem this as "Petőfi country", where their national poet was born, its prime attractions for visitors are Kiskunság National Park and the exhibition complex at Ópusztaszer.

Kiskunfélegyháza

To Hungarian ears, **KISKUNFÉLEGYHÁZA**, 30km south of Kecskemét, suggests people and paths converging on the "House of Cumania". The present town was actually created by Jazygian settlers in the 1740s, but the name is nevertheless appropriate as the Cumanian original was wiped out by the Turks. As regional capital, it is a rural foil to urbane Kecskemét, a town that lives by geese-breeding and market gardening, with storks' nests on the chimneys and draw-wells in the courtyards. Indeed, one of the more entertaining local festivals is the town's **Gastronomy Festival** in the second week of September, the highlight of which is a goose fair, incorporating, somewhat bizarrely, a goose beauty pageant.

Like many small towns on the Plain, Kiskunfélegyháza's main street follows the primary trade route of old, and its main square, Petőfi tér, is sited at the crossroads with the secondary route. On one side of the square is the majolica-encrusted **town hall** in the National Romantic style; built by József Vass and Nándor Morbitzer in 1912, its superb facade is adorned with embroidery motifs typical of the region, as are the staircase and main hall. Diagonally opposite is the white **Swan House** (Hattyuház), where Petőfi's father had a butcher's shop and the poet spent his childhood (it's now the town library), while his statue stands opposite. His life is documented with newspaper articles, maps and suchlike at the **Petőfi Ház**, directly behind the large Baroque church at Petőfi utca 7 (mid-March to Oct Wed–Fri 9am–noon; 200Ft). Five minutes' walk south, at Móra Ferenc utca 19, is a museum with exhibits on **Ferenc Móra**, writer, journalist and antiquarian, who was born in this house in 1879 (mid-March to Oct Wed–Fri 9am–noon; 200Ft).

More rewarding, however, is the **Kiskun Museum** (March–Oct Wed–Sun 9am–5pm; 250Ft), in an eighteenth-century manor house 300m north of Petőfi tér at Holló Lajos utca 9. Exhibits on the Cumanians and Jazygians and modern paintings of rural life by László Holló pale before a section devoted to the **history of prisons**, in the very cell where the famous *betyár* Sándor Rózsa languished in 1860. Amongst the many fascinating exhibits on display are some fiendish-looking torture implements, and several items made by prisoners, including musical instruments, toys, and a beautifully crafted chess set – look out, too, for the carefully preserved etchings on the walls of the cells. Down in the prison chapel, where inmates were allowed to worship each Saturday, there's a lovely collection of ecclesiastical treasures and folk art, such as chalices, vestments, scriptures and icons. The nineteenth-century wooden **windmill** in the courtyard was transported here from the village of Mindszent by the River Tisza, where Cardinal Mindszenty was born (see box, p.167). For a break from museums, you could go for a soak in the outdoor **thermal baths** at Blaha Lujza tér 1, down towards the train station (daily 9am–8pm, Fri & Sat until 11pm; 700Ft).

Practicalities

The **bus station** is on the eastern side of Petőfi tér, and the **train station** twenty minutes' walk in the opposite direction at the end of Kossuth utca. There's **information** from Tourinform, hidden away in a little courtyard on Szent János tér, opposite Petőfi tér (Mon–Fri 8am–4pm, Sat 10am–2pm; ☎76/561-420, ✉kiskunfelegyhaza@tourinform.hu), and the **post office** is next to the Kiskun museum at Holló Lajos utca 3 (Mon–Fri 8am–6pm, Sat 8am–noon). There are several **accommodation** possibilities in town, the best of which is the modern and shiny *Hotel Malom*, about 1km south of the centre at Szentesi út 23 (☎76/560-668, ⊛www.malomhotel.hu; ❺), followed by the rather old-fashioned, but homely and cheerful, *Hotel Oázis,* 500m south of the centre at Szegedi út 13 (☎76/461-427, ✉oazis_hotel@freemail.hu; ❺). Otherwise, there's the fairly basic *Mónika* (☎76/466-022; ❷) and *Borostyán* (☎76/466-785; ❷) pensions, both at Szőlő utca 1. Choices for **eating** boil down to the saloon-like *Desperádó*, next to Tourinform on Szent János tér, and *Caffe pub and pizzeria* at Kossuth utca 8.

Kiskunság National Park

The 300 square kilometres of **Kiskunság National Park** (May–Sept daily 10am–5pm; 1500Ft, includes entry to equestrian display and museum) consist of several tracts of classic *puszta* landscape, the largest of which starts 3km beyond the village of **BUGAC**. Buses from Kiskunfélegyháza and Kecskemét can drop you near the entrance to the park, where you'll find the **park office** – which can supply maps and English-language information – and the *Bugaci Karikás Csárda*, a traditional-style restaurant frequented in the main by coach parties.

From the entrance a sandy track runs 1km past flower-speckled meadows and lounging shepherds, to the **museum**, **farm** and **stables**, where *csikósok* (cowboys) in white pantaloons stage equestrian displays (May–Sept daily 12.15pm; June–Aug extra show at 3pm), riding bareback and standing up with much cracking of whips. On a hot day it is worth paying the extra 1400Ft for a **horse-drawn carriage ride** from the entrance, which also includes a short ride out into the park. In the wooden **Shepherds' Museum** (Pásztormuzeum; same hours as park), you can see felted cloaks, hand-carved pipes and a grotesque tobacco pouch made from a ram's scrotum. Among the animals bred at the **farm** are old protected species of Hungarian livestock, such as grey long-horned cattle, Merino sheep and Mangalica pigs (said to make the finest bacon). The surrounding reedy marshes that extend far beyond Bugac support diverse birdlife and flora – including rare blue globe-thistles in August – and serve as baths for water buffalo, which plod back to their barns at sunset. The office at the park entrance can give information about marked **trails** round the park.

Without your own wheels, there are two ways of getting here: the narrow-gauge **train** from Kecskemét's KK station (see p.387; 3 daily; 1hr) would be the most enjoyable method but for the two-kilometre walk from the Bugac felső terminal to the park entrance – not pleasant on a hot day – whereas **buses** from Kecskemét and Kiskunfélegyháza (4 daily, 2 at weekends; 1hr 30min from Kecskemét) drop you close to the entrance of the park – ask the driver to let you off at the nearest point. To catch the 12.15pm horse show you'll need to get the first train (leaving 7.25am), as the first bus (11am) from Kecskemét won't get you there in time; bus times do change, however, and it's worth checking timetables and park details with

Tourinform in Kecskemét. You can **stay** near the park at the countrified *Táltos Lovas Panzió* (☎76/372-633; ❹), 500m from the entrance, or the modern *Bucka Hotel* (☎76/372-511; ❹), about 1km beyond the rail terminal, which also offers smart wooden chalets (❻).

Kiskőrös

Some 50km southwest of Kecskemét, **KISKŐRÖS** deserves a mention as the **birthplace of Sándor Petőfi** (see box below), and this small town flogs this connection for all it can. Built at the end of the eighteenth century, the simple, three-roomed thatched **Petőfi House** at Petőfi tér 5 (Szulaház és Emlékmúzeum; both museums Tues–Sun 9am–5pm; 300Ft for both) is reputedly where the poet was born, and is now preserved as a museum decked out with furniture that belonged to the family, as well as displaying the carafe used for Petőfi's christening. Next door the **Petőfi Museum** houses local history displays, with the final room devoted to the poet's life and death – when local history effectively stopped, it seems. Between the two is **Translators' Park**, with busts of those who have translated Petőfi's verse into other languages (there is no English representative – yet). Nearby stands the first Petőfi **statue** in a country where every town has at least one feature named after him. Such is the cult of the poet (which the Communists tried to appropriate, but which Hungarian youth reclaimed as a symbol of rebellion) that in 1972, to mark the 150th anniversary of Petőfi's birth, Kiskőrös was re-elevated to the rank of a town, a standing it had lost in the nineteenth century.

Five minutes' walk away to the northeast at Szent István utca 23, the **Slovak Nationality House** (Szlovák tájház; Tues–Sun 9am–noon & 1–4pm), covered by the same ticket as the Petőfi museums, preserves the memory of the 700 Slovaks who settled here in 1718 as the countryside was repopulated after the retreat of the Ottomans. The colourful interior of this neat blue-and-white-painted thatched cottage has displays on how the Slovaks lived, worked and dressed at the end of the nineteenth century, and also shows how houses were

---

Sándor Petőfi

Born on New Year's Eve 1822, of a Slovak mother and a Southern Slav butcher-innkeeper father, **Sándor Petőfi** was to become obsessed with acting and poetry, which he started to write at the age of fifteen. As a strolling player, soldier and labourer, he absorbed the language of working people, writing lyrical poetry in the vernacular, to the outrage of critics. Moving to Budapest in 1844, Petőfi fell in with the young radical intellectuals who met at the *Pilvax Café*; from this time on, poetry and action were inseparable. His *Nemzeti Dal* (National Song) was declaimed from the steps of the National Museum on the first day of the 1848 Revolution ("Some noisy mob had their hurly-burly outside so I left for home," complained the director). Mindful of the thousands of landless peasants encamped outside the city, Parliament bowed to the demands of the radicals and voted for the abolition of serfdom.

During the War of Independence, Petőfi fought alongside General Bem in Transylvania, and disappeared at the battle of Segesvár (Sighişoara, Romania) in July 1849. Though he was most likely trampled beyond recognition by the Cossacks' horses (as foreseen in one of his poems), Petőfi was rumoured to have survived. In 1990, entrepreneur Ferenc Morvai announced that Petőfi had been carted off to Siberia by the Russians, married a peasant woman and later died there. The Hungarian Academy refused to support Morvai's expedition to uncover the putative grave, and it was subsequently reported that forensic analysis had proved the corpse to be that of a Jewish woman.

furnished then, including a large open fireplace in the kitchen. For a spot of relaxation, head for the town's **thermal baths**, a fifteen-minute walk east of Petőfi ter on Erdőtelki utca, where the temperature is a constant 38°C (Mon–Thurs & Sun 9am–7pm, Fri & Sat till 10pm; 800Ft), or to the small **park** 50m behind the Petőfi Museum, a small grassy space centred around a small bridge – a bizarre sight given the lack of any water – inscribed with a corny Eric Clapton quote: "Love can build a bridge".

Practicalities

From the **bus station**, it's a two-minute walk to central Petőfi tér, and from the **train station** it's a fifteen-minute walk along Kossuth utca to the centre. **Information** is available from Tourinform, housed in the ugly concrete building near the Petőfi House at Petőfi tér 4 (mid-June to Aug Mon–Fri 8am–5pm, Sat 9am–1pm; Sept to mid-June Mon–Fri 9am–4pm; ☎78/514-850, ✉kiskoros@tourinform.hu). The **post office** is on Petőfi tér (Mon–Fri 8am–6pm, Sat 8–11am).

The town has several appealing **hotels**, including the *Hotel Imperial*, out by the thermal baths at Erdőtelki utca 21 (☎78/514-400, ⓦwww.hotelimperial.hu; ⑨), the *Hotel Szarvas*, in the centre at Petőfi Sándor tér 17 (☎78/511-500, ✉szarvasfogado @szarvasfogado.hu; ⑨), which has tasteful rooms befitting a grand old building, as well as a fitness room and solarium; and the large *Vinum* hotel out on the edge of town towards Soltvadkert at Petőfi utca 106 (☎78/511-050, ⓦwww.vinumhotel.hu; ⑥). There's **camping** out by the thermal baths (☎78/312-077; May–Sept). Aside from the **restaurant** at the *Hotel Szarvas*, simple meals are served in the *Kurta Kocsma* 400m south of the centre at Csokonai utca 51.

Kiskunhalas

Thirty kilometres south of Kiskőrös, **KISKUNHALAS** is another low-key town, save during its **Grape Harvest Festival** in the second weekend of September, when folk dancing and other celebrations enliven the squares around its Art Nouveau town hall. Another more specialized attraction of Kiskunhalas is its tradition of **lace making**, a medieval industry whose revival in the 1890s owed much to local schoolteacher Maria Markovits, who studied patterns and samples from before the Turkish occupation.

A statue of Maria Markovits stands outside the **Lace House** (Csipkemúzeum; daily 9am–noon & 1–5pm; 400Ft), ten minutes' walk from the centre towards the train station at Kossuth utca 37A. The house features a treasury of tablecloths, ruffs and petticoats and other trimmings – some composed of 56 different types of stitches – as well as a workshop. Back in the centre, the **town hall** is the most architecturally impressive building, with flowers, storks and human figures etched into its rough-hewn concrete facade – note, too, the old firewatch tower protruding from one corner. The **Thorma János Museum**, opposite the town hall at Kőztársaság utca 2 (March–Nov Tues–Sun 9am–5pm; 450Ft), features local history and the artistic oeuvre of the eponymous impressionist painter, including two enormous canvases dedicated to the 1848 Revolution, *Rise Up Magyar!* and *Arad Blood Witness* – the former stars key Hungarian revolutionaries Sándor Petőfi and Jókai Mór. Other sights in town include a lovely classical **synagogue** 400m east of the town hall at Petőfi utca 1 (Raáb András has the key at Semmelweis tér 24, ☎77/423-489), and an old stone **windmill** (Sáfrik malom; April–Oct Sat & Sun 10am–6pm; 300Ft), somewhat incongruously sited on Kölcsey utca, 1km north of the centre to the right of the main road. Aside from lace making, the craft of saddlemaking is also pursued here, and **saddlemaker** Balázs Abonyi Tóth welcomes visitors to his workshop at Vas utca 1, out past the bus station. There are **thermal baths** here too, ten minutes west of the centre on Dr. Monszpart László utca (daily 7am–7pm; 650Ft).

Practicalities

Kiskunhalas is accessible by train or bus from Baja or Kiskunfélegyháza. Its **train station** lies 1km east of the centre on Kossuth utca, while the **bus station** is located just west of the centre on Május 1 tér. From here it's a two-minute walk to Proko Travel at Hősök tere 1 (Mon–Fri 9am–5pm; ☏77/421-984), where you can pick up limited **information**. If you wish to **stay**, make tracks for the *Termal Panzió*, out near the baths at Dr. Monszpart László utca 4 (☏30/990-2525, ⓦwww.termalpanziohalas.hu; ❹), which has six large and colourful rooms, some with a kitchen area. The only other **hotel** is the dowdy *Hotel Csipke*, close by on Semmelweis tér (☏77/421-455, ⓦwww.csipkehotel.hu; ❺), while the Napfény **campsite** is also out by the baths on Nagy Szeder István utca (☏77/422-590; mid-April to mid-Oct). There's nowhere decent to eat in town, but grab a coffee and pastry at the pleasant *Gábriel Cukrászda*, Bokányi Dezső ut 6.

Ópusztaszer Historical Park

The **Ópusztaszer National Historical Memorial Park** (Ópusztaszeri Nemzeti Tőrténeti Emlékpark; daily: May–Sept 9am–6pm, Oct–April 9am–4pm; 1900Ft, 900Ft park only; ⓦwww.opusztaszer.hu), just outside the village of the same name, commemorates the conquest of the seven Magyar tribes who crossed into the Carpathian Basin and spread out across the plains, each claiming a territory – an event known in Hungarian history as the *honfoglalás*, or "land-taking". The park supposedly marks the site of their first tribal "parliament" after the land-taking, in about 896 AD, although the only evidence for this comes from an anonymous writer from 300 years later. A huge memorial was erected here for the millennial anniversary celebrations of 1896, and in 1945 the Communists symbolically chose Ópusztaszer for the first distribution of land amongst the peasants.

Today, the park has some excellent displays, but reeks of nationalism, stressing the links between those early tribes and today's Hungary – the place is littered with maps of pre-World War I Hungary, which similarly covered the Carpathian Basin, as if that were the natural Hungarian "homeland". The park's most touted attraction is housed in the large round building 200m down from the entrance: the **Cyclorama**, entitled "Arrival of the Conquering Hungarians", by Árpád Feszty, is a monumental canvas 15m high and 120m long that depicts Prince Árpád leading the tribes into the Verecke pass in the Ukraine as they enter the Carpathian basin. Taking just two years to complete, it was first exhibited in 1894 in Budapest's City Park, but was badly damaged during World War II when more than half of the painting was destroyed. This most recent restoration, by a team of Polish experts, was completed in 1995. Inside the same building is an easily missable waxworks exhibition (Panoptikum; 500Ft), and a Tourinform office (same times as park; ☏62/275-257, ⓔinfo@opusztaszer.hu).

Heading up the slope from the Cyclorama past the **Árpád Memorial**, a grand Classical-style stone memorial to the leader of the Magyars set up in 1896, you reach the ruins of the thirteenth-century **Szer Monastery** – although the layers of brick covering the old remains make the place look like a modern fabrication. Excavations here have revealed a cemetery containing the remains of the first Hungarian settlers. Peeping over the trees 50m away is a series of yurta-like structures – supposedly inspired by early Hungarian architecture and crowned with symbols said to come from the early tribes – housing the **Men and Forests**

The legend of Attila the Hun

The lower reaches of the Tisza are associated with the **legend of Attila the Hun**, who died in 453 AD of a nasal haemorrhage following a night of passion with his new bride, Kriemhild. The body of the "Scourge of God" was reputedly buried in a triple-layered coffin of gold, silver and lead, and then submerged in the Tisza at an unknown spot – unknown because the pallbearers were slain before the Huns departed. Archeologists have yet to find it, but the legend gains credence from the "treasure of Attila". Thought to have belonged to a Hun general, the treasure was discovered at Nagyszentmiklós (in what is now Romania) and is currently held by Vienna's Kunsthistorisches Museum.

exhibition (Erdő és Ember), a small set of displays on forestry and wildlife with English notes. The best section of the park, however, is the **Village Museum** (Skanzen; closed in winter), which re-creates buildings from villages in southern Hungary, including a school, post office and bakery – the last two still functional. The park is the focus for craft fairs and demonstrations throughout the year, including Easter, Whitsun, August 20 and the **Hunnia**, a festival on the last Saturday of June celebrating the arrival of the all-conquering Hungarian tribes. There are also Nomadic shows during the summer (11.30am & 2.30pm; 800Ft), featuring horseriding, archery displays and the like.

Practicalities

ÓPUSZTASZER itself lies 10km east of Kistelek on the Kecskemét–Szeged road, and is linked by regular buses from Szeged. Buses stop at the top of the road that leads down to the park. Alternatively, you could try hitching from Kistelek, a stop for buses along the highway. Note that if you are travelling by train from anywhere in Hungary to Szeged or Kistelek and buy a single ticket, you can return to the same station free of charge if you get your ticket stamped at the park ticket office. On the way to the park on Árpád liget you'll find the *Szeri Csárda* restaurant and next door the basic *Szeri Camping* (☎62/275-123; April–Oct).

Szeged

SZEGED straddles the River Tisza like a provincial Budapest, as cosmopolitan a city as you'll find on the Great Plain, with a friendly atmosphere that's mainly thanks to the students from the university. The old city's eclectic good looks have been saved by placing the ugly modern housing and industry over the river, in the suburb of Újszeged. Though Kőrös folk settled here four to five thousand years ago, and the town flourished after 1225 because of its royal monopoly over the salt mines of Transylvania, Szeged's present layout dates from after the **great flood** of March 1879, which washed away all but 300 homes and compelled the population to start again from scratch. With aid from foreign capitals (after whom sections of the outer boulevard are named), the city bounced back, trumpeting its revival with huge buildings and squares where every type of architectural style made an appearance.

During Communist times **Szeged University** was at the forefront of student protests in 1956, and one of the seedbeds of the peace movement and punk rock scene in the 1980s. More recently, the wars in the former Yugoslavia led to a boom in cross-border **smuggling** and Mafia activity, which made Szeged notorious in Hungary and enriched the local economy at a time when other cities were feeling the pinch.

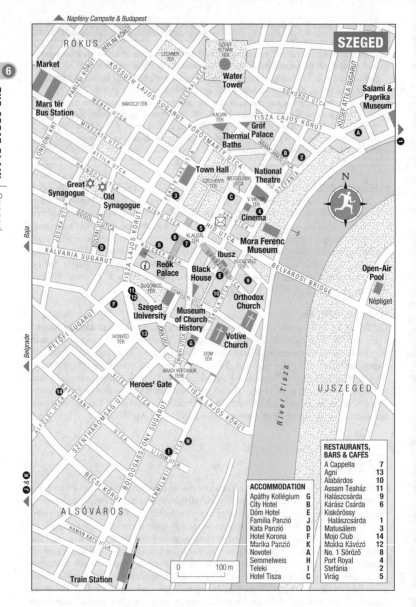

Napfény Campsite & Budapest

SZEGED

RÓKUS

Market

Mars tér
Bus Station

Great
Synagogue

Old
Synagogue

Water
Tower

Salami &
Paprika
Museum

Gróf
Palace

Thermal
Baths

Town Hall

National
Theatre

Cinema

Mora Ferenc
Museum

Ibusz

Reök
Palace

Black
House

Orthodox
Church

Szeged
University

Museum
of Church
History

Votive
Church

Open-Air
Pool

Népliget

Heroes' Gate

River Tisza

UJSZEGED

Train Station

ALSÓVÁROS

BELGRADE

Baja

Belgrade

ACCOMMODATION	
Apáthy Kollégium	G
City Hotel	B
Dóm Hotel	E
Familia Panzió	J
Kata Panzió	D
Hotel Korona	F
Marika Panzió	K
Novotel	A
Semmelweis	H
Teleki	I
Hotel Tisza	C

RESTAURANTS, BARS & CAFÉS	
A Cappella	7
Agni	13
Alabárdos	10
Assam Teaház	11
Halászcsárda	9
Kárász Csárda	6
Kiskörössy Halászcsárda	1
Matusálem	3
Mojo Club	14
Mokka Kávézó	12
No. 1 Söröző	8
Port Royal	4
Stefánia	2
Virág	5

0   100 m

Arrival and information

To get to the old city (Belváros) from the **train station**, take tram #1, while from the intercity **bus terminal** on Mars tér it's a five-minute walk. The Belváros, on the west bank of the Tisza, is encircled by Tisza Lajos körút and an outer ring boulevard, with radial avenues (*sugárút*) emanating from the centre. For a map and **information**, drop into the helpful Tourinform at Dugonics tér 2 (June to mid-Sept Mon–Fri 9am–6pm,

Sat 9am–1pm; mid-Sept to May Mon–Fri 9am–5pm; ℡62/488-690, ℮szeged@ tourinform.hu), which also operates a stall in the square (daily May–Sept 9am–9pm). It also has **bikes for rent** throughout the year (1500Ft per 3hr, 2500Ft per day). There's **internet access** at Cyber Arena at Hid utca 1 near the bridge (open 24hr), with the **post office** close by at Hid utca 3 (Mon–Fri 8am–7pm, Sat 8am–noon).

Accommodation

There's a reasonable spread of accommodation in Szeged, and you should be able to get some form of **accommodation** at any time of the year, though the city's resources can be strained during the Festival Weeks in July and August. **Private rooms** (❷–❸), from Ibusz at Oroszlán utca 3 (Mon–Fri 9am–5pm, Sat 9am–1pm; ℡62/471-177, ℮szeged@ibusz.hu), are the best value for money if you can get somewhere in the centre. Throughout July and August there are double rooms (❷–❸) available in **colleges** around Dóm tér – such as the *Apáthy István Kollégium* at Apáthy István utca 4 (℡62/545-896) and, just a little further south, the *Semmelweis* at Semmelweis utca 4 (℡62/545-042), and the *Teleki* at Semmelweis utca 5 (℡62/546-088). In addition to the campsites listed below, there is a **nudist camp**, *FKK Naturista Camping & Strand*, 10km northwest of the city in Kiskundorozsma (℡62/463-988).

Hotels and pensions

City Hotel Arany János utca 5 ℡62/543-330, ⓦwww.cityhotelszeged.hu. Distinguished by its slender, lime-green corner tower, this polished, twelve-room hotel has gorgeous, light-blue rooms with designer furnishings and a/c. ❼

Dóm Hotel Bajza utca 3–6 ℡62/423-750, ⓦwww.domhotel.hu. A real gem of a hotel secreted away on a closed-off street behind the Black House. Sophisticated, business-like rooms, with big TVs, wi-fi and large wooden desks; sauna and jacuzzi too. ❻

Familia Panzió Szentháromság utca 71 ℡62/441-122, ⓦwww.familiapanzio.hu. Large, hospitable pension south of the town centre and a 10min walk west of the train station. Two- to four-bed rooms, some with a/c. Protected parking available. ❹–❺

Kata Panzió Bolyai utca 20 ℡62/311-258, ⓦwww.katapanzio.hu. Super little pension on a quiet residential street not far from the centre, with sweet, well-equipped rooms; there's also a mini wellness centre. ❻

Hotel Korona Petőfi sgt 4 ℡62/555-787, ⓦwww.hotelkoronaszeged.hu. Nothing special from the outside, but this is a cracking hotel just a stone's throw from the centre, with large, decently furnished and good-looking rooms, all equipped with wi-fi. Triples and quads too. ❼

Marika Panzió Nyíl utca 45 ℡62/443-861, ⓦwww.marika.hu. Well-equipped pension in a charming old peasant house in the Alsóváros, 600m south of the train station, complete with a/c, minibars, protected parking and a swimming pool. ❺

Novotel Maros utca 1 ℡62/562-200, ⓦwww.novotel-szeged.hu. Polished chain hotel offering bright, spacious and smoothly furnished rooms, most of which have great views over the River Tisza. Also has a sauna and fitness room. ❽

Hotel Tisza Széchenyi tér 3 ℡62/478-278, ⓦwww.tiszahotel.hu. A hotel of sorts since 1886, this fine old building overlooking the square now harbours two categories of room; the cheaper ones are fine but poky, while the much larger, more expensive ones have parquet flooring and lovely wood-finished furnishings. ❻–❼

Campsites

Napfény Camping Dorozsmai út 4 ℡62/554-280. In the western suburbs of the city near the start of the Budapest highway (bus #78), with wooden chalets (❷). Open May–Sept.

Partfürdő Camping Középkikötő sor ℡62/430-843, ⓦwww.szegedkemping.hu. On the river bank just across the bridge in Újszeged near the *strand* and thermal baths. Has wooden chalets (❷–❸). Open May (later if the Tisza is in flood) to Sept.

The Town

Szeged's sights are all within comfortable walking distance of one another, with the majority of attractions clustered around or near to the city's main squares and along the waterfront area.

Dom tér and around

Dóm tér is the most impressive feature of the inner city. Flanked by arcades with twisted columns and busts of illustrious Hungarians, this 12,000-square-metre expanse (approximately the same size as St Mark's Square in Venice) was created in 1920 by demolishing a network of backstreets to accommodate a gigantic **Votive Church** (Mon–Sat 9am–5pm, Sun 9.30–10am, 11–11.30am & 1–6pm; 500Ft), which the townsfolk had pledged to erect after the flood. Built of brown brick in the neo-Romanesque style, its beautifully carved, thick-set portal is surmounted by a statue of the Virgin whose image recurs inside the church in peasant costume, wearing embroidered "Szeged slippers". Visitors are dwarfed by the white, blue and gold interior, where the organ, with its 10,180 pipes and five manuals, benefits from superb acoustics.

The eight-sided **Demetrius Tower** out in front dates from the eleventh century, but was largely rebuilt by Béla Rerrich, who designed the square. A chiming clock plays the folk song "Szeged, a famous town" at midday. Across from the tower, at no. 5, is a small **Museum of Church History** (Egyháztörténeti Múzeum; Tues–Sun 10am–6pm; 100Ft), which holds a fine hoard of eighteenth- and nineteenth-century church treasures, including bejewelled chalices, reliquaries and vestments. On the south side of the square crowds gather every day at 12.15pm and 5.45pm (and at 8.15pm during the summer festival) to watch the **Musical Clock** (Zenélő óra), whose figures move round to the rich sound of the bells.

In the summer rows of seats are banked opposite the Votive Church for Szeged's festival, where local operas are performed. When performances (which start with everyone standing for the national anthem) finish, the crowds flood out towards the **Heroes' Gate** (Hősök Kapuja), which links Aradi vértanúk tere with Boldogasszony sugárút. Actually a large, rather undistinguished arch, flanked by two smaller ones, the gate was raised to honour Admiral Horthy's henchmen, the "Whites", who gathered here in 1919, waiting for the Romanian army to defeat the Republic of Councils before they fanned out across Hungary to persecute Jews and "Reds" in the "White Terror". The mural inside the gate, by Aba Novak Vilmos, one of Hungary's leading interwar artists, was painted over by the Communists, who hated its glorification of Horthy and its nationalist references.

▲ Szeged

A few years ago the Aba Novak Society raised funds to remove the paint, though the figure of Horthy itself remained covered until recently. The mural itself is a rather simplistic militaristic affair, but the local people are very proud of it. Behind the Votive Church to the northeast of Dóm tér stands an eighteenth-century **Serbian Orthodox Church** (Szerb Ortodox Templom; 200Ft), worth a look for its magnificent iconostasis framed in pear wood – if the church is closed, the key can be obtained from the house directly opposite.

Dugonics tér and around

Many of the buildings to the west of Dóm tér are part of **Szeged University**, whose main building overlooks **Dugonics tér** and a Water Music Fountain where students congregate during breaks. Locally known by its Hungarian initials, JATE (pronounced "yohteh"), the university is named after the poet **Attila József**, whom it expelled in 1924 for a poem which began "I have no father, I have no mother, I have no god and I have no country" and continued "with a pure heart, I'll burn and loot, and if I have to, even shoot". Attila's bitterness was rooted in his childhood, when his mother, a poor washerwoman, died of starvation. Later he was expelled from the Communist Party for trying to reconcile Marx and Freudian psychology and, rejected by the woman he loved, finally jumped under a train at Lake Balaton (see p.200). Though unappreciated during his lifetime, Attila's poetry is now recognized as some of the best in the language. Elderly Hungarians weep upon hearing his sentimental "Mama", while anarcho-punks relish lines such as "Culture drops off me, like clothes off a happy lover".

Across from the university, on the corner of Somogyi and Kelemen utca, is the so-called **Black House** (Fekete-Ház). This Romantic-style edifice is actually painted brown and white, but the ironmonger who lived here in the nineteenth century always told peasants "You can find me in the Black House". It now houses a very missable local history **museum** (Tues–Sun 10am–5pm; 300Ft), though there are occasionally some good temporary exhibitions staged here. If you carry on up Somogyi utca and bear right onto Fekete sas utca you'll find the fabulous **Reök Palace** (Reök palota; Tues–Sat 10am–6pm; 400Ft) on the corner of Kölcsey utca. Built in 1907 for Iván Reök, a nephew of the painter Munkácsy, this Art Nouveau masterpiece by Ede Oszadszki Magyar has been beautifully restored and now functions as a regional arts and cultural centre, with rotating exhibitions each month. Even if you don't fancy taking in an exhibition, the wonderfully light and airy interior, which has retained several of its original features including the spiral stone staircase, is worth a peek. Look out for the siren over the entrance with her Medusa-like coils of hair.

Along the waterfront

Heading northwards from Dóm tér towards Roosevelt tér, you can't miss the enormous Neoclassical facade of the **Móra Ferenc Museum** (Tues–Sun 10am–5pm; 600Ft), named after the eponymous local excavator. The museum conceals a typical mix of *objets d'art* and artefacts of local significance, notably a huge painting of the great flood by Pál Vágó. More fascinating is the display on the Avars, the people displaced by the arriving Magyars – the highlights of a memorable collection include jewellery, pottery and weapons, exquisitely embossed artwork, and a double grave excavated by Ferenc himself.

Standing on the remains of the town castle just behind the museum is the **Castle Museum** (Varmúzeum; Tues–Sun 10am–5pm; 300Ft), which is a bit of a misnomer as it primarily stages temporary exhibitions. The castle once served as a prison for the outlaw Sándor Rózsa and for convicts who laboured on the river towpaths during the eighteenth century. As in Debrecen, this was a time of mass witch trials organized by the church elders, when victims were tortured to make them confess.

From here you can walk away from the river up to Vaszy Viktor tér and the **National Theatre** (Nemzeti Szinház) and the **City Cinema** (Belvárosi Mozi) – both stunning buildings in very different styles. The former, built in 1883, is a typically ostentatious piece of work by the Viennese duo Hellmer and Fellner, and features statues of József Katona and Ferenc Erkel in niches either side of the entrance.

Széchenyi tér and around

Walking up Wesselényi utca brings you to spacious, verdant **Széchenyi tér**, Szeged's inner-city park. On the far side stands the neo-Baroque **Town Hall**, rebuilt in 1883 following the great flood and likened by the poet Mihály Babits to "a lace-covered young woman dancing in the moonlight". The town hall is linked to the neighbouring council house – built at the same time on account of the visit of Franz Joseph – by a charming "Bridge of Sighs", modelled on the one in Venice. In front of the town hall stand two allegorical **fountains**, known as "The Blessed" and "The Angry", symbolizing the benevolent and destructive aspects of the River Tisza. Among the many other statues scattered throughout the park is one of Pál Vásárhelyi, underneath which is a marble plaque denoting the high-water mark in the city during the more recent flood of June 2, 1970.

A short walk south is **Klauzál tér**, a bright, Mediterranean-style piazza fringed by some fine pastel-coloured Neoclassical buildings, and setting for some of the town's most inviting cafés (see p.400). In the centre of the square stands a statue of Lajos Kossuth, who gave his last speech before his exile in 1849 from the balcony of the building at no. 5, which is now a bank. Opposite is the attractive Well of Kings, featuring four winged lions, from whence water spouts. Heading northwards from Széchenyi tér on Tisza Lajos körút are the magnificent **Anna thermal baths** (Anna Furdő; Mon–Fri 8am–8pm, Sat & Sun 6am–8pm; 900Ft), indoor steam baths built at the end of the nineteenth century and recently completely restored – the complex now comprises some ten different pools.

A five-minute walk further north from the baths brings you to newly relaid **Szent István tér**, in the centre of which stands the renovated **water tower** (Viztorony; open first Sat of each month 10am–4pm; 200Ft). Constructed in 1904, the fifty-metre tower was one of the first buildings in Hungary to utilise reinforced concrete technology, and it remains the oldest, still functioning structure of its kind in the country.

Back on the riverside, a ten-minute walk east of Szent István tér brings you to the **Salami and Paprika Museum**, situated within the Pick Salami Factory at Felső-Tisza-part 10 (Tues–Sat 3–6pm; 800Ft). The display on salami downstairs could put you off the stuff forever, but there are some good historical photos to look at, and the paprika exhibition upstairs – complete with lots of information on the healthy properties of the plant – smells marvellous. The entrance ticket has two halves: a token that entitles you to some salami samples in the restaurant at the end of your visit, and a postcard that you can send anywhere in the world for free – you just have to write it and put it in the museum postbox.

The Jewish quarter and beyond

Beyond Tisza Lajos körút, Szeged is shabbier and more utilitarian, but not devoid of sights, especially in the former **Jewish quarter** around Hajnóczy utca. The classical **Old Synagogue**, dating from 1843, bears a plaque showing the height of the water during the flood; it is now a contemporary arts centre, Alterra. Far grander and more alluring is the Secession-style **Great Synagogue** (Új Zsinagóga) with its entrance on Jósika utca (Mon–Fri & Sun: April–Sept 10am–noon &

1–5pm; Oct–March 10am–2pm; 400Ft). One of the largest synagogues in Europe, it was built between 1900 and 1903 by Lipót Baumhorn, who designed 22 synagogues throughout Hungary; this one is regarded as the finest example of his work. Its magnificent dome, executed in blue stained glass, represents the world, with 24 columns for the hours of day and night, white flowers for faith, and blue stars for the infinity of the cosmos. The stained-glass windows illustrate texts from *The Flora of the Jews*, by Rabbi Immanuel Löw, who was the Chief Rabbi here in the early part of the century.

Around the outer boulevard (bus #11 or #21), to the south, parts of the **Alsóváros** or "lower town" resemble a village, with ochre-painted cottages and rutted streets. This quarter was traditionally inhabited by paprika-growers, and centres around the **Alsóvárosi Church** on Mátyás király tér, begun in the late fifteenth century. Its reworked Baroque interior contains the *Black Madonna*, a copy of the famous Madonna of Czistochowa, and the focus of attention during the reconsecration ceremonies at the annual melon harvest festival.

The busy outdoor **market** (daily 6am–noon), on Mars tér in the Rókus quarter, is well worth a visit, as is the excellent **antiques market** on Dugonics tér, held on the third Saturday of each month. To the west of the centre (tram #3 from Dugonics tér), there's a **wildlife park** (Vadaspark; daily: June–Aug 9am–7pm; Sept–May 9am–5pm; 900Ft) with a large collection of small monkeys, parrots and South American animals. Southeast of town, across the Tisza at Lövölde utca 42, are the lovely **botanical gardens** (Füvészkert; daily: April–Oct 9am–6pm; Nov–March 9am–4pm; 500Ft), which harbour Giant Sequoia, Dawn Redwood and some five thousand plant species; take bus #70 from Mars tér and get off at the last stop. Meanwhile, on hot summer weekends people flock to the *Ligetfürdő* **open air pool** (May–Sept daily 6am–8pm; 800Ft) in Újszeged across the river, which also has thermal pools.

Eating and drinking

Szeged has a decent, though not exceptional, range of **restaurants**, and is famous for its sausages and for dishes such as *halászlé* (fish soup) and *halpaprikás* (fish in paprika sauce). The city abounds in good **drinking** spots, be they cafés, bars or clubs, the last firmly centred around the student quarters.

Restaurants

Agni Lajos Korut 76. A rarity in Hungary, this sweet little vegetarian restaurant offers more than the usual veggie standards, such as baked pumpkin with pasta and a hot Indian vegetable stew.

Alabárdos Oskola utca 13. Smart establishment incorporating a beautifully decorated formal section, where you can dine on high-quality fish (crab with chilli, French mussels, buttered salmon) and game (deer, hog) dishes; there's also an adjoining, informal seating area where you can grab a pizza.

Halászcsárda Roosevelt tér 12. Down by the waterfront, this warm and classy restaurant is almost exclusively devoted to fish, with fried Paprika catfish, crab stew with pike perch, and fish-stuffed pancakes just some of the inducements. The lovely, lime-green coloured interior, with its seductive lighting and immaculately laid tables, rounds things off perfectly.

Kárász Csárda Klauzál tér 5. Modern, two-floored place tucked away in a little courtyard just off the pretty main square, which is heavily accented towards the wet stuff, although it does feature a good selection of grilled meat dishes too. Smoking section upstairs.

Kiskörössy Halászcsárda Felső Tisza-part 336. Fish lovers should make a pilgrimage to this place on the banks of the Tisza where the Prince of Wales (later Edward VII) often came in the 1890s. Bus #73 or #73Y from Mars tér (ask the driver to tell you when to get off), then walk along the dyke and follow a road down to the right, where there are two restaurants and holiday houses amongst the trees.

Matusálem Széchenyi tér 13. Housed in an old printing works, this is an agreeably simple place with unfussy, inexpensive dishes (pastas, burgers, salads, baguettes) and an enjoyable terrace looking across to the square.

Port Royal Stéfánia 4. Buzzy, informal spot, with tables arrayed around a long, colourful bar;

the food is decent enough, dozens of different pizzas vying with lots of generously portioned meat dishes. Occasional live music too.

Drinking and nightlife

For **coffee and cakes**, most people congregate at the large and sociable *Virág* and *A Cappella Cukrászdas*, opposite each other on Klauzál tér, both of which have bustling summer terraces. Two fun places, next door to each other at Tisza Lajos Korut 60, are the *Assam Teaház*, a beautifully decorated teahouse where you can kick off your shoes and settle back into squishy floor cushions, and the *Mokka Kávézó*, which offers the best range of coffees in town. Also worth a look-in is the cosy *Stefánia*, down by the riverside park at Stefánia 9.

The best of the city centre **bars** is *No. 1 Söröző*, Kölcsey utca 11, a cool and roomy, brick-vaulted cellar joint with deep leather sofas and lamp-topped tables. Although it's a large university town, Szeged can be quiet at weekends, when many students head home; the big student night out is Thursday, known as *kis péntek* – "little Friday". A popular student hangout is the mellow *Mojo Club*, Alföld utca 1, while the *Nem Egri Borozó* at József Attila utca 6 (closed Sun) attracts a mix of locals and students. There are regular **raves and parties** at the *JATE Klub* at Toldi utca 2 behind the university, and at the *SZOTE Klub* (the medical university club) at Dom tér 13 – in July and August the music only starts after the open-air stage (see below) has finished.

Entertainment and festivals

Szeged's **concert season** runs from September to May, with events held in the National Theatre (see p.398), the ticket office for which is at Stefánia 6 (Mon–Fri 10am–5pm, Sat 10am–noon; ☎62/554-714). The city's big festival date is the **Szeged Open-Air Festival** (Szegedi Szabadtéri Játékok) throughout July and August, when Dóm tér is filled with a huge stage hosting a festival of top-rate music, opera and drama. **Tickets** are available online (ⓦwww.szegediszabadteri.hu), from the regional arts centre inside the Reök Palace (see p.397), and Tourinform. Two more low-key, but no less enjoyable, festivals are the week-long **Days of Szeged** in May, which incorporates a series of concerts, a large wine gathering on Széchenyi tér, and a bridge market on Belvárosi Hid, and the **Tisza Fish Festival** on the first weekend of September, when much consumption of fish takes place down by the river.

The Southern Plain beyond the Tisza

The **Southern Plain** east of the Tisza is sunbaked and dusty, with small towns that bore the brunt of the Turkish occupation and often suffered from droughts, giving rise to such paranoia that "witches" were burned for "blowing the clouds away" or "selling the rain to the Turks". Resettled by diverse ethnic groups under Habsburg auspices, they later attracted dispossessed Magyars from Transylvania, who displaced the existing communities of Swabians, Serbs, Slovaks and Romanians. In the 1950s, geologists scoured the region for oil, but almost every borehole struck thermal springs instead, hence the numerous **spas** in this region. The most attractive towns are **Hódmezővásárhely**, **Gyula** and **Szarvas**, while the famous stud farm at **Mezőhegyes** is another attraction.

Approaches to the region are largely determined by where you cross the river. Crossing at Szeged, the main trunk route heads towards Békéscsaba. The more northerly route from Szolnok to Debrecen is covered under the Northern Plain (see p.408).

East from Szeged

Heading on from Szeged there are two basic routes: northeast towards Békéscsaba via **Hódmezővásárhely**, or southeast through **Makó** to the Romanian border. Counting the lovely park at nearby **Mártely**, Hódmezővásárhely is better endowed with sights than Makó, but the latter is closer to the stud farm at **Mezőhegyes**, with its horseriding opportunities.

Hódmezővásárhely

HÓDMEZŐVÁSÁRHELY's tongue-twisting name can be translated as "marketplace of the beaver's field", though it's disputed whether the *hód-* prefix really derives from the Magyar word for "beaver". That aside, this long-established market town has the distinction of being the second-largest municipality in Hungary, incorporating several distant settlements. It's an appealing little town, with some worthwhile museums and plenty of fine architecture to admire. Otherwise the best time to visit is during the **St Stephen celebrations** around August 20, four days of events, including a craft market and fireworks. The other major annual event is the **Shepherd Contest** (Juhászverseny), a three-day animal fair held in April on the northeast edge of town, which is more than just a farming get-together, with horse displays, crafts fairs and entertainments.

The Town

Most of the town's sights are located around the grand, tree-filled main square, Kossuth tér, and the street leading north, Szántó Kovács János utca. Kossuth tér is dignified by several fine buildings, not least an imposing **town hall** (Mon–Fri 8am–3pm), whose magnificent banqueting hall is hung with pictures of local heroes and historical figures; ask the porter who will let you visit if the hall is free. On the other side of the square is a huge bank topped with a four-metre statue of Mercury, and the **Fekete Sas ("Black Eagle") Hotel**, a grand, vanilla-coloured edifice where merchants once gathered to trade agricultural products from all over the Balkans, storing their money in the bank and gambling the profits in the former casino opposite. It is not actually a hotel at all, but is a venue for important functions – you can, though, pop your head in and have a look.

On Szőnyi utca, a few paces along from the town hall, the **Alföldi Gallery** (Tues–Sun 10am–6pm; 400Ft) exhibits scenes of *puszta* life by local artist János Tornyai, an oeuvre recently enhanced by the discovery of 700 canvases in a Budapest attic. Work by other local artists hangs in the **Tornyai János Museum**, a five-minute walk north of Kossuth tér at Szántó Kovács János utca 16 (Tues–Sun 10am–6pm; 400Ft); its archeological collection includes a 5000-year-old statue of a fertility goddess known as "the Venus of Kökénydomb". Across the street stands a fine little Baroque **Greek Orthodox Church**, whose "Nahum iconostasis" from

Mount Athos is named after an obscure seventh-century prophet – unfortunately, however, it's currently not possible to enter, such is its poor state.

A fifteen-minute walk east of Kossuth tér, along Andrássy utca at no. 34, a futuristic building houses the **Emlékpont** (Mon–Sun 10am–6pm; 800Ft). Essentially a memorial museum paying tribute to those local citizens who lost their lives during World War II, it also documents life in the town under Communist rule in the period thereafter. Although the exhibition is thoughtfully conceived, the absence of English captioning unfortunately renders the visit a little underwhelming. A short walk north of the museum on Szent István tér is the florid Art Nouveau **synagogue** (Mon–Fri & Sun 9am–1pm), both the interior and exterior of which have been beautifully restored to the 1906 design of Gyula Müller. To the rear of the synagogue is a small exhibition commemorating those from Hódmezővásárhely who died in the Holocaust.

Hódmezővásárhely is renowned for its **pottery**, and each district of the town has a different style. The most distinctive is the black pottery based on Turkish designs, fired in a manner dating back to Neolithic times. To buy pottery or watch it being made, visit the **workshop** of Sándor Ambrus, close to the centre at Lánc utca 3 (Fazekasház; Mon–Fri 10am–6pm, Sat 10am–2pm) – to get there walk east from Kossuth tér along Andrássy utca for around 500m. There are further examples displayed in the **Csúcs Potter's House** (by appointment only; ☎36/533-317; 300Ft), twenty minutes' walk north of the centre at Rákóczi utca 101, and in the **Folk Culture House**, two thatched cottages at Árpád utca 21, near the levee (Tájház; Tues–Sat 10am–5pm; 300Ft), which also displays peasant costumes and furniture. The town's **thermal baths** complex, south of Kossuth tér at Ady Endre utca 1, includes an outdoor thermal pool and an Olympic-size indoor pool (daily 8am–8pm; 950Ft).

Practicalities

All **trains** to Hódmezővásárhely stop at two stations: Népkert, south of the centre, and the main station to the east, both of which are connected to the centre by local buses. **Buses** from Szeged run right through the centre before terminating at the main train station rather than the intercity bus terminal, in Bocskai út, where buses from elsewhere wind up.

There's plenty of **information** at Tourinform, housed in an old granary building across the road from Kossuth tér at Szőnyi utca 1 (Mon–Thurs 7.30am–4pm, Fri 7.30am–1.30pm; ☎62/249-350, ⓔhodmezovasarhely@tourinform.hu). It can also advise on **private rooms** (②), while there are dorm beds available in the Agricultural College at Petőfi utca 10 (☎62/242-413; 1500Ft), a five-minute walk east of Kossuth tér.

The best option for other **accommodation**, in a town with few possibilities, is the homely *Kenguru Panzió*, just under 1km north of the centre at Szántó Kovács János utca 78, opposite the water tower (☎62/534-841, ⓦwww .kengurugm.hu; ⑤), which has lovely little rooms, as well as a sauna and heated outdoor pool. The alternatives are the friendly if rather dull *Hotel Fáma*, behind the synagogue at Szeremlei utca 7 (☎62/222-231, ⓦwww.hotelfama.hu; ④), and the joyless and overpriced *Hotel Pelikán* next to the thermal baths at Ady Endre utca 1 (☎62/245-072, ⓔinfo@pelikanhotel.hu; ④–⑤). The town's **campsite** (☎62/245-033; April–Sept; wooden chalets ②) is next to the *Hotel Pelikán* by the thermal baths. The **post office** is on Kossuth tér (Mon–Fri 8am–7pm, Sat 8am–noon) and there's **internet access** in the cultural centre at Szántó Kovács János utca 7.

The best **restaurant** in town is the posh-looking, but inexpensive, *Bandula* at Pálffy utca 2, north of the centre near the water tower, which has a varied Hungarian menu, while the vegetarian choices are better then average. A respectable second choice is the *Bagólyvár*, near the Folk Art centre at Kaszap utca 31, offering similarly bright Hungarian dishes. A lovely spot for coffee is the charming little *Kaveház*, adjoining the Fekete Sas Hotel, while Hősök tere, south of Kossuth tér, is a popular place to hang out in the summer, with two **bars** that both have terraces running under the trees: the *Hordó Pub*, where you can also get pizza; and the *Casino Söröző*, which offers beer, food, pool tables and darts.

Mártély

From Hódmezővásárhely regular buses run 10km northwest to the village of **Mártély** beside a backwater of the Tisza, with boats for rent, hand-woven baskets for sale and a gorgeous **bird reserve** nearby. Ideal for picnics and **horseriding**, it's a nice spot in which to relax and unwind, featuring the *Tiszapart* **campsite** (✆62/228-057; May–Sept), with chalets (❷) and apartments (❸). In the first weekend of August the village's peace is disturbed by the *Mártélyi Kavalkád* festival, when there's a fair, music and other events.

Makó and Mezőhegyes

Aside from being the "onion capital" of Hungary, the faded town of **MAKÓ**, 32km south of Hódmezővásárhely on the Romanian border, is notable for its **therapeutic baths** in radioactive Maros mud, and for being the birthplace of Joseph Pulitzer, who won fame as a journalist and publisher in America in the nineteenth century and founded the Pulitzer Prize. Pulitzer left here when he was 10, and a plaque on the apartment block at Úri utca 4 (across from the town hall) marks the place where his house once stood. It was here, too, that the poet Attila József was sent to school after his mother died, had his first verses published, and made several attempts to commit suicide throughout 1912 and 1913 – he finally succeeded in 1937 when he threw himself under a train (see p.200). His former domicile is now the **Attila Memorial House** at Kazinczy utca 6 (Espersit Ház; Wed–Sun 9am–4pm; 150Ft), which keeps a selection of his letters and personal effects; while his name graces the **József Attila Museum** on the corner of Kazinczy and Megyeház utca (Wed–Sun 9am–4pm; 200Ft); a typical collection of local paintings and artefacts, this museum also documents the history of Makó's onion trade. More interesting is the handful of dwellings in the yard, containing various agricultural implements and wooden contraptions used for onion harvesting. Two buildings worth tracking down are the crenellated **Orthodox Synagogue**, near the bus station at Eötvös utca 15, and the **Onion House**, hidden away on Posta utca, just behind Széchenyi tér. Built in 1998, it's a typically outlandish structure by Imre Makovecz (see box, p.163), the dome indeed resembling the top half of an onion, and flanked by four gherkin-shaped glass pillars. The inside, which is a theatre, is no less unusual, the roof resembling something like an upturned hull of a ship – ask at reception if you want to have a look. A five-minute walk west of Széchenyi tér, on Marczibányi tér, is the large **thermal baths** complex (Mon–Fri 8am–7pm, Sat & Sun 9am–7pm; 1000Ft), which Makovecz also had a hand in, designing the indoor pool building. The town's largest annual event is, naturally enough, the three-day **Onion Festival** in mid-September, with a procession and various events on a stage at the western end of town.

Practicalities

From the **bus station** it's a ten-minute walk south to the main square, Széchenyi tér, while the **train station** lies about 500m in the opposite direction, on Lonovics sugár út. There's lots of **information** available from Tourinform, at Széchenyi tér 8 (June–Aug daily 8am–6pm; Sept–May Mon–Fri 8am–4pm; ☎62/210-708, ✉mako@tourinform.hu). The uninspiring **accommodation** possibilities boil down to the very basic, and not particularly good-value, *Bástya Hotel* at Szegedi utca 2 (☎62/214-224, ✉bastya_hotel@freemail.hu; ❹); the friendly *Karaván Panzió* in an old town house ten minutes' walk further west at Szegedi utca 16 (☎62/219-912, ✉karavanpanzio@freemail.hu; ❸); and the *Kerekes Panzió*, beyond the museums east of the centre at Megyeház utca 37 (☎62/216-687, ✉kerekespanzio@freemail.hu; ❸). There's also a pleasant **campsite** (☎62/211-914, ⓦwww.campingmako.hu; May–Sept) beside the River Maros, 500m out towards Szeged, which also has three-bedded bungalows (❷) and chalets (❸), the latter charmingly equipped with old peasant furniture; there's also a restaurant, pool, and canoes and kayaks for rent. The old Korona Hotel building in the centre of Széchenyi tér now houses a fine **restaurant** and coffee house.

Mezőhegyes

From Makó regular buses make the thirty-kilometre journey northeast to **MEZŐHEGYES**, home to a stud farm for breeding Lippizaner horses, founded in 1785. Today the **stud farm** breeds **Gidrán and Nonius horses**, the latter having been introduced from Normandy in 1810 to produce resilient cavalry chargers. There is a covered **riding school** offering horse or carriage rides (2500Ft/5000Ft per hour respectively), and you can stay at the *Hotel Nónius* in the same complex (☎68/467-321, ⓦwww.hotels.hu/nonius; ❺), which also organizes visits to the stables. A tour of the buildings and coach museum (4500Ft) is usually restricted to groups, and has to be booked in advance through the hotel, but it's always worth enquiring.

Békéscsaba, Gyula and Szarvas

Travelling by road from Szeged to Debrecen, you're almost bound to pass through **BÉKÉSCSABA**, the "sausage capital" of Hungary. Settled by the Magyars at the time of the land-taking, the region around Békéscsaba was left virtually devoid of life by the Turkish wars and the War of Independence, until it was revived by settlers from all over the Habsburg Empire, making it the most ethnically diverse town in eighteenth-century Hungary. The town itself was rebuilt by Slovaks, whose characteristic folk costumes and handicrafts are exhibited in an ornate **Slovak House** at Garay utca 21 (Szlovák Tájház; Tues–Sun 10am–noon & 2–6pm; 200Ft), which you can find by bearing off the main Szent István tér along Baross utca, and turning right.

Other oddments relating to the Slovaks can be found in the **Munkácsy Mihály Museum** at Széchenyi utca 9, a short way off the square along the Gyula road (Tues–Sun 10am–6pm; 800Ft). The museum is named after the nineteenth-century Romantic painter Mihály Munkácsy (1844–1900), several of whose large-scale biblical paintings and historical pictures are displayed here. There are also some excellent photos of the painter, alongside a superbly presented assemblage of personal effects, including his palette, sketchbook, collapsible chair and a tuft of hair – look out, too, for the beautifully carved coat hanger, in the centre of which Munkácsy painted a pair of dancers. Down in the basement is a fine ethnographic collection representing the multifarious settlers in the region, with German furniture, Slovak embroidery and clothing, Romanian and Serbian Orthodox icons, and some jewellery and woodcarvings courtesy of the Roma, all on display.

Munkácsy actually spent much of his time as a teenager at Gyulai út 5, 100m along the road, in what is now the **Munkácsy Memorial House** (Tues–Fri 9am–4pm, Sat

10am–4pm; 500Ft). This fine whitewashed porticoed domicile contains a far more representative sample of Munkácsy's work, including the celebrated *Afternoon Visit* and *Daydreaming Woman* (two pieces from his so-called drawing-room period), in addition to some splendid period furniture. If you feel like a wallow, the **Árpád thermal baths** are on the east bank of the canal at Árpád Sor 3 (daily 6am–6pm; mid-June to mid-Aug till 9pm; 1200Ft); bus #8 runs fairly close by.

If you're here in late October and have a strong stomach you could take in the **Kolbász Sausage Festival**, which celebrates *kolbász* – a crude but tasty salami-style sausage – as well as Békéscsaba's role in the meat-processing industry. Folk music and dancing events are accompanied by demonstrations of pig-slaughtering and sausage-making.

Practicalities

From the **train and bus stations** on the southern edge of town, bus #1, #1G, #2 or #7 can get you to the start of the pedestrian stretch of Andrássy út, from where it's fifteen minutes' walk to Szent István tér. Here you'll find Tourinform at no. 9 (mid-June to Aug Mon–Fri 9am–6pm, Sat & Sun 10am–7pm; Sept to mid-June Mon–Fri 8am–4pm; ☎66/441-261, ✉bekescsaba@tourinform.hu), and Ibusz next door (Mon–Fri 8am–4pm, Sat 8am–noon; ☎66/328-428, ✉i043@ibusz .hu), who can help with private rooms (❷). The **post office** is across the road at Szabadság tér 1–3 (Mon–Fri 8am–6pm, Sat 8am–noon).

Aside from **private rooms**, the choice of **accommodation** is limited to the reasonable, if slightly overpriced, *Fiume Hotel*, a restored prewar hotel across from Tourinform at Szent István tér 2 (☎66/443-243, ⓦwww.hotelfiume.hu; ❺), and the homely, and much better value, *Szlovák Hotel* (☎66/441-750, ✉szlovakhaz @mail.globonet.hu; ❺), five minutes' walk north of Szent István tér behind the church at Kossuth tér 10. For **eating**, try your luck in the *Szlovák Hotel*'s delightful restaurant, where you can sample Slovak food and draught beer surrounded by folksy decor; otherwise, there's the canalside *Halászcsárda* fish restaurant, 200m east of Szent István tér at Árpád Sor 1, or simple fare at the *Speed Pizzeria*, just off Szent István tér on Hunyadi tér, which also has a good choice of sweet and savoury pancakes. For drinks, the *Mozart café* is a quiet little bolt hole at Andrássy út 4.

Gyula

Just 20km south of Békéscsaba, en route to the Romanian border, **GYULA** is one of the prettiest towns in the Southern Great Plain region, strong in Art Nouveau buildings and with the most to show for its history. Named after a Hungarian tribal chieftain, the town was heavily fortified by the Angevins but quickly succumbed to the Turks, who held its castle for nearly 130 years. After the Turks were evicted, Gyula was rebuilt as a twin town, with Hungarian Magyargyula on one side of the Élővíz Canal, and German–Romanian Németgyula on the other. Though this distinction ceased long ago, you'll still hear German and Romanian spoken in town: Germans come here for the thermal baths and Romanians to trade. Gyula's lively character, however, is largely due to its sizeable student population, rather than its tourists.

Arrival and information

The **bus station** is a five-minute walk south of the centre on Vásárhelyi Pál utca, while the **train station** is a fifteen-minute walk north of the centre at the end of Béke sugár út. Tourinform is at Kossuth utca 7 (mid-June to mid-Sept daily 9am–5pm; mid-Sept to mid-June Mon–Fri 9am–5pm; ☎66/561-680, ✉bekes-m@tourinform.hu). The **post office** is on Eszperantó tér (Mon–Fri

8am–7pm, Sat 8am–noon), and there's **internet access** at Fókusz Pont (Mon–Fri 9am–6pm, Sat 9am–noon), at Tiborc utca 1 near the baths.

Accommodation

For a reasonably small town Gyula has an extraordinary amount of **accommodation**, with plenty of affordable hotels and pensions. Private rooms (❷) are available through Békéstourist at Vásárhelyi Pál utca 2 (Mon–Thurs 8am–4.30pm, Fri 8am–3.30pm; ☏66/463-028), and Gyulatourist, just across the bridge at Eszperantó tér 1 (June–Aug Mon–Fri 8am–5pm, Sat 9am–noon; Sept–May Mon–Fri 9am–4pm; ☏66/463-026, ✉gytour@t-online.hu); both also handle beds in colleges during the summer. The town's two **campsites**, both open year-round, are the enormous *Termál Camping* at Szélső utca 16 (☏66/463-704), which has chalets (❷) and a motel (❸), but is almost 1km from the castle, and the closer *Márk Camping* at Vár utca 5 (☏66/463-380).

Hotel Aranykereszt Eszperantó tér 2 ☏66/463-194, ✉aranykereszt5700@t-online.hu. This medium-sized hotel on the main square is fairly dated and not exactly flush with character, but its rooms are more than adequate and it's one of the cheaper options in town. ❸

Hotel Corvin Jókai utca 9–11 ☏66/362-044, 🌐www.corvin-hotel.hu. Neat, polished place harbouring shiny, green and yellow rooms, in addition to a fine restaurant, grill garden and a terrific little winery. ❻

Gyula Panzió Megyeház utca 10 ☏66/464-644, 🌐www.gyulapanzio.hu. Warm and welcoming pension midway between the centre and the baths, with bright, modern rooms. Excellent value. ❹

Halászcsárda Panzió Part utca 3 ☏66/466-303, ✉info@halaszcsarda-panzio.hu. Out towards the baths, this restful canalside guesthouse has smallish rooms with elementary furnishings, but is pretty good value. ❹

Maestro Panzió Kossuth utca 3 ☏66/560-120, ✉maestrorestaurant@yahoo.com. Across the road from the *Gyula Panzió*, this is another cracking little pension, with handsome, softly coloured rooms, all with a/c and wi-fi. ❺

The Town

Gyula's major sight is its fourteenth-century **Castle** (Vár; mid-June to Aug 9am–7pm; Sept to mid-June 9am–5pm; 1200Ft), an imposing rectangular bulk and the only brick fortress to have survived in Hungary; its walls are 3m thick and originally incorporated every defensive feature known in Europe at that time. Now fully renovated, the castle's many rooms are stuffed with documents and items relaying its history, alongside reconstructions of the castle rooms as they would have once looked, and mock-up workshops representing trades such as blacksmiths and potters. You can finish off with a walk along the ramparts, from where there are fine views of the town and surrounds. In July and August the courtyard provides a stage for the **Castle Theatre** (Várszinház; 🌐www.gyulai varszinhaz.hu), which presents historical dramas, opera, jazz and classical and folk music – there is a second stage by the lake outside the castle walls. Ferenc Erkel (see opposite) used to compose in the park beside the castle under the shade of an oak known as **"Erkel's Tree"**, which still stands.

On the north side of the castle is a **memorial to the Arad Martyrs**, commemorating the thirteen Hungarian generals executed by Austrian troops in Arad, just across the border in Romania, on October 6, 1849. Across the small lake are the popular **Castle Baths** (Várfürdő; daily 8am–8.30pm; 1650Ft, 1250Ft after 6pm), a complex of 22 thermal pools ranging in temperature from 46°C to 75°C – the latter can only be endured after you've acclimatized yourself, and then only for a very short time. There is also a large outdoor pool, likewise full of peaty-coloured water, where people lark about.

Close by, at Kossuth utca 17, is an exhibition hall called the **Dürer Terem** (Tues 1–5pm, Wed–Sat 9am–5pm, Sun 9am–1pm; 500Ft), named after the German artist Albrecht Dürer, whose jeweller father migrated from Gyula to Germany. (Their original surname was Ajtossy, from the Hungarian for "door"; Dürer has an identical root in the German word *Tür*.) Strangely, though, there is nothing related to its namesake, just a hoard of medieval weaponry.

The town's remaining sights are all east of here, clustered fairly close together either side of Béke sugárút, itself a short walk north of the main square, Eszperantó tér. The **Ladics House** at Jókai utca 4 (Ladics ház; Tues 1–5pm, Wed–Sat 9am–5pm, Sun 9am–1pm; 500Ft) is a fascinating nineteenth-century bourgeois home preserved down to the last antimacassar, though, unfortunately, lacking any information in English. Further out in the same direction, the **Erkel Museum** at Ápor Vilmos tér 7 (Erkel Ferenc Emlékház; same times and price) pays homage to Ferenc Erkel, composer of two of Hungary's most famous operas, *Hunyadi László* (1844) and *Bánk bán* (1861), and the Hungarian national anthem; exhibits in this, Erkel's birthplace, include musical scores, personal effects and his piano. The **György Kohán Museum** at Béke sugárút 35, just north of the centre (Kohán Képtár; same times and price), exhibits some of the 3000 works that its namesake bequeathed to his home town – mostly bold depictions of horses, women and houses.

Eating and drinking

For a relatively small town, there's a decent range of places to **eat and drink** in Gyula. Pick of the **restaurants** is the *Kisködmön* at Városház utca 15, a genuinely enjoyable place where you can tuck in to tasty and beautifully presented Hungarian food amidst a very folksy interior design, with waitresses suitably attired in peasant garb. Further along at Kossuth utca 3, *Patriota* is a quiet, polished little establishment offering a limited but appealing Hungarian menu, while *Maestro*, next door, has fairly standard offerings down in its cosy cellar surrounds. Down at Kossuth tér 2, the popular *Sörpince* beer cellar serves large meaty plates alongside big jugs of beer, while the decent *Skorpió Pizzeria*, a five-minute walk north at Jókai utca 17, has good pizza.

Don't miss the gorgeous *Százéves Cukrászda* at Erkel tér 1, which is the **oldest patisserie** in Hungary after *Ruszwurm*'s in Budapest, open since 1840. Furnished in the Biedermeier style and painted in shades of crème de menthe and chocolate, the "Old Lady", as it is locally known, includes a small museum of pastry-chef's utensils – it also offers some 150 types of confectionery. Run by the same management is the excellent *Kézműves* coffee house at Városház utca 21. There are several loud **drinking** spots along Kossuth utca, including *Bols Café* at no. 1 and *Bacardi* at no. 3, while the *Macho Pub*, close by at Városház utca 1, has a more party-like atmosphere.

Szarvas

Attractive **SZARVAS** ("Stag"), 45km northwest of Békéscsaba, feels peculiarly spacious, with a broad main street intersected by wide roads. The town was laid out like a chessboard in the eighteenth century by the enlightened thinker Samuel Tessedik, who served as a Lutheran priest in the town until his death in 1820. The **Samuel Tessedik Museum**, to the west of town near the bridge at Vajda Péter utca 1 (Tues–Sun 10am–4pm; 400Ft), features a better than average display of local archeological finds, agricultural implements and ceramics, though, predictably, it's all in Hungarian. Like Békéscsaba and Kiskőrös, Szarvas was populated by Slovak settlers after the withdrawal of the Turks in 1722, athough the domestic items and folk costumes on show in the **Slovak House** at Hoffmann utca 1 (Szlovák Tájház; April–Oct Tues–Sun 1–5pm; 400Ft) date from the late nineteenth century. Devotees of national tat shouldn't miss the sculpture fountain by the bridge at the western end of town, which has St Stephen's crown resting on top of what looks like a leaking pipe. A new attraction in the town – and one that brings in hordes of school parties – is the kilometre-long **Historical Memorial Way** (Történelmi Emlékút), yet another piece of Trianon nostalgia: starting from a Transylvanian-style gateway in Szent István park down by the backwater of the Kőrös, eighteen wooden sculptures, symbolizing the stations of Hungarian history up to the present day, lead up to a small windmill marking the very centre of pre-World War I Hungary.

The town's principal draw, however, is the **Arboretum**, a couple of kilometres out along the road to Mezőtúr, beside a backwater of the River Körös (daily mid-March to mid-Nov 8am–6pm, mid-Nov to mid-March 8am–3pm; closed Dec 15 to Jan 5; 500Ft). This 200-acre park contains 1600 different plants in its five arboreal collections. The oldest of the five is the *Pepikert* (Pepi Garden), laid out by Count Pál "Pepi" Bolza in emulation of the grounds of Schönbrunn Palace in Vienna. You can try your hand at catching jumping fish on excellent **boat trips** (40min; 500Ft per person) along the Körös backwater past the sights of the park and the Memorial Way; ask at the entrance of the Arboretum for departure times.

Practicalities

Tourinform at Kossuth tér 3 – the entrance is actually on Szabadszág utca (June–Sept Mon–Fri 9am–6pm, Sat 9am–1pm; Oct–May Mon–Fri 9am–4pm; ⓣ66/311-140, ⓔszarvas@tourinform.hu) – can furnish you with any **information** about the town. If you wish to **stay**, there's the very comfortably furnished *Lux Panzió* down the road from Tourinform at Szabadszág utca 35 (ⓣ66/313-417, ⓔlux@szarvas.hu; ❺), while in the park to the west of town on the banks of the backwater is the high-class *Liget Hotel* (ⓣ66/311-954, ⓦwww.ligetszarvas.hu; ❽), with fully equipped bungalows sleeping four (❼); the prices include use of the hotel's extensive wellness facilities. For **meals**, the *Lux Panzió* has a good restaurant, while across the bridge west of town on Arborétum utca, both the *Halászcsárda* and the *Ciprus Fogadó*, facing each other, have terraces looking onto the water. The *Kiszely Cukrászda* next to Tourinform serves coffee, cakes and ice cream.

The biggest events in the year are the **National Pastor Meeting and Piper Festival** held in Erzsébet liget in July, which brings together a lot of animals and music, and **Plum Day** (Szilvanap) in mid-September, when Fő tér is awash with *pálinka* and *szilvagombóc* (plum dumplings).

The Northern Plain beyond the Tisza

The **Northern Plain** has more to offer than the south, with **Hortobágy National Park**, the friendly city of **Debrecen** and picturesque villages around the headwaters of the River Tisza. In July and August, you can catch colourful **festivals** at Nagykálló, Hortobágy and Debrecen, while in September there's a carnival at Nyíregyháza. The region is also noted for its **pilgrimages**, and long history of religious fervour. Debrecen is the centre of Hungarian Protestantism, dubbed "the

Calvinist Rome", the village of Máriapócs is a focus for Greek Catholics and Roma believers, while the tomb of the "miracle rabbi" at Nagykálló is a vestige of the rich Hasidic culture that existed here before the Holocaust.

Szolnok

Sited at the confluence of the Zagyva and Tisza rivers, **SZOLNOK** has never been allowed to forget its importance as a bridgehead. Once the Mongols had stormed its castle in the thirteenth century, there was nothing to stop them riding on to Buda. In the last century, the town's seizure by the Red Army foretold its inexorable advance in 1944 and again in 1956, when it crushed the Uprising. Given this history, it's not surprising that most of Szolnok consists of unsightly postwar blocks, or that the population turned out to jeer the Soviets goodbye in 1990.

Arrival, information and accommodation

Szolnok's **bus station** is on Ady Endre utca, the street running parallel to the main thoroughfare, Baross Gábor út, and its **train station** is west of the city centre on Jubileumi tér (bus #24, #8, #7, #6 or #15). The city is sited along the main road and rail line from Budapest to Debrecen, and serves as a terminus for trains to Kiskunfélegyháza via Lakitelek, and a nexus for buses to Jászberény, Cegléd, Tiszafüred and other towns on the Plain.

There's **information** from the ever-helpful Tourinform, across from the bus station at Ságvári körút 4 (mid-June to mid-Sept Mon–Fri 8am–4pm, Sat & Sun 9am–5pm; mid-Sept to mid-June Mon–Thurs 8am–4pm, Fri 8am–3pm; ☎56/424-803, ✉szolnok-m@tourinform.hu).

There's a decent spread of **accommodation** in town, with the three best hotels located down near the banks of the Tisza. The *Tisza Hotel* at Verseghy park 2 (☎56/371-155, ⊛www.hoteltisza.hu; ⑥) is a wonderfully old-fashioned place with its own thermal bath and a fine patio overlooking the river, while, a little further along at Sóház út 4, the cracking *Hotel Sóház* (☎56/516-560, ⊛www .sohazhotel.hu; ⑤–⑥) has ultra-modern rooms equipped with a small kitchen area. Continuing west, at Mária utca 25, is the much pricier *Hozam Hotel* (☎56/510-530, ⊛www.hozamhotel.hu; ⑧), a plush four-star apartment hotel in a quiet, leafy street with off-street parking, pool and sauna. A more affordable alternative to these three is the *Pelikán Hotel*, slap-bang in the centre at Jászkürt út 1 (☎56/423-855; ④) – the ghastly-looking exterior actually conceals pleasantly refurbished rooms. Szolnok's **campsite** (☎56/424-403) is on Tiszaligeti sétány in the neglected resort area across the river (accessible by bus #15), where you'll also find the open-air **thermal baths**. Ibusz at Szapáry utca 24 (Mon–Fri 8am–5pm, Sat 9am–1pm; ☎56/423-602) handles **private rooms** (②).

The Town

Along the main axis through the centre, the **János Damjanich Museum** at Kossuth tér 4 (Tues–Sun 9am–5pm; 800Ft) bears the name of the general who trounced the Habsburg army just up the road in 1849. Of the four separate sections located within, two stand out: the archeological section, displaying some fabulous grave goods, including colourful beaded jewellery, statuettes and ceramic jugs and vases; while the no less impressive ethnographic section features some splendid folk art, such as regional peasant attire, viticultural and agricultural implements, and cottage furnishings, many of which are painted a striking "kunkék" blue, a colour peculiar to this region. The two remaining sections focus on nineteenth-century interiors and work by the Szolnok Artists' Colony, whose leading members were László Mednyánszky (1852–1919) and Adolf Fényes (1867–1945).

Heading south from the centre towards the banks of the Tisza, several Art Nouveau buildings on Szapáry utca presage Szolnok's former **synagogue** (Tues–Sun 9am–5pm), a magnificent creation by Lipót Baumhorn in the last years of the nineteenth century. Gutted during the war like so many others, it was turned into an art gallery in the 1960s, and retains some original features. On Templom út nearby stands a handsome Baroque Franciscan church (Belvárosi Nagytemplom), where **organ concerts** are held in August. Heading in the opposite direction along Sóház út you come to Szolnok's striking modern **theatre** in Tisza park.

With more time to kill, it's worth investigating the **Tabán district** beside the Zagyva, a twenty-minute walk east along the main street and off to the left. One of the oldest parts of Szolnok, it used to be a poor quarter of fishermen and bargees, but is now a quiet residential area. As a reminder of the past, one thatched house on the river side, at Tabán utca 24, has been preserved as a **Tájház** (May–Sept Thurs–Sun 1–5pm; 300Ft), with its interior as it would have looked in the 1930s, when fisherman Sándor Kovács and his family lived here; the adults slept on the bed and their six children on the dirt floor.

Eating, drinking and entertainment

For Hungarian **food**, the restaurant in the *Tisza Hotel* has a grand ambience and a riverside summer garden, while the fairly formal *Galéria*, at the end of Szapáry utca by the synagogue, offers arguably the best food in town. There's more atmosphere, however, at the *Caffé Alexander Pizzeria*, at Táncsics utca 15 opposite the theatre, and the lively *Bajnok* at Hősök tere 3. The *Irish Pub* at Szapáry utca 24 is a lively **drinking** place, and you can get coffee and cakes at the *Tünde Cukrászda*, housed in a building a few doors along with fine floral Art Nouveau decorations on its upper floors. One of the region's more intriguing festivals is the **Szolnok Goulash Festival** (gulyasfesztival) during the first or second weekend of September, when the town is taken over by food and wine to celebrate the nation's most famous dish.

Debrecen

Once upon a time, **DEBRECEN** was the site of Hungary's greatest livestock fair, and foreigners tended to be snooty about "this vast town of unsightly buildings". Even so, none denied the significance of Debrecen (pronounced "*Deb*-retzen"), both economically and as the fount of **Hungarian Calvinism**. From the sixteenth century onwards there wasn't a generation of lawyers, doctors or theologians that didn't include graduates from its Calvinist College. Indeed, Debrecen, which is the country's second most populous city (around 200,000), is still renowned for its university and teacher-training colleges.

There's plenty here to keep visitors entertained for a couple of days, with restaurants, pubs and nightlife as good as any on the Plain; moreover, the city hosts two major **festivals**, including a mega Flower Carnival. With decent public transport to the outlying towns and villages, and the completion of the M3 motorway to nearby Nyíregyháza, Debrecen also makes an ideal base for **excursions** to Hortobágy National Park and the Hajdúság and Nyírség regions.

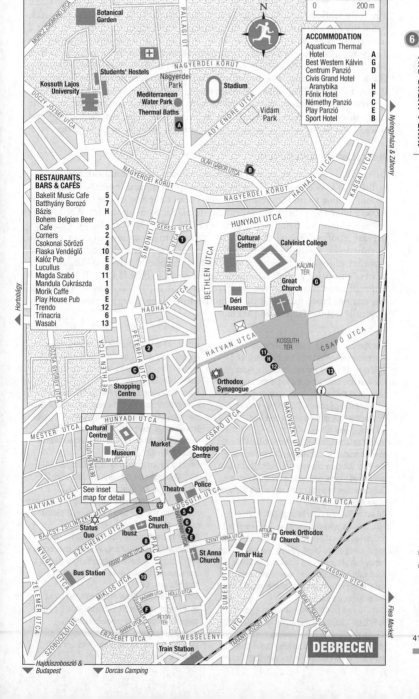

ACCOMMODATION
Aquaticum Thermal Hotel	A
Best Western Kálvin	G
Centrum Panzió	D
Civis Grand Hotel Aranybika	H
Fónix Hotel	F
Némethy Panzió	C
Play Panzió	E
Sport Hotel	B

0   200 m

N

RESTAURANTS, BARS & CAFÉS
Bakelit Music Cafe	5
Batthyány Borozó	7
Bázis	H
Bohem Belgian Beer Cafe	3
Corners	2
Csokonai Söröző	4
Flaska Vendéglő	10
Kalóz Pub	E
Lucullus	8
Magda Szabó	11
Mandula Cukrászda	1
Morik Caffe	9
Play House Pub	E
Trendo	12
Trinacria	6
Wasabi	13

Botanical Garden

Students' Hostels

Kossuth Lajos University

Nagyerdei Park

Mediterranean Water Park

Thermal Baths

Stadium

Vidám Park

PALLAGI ÚT

MÓRICZ ZSIGMOND UTCA

NAGYERDEI KÖRÚT

ADY ENDRE UTCA

DÓCZY JÓZSEF UTCA

OLÁH GÁBOR UTCA

NAGYERDEI KÖRÚT

NAGYERDEI KÖRÚT

HADHÁZI UTCA

KASSAI UTCA

HUNYADI UTCA

Cultural Centre

Calvinist College

KÁLVIN TÉR

Great Church

Déri Museum

KOSSUTH TÉR

Orthodox Synagogue

BETHLEN UTCA

SIMONYI ÚT

GERESI UTCA

EMBER P. UTCA

HATVAN UTCA

CSAPÓ UTCA

HADHÁZI UTCA

PÉTERFIA UTCA

Shopping Centre

HUNYADI UTCA

Cultural Centre

Museum

MÚZEUM UTCA

Market

Shopping Centre

See inset map for detail

BETHLEN UTCA

MÉSTER UTCA

DÓZSA GYÖRGY UTCA

HATVAN UTCA

BAJCSY-ZSILINSZKY UTCA

Status Quo

Ibusz

Small Church

Theatre

Police

KOSSUTH UTCA

BATTHYÁNY UTCA

FARAKTÁR UTCA

RÁKÓCZKY UTCA

CSAPÓ UTCA

SZÉCHENYI UTCA

PIAC UTCA

ARANY JÁNOS UTCA

St Anna Church

SZENT ANNA UTCA

ATTILA TÉR

Greek Orthodox Church

Timár Ház

NYUGATI UTCA

ZELEMER UTCA

MIKLÓS UTCA

SAGVARI UTCA

HOLLÓ UTCA

SUMEN UTCA

VÁGÓHÍD UTCA

Bus Station

PETŐFI TÉR

BARNA UTCA

ERZSÉBET UTCA

WESSELÉNYI UTCA

SZOBOSZLÓI ÚT

TARJÁN JÓZSEF UTCA

BUDAI ÉSAS UTCA

Train Station

DEBRECEN

Hajdúszoboszló & Budapest

Dorcas Camping

Flea Market

Hortobágy

Nyíregyháza & Záhony

Arrival and information

The **train station** is on Wesselényi tér, at the bottom of the main street Piac utca, while the **bus station** is west of the centre off Széchenyi utca, from where it's a ten-minute walk into the centre. There's stacks of **information** available from Tourinform at Piac utca 20 (mid-June to mid-Sept Mon–Fri 8am–8pm, Sat & Sun 9am–7pm; mid-Sept to mid-June Mon–Fri 9am–5pm; ☏52/412-250, ⓦwww.debrecen.hu). The helpful Mezon youth/student office and centre at Batthyány utca 2b (Mon–Fri 10am–6pm, Sat 10am–1pm; ☏52/415-498, ⓦwww.c3.hu/~mezon) can also assist with queries and accommodation. The **post office** is on Hatvan utca 5–9 (Mon–Fri 7am–7pm, Sat 8am–noon) and there's **internet access** at Datanet, Kossuth utca 8 (daily 8am–midnight).

Accommodation

Given the size of the city, Debrecen's choice of **accommodation** is not brilliant. It's wise to make reservations during the annual festivals, though you should be able to find something at short notice the rest of the time. Ibusz, at Révész tér 2 (May–Sept Mon–Fri 8am–6pm, Sat 8am–1pm; Oct–April Mon–Fri 8am–5pm, Sat 8am–noon; ☏52/415-555, ⓔi045@ibusz.hu), can arrange **private rooms** (❷) and flats (❹), in addition to accommodation in **college dormitories**, charging by the room, with places available on Friday and Saturday throughout the year and daily throughout July and August. The nearest **campsite** is the year-round *Dorcas camping* (☏52/541-119), some 6km south of town near Lake Vekeri, which has chalets (❷); take bus #26 from the bus station. Note that most of the hotels listed here charge a considerable fee (typically 1500–1800Ft) for parking.

Hotels and pensions

Aquaticum Thermal Hotel Nagyerdei park 1 ☏52/514-111, ⓦwww.aquaticum.hu. Plush four-star spa hotel attached to the thermal baths complex to the north of town; sparkling rooms with sofas, large plasma TVs and wi-fi. Guests receive free use of the thermal pool and swimming pool. ❽

Best Western Kálvin Kálvin tér 4 ☏52/418-522, ⓦwww.bestwestern.hu/kalvin. Clinical, business-like establishment opposite the Great Church, with good-sized rooms, each with a small kitchen area. Guests receive free use of the sauna and the pool at the Aranybika. ❼

Centrum Panzió Péterfia utca 37A ☏52/416-193, ⓦwww.panziocentrum.hu. Just one of a handful of decent pensions along this busy main street north of the Great Church. Homely, family-run place offering comfortable rooms, each with a little sink and microwave; ask for a room in the quieter building at the back. Breakfast costs extra. ❹

Civis Grand Hotel Aranybika Piac utca 11–15 ☏52/508-600, ⓦwww.civishotels.hu. Reputedly Hungary's oldest hotel, established in 1690 (though most of today's building dates from the early twentieth century), it has over 200 rooms, with those in the older wing far classier (and considerably more expensive) than those in the modern part of the hotel. Pool and sauna for guests. ❼–❾

Főnix Hotel Barna utca 17 ☏52/413-054, ⓔfonix@hnhotels.hu. Dirt-cheap option close to the train station that's really only worth it if you're looking to get away early; the rooms, with and without TV and bathroom, are old and somewhat decrepit. ❷–❸

Némethy Panzió Péterfia utca 50 ☏52/444-480, ⓔinfo@nemethypanzio.hu. Just across the road from the *Centrum Panzió*, this terrific-value pension has warm, pastel-coloured rooms with smart, modern furniture. Breakfast costs extra. ❹

Play Panzió Batthány utca 26 ☏52/411-252, ⓔpanzio@playpubhouse.hu. Pleasant guesthouse with a dozen modern but simply furnished rooms, and surprisingly quiet given that it's on the top floor of a pub. ❹

Sport Hotel Oláh Gábor utca 5 ☏52/514-444, ⓦwww.dbsporthotel.hu. Far better than the name suggests, this stylishly renovated hotel in Nagyerdei has large, well-equipped rooms; guests get one free entry to the sauna, solarium and excellent gym. ❼

The City

Arriving at the train station, your first impressions of the city – with its busy traffic and huddled masses – may make you want to get straight on the next train out. However, as you follow the old, much maligned **Piac utca** (Market Street) north up to spacious **Kossuth tér** and the Great Church, the place becomes more congenial and the buildings grander, and by the time you reach **Nagyerdei Park** and the university you'll find yourself in quiet leafy streets and another world completely.

Along Piac utca

Tram #1, running from the train station right through the centre of town to the baths and university, makes sightseeing a cinch (tickets 220Ft from the Bauhaus-style kiosk outside the station). Setting off from the station you pass the former **County Hall** at Piac utca 54, its facade crawling with Zsolnay pyrogranite statues of Haiduks (see p.417); an ornate corner house (no. 51) and the Romantic-style **Small Church**, whose bastion-like top replaced an onion dome that blew off during a storm in 1909 – hence its local name, the "Truncated church". The flesh-coloured Secessionist pile opposite, adorned with swan reliefs and statues of eagles (note, too, the gilded portal), was originally a savings bank rivalling the Gresham Building in Budapest for opulence. Debrecen's coat of arms, a phoenix arising from the ashes, appears on the **town hall** at no. 20, shortly before the road widens into the pedestrianized **Kossuth tér**.

Kossuth tér and around

Dominating Kossuth tér, the monumental **Great Church** (Nagytemplom; Mon–Fri 10am–4pm, Sat 9am–1pm, Sun noon–4pm; 400Ft) is an appropriately huge monument to the *Református* faith that swept through Hungary during the sixteenth century and still commands the allegiance of roughly one third of the population. Calvinism took root more strongly in Debrecen than elsewhere, as local Calvinists struck a deal with the Turks to ensure their security and forbade Catholics to settle here after 1552. In 1673, the Catholic Habsburgs deported 41 Calvinist priests (who ended up as galley slaves), but failed to shake the faith's hold on Debrecen. A reconciliation of sorts was achieved during the pope's visit in 1991, when he laid a wreath at their memorial. The church is a dignified Neoclassical building designed by Mihály Pollack. Its typically austere interior,

---

Witchcraft

The early Calvinists' hatred of popery was only exceeded by their animus towards pagan beliefs among the peasantry of the Great Plain, who regarded *táltos* (village wise men) with benevolence, while fearing *boszorkány*, their female counterparts. Until the eighteenth century, women accused of **witchcraft** were able to plead that they were beneficent *táltos* (for example Frau Bártha, who claimed to have learned *táltos* skills from her brother), but as the Calvinists' grip tightened this defence became untenable. Midwives were particularly vulnerable as it was popularly believed that the murder of a relative or newborn child was a prerequisite for acquiring their "magical" skills, but women in general suffered from the Calvinists' witch-hunting zeal, which also found scapegoats in herbalists, beggars and vagabonds.

Witch trials were finally banned by Maria Theresa in 1768 after some scandalous trials in Szeged when "witches" had confessions tortured out of them. By the nineteenth century the bloody deeds of Debrecen's forefathers were buried beneath platitudes eulogizing the "Calvinist Rome".

completely bare, accommodated the Diet of 1849 that declared Hungary's secession from the Habsburg Empire. The *Rákóczi-harang* – forged from cannons used in the Rákóczi War of Independence – is the largest **bell** in Hungary. From the tower you can get an excellent view of the city (same times; 300Ft).

Southwest of the church stands the **Grand Hotel Aranybika** (The Golden Bull), reputedly the oldest hotel in Hungary. Although its grandeur has faded somewhat, it's worth a peek inside to see the kitschy stained glass around the walls of the potentially magnificent glass-roofed restaurant. In front of the hotel is an exuberant 18-metre-wide glass and ceramic **fountain**, part of an effort to spruce up the square. Two days before its unveiling it was embroiled in controversy when a nymph representing the city of Debrecen was apparently stolen. It turned out that the council had removed it without consulting the artist, claiming that it was responding to popular outrage at the figure – though popular gossip has it that the figure offended the mayor's wife.

Around the back of the church on Kálvin tér stands the **Calvinist College** (Református Kollégium), where students were compelled to rise at 3am and be in bed by 9pm until the end of the eighteenth century. The college motto, inscribed over the entrance, is *orando et laborando* ("praying and working"). Though venerable in appearance, this is not the original college founded in 1538, but an enlarged nineteenth-century version. It was here that the Provisional National Assembly of left-wing and centre parties met under Soviet auspices late in 1944, unwittingly conferring legitimacy on the Soviet occupation. You can learn plenty about Calvinist Debrecen in the worthwhile **Calvinist College Museum** (Református Kollégium Múzeuma; Tues–Sat 10am–4pm, Sun 10am–1pm; 500Ft) located within the college. The first part of the museum offers a useful insight into the activities of those that lived and studied here, as well as a few items belonging to some of the college's most distinguished former members, such as Endre, Csokonai and Zsigmond. The second part is given over to the college's rich ecclesiastical history, comprising a sublime collection of goodies including Turkish embroidery, Renaissance-era communion jugs and vessels, and boat-shaped wooden grave markers particular to this region. There's also a beautiful painted ceiling panel from Mezőcsát, typical of the kind found in churches in villages and smaller market towns of the region. You can also view the **Library**, which keeps a splendid, and voluminous, collection of fifteenth- to eighteenth-century books, copper-engraved incunabula and hand-painted atlases.

The Déri Museum

The beguiling **Déri Museum** (Tues–Sun: April–Oct 10am–6pm; Nov–March 10am–4pm; 1000Ft) is fronted by statues by Ferenc Medgyessy that won a prize at the 1937 Paris Expo. Its superb ethnographic collection includes the richly embroidered shepherds' cloaks (*szűr*) which played a significant role in local courtship rituals. A herdsman would "forget" to remove his finest *szűr* from the porch when he left the house of the woman he was courting, and if it was taken inside within an hour a formal proposal could be made. Otherwise, the cloak was hung prominently on the veranda, giving rise to the expression *kitették a szűrét* ("his cloak was put out"), meaning to reject an unwanted suitor. Amongst the other must-see exhibits is a fine collection of agricultural and viticultural implements, and various items related to the many branches of industry prominent in Debrecen during the eighteenth century, the most important of which were tanners, boot-makers and furriers.

Unquestionably the museum's star turn, however, is a separate gallery containing painter **Mihály Munkácsy**'s monumental Christ trilogy. The three works, *Ecce Homo*, *Christ before Pilate* and *Golgota*, were reunited only a few years ago, but already there is a danger they will be split up again if desperate attempts to keep *Golgota* in the country come to nothing. *Ecce Homo*, an allegorical representation of good and evil, truth and falsehood, toured the world in the 1890s. Having viewed it in Dublin,

James Joyce commented: "It is a mistake to limit drama to the stage; a drama can be painted as well as sung or acted, and *Ecce Homo* is a drama." There's more artwork in the gallery of Old Masters, featuring sixteenth- to nineteenth-century paintings by some of Hungary's foremost artists, such as Kiss, Lotz and Paál.

Other sights in the centre

Given the focus on Calvinism, it's easy to overlook the existence of other faiths in Debrecen. Before the war there were over 9000 Jews (there are now around 1200) and eight synagogues, of which only two remain, in the backstreets west of Kossuth tér. The Eclectic-style **Orthodox Synagogue** on Pásti utca is so derelict that the Jewish community is negotiating with the council to turn it into a cultural centre. The nearby **Status Quo Synagogue** on Kápolnási utca, built to serve the Status Quo Jews in 1909, has been restored and may be visited by appointment (T 52/415-777). Its pale pastel decor and *bemah* are as austere as a Calvinist church, unlike the rich interiors of the synagogues of Szeged and Budapest.

If ecclesiastical architecture is your thing, consider tracking down **St Anna's Church**, a couple of blocks east of Piac utca, which is Catholic and Baroque and originally belonged to the Piarist order. Peek inside to view the fanciful Rococo decor and medallion-shaped ceiling frescoes representing venerable saints from the Árpád dynasty. Above the portal you can discern the coat of arms of its founder, Cardinal Csáky. The street on which it stands was previously called Béke útja (Avenue of Peace), which raised a mordant chuckle amongst the townsfolk, as it leads to a slaughterhouse beyond the **Greek Orthodox Church** on Attila tér. Built in 1910, this, too, has some impressive frescoes, depicting the bombing of the city in 1914. Just before you reach the church, on the right at Nagy Gál István utca 6, is the **Tanner's House** (Timár Ház; Tues–Fri 10am–5pm, Sat 10am–4pm; 400Ft), a small crafts centre where pottery, basketweaving and other skills are on display – you can buy the finished product.

Nagyerdei Park and Kossuth Lajos University

North of Kálvin tér the city turns greener and quieter, with stylish residences lining the roads to **Nagyerdei Park**. In the western section you'll find the **thermal baths** (daily: April–Oct 8am–8pm; Nov–March 8am–6pm; 1400Ft 1–8pm and at weekends, 950Ft 8am–1pm), an indoor complex fed by springs of sulphurous "brown water" (bárna-víz) rising up from beneath the park. The large dome just behind the baths is the **Mediterranean Water Park** (Mon–Thurs 11am–9pm, Fri–Sun 10am–10pm; 2200Ft for 2hr, 15Ft every min thereafter), a vast water complex with dozens of chutes, slides and jets. Elsewhere you may notice hemp growing wild; the plants are so low in THC that they're not worth smoking, but the local *táltos* have been known to boil bushels in cauldrons, to some effect.

Beyond the reedy lake and wooden footbridge rises the columned bulk of **Kossuth Lajos University**, fronted by fountains where newlyweds pose for photos. The university's **Hungarian language courses** in mid-January, late May and mid-July draw students from all over the world (T 52/489-117, W www.nyariegyetem.hu). Beyond the campus lies a **Botanical Garden** (daily April–Oct 8am–6pm; Nov–March 8am–4pm; 500Ft).

Eating, drinking and entertainment

Debrecen has a tight concentration of distinguished **restaurants**, though most tend to stick to Hungarian standards. There are plenty of convivial **cafés** around town and, thanks to a large student and local population, the city does well for **nightlife**, with many little bolt holes in and around Kossuth tér and Piac utca.

Though the great bi-monthly fairs no longer take place, Debrecen's pungent **fruit and vegetable market** (vásárcsarnok), next to the supermarket on Csapó utca (Mon–Sat 4am–3pm, Sun 4–11am), is awash with kerchiefed grannies hawking pickles, meat, soft cheese and strange herbs, the air filled with smells and Magyar interrogatives ("*Hogy a… ?*" is slang for "how much is the… ?").

Restaurants

Bohem Belgian Beer Café Piac utca 29. Simple, pub-style place serving pricey, but tasty, well-cooked and nicely presented Belgian specialities, and the draught beer is the best in town.

Corners Péterfia utca 61. Convivial, bright-red and orange cellar restaurant serving pizza, pasta, noodles, breakfasts and brunches; there's also a great daily menu (Napi menu; 11am–3pm) for 800Ft.

Csokonai Söröző Kossuth utca 21. Romantic cellar establishment with wall lamps and candle-topped tables, offering an upscale take on Hungarian favourites, in addition to a range of appealing generic dishes like lamb with rosemary, trout in soy sauce, and roasted spare ribs.

Flaska Vendéglő Miklós utca 4. Warm and homely basement restaurant decked out in peasant-style decor, serving inexpensive regional specialities such as Palóc soup, Hortobágy pancakes, stuffed cabbage and steamed lamb with pasta.

Lucullus Etterem Piac utca 41. The Medieval-themed interior is a bit over the top, but the food is genuinely first-class – fish, game and grilled meats, alongside the best veggie options in town.

Trendo Piac utca 11–15. Thoroughly modern and cool place adjoining the *Hotel Aranybika*, dishing up the likes of grilled aubergine, green mussels and creamy pastas, as well as some appetizing desserts.

Trinacria Batthyány utca 4. Colourful, trattoria-style joint harbouring a labyrinthine cellar (non-smokers can eat upstairs) offering exceptionally good pizza and pasta dishes, plus a good sideline in steaks.

Wasabi Piac utca 18. Stylish, all-you-can-eat wok and sushi restaurant. The restaurant itself – a cool brick-walled interior with white leather seating, ceiling drapes and smooth orange lighting – looks fantastic.

Drinking and nightlife

There are several very enjoyable **cafés** spotted around town, none more so than *Magda Szabó*, an elegant little coffee house next door to the *Hotel Aranybika* named after the famous Hungarian author; in summer, its wood-decked terrace is a terrific spot for people-watching. Down at Miklós utca 1, *Morik Caffé* is a gorgeous mock eighteenth-century café with oil lamps adorning the tables, while *Mandula Cukrászda*, somewhat awkwardly located at Ember Pál utca 6 up towards Nagyerdei Park, has superb cakes and ices.

For **drinking**, the coolest place is *Bázis* in the old casino inside the *Hotel Aranybika*, a hip bar with a varied programme of club and party nights, DJs and live music (Tues, Fri & Sat only). After 10pm the entrance is from the terrace around the side of the hotel on Bajcsy Zsilinszky utca. Three reliable drinking spots on Batthyány utca include the *Play House Pub* and *Kalóz Pub*, both at no. 24, and the *Batthyány Borozó*, a smaller cellar den at no. 14. Up around the corner, next to the *Csokonai* restaurant, the *Bakelit Music Café* is a loud and smoky dive that's invariably crammed. The *Klinika Mozi* at Nagyerdei körút 98 hosts **concerts** and raves with visiting DJs, as does the *El Tornádó* at Pallagi út 2 which attracts foreign students. The *Lovarda*, out at Kassai út 24, is another popular bar which also hosts regular concerts.

Festivals and events

Debrecen endeavours to dispel its austere image with several big events. In late March, the **Spring Festival** (Tavaszi Fesztivál) of music and drama coincides with events in Budapest, though Debrecen claims to have originated the custom. In early July, the week-long **Bartók International Choir Competition**, held in odd-numbered years, alternates with the biennial **International Military Bands** festival.

There's a riot of colour in mid-August for the week-long **Carnival of Flowers** (Virágkarnevál), which culminates in a superb parade on August 20 when some thirty floats laden with flowers, bands and operatically dressed soldiers trundle north from Petőfi tér, along Kossuth utca and round towards the stadium by the university (the route can change). People hang from windows en route, cheer wildly when the band plays tunes from *István a király* (*Stephen the King* – a patriotic rock opera) and surge behind the last float to the stadium, where the show continues into the late afternoon. In the evening there's a **fireworks** display outside the Great Church. The four-day **Jazz Festival** (Jazznapok) at the beginning of September is Hungary's principal such festival, featuring top Hungarian musicians and some big-name foreign acts. Finally, the **Autumn Festival** in October has classical music concerts, films and theatrical performances as the key events.

There's often something worth watching at the **Csokonai Theatre** on Kossuth utca, an exotic-looking Moorish structure named after the locally born poet, Mihály Csokonai Vitez (1773–1805); meanwhile the city's excellent **puppet theatre** (Vojtina Bábszinház) at Kalvin tér 13 has plenty to keep kids happy.

The Hajdúság

The **Hajdúság** region around Debrecen takes its name from the **Haiduk** communities who occupied eight derelict villages here during the early seventeenth century. Originally Balkan cattle drovers-cum-bandits who fought as mercenaries against the Turks, they were unfettered by feudal servitude and infamous for their ferocity and bisexuality. Their ranks were swollen by runaway serfs and homeless peasants, and they formed a guerrilla army, led by István Bocskai, which turned against the Habsburgs in the winter of 1604–5. After Bocskai achieved his ambition to be Prince of Transylvania, the Haiduk were pensioned off with land to avert further disturbance. The result was a string of settlements with names prefixed *Hajdú-*, where the Haiduk farmed, enjoyed the status of "nobles" (*natio*) and, if necessary, were mustered to fight. Chief amongst these settlements is **Hajdúszoboszló**, a rapidly expanding spa resort, which also features one of the country's largest water theme parks and a sprinkling of small museums.

Hajdúszoboszló

A spa since 1927, **HAJDÚSZOBOSZLÓ** gets about one and a half million visitors – the majority of them Poles and Germans – each year, far more than anywhere else in the Hajdúság. Surveying the wallowing, guzzling crowds in the steaming brown waters of the **Hungarospa thermal baths** (daily 7am–7pm; 1200Ft, 800Ft after 4pm), located in the Szent István Park east of town near the bus station, you might try the old Haiduk war cry, *Huj, huj, hajrá!*, to clear some space before jumping in yourself. Inside the massive pool complex is the **Aquapark** (June–Aug daily 9am–7pm; May & Sept Sat & Sun 10am–4pm; 2800Ft, 1900Ft after 4pm), containing the largest water slide in Hungary, with six chutes arranged round a twelve-metre tower. Away from the baths, things are more relaxed, with tennis courts for hire in the park, and cafés and quaint old buildings around Hősök tere, guarded by a comically fierce statue of Bocskai.

Twenty metres of **fortress wall**, part of the fifteenth-century defences, lurk behind the inevitable Calvinist church on Hősök tere. Around the corner at Bocskai utca 12, the **Bocskai Museum** (Tues–Sun 9am–1pm & 2–4pm; 150Ft) exhibits photos of nineteenth-century Haiduk villagers, and assorted military relics –

among them Bocskai's embroidered silk banner, given pride of place alongside the town's charter. Another building at no. 21 houses a folklore and ethnographic display, and there are temporary exhibitions at no. 11 (400Ft for all three museums).

Practicalities

Buses #1, #4 and #6 run from the **train station**, 2km southeast of town, into the centre, terminating at the **bus station** near the baths. Most things are on or just off the main street, Szilfákalja út, which is also Route 4 between Budapest and Debrecen. There's **information** at Tourinform, next to the Aqua Park entrance (mid-June to mid-Sept Mon–Fri 8am–6pm, Sat & Sun 9am–2pm; mid-Sept to mid-June Mon–Fri 9am–5pm, Sat 9am–noon; ☎52/558-928, ✉hajduszoboszlo@tourinform.hu).

Spa tourism is big business in Hajdúszoboszló, as the huge number of **hotels** testifies, particularly along Mátyás király sétány, the street leading away from the baths. At the top end of the scale is the *Hotel Silver* (☎52/363-811, ⓦwww .hotelsilver.hu; ❻) at no. 25, and the *Aqua Sol* right next to the baths (☎52/273-310, ⓦwww.hunguesthotels.com; ❾), both with their own thermal spas. Cheaper, less glamorous, options by the baths include the *Start Panzió* at József Attila utca 22 (☎52/365-981; ❹) and the *Admirális Panzió*, across Debreceni út at Hőforrás utca 2 (☎52/364-198; ❹). Back in the centre of town, on Hősök tere, is the modern and friendly *Puskás Panzió* (☎52/362-158, ✉puskaspanzio@enternet.hu; ❹). The *Hajdú* **campsite** beside Debreceni út (☎52/557-851; May–Sept) also has two- to six-bed chalets (❸–❺); guests receive discounted tickets to the spa. The most enjoyable **place to eat**, and preferable to the cluster of touristy places by the baths, is the rustically themed *Kemencés Csárda*, a five-minute walk from the baths at Szilfákalja út 40.

Hortobágy National Park

Petőfi compared the **Hortobágy puszta** of the central Plain to "the sea, boundless and green". In his day, this "glorious steppe" resounded to the pounding hooves of countless horses and cattle being driven from well to waterhole by mounted *csikósok* (horse-herds) and *gulyások* (cowboys), while Racka sheep grazed under the

---

Bird-watching and other wildlife

The Hortobágyi-halastó lakes (head 6km west of Hortobágy village and turn right) are great for **bird-watching** – especially storks, buzzards, mallards, cranes, terns and curlews – with lodgings at the lakeside *Öregtavi Vendégház* (☎52/589-321; ❹), bookable through Tourinform. The *Hortobágy Club Hotel* in Mata (see p.420) also arranges bird-watching excursions (15,000Ft per person for 4hr). Most trains stop at the Halastó halt, the next station west of Hortobágy. Elsewhere in the park, little ringed plovers, stone curlews and pratincoles favour dry sheep-runs, while red-footed falcons behave unusually for their species, forming loose groups in abandoned rooks' nests. Millions of migratory birds pass through in spring and autumn – the thousands of cranes that fill the skies in late September make an incredible sight and sound. There's less to see at the bird reservation southwest of Nagyiván, although large colonies of storks nest in the villages of Nagyiván and Tiszacsege till the end of August.

Wild **mammals** can be found all over the park – boars near Kecskéses in marshy thickets, otters at Árkus and by the canals and fishponds, ground squirrels near Kónya in the northern grasslands, and roe deer in the reeds, meadows and copses between Óhat and Tiszaszőlős.

surveillance of Puli dogs. Medieval tales of cities in the clouds and nineteenth-century accounts of phantom woods, or the "extensive lake half enveloped in grey mist" which fooled John Paget, testify to the occurrence of **mirages** during the hot, dry Hortobágy summers. Caused by the diffusion of light when layers of humid air at differing temperatures meet, these *délibáb* sporadically appear at certain locations – for example north of Máta, south of Kónya, and along the road between Cserepes and the *Kis-Hortobágyi Csárda*.

Over the ages tribes have raised burial mounds (*kurgán*), some dating back 4000–5000 years. One of them served as the site of a duel between Frau Bártha of Debrecen and two rival *táltos*. Nowadays, the grasslands have receded and mirages are the closest that Hortobágy gets to witchcraft, but the classic *puszta* landscape can still pass for Big Sky country, its low horizons casting every copse and hillock into high relief. Now a UNESCO World Heritage Site, the 730-square-kilometre **Hortobágy National Park** is a living heritage museum, with roaming animals and cowboys demonstrating their skills.

Hortobágy village and around

The park's main settlement, situated 35km from Debrecen en route to Tiszafüred, is **HORTOBÁGY** village. Approaching from Tiszafüred, you'll enter the village via the lovely **nine-arched stone bridge**, depicted in a famous painting by Tivadar Csontváry. Beyond here stands the much-restored **Great Inn** (Nagycsárda), or *Hortobágyi Csárda*, a rambling thatched edifice dating from 1871 that's now a touristy restaurant (see p.420). Across the road you'll find the **Herdsmen's Museum** (Pástormúzeum; daily: May–Sept 9am–6pm, April & Oct 10am–4pm, March & Nov 10am–2pm; 500Ft), whose embroidered *szűr* (cloaks), carved powder horns and other objects were fashioned by plainsmen to while away solitary hours. A few paces away, the thatched, circular **Körszín** building (same times; free) holds an exhibition on local craftsmen; between May and October, **craftsmen's workshops** (saddlers, potters, coppersmiths and the like) are held in the visitor centre (see p.420), which you can watch and participate in for free.

Across the bridge from the village and 800m down to the left, the **Hortobágy Rare Breeds Park** (Pusztai Állatpark; daily: March to mid-Nov 9am–6pm; mid-Nov to Jan 9am–4pm; 500Ft) is devoted to the distinctive breeds of the Great Plain: hairy Mangalica pigs, corkscrew-horned Racka sheep, grey horned cattle, water buffalo and kuvasz sheepdogs, with information on each in English. The park offers several excellent **nature trails** (also known as demonstration areas), for which you will need a **visitor pass** (1000Ft per day, 1800Ft per week), available from the visitor centre. Guided tours of the demonstration areas are also possible, though you should call at least two days in advance.

You can witness equestrian displays and go riding in horse-drawn carriages in the **Szálkahalom nature reserve** 7km to the east, which is more secluded, and in the *Hortobágy Club Hotel* at **Máta**, a large tourist development tacked onto the Máta stud farm. Both have displays from April till October, while the Rare Breeds Park also has displays in July and August – you can get information and tickets (2000Ft for 90min) for all programmes from the visitor centre.

The summer's main events are the **Village Days** (Falunap) at the end of May, an excuse for folk music and dancing, a craft fair and general merriment; the **International Horsemen Festival** (Nemzetközi Lovasnapok) on the first weekend of July, held in Máta; and – the biggest event of the year – the annual **Bridge Fair** (Hortobágyi Hídivásár) between August 20–23, a Magyar rodeo occasioning the sale of leatherwork, knives and roast beef, which is staged by the bridge near Hortobágy.

Practicalities

A succession of small tourist inns gives advance notice of the park to drivers approaching via the Debrecen–Füzesabony road, but **getting there** by train offers a subtler transition from farmland to *puszta*. Services from Debrecen (towards Tiszafüred and Füzesabony) are better than trains from Nyíregyháza, which leave you stranded at Óhat-Pusztakócs, several kilometres west of Hortobágy village. During summer there might even be a "nostalgia" steam train from Debrecen. Buses, calling at Hortobágy en route between Eger and Hajdúszoboszló (or direct from the latter during high season), are another option. Although cycling is the best way of getting around, some of the sites are within walking distance of train halts along the Debrecen–Tiszafüred, Tiszafüred–Karcag and Nyíregyháza–Óhat-Pusztakócs lines. **Bike rental** (2000Ft per day) is available from the *Hortobágy Club Hotel* (see below) – though you've got to get there first – or you can get the addresses of locals renting bikes from the visitor centre.

Most amenities are concentrated at the western end of Hortobágy village, at the centre of which is the excellent **Hortobágy National Park Visitor Centre** (July & Aug Mon–Fri 8am–5pm, Sat & Sun 10am–5pm; May, June, Sept & Oct Mon–Fri 8am–4pm, Sat & Sun 10am–4pm; Nov–April Mon–Fri 8am–4pm; ☎52/589-321, ⓦwww.hnp.hu), which can supply all sorts of **information** about the park, including details on **permits** and **programmes**. In the same building is a small, but very informative, **exhibition** (free) on the park's flora and fauna.

Accommodation is largely restricted to locals offering **private rooms** (❷), of which there are many – the visitor centre has a list. Other options include the very basic *Hortobágy Fogadó*, just behind the visitor centre at Kossuth utca 1 (☎52/369-137; ❸), and the *Pásztortanya Vendégfogadó* 5km west of the village by the main road (☎52/369-127, ⓔj.melko@t-online.hu; ❷), which has a good restaurant. Considerably more upmarket, the *Hortobágy Club Hotel* in Máta (☎52/369-020, ⓦwww.hortobagyhotel.hu; ❼) is a lavish resort complex with its own swimming pool, fitness centre, tennis courts and **riding school** – the room rate includes everything but the riding. The *Puszta* **campsite** is located just down the river bank from the Herdsmen's Museum (☎52/369-300; May–Oct). Despite its obvious tourist trappings, the *Hortobágyi Csárda*, across from the visitor centre, has some excellent local specialities, such as guinea fowl soup, Mangalica pork and kettle goulash.

Lake Tisza

Created by damming the upper reaches of the river, **Lake Tisza** has become an important centre for tourism, though it's nowhere near as developed as Lake Balaton – its very charm for many visitors. It has three main areas: the southern end around Kisköre and Abádszalók, where motorboats are permitted; the middle section around Tiszafüred, which is reserved for ecotourism and is slightly quieter, with fishing and bird-watching, swimming and canoeing (motorboats are banned here); and the area north of Route 33, which is a nature reserve with restricted access. If you plan to spend any length of time exploring the environs of the lake, then you might consider buying the 1:35,000 *Tisza-Tó* map, available from Tourinform.

Tiszafüred

Thirty-four kilometres west of Hortobágy, the faceless town of **TISZAFÜRED** is the largest of the Lake Tisza resorts, and a transport junction between the Plain and the Northern Uplands. From the bus and train stations, it's a fifteen-minute

▲ Bird-watching hut at Lake Tisza

walk up Vasút út and Baross utca to Kossuth tér and the main through street, Főút. The only "sights" are the **Kiss Pál Museum** on Tariczky sétány near Kossuth tér (Tues–Sat 9am–noon & 1–5pm; 260Ft), where fishing features prominently in the local history display; and the **Pottery House** (Fazekasház; Tues–Sun 9am–noon & 1–5pm; free) towards the bottom of Főút at Malom utca 12; turn right down Igari utca opposite the Calvinist church. The real lure, however, is swimming and sunbathing, either in a backwater of the Tisza twenty minutes' walk down Ady Endre út towards the lake, where you can rent canoes, or on the river itself at Tiszaörvény, accessible by regular buses from Tiszafüred. There are also **thermal baths** (daily: April–Oct 8am–7pm; Nov–March 9am–5pm; 650Ft), a few minutes' walk up Fürd őút from Tourinform.

Tourinform, at Fürd őút 21, south of Kossuth tér along the Debrecen road (mid-June to Aug Mon–Fri 8am–8pm, Sat & Sun 10am–7pm; Sept to mid-June Mon–Fri 8am–4pm; ☎59/511-123, ⓔtiszafured@tourinform.hu), can furnish you with all the **information** you might need on the lake and surrounding areas. The **post office** is at Fő út 20 (Mon–Fri 8am–5pm, Sat 8–11am). Ibusz, in the centre at Főút 30 (Mon–Fri 9am–5pm, Sat 9am–noon; ☎59/511-005), can supply **private rooms**, though it's advisable to book ahead in high season.

The town's outstanding **accommodation** is the *Tisza Balneum Thermal Hotel*, a lakeshore spa complex 200m north of Tourinform at Húszöles út 27 (☎59/886-200, ⓦwww.balneum.hu; ❾); as well as beautifully conceived rooms, with furnishings crafted from local materials, its stunning pools (free to guests; 3500Ft per day to non-guests) are far superior to the thermal baths in town (see above). It also possesses a fabulous **restaurant** with a summer terrace overlooking the lake, in addition to having **bikes** and **kayaks** for rent (both 600Ft per hr, 3500Ft per day).

There are several colourful pensions in town too, including the restful *Aurum Panzió*, a short walk south of Tourinform at Ady Endre út 29 (☎59/351-338; ❹); the delightful, thatched-roofed *Nádas Panzió*, 200m further south at Kismuhi utca 2 (☎59/511-401, ⓦwww.nadaspanzio.hu; ❹), which has cool, beautifully furnished rooms; and, 3km west of town in Tiszaörvény, the pleasant *Hableány Hotel* at Hunyadi utca 2 (☎59/353-333, ⓔhableanyhotel@dunaweb.hu; April–Dec; ❾), which also offers fishing and boat rental. Tiszafüred has several **campsites** (all open April–Oct), including *Tóparti Kemping* (☎59/351-606) and *Fortuna Camping* (☎59/352-835), both down by the lake, and *Termál Camping* opposite Tourinform on Fürdő út (☎59/352-911; cabins ④).

Szabolcs-Szatmár-Bereg county

North of Debrecen, the Plain ripples with low ridges of wind-blown sand, anchored by birches, apple groves and tobacco fields. The soft landscape of the *Nyírség* (Birch Region) makes a pleasant introduction to **Szabolcs-Szatmár-Bereg**, an area scorned by many Magyars as the "black country", mainly a disparaging reference to the region's large Roma population. More densely settled than other parts of the Plain, Szabolcs would be wholly agricultural if not for industrialized Nyíregyháza, straddling the main routes to the Northern Uplands, the Erdőhát villages and Ukraine. Historically isolated by swamps, and then severed from Transylvania and Ruthenia in 1920, the region has remained poor and backward in comparison with the rest of Hungary and was badly hit by recession in the 1990s, with unemployment levels in this region up to five times higher than in Budapest.

If your interest in **rural life** is limited, stick to **Nyíregyháza**, with its Village Museum, or **Nyírbátor**, with its striking churches – both conveying something of the character of the region. For anyone seeking the challenge of remote areas, encounters with rural Roma, or the folk customs and architecture of old Hungary, though, the county has much to offer, particularly in the **Erdőhat** region. Though sufficient accommodation and transport exists to make independent travel feasible, the only **tourist offices** are in Nyíregyháza and Vásárosnamény, both of which can supply information on the whole region, including private accommodation.

Nyíregyháza

NYÍREGYHÁZA grew into the "Big Apple" of Szabolcs county thanks to the food-processing industry developed to feed the Soviet market during the 1960s and 1970s, and the collapse of this market has hit the region badly. The town itself (population 125,000) has a surprisingly attractive core of pedestrianized squares and old buildings which have recently been smartened up, with an attractive garden suburb, **Sóstófürdő**, to the north. The best time to come is the first Saturday in September, when a **carnival** inaugurates the month-long Nyírség autumn arts festival.

Arrival and information

Arriving at the **bus or train station** on Petőfi tér, 1km south of the centre, you can catch bus #8 or #8A downtown, riding on to Sóstófürdő at the end of the line if you prefer. It is also accessible by a narrow-gauge line from Nyíregyháza's main station, the Balsa-Dombrád line. Most other buses leave from Jókai tér, in the centre. Tourinform, at Országzászló tér 6 (Mon–Fri 9am–5pm; ☎42/504-647, ⓦwww.tourinform.szabolcs.net), can supply **information** on both the town and the county as a whole. During the summer there's also a branch in the old water tower in Sóstófürdő (mid-June to Sept Mon–Fri 9am–6pm, Sat & Sun 10am–4pm; ☎42/411-193, ⓔsostofurdo@tourinform.hu). The **post office** is at Bethlen Gábor utca 4 (Mon–Fri 7am–7pm, Sat 8am–noon).

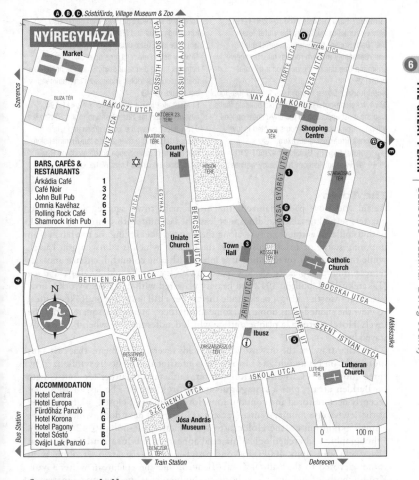

Ⓐ, Ⓑ, Ⓒ, *Sóstófürdő, Village Museum & Zoo* ▲

NYÍREGYHÁZA

Market

BARS, CAFÉS & RESTAURANTS

Árkádia Café	**1**
Café Noir	**3**
John Bull Pub	**2**
Omnia Kavéhaz	**6**
Rolling Rock Café	**5**
Shamrock Irish Pub	**4**

ACCOMMODATION

Hotel Centrál	**D**
Hotel Europa	**F**
Fürdőház Panzió	**A**
Hotel Korona	**G**
Hotel Pagony	**E**
Hotel Sóstó	**B**
Svájci Lak Panzió	**C**

0 ————— 100 m

Accommodation

There's a limited supply of **accommodation** in Nyíregyháza itself, so you might prefer to find a place out in Sóstófürdő where there are more restful alternatives. In July and August and at weekends throughout the year, you can get beds (2500Ft) or double rooms (❸) in the *Hotel Sandra*, a college 3km from the centre of town at Sóstó út 31/b (☎42/505-400, Ⓔinfo@hotelsandra.hu). There are a couple of **campsites** in Sóstófürdő; *Sóstó Camping* (☎42/500-692; May–Sept), attached to the hotel and hostel of the same name at Sóstói utca 76, also has four-bed bungalows (❸); and *Igrice Camping*, by the lake at Blaha Lujza sétány 43 (☎42/479-711; mid-May to Sept), which offers both fancy and humbler chalets (❷-❻). Tourinform has a list of **private rooms** (❷).

Hotel Centrál Nyár utca 2–4 ☎42/411-330, Ⓦwww.centralhotel.hu. Quirkily designed building close to the centre, with tidy but quite small and rather lifeless rooms, all with wi-fi. Pool, jacuzzi and sauna. ❻

Hotel Europa Hunyadi utca 2 ☎42/508-670, Ⓔinfo@europahotel.hu. Business-like hotel that's hardly sparkling with character, but the rooms are decent enough and it's fairly priced. ❹

Fürdőház Panzió Sóstófürdő ☎ 42/411-191, ⓦ www.furdohaz.hu. Up by the water tower, the "Bath House" has warm, comfortable, and reasonably modern rooms; guests receive unlimited free use of the pension's thermal baths. ❻

Hotel Korona Dózsa György utca 1 ☎ 42/409-300, ⓦ www.korona-hotel.hu. A grand old building that's also the most appealing of the city-centre options, offering large, modernish rooms painted in lovely lilac tones. Breakfast costs extra. ❻

Hotel Pagony Ujmajor ☎ 42/501-210, ⓦ www.hotelpagony.hu. Classy wellness hotel 2km northeast of town, with gorgeously furnished rooms and first-rate spa facilities. ❹

Hotel Sóstó Sóstói utca 76 ☎ 42/500-692, ⓦ www.hotelsosto.hu. Large hotel and camping complex in the centre of Sóstófürdő; the hostel-like rooms (doubles, triples and quads) are rudimentary but cheap. ❸–❹

Svájci Lak Panzió Sóstófürdő ☎ 42/411-194, ⓦ www.sostort.hu. Sister pension to the *Fürdőház*, a few paces away, the lovely green and white "Swiss Chalet" is a charismatic ten-room pension that boasts of having once accommodated Gyula Krudy and the singer Lujza Blaha. ❻

The Town

Relaid and now pedestrianized, the broad main town square, **Kossuth tér**, quarters several notable buildings, not least the late nineteenth-century **town hall**, with its pillared entrance, spread along the western side. Facing the town hall is an imposing statue of Lajos Kossuth, on the back of which is a broken gun barrel, while the pavement surrounding it is inlaid with nine colourful, circular mosaics representing the planets. A few paces away stands the old **Savings Palace** (Takarékpalota), built in 1912 and heavily plastered with fine stucco work – now a bank, it's worth taking a peek inside the cashier's hall (entrance on Rákóczi utca) to view the stained-glass dome and some more stucco. Across the square stands the lovely **Hotel Korona**, a plaque outside which denotes the date when Béla Bartók stayed here.

A further trawl of the downtown area yields several monuments that cast a bit more light on Nyíregyháza's history. Its confessional diversity is symbolized by three **churches** – Catholic on Kossuth tér, Lutheran on Luther tér, and Uniate on Bethlen utca – plus a **synagogue** at Mártirok tere 6. The last of these has recently been restored and contains some lovely murals; if closed, ask for the key at the Jewish community centre (Izraelita Hitközség) next door, which also has a small exhibition on the Holocaust (Mon–Thurs 9am–noon; ☎ 42/417-939). Ethnographic and archeological material appears in the **Jósa András Museum** (Tues–Sun 9am–4pm; 400Ft), beyond pastel-hued Országzászló tér, along with rooms devoted to the painter Gyula Benczúr and the epicurean writer Gyula Krúdy, both of whom were born in Nyíregyháza in the mid-nineteenth century. However, the most cosmopolitan place in town is the "**Comecon Market**" on Rákóczi út (not to be confused with the regular daily market on Búza tér nearer the centre), where Ukrainians, Magyars, Poles and Romanians barter and sell everything from fur hats to cars.

Sóstófürdő and the Village Museum

Nyíregyháza's chief attraction is the leafy resort of **Sóstófürdő** ("Salty Lake Bath"), 7km north of the city. Buses and trains bring you to the striking *Krudy Hotel*, from where the Village Museum is a short walk to the left, and the various baths over to the right. Just behind the *Fürdőház Panzió*, the **Aquarius Aquapark** (Mon–Fri 10am–8pm, Sat & Sun 9am–8pm; 1400Ft) is a vast complex of adventure pools and thermal baths, while the *Fürdőház Panzió* (see above) has its own year-round indoor thermal baths (Mon–Fri 2–9pm, Sat & Sun 10am–9pm; 2400Ft). Lastly, the outdoor **thermal baths** (Parkfürdő; mid-May to mid-Sept daily 9am–7pm; 1200Ft) lie a couple of hundred metres up Blaha Lujza sétány in the northernmost part of the resort.

The resort's other main draw is the outdoor **Village Museum** (Műzeumfalu; April–Oct Tues–Sun 9am–5pm; Nov–March, you can only see the exterior of the buildings; 600Ft). This *Skanzen* represents architecture from five different ethnographic regions within the county, complete with Roma dwellings set firmly at the end of the village, a form of segregation that still exists today. With clothes hanging on the washing line, tables laid and boots by the hearth, the farmsteads appear to have been abandoned by their occupants only yesterday, leaving mute testimony to their lives in a nineteenth-century Szabolcs village. In this world, the size of the barns and stables denoted a family's wealth, as did the presence of a Beam Gate opening onto the street: "A gate on a hinge, the dog is big, the farmer is great", runs an old proverb. Other clues to social standing are the knick-knacks beloved of the "sandled nobility" or petty gentry, and the placing of a bench between two windows in Orthodox households. A single communal bowl speaks volumes about life in the poorest dwellings, but it's worth buying the excellent guidebook (1200Ft), in English, to learn more. If you fancy some refreshments, there's a typical *kocsma* (pub) in the centre of the museum. If animals are your thing, the town **zoo** (daily 9am–7pm; 1600Ft), 300m down from the Village Museum, is one of the largest, and better ones, in Hungary.

Eating and drinking

Decent culinary possibilities in Nyíregyháza are desperately few and far between. The most reliable **restaurant** is the one in the *Hotel Central*, while the *Rolling Rock Café* at Luther tér 5 serves up steaks, grilled meats and the like, and also doubles as the town's liveliest bar. Although it may not immediately appeal, the very British-looking *John Bull Pub*, attached to the *Hotel Korona* at Dózsa György utca 1–3, actually has pretty decent food and a good selection of beers. Alternative **drinking** spots are the *Shamrock Irish Pub* on Korányi Frigyes utca, which also keeps a decent range of beers, while the *Sense Music Club*, at Bethlen Gábor utca 24, has regular concerts and visiting DJs. For coffee, try the *Árkádia Café* at Dózsa György utca 5; *Café Noir* next to the town hall at Kossuth tér 1; or the *Netcafé* attached to the *Europa Hotel*, which also has **internet access**.

Nagykálló and Máriapócs

"Go to **NAGYKÁLLÓ**!" used to be a popular insult east of the Tisza, referring to the large mental asylum in this small town of converging houses painted a flaky ochre. The asylum still stands at one end of the long main square, Fő tér, but such visitors as the town receives come for quite different reasons. The big attraction is the annual *Művészeti Tábor*, a **festival of Hungarian folk arts** held in a weird "barn" shaped like a Viking's helmet, amid a cluster of other buildings designed by Imre Makovecz, 2km north of the centre. The event occurs in late June and lasts about ten days; you can obtain the exact dates from Tourinform in Nyíregyháza or Vásárosnamény.

For Hasidic Jews, however, Nagykálló is a cradle of the Satmar sect, one of the largest in the diaspora (see box, p.426). Two reminders of Nagykálló's once sizeable Jewish population can be found on Nagybalkáni út, running off the other end of Fő tér from the asylum. A plaque at the top of the street on the right indicates the former Jewish school, while the Jewish cemetery 200m further down harbours the **tomb of Rabbi Isaac Taub**, one of the most revered of the Hungarian Hasidic rabbis, who was called "the miracle rabbi" and credited with writing the plaintive folk tune *Szól a kakás már* ("The cock has crowed"). Hundreds of pilgrims come in early spring (7th of Adar by the Jewish calendar) to ask for his help. To get the key to his shrine (in the red and yellow building

The Satmar Hasids

The pilgrims who come and pray at Rabbi Taub's tomb are members of the **Satmar sect**, which originated in the town of Satu Mare (Szatmár in Hungarian) in what is now Romania. Like the better-known Lubavitchers, the Satmars follow **Hasidism**, a form of Judaism founded by Jewish mystics in southern Poland in the mid-eighteenth century as a movement of spiritual renewal. Their ecstatic worship and emphasis on song and dance as an expression of joy, their strict laws on dress, diet and everyday life, and their use of Yiddish appealed to the poor village communities of Jews, and the movement won millions of adherents in Poland, Romania, Hungary and the Ukraine.

It was only because so many Hasids emigrated to the US, Canada, Britain and Australia between the 1890s and 1930s that Hasidism survives today. In Central and Eastern Europe, the distinctively dressed Yiddish-speaking Hasid communities were easy targets for the Fascists, and there was little opposition to the Holocaust from local Gentiles. With frightening ease a whole way of life was cleaned out of the region, leaving only vandalized synagogues and cemeteries. In Hungary ninety percent of provincial Jews perished, whereas about half of the Jews of Budapest survived (few of whom were Hasids). The traditions of the old country are now preserved by the descendants of emigrants, who now return to visit the tombs of the great rabbis in Nagykálló, Bodrogkeresztúr and Sátoraljaújhely.

behind the wall), try ringing Gábor Blajer (☏30/224-7349) and someone will bring the key to the grave.

MÁRIAPÓCS, off the road between Nagykálló and Nyírbátor, is a place of pilgrimage for the Orthodox and Catholic faithful, and especially for the Roma. Its **Orthodox Church** contains an icon of the Virgin that has been seen to shed tears since 1696 – though this is a replica of the original, which is now in Venice. The beautiful (though incomplete) iconostasis features some thirty icons representing scenes from the Old and New Testaments. Now that old identities are reasserting themselves across the Carpathians, Máriapócs has become a spiritual focus for ethnic Magyars and Uniate Christians in Romania, Slovakia, Ukraine and the Voivodina – in 1991, 200,000 worshippers from all round the region attended an open-air papal Mass here. **Pilgrimages** occur on August 15 (the Feast of the Assumption), and the Saturday closest to September 8, which is particularly holy to Roma. The train station is at least 3km from the village, making buses a better bet.

Nyírbátor and around

The tangled history of Trans-Carpathia has also left its mark on **NYÍRBÁTOR**, a small, sleepy town whose name recalls the **Báthori family**, a Transylvanian dynasty which veered between psychopathic sadism and enlightened tolerance. Both attributes are subtly manifest in Nyírbátor's two churches, which were equally funded by the Báthoris in an age when religious strife was the norm. The churches are a superb venue for **concerts** of choral and chamber music from mid-July to early September, the high point being the **Music Days** in August.

The Town

Sited on a grassy hillock above Báthori utca, the **Calvinist Church** was originally founded as a Catholic church in the 1480s, complete with a fourteen-seat pew that's now in the National Museum in Budapest. At the back of its web-vaulted Gothic nave lies the **tomb of István Báthori**, whose sleeping figure indicates that he died in bed, but reveals nothing of the character of this

Transylvanian Prince. Hungarian history judges him a shrewd ruler, forgiving his machinations against the Transylvanian Saxons, and the bouts of orgiastic cruelty for which István atoned by endowing churches. Scholars are less willing, however, to dismiss the tales about his cousin, the "Blood Countess" Báthori. It's possible that she, too, is buried here, as her body was reputedly removed from Aachtice after relatives of her victims protested, and it might well have been reburied in the Báthori crypt at Nyírbátor.

When the church turned *Református* in the late sixteenth century, it was obliged to erect a freestanding **wooden bell-tower**, since only Catholic churches were permitted stone belfries during the Counter-Reformation. From its wide-skirted base, the tower rises to a defiant height of 30m, with a spire like a wizard's hat sprouting four mini-towers known as *fiatorony* ("sons of the tower"), symbolizing a civic authority's right to execute criminals. Its hand-cut shingling and oak-pegged joists and beams can be inspected from the crooked stairway up to the balcony and bell chamber.

István Báthori's other legacy to Nyírbátor is located on Károlyi Mihály utca, and signposted from the main square. Paid for by the spoils of war against the Turks (who, perhaps appropriately, gutted it in 1587), the **Minorite Church** contains fantastic Baroque woodcarvings from Eperjes in Slovakia. The altars swarm with figures wearing disquieting expressions, suggestive of István's soul but actually commissioned by János Krucsay around 1730. To gain admission, ring at the side door marked *plébánia csengője*, which leads to an exhibition of photos of ancient Szabolcs churches.

Next door you'll find the **Báthori Museum** (April–Oct Tues–Sun 9am–5pm; Nov–March Mon–Fri 8am–4pm; 500Ft), where various relics with unintelligible captions trace the history of the dynasty, whose estates included most of Szatmár. Though predominantly inhabited by Hungarians, this region was bisected as a result of the Treaty of Trianon, which allotted the provincial capital (now Satu Mare) and its surroundings to Romania. Relations have been awkward, if not hostile, ever since, which partly explains the small number of border crossings in these parts.

Practicalities

Arriving at the **bus and train stations** on Ady Endre utca, it's a fifteen-minute walk down Kossuth utca to the main square, Szabadság tér. **Accommodation** in Nyírbátor boils down to the colourful and engaging *Hotel Hódi*, in a beautiful old town house just off Szabadság tér at Báthory utca 11 (☎42/283-556, ⓦwww .hotelhodi.com; ❺); the silly-looking, faux-castle like *Bástya Hotel* at Hunyadi utca 10, south of the main square (☎42/281-657, ⓔbastya2@t-online.hu; ❹); and the rudimentary *Napsugár Panzió*, by the turning towards the Minorite Church at Zrinyi Ilona út 15 (☎42/283-878; ❹). The small *Holdfény Camping* is on Széna tér (☎42/281-494; May–Aug).

The best **meals** can be had at the restaurant in the *Hotel Hódi*, or there's the agreeable and cheap *Kakukk* at Szabadság tér 21, and the *Csekő* pizzeria and patisserie, 300m west of the *Napsugár Panzió* at Bajcsy-Zsilinszky út 62. There's an outdoor **market** on the corner of Váci and Fürst utcas.

Mátészalka, Nagyecsed and Vaja

A shabby fusion of flaking estates and low yellow houses, **MÁTÉSZALKA**'s main claim to fame is that it's the birthplace of the parents of the actor **Tony Curtis**. It was also the first town in provincial Hungary to be lit by electricity – though as the carts, woodcarvings and ceramics in the **Szatmár Museum**, ten minutes' walk east of Hősök tere at Kossuth út 5 (Tues–Fri 8am–4pm, Sat & Sun 10am–3pm; 400Ft) attest, its urbanity was merely a veneer on what was, and still is, an extended village. More impressive is the outdoor display of carriages, carts and sledges – some 100 in all, making it one of the largest such collections in Europe. Back along the same street at no. 30 stands Mátészalka's old **synagogue**, now restored but still closed, a sad reminder of the now minute Jewish population of the town.

The museum and synagogue can be found by turning right off Bajcsy-Zsilinszky utca, leading east off the main square, Hősök tere, which is ten minutes' walk from the bus and train stations. If you need **to stay**, try either the *Bianco Panzió*, a five-minute walk from the stations at Kölcsey utca 27 (☎44/502-628, ⓔbianco27@freemail.hu; ❸), or the Swiss-chalet-style *Kristály Panzió*, a ten-minute walk northeast of Hősök tere at Eötvös utca 17 (☎44/312-036, ⓔkristalypanzio@gmail.com; ❹) – the *Bianco* also has a reasonable **restaurant**. More likely, though, you'll want **transport** to somewhere else. There are regular buses to Nagyecsed and Vaja (see below), and both buses (12 on weekdays, 6 at weekends) and trains (3–4 daily) to Csenger and Fehérgyarmat in the Erdőhát region. Other slow trains (5 daily) run up to Vásárosnamény and Záhony, and across the border to Carei in Romania.

The small town of **NAGYECSED**, 15km south, deserves a mention as the birthplace of the **"Blood Countess" Báthori**, the most notorious of the Báthori clan (see p.282). In the 1560s Ecsed was a palatial Renaissance court surrounded by mires and quicksands, where the family's ancestor Vid Báthori reputedly slew a dragon (hence the Báthori coat of arms, a dragon coiled around three dragon's teeth). It was here that Erzsébet Báthori spent her childhood till she was sent to marry Ferenc Nádasdy at Sárvár. Alas for sensation-seekers, nothing remains of the palace but a few stones.

A tangible relic of the past is the splendidly restored **fortified manor** (Vaj-kastély; April–Oct Tues–Sun 10am–6pm; Nov–March Mon–Fri 8am–4pm; 500Ft) 14km northwest of Mátészalka in **VAJA**, the feudal seat of Ádám Vaj, an early supporter of Rákóczi's campaign against the Habsburgs. Once within the thick-set walls, and having donned a pair of felt slippers, there's plenty to see, including lots of painted furniture – trousseau chests, inlaid tables and carved wardrobes – portraits of the Vaj dynasty, the grand meeting hall (the *Rákóczi-terem*), and an exhibition on the Hungarian War of Independence. There's simple **accommodation** in the neighbouring Gate building, for which you should call in advance (☎44/385-297; ❶).

The Erdőhát

The **Erdőhát** is Hungary's most isolated region, a state imposed by nature and confirmed by history. Meandering and flooding over centuries, the headwaters of the Tisza and its tributaries carved out scores of enclaves beneath the flanks of the Subcarpathians, where dense oak forests provided acorns for pig-rearing and ample timber for building. Though invaders were generally deterred by the Escedi Swamp and similar obstacles, scattered communities maintained contact with one another through their intricate knowledge of local tracks and waterways. When the borders came down like shutters in the twentieth century, people were suddenly restricted to three tightly controlled frontier crossings into the Ukraine, which have been only partially relaxed since the demise of Communism.

If you're interested in rural customs and architecture that's almost extinct elsewhere in Hungary, the Erdőhát **villages** are well worth the effort. Although neither is particularly enticing, the two small towns of Fehérgyarmat and Vásárosnamény serve as jumping-off points for the region, while public

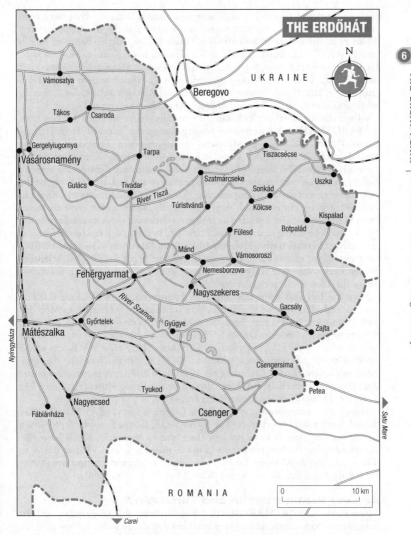

transport links are surprisingly good in these parts, with fairly frequent bus services on weekdays.

Fehérgyarmat and Vásárosnamény

Much of the southern Erdőhát is accessible from **FEHÉRGYARMAT**, a small, rather nondescript town whose main street is one long park. The train station is ten minutes' walk south of the centre, while the bus station is at the foot of the main street along Móricz Zsigmond út. Its only sights are a Calvinist church with a fine **medieval tower** topped by a superb Transylvanian wooden spire, and, 300m beyond here at Vörösmarty utca 1, the **Szatmár–Bereg National Conservation Museum** (Mon–Fri 9am–2pm; free), with a collection of paintings and photos of the local flora and fauna. The only **accommodation** is the utterly grotty *Hotel Szamos* (℡44/362-211; ❷) next to the bus station and the *Szarkafészek Panzió* 400m away at Rákóczi utca 40 (℡44/362-300; ❷), so you'd do better staying in one of the villages. **Buses** fan out to Tivadar (Mon–Fri 7 daily, Sat 3, Sun 1), Gyügye (Mon–Fri 8 daily, Sat 4, Sun 1), Tűristvándi & Szatmárcseke (Mon–Fri 7 daily, Sat 3), Tiszacéscse (Mon–Fri 5 daily, Sat 2), Vásárosnamény (Mon–Fri 5 daily, Sat 3, Sun 1) and Csenger & Csengersima (Mon–Fri 3 daily, Sat 2, Sun 1), while **trains** to Zajta (2–3 daily) can drop you at Nagyszekeres or Gacsály.

Villages in the northern Erdőhát are generally easier to reach by bus from **VÁSÁROSNAMÉNY**, an erstwhile trading post on the "salt road" from Transylvania. The excellent **Beregi Museum**, in the renovated Tomcsányi Castle at Szabadság tér 26 (April–Oct Tues–Fri 8.30am–4.30pm, Sat & Sun 8am–4pm; Nov–March Mon–Fri 8am–4pm; 400Ft), sheds fascinating light on the region's history, with colourful displays of local embroidery and folk art (look out for the exquisitely carved sticks used for spinning, known as *Guzsaly*), a room devoted to Erdőhát funerary customs, and, most impressively, some superb cast-iron stoves from Munkachevo; you'll need to wear slippers over your shoes, available from the box by the door saying *papucs kötelező*. Elsewhere in town, you can have a splash at the **Szliva Thermal Baths** (Mon–Fri 10am–9pm, Sat & Sun 9am–8pm; 1000Ft), back out on the road towards Tákos on Beregszászi ut, or the seasonal **Atlantika Water Park** (May–Aug daily 9am–6.30pm; 2000Ft), a bit further beyond, just across the Tisza in Gergelyiugornya.

From the **bus and train stations**, it's a twenty-minute walk along Rákóczi utca to Szabadság tér and the Tourinform office at no. 9 (June–Aug Mon–Fri 9am–5pm, Sat 9am–1pm; Sept–May Mon–Fri 8am–4pm; ℡45/570-206, ✉vasarosnameny@tourinform.hu). There are three **hotels** in town, by far the best of which is the tidy and good-value *Winkler Ház Panzió* at Rákóczi utca 5 (℡45/470-945, ⊛www.winklerhaz.hu; ❹). The alternatives are the grey *Marianna Center Hotel* at Szabadság tér 19 (℡45/470-401, ✉marianc@enternet .hu; ❸) and the similarly dull *Feher Hotel*, near the Bereg Museum at Bereg köz 1–4 (℡45/471-073, ⊛www.hotelfeher.hu; ❹).

There's also a **campsite** across the Tisza in Gergelyiugornya (℡45/371-076; May to mid-Sept), a small resort whose holiday homes are all raised on stilts as protection against flooding; hourly buses run here from June to August 25. The *Winkler Ház Panzió* easily has the best **restaurant** in town. **Buses** run from Vásárosnamény to Tákos and Csaroda (Mon–Fri 8 daily, Sat & Sun 3), Fehérgyarmat and Tarpa (Mon–Fri 6 daily, Sat & Sun 3), and Nyiregyháza (Mon–Fri 7 daily, Sat 3).

Around Szatmárcseke and Túristvándi

The cemetery at **SZATMÁRCSEKE**, 20km northeast of Fehérgyarmat, contains a number of boat-shaped oaken **grave markers** (*kopjafa*), probably representing the ships that were supposed to transport the souls of the dead to the other world in ancient Finno-Ugric mythology. Beside the entrance is a map indicating Hungarian populations around the world, while nearby is the mausoleum of **Ferenc Kölcsey**, born locally in 1790, who penned the words to Hungary's national anthem. Between April and October, visitors can **stay** at the *Kölcsey Fogadó*, Honvéd utca 6 (℡44/377-868; ❷), which has a **restaurant** attached.

A few kilometres to the south, **TÚRISTVÁNDI** has a picturesque **wooden watermill** (daily 8am–6pm; 250Ft), whose workings are demonstrated should a group of tourists materialize. The key to the mill is kept at the house on the corner, across the main road.

Other fine examples of wooden architecture used to grace Nemesborzova, Vámosoroszi and Botpálad, until they were removed to Szentendre's Village

Museum in the 1970s. However, **TISZACSÉCSE** retains the thatched cottage (Tues–Sun 10am–6pm; 300Ft) where the novelist and critic **Zsigmond Móricz** was born in 1879, and also affords fine views across the plain towards the Carpathian mountains.

The southern Erdőhát

The southern Erdőhát is notable for its beautiful churches, folksy adaptations of Gothic or Baroque architecture. Slow trains bound for Zajta can drop you off at **NAGYSZEKERES** or **GACSÁLY**, whose churches feature striking wooden **bell-towers**. The tiny **church** in **GYÜGYE** has a coffered ceiling decorated with astrological symbols (illuminated in turn by a sunbeam during the course of the year, so the priest says), but it has been closed for repair for a while, and no one knows when it will open again. If you want to take the chance, Gyügye is easily reached by bus from Fehérgyarmat, or you can walk there in an hour from Nagyszekeres.

Committed church buffs might also visit **CSENGER**, where the **Catholic Church** dates from the Middle Ages. Built of red and black brick, it similarly features a superb coffered ceiling with folk Baroque paintings; ask at the parish office next door for the key if it is closed. Csenger used to be in the centre of Szatmár county until the 1920 Trianon Treaty put a border between the village and the old county seat, now Satu Mare in Romania. The road and the railway now end abruptly, and the place is served by a branch line down from Mátészalka; the last train back leaves at 6.30pm. By rights, Csenger should be a dead-end sort of village, but a few years ago the town's mayor started a local revival by calling in the architect Imre Makovecz and giving him a free hand with a sweep of land in the centre; today the school, church, sports hall, library and numerous other buildings all display the distinctive Makovecz exuberance. Csenger's history is captured in the enchanting **Local History Museum** opposite the church at Hősök tere 3 (Helytörténeti Múzeum; Tues–Sun 9am–5pm; 400Ft), a very personal collection of the museum director, which re-creates a typical room of a wealthy peasant household using his grandparents' furniture and photographs; don't miss the wooden ice skates. Should you need **accommodation**, there's the *Barcsay Panzió* at Hősök tere 11 (T 44/341-335; ❷) and there are also camping facilities in the museum's garden.

Although **CSENGERSIMA**, a few kilometres north, has been designated a 24-hour **crossing into Romania** – it also happens to be one of the least crowded – the Romanian officials at Petea may refuse to admit travellers after dark. There are five **buses** daily (1 on Sun) between Csengersima and Fehérgyarmat, but none across the border.

North of the Tisza

Another clutch of villages lies north of the Tisza, in the region known as *Bereg*. While some are only accessible from Vásárosnamény, others, such as Csaroda and Tákos, can also be reached from Fehérgyarmat.

Nine kilometres east of Vásárosnamény, **TÁKOS** harbours a tiny wattle-and-daub **Protestant church** (200Ft), dubbed the "bare-footed Notre Dame". Entranced via an exquisite thick-set wooden porch, and not much bigger than the size of a house, the church's quaint interior features bold floral designs on its gallery, pews and walls and a coffered ceiling painted by Ferenc Asztalos in 1766. As in most village churches, the men sit up front and the women at the back. The church is usually closed, but you can get the key from the lady living at Bajcsy-Zsilinszky utca 29, 200m down the road; she might also be able to help with **accommodation**. She herself needed it in the big floods of 2001, which severely damaged her house and threatened to cause lasting damage to the church too.

One of the oldest, and loveliest, churches in the region lies 2km to the east in **CSARODA**. Sited on a small rise, and surrounded by trees and thatched cottages, the shingled, thirteenth-century **Gothic Church** was originally built as a Catholic church in the eleventh century, and later decorated with frescoes of various "smiling saints", although not all of them look very cheerful. In 1552 the building was turned into a Calvinist church, and red and blue floral designs similar to those found on shepherds' cloaks were added. These were later painted over, remaining hidden from view until the 1960s when, so the story goes, restorers brought them back to life by covering them overnight with raw minced meat. Nearby stands a shingled wooden belfry dating from 1855. In theory the church is open from 10am to 6pm daily (200Ft), but if it's closed, you can get the key from Alkotmány utca 13. If you want to **stay** here, the *Székely Panzió*, close to the church at József Attila utca 54 (☏45/484-830; ❸), is a lovely three-room guesthouse – two rooms with a shared bathroom and the other en suite.

The restorers have also been at work in **TARPA**, some 10km to the southeast, where a large horizontal "dry" **mill** (száraz-malom) with an intricate conical roof stands amongst the cottages on Árpád utca. It can only usually be viewed from the outside, but if you wish to enter properly, call ☏70/319-7188. The **Protestant church**, a short walk away at Kossuth utca 13, retains some interesting features, notably some recently discovered frescoes on the north wall (including one of St George and the Dragon), and the original six-hundred-year-old wooden door, carved from a single piece of wood. There's **accommodation** here at the pleasant *Pálma Panzió* (☏45/488-124; ❷), in the centre of the village at Kossuth utca 25, and the *Kuruc Vendéglő* (☏45/488-121; ❷) immediately next door, where you can also get a decent lunch. Another formidable-looking **wooden bell-tower** can be found in **VÁMOSATYA**, 8km northwest of Csaroda.

Around Kisvárda and Záhony

The fruit-growing area northeast of Nyíregyháza is called the *Rétköz* (Meadow Land) or *Tiszakanyár* (Tisza Bend). Though pretty to drive through, there is little

Into the Ukraine

Obtaining **Ukrainian visas** is an uncertain business, best done at the Ukrainian Embassy in Budapest or elsewhere – leave several days for the process – and *not* at the border. The **road crossing** is a narrow bridge, easily found by following the traffic, but notorious for robberies and car thefts. Even customs at Chop on the Ukrainian side may be out to extort cash or confiscate desirable items. The reason for this becomes apparent once you enter Trans-Carpathia, the mountainous region traditionally known as **Ruthenia**, control of which has passed from Hungary to Czechoslovakia to the USSR to the Ukraine within the last eighty years. This forgotten corner of Central Europe is as poor and backward as Albania, with a tradition of emigration that took Andy Warhol and Robert Maxwell to their adoptive countries. Its ethnic mix includes Hungarians, Slovaks, Roma and Romanians, not to mention a large number of Ruthenians (*Rusyns*), who cling to their Uniate faith.

The main road and rail line run through **Uzhgorod** (also a border crossing into Slovakia), known as **Ungvár** to its Hungarian-speaking inhabitants. Another road heads east to **Mukachevo** (*Munkács*), the site of a last-ditch battle against the Habsburgs during the Kuruc War. From here, the road continues across the mountains towards the Ukrainian city of Lvov, via the **Verecke Pass** through which Árpád led the Magyar tribes into the Carpathian Basin.

to attract visitors beyond Kisvárda, midway along the road and train line to Záhony, the only border crossing into Ukraine.

Kisvárda
KISVÁRDA is a backwater **spa** with a **ruined castle** used for staging plays in the summer. The **theatre festival** in early June (Határontúli Magyar Színházak Fesztiválja), for Hungarian minorities living in the neighbouring countries and further afield, attracts some very good companies. Despite being undamaged in the war, a random selection of buildings along the main street has been replaced by ugly modern structures, spoiling the look of Fő utca, which leads to the main square. Just off Fő tér at Csillag utca 5 stands an old **synagogue** with an ornamental ceiling and stained-glass windows, housing the **Rétköz Museum** of local history (April–Sept Tues–Sun 9am–noon & 1–4pm; 300Ft). For **accommodation** there is the *Bástya Panzió* at Krucsay Marton út 2, in the centre of town (☎45/421-100; ❷), with en-suite bathrooms.

Záhony and Zsurk
ZÁHONY is the "front line" between relatively prosperous, westernized Hungary and the impoverished masses of the former Soviet Union. When travel restrictions were eased in 1990, people flooded in from Ukraine and Russia to trade goods for foodstuffs at the **"free" market** on the edge of town, until controls were reimposed the following year. Since then, spivs and dealers from Hungary and Poland drive across the border to do business in Uzhgorod, using Záhony as a base. Unless you relish hobnobbing with such characters, however, the only reason to come here is another picturesque **church** with a wooden belfry, in the nearby village of **ZSURK**.

Should either prospect appeal, it's possible to stay at the *Európa Panzió* at Ady Endre út 4, near the station in Záhony (☎45/425-835; ❷). There are **trains** from here down to Nyíregyháza and Debrecen, but you are not allowed to board international expresses running in either direction.

Travel details

Trains

Baja to: Bátaszék (12 daily; 20min); Budapest (2 daily; 4hr); Kiskunhalas (8 daily; 2hr).
Békéscsaba to: Budapest (every 1–2hr; 3hr); Szeged (11 daily; 2hr).
Debrecen to: Budapest (hourly; 2hr 30min–3hr 30min); Hortobágy (9 daily; 1hr); Mátészalka (8 daily; 1hr 20min); Nyírbátor (8 daily; 1hr); Nyíregyháza (every 30–45min; 30–45min).
Kalocsa to: Kiskőrös (4 daily; 1hr).
Kecskemét to: Budapest (10 daily; 1hr 30min); Bugac (3 daily; 1hr); Kiskunfélegyháza (every 1–2hr; 20min); Szeged (12 daily; 1–2hr).
Kiskőrös to: Kalocsa (4 daily; 1hr).
Kiskunfélegyháza to: Budapest (10 daily; 1hr 45min); Kecskemét (every 1–2hr; 20min); Szeged (every 1–2hr; 45min–1hr).
Kiskunhalas to: Baja (8 daily; 1hr 30min).
Mátészalka to: Csenger (5 daily; 1hr); Vásárosnamény (6 daily; 30min); Záhony (6 daily; 1hr 30min).
Nyírbátor to: Záhony (5 daily; 45min).
Nyíregyháza to: Budapest (every 1–2hr; 3hr–3hr 30min); Debrecen (every 30–45min; 30–45min); Mátészalka (8 daily; 1hr 15min); Nagykálló (8 daily; 15min); Nyírbátor (7 daily; 1hr).
Szeged to: Békéscsaba (11 daily; 2hr); Budapest (10 daily; 1–2hr); Hódmezővásárhely (12 daily; 30–45min); Kiskunfélegyháza (every 30–45min; 45min–1hr).

Buses

Baja to: Budapest (10 daily; 3hr 15min); Hajos (4 Mon–Fri; 40min); Kalocsa (hourly; 1hr); Kecskemét (8 daily; 2hr 40min); Kiskőrös (6 daily;

1hr 15min); Mohács (10 daily; 40min); Pécs
(10 daily; 2hr); Szeged (every 1–2hr; 2hr 15min);
Szekszárd (10 daily; 40min).

Békéscsaba to: Budapest (3 daily; 4hr); Debrecen
(9 daily; 3hr); Eger (2 daily; 5hr); Gyula (every
30–60min; 1hr); Kecskemét (5 daily; 2hr 30min);
Miskolc (1 daily; 5hr); Pécs (1 daily; 6hr 30min);
Szeged (8 daily; 1hr 45min).

Debrecen to: Békéscsaba (10 daily; 3hr 30min);
Eger (7 daily; 3hr); Gyula (3 daily; 3hr);
Hajdúszoboszló (every 30–40min; 45min);
Hortobágy (6 daily; 1hr); Miskolc (every 30–90min;
2hr); Nyíregyháza (5 daily; 1hr); Szeged (3 daily;
5hr); Tiszafüred (6 daily; 1hr 45min); Tokaj
(2 daily; 1hr 30min).

Gyula to: Békéscsaba (every 30min–1hr; 1hr);
Debrecen (3 daily; 2hr); Mako (6 daily; 2hr);
Mezohegyes (4 daily; 1hr 30min); Szarvas (Mon–Fri
6 daily; 1hr 15min); Szeged (6 daily; 2hr).

Hajdúszoboszló to: Debrecen (hourly; 45min);
Eger (1 daily; 3hr 15min); Hajdúböszörmény
(2 daily; 1hr); Miskolc (5 daily; 2hr 45min).

Hódmezővásárhely to: Békéscsaba (8 daily; 1hr
20min); Csongrad (8 daily; 45min); Kecskemét
(4 daily; 1hr 45min); Kiskunfélegyháza (5 daily;
1hr 15min); Mako (1–2hr; 45min); Mártely (every
60–90min; 20min); Szeged (every 40min–1hr;
30min).

Hortobágy to: Debrecen (5 daily; 1hr); Eger
(1 daily; 2hr 15min); Hajdúszoboszló (1 daily;
1hr 15min); Tiszafüred (5 daily; 1hr).

Kalocsa to Baja (every 40min–1hr 30min; 1hr);
Budapest (10 daily; 2hr 30min); Hajos (Mon–Fri

9 daily, Sat & Sun 4 daily; 30min); Szeged (4 daily;
2hr 30min); Székesfehérvár (2 daily; 3hr);
Szekszárd (6 daily; 1hr).

Kecskemét to: Budapest (every 1hr–1hr 30min;
1hr 45min); Bugac (Mon–Fri 5 daily, Sat & Sun
2 daily; 45min); Dunafoldvár (8 daily; 1hr 10min);
Eger (3 daily; 4hr); Gyöngyös (4 daily; 3hr);
Jászberény (7 daily; 2hr); Kiskőrös (Mon–Fri 10
daily, Sat & Sun 4 daily; 1hr); Kiskunfélegyháza
(every 40min–1hr; 45min); Szeged (8 daily; 1hr
30min).

Kiskunfélegyháza to: Bugac (Mon–Fri 9 daily,
Sat & Sun 4 daily; 30min); Kecskemét (hourly;
45min); Kiskunhalas (5 daily; 1hr 20min); Szeged
(9 daily; 1hr).

Nyírbátor to: Máriapócs (7 daily; 25min);
Máteszalka (2 daily; 30min); Nagykálló (4 daily;
40min); Nyíregyháza (Mon–Fri 4 daily; 1hr).

Nyíregyháza to: Debrecen (5 daily, 3 at weekends;
1hr); Miskolc (3 daily except Sun; 2hr); Szeged
(2 weekly; 6hr); Tokaj (2 daily; 1hr 15min).

Szeged to: Baja (8 daily; 2hr 15min); Békéscsaba
(7 daily; 2hr); Budapest (7 daily; 3hr); Debrecen
(2 daily; 5hr); Gyula (5 daily; 2hr);
Hódmezővásárhely (hourly; 1hr 30min); Kecskemét
(10 daily; 1hr 30min); Őpusztaszer (10 daily;
45min); Pécs (7 daily; 3hr 15min); Tiszafüred
(2 daily; 5hr).

Szolnok to: Eger (3 daily; 2hr 30min); Tiszafüred
(6 daily; 1hr 30min).

Tiszafüred to: Debrecen (7 daily; 1hr 45min);
Hodmezővásárhely (2 daily; 4hr 30min); Miskolc
(Mon–Fri 3 daily; 1hr 30min); Szeged (2 daily; 5hr).

Contexts

Contexts

History

The region of the Carpathian basin known as Hungary (Magyarország) changed hands many times before the Magyars arrived here at the end of the ninth century, and its history is marked by migrations, invasions and drastic changes, as Asia and Europe have clashed and blended. Over the centuries, borders have shifted considerably, so geographical limits as well as historical epochs are somewhat arbitrary. Transylvania, an integral part of Hungary for hundreds of years, was lost to Romania in 1920, and the plight of its Magyar minority remains a contentious issue, while the situation of ethnic Hungarians in Serbia and Slovakia is also a cause for national concern.

Prehistory

Although recorded history of the area now covered by Hungary begins with the arrival of the Romans, archeological evidence of **Stone Age** (30,000–8000 BC) humans has been found in the Istállóskő and Pilisszántó caves in northern Hungary, suggesting that the earliest inhabitants lived by gathering fruit and hunting reindeer and mammoths. The end of the Ice Age created favourable conditions for the development of agriculture and the domestication of animals, which spread up through the Balkans in the Neolithic era, and was characteristic of the **Kőrös culture** (5500–3400 BC): clans living alongside the River Tisza, herding sheep and goats and worshipping fertility goddesses. As humans became more settled and spread into Transdanubia, evidence survives of mounds (*tell*) full of artefacts, apparently leading towards the rise of the **Lengyel culture** around Lake Balaton.

During the Bronze Age (2000–800 BC), warlike tribes arrived from the Balkans and steppes, introducing cattle and horses. Subsequent migrants brought new technology – iron came with the Cimmerians, and the Asiatic Scythians (500–250 BC) brought the potter's wheel and manufactured goods from Greek traders on the Black Sea coast – while the Celts, who superseded them in the early third century BC, introduced glassblowing and left mournful sculptures and superb jewellery (most notably the gold treasures of Szárazd-Regöly), before being subdued by the Romans.

The Romans

The **Roman conquest** was initiated by Augustus at the beginning of the Christian era, primarily to create a buffer zone in **Pannonia** between the empire and the barbarians to the east. By the middle of the first century AD, Roman rule extended throughout Transdanubia, from the Sava to the Danube; fortified with castra, the river formed the limes or military frontier. Trade, administration and culture grew up around the garrison towns and spread along the roads constructed to link the imperial heartland with the far-flung colonies in Dacia (Romania) and Dalmatia (Yugoslavia). Pécs, Sopron, Szombathely and Buda were all Roman towns, as archeological finds have revealed. Some of the best-preserved Roman remains are found in these towns, including Buda's amphitheatre and baths, the ruins of Gorsium near Székesfehérvár, and Szombathely's Temple of Isis.

During the fourth century the Romans began to withdraw from Pannonia, handing over its defence to the Vandals and Jazygians who lived beyond the Danube. In 430 these people fell under the invading **Huns**, whose empire reached its zenith and then fragmented with the death of Attila in 453. Other warring tribes – Ostrogoths, Gepidae and Langobards – occupied the region for the next 150 years, before being swept aside by the **Avars**, whose empire survived until the beginning of the eighth century, when the region once again came up for grabs for any determined invader.

The Magyars

The **Magyars**' origins lie in the Finno-Ugric peoples who dwelt in the snowy forests between the Baltic and the middle Urals. Around the first century AD, some of these tribes migrated south across the Bashkiran steppes and fell under the influence of Turkic and Persian culture, gradually becoming tent-dwelling nomadic herders who lived on a diet of mare's milk, horse flesh, fish and berries. Some archeologists believe that they mingled with the ancient Bulgars north of the Caspian Sea (in a land known as "Magna Bulgaria"), before the majority fled from marauding Petchenegs in about 750 and moved westwards to settle on the far bank of the River Don in the so-called Etelköz region, around the year 830. Ties with the Huns and Avars have been postulated, including a common language, but there's more evidence to link the seven original Magyar tribes with three Kavar tribes, known collectively as the Onogur, or "Ten Arrows".

Overpopulation and Petcheneg attacks forced the Onogur to move westwards in 889, and tradition has it that the seven Magyar chieftains elected **Árpád** as their leader, pledging fealty to his heirs with a blood oath. Accompanied by smaller Kun (or Cuman) tribes, the Onogur entered the Carpathian basin in 896, and began the **"land-taking"** (honfoglalás) or conquest of the region. Six Magyar tribes settled west of the Danube and in the upper Tisza region, the seventh took the approaches to Transylvania, while the lower Tisza and the northern fringes of the Plain went to the Kuns and Kavars. The Magyars continued to raid for the next seventy years, striking terror as far afield as Constantinople and Orleans (where people thought them to be Huns), until a series of defeats persuaded them to settle for assimilating their gains.

Civilization developed gradually, after Árpád's great-grandson **Prince Géza** established links with Bavaria and invited Catholic missionaries to Hungary. His son **Stephen (István)** took the decisive step of applying to Pope Sylvester for recognition, and on Christmas Day in the year 1000 was crowned as a Christian king and began **converting** his pagan subjects with the help of Bishop Gellért. Royal authority was extended over the non-tribal lands by means of the *megye* (county) system, and defended by fortified *vár* (castles); artisans and priests were imported to spread skills and the new religion; and tribal rebellions were crushed. Stephen was subsequently credited with the foundation of Hungary and canonized after his death in 1038. His mummified hand and the Crown of St Stephen have since been revered as both holy and national relics.

The Middle Ages

Succession struggles raged for decades following Stephen's death, and of the sixteen kings who preceded Andrew II (1205–35) only the humane László I (also canonized), Kálmán "the Booklover" and Béla III contributed anything significant to Hungary's development. Fortunately, invasions were few during the eleventh and twelfth centuries, and **German and Slovak immigrants** helped double the population to about two million by 1200. Parts of **Transylvania** were settled by the Magyars and Székely, perhaps before the second half of the eleventh century, when the "lands of St Stephen" were extended to include **Slavonia** (between the Sava and Drava rivers) and the unwillingly "associated" state of **Croatia**. The growth in royal power caused tribal leaders to rebel in 1222, when Andrew II was forced to recognize the "noble" status and rights of **the Natio** – landed freemen exempt from taxation – in the "Golden Bull", a kind of Hungarian Magna Carta.

Andrew's son **Béla IV** was trying to restore royal authority when disaster struck from the east – the **Mongol invasion** of 1241, which devastated Hungary. Hundreds of towns and villages were sacked; refugees fled to the swamps and forests; crops were burned or left unharvested; and famine and plague followed. Population losses ranged from sixty to one hundred percent on the Plain and twenty percent in Transdanubia, and after the Mongol withdrawal a year later (prompted by the timely death of the Khan) Hungary faced a mammoth task of **reconstruction** – the chief achievement of Béla's reign, to which foreign settlers made a large contribution. Renewed domestic feuding (complicated by foreign intervention and the arrival of more Cuman tribes) dogged the reign of Andrew III, and worsened when he died heirless in 1301, marking the **end of the Árpád dynasty**.

Foreign rule

Foreign powers advanced their own claimants, and for a while there were three competing kings, all duly crowned. **Charles Robert** of the French Angevin (or Anjou) dynasty eventually triumphed in 1310, when his rivals went home in disgust; and despite colonial skirmishes with Venice, Serbia and Wallachia, Hungary itself enjoyed a period of peace, while the Mongols and other great powers were occupied elsewhere. Gold mines in Transylvania and northern Hungary – the richest in Europe – stabilized state finances and the currency. Charles's son **Louis the Great** reigned (1342–82) during a period of expansion, when the population rose to three million; and by war and dynastic aggrandizement crown territory grew to include Dalmatia, the Banat, Galicia and (in theory) Poland. Louis, however, sired only daughters, so that after his demise another foreigner ascended the throne in 1395 – **Sigismund of Luxembourg**, Prince of Bohemia, whom the nobles despised as the "Czech swine". His extravagant follies and campaigns abroad were notorious, and while Sigismund recognized the growing threat of the Turks he failed to prevent their advance up through the Balkans.

During the fourteenth century, the realm contained 49 boroughs, about 500 market towns and 26,000 villages. Everyone benefited from peace and expanded trade, but the rewards weren't shared evenly, for the Angevins favoured towns and guilds, and, most of all, the top stratum of the Natio, on whom they depended for troops (*banderia*) when war posed a threat. The burden fell upon the **peasantry**, who lacked "free" status and were compelled to pay *porta* (gate tax) to the state, tithes to the church, and one ninth of their produce to the landlords – plus extra taxes and obligations during times of war, or to finance new royal palaces.

Sigismund died in 1447 leaving one daughter, Elizabeth, just as **the Turks** were poised to invade and succession struggles seemed inevitable. The Turks might have taken Hungary then, but for a series of stunning defeats inflicted upon them by **János Hunyadi**, a Transylvanian warlord of Vlach (Romanian) origin. The lifting of the siege of Nándorfehérvár (Belgrade) in 1456 checked the Turkish advance and caused rejoicing throughout Christendom – the ringing of church bells at noon was decreed by the pope to mark this victory – while Hunyadi rose to be Voivode or Prince of

Transylvania, and later regent for the boy king László. Following Hunyadi's death, László's early demise, and much skulduggery, Mihály Szilágyi staged a coup and put his nephew Mátyás (Matthias), Hunyadi's son, on the throne in 1458.

Renaissance and decline

Mátyás Corvinus is remembered as the **"Renaissance King"** for his statecraft and multiple talents (including astrology), while his second wife **Beatrice** of Naples lured humanists and artists from Italy to add lustre to their palaces at Buda and Visegrád (of which some remains survive). Mátyás was an enlightened despot renowned for his fairness: "King Mátyás is dead, justice is departed", people mourned. By taxing the nobles (against every precedent) he raised a standing force of 30,000 mercenaries called the Black Army, which secured the realm and made Hungary one of Central Europe's leading powers. However, when he died in 1490 leaving no legitimate heir, the nobles looked for a king "whose plaits they could hold in their fists".

Such a man was Ulászló II (whose habit of assenting to any proposal earned him the nickname "King Okay"). Under his rule the Black Army and its tax base were whittled away by the Diet, which met to approve royal decrees and taxes, while the nobility filched common land and otherwise increased their exploitation of the peasantry. Impelled by poverty, many joined the crusade of 1514, which, under the leadership of **György Dózsa**, turned into an **uprising against the landlords**. Its savage repression (over 70,000 peasants were killed and Dózsa was roasted alive) was followed by the **Werbőczy Code** of 1517, binding the peasants to "perpetual serfdom" on their masters' land and 52 days of *robot* (unpaid labour) in the year.

Hungary's decline accelerated as corruption and incompetence bankrupted the treasury, forts along the border crumbled and the revived *banderia* system of mobilization disintegrated. Ulászló's son Louis II was only nine when crowned, and by 1520 the Turks, under Sultan Süleyman "the Magnificent", had resumed their advance northwards, capturing the run-down forts in Serbia. In August 1526 the Turks crossed the Drava and Louis hastened south to confront them at the **battle of Mohács** – a catastrophic defeat for the Magyars, whose army was wiped out together with its monarch and commanders.

Turkish conquest: Hungary divided

After sacking Buda and the south, the Turks withdrew in 1526 to muster forces for their real objective, Vienna, the "Red Apple". To forestall this, Ferdinand of Habsburg proclaimed himself king and occupied western Hungary, while in Buda the nobility put **János Zápolyai** on the throne. Following Zápolyai's death in 1541 Ferdinand claimed full sovereignty, but the Sultan occupied Buda and central Hungary, and made Zápolyai's young son ruler of Transylvania. Thereafter Transylvania became a semi-autonomous principality, nominally loyal to the Sultan and jealously coveted by the Habsburgs. The tripartite **division of Hungary** was formally recognized in 1568. Despite various official or localized truces, warfare became a feature of everyday life for the next 150 years, and national independence was not recovered for centuries.

Royal Hungary – basically western Transdanubia and the north – served as a "human moat" against the Turkish forces that threatened to storm Austria and Western Europe, who were kept at bay by Hungarian sacrifices at Szigetvár, Kőszeg and other fortresses. Notwithstanding constitutional arrangements to safeguard the Natio's privileges, real power passed to the Habsburg chancellery and war council, where the liberation of Hungary took second place to Austria's defence and aggrandizement, and the subjugation of Transylvania.

Turkish-occupied Hungary – Eyalet-i Budin – was ruled by a Pasha in Buda, with much of the land either deeded to the Sultan's soldiers and officials, or run directly as a state fief (*khasse*). The peasants were brutally exploited, for many had to pay rent to both their absentee Magyar landlords and the occupying Turks. Their plight is evident from a letter to a Hungarian lord by the villagers of Batthyán: "Verily, it is better to be Your Lordship's slaves, bag and baggage, than those of an alien people." Peasants fled their villages on the Alföld to the safer fields around the expanding "agro-towns" of Debrecen and Szeged, the nexus of the cattle trade which gradually supplanted agriculture, while neglect and wanton tree-felling transformed the Plain into a swampy wasteland – the *puszta*.

The Voivodes of **Transylvania** endeavoured to provoke war between the Habsburgs and Turks, in order to increase their independence from both and satisfy the feudal Nationes. The latter, representing the elite of the region's Magyars, Saxons and Székely, combined to deny the indigenous Vlachs political power, while competing amongst themselves and extending the borders of Transylvania (then much bigger than today). István Bocskai's Hajdúk forces secured the Szatmár region and Gábor Bethlen promoted economic and social development, but Prince György Rákóczi II aimed too high and brought the wrath of the Sultan down on Transylvania.

Religion was an additional complicating factor. The Protestant Reformation gained many adherents in Hungary during the sixteenth century, and, while religious toleration was decreed in Transylvania in 1572, in Royal Hungary the Counter-Reformation gathered force under Habsburg rule. The Turks, ironically, were indifferent to the issue and treated all their Christian subjects (Rayah) with equal disdain. After the expulsion of the Turks, Protestant landowners were dispossessed in favour of foreign servants of the crown – a major cause of subsequent anti-Habsburg revolts.

Habsburg rule

After heavy fighting between 1683 and 1699, a multinational army evicted the Ottomans, and the Turks relinquished all claims by signing the **Peace of Karlowitz**. Yet for many years peace remained a mirage, for the Hungarians now bitterly resented Habsburg policy and their plundering armies. The **Kuruc revolt** (1677–85) led by **Imre Thököly** was but a prelude to the full-scale **War of Independence** of 1703–11, when peasants and nobles banded together under **Ferenc Rákóczi II**, György's grandson, and initially routed the enemy. Ultimately, however, they were defeated by superior Habsburg power and the desertion of their ally, Louis XIV of France, and peace born of utter exhaustion came at last to Hungary.

Habsburg rule combined force with paternalism, especially during the reign of Empress **Maria Theresa** (1740–80), who believed the Hungarians to be "fundamentally a good people, with whom one can do anything if one takes them the right way". The policy of "impopulatio" settled thousands of Swabians, Slovaks, Serbs and

Romanians in the deserted regions of Hungary, so that, in areas such as the "Military Border" along the Sava, Magyars became a minority. By the end of the eighteenth century they formed only 35 percent of the population of the huge kingdom. For the aristocrats it was an age of glory: the Esterházy, Grassalkovich and Batthyány families and their lesser imitators commissioned over 200 palaces, and Baroque town centres flourished. Yet the masses were virtually serfs, using medieval methods that impoverished the soil, and mired in isolated villages. Cattle, grain and wine – Hungary's main exports – went cheap to Austria, which tried to monopolize industry.

The **Germanization** of culture, education and administration was another feature of Habsburg policy. Yet, though the richest nobles and most of the urban bourgeoisie chose the Habsburg style, the petty gentry and peasantry clung stubbornly to their Magyar identity. The ideals of the **Enlightenment** found growing support among intellectuals, and the revival of the **Magyar language** became inseparable from nationalist politics. **Ferenc Kazinczy**, who refashioned Hungarian as a literary language and translated foreign classics, was associated with the seven **Jacobin conspirators**, executed for plotting treason against the Habsburgs in 1795.

The nineteenth century: nationalism and reform

Magyar nationalism, espoused by sections of the Natio, became increasingly vocal during the early nineteenth century. Hungary's backwardness was a matter for patriotic shame and self-interested concern, especially after the occurrence of peasant riots in the impoverished, cholera-ridden Zempléni, and the publication of *Hitel* ("Credit"), written by Count István Széchenyi, which scathingly indicted the country's semi-feudal economy. However, most nobles were determined to preserve their privileges. One wrote that "God himself has differentiated between us, assigning to the peasant labour and need, to the lord abundance and a merry life". Moreover, national liberation was seen in exclusively Magyar terms – the idea that non-Magyars within the multinational state might wish to assert their own identity was regarded as subversive.

The **Reform Era** (roughly 1825–48) saw many changes. Business, the arts and technology were in ferment, with Jews playing a major role in creating wealth and ideas (although they remained second-class citizens). The **Diet** became increasingly defiant in its dealings with Vienna over finances and laws, and parliamentarians like Ferenc Deák, Count Batthyány and Baron Eötvös acted in the shadow of the "giants" of the time, Széchenyi and Kossuth, who expounded rival programmes for change. Count **István Széchenyi**, the landowning, Anglophile author of *Hitel*, was a tireless practical innovator, introducing silkworms, steamboats and the Academy, as well as an unprecedented tax on the Natio to pay for the construction of his life's monument, the Chain Bridge (Lánchíd) linking Buda and Pest. His arch rival was **Lajos Kossuth**, small-town lawyer turned Member of Parliament and editor of the radical *Pesti Hirlap*, which scandalized and delighted citizens. Kossuth detested the Habsburgs, revered "universal liberty", and demanded an end to serfdom and censorship. Magyar chauvinism was his blind spot, however, and the law of 1840, his greatest pre-revolutionary achievement, inflamed dormant nationalist feelings among Croats, Slovaks and Romanians by making Magyar the sole official language – an act for which his ambitions would later suffer.

Revolution

The fall of the French monarchy precipitated a crisis within the Habsburg Empire, which Kossuth exploited to bring about the **1848 Revolution** in Hungary. The emperor yielded to demands for a constitutional monarchy, universal taxation, wider voting rights and the union of Transylvania with Hungary; while in Budapest the nobles took fright and abolished serfdom when the poet **Sándor Petőfi** threatened them with thousands of peasants camped out in the suburbs. However, the slighted nationalities rallied against the Magyars in Croatia and Transylvania, and the reassertion of Habsburg control over Italy and Czechoslovakia closed the noose. The new emperor Franz Josef declared that Hungary would be partitioned after its defeat, in reaction to which the Debrecen Diet declared **Hungarian independence** – a state crushed by August 1849, when Tsar Nicholas of Russia sent armies to support the Habsburgs, who instituted a reign of terror.

Gradually, brute force was replaced by a **policy of compromise**, by which Hungary was economically integrated with Austria and given a major shareholding in the Habsburg Empire, henceforth known as the "Dual Monarchy". The compromise (Ausgleich) of 1867, engineered by **Ferenc Deák**, brought Hungary prosperity and status, but tied the country inextricably to the empire's fortunes. Simmering nationalist passions would henceforth be focused against Hungary as much as Austria, and diplomatic treaties between Austria and Germany would bind Hungary to them in the event of war. In 1896, however, such dangers seemed remote, and people celebrated **Hungary's millennial anniversary** with enthusiasm.

World War I and its aftermath

Dragged into **World War I** by its allegiance to the Central Powers, Hungary was facing defeat by the autumn of 1918. The Western or Entente powers decided to dismantle the Habsburg Empire in favour of the "**Successor States**" – Romania, Czechoslovakia and Yugoslavia – which would acquire much of their territory at Hungary's expense. In Budapest, the October 30 "Michaelmas Daisy Revolution" put the Social Democratic party of **Mihály Károly** in power, but his government avoided the issue of land reform, attempted unsuccessfully to negotiate peace with the Entente, and finally resigned when France backed further demands by the Successor States.

On March 21, 1919, the Social Democrats agreed on cooperation with the **Communists**, who proclaimed a **Republic of Councils** (Tanácsköztársaság) led by **Béla Kun**, which ruled through local Soviets. Hoping for radical change and believing that "Russia will save us", many people initially supported the new regime, but enforced nationalization of land and capital, and attacks on religion, soon alienated the majority. Beset by the Czech Legion in Slovakia and by internal unrest, the regime collapsed in August before the advancing Romanian army, which occupied Budapest.

The rise of fascism

Then came the **White Terror**, as right-wing gangs spread out from Szeged, killing "Reds" and Jews, who were made scapegoats for the earlier Communist "Red Terror". **Admiral Miklós Horthy** appointed himself regent and ordered a return to "traditional values" with a vengeance. Meanwhile, at the Paris Conference, Hungary was obliged to sign the **Treaty of Trianon** (July 4, 1920), surrendering two-thirds of its historic territory and three-fifths of its total population (three million in all) to the Successor States. The bitterest loss was Transylvania, whose 103,093 square kilometres and 1.7 million Magyars went to Romania – a devastating blow to national pride.

During the **1920s and 1930s,** campaigning for the overturn of the Trianon diktat was the "acceptable" outlet for politics, while workers' unions were tightly controlled and peasants struggled to form associations against the landlords and the gendarmerie, who rigged ballots and gerrymandered as in the old days. Politics were dominated by the Kormánypárt (Government Party) led by Count Bethlen, representing the Catholic Church and the landed gentry, which resisted any changes that would threaten their power. Social hardships increased, particularly in the countryside where the landless **peasantry** constituted "three million beggars" whose misery concerned the **Village Explorers** (Falukutató), a movement of the literary intelligentsia ranging across the political spectrum. With the Social Democrats co-opted by conservatism and the Communist Party illegal, many workers and disgruntled petits bourgeois turned to the **radical right** to voice their grievances, and were easily turned against Jews and the "Trianon Powers".

Resentment against France, Britain and Romania predisposed many Hungarians to admire **Nazi Germany**'s defiance of the Versailles Treaty – a sentiment nurtured by the Reich's grant of credits for **industrialization**, and Nazi sympathizers within Volksdeutsche communities, commerce, the civil service and the officer corps. The rise of **anti-Semitism** gave power to nationalist politicians like **Gyula Gömbös**. At the same time, Hungary's belated industrial growth was partly due to the acquisition of territory from Czechoslovakia, following Germany's dismemberment of the latter. The annexation of Austria made the Reich militarily supreme in Central Europe, and Hungary's submission to German hegemony almost inevitable.

World War II

With the outbreak of **World War II**, the government's pro-Nazi policy initially paid dividends. Romania was compelled to return **northern Transylvania** in July 1940, and Hungary gained additional territory from the invasion of Yugoslavia a year later. Hoping for more, Premier Bárdossy committed Hungary to the Nazi invasion of the USSR in June 1941 – an act condemned by the former prime minister, Teleki (who had engineered the recovery of Transylvania), as the "policy of vultures". The Hungarian Second Army perished covering the retreat from Stalingrad, while at home, Germany demanded ever more foodstuffs and forced labour. As Axis fortunes waned Horthy prepared to declare neutrality, but Hitler forestalled him with "Operation Margarethe" – the outright **Nazi occupation of Hungary** in March 1944.

Under Sztójay's puppet government, Hungarian Jews were forced into ghettos to await their deportation to Auschwitz and Belsen, a fate hindered only by the heroism of the underground, a handful of people organized by the Swedish diplomat Raoul Wallenberg, and by the manoeuvring of some Horthyite politicians. Mindful of Romania's successful escape from the Axis in August, Horthy declared a surprise armistice on October 15, just as the Red Army crossed Hungary's eastern border. In response, Germany installed a government of the native **Arrow Cross Fascists**, or Nyilas, led by Ferenc Szálasi, whose gangs roamed Budapest extorting valuables and murdering people, while the Nazis systematically plundered Hungary. They blew up the Danube bridges and compelled the Russians to take Budapest by storm – a siege that reduced much of Buda to ruins. Meanwhile in Debrecen, an assembly of anti-Fascist parties met under Soviet auspices to nominate a **provisional government**, which took power after the Germans fled Hungary in April 1945.

The Rákosi era

In the November 1945 **elections** the Smallholders' Party won an outright majority, but the Soviet military insisted that the Communists and Social Democrats (with seventeen percent of the vote) remain in government. **Land reform** and limited **nationalization** were enacted, while the Communists tightened their grip over the Ministry of the Interior (which controlled the police) and elections became increasingly fraudulent. **Mátyás Rákosi**, Stalin's man in Hungary, gradually undermined and fragmented the "bourgeois" parties with what he called "salami tactics" (chopping his opponents into small groups and then swallowing them), and by 1948, officially called the **"Year of Change"**, the Communists were strong enough to coerce the Social Democrats to join them in a single **Workers' Party**, and neutralize the Smallholders. Church schools were seized, Cardinal Mindszenty was jailed for "espionage" and the peasants were forced into collective farms. More than 500,000 Hungarians were imprisoned, tortured or shot in native concentration camps like Recsk, or as deportees in the Soviet Union – victims of the **ÁVO** secret police (renamed the ÁVH in 1949), who spread terror throughout society.

Soviet culture and the personality cults of Rákosi (known as "Baldhead" or "Asshole" to his subjects) and Stalin were imposed on the country, and Hungarian classics such as the *Tragedy of Man* were banned for failing to meet the standards of Socialist Realism. Under the 1949 **Five Year Plan**, heavy industry took absolute priority over agriculture and consumer production. To fill the new factories, peasants streamed into towns and women were dragooned into the labour force. Living standards plummeted, and the whole of society was subjected to the laws and dictates of the Party. "Class conscious" workers and peasants were raised to high positions and "class enemies" were discriminated against, while Party officials enjoyed luxuries unavailable to the populace, who suffered hunger and squalor.

Although the Smallholders retained nominal positions in government, real power lay with Rákosi's clique, known as the "Jewish Quartet". As elsewhere in Eastern Europe at this time, Hungary saw bitter **feuds within the Communist Party**. In October 1949, the "Muscovites" purged the more independently minded "national" Communists on the pretext of "Titoism". The former Interior Minister **László Rajk** was executed, and his friend and successor (and, later, betrayer), **János Kádár**, was jailed and tortured with others during a second wave of purges. Two years later, following Stalin's death in March 1953, Kremlin power struggles resulted in a more moderate Soviet leadership and the abrupt replacement of Rákosi by **Imre Nagy**. His **"New Course"**, announced in July, promised a more balanced industrial strategy and eased pressure on the peasants to collectivize, besides curbing the ÁVH terror. Nagy, however, had few allies within the Kremlin, and in 1955 Rákosi was able to strike back, expelling Nagy from the Party for "deviationism", and declaring a **return to Stalinist policies**. This brief interlude, however, had encouraged murmurings of resistance.

1956: the Uprising

The first act of opposition came from the official Writers' Union, who, in their November Memorandum, objected to the rule of force. The Party clamped down, but also began to rehabilitate the Rajk purge victims. During June **1956** the intellectuals' **Petőfi circle** held increasingly outspoken public debates, and **Júlia Rajk** denounced "the men who have ruined this country, corrupted the Party, liquidated thousands and driven millions to despair". Moscow responded to the unrest by replacing Rákosi with **Ernő Gerő**, another hardliner – a move which merely stoked public resentment. The mood came to a head in October, when 200,000 people attended Rajk's reburial, Nagy was readmitted to the Party, and **students** in Szeged and Budapest organized to demand greater national independence and freedom.

In Poland, Gomulka's reform Communists had just won concessions from the Kremlin, and Budapest students decided to march on October 23 to the General Bem statue, a symbol of Polish-Hungarian solidarity. Patriotic feelings rose as about 50,000 people assembled, the procession swelling as it approached Parliament. A hesitant speech there by Nagy failed to satisfy them, and students besieged the Radio Building on Bródy utca, demanding to voice their grievances on the airwaves. In response, the ÁVH guards opened fire, killing many. Almost immediately, this triggered a city-wide **Uprising** against the ÁVH. The regular police did little to control it, and when Soviet tanks intervened, units of the Hungarian army began to side with the insurgents.

Over the next five days fighting spread throughout Hungary, despite Nagy's reinstatement as premier and pleas for order. **Revolutionary councils** sprang up in towns and factories and free newspapers appeared, demanding "Ruszkik haza" (Russians go home), free elections, civil liberties, industrial democracy and neutrality. Intellectuals who had led the first protests now found themselves left behind by uncontrollable dynamism on the streets. The Party leadership temporized, reshuffled the cabinet and struggled to stay in control, as all the "old" parties reappeared and the newly liberated Cardinal Mindszenty provided a focus for the resurgent Right.

The negotiated **Soviet withdrawal**, beginning on October 29, was merely a delaying tactic, while the Russians regrouped in the countryside before bringing in fresh troops from Romania and the USSR. On November 1, Nagy announced Hungary's withdrawal from the Warsaw Pact and asked the UN to support **Hungarian neutrality**; that night, Kádár and Ferenc Münnich slipped away from Parliament to join the Russians, who were preparing to crush the "counter-revolution". America downplayed Hungary in the United Nations while the Suez crisis preoccupied world attention, but the CIA-sponsored **Radio Free Europe** encouraged the Magyars to expect Western aid. At dawn on November 4, once Budapest and other centres had been surrounded with tanks under cover of a snowstorm, the **Soviet attack** began.

Armed resistance was crushed within days, but the workers occupied their factories and proclaimed a **general strike**, maintained for months despite **mass arrests**. Deprived of physical power, the people continued to make symbolic protests like the "Mothers' March" in December. Inexorably, however, the Party and ÁVH apparatus reasserted its control. Over 200,000 **refugees** fled to the West, while at home thousands were jailed or executed, including Nagy and other leading "revisionists", shot in 1958 after a secret trial.

Kádár's Hungary

In the aftermath of the Uprising, the new Party leader **János Kádár** ruthlessly suppressed the last vestiges of opposition. After the mid-1960s, however, his name came to be associated with the **gradual reform** of Hungary's social and economic system from a totalitarian regime to one based, at least in part, on **compromise**. Kádár's famous phrase, "Whoever is not against us is with us" (a reversal of the Stalinist slogan), invited a tacit compact between Party and people. Both had been shaken by the events of 1956, and realized that bold changes – as happened in Czechoslovakia in 1967 and 1968 – only invited Soviet intervention, justified by the Brezhnev doctrine of "limited sovereignty".

Having stimulated the economy by cautious reforms in the structure of pricing and management, and overcome opposition within the Politburo, Kádár and Resző Nyers announced the **New Economic Mechanism** (NEM) in 1968. Though its impact on centralized planning was slight, the NEM was accompanied by measures to promote "socialist legality" and make merit, rather than class background and Party standing, the criterion for promotion and higher education.

While generally welcomed by the populace, these reforms angered "New Left" supporters of either Dubcek's "Socialism with a human face" in Czechoslovakia or the Chinese Cultural Revolution, and also, more seriously, conservatives within the Party. With backing from Moscow, they watered down the NEM and ousted Nyers, its leading advocate, from the Politburo in 1973, expelling Hegedüs and other "revisionist sociologists" from the Party later.

Following a power struggle, Kádár was able to reverse the reactionary tide, and reduce constraints on the so-called "second economy". While structural reforms were extremely limited, consumerism, a private sector and even "forint millionaires" emerged during the **1970s**, when Hungary became a byword for **affluence** within the Socialist bloc – the "happiest barracks in the camp", as the joke had it. Mechanics and other artisans with marketable skills were able to moonlight profitably, as demonstrated by the boom in private home-building; and workers and unions acquired some say in the management of their enterprises. This **"market socialism"** attracted the favours of Western politicians and bankers, and before perestroika the "Hungarian model" seemed to offer the best hope for reform within Eastern Europe.

In the **1980s**, however, economic and social problems became increasingly obvious, ranging from thirty percent **inflation**, whose effect was felt hardest by the **"new poor"** living on low, fixed incomes, to Hungary's $14.7 billion **foreign debt** (per capita, the largest in Eastern Europe). Despite reformist rhetoric, vested interests successfully resisted the logic of the market, whose rigorous application would entail drastic lay-offs and mass **unemployment** in towns dominated by the unprofitable mining and steel industries. Although frank analyses of Hungary's economic plight started appearing in the media during the mid-1980s, other issues ran up against the limits of state tolerance. These included fears for **the environment** in the wake of Chernobyl and the decision to build a dam at Nagymaros; an unofficial **peace movement** that was quickly driven back underground; and any discussion of the Party's "leading role" or Hungary's alliance with the Soviet Union. Discussion of such topics could only be found in **samizdat** (underground) magazines such as *Beszélő*, whose publishers were harassed as dissidents. Although in 1983 the Party announced that "independents" could contest elections, it proved unwilling to let them enter Parliament, as demonstrated by the gerrymandering used against László Rajk in 1986.

Yet the need for change was becoming evident even within the Party, where the caution of the "old guard" – Kádár, Horváth and Gáspár – caused increasing frustration among **reformists**, who believed that Hungarians would only accept income tax and economic austerity if greater liberalization seemed a realistic prospect. Happily, this coincided with the advent of **Gorbachev**, whose interest in the Hungarian model of socialism and desire to bring a new generation into power was an open secret.

The end of Communism

The **end of Communism in Hungary** was so orderly that it can hardly be termed a revolution, but it did set in motion the collapse of hardline regimes in East Germany and Czechoslovakia. Prefiguring the fate of Gorbachev, the politicians who created an opening for change hoped to preserve Communism by reforming it, but were swept away by the forces which they had unleashed.

At the **May 1988 Party Congress**, Kádár and seven colleagues were ousted from power by a coalition of radical reformers and conservative technocrats. The latter backed **Károly Grósz** as Kádár's successor, but his lacklustre performance as Party leader enabled the reformists to shunt him aside in July 1989, forcing conservatives and hardliners onto the defensive. As the ascendancy of **Imre Pozsgay**, **Rezső Nyers**, **Miklós Németh** and **Gyula Horn** became apparent there was a "traffic jam on the road to Damascus" as lesser figures hastened to pledge support for reforms.

In mid-October 1989, the Communist Party formally reconstituted itself as the **Hungarian Socialist Party (MSzP)**, dissolved its private militia and announced the **legalization of opposition parties** as a prelude to free elections. To symbolize this watershed, the People's Republic was renamed the **Republic of Hungary** in a ceremony broadcast live on national television, on the thirty-third anniversary of the Uprising.

Meanwhile, the Iron Curtain was unravelling with astonishing speed. In May, Hungary began dismantling the barbed wire and minefields along its **border** with Austria, and thousands of **East Germans** seized their chance to escape to the West, crossing over via Hungary at a rate of two hundred every day. Despite protests from the Honecker regime, Hungary refused to close the border or deport would-be escapees back to the DDR, and allowed 20,000 refugees encamped in the West German embassy in Budapest to leave the country. After the DDR sealed its own borders, frustration spilled over onto the streets of Leipzig and Dresden, where mass demonstrations led to the **fall of the Berlin Wall** (November 9, 1989) and the ousting of Erich Honecker. A week later, the brutal repression of a pro-democracy demonstration in Prague's Wenceslas Square set in motion the "**Velvet Revolution**" in Czechoslovakia, which overturned forty years of Communist rule in ten days. The *annus mirabilis* of 1989 climaxed with the **overthrow of Ceaușescu** in Romania on December 22.

The 1990s

After such events Hungary's first **free elections** since 1945, in 1990, seemed an anticlimax. During the first round of voting on March 6, Pozsgay and the Socialist Party were obliterated, while two parties emerged as frontrunners. The **Hungarian Democratic Forum** (MDF), founded at the Lakitelek Conference of 1987, articulated populist, conservative nationalism, encapsulated in the idea of "Hungarianness", whereas the rival Alliance of **Free Democrats** (SzDSz) espoused a neo-liberal, internationalist outlook, similar to that of the **Federation of Young Democrats** (Fidesz). Two prewar parties revived under octogenarian leaders also participated, namely the **Smallholders' Party** (under the slogan "God, Home, Family, Wine, Wheat and Independence") and the **Christian Democrats**.

Despite being diminished by voter apathy, the **1990 elections** unceremoniously swept the reformist Communists out of power. Their place was taken by a centre-right coalition dominated by the Hungarian Democratic Forum (MDF) and its prime minister **Jozsef Antall**. A born politician with a schoolmasterly style, Antall relished the opportunity to take a role he had longed for but never expected to get during the Communist years. The model for his Hungary was its prewar state, with the restoration of the **traditions** and the **social hierarchies** that had prevailed at that time. Very much a moderate, his policies rested on the belief that over forty years of Communism had destroyed the true values of Hungarian society. However, not everyone wanted the **Catholic Church** to return to the dominant social position it had enjoyed before the war, and his party's proud belief in restoring the Hungarian nation to its former position sounded to Hungary's neighbours like a revanchist claim on the lost lands of Trianon – an interpretation that was strengthened by Antall's failure to distance himself from the ultra-right-wing nationalism advocated by **István Csurka**.

After Antall's death in 1993, his successor Peter Boross was unable to turn the economy around, and the **1994 elections** saw the **return to power** of the Socialists (reform Communists), assisted by sympathetic media that presented the outgoing government as amateurish and arrogant. To guard against accusations of abusing power as their Communist predecessors had done, the Socialists also brought the Free Democrats into the government. The government's **corruption** became blatant, however, and, though their austerity policies succeeded in bringing an economic upturn, living standards did not improve for most people.

Despite this, the government still rode high in the opinion polls, helped by the fact that the opposition was in disarray. After its poor showing in the 1994 elections, Fidesz had been repositioned by its leader **Viktor Orbán** to the right of centre, bidding to become the focus of opposition to the Socialist-led government. Orbán adopted phrases about the need to revive national culture that would appeal to the right, and renamed the party Fidesz-Hungarian **Civic Party** (the word for civic – **polgári** – also evokes notions of bourgeois middle-class values). It still seemed, however, that Orbán needed more time to mature as a potential prime minister.

Then, in early 1998, the Socialists committed their biggest blunder, announcing that Hungary would go ahead with building the controversial **Nagymaros dam**. It was the revenge of Gyula Horn: as a leading figure in the old Communist Party he had given full support to the dam, but it had been condemned as undemocratic; now as prime minister of a democratically elected government he could give the go-ahead. At first it looked as if he had got away with it, but as the May **1998 elections** approached, public disillusionment mounted. Fidesz's win by a narrow margin came as a surprise to many people – though it was not as unexpected as Csurka's extreme right-wing Hungarian Justice and Life Party (MIÉP) breaking the four percent threshold to get into Parliament. Orbán, given the chance to be the youngest premier in Hungarian history, set about talks with the MDF and Smallholders with alacrity in order to form a **coalition** – despite the fact that the prospect of government with the unpredictable Torgyán and his Smallholders worried many Fidesz supporters. Orbán, however, bit the bullet.

Hungary's first major step into the wider European arena came the following year on March 12, 1999 when, just twelve days before NATO allies were due to begin a bombing campaign against Yugoslavia, Hungary was formally **admitted into NATO**. Whilst delighted at receiving the recognition it had long coveted, the timing was awkward to say the least. With the country now a fully fledged member, it was placed in the rather dubious position of having to play an active role in the campaign, if only as a base from which allied aircraft could fly – convenient for the allies, not so for Hungarians who were distinctly nervous at the prospect. Not only was Hungary a neighbouring country – one of the few with which Serbia was on good terms – but there was also the very delicate question of the large Hungarian minority living in the Serbian province of Vojvodina, which borders southern Hungary. However, despite very real fears of a backlash against Hungarians living there, it turned out that most Serbs were far too concerned with surviving the bombs to be bothered about stirring up further trouble. In the event, the bombing lasted eleven weeks, and aside from the odd stray cruise missile, Hungarians were not too troubled.

Europe and the new millennium

Back on the domestic front, few predicted anything other than another Orbán victory in the **2002 parliamentary elections**, thanks to an upwardly mobile economy, steadily falling inflation and low unemployment levels. However, in what was the most spitefully contested election since the end of Communism, the Orbán-led Fidesz-MDF coalition was surprisingly ousted by a centre-left alliance – comprising a combination of the Hungarian Socialist Party (MSzP) and the Alliance of Free Democrats (SzDSz) – whose margin of victory was just ten seats. Rejecting Orbán's media-savvy, aggressive style and attendant nationalist overtures, the Hungarian electorate – in an unprecedented post-Communist turnout of more than 70 percent – instead opted for a return to the same coalition that had governed, albeit largely ineffectively, between 1994 and 1998. The new premier was **Peter Medgyessy**, a former banker and an altogether less charismatic figure than Orbán. Medgyessy's past, however, was discovered to be rather more colourful when it was revealed just a few months later that he had, alongside ten other government ministers, worked as an agent for the country's Moscow-linked secret service, though he was quick to deny any links to the KGB.

Internationally, at the tail end of the same year, Hungary saw final accession negotiations to the European Union wrapped up, with referendums held the following April. Although the turnout was disappointingly low, support was more or less unequivocal, with 84 percent of voters in favour. A little over a year later, on May 1, 2004, Hungary, alongside nine other former Eastern bloc countries, was **admitted to the EU**. While most Hungarians remain fervently committed to membership, believing that they will benefit under Europe's protective mantle, there are several areas of deep concern, such as the desire of most Hungarians to limit foreign ownership, which goes against EU directives, and apprehension over the distribution of agricultural subsidies.

With the euphoria surrounding the country's accession having barely died down, domestic problems were brewing. A poor showing in the European elections, combined with bitter party infighting and barely disguised dissatisfaction at Medgyessy's performance as prime minister, resulted in the premier's **shock resignation** in August 2004. His successor was sports minister and millionaire businessman, **Ferenc Gyurcsány**, whose task it was to revive the party's ailing fortunes in time for the elections in 2006.

In the event, Gyurcsány and the ruling Socialists once again comfortably defeated Orbán and his Fidesz party in the **2006 elections**, the first occasion since the end of Communist rule that a governing party had won consecutive terms. However, what occurred in the aftermath of the election proved to be far more exciting than anything that happened during it. In a tape of a private party speech given by Gyurcsány just after the election (broadcast on national radio a few months later), the prime minister openly admitted to lying to voters in the run-up to the election, in particular about the country's ailing economy. In the speech Gyurcsány reveals that both he and his "boneheaded government" had "lied morning, noon and night" in order to secure electoral victory. His subsequent refusal to resign prompted mass protests in front of Budapest's parliament building, which continued throughout September and into October. As the demonstrations grew, so they became increasingly inflamed, culminating in particularly violent clashes on the **fiftieth anniversary of the 1956 Uprising** on October 23. For several nights thereafter, running battles between protesters and police – whose use of tear gas, rubber bullets and water cannons subsequently drew charges of excessive force – brought the city to a virtual standstill. In one of the more surreal moments, a tank that had been on display as part of the commemorations was commandeered by a protester and driven down one of the main city boulevards towards police lines. Orbán and his party also came in for some heavy criticism, with accusations that, in addition to staging their own high-profile rallies, they had been responsible for orchestrating the protests. In the event, and after narrowly securing a vote of confidence, Gyurcsány survived.

Whilst the premier's candid gaffe may have been the spark for the clashes, there had already been growing widespread public disenchantment at the country's deepening economic crisis. Reckless government spending – largely financed with foreign currency loans – and unsustainable public sector wage increases, allied to high levels of personal debt (many loans had been taken out in Swiss francs and euros, and following the dramatic collapse of the forint against both currencies, many found themselves with rising debt payments), had contrived to create a critical state of affairs. As similarly violent clashes between police and protesters erupted in Budapest the following year – in March, on the occasion of the anniversary of the 1848 Revolution, and then again in September on the next anniversary of the Uprising – the country's economic situation had reached crisis point. Only a multi-billion-dollar bail-out in late 2008 from the International Monetary Fund and European Central Bank averted the total collapse of the national currency. In a somewhat surprising turn of events, Gyurcsány resigned from his post in March 2009, stating that he could do no more to further the country's economic reforms. Replacing him as prime minister was the little-known **Gordon Bajnai**, who had hitherto been serving as the government's economic minister.

Books

Whilst Hungarian travelogues are relatively few and far between, there are plenty of books on the country's history and politics, with some particularly fine accounts of the 1956 Uprising, and the changes of 1989. There are also several particularly memorable accounts of the Holocaust.

Hungary has a fabulously rich literary heritage, and approach to the genre has greatly improved in recent years, thanks in no small part to the success of authors such as the Nobel-prize-winning Imre Kertész, and the wider availability of translations of works by the likes of Antal Szerb, Sándor Márai and Péter Esterházy.

Worth consulting is the respected *Hungarian Quarterly* (⨂www.hungarianquarterly .com), which features extensive translations of Hungarian fiction and poetry, while *Hungarian Literature* (Babel Guides) is an informative guide to the best Hungarian fiction, drama and poetry in translation, also with selected excerpts. Most of Budapest's better bookshops have a good range and can take orders, whilst works by nineteenth-century authors such as Mór Jókai are most likely found in secondhand bookshops (see Budapest "Listings").

Travel writing

Patrick Leigh Fermor *A Time of Gifts* and *Between the Woods and the Water*. In 1934 the young Leigh Fermor started walking from Holland to Turkey, reaching Hungary in the closing chapter of *A Time of Gifts*. In *Between the Woods and the Water* the Gypsies and rusticated aristocrats of the Great Plain and Transylvania are superbly evoked. Lyrical and erudite.

Ruth Gruber *Jewish Heritage Travel: A Guide to Central and Eastern Europe*. The most comprehensive guide to Jewish sights in Hungary (amongst other countries), as well as lively historical accounts of pre-World War II Jewish communities and cultures.

Brian Hall *Stealing from a Deep Place*. In 1982 Hall cycled through Hungary, Romania and Bulgaria and came up with this engaging portrayal of rural life in southeastern Europe. The

account of the several months he spent in Budapest is particularly absorbing.

Gyula Illyés *People of the Puszta*. An unsentimental, sometimes horrifying, immersion in the life of the landless peasantry of prewar Hungary, mainly in Transdanubia. Illyés, one of Hungary's greatest writers, was born into such a background, and the book breathes authenticity.

Claudio Magris *Danube*. Magris undertakes an epic voyage along the course of Europe's most romantic river, blending travel narrative, history and anecdote to wonderful effect.

Walter Starkie *Raggle-Taggle*. The wanderings of a Dublin professor with a fiddle, who bummed around Budapest and the Plain in search of Gypsy music in the 1920s. First published in 1933 and last issued in 1973.

History, politics and society

Judit Frigyesi *Béla Bartók and Turn-of-the-century Budapest*. Placing Bartók in his cultural milieu, this is an excellent account of the

Hungarian intellectual world at the beginning of the twentieth century.

András Gerő *Modern Hungarian Society in the Making: The Unfinished Experience*.

A good collection of essays setting Hungary in the context of the Eastern European environment.

Jörg K Hoensch *A History of Modern Hungary 1867–1994*. A good history of the country on its way from tragedy to tragedy, but with a happy(ish) outcome.

László Kontler *Millennium in Central Europe: A History of Hungary*. Another very thorough and reliable history of the country, although its slightly archaic wording lets it down.

Paul Lendvai *The Hungarians: 1000 Years of Victory in Defeat*. Refreshing and authoritative book on Hungary's complex history, with particularly stimulating accounts of the Treaty of Trianon and the subsequent Nazi and Communist tyrannies – fascinating pictures, too. Lendvai's *One Day that Shook the World* is a superb, first-hand account of the 1956 Uprising.

Bill Lomax *Hungary 1956*. Still one of the best – and shortest – books on the Uprising, by an acknowledged expert. Lomax also edited *Eyewitness in Hungary*, an anthology of accounts by foreign Communists (most of them sympathetic to the Uprising) that vividly depicts the elation, confusion and tragedy of the events of October 1956.

John Lukács *Budapest 1900*. Excellent and very readable account of the politics and society of Budapest at the turn of the twentieth century, during a golden age that was shortly to end.

Jonathan Matthews *Explosion – Hungarian Revolution*. The author, a journalist with Radio Free Europe at the time, provides another illuminating ringside account of the revolution in this voluminous tome, which also features some excellent photos.

George Mikes *A Study in Infamy*. Better known in the West for his humorous writings, Mikes here exposes the activities of the secret police during the Rákosi era. Based on captured documents which explain their methods of surveillance and use of terror as a political weapon.

Miklós Molnár *A Concise History of Hungary*. Dry but comprehensive thousand-year history of Hungarian land, people, culture and economy, right up until the 1998 elections.

Victor Sebestyen *Twelve Days*. This fascinating, blow-by-blow account of those tumultuous days in 1956 is a lucid and engrossing read, with detailed background coverage of the events leading up to the Uprising as well as an in-depth look at its aftermath.

Michael Stewart *The Time of the Gypsies*. Based on anthropological research in a Gypsy community in Hungary, this superb book presents Gypsy culture as a culture, and not as a parasitic body on society, as it is widely perceived in Hungary and elsewhere.

Peter Sugar (ed) *A History of Hungary*. A useful, not too academic, survey of Hungarian history from pre-Conquest times to the close of the Kádár era, with a brief epilogue on the transition to democracy.

Literature

Anthologies

Loránt Czigány (ed) *The Oxford History of Hungarian Literature from the Earliest Times to the Present*. Probably the most comprehensive collection in print to date. In chronological order, with good coverage of the political and social background.

György Gömöri (ed) *The Colonnade of Teeth*. A strange title, but a very satisfactory introduction to the work of the country's finest twentieth-century poets.

Michael March (ed) *Description of a Struggle*. A collection of contemporary Eastern European prose, featuring four pieces by Hungarian writers including Nádas and Esterházy.

George Szirtes (ed) *Leopard V: An Island of Sound*. Superbly compiled anthology featuring the cream of Hungarian prose and poetry from the end of World War II through to 1989, including Márai, Esterházy and Nagy.

Poetry

🏃 **Endre Ady** *Poems of Endre Ady*. Arguably the finest Hungarian poet of the twentieth century, Ady's allusive verses are notoriously difficult to translate, but here, the linguist and poet Anton Nyerges has succeeded brilliantly. *Explosive Country* is a collection of essays about his homeland.

George Faludy *Selected Poems, 1933–80*. Fiery, lyrical poetry by a victim of both Nazi and Soviet repression. Themes of political defiance, the nobility of the human spirit, and the struggle to preserve human values in the face of oppression predominate. The author's cheerfully resigned biographical account of the 1940s and 1950s and the prison camps of the period, *My Happy Days in Hell*, is also worth reading.

Attila József *Selected Poems*. Alongside Ady, József remains Hungary's most celebrated poet, as demonstrated here with a fine selection of hugely affecting poems by the tragic realist who committed suicide in 1937.

Ágnes Nemes Nagy *The Night of Akhenaton: Selected Poems*. Nagy is a major postwar poet, who often speculates on knowledge and the role of poetry in trying to impose order on the world. Fine translations by the ubiquitous George Szirtes.

Miklós Radnóti *Under Gemini: the Selected Poems of Miklós Radnóti, with a Prose Memoir*; *Foamy Sky: the Major Poems*. The two best collections of Radnóti's sparse, anguished poetry. His final poems, found in his coat pocket after he had been shot on a forced march to a labour camp, are especially moving.

Fiction

🏃 **Miklós Bánffy** *The Transylvanian Trilogy*. Bánffy's celebrated trilogy (*They Were Found Wanting, They Were Divided, They Were Counted*) is a vivid portrayal of the vanished world of pre-World War I Hungary as seen through the eyes of a pair of aristocratic Transylvanian cousins.

Géza Csáth *The Magician's Garden and Other Stories* and *Opium and Other Stories*. Disturbing stories written in the magic realist genre. The author was tormented by insanity and opium addiction, finally killing his wife and then himself in 1918.

Péter Esterházy *Celestial Harmonies*. Written by a descendant of the famous aristocratic family, this dense, demanding novel chronicles the rise of the Esterházys during the Austro-Hungarian Empire, and their subsequent downfall under Communism. Other works include *The Glance of Countess Hahn-Hahn (Down the Danube), Helping Verbs of the Heart, A Little Hungarian Pornography* and *She Loves Me*.

Tibor Fischer *Under the Frog, A Black Comedy*. The fictional adventures of two young Hungarian basketball players between the end of World War II and the 1956 Uprising, by the English-born son of Hungarian survivor émigrés. Witty and enjoyable.

🏃 **Imre Kertész** *Fateless*. Drawing from his own experiences as an Auschwitz survivor, this beautifully moving, Nobel-prize-winning book tells the tale of a young boy's deportation to, and survival in, a concentration camp. Kertész also wrote the screenplay for the 2005 film version.

Dezso Kosztolányi *Skylark*. A short and tragic story of an old couple and their beloved child by one of Hungary's top writers of the twentieth century, in a masterly translation by Richard Aczél and Anna Édes.

Gyula Krúdy *Adventures of Sinbad*. Stories about a gourmand and womanizer by a popular Hungarian author with similar interests to his hero. Good translation.

🏃 **Sándor Márai** *Embers*. Atmospheric and moving tale about friendship, love and betrayal by one of Hungary's most respected pre-World War II writers. *Esther's Inheritance* and *The Rebels* are equally beautiful reads.

Zsigmond Móricz *Be Faithful Unto Death*. This book, by a major figure in late nineteenth-century Hungarian literature, tells the tale of a young boy growing up in a boarding school

in Debrecen, and is helpful in understanding the way Hungarians see themselves – both then and now.

Péter Nádas *A Book of Memories*. This novel about a novelist writing about a novel caused a sensation when it appeared in 1998. A Proustian account of bisexual relationships, Stalinist repression and modern-day Hungary in a brilliant translation by Iván Sanders.

Giorgio and Nicola Pressburger *Homage to the Eighth District*. Evocative tales of Jewish life in Budapest, before, during and after World War II, by twin brothers who fled Hungary in 1956.

🏃 **Magda Szabó** *The Door*. A beautiful and poignant story by one of Hungary's foremost female writers, which tells of the deepening relationship between a writer and her housekeeper.

🏃 **Antal Szerb** *Journey by Moonlight*. This recently translated Hungarian classic, written in 1937, tells the story of a Hungarian businessman on honeymoon in Italy who embarks upon a mystical and dazzling journey through the country. Superbly translated by Len Rix, as is Szerb's excellent *Pendragon Legend*, a mysterious, and often humorous, tale of a young Hungarian scholar's involvement with an aristocratic family in North Wales.

Biography and autobiography

John Bierman *The Secret Life of Laszlo Almasy: the Real English Patient*. Engaging, if somewhat dry, portrayal of Laszlo Almasy, the enigmatic Hungarian explorer, soldier and spy. For most people, Almasy first came to light as the fictional character in Michael Ondaatje's Booker-winning novel (and later an Oscar-winning film), *The English Patient*.

Magda Dénes *Castles Burning: A Child's Life in War*. A moving biographical account of the Budapest

ghetto and postwar escape to France, Cuba and the United States, seen through the eyes of a Jewish girl. The author died in December 1966, shortly before the book she always wanted to write was published.

Paul Hoffmann *The Man Who Loved Only Numbers: the Story of Paul Erdöss and the Search for Mathematical Truth*. The amazing story of a Hungarian-born mathematician who became a legend. Totally dedicated to his goal, he wandered from friend to friend with his possessions in a few carrier bags, concerned with nothing but mathematics. Affectionate, engaging account of this genius and his world.

Erno Szép *The Smell of Humans*. In this superb and harrowing memoir of the Holocaust in Hungary, the author reflects upon his time interned in a forced labour camp.

Marcus Tanner *The Raven King*. This compelling true story charts the deeds of the fifteenth-century Hungarian warrior-king and renowned bibliophile, Matthias Corvinus (aka the Raven King), and his attempt to amass one of the finest libraries in all of Europe. The library's subsequent disappearance at the hands of the Ottomans led to an intriguing quest to rediscover it some time later. Superbly researched.

Béla Zsolt *Nine Suitcases*. Originally published in serial form in 1946, this recently translated English version of the author's experiences in the ghetto of Nagyvárad and as a forced labourer in the Ukraine is one of the most powerful accounts of the Holocaust. Intriguingly, it was at Bergen-Belsen that the author met a young boy who would become the book's translator, Ladislaus Lob.

Foreign writers on Hungary

Heinrich Böll *And Where Were You, Adam*. A superb short novel by one of the major postwar German novelists, consisting of loosely connected and semi-autobiographical short stories describing the panic-stricken retreat of Hitler's forces from the *puszta* before the Red Army in 1944.

Hans Habe *Black Earth*. The story of a peasant's commitment to the Communist underground and his disillusionment with the Party in power; a good read.

Cecilia Holland *Rakossy* and *The Death of Attila*. Two well-crafted historical romances: *Rakossy* is a bodice-ripping tale of a shy Austrian princess wed to an uncouth Magyar baron, braving Turkish hordes on the Hungarian marches; *The Death of Attila* evokes the Huns, Romans and Goths of the Dark Ages, pillaging around the Danube.

Miscellaneous

Györgyi Éri et al *A Golden Age: Art and Society in Hungary 1896–1914*. Hungary's Art Nouveau age in a beautiful coffee-table volume.

János Gerle et al *Budapest: An Architectural Guide*. The best guide to the city's twentieth-century architecture, covering almost 300 buildings.

Gerard Gorman *Birds of Hungary*. The best book on the country's ornithological picture by a resident expert. His *Birding in Eastern Europe* also has good coverage of Hungary's birds.

Rogan Taylor & Klára Jamrich (eds) *Puskás on Puskás*. This marvellous book both depicts the life of one of the world's greatest footballers, and gives a fascinating insight into postwar Communist Hungary.

Ray Keenoy *Eminent Hungarians*. Everything you need to know about Hungary's most renowned historical and contemporary figures – from Lajos Kossuth to Harry Houdini.

Stephen Kirkland *The Wines and Vines of Hungary*. The definitive book on Hungarian wine.

George Lang *The Cuisine of Hungary*. A well-written and beautifully illustrated work on Hungarian cooking.

Dora Wieberson et al *The Architecture of Historic Hungary*. Comprehensive survey of Hungarian architecture through the ages.

Music

H ungarian classical **music** enshrines the trinity of Liszt, Bartók and Kodály: Liszt was the founding father, Bartók one of the greatest composers of the twentieth century, and Kodály (himself no slouch at composition) created a widely imitated system of musical education. When you also take into account talented Hungarian soloists like Perényi, it's clear that this small nation has made an outstanding contribution to the world of classical music. After classical, the musical genres most readily associated with Hungary are Gypsy and folk, both of which have some excellent exponents, the former led by the likes of violinist Roby Lakatos and cimbalom player Kálmán Balogh, and the latter by Muzsikás and the wonderful singer Márta Sebestyén. The increasing popularity of jazz is manifest in the growing number of clubs in Budapest and other larger cities, as well as several terrific summer jazz festivals held around the country. Meanwhile, Hungarian popular music, whilst not exactly cutting-edge, is becoming more adventurous as a new generation of DJs and bands soaks up the influence of Western European and American artists.

Classical music

Franz Liszt (1811–86), who described himself as a "mixture of Gypsy and Franciscan", cut a flamboyant figure in the salons of Europe as a virtuoso pianist and womanizer. His *Hungarian Rhapsodies* and other similar pieces reflected the "Gypsy" side to his character and the rising nationalism of his era, while later work like the *Transcendental Studies* (whose originality has only recently been recognized) invoked a visionary "Franciscan" mood. Despite his patriotic stance, however, Liszt's first language was German (he never fully mastered Hungarian), and his expressed wish to roam the villages of Hungary with a knapsack on his back was a Romantic fantasy.

That was left to **Béla Bartók** (1881–1945) and **Zoltán Kodály** (1882–1967), who began exploring the remoter districts of Hungary and Transylvania in 1906, collecting peasant music. Despite many hardships and local suspicion of their "monster" (a cutting stylus and phonograph cylinders), they managed to record and catalogue thousands of melodies, laying down high standards of musical ethnography, still maintained in Hungary today, while discovering a rich source of inspiration for their own compositions. Bartók believed that a genuine peasant melody was "quite as much a masterpiece in miniature as a Bach fugue or a Mozart sonata...a classic example of the expression of a musical thought in its most conceivably concise form, with the avoidance of all that is superfluous".

Bartók created a personal but universal musical language by reworking the raw essence of Magyar and Finno-Ugric folk music in a modern context – in particular his six String Quartets – although Hungarian public opinion was originally hostile. Feeling misunderstood and out of step with his country's increasingly pro-Nazi policies, Bartók left Hungary in 1940, dying poor and embittered in the United States. Since then, however, his reputation has soared, and the return of his body in 1988 occasioned national celebrations, shrewdly sponsored by the state.

Kodály's music is more consciously national: Bartók called it "a real profession of faith in the Hungarian soul". His *Peacock Variations* are based on a typical Old Style pentatonic tune and the *Dances of Galanta* on the popular music played by Gypsy bands. Old Style tunes also form the core of Kodály's work in musical education: the "Kodály method" employs group singing to develop musical skill at an early age. His ideas have made Hungarian music teaching among the best in the world, and Kodály himself a paternal figure to generations of children.

For others Kodály was a voice of conscience during the Rákosi era, writing the *Hymn of Zrínyi* to a seventeenth-century text whose call to arms against the Turkish invasion – "I perceive a ghastly dragon, full of venom and fury, snatching the crown of Hungary…" – was tumultuously acclaimed as an anti-Stalinist allegory. Its first performance was closely followed by the Uprising, and the *Hymn* was not performed again for many years; nor were any recordings made available until 1982.

Gypsy music

In recent years **Gypsy or Roma music** has really made a mark on the Hungarian music scene. Played on anything from spoons and milk jugs to guitars, Roma music ranges from haunting laments to playful wedding songs – as can be seen in French director Tony Gatliff's excellent film *Latcho Drom*, which explores Roma music from India to Spain. The most exciting artist around in the field of Gypsy music is the wizard violinist **Roby Lakatos**. A seventh-generation descendant of János Bihari (aka "King of the Gypsy Violinists"), Lakatos began playing the violin aged 5, graduated from Budapest with a First in classical violin and then, at the age of 18, formed his own orchestra in Brussels. He has since become one of the foremost violinists in the world. Fusing traditional Hungarian Gypsy sounds with elements of classical and jazz, the charismatic Lakatos and his band – which, unusually for a Gypsy band, includes piano and guitar – are an extraordinary proposition live, rarely failing to dazzle with their electric, often improvised performances. At one stage a regular at Les Ateliers in Brussels, Lakatos now tours extensively around the world and was a huge hit at the London Proms.

Although not Roma, another major star, and the one musician who could justifiably claim to be in the same league as Lakatos, is **Félix Lajkó**, a Hungarian virtuoso violinist from Vojvodina in Serbia, whose eccentric fusion of Gypsy, jazz and folk inspires a devout following. Not too far behind these stand-out musicians is **Kálmán Balogh**, one of the world's foremost exponents of the cimbalom, a hammer dulcimer (stringed instrument) played with little mallets. A mesmerizing virtuoso performer, Balogh also tours regularly with his Gypsy Cimbalom Band, who bring a strong, jazz-influenced sound to proceedings. The next generation of Hungarian Gypsy musicians is currently being led by **Bela Lakatos and the Gypsy Youth Band**, a wonderfully talented five-piece collective whose predominantly vocal sound is complemented by guitar and mandolin, and a percussive element comprising sticks, spoons, metal cans and the like. Other well-established Roma artists in Hungary to keep an eye out for include Romano Drom, Andro Drom, the Szilvási Folk Band, and Kalyi Jag – all these groups tour extensively and are the focal point of most Roma festivals in Hungary and abroad.

None of the above, however, has much in common with the "Gypsy music" which you will see advertised at touristy restaurants, known in Hungarian as **Magyar nóta** – although that is not to say it should be avoided. Consisting of a series of mid-nineteenth-century Hungarian ballads traditionally played by Roma musicians, Magyar nóta is usually performed by one or two violinists, a bass player and a guy on the cimbalom. The more famous restaurants boast their own musical dynasties, such as the Lakatos family, who have been performing this sort of music for over a century. In the past, wandering self-taught artists like János Bihari, Czinka Panna and Czermak (a nobleman turned vagabond) were legendary figures. Hungarian diners are usually keen to make requests or sing along when the *prímás* (band leader) comes to the table, soliciting tips. If approached yourself, it is acceptable (though rather awkward) to decline with a *"nem köszönöm"*, but if you signal a request to the band, you have to pay for it.

Folk music

Hungarian folk music (*Magyar népzene*) originated around the Urals and the Turkic steppes over a millennium ago, and is different again from Gypsy or Roma music. The haunting rhythms and pentatonic scale of this "Old Style" music (to use Bartók's terminology) were subsequently overlaid by "New Style" European influences – which have been discarded by more modern enthusiasts in the folk revival centred around Táncház. These "Dance Houses" encourage people to learn traditional dances – with much shouting, whistling, and slapping of boots and thighs.

The two biggest names to emerge from the Táncház movement were **Muzsikás** and **Márta Sebestyén**, who have been regular collaborators for years. A four-piece ensemble comprising bass, violin and flute, Muzsikás (pronounced *Mu-zhi-kash*) started out in the early 1970s by exploring the musical archives of village folk music, from which they derived their own distinctive repertoire, combining traditional Hungarian music with the sounds of Transylvania, across the border in Romania – whilst their recorded output is not that prolific, they do tour regularly, both at home and abroad.

Unquestionably Hungary's finest folk singer, and one of the best in Europe, Sebestyén's gorgeous and distinctive voice has seen her become firmly established on the world music scene in recent years, a reputation that was sealed after she featured on the soundtrack to the film *The English Patient*. Aside from her regular appearances with Muzsikás, Sebestyén has also guested with **Vujicsics**, a marvellous seven-strong ensemble from Pomáz near Szentendre who specialize in Serbian and Croatian folk melodies. A somewhat more unorthodox outfit are the Transylvanians, a group of four young German-based Hungarians whose frenetic blend of folk, classical, rock and techno (termed speedfolk) pretty much defies any standard form of categorization. Other folk artists to watch out for include the Ökrős Ensemble, who play folk music from Transylvania, the Slovakian-based Hungarian group Ghymes, and the superb Budapest Klezmer outfit Da Naye Kapelye.

Popular music and jazz

Budapest has undergone a **popular music** revival in the last few years: radio stations and music magazines have taken off and the city has become part of the international tour circuit – the Sziget Festival each August (see p.132) is now unquestionably one of the premier music gatherings on the continent. This has all had a knock-on effect on local music, which ranges from instrumental groups (Korai Öröm and Másfél) to techno-inspired performers like Anima Sound System. Heaven Street Seven call their version of guitar pop Dunabeat, while Quimby is the Hungarian equivalent of Tom Waits. The controversial, and one-time underground, local radio station **Tilos Rádió** has done much to promote **DJs**, and there is now a host of them around the country. Some like Tommy Boy and Schultz play run-of-the-mill **techno**, while others like Palotai and Mango do a lot of wild mixing using a mass of sources and sounds. Bestiák are a sort of Magyar Girls Aloud and Ganszta Zoli looks to LA gangster rap for his inspiration. A rather more unlikely figure on the Hungarian pop scene is Uhrin Benedek, a septuagenarian, wig-enhanced, former warehouse worker who, since an appearance at the Sziget Festival, has gained a cult following for his extremely bizarre, and somewhat less than tuneful, songsmithery.

Jazz has always had a devout, but small, following in the country and more and more clubs and bars offer live jazz. There are excellent summer jazz **festivals** in Miskolc, Salgótarján and Sárospatak, but the biggest and best is in Debrecen. Dés, Mihály Dresch, Aladár Pege and the Benkó Dixieland Band have all achieved success outside Hungary, as has György Szabados, who works on the interface between jazz and classical music. Another name worth checking out is Béla Szakcsi Lakatos, a jazz pianist who frequently plays in Budapest clubs.

Discography

Many of the recordings listed below can be bought from Passion Music in the UK (⊛ www.passiondiscs.co.uk). In Hungary, good-quality **records and CDs** produced by Hungaroton (⊛ www.hungaroton.hu) retail for half or a third of what you'd pay abroad, which makes it well worth rooting through record shops (*lemezbolt*). After Western and Hungarian **pop**, the bulk of their stock consists of **classical music**. A full discography of the works of Liszt, Bartók and Kodály, directors like Dohnányi and Doráti, and contemporary Hungarian soloists and singers would fill a catalogue, but look out for the following names: pianists András Schiff, Zoltán Kocsis (who also conducts) and Dezső Ránki; the cellist Miklós Perényi; the Liszt Ferenc Chamber Orchestra, the Budapest Festival Orchestra and the Hungarian Radio and TV Symphony; conductors Iván Fischer and Tamás Vasáry; and singers Mária Zádori, Ingrid Kertesi, Andrea Rost, Adrienne Csengery, József Gregor, Kolos Kovats and László Polgar, the last two excellent bass singers.

For those who like contemporary music, the grand old man of the modern Hungarian scene is György Kurtág, while Tibor Szemző produces meditative works, one of which, *Tractatus*, inspired by German philosopher Ludwig Wittgenstein, is quite extraordinary. If you're into ethnomusic, then László Hortobágyi's "Gaia" music is worth listening to.

Folk and Gypsy music can be bought at all record stores, though you should be warned that a CD with a picture of a Gypsy orchestra all dressed up in red waistcoats is of the "*nóta*" variety – it's worth asking to listen before you buy. As well as the artists listed below, there are hundreds of great recordings in the above fields. The following simply offer an introduction.

Individual artists

Kálmán Balogh *Roma Vándor* (M&W, Netherlands). On this live recording, the virtuoso of the cimbalom turns this staple of Hungarian Gypsy restaurant bands into something much more than entertainment for eating. Recorded with artistic director Romano Kokalo, *Gipsy Colours* (Fonó,

Budapest) is a fabulous selection of Balkan-inspired dance tunes.

Félix Lajkó *Remény (Hope)*, *Félix* (both Tilos), *Lajkó Félix and Band* (Fonó). The best recordings so far of this Hungarian virtuoso violinist from Subotica in northern Serbia – *Hope*, his most recent CD, is a marvellous record featuring previously unreleased concert recordings alongside pieces from the soundtrack to *Othello*, while *Félix* is a collection of his work from various projects and festivals between 1997 and 2002. He also features with the Boban Markovic Orchestra, the fantastic Serbian Gypsy ensemble, on the CD *Srce Cigansko*, which combines typically rumbustious Serbian brass with Lajkó's violin to marvellous effect.

Roby Lakatos Earlier works include *Lakatos* (Deutsche Grammophon), which features new workouts of favourites by the likes of Brahms alongside traditional Hungarian folk songs; *Lakatos: Live from Budapest* (Deutsche Grammophon), a homecoming concert in Budapest's Thália Theatre in 1999; and *As Time Goes By* (Deutsche Grammophon) is a recording of popular soundtracks from the movies, including the gorgeous "Djelem, Djelem" from Emir Kusturica's memorable *Time of the Gypsies*. His most recent albums (all on the Avanti label) are *Firedance*, a sizzling record exploring Gypsy themes from around the world; *Klezmer Karma*, a funky, Jewish-influenced recording featuring performances by Miriam Fuks and the Franz Liszt Chamber Orchestra; and *Roby Lakatos with Musical Friends*, an all-jazz project boasting some stellar guests such as Stephane Grappelli and Marc Fossett.

Márta Sebestyén *Kismet* (Hannibal). On this wide-ranging album, Hungary's leading Tánchaz singer draws upon various folk traditions, with Bosnian, Hindi and Irish songs, among others; otherwise, Sebestyén is best known for her recordings with the folk group Muzsikás (see p.459), while her international star has risen thanks to significant contributions to the Grammy-award-winning Deep Forest album *Boheme* and the film *The English Patient*.

Groups

Bela Lakatos and The Gypsy Youth Project *Introducing* (World Music Network). Lively and refreshing debut album from this superbly talented outfit, with songs pertaining to rural Roma life. Wonderful vocals and some fabulous instrumental improvisation.

Di Naye Kapelye The band's three albums to date are the eponymous *Di Naye Kapelye*, *A Mazeldiker Yid* and *Traktorist* (all Oriente Musik), all terrific, and typically exuberant, Klezmer recordings, which make for immensely enjoyable listening. *Traktorist* features a wonderfully jolly Communist-era ode to the Yiddish tractor.

Jánosi Ensemble *Jánosi Együttes* (Hungaroton). A young group performing "authentic" versions of some of the folk tunes that Bartók borrowed in his compositions – a record that makes a bridge between classical and folk music.

The Kalamajka Ensemble *Bonchidától Bonchidáig* (Hungaroton). Another leading Tánchaz group, this terrific ensemble plays Transylvanian and Csángó ballads and dances.

Muzsikás *The Bartók Album* (Hannibal). Featuring Márta Sebestyén and the Romanian violinist Alexander Balanescu, this manages to set the music of Bartók in its original context – three of Bartók's violin duos are presented alongside original field recordings and recordings of his transcriptions by Muzsikás. *Morning Star* (Hannibal) is another fine Muzsikás volume – interestingly, their record company recommended slight changes and a softening of edges for this foreign edition of *Hazafelé* (Hungaroton), the original Hungarian recording. Their latest release, 2004's *Live at the Liszt Academy of Music*, which again stars Sebestyén, is a compilation of recordings taken from successive appearances at the Budapest Spring Festival.

Transylvanians *Denevér* (Mega) and *Igen!* (Westpark). On these two recent albums, this exceptional group of young musicians showcase their full range of talents – the latter features the wonderful voice and terrific bass playing of the front woman, Isabel Nagy.

Vujicsics Ensemble *Serbian Music from South Hungary* (Hannibal). More complex tunes than most Magyar folk music, with a distinct Balkan influence. Two more recent albums, both featuring Márta Sebestyén, are *25 – Live at the Academy of Music* (R-E-Disc 005), a concert in Budapest celebrating the group's twenty-fifth anniversary, and *Podravina* (R-E-Disc 004), a selection of Croatian dance melodies.

János Zerkula and Regina Fikó *Este a Gyimesbe Jártam* (Hungaroton). Music from the Csángó region; sparser, sadder and more discordant than other Transylvanian music.

Compilation albums

Magyar népzene 3 (Hungarian folk music; Hungaroton). A four-disc set of field recordings covering the whole range of folk music, including Old and New Style songs, instrumental and occasional music, that's probably the best overall introduction. In the West, the discs are marketed as "Folk Music of Hungary Vol.1".

Magyar hangszeres népzene (Hungarian Instrumental Folk Music; Hungaroton). A very good three-disc set of field recordings of village and Gypsy bands, including lots of solos.

VII. Magyarországi Táncház Találkozó. One of a series, the *Seventh Dance House Festival* (Hungaroton) features a great mixture of dances, ballads and instrumental pieces from all over Hungary. The *Tenth Dance House Festival* collection (Hungaroton) is also especially good.

Rough Guide to Hungarian Music (World Music Network). Despite one or two obvious omissions, this is an otherwise excellent introduction to the many wildly differing sounds of Hungarian music.

Rough Guide to the Music of Eastern Europe (World Music Network). Although most of the songs on this CD are from the Balkans, there is a healthy representation from Hungary, featuring songs by Márta Sebestyén, Vízöntő and Kálmán Balogh and the Gypsy Cimbalom Band.

Rough Guide to the Music of Hungarian Gypsies (World Music Network). All the big-hitters are here on this marvellous and thoroughly comprehensive introduction to the many strands of Hungarian Gypsy music – the highlight is a ripping tune by Mitsou performed with the brilliant Romanian band Fanfare Ciocarlia.

Rough Guide Music of the Gypsies (World Music Network). From India to Spain, this is a fantastic introduction to Gypsy music worldwide, with Hungary represented by Kálmán Balogh and the József Lacatos Orchestra. Also worth checking out is the *Rough Guide to Klezmer Revival* (RGNET 1203), which features a track by Di Naye Kapelye.

Táncházi muzsika (Music from the Táncház; Hungaroton). A double album of the Sebö Ensemble playing Táncház music from various regions of Hungary. Wild and exciting rhythms.

Language

Language

Hungarian

H ungarian is a unique, complex and subtle tongue, classified as belonging to the Finno-Ugric linguistic group, which includes Finnish and Estonian. If you happen to know those languages, however, don't expect it to be a help – there are some structural similarities, but lexically they are totally different. In fact, some scholars think the connection is completely bogus, and have linked Hungarian to the Siberian Chuvash language and a whole host of other pretty obscure tongues. Basically the origins of Hungarian remain a total mystery, and though a few words from Turkish have crept in, together with some German, English and (a few) Russian neologisms, there is not much that the beginner will recognize.

Consequently, foreigners aren't really expected to speak Hungarian, and natives are used to being addressed in German, the lingua franca of tourism. It's understood by older people, particularly in Transdanubia, and by many students and business people, besides virtually everyone around Balaton or in tourist offices. For a brief visit it's probably easier to brush up on some German for your means of communication. A few basic Magyar phrases can make all the difference, though. Hungarians are intensely proud of their language, and as a nation are surprisingly bad at learning anyone else's. However, English is gaining ground rapidly, and is increasingly widely understood.

Basic grammar

Although its rules are complicated, it's worth describing a few features of **Hungarian grammar**, albeit imperfectly. Hungarian is an agglutinative language – in other words, its vocabulary is built upon **root-words**, which are modified in various ways to express different ideas and nuances. Instead of prepositions – "to", "from", "in", etc – Hungarian uses **suffixes**, or tags added to the ends of genderless **nouns**. The change in suffix is largely determined by the noun's context: for example the noun "book" (*könyv*) will take a final "*et*" in the accusative (*könyvet*); "in the book" = *könyvben*; "from the book" = *könyvből*. It is also affected by the rules of vowel harmony (which take a while to get used to, but don't alter meaning, so don't worry about getting them wrong). Most of the nouns in the vocabulary section below are in the nominative or subject form – that is, without suffixes. In Hungarian, "**the**" is *a* (before a word beginning with a consonant) or *az* (preceding a vowel); the word for "**a/an**" is *egy* (which also means "one").

Plurals are indicated by adding a final "k", with a link vowel if necessary, giving -*ek*, -*ok* or -*ak*. Nouns preceded by a number or other indication of quantity (eg: many, several) do *not* appear as plural: eg *könyvek* means "books", but "two books" is *két könyv* (using the singular form of the noun).

Adjectives precede the noun (*a piros ház* = the red house), adopting suffixes to form the comparative (*jó* = good; *jobb* = better), plus the prefix *leg* to signify the superlative (*legjobb* = the best).

Negatives are usually formed by placing the word *nem* before the verb or adjective. *Ez* (this), *ezek* (these), *az* (that) and *azok* (those) are the **demonstratives**.

Pronunciation

Achieving passably good **pronunciation**, rather than grammar, is the first priority (see below for general guidelines). **Stress** almost invariably falls on the first syllable of a word and all letters are spoken, although in sentences the tendency is to slur words together. Vowel sounds are greatly affected by the bristling **accents** (that actually distinguish separate letters) which, together with the "double letters" *cs*, *gy*, *ly*, *ny*, *sz*, *ty* and *zs*, give the Hungarian **alphabet** its formidable appearance.

A o as in h**o**t

Á a as in f**a**ther

B b as in **b**est

C ts as in ba**ts**

CS ch as in **ch**urch

D d as in **d**ust

E e as in y**e**t

É ay as in s**ay**

F f as in **f**ed

G g as in **g**o

GY a soft dy as in **due**

H h as in **h**at

I i as in b**i**t, but slightly longer

Í ee as in s**ee**

J y as in **y**es

K k as in si**ck**

L l as in **l**eap

LY y as in **y**es

M m as in **m**ud

N n as in **n**ot

NY ny as in o**ni**on

O aw as in s**aw**, with the tongue kept high

Ó aw as in s**aw**, as above but longer

Ö ur as in f**ur**, with the lips tightly rounded but without any "r" sound

Ő ur as in f**ur**, as above but longer

P p as in si**p**

R r pronounced with the tip of the tongue like a Scottish "**r**"

S sh as in **sh**op

SZ s as in **s**o

T t as in si**t**

TY ty as in **Tue**sday or pret**ti**er, said quickly

U u as in p**u**ll

Ú oo as in f**oo**d

Ü u as in the German "**ü**ber" with the lips tightly rounded

Ű u as above, but longer

V v as in **v**at

W v as used in "**V**alkman," "**v**hiskey" or "WC" (vait-say)

Z z as in **z**ero

ZS zh as in me**as**ure

Words and phrases

Basics

Do you speak…?	… beszél…	you're welcome	szívesen
English	angolul!	~~hello/goodbye (informal)~~	szia
German	németül	goodbye	viszontlátásra
French	franciául	see you later (informal)	viszlát
yes	igen	good morning	jó reggelt
OK	jó	good day	jó napot
no/not	nem	good evening	jó estét
I (don't) understand	(nem) Értem	good night	jó éjszakát
please	kérem	How are you? (informal)	Hogy vagy?
excuse me	bocsánat	(more formal)	Hogy van?
Two beers, please	Két sört kérek	Could you speak	Elmondaná
thank you (very much)	köszönöm (szépen)	more slowly?	lassabban?

What do you call this?	Mi a neve ennek?	the day before yesterday	tegnapelőtt
Please write it down	Kérem, írja le	in the morning	reggel
today	ma	in the evening	este
tomorrow	holnap	at noon	délben
the day after tomorrow	holnapután	at midnight	éjfélkor
yesterday	tegnap		

L LANGUAGE | Words and phrases

Questions and requests

Legyen szíves ("Would you be so kind") is the polite formula for attracting someone's attention. Hungarian has numerous interrogative modes whose subtleties elude foreigners, so it's best to use the simple *van?* ("is there?"), to which the reply might be *nincs* or *nincsen* ("there isn't"/"there aren't any"). In shops or restaurants you will immediately be addressed with the one-word *tessék,* meaning "Can I help you?", "What would you like?" or "Next!". To order in restaurants, shops and markets, use *kérek* ("I'd like…") plus accusative noun; *Kérem, adjon azt* ("Please give me that"); *Egy ilyet kérek* ("I'll have one of those").

I'd like/we'd like	Szeretnék/szeretnénk	Do you have a student discount?	Van diák kedvezmény?
Where is/are…?	Hol van/vannak…?	Is everything included?	Ebben minden szerepel?
Hurry up!	Siessen!	I asked for…	Én…-t rendeltem
How much is it?	Mennyibe kerül?	The bill please	Fizetni szeretnék
per night	egy éjszakára	We're paying separately	Külön-külön fizetünk
per week	egy hétre	what?	mi?
a single room	egyágyas szoba	why?	miert?
a double room	kétágyas szoba	when?	mikor?
hot (cold) water	meleg (hideg) víz	who?	ki?
a shower	egy zuhany		
It's very expensive	Ez nagyon drága		
Do you have anything cheaper?	Van valami olcsóbb?		

Some signs

entrance	bejárat	shop	bolt
exit	kijárat	market	piac
push	tólni	room for rent	szoba kiadó or Zimmer frei
pull	húzni		
arrival	érkezés	hospital	kórház
departure	indulás	pharmacy	gyógyszertár
open	nyitva	(local) police	(kerületi) rendőrség
closed	zárva	caution/beware	vigyázat!/vigyázz!
free admission	szabad belépés	no smoking	tilos a dohányzás/ dohányozni tilos
women's toilet	női (or WC – "vait-say")	no bathing	tilos a fürdés/füredni tilos
men's toilet	férfi mosdó (or WC – "vait-say")		

Directions

Where's the…?	Hol van a…?	towards	felé
campsite	kemping	on the right (left)	jobbra (balra)
hotel	szálloda/hotel	straight ahead	egyenesen előre
railway station	vasútállomás	(over) there/here	ott/itt
bus station	buszállomás	Where are you going?	Hova megy?
bus-stand	kocsiállás	Is that on the	Az a…úton?
(bus or train) stop	megálló	way to…?	
inland	belföldi	I want to get	Le akarok szállni
international	külföldi/nemzetközi	out at…	…-on/en
Is it near (far)?	Közel (messze) van?	Please stop here!	Itt álljon meg!
Which bus goes	Melyik busz	I'm lost!	Eltévedtem!
to…?	megy…-ra/re?	arrivals	érkező járatok
A one-way ticket	Egy jegyet kérek…		(or érkezés)
to…please	-ra/re csak oda.	departures	induló járatok
A return ticket to…	Egy retur		(or indulás)
	jegye…-ra/re	to/from	hova/honnan
Do I have to change	Át kell szállnom?	change	átszállás
trains?		via	át

Descriptions and reactions

and	és	small	kicsi
or	vagy	quick	gyors
nothing	semmi	slow	lassú
perhaps	talán	now	most
very	nagyon	later	később
good	jó	beautiful	szép
bad	rossz	ugly	csúnya
better	jobb	Help!	Segítség!
big	nagy	I'm ill	beteg vagyok

Numbers

1	egy	15	tizenöt
2	kettő	16	tizenhat
3	három	17	tizenhét
4	négy	18	tizennyolc
5	öt	19	tizenkilenc
6	hat	20	húsz
7	hét	21	huszonegy
8	nyolc	30	harminc
9	kilenc	40	negyven
10	tíz	50	ötven
11	tizenegy	60	hatvan
12	tizenkettő	70	hetven
13	tizenhárom	80	nyolcvan
14	tizennégy	90	kilencven

100	száz	800	nyolcszáz
101	százegy	900	kilencszáz
150	százötven	1000	egyezer
200	kettőszáz	half	fél
300	háromszáz	a quarter	negyed
400	négyszáz	each/piece	darab (db)
500	ötszáz	10 grams (common	deka
600	hatszáz	unit for fruit and veg)	
700	hétszáz	100 grams	tíz deka

Time, days and dates

Luckily, the 24-hour clock is used for timetables, but on cinema programmes you may see notations like 1/4, 3/4, etc. These derive from the spoken expression of time which, as in German, makes reference to the hour approaching completion. For example 3.30 is expressed as *fél négy* – "half (on the way to) four"; 3.45 – *háromnegyed négy* ("three quarters on the way to four"); 6.15 – *"negyed hét"* ("one quarter towards seven"), etc. However, "...o'clock" is...*óra*, rather than referring to the hour ahead. Duration is expressed by the suffixes *-tól* ("from") and *-ig* ("to"); minutes are *perc*; to ask the time, say *"Hány óra?"*.

Sunday	vasárnap	on Monday	hetfőn
Monday	hétfő	on Tuesday	kedden etc. but note:
Tuesday	kedd	on Sunday	vasárnap
Wednesday	szerda	day	nap
Thursday	csütörtök	week	hét
Friday	péntek	month	hónap
Saturday	szombat	year	év

Hungarian food and drink terms

The food categories below refer to the general divisions used in menus. In cheaper places you will also find a further division of meat dishes: ready-made dishes like stews (*készételek*) and freshly cooked (in theory) dishes such as those cooked in breadcrumbs or grilled (*frissensültek*).

Tészták is a rogue pasta-doughy category that includes savoury dishes such as *túróscsusza* (pasta served with cottage cheese and a sprinkling of bacon), as well as sweet ones like *somlói galuska* (cream-and chocolate-covered sponge).

Basics

bors	pepper	mustár	mustard
cukor	sugar	rizs	rice
ecet	vinegar	só	salt
Egészségedre!	Cheers!	tejföl	sour cream
Jó étvágyat!	Bon appétit!	tejszín	cream
kenyér	bread	vaj	butter
kifli	croissant-shaped roll	zsemle or	bread rolls
méz	honey	péksütemeny	

Cooking terms

comb	leg	jól megfőzve	well done (boiled)
mell	breast	pörkölt	stewed slowly
angolosan	(English-style) underdone/rare	rántott	deep fried in breadcrumbs
főtt	boiled	roston sütve	grilled
főzelék	basic vegetable stews	sülve	roasted
jól megsütve	well done (fried)	sült/sütve	fried

Soups (levesek)

bakonyi betyárleves	"Outlaw soup" of chicken, beef, noodles and vegetables, richly spiced	halászlé	a rich paprika fish soup often served with hot paprika
		húsleves	meat consommé
csirke-aprólék leves	mixed vegetable and giblet soup	jókai bableves	bean soup flavoured with smoked meat
erőleves	meat consommé often served with noodles (tésztával or metélttel), liver dumplings (májgombóccal), or an egg placed raw into the soup (tojással)	kunsági pandúrleves	chicken soup seasoned with nutmeg, paprika and garlic
		lencseleves	lentil soup
		hideg meggyleves	delicious chilled sour cherry soup
		palócleves	mutton, bean and sour cream soup
		paradicsomleves	tomato soup
gombaleves	mushroom soup	tarkonyos borjúraguleves	lamb soup flavoured with tarragon
gulyásleves	goulash in its original Hungarian form as a soup, sometimes served in a small kettle pot (bográcsgulyás)	ujházi tyúkleves	chicken soup with noodles, vegetables and meat
		zöldségleves	vegetable soup

Appetizers (előételek)

These comprise both hot (*meleg*) and cold (*hideg*) dishes.

füstölt csülök tormával	smoked knuckle of pork with horseradish	rakott krumpli	layered potato casserole with sausage and eggs
hortobágyi palacsinta	pancake stuffed with minced meat and served with creamy paprika sauce	rántott gomba	mushrooms fried in breadcrumbs, sometimes stuffed with sheep's cheese (juhtúróval töltött)
körözött	a paprika-flavoured spread made with sheep's cheese and served with toast	rántott sajt, Camembert, karfiol	Camembert or cauliflower fried in breadcrumbs
libamáj	goose liver		

| tatárbeefsteak | raw mince that you mix with an egg, salt, pepper, butter, paprika and mustard and spread on toast | velőcsont fokhagymás pirítóssal | bone marrow spread on toast rubbed with garlic, a special delicacy associated with the gourmet Gyula Krúdy |

Salads (saláták)

Salads are often served in a vinegary dressing, although other dressings include blue cheese (*rokfortos*), yogurt (*joghurtos*) or French (*francia*).

csalamádé	mixed pickled salad	paradicsom saláta	tomato salad
fejes saláta	lettuce	uborka saláta	cucumber which can be gherkins (csemege or kovászos) or the fresh variety (friss)
idénysaláta	fresh salad of whatever is in season		
jércesaláta	chicken salad		

Fish dishes (halételek)

csuka tejfölben sütve	fried pike with sour cream	ponty	carp
fogas	a local fish of the pike-perch family	ponty filé gombával	carp fillet in mushroom sauce
fogasszeletek Gundel modra	breaded fillet of fogas	rántott pontyfilé	carp fillet fried in breadcrumbs
harcsa	catfish	rostélyos töltött ponty	carp stuffed with bread, egg, herbs and fish liver or roe
kecsege	sterlet (small sturgeon)		
nyelvhal	sole	süllő	another pike-perch relative
paprikás ponty	carp in paprika sauce		
pisztráng	trout	sült hal	fried fish
pisztráng tejszínes mártásban	trout baked in cream	tonhal	tuna

Meat dishes (húsételek)

baromfi	poultry	marha	beef
bécsi szelet	Wiener schnitzel	nyúl	rabbit
bélszin	sirloin	őz	venison
bélszinjava	tenderloin	pulyka	turkey
csirke	chicken	sertés	pork
fácán	pheasant	sonka	ham
fasírt	meatballs	vaddisznó	wild boar
hátszin	rumpsteak	vadételek	game
kacsa	duck	virsli	frankfurter
kolbász	spicy sausage	borjúpörkölt	closer to what foreigners mean by "goulash", veal stew seasoned with garlic
liba	goose		
máj	liver		

cigányrostélyos	"Gypsy-style" steak with brown sauce	rablóhús nyárson	kebab of pork, veal and bacon
csikós tokány	strips of beef braised in bacon, onion rings, sour and tomato sauce	sertésborda	pork chop
		sült libacomb tört burgonyával és párolt káposztával	grilled goose leg with potatoes, onions and steamed cabbage
csülök	knuckle of pork	töltött-káposzta	cabbage stuffed with meat and rice, in a tomato sauce
erdélyi rakott-káposzta	layers of cabbage, rice and ground pork baked in sour cream (a Transylvanian speciality)		
		töltött-paprika	peppers stuffed with meat and rice, in a tomato sauce
hagymás rostélyos	braised steak piled high with fried onions	vaddisznó borók amártással	wild boar in juniper sauce
pacal	tripe, often served in a paprika sauce	vasi pecsenye	fried pork marinated in milk and garlic
paprikás csirke	chicken in paprika sauce		

Sauces (mártásban)

bormártásban	in a wine sauce	tárkonyos mártásban	in a tarragon sauce
ecetes tormával	with horseradish	tejszínes paprikás mártásban	in a cream and paprika sauce
fokhagymás mártásban	in a garlic sauce	vadasmártásban	in a brown sauce (made of mushrooms, almonds, herbs and brandy)
gombamártásban	in a mushroom sauce		
kapormártásban	in a dill sauce		
meggymártásban	in a morello cherry sauce	zöldborsós	in a green pea sauce
paprikás mártásban	in a paprika sauce	zöldborsosmártásba	in a green peppercorn sauce

Accompaniments (köretek)

galuska	noodles	burgonya	served with parsley
hasábburgonya	chips/French fries	rizs	rice
krokett	potato croquettes	zöldköret	mixed vegetables (often of frozen origin)
petrezselymes	boiled potatoes		

Vegetables (zöldségek)

bab	beans	kukorica	sweetcorn
borsó	peas	lecsó	a tomato-green pepper stew, a popular ingredient in Hungarian cooking
burgonya/krumpli	potatoes		
fokhagyma	garlic		
gomba	mushrooms		
hagyma	onions	padlizsán	aubergine/eggplant
káposzta	cabbage	paprika (édes/erős)	peppers (sweet/hot)
karfiol	cauliflower	paradicsom	tomatoes
kelkáposzta	savoy cabbage	sárgarépa	carrots
		spárga	asparagus

spenot	spinach	zöldborsó	peas
uborka	cucumber	zukkini	courgette
zöldbab	green beans		

Fruit and nuts (gyümölcs)

alma	apple	dió	walnut
bodza	elderflower	eper	strawberry
citrom	lemon	füge	fig
(görög) dinnye	(water) melon		
körte	pear	őszibarack	peach
málna	raspberry	sárgabarack	apricot
mandula	almond	szilva	plum
meggy	morello cherry	szőlő	grape
mogyoró	hazelnut	tök	marrow or pumpkin/
narancs	orange		squash

Cheese (sajt)

füstölt sajt	smoked cheese	trappista	rubbery, Edam-type
juhtúró	sheep's cheese		cheese
márvány	Danish blue cheese	túró	curd cheese

Drinks

ásványvíz	mineral water	sima (csap) víz	ordinary (tap) water
bor	wine	sör	beer
gyümölcslé	fruit juice		
narancslé	orange juice		
Pálinka	schnapps-like fruit brandy, which comes in a large range of flavours		

Glossary

ÁFA Goods tax, equivalent to VAT

alföld Plain; usually refers to the Great Plain (*Nagyalföld*) rather than the Little Plain (*Kisalföld*) in northwestern Hungary

állatkert zoo

áruház department store

autóbuszállomás bus station

ÁVO The dreaded secret police of the Rákosi era, renamed the ÁVH in 1949

barlang cave

Belváros Inner town or city, typically characterized by Baroque or Neoclassical architecture

borkostoló wine tasting

borozó wine bar

botanikuskert botanical garden

büfé snack bar

castrum (Latin) a Roman fortification

cigány Gypsy (can be abusive); hence *cigánytelep*, a Gypsy settlement; and *cigányzene*, Gypsy music

csárda inn; nowadays, a restaurant with rustic decor

csárdás traditional wild dance to violin music

csikós (plural *csikósok*) *puszta* horse herdsman; a much romanticized figure of the nineteenth century

cukrászda cake shop

djami or **dzami** mosque

domb hill

Duna River Danube

Erdély Transylvania; for centuries a part of the Hungarian territories, its loss to Romania in 1920 still rankles

erdő forest, wood

erőd fortification

étterem restaurant

falu village

fogadó inn

folyó river

forrás natural spring

fürdő public baths, often fed by thermal springs

gyógyfürdő mineral baths with therapeutic properties

hajdúk cattle-drovers turned outlaws, who later settled near Debrecen in the Hajdúság Region

hajó boat

hajóállomás boat landing stage

halászcsárda/halászkert fish restaurants

ház house

hegy hill or low mountain (**hegység** = range of hills)

híd bridge

ifjúsági szálló youth hostel

iskola school

kápolna chapel

kapu gate

kastély manor house or stately home, country seat of noble families

kávéház coffee house

kert garden, park

kerület (ker.) district

kiállítás exhibition

kincstár treasury

kirakodó vásár fair, craft or flea market

kollégium student hostel

komp ferry

körút (krt.) literally, ring; normally a boulevard around the city centre. Some cities have semicircular "Great" and "Small" boulevards (Nagykörút and Kiskörút) surrounding their Belváros

kőtár lapidarium

köz alley, lane; also used to define geographical regions, eg the "Mud strip" (*Sárköz*) bordering the Danube

kulcs key

kút well or fountain

lakótelep high-rise apartment buildings

liget park, grove or wood

lovarda riding school

Magyar Hungarian (pronounced "*mod*-yor")

Magyarország Hungary

Malév Hungarian national airline

MÁV Hungarian national railways

megálló a railway station or bus stop

megye county

műemlék historic monument, protected building

művelődési ház/központ arts centre

palota palace; *Püspök-palota*, a Bishop's residence

pályaudvar (pu.) rail terminus

panzió pension

patak stream

pénz money

piac outdoor market

pince cellar; a **Bor-Pince** contains and serves wine

puszta another name for the Great Plain, coined when the region was a wilderness

rakpart embankment or quay

rév ferry

rom ruined building; sometimes set in a garden with stonework finds, a *Romkert*

Roma The Romany word for Gypsy, preferred by many Roma in Hungary

sétány "walk" or promenade

skanzen outdoor ethnographic museum

söröző beer hall

strand beach, or any area for sunbathing or swimming

szabadtér open-air; as in *színház* (theatre) or *múzeum* (museum)

szálló or szálloda hotel

szent saint

sziget island

szüret grape harvest

tájház old peasant house turned into a museum

táncház venue for Hungarian folk music and dance

temető cemetery

templom church

tér square; *tere* in the possessive case, as in Hősök tere, "Heroes' Square"

terem hall

tó lake

torony tower; as in *Tv-Torony*, television tower, and *Víztorony*, water tower

túristaház tourist hotel

turista térkép hiking map

üdülőház holiday home or workers' hostel

út road; in the possessive case, *útja*, eg *Mártírok útja*, "Road of the Martyrs"

utca (u.) street

vár castle; *várrom*, castle ruin

város town; may be divided into an inner Belváros, a lower-lying *Alsóváros* and a modern *Újváros* section

városháza town hall

vásár market

vásárcsarnok market hall

vasútállomás train station

vendéglő a type of restaurant

völgy valley; *Hűvösvölgy*, "Cool Valley"

Zsidó Jew or Jewish

zsinagóga synagogue

Travel
store

www.roughguides.com

478

Nicaragua Central America on a Budget
Niger West Africa
Nigeria West Africa
Norway Europe on a Budget, Norway, Scandinavia
Panama Central America on a Budget, Costa Rica & Panama Map, Panama
Paraguay South America on a Budget
Peru Peru, Peru Map, South America on a Budget
Philippines The Philippines, Southeast Asia on a Budget,
Poland Europe on a Budget, Poland
Portugal Algarve DIR, The Algarve Map, Europe on a Budget, Lisbon DIR, Lisbon Map, Madeira DIR, Portugal, Portugal Map, Spain & Portugal Map
Puerto Rico The Caribbean, Puerto Rico
Romania Europe on a Budget, Romania
Russia Europe on a Budget, Moscow, St Petersburg
St Kitts & Nevis The Caribbean
St Lucia The Caribbean
St Vincent & the Grenadines The Caribbean
Scotland Britain, Camping in Britain, Edinburgh DIR, Europe on a Budget, Scotland, Scottish Highlands & Islands
Senegal West Africa
Serbia Montenegro Europe on a Budget
Sierra Leone West Africa
Singapore Malaysia, Singapore & Brunei [1 title], Singapore, Singapore DIR, Southeast Asia on a Budget
Slovakia Czech & Slovak Republics, Europe on a Budget
Slovenia Europe on a Budget, Slovenia
South Africa Cape Town & the Garden

Route, South Africa, South Africa Map
Spain Andalucía, Andalucía Map, Barcelona, Barcelona DIR, Barcelona Map, Europe on a Budget, Ibiza & Formentera DIR, Gran Canaria DIR, Madrid DIR, Lanzarote & Fuerteventura DIR Madrid Map, Mallorca & Menorca, Mallorca DIR, Mallorca Map, The Pyrenees, Pyrenees & Andorra Map, Spain, Spain & Portugal Map, Tenerife & La Gomera DIR
Sri Lanka Sri Lanka, Sri Lanka Map
Suriname South America on a Budget
Sweden Europe on a Budget, Scandinavia, Sweden
Switzerland Europe on a Budget, Switzerland
Taiwan Taiwan
Tanzania Tanzania, Zanzibar
Thailand Bangkok, Southeast Asia on a Budget, Thailand, Thailand Map, Thailand Beaches & Islands
Togo West Africa
Trinidad & Tobago The Caribbean, Trinidad & Tobago
Tunisia Tunisia, Tunisia Map
Turkey Europe on a Budget, Istanbul, Turkey, Turkey Map
Turks and Caicos Islands The Bahamas, The Caribbean
United Arab Emirates Dubai DIR, Dubai & UAE Map [1 title]
United Kingdom Britain, Devon & Cornwall, Edinburgh DIR England, Europe on a Budget, The Lake District, London, London DIR, London Map, London Mini Guide, Scotland, Scottish Highlands

& Islands, Wales, Walks In London & Southeast England
United States Alaska, Boston, California, California Map, Chicago, Colorado, Florida, Florida Map, The Grand Canyon, Hawaii, Los Angeles, Los Angeles Map, Los Angeles and Southern California, Maui DIR, Miami & South Florida, New England, New England Map, New Orleans & Cajun Country, New Orleans DIR, New York City, NYC DIR, NYC Map, New York City Mini Guide, Oregon & Washington, Orlando & Walt Disney World® DIR, San Francisco, San Francisco DIR, San Francisco Map, Seattle, Southwest USA, USA, Washington DC, Yellowstone & the Grand Tetons National Park, Yosemite National Park
Uruguay South America on a Budget
US Virgin Islands The Bahamas, The Caribbean
Venezuela South America on a Budget
Vietnam Southeast Asia on a Budget, Vietnam, Vietnam, Laos & Cambodia Map [1 Map],
Wales Britain, Camping in Britain, Europe on a Budget, Wales
First-Time Series FT Africa, FT Around the world, FT Asia, FT Europe, FT Latin America
Inspirational guides Earthbound, Clean Breaks, Make the Most of Your Time on Earth, Ultimate Adventures, World Party
Travel Specials Camping in Britain, Travel with Babies & Young Children, Walks in London & SE England

For more information go to www.roughguides.com

Books change lives

Book Aid International
www.bookaid.org

Poverty and illiteracy go hand in hand. But in sub-Saharan Africa, books are a luxury few can afford. Many children leave school functionally illiterate, and adults often fall back into illiteracy in adulthood due to a lack of available reading material.

Book Aid International knows that books change lives.

Every year we send over half a million books to partners in 12 countries in sub-Saharan Africa, to stock libraries in schools, refugee camps, prisons, universities and communities. Literally millions of readers have access to books and information that could teach them new skills – from keeping chickens to getting a degree in Business Studies or learning how to protect against HIV/AIDS.

What can you do?

Join our Reverse Book Club and with your donation of only £6 a month, we can send 36 books every year to some of the poorest countries in the world. For every two pounds extra you can give, we can send another book!

Support Book Aid International today!

 Online. Go to our website at **www.bookaid.org**, and click on 'donate'

 By telephone. Start a Direct Debit or give a donation on your card by calling us on 020 7733 3577

So now we've told you about the things not to miss, the best places to stay, the top restaurants, the liveliest bars and the most spectacular sights, it only seems fair to tell you about the best travel insurance around

WorldNomads.com
keep travelling safely

Recommended by Rough Guides

Small print and
Index

A Rough Guide to Rough Guides

Published in 1982, the first Rough Guide – to Greece – was a student scheme that became a publishing phenomenon. Mark Ellingham, a recent graduate in English from Bristol University, had been travelling in Greece the previous summer and couldn't find the right guidebook. With a small group of friends he wrote his own guide, combining a highly contemporary, journalistic style with a thoroughly practical approach to travellers' needs.

SMALL PRINT

The immediate success of the book spawned a series that rapidly covered dozens of destinations. And, in addition to impecunious backpackers, Rough Guides soon acquired a much broader and older readership that relished the guides' wit and inquisitiveness as much as their enthusiastic, critical approach and value-for-money ethos.

These days, Rough Guides include recommendations from shoestring to luxury and cover more than 200 destinations around the globe, including almost every country in the Americas and Europe, more than half of Africa and most of Asia and Australasia. Our ever-growing team of authors and photographers is spread all over the world, particularly in Europe, the US and Australia.

In the early 1990s, Rough Guides branched out of travel, with the publication of Rough Guides to World Music, Classical Music and the Internet. All three have become benchmark titles in their fields, spearheading the publication of a wide range of books under the Rough Guide name.

Including the travel series, Rough Guides now number more than 350 titles, covering: phrasebooks, waterproof maps, music guides from Opera to Heavy Metal, reference works as diverse as Conspiracy Theories and Shakespeare, and popular culture books from iPods to Poker. Rough Guides also produce a series of more than 120 World Music CDs in partnership with World Music Network.

Visit www.roughguides.com to see our latest publications.

Rough Guide travel images are available for commercial licensing at www.roughguidespictures.com

Rough Guide credits

Text editor: Ann-Marie Shaw
Layout: Ankur Guha
Cartography: Ashutosh Bharti
Picture editor: Emily Taylor
Production: Rebecca Short
Proofreader: Jan McCann
Photographer: Michelle Grant
Editorial: Ruth Blackmore, Andy Turner, Keith
Drew, Edward Aves, Alice Park, Lucy White,
Jo Kirby, James Smart, Natasha Foges, Róisín
Cameron, James Rice, Emma Traynor, Emma
Gibbs, Kathryn Lane, Monica Woods, Mani
Ramaswamy, Harry Wilson, Lucy Cowie, Alison
Roberts, Joe Staines, Peter Buckley, Matthew
Milton, Tracy Hopkins, Ruth Tidball; **Delhi**
Madhavi Singh, Karen D'Souza, Lubna Shaheen
Design & Pictures: **London** Scott Stickland,
Dan May, Diana Jarvis, Mark Thomas, Nicole
Newman, Sarah Cummins; **Delhi** Umesh
Aggarwal, Ajay Verma, Jessica Subramanian,
Pradeep Thapliyal, Sachin Tanwar, Anita Singh,
Nikhil Agarwal, Sachin Gupta.
Production: Liz Cherry

Cartography: **London** Ed Wright, Katie Lloyd-
Jones; **Delhi** Rajesh Chhibber, Rajesh Mishra,
Animesh Pathak, Jasbir Sandhu, Karobi Gogoi,
Alakananda Bhattacharya, Swati Handoo,
Deshpal Dabas
Online: **London** Faye Hellon, Jeanette Angell,
Fergus Day, Justine Bright, Clare Bryson, Aine
Fearon, Adrian Low, Ezgi Celebi; **Delhi** Amit
Verma, Rahul Kumar, Narender Kumar, Ravi
Yadav, Debojit Borah, Rakesh Kumar, Ganesh
Sharma, Shisir Basumatari
Marketing & Publicity: **London** Liz Statham,
Louise Maher, Jess Carter, Vanessa Godden,
Vivienne Watton, Anna Paynton, Rachel
Sprackett, Laura Vipond; **New York** Katy Ball,
Judi Powers; **Delhi** Ragini Govind
Reference Director: Andrew Lockett
Operations Assistant: Becky Doyle
Operations Manager: Helen Atkinson
Publishing Director (Travel): Clare Currie
Commercial Manager: Gino Magnotta
Managing Director: John Duhigg

Publishing information

This seventh edition published March 2010 by
Rough Guides Ltd,
80 Strand, London WC2R 0RL
14 Local Shopping Centre, Panchsheel Park,
New Delhi 110017, India
Distributed by the Penguin Group
Penguin Books Ltd,
80 Strand, London WC2R 0RL
Penguin Group (USA)
375 Hudson Street, NY 10014, USA
Penguin Group (Australia)
250 Camberwell Road, Camberwell,
Victoria 3124, Australia
Penguin Group (Canada)
195 Harry Walker Parkway N, Newmarket, ON,
L3Y 7B3 Canada
Penguin Group (NZ)
67 Apollo Drive, Mairangi Bay, Auckland 1310,
New Zealand
Cover concept by Peter Dyer.

Typeset in Bembo and Helvetica to an original
design by Henry Iles.
Printed in Singapore
© Norm Longley, 2010
Maps © Rough Guides

496pp includes index
A catalogue record for this book is available from
the British Library
ISBN: 978-1-84836-049-5

The publishers and authors have done their best
to ensure the accuracy and currency of all the
information in **The Rough Guide to Hungary**,
however, they can accept no responsibility for
any loss, injury, or inconvenience sustained by
any traveller as a result of information or advice
contained in the guide.

1 3 5 7 9 8 6 4 2

Help us update

We've gone to a lot of effort to ensure that the
seventh edition of **The Rough Guide to Hungary**
is accurate and up-to-date. However, things
change – places get "discovered", opening hours
are notoriously fickle, restaurants and rooms raise
prices or lower standards. If you feel we've got it
wrong or left something out, we'd like to know,
and if you can remember the address, the price,
the hours, the phone number, so much the better.

Please send your comments with the subject
line "**Rough Guide Hungary Update**" to ©mail
@roughguides.com. We'll credit all contributions
and send a copy of the next edition (or any other
Rough Guide if you prefer) for the very best
emails.
Have your questions answered and tell others
about your trip at ®www.roughguides.com

www.roughguides.com

Acknowledgements

Norm Longley: Very special thanks to Annie for her diligent and enthusiastic editing, not to mention her inordinate patience during the course of writing this book; Monica for her continued support; Charles, Dan and Tim; Karin Jones, Endre Kardos and Viktor Hajko at the Hungarian Tourist Board in London; and Olga Patkai in Budapest. Thanks are also due to: Gábor Törő csik in Eger; László Köteles in Komlóska; Lavrik Wiersum in Sarospatak; Judit Marcziné Szappanos in Sarospatak; Ádám Tornay in Budapest; Melinda Sellyei-Barócsi in Szilvásvárad. Most of all, to Tim for being such a sterling friend; Christian for her support; and Luka.

Dan Richardson: Thanks to Gordon Cross and Josey Walker for a great time in Budapest.

Charles Hebbert: Firstly, thanks to Rachel Appleby and Rozgonyi Zoltan for their additional research; and Bakonyi Ági, Biber Kriszta, Fenyő Krisztina, Gyene Gyöngyvér, Judith Heywood, Lő rinc Anna, Lucy Mallows, Alison Murchie, Nádori Péter, Pallai Peter, Helen Percival, Persanyi Miklos, Pulay Gergő, Szűcs Julia, Tolnai Lea and of course Caroline, Molly and Fergus.

Readers' letters

Thanks to all the readers who have taken the time to write in with comments and suggestions (and apologies if we've inadvertently omitted or misspelt anyone's name):

Clare Abbott, Fergal Beirne, Micaela Blitz, G. Brewster, Marsha Brown, Hilary Clare, Mererid Puw Davies and Dan Gibson, I. Doak, Jane Doy, Katalin and Shaun Fisher, Edward Garston, Bren & Rob Golder, Kati Havasi, Mark Hilton, Geoff Holden, Ray and Ree Holmes, Mike Hounsell, Anita Isalska, Ryan James, Marion Janner, Andre Jordan, Mary Kauffman, Katherine Lieb, Steve Locke, Tiffany Madigan, Sue Middleton, Laura Mózes and Mark Kristóf, William Mulholland and Jan Hughes, Leslie Proudfoot, Gemma Rogers, Michel Rorai, Linda Shannon, Mirjam Schiffer, Frank Paul Silye, Bob Telfer, Melanie Trull, R. Vieira, Tom Walsh, Ronelle Ward, Wayne.

Photo credits

All photos © Rough Guides except the following:

Full page
Girls at folk dancing festival, Debrecen © Walter Bibikow/Vladpans/eStock Photo

Introduction
Matryoshka nesting dolls © Walter Bibikow/Vladpans/eStock Photo
Detail of Pécs Cathedral © Douglas Pearson/Corbis
Danube River town view © Walter Bibikow/Vladpans/eStock Photo
Esztergom Cathedral and Monument © Stephen L Saks/Pictures Colour Library
Budapest Parliament © SIME/4Corners

Things not to miss
02 Waterslide at Siófok resort © Mike Goldwater/Alamy
03 Széchenyi tér, Pécs © Doug Pearson/PhotoLibrary
04 Aggtelek Cave © Alberto Paredes/Alamy
05 Traditional Csikos horseman with horse © Tibor Bognar/Corbis
06 Spring Festival © Courtesy of The Budapest Spring Festival
07 Busojaras Carnival © Laszlo Toth/Rex Features
08 Springtime in Bukk Hills National Park © Walter Bibikow/PhotoLibrary
10 Barrels of Tokaji wine in cellar © Georgia Glynn Smith/PhotoLibrary
11 Eger © Mattes Mattes/PhotoLibrary
13 Fire Tower in Sopron © Yoshio Tomii/PhotoLibrary
14 Putti at Esterházy Palace © Michael St. Maur Sheil/Corbis
15 Woman wearing traditional clothing, Hollókő © Sandro Vannini/Corbis

Bathing matters colour section
Lake Balaton, Heviz thermal lake © Hemis/Alamy
Bath house in Budapest © Mark Downey/Masterfile
Héviz, Balaton © FAN travelstock/Alamy

Food and drink colour section
Harvesting in Kiraly-Hegy vineyard © Herbert Lehmann/Photolibrary
Gastronomy festival, Budapest © Daniel Kerek/Alamy

Black and whites
p.182 A swimmer plunges into the water of Lake Balaton © EPA/Corbis
p.199 Lake Balaton; a young couple at a club in Siófok © Mike Goldwater/Alamy
p.220 Keszthely Festetics Palace © PCL
p.236 The library of Pannonhalma © Michael Runkel/Alamy
p.248 View of Kakinczy Street, Győr © Adalberto Rios Szalay/Photolibrary
p.272 Fountain in the historic centre of Kőszeg © Egmont Strigl/Photolibrary
p.304 Siklós © Danita Delimont/Alamy
p.320 Narrow-gauge railway © Image Service s.r.o/Alamy
p.324 Royal Mansion, Gödöllő © Walter Bibikow/Photolibrary
p.342 Lipizzana horses © Angelika Ciesniarska /Alamy
p.357 Vineyard in Tokaji © Georgia Glynn Smith/Photolibrary
p.370 A traditional Hungarian horseman on the Great Plain © Reuters/Corbis
p.383 Kecskemét © P Narayan/Photolibrary
p.396 Szeged © Jesus Rodriguez/Photolibrary
p.421 Bird-watching hut in Tisza Lake © Alberto Paredes/Alamy

ROUGH
GUIDES

SMALL PRINT

Selected images from our guidebooks are available for licensing from:

ROUGH**GUIDES**PICTURES.COM

Index

Map entries are in colour.

Map symbols

maps are listed in the full index using coloured text

– – –	Chapter division boundary	P	Parking
– – – –	International boundary	♦	Point of interest
▬▬▬	Motorway	@	Internet café
═══	Major road	ⓘ	Tourist office/information point
══	Minor road	⊠	Post office
▬▬	Pedestrianized street	♀	Museum
▥▥▥	Steps	⊙	Statue
╼╾	Railway	Å	Campsite
– – – – –	Footpath	⌂	Cave
───	River	∴	Ruin
— —	Ferry	∩	Arch
▬▬▬	Wall	⚲	Lighthouse
■━■	Gate	✡	Synagogue
╳	Bridge	☪	Mosque
✕	Level crossing	⚑	Church (regional maps)
⚞	Mountain range	✛	Church (town maps)
▲	Mountain peak	▩	Building
⸰⸰⸰	Swamp	▢	Market
⸰⸰⸰	Viewpoint	◯	Stadium
✈	Airport	+⌐+	Cemetery
Ⓜ	Metro station	▨	Park/forest
★	Bus stop	▨	Beach